Stephen M. Miller's

Illustrated
BIBLE
Dictionary

Presented to Library of
Trinity United Methodist Church
New Kingstown, PA
by
Leonard W. Tritt
March 2015

BARBOUR
PUBLISHING

THIS ISN'T YOUR NORMAL BIBLE DICTIONARY.

It's your Bible dictionary on training wheels.

Try not to feel intellectually insulted.

I do occasionally use big words. *Intellectually* requires two hands to count the number of syllables.

This is a Bible dictionary especially for Bible newcomers. Lifers can read it, too. I'm okay with that. But as I wrote the entries, I didn't give one snapping synapse of energy to what lifelong Christians might want to read. There are wonderful Bible dictionaries for them, mini encyclopedias packed full of details both interesting and boring.

I didn't figure Bible newbies needed another one of those.

What I figure they do need is some basic Bible info that's fast-paced, fun to read, and hard to put down. Info about Bible-time people, places, customs, sharp objects, and anything else in Scripture that raises an eyebrow or drops a jaw.

Illustrated Bible Dictionary doesn't have everything you'd ever want to know about anything in the Bible. But it does have the first thing you'd want to know about many things.

I'd be delighted if you could think of this book as one of your first stops in Bible study.

Let me tell you a trade secret.

When I research in prep for writing easy-reading Bible reference books like this, I read lots of stuff. I'm surrounded by stacks of books. If my research were a Terminator movie, it would be called *Terminator: Rise of the Books*. Here's my secret: When I'm reading, I start with the simple stuff. In time, I work my way up to the industrial-strength biblical scholarship.

I think that's a good plan for just about anyone trying to learn a thing or two about the Bible.

I hope you agree. But it won't bum me out if you have a better approach. I haven't cornered the market on good ideas, regardless of what my beloved mother continues to tell me.

A NOTE ABOUT CROSS REFERENCES

To make this book as helpful as possible, we've added a lot of cross references. If you see a word in SMALL CAPS within an entry, it means that word or phrase has its own entry in the *Illustrated Bible Dictionary*.

A WORD OF THANKS

It takes me about a year to research and write a book like this.

It takes a team of people to help me pull it off. I couldn't do it by myself. I'd like to thank a few notables.

Wife. Linda has supported me in this risky business of full-time freelance writing—for about two decades. I'd still be working for the man if it weren't for her. And by *the man*, I don't mean God. I mean bosses who think they're god. You know what I mean. Unless, of course, you're the boss. In which case you don't have a clue. (See why I'm a freelancer?)

Agent. Steve Laube doesn't just sell my ideas to publishers, he's my professional guide. He gives me advice. Some of it is welcome, like a double-fisted handshake. Some of it is painful—or worse, embarrassing—like a kick in the keister. Both are necessary, sad to say.

Editor. Paul Muckley has a tough job. He lives and works and breathes in no-man's land, as far as I'm concerned. It's the scorched earth between the author and the production department. There's a reason it's scorched. Authors want a top-quality book. That requires two ingredients that no production department seems to have enough of: time and money. If a book turns out well and no blood is shed, it's the editor's doing.

Designer. The folks at Faceout Studio gave this book its good looks. What they got from me was a mess of words, a stack of pictures, and a hearty "Hi-yo, Silver! Away!" At trail's end, once the dust settled, what they pulled out of their saddlebag was a work of art. At least in the design. The words weren't their fault.

God bless them, every one.

Steve

Stephen M. Miller
StephenMillerBooks.com

AARON

(AIR un)

1400s BC or 1200s BC (debated)

"What about your brother, Aaron the Levite?"
Exodus 4:14

- Big brother of Moses
- First high priest of Jews
- Family dynasty of priests lasts about 1,000 years
- Moses' spokesman to Pharaoh
- Okayed golden calf idol

AARON WAS 83 YEARS OLD when he teamed up with his 80-year-old little brother, MOSES, to deliver GOD's demand to the king of EGYPT: "Let my people go" (Exodus 5:1).

The king—known only in the BIBLE by his title, PHARAOH—used the JEWS as slave labor to build cities.

It took 10 plagues, including DISEASE and crop disasters, before the brothers could convince Pharaoh that God meant business. Once freed and out of Egypt, the Jews camped for about a year at the foot of MOUNT SINAI. While Moses was up on the mountain getting the 10 COMMANDMENTS, he was gone so long that many figured he wasn't coming back. They said to Aaron, "Make us some GODS who can lead us" (Exodus 32:1). Aaron collected GOLD and molded it into a calf, which the people worshiped in what reads like a drunken orgy.

When Moses came and asked Aaron what happened, Aaron said he simply threw the gold into the fire, "and out came this calf!" (Exodus 32:24).

Yeah, right.

God ordered the worshipers punished. About 3,000 were executed. God not only spared Aaron, but he appointed him ISRAEL's first HIGH PRIEST—leader of their worship rituals. Aaron's sons became associate PRIESTS. All priests had to come from Aaron's descendants. Aaron's tribe—known as LEVITES, descended from JACOB's son LEVI—served as WORSHIP assistants, helping the priests and taking care of the TENT worship center.

ISRAEL'S FIRST HIGH PRIEST, Aaron ministered in a portable worship center called the Tabernacle. It was a tent sanctuary with a courtyard surrounded by a curtain wall. Jews offered their animal sacrifices at the altar in the courtyard.

AARON'S ROD

Aaron's staff. . .sprouted, budded, blossomed, and produced ripe almonds!
Numbers 17:8

GOD USED AARON'S WALKING STAFF to produce several MIRACLES during the Jewish EXODUS out of EGYPT. The most famous: bringing the dead stick to life, sprouting ALMOND blossoms and nuts.

Rebellious JEWS sparked that miracle. They insisted on serving as WORSHIP leaders—an honor GOD assigned only to the tribe of LEVI. In response to their bold demand, God ordered the leader from each of ISRAEL's 12 tribes to give his wooden staff to MOSES. Each staff, inscribed with the tribe's name, rested overnight in the

TENT worship center. The next morning, the only staff to show a SIGN from God was Aaron's almond-loaded stick, representing the tribe of Levi.

On God's order, Moses permanently stored the staff inside Israel's most holy relic: the ARK OF THE COVENANT, a chest that also held the 10 COMMANDMENTS.

In earlier miracles, to convince Egypt's king to free the Jews, Aaron's staff:

- changed into a SNAKE
- turned the NILE RIVER red
- cued the PLAGUE of frogs
- cued the plague of gnats

ABBA

(AB ah) or (AH bah)

"Abba, Father," he cried out. . . . "Please take his cup of suffering away from me."
Mark 14:36

A TENDER WORD for "FATHER," much like "daddy" or "papa." It's ARAMAIC, a language JEWS learned while EXILED in BABYLON, now Iraq, about 500 years earlier.

ABEDNEGO (see SHADRACH)

ABEL

(A bull)

Before 4000 BC

Cain attacked his brother, Abel, and killed him.
Genesis 4:8

- Son of Adam and Eve
- World's first murder victim

WITH FOUR SOULS on the planet, jealously caused the first MURDER.

CAIN, oldest son of ADAM AND EVE, killed his little brother. Apparently, Cain thought GOD loved Abel best. God accepted Abel's SACRIFICE of "the best of the FIRST-BORN lambs" but rejected Cain's offering of "some of his crops" (Genesis 4:3–4).

A MERRY WIDOW, Abigail buries a fool of a husband whose rude behavior nearly got their entire household killed. She promptly marries David, who had planned to do the killing.

ABIB

(A bib)

On this day in early spring, in the month of Abib, you have been set free. Exodus 13:4

ABIB is the Canaanite name for the first month on the Jewish CALENDAR, when EGYPT freed its Jewish slaves. JEWS later called it Nisan, a month that usually stretches over parts of March and April.

ABIGAIL

(AB uh gay ill)

About 1000 BC

They told Abigail, "David has sent us to take you back to marry him." 1 Samuel 25:40

- Second of King David's eight wives
- Saved her former husband by apologizing for him

BEAUTIFUL AND SENSIBLE Abigail saved her jerk of a first husband, NABAL, from certain DEATH—only to watch him die of shock after he sobered up and found out what had happened.

DAVID and his men were refugees, hiding from King SAUL. Nabal was a rich SHEPHERD who owned 4,000 SHEEP and GOATS. David's men voluntarily protected the flock while camping in the area.

During the annual sheepshearing, a time of prosperity and partying, David sent messengers to ask Nabal for food. Drunken Nabal refused, insulting David's men. David responded to the shearing party with a raiding party. Abigail intercepted the SOLDIERS—bringing them supplies as an apology. When she later told Nabal about this, he died, perhaps of a stroke or a heart attack. David promptly married the WIDOW.

ABIMELECH

(uh BIM uh leck)

About 2100 BC

King Abimelech of Gerar sent for Sarah and had her brought to him at his palace. Genesis 20:2

- Tried to marry Abraham's wife, Sarah

A CANAANITE KING in what is now southern ISRAEL, Abimelech took ABRAHAM's wife SARAH into his HAREM. Honest mistake. Abraham had told everyone in the area that Sarah was his sister. He was afraid if they knew she was his WIFE, they'd kill him to get her—she was that beautiful. GOD revealed the truth to Abimelech in a DREAM. Abimelech released Sarah, made peace with Abraham, and showered the couple with GIFTS.

ABNER

(AB nur)

About 1050 BC

The commander of Saul's army was Abner. 1 Samuel 14:50

- Introduced young David—future giant-killer—to King Saul
- Accused of sleeping with one of the royal wives; no denial
- Traitor who plotted to turn Saul's army over to David

A COUSIN OF KING SAUL—their fathers were brothers—Abner served as SAUL's bodyguard and ARMY commander. After Saul died in battle, Saul's son and successor, ISHBOSHETH, accused Abner of sleeping with one of the royal wives. Without denying it, Abner stormed off to the enemy camp of DAVID, vowing to give him Saul's old army. Never got a chance. On his way home, David's commander, JOAB, murdered him—blood vengeance. Abner had killed Joab's little brother in battle.

ABRAHAM

(A bruh ham)

2100s BC

"You will be called Abraham, for you will be the father of many nations." Genesis 17:5

- Father of Jews, through son Isaac
- Father of Arabs, through son Ishmael
- Offered Isaac to God in near-fatal sacrifice
- Revered by Jews, Christians, Muslims

IT SEEMS ODD to some folks that the father of the Jews was an Iraqi.

That's where Abraham grew up, in a bustling EU-PHRATES RIVER town about 200 miles (about 300 km) south of Baghdad. The city was UR—beating heart of the world's first known empire: SUMER.

His NAME was Abram then. He married his half sister Sarai; they had the same father, TERAH, but different mothers.

For some reason that the Bible writer didn't bother to mention, Terah uprooted his entire extended FAMILY. His plan: trade city life for a country life upgrade. It was the boonies or bust, as he headed some 1,000 miles (1,600 km) west for what is now Israel—in those days called CANAAN, a lightly populated haven for nomadic herders.

Traveling northwest along the Euphrates riverfront trade route, Terah's CARAVAN stopped at HARAN, a city in what is now south Turkey—over halfway to Israel. He settled there.

After Terah died, GOD told 75-year-old Abram to finish what his father started: "Go to the land that I will show you." God showed him Canaan, promising: "I will make you into a great nation" (Genesis 12:1–2).

A bold promise to an old man with no kids and an infertile, 66-year-old WIFE.

Sarai wasn't the only thing infertile. So was Canaan—deep in DROUGHT.

Shortly after arriving, Abram moved south to the drought-resistant NILE RIVER valley in EGYPT.

There Abram worried that the good looks of his lady love might land him on a mummy's slab—gutted, dried, and nicely salted.

"Look, you are a very beautiful woman," Abram told Sarai. "When the Egyptians see you, they will say, 'This is his wife. Let's kill him; then we can have her!' " (Genesis 12:11–12).

Sure enough, Sarai ended up in Pharaoh's HAREM—perhaps getting prepped for her honeymoon night. God unleashed some kind of PLAGUE on the king's household. Somehow, the king traced the misery back to Sarai, concluding that she wasn't just Abram's sis, she was also his wife.

Abram and Sarai were promptly escorted out of Egypt. But they got to keep a wealth of GIFTS the king had previously given Abram, including SERVANTS. Perhaps that's where they picked up HAGAR, Sarai's Egyptian servant—and future mother of Abram's first child, ISHMAEL.

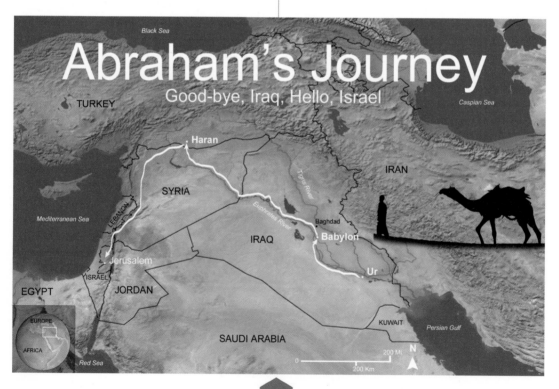

Abraham's Journey
Good-bye, Iraq, Hello, Israel

8

Back in Canaan, just across Egypt's border, Abram repeated the half-truth about Sister Sarai, this time with King ABIMELECH of GERAR. And with even better results. Abram got to keep the king's gifts. Plus a settlement. And a peace treaty, which allowed him to live nearby.

ABRAHAM'S BOYS

A decade after arriving in Canaan, 76-year-old Sarai reached a conclusion: she couldn't have kids.

A late-dawning news flash like that might leave some wondering if the chiseled curves of her good looks were counterbalanced by the lethargic learning curve of a slow-minded soul.

In keeping with a custom of the day, Sarai offered her husband a surrogate. Abram would impregnate Sarai's personal slave, Hagar. The child would belong to Abram and Sarai.

Ishmael was born.

Fourteen years later, so was ISAAC—to 90-year-old Sarai. By that time, God had renamed Sarai as SARAH. It happened some nine months earlier. God had appeared to Abram and renamed both of them. It was part of a CONTRACT God made with the man now called Abraham, HEBREW for "father of many." Sometimes in ancient agreements between a ruler and a subject, the ruler gave his subject a new, relevant name—as a way to publicly validate the contract and to remind everyone who was boss.

Abraham's contract obligation: Circumcise all males in the family—including each newborn on the eighth day of life. "From GENERATION to generation" (Genesis 17:12).

God's contract promise: Sarah would give BIRTH to Abraham's SON. That son would produce descendants who would grow into many nations. The "entire land of Canaan. . .will be their possession forever" (Genesis 17:8).

Once Sarah had her own son, she wanted Ishmael gone: "I don't want him to inherit anything. It should all go to my son" (Genesis 21:10 CEV).

By custom, the oldest son became the alpha male when the FATHER died. Alpha got twice the INHERITANCE of any other son—and he led the extended family like a chief leads a tribe.

God told Abraham to do as Sarah wanted. But he assured Abraham, "I will also make a nation of the descendants of Hagar's son because he is your son,

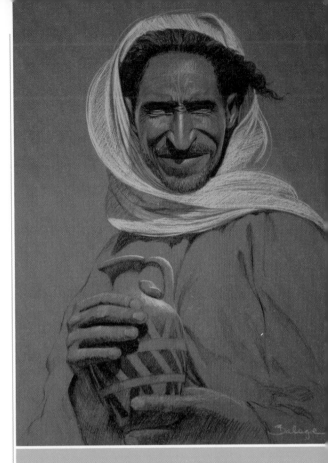

ABRAHAM HAD TO WAIT 86 years to become a father—and at that, with a surrogate mother. He didn't have a son with his own wife until age 100. That's when Sarah gave birth to Isaac.

ABE, THE SHORT STORY

- Grew up as Abram in Ur, a city in Iraq
- Married half sister, Sarai
- Moved to Haran, a city in Turkey
- Age 75, moved to Canaan, today's Israel
- Moved temporarily to Egypt to escape drought
- Rescued nephew Lot from raiders
- Age 86, had son Ishmael with slave woman Hagar
- God renamed Abram as Abraham, Sarai as Sarah
- Age 99, circumcised himself in covenant with God
- Age 100, had son Isaac with Sarah
- Nearly sacrificed Isaac to God
- Wife Sarah died at age 127
- Abraham died about 40 years later, at age 175

too" (Genesis 21:13). Though Isaac's family would produce the 12 TRIBES OF ISRAEL, Ishmael's family produced a dozen tribes of his own—nations scattered throughout the Middle East from what is now Egypt to Syria (Genesis 25:18).

ABRAHAM'S TEST OF FAITH is to sacrifice his son and burn the body on a stone altar. Fortunately for everyone, an angel stops him at the last moment.

ABRAHAM'S BIGGEST TEST OF FAITH

In perhaps the most bizarre request God made of anyone in the BIBLE, he told Abraham:

> *"Take your son, your only son—yes, Isaac, whom you love so much—and go to the land of Moriah. Go and sacrifice him as a burnt offering on one of the mountains, which I will show you." Genesis 22:2*

A burnt offering is slaughtered, dismembered, and burned on a stone ALTAR.

Jewish legend says Isaac was 37 at the time, and that the shock of God's request—which Abraham agreed to honor—killed Sarah at age 127.

Jewish tradition also places MORIAH at JERUSALEM, adding that the stone of Isaac's SACRIFICE has survived as the massive flat rock on the hilltop. This rock is now enshrined as the centerpiece inside a 1,300-year-old Muslim worship center that has become Jerusalem's most famous landmark: the Dome of the Rock. This is where many say the Jewish TEMPLE once stood, before Romans destroyed it in AD 70.

Jerusalem would have been about the right distance from Abraham's home in BEERSHEBA. The Bible says they walked for three days. Jerusalem is about a three-day walk north, some 45 miles (72 km).

An ANGEL, or perhaps the LORD himself, stopped Abraham at the last second, saying, "Now I know that you truly fear God. You have not withheld from me even your son, your only son" (Genesis 22:12).

As if God wouldn't have known it otherwise.

Most Bible experts say this test of Abraham's FAITH wasn't for God's benefit. It was a message for the rest of us. They speculate that the odd story is a kind of living parable to foreshadow another heart-wrenching Father-Son story. What Abraham was willing to do, God did. He sacrificed his only Son, Jesus.

ABRAHAM TO THE RESCUE

Abraham's nephew, LOT, had made the trek with him down from Haran. But they parted company after their herds grew too large to share the same pastures and wells.

Lot moved to the city of Sodom—just in time for a WAR. Invaders defeated Sodom and their allied kingdoms, taking Lot captive. Abraham mustered a militia of 318 men born into his household, perhaps from his extended family and servants. They tracked the raiders and crushed them in a night attack, recovering Lot along with all the other captives and the possessions the invaders had taken.

A WIFE FOR ISAAC, A TOMB FOR ABRAHAM

When Sarah died, Isaac was 37 years old and still a bachelor. Abraham sent his most trusted servant on a mission to find Isaac a wife. The servant came back with REBEKAH, granddaughter of Abraham's brother. That means Isaac married the daughter of a cousin; Rebekah was his second cousin.

Abraham lived long enough to see his grandsons, ESAU and JACOB, grow into teenagers. They were about 15 years old when Abraham died at age 175. Their father, Isaac, and their uncle, Ishmael, buried Abraham with Sarah.

BURIAL was in a cave called MACHPELAH in what is now the West Bank city of HEBRON. Muslims later built a mosque over the cave. Today Muslims worship there. So do Jews, with restrictions. Jews consider this burial site of Abraham, Isaac, and Jacob the second holiest site on earth, after the Western Wall, a stone retaining wall that shored up the hilltop where the Jerusalem Temple once stood.

ABRAHAM'S BOSOM

The beggar died, and was carried by the angels into Abraham's bosom. Luke 16:22 KJV

JESUS USED THIS PHRASE in a PARABLE to describe where godly people went after they died. They went to be by ABRAHAM's side. Jesus also called the place PARADISE (Luke 23:43).

ABSALOM

(AB suh lum)

About 1000 BC
The king [David]. . .cried, "O my son Absalom! . . . If only I had died instead of you!"
2 Samuel 18:33

- Son of King David
- Murdered his half brother
- Led a coup against his father
- His long hair got him killed

SECOND IN LINE to succeed his father as KING, Absalom orchestrated the MURDER of the heir apparent, his half brother AMNON. Politics wasn't the motive. REVENGE was.

Amnon had raped Absalom's full sister, TAMAR, and DAVID had done nothing to punish him.

Two years later Absalom invited Amnon to a sheep-shearing festival, got him drunk, ordered his SERVANTS to kill him, and then fled to his maternal grandparents in a small city-nation in what is now Syria.

After three years of self-imposed exile, he returned home at David's invitation. Yet he had to wait another two years before the elderly David would see him. By that time, Absalom was livid. Absalom courted the crowds, walking among them and treating them like dear friends—and dissing David's administration.

When Absalom finally declared himself king, he had enough supporters that David fled JERUSALEM. But in the battle that followed, David's seasoned SOLDIERS overpowered Absalom's men. As Absalom tried to escape on his MULE, some low-hanging branches of an OAK tree snagged him by his thick HAIR, yanked him off the critter, and left him dangling in midair like a royal bull's-eye.

Three DAGGERS to the heart—courtesy of David's commander, JOAB—ended his run at the throne.

see painting, page 12

ABSTINENCE

"Abstain from eating food offered to idols." Acts 21:25

ONE WAY TO RECOGNIZE JEWS was to watch what they didn't do. Observant JEWS abstained from:

- working on the Sabbath
- worshiping idols
- eating meat pink with blood
- eating food identified as not kosher, such as shellfish

When CHRISTIANITY began as a Jewish movement, many Jews tried to impose these and other Jewish laws on non-Jewish converts. CHURCH leaders offered a compromise. They asked Christians to abstain from sexual IMMORALITY and from food offered to idols or with blood in it. Only abstinence from sexual immorality stuck. In time, Christians felt free to eat any food they wanted, whether it was kosher or not.

ABYSS (see BOTTOMLESS PIT)

ACACIA GROVE Map 1 E5
(a KAY shuh)

Joshua secretly sent out two spies from the Israelite camp at Acacia Grove.
Joshua 2:1

- Last camp on the Exodus

JEWS USED THIS CAMP as a staging ground for the invasion JOSHUA launched into the PROMISED LAND. Many archaeologists link it to a ruin, Tell el-Hammam, about 10 miles (16 km) east of the JORDAN RIVER in what is now Jordan. Earlier, some of the JEWS camped there engaged in SEX rituals with local women "in the worship of BAAL" (Numbers 25:3).

ACACIA WOOD
(a KAY shuh)

"Build a chest of acacia wood. . . . Cover it inside and out with pure gold. . . . When I give you the Ten Commandments. . .put them inside." Exodus 25:10–11, 16 CEV

A HARDWOOD TREE, it was the most common source of wood in the Sinai and in what is now southern ISRAEL. Jewish carpenters during the EXODUS used it to

ABSALOM'S COUP against his father, David, ends when an oak tree snags him by his long locks, yanking him off his mule. When enemy soldiers find him dangling there, they know what to do.

build the frame for the tent WORSHIP center as well as ISRAEL's most sacred relic: the chest known as the ARK OF THE COVENANT.

ACCAD (see AKKAD)

ACCENTS

"You must be one of them; we can tell by your Galilean accent." Matthew 26:73

PHONETICS BECAME FATAL when travelers in wartime carried their accents with them.

One Jewish leader, JEPHTHAH, waged WAR on the Jewish tribe of EPHRAIM; they had insulted him. Ephraim JEWS had trouble pronouncing words with *sh* in them. So when Jephthah caught people he thought came from Ephraim, he ordered them to say "SHIBBO-LETH" (Judges 12:6). When they managed only "Sibbo-leth," he killed them—42,000 of them.

At the trial of Jesus, a SERVANT of the HIGH PRIEST in JERUSALEM spotted PETER as a Galilean DISCIPLE—because of Peter's northern accent.

One ancient Jewish story confirms the northern accent. The writer tells of a southern Jew insulting the accent of a Galilean who wanted to buy some wool. Apparently Galileans dropped their *h*'s.

"You stupid Galilean," the southerner said, without a trace of southern hospitality. "Do you mean a donkey (ham r), wine (hamar), wool, ('amar), or a lamb (immar)?"
Babylonian Talmud, *Erubin* 53b

ACCO
Map 4 B4

(ACK oh)

The tribe of Asher failed to drive out the residents of Acco. Judges 1:31

ONE OF CANAAN'S BUSIEST CITIES, Acco was just north of what is now Haifa, Israel. The apostle PAUL visited there during his third missionary trip, when it was called Ptolemais (Acts 21:7)—after the Egyptian king who rebuilt it: PTOLEMY. Crusaders captured it a thousand years later and called it Acre. Today it's a ruin known as Tell el-Fukhkhar.

ACCUSER

Members of the heavenly court came to present themselves before the LORD, and the Accuser, Satan, came with them. Job 1:6

ACCUSER is the English translation of the HEBREW word *SATAN*. As it appears in the BIBLE, *Satan* can refer to the devil, humans, ANGELS—and even to GOD, when he accuses people of sinning or when he opposes them (see Numbers 22:22).

ACHAIA
Map 3 B3

(uh KAY yah)

Paul felt compelled by the Spirit to go over to Macedonia and Achaia. Acts 19:21

- Roman province where Paul started the church in Corinth, Greece

ON HIS SECOND MISSIONARY TRIP, PAUL decided to take the story of Jesus into what is now Europe. He left Turkey and sailed a short distance to MACEDONIA in what is now northern Greece. Passing quickly through, and starting churches in a couple of towns along the way, he settled for about a year and a half in CORINTH, a busy port town in southern GREECE.

ACHAN

(A kin)

About 1400 BC or 1200s BC (debated)
All the Israelites stoned Achan and his family and burned their bodies. Joshua 7:25

ACHAN'S GREED got 36 of JOSHUA's warriors killed during the Jewish invasion of what is now ISRAEL.

JEWS had destroyed the border town of JERICHO. They were supposed to take nothing but leave everything as an offering to GOD. Achan, one of the Jews, took a ROBE imported from what is now Iraq, along with 200 SILVER coins and a GOLD bar.

For this, the BIBLE says, God allowed the Jews to lose their next battle. When Achan eventually confessed, Joshua ordered him and his entire FAMILY killed and burned, with all of his property. For coveting what the people of Jericho had, Achan got what they got. Dead.

ACHOR

(A core)

They led them off to the Valley of Achor. . . .
And all Israel stoned him. Joshua 7:24–25 MSG

ACHOR is HEBREW for "Trouble." That's what ACHAN brought on his fellow JEWS by stealing battlefield booty from JERICHO. The BIBLE says GOD allowed JOSHUA'S ARMY to lose their next battle because of Achan's disobedience. So the Jews executed Achan in a valley, which they named Valley of Trouble.

ACTS, BOOK OF

Famous sound bite: "The Holy Spirit will come upon you and give you power. Then you will tell everyone about me in Jerusalem, in all Judea, in Samaria, and everywhere in the world." Jesus to his disciples. Acts 1:8 CEV

ACTS IS THE STORY of how Jesus' followers started the CHRISTIAN movement after Jesus left the planet.

- Writer: Unknown. Church leaders in the AD 100s said a non-Jewish physician named Luke—one of the apostle Paul's associates—wrote Acts as a sequel to his story about Jesus, the Gospel of Luke. Both books are addressed to a mystery man: Theophilus. Some scholars speculate he was a Roman official Luke was trying to convince that CHRISTIANITY wasn't a threat to the Roman Empire.
- Time: The story covers more than 30 years, from the early AD 30s until the AD 60s. Many Bible experts guess Luke wrote the book in the AD 70s or 80s.

- Location: The story takes place in several countries of the Middle East and Europe, starting in Jerusalem and moving into Egypt, Syria, Lebanon, Turkey, Cyprus, Greece, and Italy.

BIG SCENES

Jesus leaves. Jesus ascends into the sky from the MOUNT OF OLIVES, after telling his DISCIPLES to wait in JERUSALEM for the HOLY SPIRIT to fill them with power to spread his story throughout the world. *Acts 1*

Holy Spirit arrives. Filled with the Spirit, Jesus' disciples tell Jerusalem crowds about the RESURRECTION of Jesus—backing up their words with MIRACLES of HEALING and speaking in foreign languages they had never learned. Some 3,000 JEWS join the emerging Christian movement. *Acts 2*

Persecution scatters the Christians. A Jewish mob kills STEPHEN, a CHURCH leader. King HEROD AGRIPPA I kills JAMES, a disciple of Jesus. Many Christians flee the Jerusalem area, taking their religion with them. *Acts 6–8, 12*

Paul converts and becomes a missionary. Jesus appears to PAUL who's on his way to arrest Christians in DAMASCUS. Convinced of Jesus' resurrection, Paul converts and starts spreading the Christian teachings. He makes three missionary trips into TURKEY and GREECE and writes almost half the books in the NEW TESTAMENT. *Acts 9–20*

Paul arrested. A mob of Jerusalem Jews attack Paul. Roman soldiers arrest him. He's held for two years before appealing for a trial before CAESAR—his right as a Roman CITIZEN. The book ends with Paul in ROME waiting for trial. *Acts 21–28*

ADAM AND EVE

(ADD um) (EEV)

Before 4000 BC
The man—Adam—named his wife Eve.
Genesis 3:20

- Humanity's first couple
- Kicked out of the Garden of Eden for sinning

APPARENTLY SAVING THE BEST FOR LAST, God created humans on the last day of CREATION: day six.

HOLY SPIRIT FIRE sparks the Christian movement. Literally. When the Spirit descends on the awaiting followers of Jesus, "what looked like flames or tongues of fire appeared and settled on each of them" (Acts 2:3).

STEPHEN M. MILLER'S ILLUSTRATED BIBLE DICTIONARY

Adam first. Eve next. God declared them "very good." A notch up from the "good" rating he gave all other creations.

Their job description: "Be fruitful and multiply. Fill the earth and govern it" (Genesis 1:28).

Their one and only rule: "You may freely eat the FRUIT of every tree in the garden—except the tree of the knowledge of good and evil. If you eat its fruit, you are sure to die" (Genesis 2:16–17).

Of course, they ate the FORBIDDEN FRUIT.

A SNAKE—identified in REVELATION as SATAN—convinced Eve that God was lying about the fruit. The creepy critter said if Eve ate it she'd be as wise as God—eyes opened. She bit. And she convinced Adam to do the same.

All they seemed to realize with their newfound insight, however, was that they had disobeyed God—and they were stark naked.

God banished them from their paradise homeland, known as the Garden of EDEN. He sentenced Adam to a lifetime of hard labor: fighting weeds to grow crops. He sentenced Eve to childbirth. Worse, as God had warned them, they are now doomed to die: "You were made from dust, and to dust you will return" (Genesis 3:19).

The couple had three sons—CAIN, ABEL, and SETH—along with "other sons and daughters" (Genesis 5:4). The BIBLE says Adam died at age 930.

EVICTED, Adam and Eve get an armed escort out of the Garden of Eden. God had given them just one rule to obey: don't eat the forbidden fruit. It was one rule too many.

ADAM, CITY OF

Map 1 E5

(ADD um)

The river stopped flowing, and the water started piling up at the town of Adam.
Joshua 3:16 CEV

JUST AS THE BIBLE SAYS God parted the WATER for JEWS fleeing Egyptian SLAVERY during the EXODUS, the Bible adds that GOD parted the water when they arrived in the PROMISED LAND now called ISRAEL.

JOSHUA led them across the JORDAN RIVER during springtime flooding. The water had topped the riverbank. Fortunately, something upstream dammed the river, allowing the Jews to cross.

Some archaeologists identify Adam as a Jordanian ruin called by a similar-sounding Arabic name: Damiyeh. It's about 20 miles (32 km) upstream from JERICHO. EARTHQUAKES have occasionally shaken loose the dirt cliffs alongside the Jordan River, temporarily blocking it. In 1927 a quake dropped part of the 150-foot-high (45 m) cliffs near Damiyeh, damming the river for 21 hours.

see map, page 249

ADOPTION

God decided in advance to adopt us into his own family by bringing us to himself through Jesus Christ. Ephesians 1:5

ADOPTING someone else's CHILDREN is rarely reported in the OLD TESTAMENT. One famous exception: an Egyptian king's daughter adopted baby MOSES when she found him seemingly abandoned (Exodus 2:10).

Ancient Iraqi laws from several centuries before Moses—the CODE OF HAMMURABI—include laws about adoption. Roman law allowed people to adopt adults as well as children. The adopted person had full legal IN-HERITANCE rights, as though born into the FAMILY.

The apostle PAUL used *adoption* as a metaphor to describe a person's relationship to GOD. Because of God's compassion, Bible writers say, a stranger who doesn't know God can actually become part of his family.

ADULLAM
Map 1 C6

(ADD duh luhm)

David. . .escaped to the cave of Adullam.
1 Samuel 22:1

ON THE RUN from King SAUL, who became insanely jealous about DAVID's rising popularity, David chose a cave near the city of Adullam as his hideout. David knew the area because it was about 13 miles (21 km) from his BETHLEHEM hometown. He may have grazed his father's SHEEP in the nearby fields and sheltered them in some of the many caves that pocketed the hills.

ADULTERY

"You must not commit adultery."
Exodus 20:14

OF ISRAEL'S 10 COMMANDMENTS—the bedrock foundation on which all Jewish laws are built—the law prohibiting adultery shows up at number SEVEN. MOSES declared adultery a capital offense: "Both the man and the woman who have committed adultery must be put to death" (Leviticus 20:10).

Jesus, however, introduced another option: FORGIVENESS.

Jewish leaders brought him a woman caught in the act of adultery. They asked him if they should stone her. Jesus said that anyone who hasn't sinned sometime in his life could go ahead and throw the first stone.

Stunned speechless, the crowd gradually dispersed.

"Where are your accusers?" Jesus asked the woman. "Didn't even one of them condemn you?"

"No, LORD," she said.

"Neither do I," Jesus replied. "Go and SIN no more" (John 8:10–11).

In his famous SERMON ON THE MOUNT, Jesus seemed

to level sin's playing field—equating adultery to what many folks would say is the lesser offense of lust. "Anyone who even looks at a woman with lust has already committed adultery with her in his heart" (Matthew 5:28).

Both are hurtful. Both are sinful. Both can be forgiven.

AGAG

(A gag)

Samuel cut Agag to pieces before the LORD.
1 Samuel 15:33

FAILURE TO EXECUTE King Agag produced a pivotal moment in Jewish history: the beginning of the end of SAUL, ISRAEL's first KING.

Agag ruled the Amalekites, a race of Canaanites descended from ESAU. They lived in what is now southern Israel. They were the first to attack and drive back MOSES and the JEWS during the EXODUS.

GOD ordered Saul to kill all the Amalekites and destroy their possessions. When Saul spared the king and kept whatever he wanted as WAR treasures, SAMUEL executed Agag and announced tragic news about Saul. "Because you have rejected the command of the LORD, he has rejected you as king" (1 Samuel 15:23).

Samuel never met with Saul again.

AGING

Don't be harsh or impatient with an older man. Talk to him as you would your own father. 1 Timothy 5:1 MSG

BIBLE WRITERS told people to show compassion and respect for the elderly.

In Bible times there was no national safety net to protect the elderly. So the apostle PAUL urged families to look after their own, and for churches to pick up the slack when families failed to do their job:

"Take care of any WIDOW who has no one else to care for her. But if she has CHILDREN or grandchildren, their first responsibility is to show godliness at home and repay their parents by taking care of them. This is something that pleases GOD" (1 Timothy 5:3–4).

AHAB

(A hab)

Ruled about 875–854 BC

Ahab the son of Omri did evil in the sight of the Lord, more than all who were before him.
1 Kings 16:30 NKJV

- Seventh king of the northern Jewish nation of Israel
- Married Jezebel, the prophet-killer

A GIFTED MILITARY LEADER who fought off two Syrian invasions and helped temporarily stop the advancing Assyrian Empire, Ahab picked a rotten WIFE: JEZEBEL.

She was a PRINCESS from ISRAEL's next-door neighbor to the north: PHOENICIA, now Lebanon.

Ahab did nothing to stop Jezebel when she went on a crusade to wipe out the Jewish religion by executing Israel's PROPHETS. On the other hand, he didn't interfere when the prophet ELIJAH retaliated by ordering the execution of Jezebel's sacred cows: 850 prophets and priests devoted to Canaanite gods BAAL and ASHERAH.

A second-generation KING, Ahab inherited the throne from his father OMRI, whose name is carved in stone— the Moabite Stone. This stone tells how he oppressed the neighboring country of MOAB in what is now Jordan.

Ahab died in battle when an arrow penetrated a seam in his ARMOR.

Ahab's FAMILY dynasty ended when a Jewish commander named JEHU launched a coup, killing Ahab's son, JORAM, along with the queen mother, Jezebel.

AHASUERUS

(see XERXES I)

IN NEED OF VEGGIES, King Ahab offers to buy Naboth's vineyard. It's beside the king's summer palace, making it a handy place to plant a garden. When Naboth refuses to sell, Queen Jezebel arranges his execution and takes the property.

AHAZ

(A has)

Ruled about 742–727 BC

Ahab. . .sacrificed his son in the fire to another god. **2 Kings 16:2–3** NIRV

- Father of saintly King Hezekiah
- King of the southern Jewish nation of Judah
- Sacrificed one of his sons to an idol
- Jews refused to bury him in the royal cemetery

ONE OF THE MOST HATED KINGS in Jewish history, Ahaz came to the throne at age 20, after his father Jotham died.

During Ahaz's 16-year reign, he managed to weave idolatry into the Jewish culture. He even served as idolatry's poster child, sacrificing one of his own sons perhaps to MOLECH, a regional god whose worship involved burning babies to death.

Ahaz's big political mistake was to call on the Assyrian Empire to help him fight off a military threat from the neighboring nations. "When King Tiglath-pileser of Assyria arrived, he attacked Ahaz instead of helping him" (2 Chronicles 28:20). The invader also levied a heavy TAX on Judah, forcing Ahaz to scavenge valuables from the Jerusalem Temple, the palace, and the homes of officials.

AI
Map 1 D5

(A eye)

Men of Ai chased the Israelites from the town. Joshua 7:4–5

- Handed Joshua his first defeat
- Ambushed, defeated in Joshua's second attack
- Joshua executes entire population: 12,000

JOSHUA'S INVASION FORCE destroyed the border town city of Jericho after the walls collapsed. Cocky, the Jews scouted Ai, a city deeper into what is now Israel and decided to send only 3,000 soldiers.

The Jews lost and ran for their lives. Joshua said they lost because one of them had disobeyed God by taking valuables from Jericho. Joshua executed the man—Achan—and then led the next attack, adding some trickery.

He faked another retreat. Ai's army charged out to pursue. A Jewish militia in hiding then attacked the undefended city and burned it. Then it went after Ai's army, trapping it between two waves of Jewish warriors.

Ai's location remains uncertain. Several ruins are contenders, including et-Tell and Khirbet Nisya, each about 10 miles (16 km) west of Jericho.

AIJALON
Map 1 B5

(A jah lon)

"Let the sun stand still over Gibeon, and the moon over the valley of Aijalon." Joshua 10:12

- Joshua orders the sun and moon to stop during a battle
- Joshua's militia wins the fight

SOME 15 MILES (24 km) west of Jericho, residents of a hilltop village called Gibeon found themselves surrounded by a coalition of five armies. It seems their neighbor cities were upset with them for making a peace treaty with Joshua and the Jewish invaders. Gibeon sent a messenger who convinced Joshua to come to their rescue.

Joshua led his men on an all-night, forced march up out of the Jordan River valley where they were camped, into the hills of Gibeon.

There, Joshua prayed a mystifying PRAYER that seems to ask the sun and moon to defy the laws of physics: sun stop over Gibeon; moon stop over Aijalon Valley about 10 miles (16 km) further west.

Some Bible experts say that when Joshua led the attack with that two-line prayer, he was driving with a poetic license. Others say the Hebrew word translated "stand still" or "stop" can mean "stop shining"—as in cue the shade for the exhausted Jewish warriors.

Clouds blanketed the sky, the Bible reports. A hailstorm killed most of the enemies.

AKKAD
Location Uncertain

(A cad) or (ACK add)

Nimrod first ruled in Babylon, Erech, and Accad, all of which were in Babylonia. Genesis 10:10 CEV

SPELLED ACCAD in some Bibles, it was a famous city in what is now Iraq. Sargon the Great (about 2270–2215) ruled much of the Middle East from this headquarters perhaps a century or two before Abraham's time. Akkad's location is uncertain, but some scholars place it along the banks of the Euphrates River outside Baghdad.

ALABASTER

(al uh BASS ter)

While Jesus was there, a woman approached him with an alabaster jar filled with expensive perfume. Matthew 26:7 NCV

STONE-LIKE MINERAL, alabaster is soft enough to carve into ornate jars, figurines, and statues. Often white and translucent, it's actually fine-textured gypsum. Alabaster was common throughout the Middle East.

Canaanites in what is now ISRAEL once mined it in the JORDAN RIVER valley. The GOSPELS of MATTHEW, MARK, and LUKE all tell of a woman pouring scented oil on Jesus from an alabaster jar.

ALEXANDER

(al ex AN der)

Alexander the coppersmith did me [Paul] much harm. 2 Timothy 4:14

1. ALEXANDER THE GREAT (356–323 BC). The BIBLE doesn't specifically name this Greek king who overthrew the Persian Empire and turned the Middle East into his own Greek Empire. But many scholars say he's strongly hinted at in a prophecy by DANIEL.

"The shaggy male GOAT represents the king of GREECE, and the large horn between his eyes represents the first king of the Greek Empire. The four prominent horns that replaced the one large horn show that the Greek Empire will break into four kingdoms, but none as great as the first" (Daniel 8:21–22).

When Alexander died on a military campaign at age 33, his generals carved up the empire among themselves: three main kingdoms and one assortment of smaller kingdoms.

2. ANTI-PAUL ALEXANDER (first century AD). Alexander shows up twice in the NEW TESTAMENT as an opponent of the apostle PAUL. He might have been one man, or two. Paul, writing LETTERS to his colleague TIMOTHY, said that the FAITH of Alexander "has been shipwrecked" (1 Timothy 1:19), and that Alexander the coppersmith—possibly the same man—"fought against everything we said" (2 Timothy 4:15).

ALEXANDRIA

Map 2 H7

(al ex AN dree uh)

Apollos, an eloquent speaker who knew the Scriptures well, had arrived in Ephesus from Alexandria in Egypt. Acts 18:24

- Capital of Egypt for almost 1,000 years
- Home to largest library in ancient world
- Jews commissioned to translate their Bible into Greek

ALEXANDRIA was a scholar's paradise and the seaside hometown of APOLLOS, a Jewish CHRISTIAN preacher who drew high praise from NEW TESTAMENT writers.

ALEXANDER the Great founded the city after

ON THE BATTLEFIELD, Alexander the Great and his Greek army overpower the Persian forces of King Darius at the Battle of Issus in Turkey, 333 BC. This is part of a larger battle scene in a first-century mosaic from Pompeii.

he conquered Egypt in 332 BC. Not so humbly, he named it after himself. Located on the MEDITERRANEAN SEA's southern coast, where the NILE RIVER empties, Alexandria remained Egypt's capital until Muslim Arabs conquered it in AD 642.

A large community of JEWS lived in the city. Some scholars speculate that this is where JOSEPH hid with his FAMILY—MARY and baby Jesus—when King HEROD ordered the slaughter of BETHLEHEM boys.

The city is perhaps most famous for its massive library. Egyptian kings were so proud of it that they commissioned books to add to its holdings. One king arranged for a team of Jewish scholars to begin translating their sacred writings into GREEK, the international language of the day. The result: the BIBLE's first known translation, called the SEPTUAGINT.

ALMOND

(ALL mond)

Your hair will turn as white as almond blossoms. **Ecclesiastes 12:5** CEV

ISRAEL'S FIRST TREE TO BLOOM, almonds pop their white and pink blossoms as early as January. Some trees never make it beyond shrub height, thanks to hungry GOATS that keep them well pruned. Almond trees were valued in Bible times for their nuts. JACOB

AN ALMOND NUT ripens on the tree. Aaron's staff, made of almond wood, comes to life with blooms and nuts—a sign from God to prove Aaron is Israel's rightful worship leader.

sent some almonds as a GIFT to the Egyptians (Genesis 43:11). But the most famous almond reference in the BIBLE describes AARON's ROD miraculously budding.

A

ALMS

(see CHARITY)

ALOE

(AL oh)

I've perfumed my bed with myrrh, aloes, and cinnamon. **Proverbs 7:17**

THE BIBLE seems to identify two different plants as "aloe." According to some scholars, aloe written in the New Testament GREEK language refers to *Aloe vera*—nicknamed the burn plant because people apply it to burns. This would include the aloe that Jesus' followers used to preserve his body until they could give him a proper BURIAL (John 19:39). The ancients also used its juices in INCENSE and PERFUME for EMBALMING, and as a laxative.

Aloe written in the Old Testament HEBREW language refers to eaglewood, *Aquilaria agallocha*. It was expensive tree sap imported from India, also used for incense, perfume, and embalming.

ALPHA AND OMEGA

(AL fuh) (oh MAY guh)

"I am the Alpha and the Omega, the First and the Last, the Beginning and the End." **Revelation 22:13**

GREEK VERSION of *A* and *Z*—the first and last letters of the GREEK alphabet. REVELATION uses these letters to describe GOD as "the one who is, who always was, and who is still to come" (Revelation 1:8).

(ALL tur)

"Build for me an altar made of earth, and offer your sacrifices. . . . If you use stones. . . use only natural, uncut stones."
Exodus 20:24–25

A BIT LIKE A STONE-RINGED CAMPFIRE,

ancient altars were often just a small mound of dirt or ROCKS for a fire. JEWS and people of many other religions would slaughter an ANIMAL, cut it to pieces, and burn it on the altar as an offering to GOD or other deities. MOSES told the Jews that the smoke of a burnt offering "is a pleasing aroma, a special GIFT presented to the LORD" (Exodus 29:18).

When the Jews consolidated their WORSHIP to one central location—first at the TENT worship center during the EXODUS out of EGYPT, and later at the TEMPLE in JERUSALEM—they built a large altar for each facility.

The portable altar the Jews used during the Exodus was framed in wood, plated with BRONZE, and topped with grating a bit like a barbecue grill. The altar stood as a square that measured 7.5 feet on all four sides, rising 4.5 feet high (2 by 1.5 m). A "horn" stuck up on the top from each corner, perhaps to help hold the wood or meat in place, some speculate.

Jerusalem's bronze altar towered three times larger. It stood as a square measuring 30 feet on all four sides and standing 15 feet high (9 by 4.5 m).

Romans destroyed the Temple and the altar in AD 70, crushing a Jewish revolt. This abruptly ended the Jewish sacrificial system. Jews never rebuilt the Temple. A 1,300-year-old Muslim shrine—the Dome of the Rock—now sits on the site.

HOLY LAND TOURISTS pass a horned altar at Beersheba. It's unclear what purpose the horned corners provided. One guess: to hold the firewood and sacrificial meat in place on the top.

STEPHEN M. MILLER'S ILLUSTRATED BIBLE DICTIONARY

AMBASSADORS

(am BASS uh door)

Hanun seized David's ambassadors and shaved off half of each man's beard, cut off their robes at the buttocks, and sent them back to David in shame. 2 Samuel 10:4

JUST LIKE AMBASSADORS TODAY, ambassadors in Bible times delivered messages for their national leaders—and sometimes got indelicately booted out of the host country.

The most notable boot in the backside came to DAVID's ambassadors among the Ammonites, in what is now Jordan. AMMON's king had died, and David sent envoys to express his sympathy. The new king of Ammon—son and successor of the dead king—figured the JEWS were spies scouting out the new king's weaknesses. So he expelled them, after shaving off half of each man's BEARD and hacking their ROBES high enough to leave their rear ends exposed.

WAR followed. David won.

AMEN

(A men)

"Cursed is anyone who denies justice to foreigners, orphans, or widows. And all the people will reply, 'Amen.' "
Deuteronomy 27:19

IT'S A HEBREW WORD most commonly heard today at the end of a PRAYER. Reasonable English translations: "Absolutely," "Right on," "So be it," "Well, that's the truth if I ever heard it."

AMMON

Map 1 G5

(AM un)

"I'm not giving you any of the land of the People of Ammon." God to Israelites,
Deuteronomy 2:19 MSG

ISRAEL'S NEIGHBOR nation to the east, Ammon controlled land across the JORDAN RIVER in what is now the Arab country of Jordan.

The BIBLE identifies Ammonites as descendants of INCEST between ABRAHAM's nephew LOT and one of Lot's own daughters. After GOD destroyed their hometown of Sodom, Lot's daughters thought everyone else was dead. So to repopulate the land, they got their father drunk and became pregnant by him. One son, Ben-ammi, produced the Ammonites (Genesis 19:38).

During the time of the famous JUDGES—heroic warriors like GIDEON and SAMSON—Ammonites raided ISRAEL for 18 years. A hero rose to the occasion and stopped them. His name was JEPHTHAH.

Later, Jewish KINGS SAUL and DAVID both defeated the Ammonites in battle. King SOLOMON—a lover, not a fighter—married at least one Ammonite woman (1 Kings 11:1).

Today's capital city of Jordan—Amman—preserves the name of this ancient nation and is built over the ruins of its capital.

AMNON

(AM nahn)

About 1000 BC
Amnon was obsessed with his sister Tamar.
2 Samuel 13:2 MSG

- King David's oldest son
- Raped his half sister
- Murdered by the raped woman's full brother

PRINCE AMNON, King DAVID's oldest son and presumed successor, fell in lust with one of his half sisters: TAMAR. They had the same father, David, but different mothers.

It was a fatal attraction.

Amnon targeted her like a thief targets a mark, hatching a plot to rob the PRINCESS of her virginity. He faked sickness and then asked her to bring food into his bedroom. There he raped her.

Disgust became his afterglow. "Amnon's love turned to hate, and he hated her even more than he had loved her" (2 Samuel 13:15).

Amnon ordered his SERVANT to throw her out—damaged goods. She moved out of the PALACE where the king's VIRGIN daughters lived. She moved in with her full brother ABSALOM. There's no record that she ever married.

King David did nothing to punish Amnon. Jewish

law required either death or a WEDDING—with the rapist never allowed to DIVORCE his former victim (Deuteronomy 22:25–29).

It took two years for Absalom to settle the score. He invited Amnon to a party and then partied him to death. Got him drunk. Had him murdered.

AMORITE

(AM or rite)

"I will lead you to a land flowing with milk and honey—the land where the Canaanites, Hittites, Amorites. . .now live." Exodus 3:17

DESCENDANTS of NOAH's grandson CANAAN, the Amorites were a race of people scattered in cities and camps throughout the Middle East. Many lived in what is now ISRAEL (then known as Canaan), along with LEBANON and SYRIA. Jews killed many of them when JOSHUA led the Jews home from SLAVERY in EGYPT. Others lived among the Jews. Scattered abroad, surviving Amorites apparently were assimilated into Jewish and Arab nations over the centuries.

AMOS

(A muhs)

Ministered about 760 BC

Amos replied, "I'm not a professional prophet. . . . I'm just a shepherd, and I take care of sycamore-fig trees." Amos 7:14

- Part-time prophet, full-time shepherd and farmer
- The go-to prophet for people looking for quotable words about justice
- Put exploitive power brokers in their place, at the bottom of the barrel

IMAGINE A MEXICAN jalapeño farmer showing up in Washington DC to announce the fall of America. Amos is the Mexican.

Actually, Amos was a SHEPHERD and a FIG farmer from the southern Jewish nation of JUDAH. He lived in the tiny village of TEKOA, about 10 miles (16 km) south of JERUSALEM. On GOD's orders, he traveled up to the northern Jewish nation of ISRAEL, where the rich and powerful were wallowing through a GENERATION-long stretch of PEACE and prosperity.

Amos said the rich got high and mighty by climbing on the backs of the POOR and the helpless. He warned that JUDGMENT DAY was coming. Israel would fall.

Amos may have lived to see it. Assyrian invaders from what is now Iraq erased Israel from the political map in 722 BC and repopulated the land with their own settlers.

AMOS, BOOK OF

(A muhs)

Famous sound bite: "They walk on poor people as if they were dirt, and they refuse to be fair to those who are suffering." Amos 2:7 NCV

PART-TIME PROPHET Amos warns the movers and shakers of ISRAEL that GOD is sick of the way they exploit the POOR and the way they SIN like it's no big deal. In fact, it's a deal breaker. They're going to find out what it's like to be poor and homeless—if they're lucky enough to survive what it's like to be dead.

- Writer: Amos, a shepherd and farmer
- Time: Amos delivered his message sometime during the reign of Israel's King Jeroboam II (about 786–746 BC) and Judah's King Uzziah (about 792–742 BC).
- Location: Amos lived in the small village of Tekoa, about 10 miles (16 km) south of Jerusalem, in the southern Jewish nation of Judah. He took his message on the road, traveling to the northern Jewish nation of Israel. There he warned people in the capital city of Samaria and at their worship center in Bethel.

BIG SCENES

The end is near. Amos announces God's judgment on both Jewish nations along with their Arab neighbors. In time, God will punish them all—JUDAH and Israel, along with their neighbors in what is now SYRIA, Jordan, LEBANON, and Saudi Arabia. The punishment: DESTRUCTION. *Amos 1*

Sins of the Jews. Amos levels God's charges against JEWS in both nations, north and south. These Jews:

- reject God laws
- sell poor folks into SLAVERY to recoup DEBTS as tiny as the price of a pair of SANDALS
- help themselves to the helpless, exploiting and oppressing them
- commit sex sins (Amos 2)

Fat cows headed for slaughter. Zeroing in on the northern Jewish nation of Israel, Amos paints a picture of their future in EXILE: "Listen to me you fat cows. . .you WOMEN who oppress the poor. . .you will be dragged away like a fish on a hook!" *Amos 4*

Repent. Amos sings a funeral song for dead Israel. He says God is going to execute this nation of repeat offenders. Their crimes: worshiping IDOLS, exploiting the poor, buying off JUDGES—all while living as HYPOCRITES who pretend to observe Jewish WORSHIP rituals and festivals. Their only hope is to plead for God's MERCY. *Amos 5*

Israel's makeover. Even if Israel refuses to repent, God vows a comeback. "I will restore the fallen house of DAVID. I will repair its damaged walls. From the ruins I will rebuild it and restore its former GLORY." *Amos 9*

AMULET
(see CHARM)

ANAB
Map 1 C6

(A nab)

1400s or 1200s (debated)
Joshua destroyed all the descendants of Anak, who lived in. . .Anab. Joshua 11:21

- Hometown of giants

ANAB was one of several towns where a race of GIANTS lived, in what is now southern Israel. These tall people helped spook JEWS of the EXODUS away from the PROMISED LAND. JOSHUA defeated them when he led the next GENERATION of Jews into ISRAEL. The site is a ruin called Khirbet Anab about 30 miles (50 km) south of JERUSALEM.

ANANIAS
(an a NI us)

About AD 35
Ananias went and found Saul. He laid his hands on him. . . . Instantly something like scales fell from Saul's eyes, and he regained his sight. Acts 9:17–18

A CHRISTIAN IN DAMASCUS, Ananias healed Saul, who had come to town to arrest followers of Jesus. Saul, on his journey, saw a VISION of Jesus that left him blind. After his HEALING, Saul—better known by his GREEK name, PAUL—joined the CHRISTIAN movement.

ANANIAS AND SAPPHIRA
(an a NI us) (suh FI ruh)

First century AD
Ananias and his wife Sapphira also sold a piece of property. But they agreed to cheat and keep some of the money for themselves. Acts 5:1–2 CEV

WHEN THE CHRISTIAN MOVEMENT was just getting started, compassionate Christians sold some of their property and donated the MONEY to the DISCIPLES—for distribution to POOR people in the CHURCH. Ananias and his WIFE, Sapphira, gave an offering, too. But theirs was self-serving. They wanted some recognition. They got dead instead.

They told the disciples that they were donating all the proceeds from the sale. But they kept part of the cash. PETER called them on it, one at a time. They died instantly, one at a time.

The writer of ACTS, thought by many to be the physician LUKE, didn't say what killed them. But he did say their DEATH put the fear of GOD into everyone who heard what happened.

ANATHOTH

See Jerusalem, Map 1 C6

(AN uh thoth)

"Why have you done nothing to stop Jeremiah from Anathoth, who pretends to be a prophet?" Jeremiah 29:27

HOMETOWN of the prophet JEREMIAH on the outskirts of JERUSALEM, Anathoth rested about 3 miles (5 km) northeast. While Babylonian invaders from what is now Iraq were laying SIEGE to Jerusalem, which they would soon destroy, Jeremiah bought a plot of land in Anathoth. He did it to make a point: "Someday people will again own property here" (Jeremiah 32:15).

ANCESTORS

David died and was buried with his ancestors in the City of David. 1 Kings 2:10

JEWS SPOKE RESPECTFULLY of their ancestors. FAMILY heritage was important. That's why there are so many family trees in the BIBLE. JEWS' genealogies linked them to their:

- property rights (land stayed in the family)
- social status (royalty were royalty and others weren't)
- jobs (PRIESTS had to belong to the tribe of LEVI)

When some Jews returning from Babylonian EXILE in what is now Iraq couldn't prove their ancestral link to Levi, they were disqualified as priests (Ezra 2:62).

In revering their ancestors, Jews weren't allowed to go overboard—diving into ancestor worship. People in some religions throughout the Middle East deified their ancestors and sought advice from dead relatives. But for Jews, there was only one Spirit they could WORSHIP: "You must not have any other god but me" (Exodus 20:3).

Some Jews broke that law. GOD said they defiled his NAME by "honoring the relics of their kings who have died" (Ezekiel 43:7).

ANCHOR

The sailors couldn't turn the ship into the wind. . . . So they lowered the sea anchor to slow the ship. Acts 27:15, 17

CARGO SHIPS often carried several anchors. Some were hacked of stone, with a hole chiseled through to hold a ROPE. Others were wooden beams imbedded with metal.

Jewish writers seldom used seafaring lingo in an upbeat way, because most were landlubbers: SHEPHERDS and farmers. In one exception, a writer calls FAITH in GOD "a strong and trustworthy anchor for our SOULS" (Hebrews 6:19).

A STONE ANCHOR from about the time of Abraham, some 4,000 years ago, was recovered off the coast Egypt.

ANDREW

(AN droo)

First century AD

Andrew went to find his brother, Simon [Peter], and told him, "We have found the Messiah." John 1:41

- One of Jesus' 12 disciples
- Brother of Peter
- Introduced Peter to Jesus

ANDREW made his living as a fisherman, working with his brother Simon PETER in the FISHING village of CAPERNAUM, on the Sea of GALILEE's north shore. He was also a follower of JOHN THE BAPTIST—until John pointed out Jesus as the MESSIAH. Andrew then became a follower of Jesus and recruited his brother. In time, Jesus approached both brothers while they were fishing and invited them to join his inner circle of DISCIPLES: "Come, follow me, and I will show you how to fish for people!" (Matthew 4:19).

ANGELS

Angels are only servants—spirits sent to care for people who will inherit salvation. Hebrews 1:14

ANGELS are spirit beings who serve GOD.

Among their jobs:

- Delivering God's messages to people. "God sent the angel GABRIEL to NAZARETH, a village in GALILEE, to a VIRGIN named MARY" (Luke 1:26–27).
- Attending to matters in heaven. "I heard the voices of thousands and millions of angels around the THRONE. . . . And they sang in a mighty chorus" (Revelation 5:11–12).
- Serving in an angelic army. "I saw the LORD sitting on his throne with all the armies of HEAVEN around him" (1 Kings 22:19).

Many scholars speculate there are different levels of angels. That's because some Bible writers use unique words to describe the angelic beings: CHERUBIM, SERAPHIM, archangels.

Though artists often portray angels with wings, the BIBLE doesn't. Not usually. Reporting their VISIONS, prophets EZEKIEL and ISAIAH talk about winged cherubim and seraphim. But the angels who come to earth with a message to deliver or a job to do seem to look human. When two walked into Sodom, LOT mistook them for travelers passing through town (Genesis 19:1–2).

The idea for wings may have come from simple reasoning, some guess—as in "How else could someone get from God's home above to earth below?"

In some reports, angels seem to glow like beings of light:

At Jesus' birth: "That night in the fields near BETHLEHEM some shepherds were guarding their sheep. All at once an angel came down to them from the Lord, and the brightness of the Lord's glory flashed around them" (Luke 2:8–9 CEV).

At Jesus' resurrection: "An angel of the Lord came down from heaven, rolled aside the stone, and sat on it. His face shone like lightning, and his CLOTHING was as white as snow" (Matthew 28:2–3).

GUARDIAN ANGELS?

Some say that everyone has a guardian angel.

Most scholars say that's a stretch—a presumption based mainly on something Jesus said to emphasize how important CHILDREN are to God: "Don't look down on any of these little ones. For I tell you that in heaven their angels are always in the presence of my heavenly FATHER" (Matthew 18:10).

Other references seem to talk about angels with specific assignments:

- "MICHAEL, the ARCHANGEL. . .stands guard over your nation [Israel]" (Daniel 12:1).
- "The SEVEN stars are the angels of the seven churches" (Revelation 1:20).

Some JEWS in Jesus' century did seem to believe in guardian angels. When PETER showed up at the front door of a HOUSE were Christians were praying for his release from jail, some inside couldn't believe they got

▲ GUARDIAN ANGELS don't show up in the Bible. At least that's not what they're called. But some Jews in Bible times seemed to believe that people had angels assigned to them. Jesus hinted that children have angels watching them from heaven.

STEPHEN M. MILLER'S ILLUSTRATED BIBLE DICTIONARY

such a quick answer to PRAYER. They said, "It must be his angel" (Acts 12:15).

Most scholars don't seem to read these passages and jump to the conclusion that everyone has a guardian angel. Some figure that when it comes to taking care of his children, God doesn't need to delegate. Jesus: "Not a single sparrow can fall to the ground without your Father knowing it. . . . So don't be afraid; you are more valuable to God than a whole flock of sparrows" (Matthew 10:29, 31).

ANIMALS

God said, "Let the earth produce every sort of animal." Genesis 1:24

ON THE SIXTH and final workday of CREATION, GOD made animals followed by humans.

Exactly what animals show up in the BIBLE is sometimes unclear. Bible translators occasionally disagree over how to translate the ancient terms. An "owl" in the New Living Translation of Isaiah 14:23 becomes a "hedgehog" in the English Standard Version and a "porcupine" in the New King James Version. The HEBREW word remains that obscure.

Some Christians who argue for a young earth, insisting that humans and dinosaurs lived at the same time, point to another obscure word as evidence: "BEHEMOTH. . .his strength is in his hips. . . . He moves his tail like a CEDAR" (Job 40:15–17 NKJV). The New Revised Standard Version, a translation many Bible scholars prefer, says the animal's tail gets "stiff like a cedar." The *Harper Collins Study Bible*, drawing from the NRSV, speculates that the animal was a crocodile—unless "tail" is a polite way of referring to the animal's sex organ.

The laws of MOSES allowed JEWS to give God sacrificial offerings of only a few animals: usually CATTLE, SHEEP, and GOATS. The POOR could sacrifice less expensive animals: DOVES or pigeons.

Moses also prepared a detailed list of what kinds of animals Jews could and couldn't eat. KOSHER FOOD included most of the common domesticated animals, some BIRDS, and any fish with scales. Not kosher: scavenger birds, shellfish, and animals found dead.

ANNUNCIATION

(a NUN see A shun)

Gabriel appeared to her and said, "Greetings, favored woman! The Lord is with you!" Luke 1:28

IN CHRISTIAN CIRCLES, *Annunciation* usually refers to the ANGEL GABRIEL's announcement to MARY that she's going to give BIRTH to Jesus, "the Son of the Most High" (Luke 1:32). Many Christians—especially Catholics, Anglicans, and Orthodox—commemorate this day every March 25, nine months before Christmas.

ANOINT

"Anoint him by pouring the anointing oil over his head." Exodus 29:7

PEOPLE IN BIBLE TIMES got OLIVE OIL applied to their bodies mainly for one of three reasons:

- ritual, to declare GOD's approval of a new KING, PRIEST, or PROPHET
- hospitality, to cool people and moisten their skin in a hot, dry land
- embalming, to cover the smell of decay during BURIAL

Some oils were scented and used after bathing. Before ESTHER's honeymoon night with the king, she spent a year in beauty treatments—including six months of having her skin "rubbed with olive oil and MYRRH" (Esther 2:12 CEV).

When it came time for AARON to become ISRAEL's first HIGH PRIEST, and later for SAUL to become the first king, each man was anointed by a noted spiritual leader: MOSES for Aaron and the prophet SAMUEL for Saul.

The HEBREW word for someone anointed this way and devoted to serving God is *MESSIAH*. In Greek, the language of the NEW TESTAMENT, the word is *CHRIST*.

Among Christians, both words became inseparably linked to Jesus, God's promised "Anointed One" (Daniel 9:26).

See also OINTMENT, PERFUME.

STEPHEN M. MILLER'S ILLUSTRATED BIBLE DICTIONARY

(AN tie christ)

You have heard that the Antichrist is coming, and already many such antichrists have appeared. 1 John 2:18

SOME END-TIME SPECIALISTS describe the Antichrist as an evil leader who will one day rule the world. But many scholars say that's not how the BIBLE uses the word.

Antichrist shows up as a brief note in two short LETTERS by JOHN. There, the word refers simply to anyone who denies the basic CHRISTIAN teachings:

"Anyone who denies the FATHER and the Son is an antichrist" (1 John 2:22).

"If someone claims to be a prophet and does not acknowledge the truth about Jesus, that person is not from God. Such a person has the spirit of the Antichrist, which you heard is coming into the world and indeed is already here" (1 John 4:3).

Many scholars say that the portrayal of an end-time tyrant began in the Middle Ages when preachers starting piecing together disconnected parts of the Bible to form a composite image. They linked:

- what JOHN said about antichrists
- with what PAUL said about a mysterious "man of lawlessness" (2 Thessalonians 2:3).
- and what JOHN OF REVELATION said about a beast who waged WAR "against God's HOLY people" (Revelation 13:7).

ANTIOCH

Map 3 M5, I4

(AN tee ahk)

Paul and Barnabas traveled inland to Antioch of Pisidia. Acts 13:14

- Paul helped start churches in two cities called Antioch

1. ANTIOCH, PISIDIA. While copastoring a mainly non-Jewish CHURCH in Syria, PAUL and BARNABAS took a temporary leave of absence so they could do some missionary work. They took the story of Jesus on the road to the Mediterranean island of CYPRUS—where Barnabas was born—and then on to what is now Turkey. One of several cities where they preached in Turkey and planted a church was Antioch in a small territory called PISIDIA, in the Roman province of GALATIA.

JEWS initially invited the PREACHING pair to talk in the SYNAGOGUE. But after the Jewish leaders saw the crowds that the two drew, they got jealous and incited a mob that drove them out of town. Paul returned to the city on both of his follow-up missionary trips. He also wrote the LETTER of GALATIANS to Christians in this province.

2. ANTIOCH, SYRIA. Paul and Barnabas co-pastored a predominately non-Jewish congregation in this riverside city—considered by some experts in Roman history to be the third-largest city in the ROMAN EMPIRE, after ROME and ALEXANDRIA, EGYPT. Population estimate: half a million.

JERUSALEM Jews scattered this far north, some 300 miles (about 500 km), to escape the Jewish PERSECUTION of Christians that began with the STONING to death of STEPHEN, a church leader in Jerusalem.

DISCIPLES sent Barnabas up to MINISTER in the church. He soon recruited Paul to help him. It was here that believers, previously known as followers of THE WAY, were first called Christians.

During a prayer service among the church leaders, the HOLY SPIRIT somehow convinced the men that Paul and Barnabas needed to take the story of Jesus abroad. That began the first of Paul's three missionary trips, stretching perhaps a decade, and ending with churches planted throughout CYPRUS, Turkey, and GREECE.

The city today is in Antakya (also called Hatay), Turkey.

APHEK

Map 1 B5

(A fek)

The Israelite army was camped near Ebenezer, and the Philistines were at Aphek. **1 Samuel 4:1**

- Philistines captured Israel's most sacred object at Aphek

TWICE, PHILISTINES used this village near what is now Tel Aviv as a staging ground to launch successful military campaigns against the JEWS. In the first battle, they captured ISRAEL's most sacred relic: the ARK OF THE COVENANT, a GOLD-plated chest that held the TEN COMMANDMENTS. In the second battle, they overran the ARMY of King SAUL, killing him and several of his sons.

APOCALYPTIC WRITING

(uh POCK uh LIP tick)

This is a revelation [apocalypse] from Jesus Christ. . .to his servant John. **Revelation 1:1**

- Highly symbolic style of writing used in Revelation

LIKE A CODED MESSAGE, apocalyptic literature revealed its meaning only to readers who knew how to decode the symbols. *Apocalypse* comes from a GREEK word that means "REVELATION." The last book of the BIBLE, Revelation, takes its name from this word.

Apocalyptic lit is a genre of writing as distinct as POETRY or parables. It was popular among JEWS and Christians during the turbulent centuries when the ROMAN EMPIRE occupied much of the Middle East—from about 200 BC–AD 200.

The symbolic lingo allowed writers to criticize people in power without putting themselves or their readers at risk. When JOHN OF REVELATION wrote "BABYLON is fallen" (Revelation 18:2), most Romans wouldn't have known he was talking about ROME. But John's readers knew. "Babylon" was a code word for Rome, because both empires had invaded ISRAEL and leveled JERUSALEM—the Babylonian Empire from

what is now Iraq in 586 BC, and the Roman Empire in AD 70.

Revelation is the only book in the Bible that many scholars say is entirely apocalyptic. But many scholars agree that some apocalyptic lit shows up in the bizarre VISIONS of DANIEL.

APOCRYPHA

(see BIBLE)

APOLLOS

(uh PAH los)

First century AD

Who is Apollos? Who is Paul? We are only God's servants through whom you believed the Good News. **1 Corinthians 3:5**

- Gifted preacher and debater

GIVEN WHAT THE BIBLE SAYS about Apollos, he might have been a traveling TEACHER who earned his living on the big-city lecture circuit. He was a Jew from an Egyptian town famous for producing smart JEWS: ALEXANDRIA, the kosher Oxford of its day.

Apollos was also a CHRISTIAN. He showed up in EPHESUS, teaching others about Jesus. There the teacher got tutored by a couple of laypeople who had studied under the apostle PAUL. "PRISCILLA AND AQUILA. . .took him aside and explained the way of GOD even more accurately" (Acts 18:26).

An "eloquent speaker," he "refuted the Jews with powerful arguments in public debate. Using the SCRIPTURES, he explained to them that Jesus was the MESSIAH" (Acts 18:24, 28).

Apollos moved to CORINTH, where he developed a following that seemed to evolve into a rift—though there's no hint that he encouraged it. Christians in Corinth split into groups favoring different leaders, including Paul, Apollos, PETER, and Jesus. Paul wrote the congregation, pleading for unity and saying that Jesus alone is the bedrock on which their FAITH is built.

APOSTASY

(see BACKSLIDER)

TO CHANNEL SPRINGWATER from the Carmel Mountains into Caesarea, Herod the Great built this aqueduct that stretched about 10 miles (16 km).

APOSTLE

(uh POS uhl)

Jesus chose twelve men and called them apostles. He wanted them to be with him, and he wanted to send them out to preach.
Mark 3:14 NCV

- Title of Jesus' original 12 disciples
- Highest office of leaders in the early church

IT'S A GREEK WORD. It means "messenger." When Jesus invited a dozen men to become his DISCIPLES, he called them apostles. He probably picked that word because it described what he wanted them to do: spread the word about his life and his teachings.

After Jesus returned to HEAVEN, the disciples decided to replace JUDAS ISCARIOT. He had committed suicide after betraying Jesus to Jewish leaders who orchestrated Jesus' CRUCIFIXION.

Apostle candidates had to come from a select group: "Men who were with us the entire time we were traveling with the LORD Jesus—from the time he was baptized by JOHN until the day he was taken from us" (Acts 1:21–22).

PAUL didn't fit this definition, yet he called himself an apostle. When others argued with him about it, he referred them to credentials he said qualified him:

- "I was not appointed by any group of people or any human authority, but by JESUS CHRIST himself and by GOD the FATHER, who raised Jesus from the dead" (Galatians 1:1).
- "I certainly gave you proof that I am an apostle. For I patiently did many signs and wonders and MIRACLES among you" (2 Corinthians 12:12).

When Paul made a list of various leaders in the CHURCH, he put apostles at the top: "These are the gifts Christ gave to the church: the apostles, the PROPHETS, the EVANGELISTS, and the PASTORS and teachers" (Ephesians 4:11).

Because apostles, by either definition—Paul's or the disciples'—had to have personally seen the resurrected Jesus, the title didn't make the jump to the next generation.

APPIAN WAY

Map 2 D5

(AP ee un)

Brothers and sisters in Rome had heard we were coming, and they came to meet us at the Forum on the Appian Way. **Acts 28:15**

ONE OF THE MAIN ROADS out of ROME, the Appian Way ran south along Italy's western coastline. PAUL traveled on this ROAD when Roman soldiers escorted him to Rome for trial. Spartacus and 6,000 other rebel slaves were crucified along this road in 71 BC. Parts of the road survive today.

AQUEDUCT

(ACK qua duct)

Assyrians took up a position beside the aqueduct that feeds water into the upper pool. Isaiah 36:2

AN ANCIENT VERSION of a waterline, an aqueduct was a channel that carried WATER from a supply source—such as a spring in the hills—to a site that needed the water, such as a city.

King HEZEKIAH built an underground channel to bring water into a Jerusalem POOL from a spring outside the city walls. King HEROD built an above-ground aqueduct that brought fresh spring water from the Carmel Mountains into the harbor town of CAESAREA, some 10 miles (16 km) south.

AQUILA

(see PRISCILLA AND AQUILA)

AR

Location Uncertain

"Do not bother the Moabites, the descendants of Lot. . . . I have given them Ar as their property." Deuteronomy 2:9

CITY, region, or perhaps both, Ar was located in what is now the Arab country of Jordan. GOD told MOSES not to let the JEWS pick a WAR with them while traveling through their land on the way to CANAAN, now called ISRAEL.

ARABAH

Map 3 M9

(AIR uh buh)

"We avoided the road through the Arabah Valley that comes up from Elath and Ezion-geber." Deuteronomy 2:8

LOOKING MORE LIKE MARS than Earth, the Arabah is 100 miles (160 km) of barren rift valley. It stretches from Israel's DEAD SEA south to the RED SEA. That's how most people use the term today. Others take the Arabah further north, saying it includes the entire rift valley—all the way up to MOUNT HERMON in north Israel. The JORDAN RIVER flows along this break in the earth's crust, a rift that has spawned many EARTHQUAKES.

ARABIA

Map 2 K9

(uh RAY bee uh)

All the kings of Arabia and the governors of the provinces also brought gold and silver to Solomon. 2 Chronicles 9:14

- Homeland of the queen of Sheba

SURROUNDED BY WATER on three sides—RED SEA, Persian Gulf, Indian Ocean—the Arabian Peninsula is a million square miles (2.6 million square km) of DESERT that could do with some water inland. That's more than a fourth the size of the United States.

Saudi Arabia makes up most of the land. The QUEEN OF SHEBA, many scholars say, probably came from Yemen at the southern tip of the region.

Desert kingdoms in Arabia mined GOLD and SILVER, which they traded in ISRAEL for products such as WINE, OLIVE OIL, and WHEAT.

ARAD
Map 1 C6

(A rad)

The Canaanite king of Arad, who lived in the Negev. . .attacked the Israelites and took some of them as prisoners. Numbers 21:1

- Defeated Jews during the Exodus
- Later wiped out by Joshua's militia

MOSES AND THE JEWS had just finished serving GOD's sentence of 40 years in the badlands when a Canaanite king launched a surprise attack from Arad. That's a desert city about 35 miles (56 km) south of JERUSALEM. The JEWS vowed to annihilate the town when it came time to invade—a promise JOSHUA helped them keep (Joshua 12:14).

ARAM
Map 2 J6

(AIR um)

The king of Aram had issued these orders. . . "Attack only the king of Israel. Don't bother with anyone else!"
1 Kings 22:31

- Ancient name of what is now roughly Syria

SCATTERED THROUGHOUT SYRIA, a nation of Aramean NOMADS settled in villages and camps. DAMASCUS was the most important of those villages.

Each tribe lived independent of the others much of the time. But they teamed up when threatened. They did that to repel an invasion force of Assyrians from what is

now Iraq. Sometimes they allied with one of the Jewish nations. But often they targeted the JEWS as their enemy or as a supply source they could raid for harvesttime crops, livestock, or slaves.

Perhaps one of their most influential contributions to history was their language: ARAMAIC. Jews picked it up and used it in Jesus' day.

ARAMAIC

(air uh MAY ick)

"I heard a voice saying to me in Aramaic, 'Saul, Saul, why are you persecuting me?'"
Acts 26:14

- Syrian language of Jesus

LIKE ENGLISH IS TODAY, Aramaic was one of the international languages of Bible times—and possibly the preferred language of Jesus. GOSPEL writers preserved some of Jesus' Aramaic phrases: "Holding her hand, he said to her, '*Talitha koum,*' which means 'Little girl, get up!' " (Mark 5:41).

Aramaic came from ARAM, in what is now Syria. But it spread throughout the Middle East, from what is now EGYPT to Iran. In fact, it became the official language used in the palaces of PERSIA, the Iranian-based empire that freed the JEWS taken captive in 586 BC by the Babylonian Empire (in today's Iraq). There, in EXILE for a GENERATION, is where many Jews picked up the language.

ARCHANGEL

(ARK ain gel)

The Lord himself will come down from heaven with a commanding shout, with the voice of the archangel, and with the trumpet call of God. 1 Thessalonians 4:16

- Top-tier category of angels

IF SOME BIBLE EXPERTS are right—that there are different levels of ANGELS—archangels are GOD's top-of-the-line model. Best of the best. Like "MICHAEL, one of the archangels" (Daniel 10:13).

GABRIEL also sounds like one of them, declaring to

the VIRGIN MARY, "I stand in the very presence of God. It was he who sent me to bring you this good news!" (Luke 1:19).

One book included in Catholic and Orthodox Bibles hints of seven archangels: "I am Raphael, one of the seven angels who stand ready and enter before the GLORY of the Lord" (Tobit 12:15 NRSV).

AREOPAGUS
See Athens, Map 3 B4

(air ee AH pay gus)

Paul stood before the meeting of the Areopagus and said, "People of Athens, I can see you are very religious." Acts 17:22 NCV

- Athens hilltop where philosophers laughed at Paul

WHILE PASSING THROUGH ATHENS on his second CHURCH-planting missionary trip, PAUL was in-

ON THIS ROCK HILLTOP known both as the Areopagus and Mars Hill, Paul told a group of Athens philosophers about Jesus. When he got to the part about Jesus rising from the dead, the laughter began. Paul soon moved on to Corinth.

vited to speak to a gathering of philosophers. They met on a flat-topped outcropping of stone that rose some 370 feet (113 m)—looking a bit like a natural stage in the middle of the city. The site was called Areopagus, also known as Mars Hill, named after the god of war: Ares for the Greeks and Mars for Romans.

The philosophers seemed interested in what Paul had to say about GOD until he reported that Jesus rose from the dead. At that point, some of them burst into laughter. At least one man, however, believed him: Dionysius.

ARIMATHEA
Map 4 C5

(air uh mah THEE uh)

Joseph of Arimathea took a risk and went to Pilate and asked for Jesus' body. Mark 15:43

- Hometown of the rich man who buried Jesus

A CITY of unknown location, Arimathea was the home of Joseph, a member of the Jewish high council called the SANHEDRIN. This council had sentenced Jesus to death, apparently against the wishes of JOSEPH OF ARIMATHEA. After Jesus' CRUCIFIXION, he got Governor PILATE's permission to bury Jesus.

ARK OF THE COVENANT

"I [God] will meet with you [Moses] there. . . over the Ark of the Covenant. From there I will give you my commands for the people of Israel." Exodus 25:22

- Gold-covered chest that held the 10 Commandments
- Israel's most sacred relic
- Once used as a magical war charm
- Captured by Philistines, though later returned
- Lost in history, perhaps taken by Babylonians from Iraq

DURING THE JEWISH EXODUS out of SLAVERY in EGYPT, GOD gave MOSES instructions for setting up the

Jewish religion. The Jews built a tent WORSHIP center called the TABERNACLE—a traveling temple. Inside the TENT's most sacred room, they were to keep their most sacred object: a chest that held their most revered laws chiseled in stone, the 10 COMMANDMENTS.

Jewish artisans built this chest—the Ark of the Covenant—out of ACACIA WOOD. It measured roughly four feet long by two feet wide and high (122 by 61 cm), plated inside and out with GOLD. They built the lid of solid gold and crowned it with two winged CHERUBIM facing each other. Jews called the lid the "MERCY SEAT" because it represented God's THRONE on earth. Here is where Moses would come to get God's instructions.

PRIESTS carried the chest on wooden poles covered in gold as they led the EXODUS caravan. They even carried it into battle, as a reminder that God was with them.

After arriving in what is now ISRAEL, the Jews once brought the ark into a battle they were losing against the PHILISTINES. They hoped it would change their luck—as a last resort. It didn't. Philistines overran the Jews and captured the chest. The Philistines returned it several months later after realizing that a PLAGUE seemed to accompany the chest as it traveled from city to city on a "war trophy" tour.

After King SOLOMON built the Jerusalem TEMPLE, he moved the chest into the holiest room, where it remained for several centuries. Once a year—on *Yom Kippur* (the DAY OF ATONEMENT)—the HIGH PRIEST went into the room to sprinkle the chest with BLOOD from a SACRIFICE offered for the sins of ISRAEL.

No one seems to know what happened to the chest. Many scholars say the Babylonian invaders probably stole it when they looted and destroyed Jerusalem and the Temple in 586 BC.

One competing legend, however, preserved in Catholic and Orthodox Christian Bibles, says the prophet JEREMIAH—an eyewitness to the Temple's destruction—buried the chest in a cave on the mountain where Moses died. Then Jeremiah "sealed up the entrance" (2 Maccabees 2:5 NRSV), promising that God would one day reveal the location.

Many Bible experts argue that this legend doesn't track with what Jeremiah predicted earlier. He said when the Jews returned from EXILE in BABYLON, "people will not talk about the ark of the covenant of the LORD anymore. It will never enter their minds. They will not remember it. The ark will not be missed" (Jeremiah 3:16 NIrV).

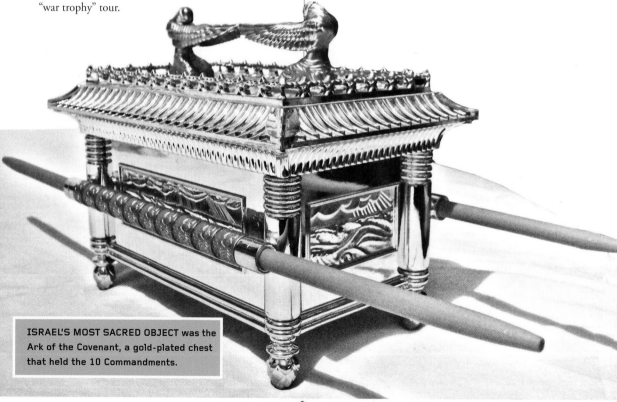

ISRAEL'S MOST SACRED OBJECT was the Ark of the Covenant, a gold-plated chest that held the 10 Commandments.

A MODEL OF NOAH'S ARK on display in the Creation Museum in Kentucky adds dinosaurs to the ship's manifest. The barge stretched about the length of one and a half football fields—half the length of many modern cruise ships.

ARK OF NOAH

"Build a large boat. . . . I am about to cover the earth with a flood." Genesis 6:14, 17

- Barge that saved Noah's family and animals from a massive flood

NOAH'S ARK looked more like a black barge than a SHIP. NOAH waterproofed it inside and out with TAR.

Parked on a football field, it would extend past both end zones, cover half the width of the playing field, and rise almost as high as the top of the goalposts: 150 by 25 by 15 yards (137 by 23 by 14 m).

Noah topped the barge with a roof, which overhung an 18-inch (46-cm) opening on all sides. The opening—like a row of open windows—provided light and ventilation.

The BIBLE says the barge held Noah's FAMILY of eight souls along with thousands of ANIMALS—for about a year. The RAIN fell for only 40 days, but it took months for the WATER to recede. Five months after the rain began, the barge plowed to a stop on a slope somewhere in the Ararat mountain range. It took another seven months for the water to recede enough for the people and animals to leave the barge.

Christians debate whether the FLOOD covered the entire earth or just the region. Archaeologists confirm that floods have wiped out ancient cities in the TIGRIS and EUPHRATES RIVER valleys. This is where civilization supposedly began, in a section of the Middle East known as the Fertile Crescent.

A

ARMAGEDDON

See Jezreel Valley, Map 1 B4

(are muh GED un)

Demonic spirits gathered all the rulers and their armies to a place with the Hebrew name Armageddon. Revelation 16:16

- Staging ground for demon-inspired rulers of earth prepping for war against God

WRITING IN THE LAST BOOK of the BIBLE, a man named JOHN reported a bunch of VISIONS he said he experienced. Most are bad news for planet Earth. One in particular, many Christians insist, sounds like a horrifying battle between the forces of good and evil—fought in Israel.

Armageddon is a place name that hasn't shown up anywhere but in John's LETTER of REVELATION. Bible experts say it's the English version of what sounds like a two-word phrase in HEBREW: *Har Megiddo*, which means MEGIDDO Hill.

Megiddo was an ancient hilltop fortress in northern Israel. It guarded the vast JEZREEL VALLEY, along with the main pass south through the Carmel Mountains. This pass connected southland kingdoms in EGYPT, ISRAEL, and ARABIA with northern nations such as Italy, GREECE, and SYRIA.

The Jezreel Valley, which has hosted scores of major battles throughout the centuries, drew high praise from Napoleon as the "perfect battlefield."

John said that in his vision he saw a DROUGHT dry up the EUPHRATES RIVER that runs through Syria and Iraq, emptying into the Persian Gulf. John said rulers from the east seized the opportunity to march their troops west across the dry riverbed. DEMONS recruited rulers worldwide "for battle against the LORD on that great JUDGMENT DAY of GOD the Almighty" (Revelation 16:14).

John didn't report what happened, instead moving on to his next vision. But many students of REVELATION link Armageddon to battle scenes in other visions of John:

- 200 million–man army. "I heard the size of their ARMY, which was 200 million mounted troops" (Revelation 9:16).

- Attack God's people. "They will surround the camp of God's people and the city that his people love" (Revelation 20:9 CEV).
- Bloodbath. "Blood flowed. . .in a stream about 180 miles [296 km] long and as high as a horse's bridle" (Revelation 14:20).

Yet many scholars say those scattered details may have nothing to do with Armageddon, adding that those scenes are only symbols of God's inevitable judgment. Others read the details literally and warn of a coming mother of all battles.

ARMOR

Goliath. . .wore a bronze helmet, and his bronze coat of mail weighed 125 pounds [57 kg]. He also wore bronze leg armor.
1 Samuel 17:4-6

SOLDIERS in Bible times wore body armor made from a wide range of materials. Some soldiers in early Middle Eastern history wore helmets and shirts made of LEATHER or cloth, stitched in layers. Some added metal studding.

To better protect against arrows and the slashes of a SWORD, weapon manufacturers developed metal shirts. Some were coats of mail, looking like loosely woven threads of metal. Others looked more like fish scales, each shirt stitched with hundreds of metal scales.

For added protection, some soldiers such as GOLIATH were accompanied by an armor bearer—someone who carried the soldier's SHIELD. When King SAUL was dying from a battlefield wound, he told his armor bearer to finish him—an order the soldier couldn't bring himself to obey (1 Samuel 31:4).

ARMS (see WEAPONS)

ARMY

When Abram heard that his nephew Lot had been captured, he mobilized the 318 trained men who had been born into his household. Then he pursued Kedorlaomer's army.
Genesis 14:14

SOME OF THE EARLIEST ARMIES in the BIBLE were more like minutemen militia—part-time warriors called to fight on short notice.

On a mission to rescue his nephew from raiders, ABRAHAM gathered from among his SERVANTS "318 trained men"—perhaps trained to fight when necessary. JOSHUA's invasion force was a militia of former slaves and sons of slaves. ISRAEL's first KING, SAUL, rallied a militia of herders and farmers when enemies threatened the nation. That may be why they were no match for the PHILISTINES, who defeated them and killed Saul.

DAVID seems to have been the first Jewish king to field a professional army, which included mercenaries.

As nations grew into empires, armies grew more specialized. Assyrians from what is now Iraq made the expensive leap from part-time soldiers to professional warriors—full-time fighters who terrorized the Middle East. This was an army of specialists: ground troops, cavalry, charioteers, archers, slingers, engineers who built roads, messengers riding Pony Express style, and supply soldiers hauling food and WEAPONS on wagons and CAMELS.

ARNON RIVER   Map 1 E6

(R nahn)

The women of Moab are left like homeless birds at the shallow crossings of the Arnon River. Isaiah 16:2

SNAKING BELOW a spectacular gorge up to three miles wide and half a mile deep (about 5 by 1 km), the Arnon River cuts west across the Arab country of Jordan and empties into the DEAD SEA. Today called Wadi Mojib, it provided a natural boundary between the nation of Ammon in the north and MOAB in the south. Because it was hard to cross, most travelers opted for the CARAVAN route about 15 miles (24 km) east: the KING's HIGHWAY.

ARROW
(see Bow and Arrow)

ARTAXERXES
(art tah ZURK zees)

Ruled 465–425 BC

King Artaxerxes. . .asked me, "Why are you looking so sad?" Nehemiah 2:1–2

- Persian king who let Nehemiah rebuild Jerusalem's walls
- Son of King Xerxes, Esther's husband

NEHEMIAH, a Jewish WINE STEWARD who served Persian King Artaxerxes, heard that the JEWS still hadn't rebuilt JERUSALEM's walls—a century after they had returned from EXILE. It depressed him. Artaxerxes noticed. This king, who ruled in what is now Iran, not only granted NEHEMIAH a leave of absence to oversee the rebuilding project, but he also provided an armed escort along with some supplies.

ARTEMIS
(ART tuh miss)

Their anger boiled, and they began shouting, "Great is Artemis of the Ephesians!" Acts 19:28

- Greek goddess and daughter of Zeus
- Patron goddess of Ephesus
- Her Ephesus temple was one of Seven Wonders of the World
- The reason Paul was run out of town

ALSO KNOWN by her Roman name, DIANA, she was the goddess of HUNTING who was said to protect ANIMALS from cruel treatment. She was also the go-to god for women in childbirth. Citizens of EPHESUS, in what is now Turkey, maintained a massive temple devoted to her—it was considered one of the Seven Wonders of the World.

When PAUL arrived in Ephesus, his PREACHING converted so many people that it hurt the local economy, which was based in part on manufacturing and selling figurines of Artemis. A silversmith named DEMETRIUS owned one of the large manufacturing businesses. He sparked a riot, accusing Paul of disrespecting Artemis. The uproar convinced Paul to move on.

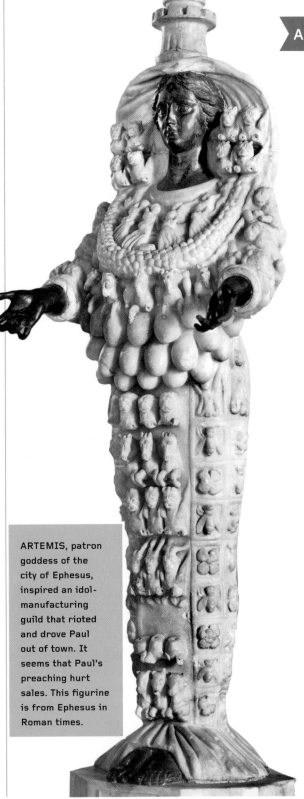

ARTEMIS, patron goddess of the city of Ephesus, inspired an idol-manufacturing guild that rioted and drove Paul out of town. It seems that Paul's preaching hurt sales. This figurine is from Ephesus in Roman times.

ASA

(A suh)

Reigned about 913–873 BC

Asa did what was pleasing in the LORD's sight. . . . He banished the male and female shrine prostitutes from the land and got rid of all the idols. 1 Kings 15:11–12

- Destroyed shrines devoted to idols

THIRD KING of the southern Jewish nation of JU-DAH, Asa ruled for 41 years. He fired his grandmother, Maacah, who was a granddaughter of King DAVID's son ABSALOM. She had been serving as queen mother. But she fed JERUSALEM's idolatry frenzy by erecting an obscene pole that people used in fertility rituals. Not kosher.

When King BAASHA of the northern Jewish nation of ISRAEL invaded Judah and captured the city of RAMAH only about 5 miles (8 km) north of Asa's capital in Jerusalem, Asa hired the Syrians to drive off Baasha's ARMY. Asa's fee: everything in the TEMPLE treasury.

ASAPH

(A saf)

About 1000 BC

The men chosen to play the cymbals were Heman. . .Asaph. . .and Ethan. 1 Chronicles 15:17 CEV

- Played in Israel's worship band
- Wrote a dozen psalms

A MEMBER OF THE LEVITE TRIBE, which served as ISRAEL's WORSHIP leaders, Asaph played CYM-BALS during worship events. That included when King DAVID led a procession that brought Israel's most sacred object to JERUSALEM: the ARK OF THE COVENANT, containing the 10 COMMANDMENTS. When Asaph wasn't playing heavy metal, he apparently wrote MUSIC. PSALMS 50 and 73–83 are credited to him.

HIGH AND LIFTED UP, Jesus ascends to heaven while his disciples watch from the Mount of Olives. About a week later, the Holy Spirit arrives, giving the disciples courage to take the story of Jesus public—even to the Jewish leaders who had orchestrated his execution.

ASCENSION OF JESUS

About AD 33

"Tell everyone about me. . . ." After Jesus had said this and while they [the disciples] were watching, he was taken up into a cloud. Acts 1:8–9 CEV

FORTY DAYS after his CRUCIFIXION, Jesus led his followers to the MOUNT OF OLIVES—a ridge beside

JERUSALEM, just across the narrow KIDRON VALLEY. A half-mile (1 km) walk from town. There he gave them their marching orders: They were to stay in Jerusalem until GOD filled them with power and boldness from the HOLY SPIRIT. Then they were to tell everyone about Jesus, "to the ends of the earth" (Acts 1:8). As soon as he said this, he ascended into the sky and disappeared in a cloud.

Straining to see him even after he was gone, the DISCIPLES were interrupted by two white-robed men with a news flash: "Jesus has been taken from you into HEAVEN, but someday he will return from heaven in the same way you saw him go!" (Acts 1:11).

ASHDOD Map 1 A6

(ASH dodd)

After the Philistines captured the Ark of God, they took it. . .to the town of Ashdod. . . and placed it beside an idol of Dagon."
1 Samuel 5:1–2

- One of five key Philistine cities
- Idol to Dagon crumbled beside Ark of the Covenant
- Captured by Assyrians in 712 BC
- Israel's fifth-largest city today, population 207,000

WHEN PHILISTINES overran the Jewish ARMY and captured ISRAEL's most sacred object, the ARK OF THE COVENANT chest that held the 10 COMMANDMENTS, they carried their war trophy back to Ashdod. Located near the Mediterranean coast, 20 miles (32 km) south of today's Tel Aviv, Ashdod was a leading town of the Philistine nation—and home to a temple devoted to their god DAGON.

PHILISTINES made the mistake of parking the Ark inside Dagon's temple beside an idol of him. By the next morning, the statue had fallen face down before the Ark. It did that for two days in a row. The Philistines sent the Ark to another town—where a PLAGUE of tumors broke out. A pattern was developing. Within seven months, Philistines returned the Ark to the JEWS—with GOLD offerings to honor GOD.

ASHER Map 1 C3

(ASH ur)

A

1800s BC

The sons of Zilpah, Leah's servant, were Gad and Asher. Genesis 35:26

- One of Jacob's 12 sons
- Father of the Jewish tribe of Asher

SON OF A SURROGATE mother, Asher was the product of what sounds like a baby-making contest in Jacob's FAMILY. Jacob's two wives were sisters LEAH and RACHEL, each competing for his affection by giving him sons. Each offered him not only their bodies, but the bodies of their personal SERVANTS as well. Asher's birth mother was Leah's servant, Zilpah. But according to the custom of the day, Asher belonged to JACOB and Leah.

When JOSHUA led the JEWS back home from SLAVERY in EGYPT, Asher's descendants got a small but fertile swath of land along what is now ISRAEL's northern coast. The land is perfect for growing OLIVES and GRAPES, two of Israel's most important crops.

ASHERAH

(uh SHEER uh)

"Summon all Israel to join me at Mount Carmel, along with the 450 prophets of Baal and the 400 prophets of Asherah who are supported by Jezebel." Prophet Elijah to King Ahab, 1 Kings 18:19

- Fertility goddess
- A favorite of evil Queen Jezebel
- Humiliated in a contest hosted by Elijah

DIVINE LOVER of Canaan's top god El, Asherah was worshiped throughout the ancient Middle East as a fertility goddess who knew what she was doing—since she was the mother of 70 GODS. Though some writings link her to El, others such as the BIBLE link her to BAAL, as though El took a new name or got bumped aside.

ISRAEL's queen JEZEBEL tried to replace the Jewish religion by killing God's PROPHETS and throwing her support behind the prophets of Baal and Asherah. ELIJAH dealt Jezebel a huge blow when he defeated her prophets in a contest to call down fire from the sky. The JEWS mobbed and killed 850 of them after Elijah won.

The Bible says shrines devoted to Asherah included sacred poles described as "obscene" (1 Kings 15:13). No one seems to know what purpose the poles served.

ASHES

Tamar tore her robe and put ashes on her head. 2 Samuel 13:19

JUST AS SOME PEOPLE today wear black clothes when they're MOURNING, people in Bible times blackened themselves with ashes. It was a way to express sorrow or humiliation.

Ashes seemed like a perfect metaphor to express loss, since ashes are all that's left after complete DESTRUCTION.

JOB, after losing his CHILDREN, his health, and his herds, "sat among the ashes" (Job 2:8). King DAVID's daughter, TAMAR, covered herself in ashes after her half-brother raped her.

ASHKELON

Map 1 A6

(ASH kah lawn)

Samson went down to the city of Ashkelon and killed thirty of its men. Judges 14:19 NCV

- Largest Philistine city

THE ONLY MAJOR PHILISTINE CITY with a beach, Ashkelon was the largest and the busiest of the top five. That's partly because it sat on the main coastal trade route to EGYPT: the Way of the Sea.

The city is most famous because of SAMSON. He bet his 30 Philistine WEDDING guests a change of clothes that they couldn't solve a RIDDLE he told them. They got the answer from his BRIDE—by threatening to kill her. Livid, Samson stormed off to Ashkelon where he killed and stripped 30 PHILISTINES to pay off his DEBT. Today the city lies about 30 miles (50 km) south of Tel Aviv, and just north of the Palestinian Gaza Strip.

ASHURBANIPAL

(ASH ur BAN up pul)

Ruled about 668–626 BC

The great King Ashurbanipal, who is worthy of honor, forced them to leave. He settled them in the city of Samaria. Ezra 4:10 NIrv

- Last great king of the Assyrian Empire
- Created first known library in Middle East: clay tablets
- Captured Jewish king Manasseh

HE SHOWS UP in the BIBLE just once—as a passing reference in a LETTER of complaint. Non-Jews had moved to what is now northern ISRAEL, apparently on orders of Ashurbanipal some 200 years earlier. The land was available because Assyrians had defeated and deported the Jews. But now with Persians in charge, the Jews were free and coming back to reclaim their land. Non-Jews living there wrote a letter of complaint to the new king of the Middle East, ARTAXERXES of the Persian Empire.

Records from Ashurbanipal's library claim he captured King MANASSEH. The Bible confirms that "the Assyrian armies. . .took Manasseh prisoner. They put a RING through his nose, bound him in BRONZE chains, and led him away to BABYLON" (2 Chronicles 33:11).

ASIA

Map 3 F3

(A sha)

People throughout the province of Asia—both Jews and Greeks—heard the word of the Lord. Acts 19:10

- Roman province in west Turkey

ASIA didn't include China and Japan. Not in Bible times. Romans gave that name to a province on the western end of what is now Turkey. Before that, it was known as the kingdom of Pergamos, headquartered in the city of PERGAMUM and ruled by a dynasty known as "the kings of Asia." Romans moved the capital to EPHESUS, where PAUL spent about three years starting a CHURCH.

ASSYRIAN KING Ashurbanipal hunts lions in style, riding in a chariot and protected by attendants. The art is from his palace and dates to his reign in the mid-600s BC.

ASIA MINOR
Map 3 I3

(A sha)

"Artemis will be weakened. Now she is worshiped through all of Asia Minor and the whole world." Acts 19:27 NIrV

- Turkey

IT'S THE TURKISH PENINSULA, surrounded on three sides by water: Black Sea in the north, Aegean Sea in the west, MEDITERRANEAN SEA in the south. It's also known as Anatolia.

ASPHALT
(see TAR)

ASSASSINS

"Aren't you the Egyptian who led a rebellion. . . and took 4,000 members of the Assassins out into the desert?" Roman solider to Paul, Acts 21:38

WHEN THE ROMAN EMPIRE occupied the Jewish homeland, a group of militant JEWS fought for independence by assassinating Romans along with Jewish collaborators. They earned the name *Sicarii*, which means "DAGGER men." They preferred daggers, which were easy to hide, easy to use, and lethal. These assassins could find their targets in a crowd, stab them, and walk away.

Romans once arrested the apostle PAUL in JERUSALEM, thinking he was a leader of one band of rebels.

In other Bible stories, assassins were:

- independent contractors—killers for hire (2 Kings 14:19)
- people who didn't like their leaders and decided to kill them (2 Kings 12:20)

43

ASSHUR (OR ASHUR)

(ASH ur)

The Tigris, flowed east of the land of Asshur.
Genesis 2:14

- Descendant of Noah's son Shem
- Ancestor of the Assyrians
- Ancient name of Assyria in what is now Iraq
- Name of Assyrian god

ASSHUR, a descendant of NOAH's son SHEM, is considered the father of what is now Iraq—land on the west side of the TIGRIS RIVER.

ASSYRIA

(uh SEER ee uh)

Peak power 800s–612 BC

- World's first superpower
- Based in what is now Iraq
- Terrorized Middle East off and on for centuries
- Wiped Israel off the world map in 722 BC

THE LOST TRIBES of Israel are lost because of Assyria.

Based in what is now northern Iraq, with NINEVEH as one of its capitals, the Assyrian Empire erased the northern Jewish nation of Israel from the map. They EX-ILED Jewish survivors, who were never heard from again. And they repopulated the Jewish homeland with their own settlers.

That's the BIBLE's headline about the world's first megaempire.

About the time some Bible experts say MOSES lived—in the 1400s BC—Assyria emerged as a kingdom of cities and tribes in northern Iraq and neighboring parts of Turkey and SYRIA. But it wasn't until after King SOLOMON died, when Israel split into two nations, that Assyria got greedy—or religious, if you believe their king Ashurnasirpal II (reigned 883–858 BC). He said he started conquering neighbor nations to enlighten them about Assyria's chief god, Ashur. But based on the taxes he imposed on those conquered nations, some say he wanted to lighten them. Of GOLD. And SILVER. And anything else that would fund his empire.

Israel died because their king, HOSHEA, made the mistake of not paying his Assyrian taxes. He joined a

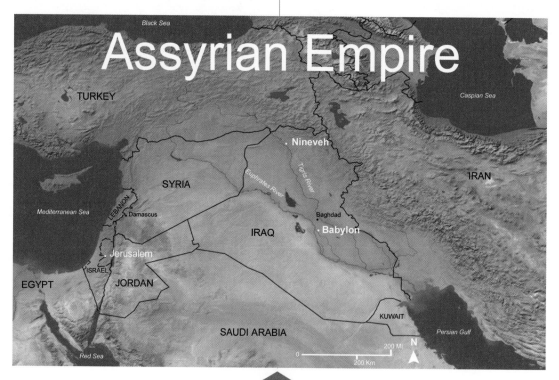

rebel movement that challenged Assyria's new king, SHALMANESER V (ruled 726–721 BC). Hoshea and his allies apparently figured Shalmaneser was more interested in hanging out in his palace than in fighting wars and collecting taxes.

Wrong.

"In the ninth year of Hoshea's reign the king of Assyria captured SAMARIA and took the people into exile in Assyria" (2 Kings 17:6 MSG).

ASTROLOGY

(as STRAH luh gee)

"Disaster strikes. . . . Call in the astrologers and stargazers. . . . Surely they can work up something! Fat chance." Isaiah 47:11, 13–15 MSG

- A unique star led wise men to Bethlehem
- Prophets portrayed it as unreliable

JUST AS GRAVITATIONAL PULL from the sun and moon can affect ocean tides, astrologers have argued the movement of stars and planets can affect human beings, who are more than 50 percent water.

PROPHETS mocked astrologers and lumped them with "magicians, enchanters, sorcerers" (Daniel 2:2).

ATHALIAH

(ath uh LIE uh)

Ruled about 842–837 BC

As soon as Athaliah heard that her son King Ahaziah was dead, she decided to kill any relative who could possibly become king. 2 Kings 11:1 CEV

- Daughter of King Ahab
- Queen of Judah
- Killed her grandkids so she could be queen

SHE SOUNDS like the daughter of ISRAEL's queen of mean, JEZEBEL. And she may have been. But the BIBLE identifies her only as the daughter of King AHAB, husband of Jezebel and perhaps other women.

A PRINCESS from Ahab's northern nation of Israel, Athaliah married a KING from the southern Jewish nation of JUDAH. In time, her son became king. But he picked

the wrong time to visit his counterpart in Israel—during a military coup. Both kings died in a sneak attack, killed by JEHU. When Athaliah got the word that her son was dead, she wiped out everyone in her FAMILY and declared herself ruler of Judah.

Killer Granny missed one grandson: JOASH, a baby. The HIGH PRIEST, Jehoiada, hid Joash at the TEMPLE until the boy reached age seven. Then the priest invited the commanders and palace guards to the Temple and introduced them to the boy king. With their approval and protection the priest declared Joash king—to cheering crowds at the Temple.

When Athaliah realized what was happening, she yelled "Treason!" On the priest's order, soldiers executed her.

ATHEIST

(ATH ee ist)

Ever since the world was created, people have seen the earth and sky. Through everything God made, they can clearly see his invisible qualities. . . . So they have no excuse for not knowing God. Romans 1:20

ATHEISTS are folks who deny the existence of GOD. The GREEK word for "atheists," *atheoi*, shows up only once in the BIBLE. Most modern Bible translations skip the word, though, and translate the idea instead: people "without God and without hope" (Ephesians 2:12).

ATHENS

Map 3 B4

(ATH inns)

Inhabited before 3000 BC

All the Athenians as well as the foreigners in Athens seemed to spend all their time discussing the latest ideas. Acts 17:21

- Birthplace of democracy
- Philosopher's paradise
- Laughed Paul out of town

BY THE TIME the apostle PAUL arrived in Athens in about AD 50, the town had earned itself a reputation as the world's best hangout for brainiacs. It was there that forward thinkers had invented democracy 500 years earlier.

45

Paul wasn't impressed.

He was bummed—"deeply troubled by all the IDOLS he saw everywhere in the city" (Acts 17:16).

He had stopped in Athens on a layover, waiting for his associates to catch up with him so he could move on down the Greek coast, where he would start a CHURCH in CORINTH. While waiting, he went to the local SYNAGOGUE. There he talked with JEWS and GOD-loving non-Jews about Jesus. He talked with some philosophers, too. His new-fangled ideas about the MESSIAH intrigued the people. He ended up addressing a meeting of philosophers.

Paul had them at hello, offering to tell them about the "Unknown God"—a name inscribed on one of the city's sacred altars.

He lost them when he said this God raised Jesus from the dead.

Many Greeks taught that the SOUL was immortal. But no respected Greek said the body was immortal. The idea that a corpse could rise from a slab, and then walk, talk, and eat—that was stand-up comedy. Many laughed at Paul. Some believed, though apparently not enough to keep him in town.

ATHLETICS

Run to win! All athletes are disciplined in their training. They do it to win a prize.
1 Corinthians 9:24–25

AFTER VISITING CORINTH, the apostle PAUL started referring to athletic contests to make spiritual points. That's probably no coincidence. Athletes met on the Corinthian isthmus every two years. There they competed in Olympic-style events called the Isthmian GAMES. Bible-era art shows athletes in what may have been some of the more popular events: footraces, wrestling, boxing, and CHARIOT racing.

Paul told his close friend, TIMOTHY, PASTOR of the CHURCH at EPHESUS, "Athletes cannot win the prize unless they follow the rules" (2 Timothy 2:5). He also wrote Christians at CORINTH, comparing a track meet to the RACE of life. He said athletes run their race for "a prize that will fade away. . .we do it for an eternal prize" (1 Corinthians 9:25).

ATONEMENT

(uh TONE ment)

Priests then killed the goats as a sin offering. . .to make atonement for the sins of all Israel. 2 Chronicles 29:24

- Spiritually clean slate

ATONEMENT is religious tech talk. It refers to the kind of do-over some first-time offenders get when their criminal records are "expunged"—destroyed.

GOD set up a sacrificial system in OLD TESTAMENT times that gave JEWS a fresh start after they sinned—assuming they didn't commit a capital offense like MURDER, which required the death penalty.

In a way, Jewish offenders would plead guilty by admitting their SIN. They would take an ANIMAL to the WORSHIP center and SACRIFICE it. As God explained to MOSES, "I have given you the BLOOD on the ALTAR to purify you, making you right with the LORD" (Leviticus 17:11).

NEW TESTAMENT writers said the sacrificial death of Jesus changed the way God forgives people. Atonement 2.0. "We are made fit for God by the once-for-all sacrifice of Jesus" (Hebrews 10:10 MSG).

In other words, folks don't have to sacrifice SHEEP and GOATS to get forgiven. PAUL told Christians in ROME that God "declares sinners to be right in his sight when they believe in Jesus" (Romans 3:26).

ATTALIA   Map 3 H4

(at uh LIE uh)

They [Paul and Barnabas] preached the word in Perga, then went down to Attalia.
Acts 14:25

MODERN-DAY ANTALYA, Attalia was a seaport city in south Turkey. PAUL and BARNABAS passed through there on their first missionary trip. With its subtropical climate, it was swampy and humid in Paul's day—a great place to get malaria.

AUGUSTUS

(uh GUS tus)

Ruled 27 BC–AD 14

And it came to pass in those days, that there went out a decree from Caesar Augustus that all the world should be taxed. Luke 2:1 KJV

- Emperor of Roman Empire
- Census he ordered led to Jesus' birth in Bethlehem
- Adopted son of Julius Caesar
- Defeated armies of Antony and Cleopatra

BY ORDERING A CENSUS, Caesar Augustus helped fulfill a 700-year-old prophecy:

> *"Bethlehem, you might not be an important town in the nation of Judah. But out of you will come a ruler over Israel for me"* (Micah 5:2 NIRV).

Joseph had to check in at his ancestral hometown: Bethlehem, hometown of his most famous ancestor, King David. He took his wife, Mary, with him. She gave birth to Jesus in that tiny, hilltop village.

CAESAR AUGUSTUS ordered the census that sent Joseph and Mary to Bethlehem, where Mary gave birth to Jesus.

AVENGER

"The victim's nearest relative. . .the avenger must put the murderer to death."
Numbers 35:19

BEFORE JEWS HAD KINGS, courts, and executioners, city leaders heard arguments for and against defendants. Jewish law demanded that if a person was found guilty of murder, the city leaders had to turn the convict over to the executioner: a family member of the victim— known as the avenger. This avenger is the person who had accepted the job of making sure justice was served.

People who killed someone unintentionally could flee to one of six cities of refuge scattered throughout the Jewish homeland. There they could escape the avenger long enough to seek a fair trial. But if convicted of murder, they found themselves at the mercy of the victim's family in a day when the rule of thumb was "a life for a life, an eye for an eye, a tooth for a tooth" (Exodus 21:23–24).

See also City of Refuge.

AZARIAH

(as zar I uh)

Azariah was called Abednego. Daniel 1:7

AN ALL-TOO-COMMON Jewish name in ancient times, "Azariah" IDs nearly 30 different men in the Bible. Ironically, perhaps the most famous of them isn't best known by that name. People who know their Bible stories remember him as one of three Jews who survived execution in a furnace: Shadrach, Meshach, and Abednego. Those were their Babylonian names. "Azariah" is also another name for Uzziah, king of Judah.

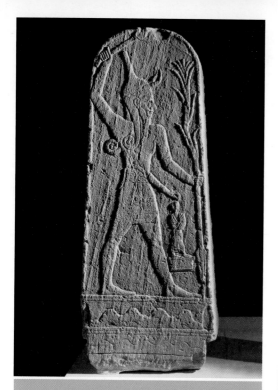

BAAL packs a lightning bolt, as god of weather. Yet he didn't send fire from heaven when Elijah challenged Baal's prophets to a duel: God vs. Baal. Elijah said Baal may have been using the toilet.

people worshiped him was to entertain him with SEX rituals. Gross as it sounds, they taught that the RAIN was his semen. They apparently figured if they could stimulate him enough, he'd send the rain.

ISRAEL's queen of mean, JEZEBEL, tried to execute all of God's PROPHETS and replace them with prophets devoted to her preferred GODS: Baal and ASHERAH. God's prophet ELIJAH challenged them to a contest of the gods—one that favored thunderbolt-toting Baal. The prophets would build an ALTAR, sacrifice an ANIMAL, and then call down fire from heaven to burn the sacrifice.

Lone Elijah succeeded where 450 prophets of Baal and 400 prophets of Asherah failed. Afterward, the Jewish crowd who came to watch executed Jezebel's prophets (1 Kings 18:40).

BAAL-HAZOR   Map 1 D5

(BAY ul HAY zor)

Absalom's sheep were being sheared at Baal-hazor near Ephraim. 2 Samuel 13:23

- Where Absalom had his half brother murdered

THIS IS WHERE King DAVID's oldest son, AMNON, paid with his life for raping his half sister TAMAR. Avenging Tamar's honor was her full brother ABSALOM. He waited two years then invited Amnon to a sheepshearing festival in the hills about 12 miles (19 km) northeast of King David's capital city, JERUSALEM. Today Baal-hazor is the West Bank site known in Arabic as *Jebel el-Asur*, Mountain of Hazor. There Absalom ordered his SERVANTS to wait until Amnon got drunk and then to kill him.

BAAL

(BAY ul)

Elijah said to them, "I am the only prophet of the LORD who is left, but Baal has 450 prophets." 1 Kings 18:22

- God of fertility in families, fields, flocks
- 450 prophets of Baal executed after losing contest with God's prophet
- A preferred god of Queen Jezebel

BAAL, a god worshiped throughout the ancient Middle East, carried a rod that looked like a thunderbolt. That's how some ancient artists portrayed him in stone engravings and figurines.

He could have accessorized a thunderbolt quite nicely since he was the god of rainstorms. Canaanites in what is now ISRAEL said he was the go-to god for growing just about anything: crops, herds, or a house full of kids.

Some Bible experts speculate that one of the ways

BAAL-PEOR   Location Uncertain

(BAY ul PEE or)

"You saw for yourself what the LORD did to you at Baal-peor. There the LORD your God destroyed everyone who had worshiped Baal." Deuteronomy 4:3

- Mountain where Balaam blessed Exodus Jews
- Where Moabite women seduced Jewish men

AT A MOUNTAIN known as Baal-peor, somewhere east of the JORDAN RIVER in what is now Jordan, the JEWS following MOSES on their final leg to the PROMISED LAND experienced a MIRACLE one day and a PLAGUE another.

Miracle: MOAB's king hired a seer named BALAAM to stand on the mountain and pronounce a CURSE on the approaching Jews. Balaam blessed them instead.

Plague: Afterward crowds of Moabite women seduced Hebrew men into what was probably ritual SEX, to worship the fertility god BAAL of Peor. GOD sent a plague on the Jews, killing 24,000.

BAASHA

(BAY ah sha)

Ruled about 900–877 BC

Baasha killed Nadab. . .and succeeded him as king. 1 Kings 15:28 TNIV

- King of the northern Jewish nation of Israel
- Became king by assassinating previous king

THIRD KING of the northern Jewish nation of ISRAEL, Baasha started the violent tradition of replacing kings by murdering them. He became king by killing the son and successor of Israel's founding KING—killing Nadab, son of JEROBOAM I. It might seem fitting that Baasha's dynasty ended when his own son and successor, Elah, was assassinated.

BABEL, TOWER OF

(BAY bull)

"Come, let's build a great city for ourselves with a tower that reaches into the sky. This will make us famous." Genesis 11:4

THE TOWER OF BABEL was probably a stair step pyramid called a ZIGGURAT, some Bible experts speculate. A temple crowned the top. A couple of dozen have survived the ages—some dating as far back as about 2200 BC, perhaps a century before ABRAHAM. That puts them during the world's first known empire: SUMER, in what is now Iraq.

The BIBLE says people all spoke the same language when they settled in what is now southern Iraq. There

they decided to build a TOWER in honor of themselves.

GOD vetoed their plans. He made them speak in different languages. That put the skids on the construction job, since they couldn't understand each other.

The Bible says that's how the city came to be called *Babylon*, which sounds like the HEBREW word for "confusion." When they tried to talk, all they could do was babble on. The citizens scattered abroad by language groups.

BABYLON'S BEST YEARS, under King Nebuchadnezzar, became the Jewish nation's worst. Babylon invaded the Jewish homeland, leveled Jerusalem, and deported the Jews. The Jewish nation was gone.

BABYLON   Map 2 L7

(BABB uh lawn)

Peak power 605–562 BC

"The time is coming when everything in your palace. . .will be carried off to Babylon." 2 Kings 20:17

- Created world's first known set of laws: Code of Hammurabi (see photo, page 116)
- Overpowered world's first superpower: Assyrian Empire
- Ruled by King Nebuchadnezzar (605–562 BC)
- Wiped the Jewish nation off the map (586 BC)
- Leveled Jerusalem, exiled Jewish survivors
- Defeated by Persian Empire (539 BC)

ONE OF THE GREATEST CITIES in the ancient world—and reportedly home to one of the Seven Wonders of the World—Babylon now lies in ruins on the outskirts of greater Baghdad, some 55 miles (88 km) south.

In Bible times, Babylon was both a city and an empire. Its "Wonder" was the Hanging Gardens—a forest-covered artificial mountain. King NEBUCHADNEZZAR reportedly built it for his queen, a mountain woman who had moved to the pancake plains of Iraq from her home in the hills of Iran. Think Rocky Mountain gal moving to Kansas. And regretting it.

Archaeologists say prehistoric people lived in Babylon as early as 5000 BC, though the name doesn't show up until the 2200s BC—perhaps a century before ABRAHAM.

At least 300 years before MOSES gave JEWS the 10 COMMANDMENTS and hundreds of other rules, a lawgiver king named Hammurabi (ruled 1792–1750 BC) conquered city kingdoms throughout what is now southern

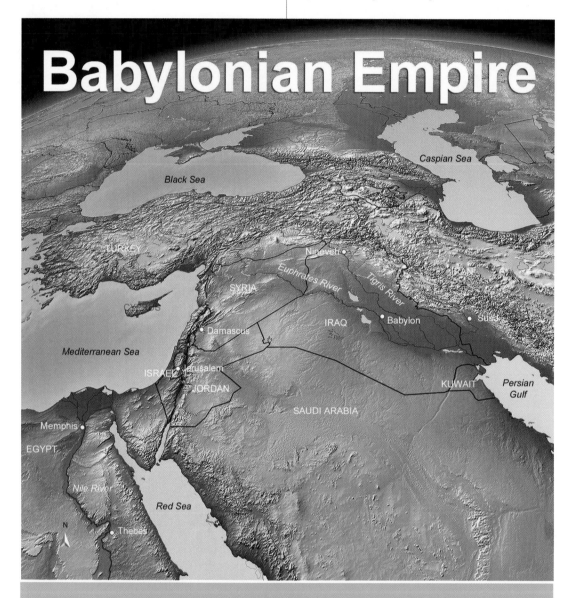

▲ A MIDDLE EAST SUPERPOWER, the Iraqi-based Babylonian Empire dominated the Fertile Crescent from the Persian Gulf to the Nile River.

Iraq. He declared his hometown of Babylon capital of his growing empire.

Hammurabi's dreams for Babylon—both the city and the empire—died with him. Regional tribes squabbled for power. Assyrians in northern Iraq eventually gained the advantage and emerged as the world's first superpower—controlling and bullying much of the Middle East.

Civil wars erupted, eroding ASSYRIA's power—enough that in 612 BC the Babylonians were able to destroy the Assyrian capital of NINEVEH. They hunted down the retreating Assyrian ARMY and finished it off at the battle of CARCHEMISH in what is now southern Turkey, near the Syrian border.

The victorious king would become Babylon's strongest and most famous ruler: Nebuchadnezzar.

Under his rule, the city of Babylon never looked better.

Babylon's eye-catching landmark was a 30-story ZIGGURAT—a pyramid-like TOWER topped with a blue temple devoted to the nation's god, Marduk. Massive double walls and a ditch surrounded the city of 4 square miles (10 square km). The EUPHRATES RIVER ran through the heart of the town, providing a reliable source of fresh WATER.

Like the Assyrians, Babylonians ran a protection racket. They bullied nations throughout the Middle East into paying taxes. When the nations refused, the rebels paid a high price. JUDAH—the last surviving Jewish nation—got wiped off the world map in 586 BC, compliments of Nebuchadnezzar's army. JERUSALEM and its majestic TEMPLE got leveled. Surviving Jews were deported to Babylon, so they couldn't resurrect their nation.

Some 50 years later, though, Babylon fell to an invasion force of Persians and Medes from what is now Iran. Then PERSIA fell to the Greeks, led by ALEXANDER the Great (336–323 BC). Impressed with Babylon, Alexander planned to renovate the city. He died trying, at age 33. He may have partied himself to death, some say. He got sick after a prolonged bout of drinking and eating.

BACKSLIDER

If you know people who have wandered off from God's truth, don't write them off. Go after them. Get them back and you will have rescued precious lives from destruction.
James 5:19–20 MSG

BACKSLIDER is Christian tech talk for a person who once claimed to be CHRISTIAN but who left the FAITH. Some CHURCH groups say the person was never a Christian to begin with, because "once saved, always saved"—more tech talk.

These Christians base their argument on selected Bible verses, including something Jesus said: "My sheep listen to my voice. . . . I give them ETERNAL LIFE, and they will never perish. No one can snatch them away from me" (John 10:27–28).

Others say GOD gives us the freedom to walk away if we want to.

See also FREE WILL, PREDESTINATION.

BAG

She gave him some milk from a leather bag.
Judges 4:19

BAGS in Bible times were stitched together from cloth or LEATHER. People used small bags like purses to carry

GOATSKIN BAG on her back, a Bethlehem woman carries water in the 1930s much as folks did in Bible times.

MONEY or ammo sacks to carry stones for a slingshot. They used large bags to carry GRAIN or vegetables. Folks carried WATER and WINE canteen-style in leather bags such as waterproof goatskins sewn tight.

BAKING

For bread they baked flat cakes from the dough without yeast. Exodus 12:39

BREAD was the main food in Bible times. Baking it was woman's work—except in towns that had bakeries. In most cases, though, each FAMILY baked its own BREAD.

WOMEN used flat stones to grind WHEAT or BARLEY kernels into powdery FLOUR. They mixed the flour with water, OLIVE OIL, SALT, and yeast, though they would skip the yeast if they were making flat bread. After shaping the bread and letting it rise, they would slide it like a pizza onto a tray in a clay oven. The oven was usually shaped like a wart sitting on the ground, rising about 3 feet (1 m) high. The oven pulled double duty, working sometimes as a KILN to harden POTTERY.

See also COOKING.

BALAAM

(BAY lum)

1400s BC or 1200s BC (debated)

Balak's messengers. . .set out with money to pay Balaam to place a curse upon Israel.
Numbers 22:7

- Respected as a seer with power to change the future
- Hired to curse Israel, he blessed them instead
- Name found on ancient inscription, 700 BC
- Died in company of idol worshipers

BALAAM was a hired gun who used words instead of bullets.

Some folks—kings included—thought he could wipe out an entire nation with little more than a sentence. All he had to do was put a CURSE on them.

Balaam enjoyed a whopper of a reputation—one that carried his name at least 400 miles (644 km). That's how far south he traveled, hired to put a curse on MOSES and the JEWS of the EXODUS who were headed to what is now ISRAEL.

▲ BAKING ALL-NATURAL BREAD, even the oven is natural. It's made from dirt, in this photo from the 1930s. People in Bible times used similar ovens, in a process that resembles making pizzas today.

Balaam lived near the EUPHRATES RIVER on the border of what is now Turkey and Syria. But he was hired by King BALAK of MOAB, in what is now Jordan, to put a curse on the approaching Jews. Only then would King Balak feel good about unleashing his ARMY on such a massive invasion force.

GOD sent an ANGEL to block Balaam's path. At first, only Balaam's DONKEY could see the angel. It's a tad funny that with God's help a jackass could see what a famous seer couldn't. The donkey stopped. Balaam beat the animal. The donkey talked: "Have I ever done anything like this before?" (Numbers 22:30). Then Balaam saw the angel.

At the angel's command, Balaam refused to curse the Jews. He blessed them instead, four times, predicting their victory.

Balaam was dead right.

He died in a battle when the Jews attacked Moab's neighboring nation of MIDIAN. It was a punitive action for luring some Jews into SEX rituals for an idol (Numbers 25).

Archaeologists found evidence of Balaam: a 2,700-year-old plaster inscription that describes Balaam as "seer of the GODS." It's written in a language that seems like a mixture of Canaanite and ARAMAIC—languages that would have been spoken in the area where Balaam's story played out.

BALAK

(BAY lack)

1400s BC or 1200s BC (debated)

Then Balak said to Balaam, "What have you done to me?" Numbers 23:11 NKJV

- King of Moab in what is now Jordan
- Hired a seer to put curse on the Jews

WHEN MOSES led the JEWS out of EGYPT, northward through what is now Jordan, they intended to pass peacefully through MOAB. But Moab's king, Balak, apparently feared that this massive swarm of humanity would turn mean and loot the country. So he hired a seer, BALAAM, to put a CURSE on the Jews—intending to attack them afterward. Balaam blessed the Jews instead, at GOD's insistence. Balak quickly backed off his WAR plans.

BALANCES

"You cheat others by using dishonest scales."
Amos 8:5 NIrV

BALANCE SCALES show up in Egyptian pictures from 7,000 years ago. People used them to measure precious metals such as GOLD and SILVER, along with food they were buying or selling.

If someone wanted to buy a pound of FLOUR, for example, the MERCHANT would put a one-pound weight in the pan on one side of the SCALE. Then he poured flour into the pan on the opposite scale until the scale leveled out.

If merchants wanted to cheat customers—and PROPHETS said that happened all too often—they could use a smaller weight that they labeled with a lie, saying it weighed one pound. So the customer might get just three-fourths of a pound of flour, while paying for a pound.

BALANCE SCALES from Pompeii, in New Testament times. It was possible for merchants to cheat customers by rigging the scales or by using mislabeled counterweights.

BALDNESS

> *Elisha. . .went up to Bethel. . . . A group of boys from the town began mocking and making fun of him. "Go away, baldy!" they chanted.* 2 Kings 2:23

BALDNESS was nothing to brag about in Bible times, if the metaphors it generated are any clue.

- Poverty: "Her elegant HAIR will fall out" (Isaiah 3:24).
- Sorrow: "They will wail. . .shaving their heads in sorrow" (Isaiah 15:2).
- Regret: "SHAVE your heads in sorrow for your sins" (Isaiah 22:12).

When a bunch of boys teased the prophet ELISHA about his bald head, he put a CURSE on them. Suddenly, two bears charged out of the woods and mauled 42 of the boys.

BALM

> *"Stuff your packs with the finest products from the land you can find and take them to the man as gifts—some balm and honey, some spices and perfumes."* Genesis 43:11 MSG

FRAGRANT SAP from the balsam tree (*Commiphora gileadensis*) produced balm. People mixed it with OLIVE OIL to make PERFUME. They also used it in creams to treat wounds—as illustrated by one prophet's sarcasm: "Is there no balm in GILEAD? Is there no physician there?" (Jeremiah 8:22 TNIV). JOSEPH's brothers used balm as currency to buy GRAIN from EGYPT when there was a DROUGHT in ISRAEL.

BANKING

> *"Why didn't you deposit my money in the bank? At least I could have gotten some interest on it."* Luke 19:23

THERE WASN'T MUCH PROFIT in Jew-on-Jew banking.

The problem? One of the laws MOSES gave them:

> *"If you lend money to any of my people who are in need, do not charge interest as a money lender would. If you take your neighbor's cloak as security for a loan, you must return it before sunset."* (Exodus 22:25–26).

Banking as we know it developed a few centuries before Jesus, partly because of the invention of coins. Earlier, livestock, crops, and other products served as currency.

JEWS apparently picked up the banking trade sometime after their 586 BC EXILE in what is now Iraq. Over the centuries, they saw banking at work among Babylonians, Persians, Greeks, and Romans.

Most Jewish bankers apparently honored their law, refusing to charge interest to fellow Jews. They made their profit on non-Jews. Others created loopholes around the law. For example, they would give a LOAN to a fellow Jew in exchange for a limited amount of the profit—which they didn't call interest.

Banking was common enough in Jesus' day that he referred to it in a PARABLE about a SERVANT who buried his master's MONEY rather than risk losing it in an investment.

BANQUET

> *"Queen Esther invited only me [Haman] and the king himself to the banquet she prepared for us."* Esther 5:12

WE'D CALL THEM dinner parties. In Bible times, people hosted them for lots of reasons:

- Honor a guest.
- Celebrate a wedding.
- Rejoice on the big paydays of harvest or sheepshearing.

Kings sometimes hosted a banquet just to show off their how rich they were. Persian King XERXES threw a six-month bash for all of his top officials.

His WIFE, Queen ESTHER, later hosted a private banquet for him and his prime minister, HAMAN—to out Haman as a Jew-killer plotting a holocaust. Since Esther was a Jew, the king decided to kill Haman before Haman killed her.

Jesus' first MIRACLE took place at a WEDDING banquet. He turned water into WINE (John 2:1–11).

Jesus also worked banquets into some of his PARABLES. Perhaps the most famous: the story of the PRODIGAL SON. When the bad boy came home, the FATHER was so happy to see him that he said, "Kill the calf we have been fattening. We must celebrate with a feast" (Luke 15:23).

BAPTISM

"I [John the Baptist] baptize with water those who repent of their sins and turn to God." Matthew 3:11

CHRISTIANS get baptized in WATER: immersed, sprinkled, or poured—different churches use different techniques. Baptism symbolizes that GOD has washed away the person's sins.

It is one of CHRISTIANITY's most important rituals, along with the LORD'S SUPPER, which is also known as COMMUNION or Mass.

JOHN THE BAPTIST was the first to baptize people. He reserved baptism for those who repented of their sins and promised to devote themselves to God.

Though John's ritual was unique, JEWS would have

BAPTISM IN A BELL. Aboard the USS *Kitty Hawk* aircraft carrier, Chaplain Michael L. Schutz baptizes Ellen Bernard in the ship's bell. It's a navy tradition.

seen the similarities with other PURIFICATION rituals. Jews could become spiritually contaminated and unfit to WORSHIP in the TEMPLE if, for example, they touched a corpse. To cleanse themselves, they had to take a ritual BATH. Jews in the QUMRAN community that created the famous DEAD SEA SCROLLS took ritual baths every day.

John's baptism, however, wasn't a ritual purification. The person was pure before hitting the water. Baptism was more like a wet badge of courage. Dripping, people pledged their allegiance to God and declared war on SIN.

John baptized his relative Jesus. Scholars can only guess why Jesus allowed himself to be baptized, since the BIBLE says, "He never sinned" (1 Peter 2:22). Jesus explained, "It should be done, for we must carry out all that God requires" (Matthew 3:15). Perhaps God wanted him to serve as an example for others, some scholars guess.

From day one—the day Jesus' DISCIPLES launched the CHRISTIAN movement—these leaders baptized anyone who wanted to join the CHURCH, as though it's part of the induction ceremony. "Those who believed what PETER said were baptized and added to the church that day—about 3,000 in all" (Acts 2:41).

Some Christians say baptism is a requirement for anyone becoming a Christian. Others say that FAITH in Jesus is our saving grace (John 3:16).

BARABBAS

(bah RABB us)

First century AD

Barabbas was in prison for taking part in an insurrection in Jerusalem against the government, and for murder. Luke 23:19

▪ Murderer released instead of Jesus

ROMAN GOVERNOR Pilate gave his Jewish crowd a choice. In honor of PASSOVER, he would release one prisoner: Jesus, a pacifist RABBI—or Barabbas, a murderer, robber, and revolutionary. PILATE was trying to manipulate the frenzied crowd into letting him free Jesus, whom he considered innocent. Didn't work. The crowd picked Barabbas. All four GOSPELS—MATTHEW, MARK, LUKE, and JOHN—report this story.

A FUNERAL PORTRAIT of a man from Roman times. Barabbas—a murderer—would likely have been one dead Jew had it not been for Jesus. When the Roman governor offered the Jewish crowd a choice of which criminal to free as a goodwill gesture on Passover, the crowd chose the murderer over the rabbi.

BARAK

(BAY rack)

1100s BC

Barak called together the tribes. . .10,000 warriors went up with him. Deborah also went. Judges 4:10

- Commander of Israelite army
- Refused to go to war unless Deborah went with him

CHICKENHEARTED GENERAL, Barak refused to go to WAR unless a woman went with him.

That's the headline most remember, though it might be a bit unfair.

The woman he wanted at his side wasn't just his boss, who had declared war. She was DEBORAH, a prophet. Typically, Jewish generals wanted assurance that GOD was going with them into battle. There's no better assurance than to take God's spokesperson along for the ride.

Deborah wasn't flattered.

"Very well," she replied, "I will go with you. But you will receive no honor in this venture, for the LORD's victory over SISERA will be at the hands of a woman" (Judges 4:9).

Sisera was the enemy commander. He died at the hands of a woman who knew how to accessorize a TENT peg and a hammer. Sisera, on the run from a lost battle, sought refuge in the tent of this woman, JAEL, a nomad.

Jael apparently pegged him as an enemy, so she pegged him literally. While he slept, she hammered the tent peg into his temple.

BAR-JESUS

(BAR GEES us)

First century AD

Barnabas and Saul. . .sailed for the island of Cyprus. . .where they met a Jewish sorcerer, a false prophet named Bar-Jesus. Acts 13:4, 6

BAR-JESUS urged the Roman governor of CYPRUS, SERGIUS PAULUS, to ignore missionaries BARNABAS and Saul (better known as PAUL). "You son of the devil," Saul replied. "You will be struck blind" (Acts 13:10–11). And he was. That got the GOVERNOR's attention. He became the first Roman official on record to convert to CHRISTIANITY.

BARLEY

(BAR lee)

Ruth gathered barley there all day, and when she beat out the grain that evening, it filled an entire basket. Ruth 2:17

A POOR MAN'S WHEAT. That's barley. It tastes so bland that when people mixed up a batch of barley BREAD, they usually added FLOUR from another GRAIN, such as the more expensive WHEAT. Barley had a couple advantages over wheat:

- harvested first, in late April and May
- heartier, and more likely to survive heat and DROUGHT.

Jesus fed a crowd of thousands with just "five barley loaves and two fish" (John 6:9). RUTH married a farmer named BOAZ after he let her take the leftovers from his barley HARVEST.

BARN

"I'll tear down my barns and build bigger ones. Then I'll have room enough to store all my wheat." Luke 12:18

BARNS in the BIBLE weren't like barns today, built to house ANIMALS and hay. They were storage sheds built to hold GRAIN and other produce—more like silos or granaries.

BARNABAS

(BARN uh bus)

First century AD

Joseph was one of the followers. . . . The apostles called him Barnabas, which means "one who encourages others." Acts 4:36–37 CEV

- Paul's missionary colleague
- Pastored the group first called "Christians"
- Sold land and gave the money to the poor
- Split with Paul over a second mission trip

BEFORE PAUL took the story of Jesus to non-Jews, Barnabas was already on the job.

The DISCIPLES had heard about a group of believers in ANTIOCH, SYRIA, about 300 miles (about 500 km) north of JERUSALEM. So they sent Barnabas to check it out. They trusted him partly because he had sold some land and then donated the MONEY to help the POOR.

Barnabas ended up leading the CHURCH and recruiting PAUL to help. "It was at Antioch that the believers were first called Christians" (Acts 11:26).

During a prayer meeting, they felt compelled by the HOLY SPIRIT to take the story of Jesus on the road. So the two of them sailed first to Barnabas's homeland: the island of CYPRUS. There they started churches and converted the Roman governor, SERGIUS PAULUS. Then they moved on to the area near where Paul grew up, in what is now southern Turkey.

After returning to Antioch, Barnabas and Paul agreed to go on a second trip. Barnabas insisted on taking his cousin, JOHN MARK. Paul refused, apparently because John Mark had abandoned them during the first trip. So Barnabas and John Mark returned to Cyprus, while Paul and a new partner named SILAS returned to Turkey.

BARREN

(see INFERTILITY)

BARTHOLOMEW

(bar THAH lah mew)

First century AD

Here are the names of the twelve apostles. . . Bartholomew. Matthew 10:2-3

ONE OF JESUS' original dozen DISCIPLES, Bartholomew shows up in several lists of the disciples but nowhere else in the BIBLE. Some scholars speculate that he also went by the name NATHANAEL, sometimes identified as one of the disciples (John 21:2). The link: in the list of disciples, Bartholomew's NAME follows PHILIP—and Philip introduced Nathanael to Jesus (John 1:45–51). Eusebius, a church historian writing in the AD 300s, said Bartholomew took the story of Jesus to India.

BARTIMAEUS

(bart tuh ME us)

First century AD

A blind beggar named Bartimaeus. . .was sitting beside the road. Mark 10:46

SITTING on the JERICHO roadside, a blind beggar named Bartimaeus heard that Jesus was passing by. In fact, it would be for the last time. Jesus was headed to JERUSALEM, where he would be crucified in a few days. "Jesus, Son of DAVID," Bartimaeus called out, "have MERCY on me!" (Mark 10:47). Jesus called him over and healed him on the spot.

BARUCH

(BARE uhk) or (BAY ruke)

600s–500s BC

As Jeremiah dictated all the prophecies that the LORD had given him, Baruch wrote them on a scroll. Jeremiah 36:4

- Scribe who copied the prophecies of Jeremiah, twice

WHEN THE PROPHET JEREMIAH wanted to write down the prophecies GOD gave him, he turned to a pro.

Baruch was a professional writer at a time when most folks couldn't read or write. People went to Baruch the way folks today go to a lawyer when they need something written that no one wants to read.

That's a fit comparison, given what happened when a SERVANT named Jehudi read the prophecies aloud to King JEHOIAKIM: "Each time Jehudi finished reading three or four columns, the king took a KNIFE and cut off that section of the SCROLL. He then threw it into the fire, section by section, until the whole scroll was burned up" (Jeremiah 36:23).

Jeremiah dictated a second, longer version—apparently the one we now have, with some add-on bad news for the king (Jeremiah 36:29–31).

Baruch is one of those rare Bible characters whose name has shown up in an archaeological discovery.

SCRIBES sealed private LETTERS with a glob of wax or clay pressed with an imprint of their name or an identifying mark. Among 250 ancient clay SEAL impressions found in Israel in 1975, one reads like it may have belonged to Baruch. The BIBLE identifies the scribe as "Baruch son of Neriah" (Jeremiah 32:12). The seal impression reads: "Belonging to Berekyahu son of Neriyahu the scribe," possibly reflecting the longer, formal names of Baruch and his father.

Many scholars say the seal is a forgery. Others say they disagree.

THE SEAL OF BARUCH, the scribe who helped Jeremiah write a Bible book of prophecy, may have made this impression onto clay. It contains what seems to be his full name, his job title, the name of his father as the Bible reports it, and even part of a fingerprint.

BASHAN

Map 1 E3

(BAY shun)

"Let them graze in the fertile pastures of Bashan." Micah 7:14

AMOS knew how to insult rich women:

"You are already as fat as the cows in Bashan." AMOS 4:1 NIRV

AMOS, a prophet, wasn't fond of how rich folks exploited the POOR. So he compared rich WOMEN to cows grazing in primo pastures of a fertile plateau east of the SEA OF GALILEE: Bashan. That's in what is now southern Syria. Bashan, rich in volcanic soil, earned a reputation for its lush grain fields and grasslands.

BASIN

They made the bronze basin and its bronze stand from the mirrors of the women.
Exodus 38:8 TNIV

MOST HOUSEHOLDS had wash basins or BOWLS made of POTTERY or metal. People used them for washing or for holding food. But in the BIBLE, most references to basins refer to some of the sacred furnishings at the WORSHIP CENTER: huge water basins that PRIESTS used to draw water to purify themselves and to wash the BLOOD and guts off sacrificial ANIMALS.

During the EXODUS out of EGYPT, Jewish artisans made the worship basin out of the polished BRONZE that WOMEN used as MIRRORS. SOLOMON's massive TEMPLE included one huge round basin called the Sea—15 feet across and 7.5 feet deep (4.6 by 2.3 m)—along with 10 smaller, portable basins (1 Kings 7:23, 27).

BASKET

One night some followers of Saul helped him leave the city by lowering him in a basket through an opening in the city wall.
Acts 9:25 NCV

LIGHTWEIGHT, baskets were the perfect container for carrying anything from harvested crops to severed heads. Much easier to tote than a pot made of heavy clay or metal.

People made baskets from various plants: tree twigs, straw, PAPYRUS reeds.

There are two especially famous baskets in the BIBLE:

Baby in a basket, to go. The most famous basket in the Bible floated baby MOSES in the NILE RIVER. Moses' mother, JOCHEBED, "got a basket made of papyrus reeds and waterproofed it with TAR" (Exodus 2:3). PHARAOH's daughter found Moses and adopted him.

Jew in a basket, to go. Saul, better known as the apostle PAUL, escaped from DAMASCUS when friends put him in a basket and lowered him over the city wall. He was running from radical JEWS waiting for him at the city gates, hoping to murder him—punishment for his recent CONVERSION to CHRISTIANITY.

Pharaoh's daughter went down to the Nile River to take a bath. Exodus 2:5 NIrv

IF YOU COULD TAKE A BATH in dirt, the Middle East would be the place to go. But if you need water, you'll find it in short supply there.

Some people were lucky enough to live by a river or a lake: NILE RIVER, JORDAN RIVER, SEA OF GALILEE. They could, and did, bathe there. In EGYPT, PHARAOH's daughter was taking a bath in the Nile when she found baby MOSES floating in a BASKET.

For nearly everyone else, there was what amounts to a sponge bath: one rag, one bowl of water, one naked human. Cue BATHSHEBA.

Jewish law, however, required a full immersion ritual bath to cleanse spiritual contamination—such as from touching a corpse or having a menstrual period or a wet dream (Leviticus 15). The bath, called a *mikvah* (MICK vuh), had to be in "living WATER," meaning water that flowed—as in a lake, river, or an underground spring. No water from stagnant ponds or mud puddles after a rain.

BATHSHEBA

(bath SHE bah)

About 1000 BC

Bathsheba. . .sent a message to David. It said, "I'm pregnant." 2 Samuel 11:5 NIrv

- Mother of King Solomon
- Wife of King David
- Committed adultery with King David
- Got pregnant with David's child

NAKED, Bathsheba walked onto the BIBLE stage—apparently not realizing she had an audience.

She was taking an afternoon BATH at her home in JERUSALEM. Not just any bath. This was a Jewish cleansing ritual required one week after a woman's monthly menstrual flow stopped. That means by bath's end, she wasn't just fresh and fragrant. She was fertile.

Her husband, URIAH, was a member of King DAVID's Special Forces—a group called The Thirty. He was away fighting a WAR in what is now Jordan.

Bathsheba may have bathed inside her walled COURT-YARD. Or perhaps in the HOUSE, with windows open for a breeze in the afternoon heat. Wherever it was, David had the angle. He was walking on the deck-like ROOF of his PALACE after a siesta, catching some air—and an eyeful.

David already had at least seven wives. But he couldn't seem to resist Bathsheba—gorgeous, naked, and dripping wet. He sent a messenger to invite her to his place.

The Bible doesn't say if the SEX was consensual—or the reluctant compliance of a lowly lady serving the alpha male.

She got pregnant. David ordered Uriah home from the front lines, hoping he would have sex with Bathsheba so he'd think the child was his. Uriah refused to partake of the loving while his comrades fought for their lives. That decision killed him. David ordered Uriah back to battle with a sealed note telling his commander to send him on a suicide mission.

David married the grieving WIDOW.

He repented, after the prophet NATHAN confronted him about this SIN.

GOD forgave David. But Bathsheba's son died. Bathsheba later gave BIRTH to SOLOMON—the PRINCE who would become ISRAEL's next KING.

BATH TIME FOR BATHSHEBA. What King David saw wasn't just a married woman bathing. It was a ritual bath—a cleansing after her menstrual period. That means she wasn't just clean. She was fertile.

BATTERING RAM

> "Cut down the trees for battering rams.
> Build siege ramps against the walls of
> Jerusalem." Jeremiah 6:6

INVADERS tried breaking through stone walls and wooden gates of a city by pummeling them with log battering rams—some tipped with metal points, others with a wrecking ball. Perhaps the most effective rams were those protected inside armored towers on wheels. Soldiers rolled the tank-like tower into position at the base of the city wall. Inside the tower, the ramming log dangled from a ROPE. Soldiers would rock the log back and forth in a pendulum motion until it gained max momentum before crashing into its target.

KNOCK, KNOCK. This is the view from the back door of a Roman-style battering ram, which is mounted on wheels. The front of the ram is mostly sealed to protect the men inside who swing the log against a city gate or wall.

BEARD

> Hanun arrested David's officers. To shame
> them he shaved off half their beards.
> 2 Samuel 10:4 NCV

JEWISH MEN wore beards. It wasn't a fashion statement. It was law: "Do not. . .trim your beards" (Leviticus 19:27). Ancient pictures of JEWS confirm that the men wore beards. One picture from the 800s BC shows JEHU, king of ISRAEL, bowing before King SHALMANESER of ASSYRIA, in what is now Iraq. Another shows bearded Jewish delegates standing before Assyrian King SENNACHERIB and the conquered Jewish city of LACHISH.

Going beardless was shameful. King Hanun from what is now Jordan shaved off half the beards of AMBASSADORS King DAVID sent. Hanun thought they were spies. David allowed the men to go into hiding until their beards grew back. And he launched a punitive attack against Hanun.

BEASTS OF REVELATION

> I saw a beast rising up out of the sea. . . .
> Then I saw another beast come up out of the
> earth. Revelation 13:1, 11

THERE ARE TWO BEASTS in Revelation, a book written in a highly symbolic genre of literature called APOCALYPTIC.

The first comes by sea. Many scholars link this beast to the ancient ROMAN EMPIRE—based across the MEDITERRANEAN SEA in Italy. Others say it refers to a similarly vicious end-time empire, or to an end-time ANTICHRIST.

The second comes from the earth. It's often linked to a FALSE PROPHET mentioned elsewhere in REVELATION. This prophet fooled people by performing MIRACLES. Scholars who read Revelation as more about Roman history than the future say this beast more likely represents Emperor NERO, the first emperor to persecute Christians.

See also MARK OF THE BEAST.

BEATING

Five different times the Jewish leaders gave me thirty-nine lashes. Three times I was beaten with rods.
2 Corinthians 11:24–25

PUBLIC BEATING was a form of punishment—often dished out to a victim tied to a post. Jewish law set a limit: "Never give more than forty lashes" (Deuteronomy 25:3). Floggers often limited it to 39, though, to make sure they didn't break the law with a miscount.

Romans didn't seem to observe any such limit. Some Romans beat their victims with rods, as the apostle PAUL reported. Others used whips with half a dozen LEATHER lashes or more, each embedded with chunks of metal or bone—to rip the skin and muscle. That's likely the kind of beating Jesus got shortly before Romans nailed him to a CROSS.

BEATITUDES

Blessed are the poor in spirit: for theirs is the kingdom of heaven. Matthew 5:3 KJV

JESUS started his famous SERMON ON THE MOUNT with a list of promises—assurances that those who are suffering now have every reason to hope for a better future.

- for the POOR: HEAVEN belongs to them
- for the grieving: comfort
- for the humble: GLORY
- for the exploited: justice
- for merciful souls: MERCY
- for godly souls: life with GOD
- for peacemakers: adoption by God
- for those who do what is right: heaven

BED

Og. . . His bed, made of iron, was over thirteen feet long and six wide [4 by 2 m].
Deuteronomy 3:11 MSG

BED was the floor. Clothes were the mattress—and the covers. At least that's how it was for most folks in Bible times, scholars say. Generally, everyone slept in the main room of the HOUSE. Only the wealthier people had beds and bedrooms. A TOMB in JERICHO turned up a wooden bed frame from the 800s BC, during the time of King AHAB and JEZEBEL. It had rope marks, suggesting it may have worked a bit like a hammock.

Excavations at Ahab's PALACE turned up IVORY decorations reported in the BIBLE: "the palace he built and furnished with ivory" (1 Kings 22:39 CEV). Some of the ivory may have decorated beds, prompting AMOS to condemn the luxury of "you who sprawl on ivory beds" (Amos 6:4).

FORTY WINKS. This Roman bed from New Testament times was reassembled from fragments: wood, glass, bone, and ivory inlays.

BEELZEBUB

(be EL zee buhb)

"Jesus is driving out demons by the power of Beelzebub, the prince of demons."
Luke 11:15 NIrV

A NICKNAME FOR SATAN, Beelzebub comes from the HEBREW term *Baal-zebub*. It means "Lord of the

Flies." Originally it may have been a flattering way of talking about the Canaanite god BAAL, as "lord of heaven." But JEWS, unimpressed with Baal, lowered his altitude.

See also SATAN.

BEER   Location Uncertain

> *Wine causes you to make fun of others, and beer causes you to start fights.*
> **Proverbs 20:1** NIRV

1. THE DRINK. In the beginning, there was beer. At least in the beginning of civilization. People of SUMER—the first known empire, in what is now southern Iraq—brewed beer from BARLEY more than 4,000 years before ABRAHAM came along.

Pictures in Egyptian tombs show how they processed barley into beer several centuries before Abraham and about 1,000 years before MOSES arrived to free the JEWS from SLAVERY.

Egyptians crushed the GRAIN, mixed it with water, and dried it into cakes. Afterward, they crumbled the cakes, mixed it with water again, and waited for it to grow a kick.

Bible sages warned that too much beer could turn a mild man mean and a smart man stupid.

2. THE PLACE. Jews on the EXODUS sang a happy beer SONG—in a Hebrew sort of a way.

Beer is a HEBREW word. It means "WELL." When Moses led the Jews north through what is now the arid nation of Jordan, they got thirsty. GOD told them to dig a well. When they struck WATER, they struck up a song: "Spring up, O well!" (Numbers 21:17 NIV).

BEER-LAHAI-ROI   Map 1 A8

(BEE air la HI roy)

> *That well was named Beer-lahai-roi (which means "well of the Living One who sees me"). Genesis 16:14*

BEER-LAHAI-ROI is the WELL where an ANGEL of GOD met runaway HAGAR, who was pregnant with ABRAHAM's son, ISHMAEL.

Hagar was the SERVANT of Abraham's WIFE, Sarah. Hagar was also a surrogate mother for the couple, since SARAH couldn't have children. When Hagar got pregnant, tensions rose between the women. Sarah treated Hagar so harshly that she ran away. An angel sent Hagar home with a promise: "I will give you more descendants than you can count" (Genesis 16:10).

BEERSHEBA   Map 1 B7

(beer SHE buh)

> *Jacob left Beersheba, and his sons took him to Egypt. . .in the wagons Pharaoh had provided for them. Genesis 46:5*

ABRAHAM CALLED IT HOME. So did his son, ISAAC, and his grandson, JACOB. There's a reason. All three were herders. The plains of Beersheba some 45 miles (72 km) south of JERUSALEM hosted them nicely, with a WELL and wintertime grazing. Summer grazing wasn't far north. The city that grew up there is now called Be'er Sheva, nicknamed "Capital of the NEGEV." Population about 200,000.

BEGGING

> *As they approached the Temple, a man lame from birth was being carried in. . .so he could beg from the people going into the Temple. Acts 3:2*

TWO BIG POINTS the BIBLE makes about begging.

Beggars live at the bottom of life's barrel. One book in the Catholic and Orthodox Bible, but not the Protestant, says "It is better to die than to beg" (Sirach 40:28 NRSV). One songwriter uses begging as a CURSE: "May his children wander as beggars" (Psalm 109:10).

Beggars deserve compassion. Bible writers consistently ask people to show MERCY to the POOR, especially those at greatest risk: "When widows and CHILDREN who have no parents are in trouble, take care of them" (James 1:27 NIRV). Jesus made a similar point in a PARABLE about a dead beggar ending up in PARADISE, while the dead rich guy who had ignored the beggar ended up in HELL (Luke 16:19–30).

see photo, page 64

WITH A CANE, a can, and an icon of the Virgin Mary and baby Jesus, a woman bows to passersby, hoping for a donation. See "Begging," page 63.

BEHEMOTH

(Be HEE muhth)

"Look at the behemoth. . . . Its tail sways back and forth like a cedar tree." Job 40:15, 17 NIrV

A MYSTERIOUS CRITTER, the behemoth was some kind of beast that GOD pointed out as a way of convincing JOB to trust him. Guesses about exactly what the behemoth was range from hippo, to crocodile, to dinosaur—a favorite of some Christians who say humans and dinos lived at the same time, a few thousand years ago.

BELIEVER

(see CHRISTIAN)

BELLS

"Aaron will wear this robe. . .and the bells will tinkle as he goes in and out of the LORD's presence in the Holy Place." Exodus 28:35

THE HIGH PRIEST came with bells on. That's how ISRAEL's top WORSHIP leader was supposed to enter the LORD's presence when he stepped into the most sacred rooms of the worship center.

AARON, Israel's first HIGH PRIEST, wore a ROBE hemmed in golden bells. Outside the TENT worship center, others could hear the bells and know that he was still alive in the Lord's presence.

Some farmers laced bells onto the harnesses of their horses (Zechariah 14:20). They served as a warning for people and critters to get out of the way. Think: honking horn.

BELSHAZZAR

(bell SHAZ ur)

Coruler about 545–539 BC

King Belshazzar was very frightened. His face turned white, his knees knocked together. Daniel 5:6 NCV

- Saw God's handwriting on the wall
- Coruler of Babylon with father, Nabonidus
- Partied with cups stolen from Jerusalem Temple

LAST KING of the once-great Babylonian Empire, Belshazzar died partying.

He threw a feast for a thousand NOBLES, along with his HAREM of wives and CONCUBINES. Many drank themselves into a drunk—using GOLD and SILVER cups that the Babylonians from what is now Iraq had stolen from the Jerusalem TEMPLE about 50 years earlier.

During the party a disembodied hand wrote on the PALACE wall a four-word coded warning: "Numbered. Numbered. Weighed. Divided."

The prophet DANIEL decoded it: "GOD has your number. Your number's up. You've been weighed and found wanting. Your kingdom is getting carved up."

An invasion force of Persians and Medes from what is now Iraq marched into the city that night, killing Belshazzar.

BELT

"He [Elijah] was hairy and had a leather belt around his waist." 2 Kings 1:8 CEV

WITHOUT A BELT, a ROBE could turn into a parachute on a windy day—exposing everything no one wants to publicize. Men and women wore dress-like robes in Bible times. Robes extended to the ankles, tunics to the knees. A belt of LEATHER, cloth, or ROPE secured the robe or tunic around the waist.

BENEDICTION

(ben uh DICT shun)

"May the LORD bless you and protect you. May the LORD smile on you and be gracious to you." Numbers 6:24–25

PART PRAYER AND PART WISH, a benediction invokes the BLESSING of GOD on someone. Several New Testament LETTERS end with such a PRAYER: "May the GRACE shown by the LORD JESUS CHRIST, and the love that God has given us, and the sharing of life brought about by the HOLY SPIRIT be with you all" (2 Corinthians 13:14 NIrv).

KING BELSHAZZAR sees the handwriting on the wall. By morning he'll be dead.

BEN-HADAD

(ben HAY dad)

800s BC

Hazael got a thick blanket; he soaked it in water and held it over Benhadad's face until he died. Hazael then became king.

2 Kings 8:15 CEV

- King in what is now Syria
- Suffocated under a wet blanket

BEN is HEBREW lingo for SON. Ben-Hadad was the son of HADAD. The BIBLE mentions four. Perhaps the most famous is Ben-Hadad II (ruled about 865–842 BC). His soldiers attacked ISRAEL many times before King AHAB defeated them and recaptured cities the invaders had taken.

The most interesting is his son, Ben-Hadad III (ruled about 842–797 BC). He died under a wet blanket. When he got sick he sent a SERVANT, HAZAEL, to ask the prophet ELISHA if he'd get well. Bad decision. Elisha said the king would die and Hazael would replace him. Hazael fulfilled that prophecy himself, with the help of a wet blanket.

BENJAMIN

(BEN juh muhn)

1800s BC

Jacob exclaimed, "You are robbing me of my children! Joseph is gone! Simeon is gone! And now you want to take Benjamin, too."

Genesis 42:36

- Youngest son of Jacob
- Father of Israel's tribe of Benjamin

YOUNGEST of JACOB's dozen sons, Benjamin was born into tragedy. His mother, RACHEL, died giving BIRTH to him. With her last breath she named him Ben-oni, which means "son of my sorrow." Jacob renamed him Benjamin, "son of my right hand."

Jacob loved Rachel more than his other three wives. He loved her two CHILDREN—JOSEPH and Benjamin—more than the others. He was devastated when his other sons, who had sold Joseph to slave traders, led Jacob to believe a wild ANIMAL had eaten the boy.

Joseph became a top administrator in EGYPT. Many years later, his older brothers came down to buy Egyptian GRAIN during a DROUGHT. Without revealing his identity, Joseph accused them of being spies and demanded they prove their story about their FAMILY by going and getting Benjamin.

Elderly Jacob refused at first, since Benjamin was all he had left of Rachel. But as the drought dragged on, he was forced to comply. It led to a happy reunion, with Jacob moving his family to Egypt to weather out the drought.

BENJAMIN, TRIBE OF

Map 1 D5

(BEN juh muhn)

The tribes of Israel sent men throughout the tribe of Benjamin demanding, "What is this evil thing some of your men have done?"

Judges 20:12 NCV

- One of the smallest of Israel's 12 tribes
- Nearly wiped out for refusing to punish rapists

RAPE is the tribe's claim to shame. A gang of men raped to death a traveler's WIFE as the couple passed through the tribal area. The other tribes demanded justice, but Benjamin's leaders refused. So the other tribes attacked and nearly annihilated Benjamin but later allowed Benjamin's few surviving men to steal women from other tribes—to repopulate their own tribe.

That was big-time irony, given that the whole mess ended the way it started: when men from Benjamin wanted a woman, they took her.

On a map of ISRAEL's dozen tribes, Benjamin's tiny strip looks like the JORDAN RIVER sticking out its tongue at the MEDITERRANEAN SEA. Benjamin's territory ran above JERUSALEM, about 20 miles westward from the river and some 10 miles north and south at its widest (32 by 16 km).

BERNICE

(burn NEECE)

First century AD

King Agrippa arrived with his sister, Bernice, to pay their respects to Festus. Acts 25:13

GREAT-GRANDDAUGHTER of HEROD THE GREAT (reigned 37–4 BC), Bernice married her uncle—and when he died she reportedly had a lifelong incestuous affair with her brother, King HEROD AGRIPPA II (AD 28–93). She and her brother met with the apostle PAUL while Paul was under arrest in CAESAREA, Agrippa's capital of Roman territory in what is now northern Israel and parts of Syria and Jordan.

BESTIALITY

(BEST chee AL uh tee) or
(BEAST chee AL uh tee)

"Anyone who has sex with an animal must be put to death." Exodus 22:19 NIRV

SEX WITH ANIMALS—not kosher. Worse, a capital offense under Jewish law.

BETHANY
Map 4 D5 / Location Uncertain

(BETH uh nee)

Jesus arrived in Bethany, the home of Lazarus. . . . Mary took a twelve-ounce jar [327 g] of expensive perfume made from essence of nard, and she anointed Jesus' feet with it, wiping his feet with her hair.
John 12:1, 3

- Jesus raised Lazarus from the dead here
- Jesus began his Palm Sunday donkey ride
- Jesus ascended into heaven
- Mary anointed Jesus with oil
- Hometown of sisters/brother Mary, Martha, Lazarus

1. BETHANY NEAR JERUSALEM. For a little burg, Bethany served up some big scenes in Jesus' ministry.

Hometown of sisters Mary and MARTHA and their brother LAZARUS, the village seemed to serve as Jesus' headquarters during that last week before his CRUCIFIXION.

Bethany nestled itself into the eastern slopes of a ridge of hills called the MOUNT OF OLIVES, about 2 miles (3 km) east of JERUSALEM. Travelers arriving from JERICHO would pass through Bethany before cresting the Mount of Olives and catching sight of Jerusalem across the narrow KIDRON VALLEY.

Today Bethany is a West Bank village named after its most famous resident: *Al-Ayzariyyah*, Arabic for "Place of Lazarus." Population: about 17,000.

The main tourist attraction—visited by many Christians—is Lazarus' Tomb. This dungeon-like TOMB 22 winding steps below ground has a tradition dating back to at least the AD 300s, when ROME first legalized CHRISTIANITY. Christians marked the spot by building a CHURCH over it.

2. BETHANY EAST OF THE JORDAN RIVER. Jesus was visiting here, in what is now Jordan, while Lazarus lay dying in Bethany near Jerusalem. This is the same place JOHN THE BAPTIST baptized people: "in Bethany, an area east of the JORDAN RIVER" (John 1:28).

The exact location is uncertain. But a church tradition dating to at least the AD 200s says John baptized Jesus near a monastery about five miles (eight km) north of where the Jordan River empties into the DEAD SEA. If that was Jordan's Bethany, the same-name villages were about 20 miles (32 km) apart, roughly a one-day walk.

BETHEL
Map 1 C5

(BETH uhl)

Jacob named the place Bethel (which means "house of God"), because God had spoken to him there. Genesis 35:15

- Abraham built an altar when arriving in Canaan
- Jacob had a dream of a stairway to heaven
- Where Jews of Israel worshiped a golden calf

JACOB SLEPT HERE. Head on a rock, he had a strange DREAM at this sacred site where his grandfather

ABRAHAM had set up camp decades earlier, after arriving in what is now ISRAEL. JACOB saw a stairway to HEAVEN. And he heard GOD promise to give him this land and fill it with "descendants. . .as numerous as the dust of the earth!" (Genesis 28:14).

Bethel was a crossroads town, with trails pointing in all four directions: north to SAMARIA, south 12 miles (19 km) to JERUSALEM, east to JERICHO, and west to the MEDITERRANEAN SEA.

During the time of the heroic JUDGES like GIDEON and SAMSON, Bethel served as a kind of capital and a staging ground for Jewish armies preparing for battle. The prophet and circuit-walking judge SAMUEL visited the city regularly to hold COURT. And for a time, JEWS kept their most sacred object there: the ARK OF THE COVENANT, a chest that held the 10 COMMANDMENTS (Judges 20:27).

When the Jewish nation split, the northern Jewish nation of ISRAEL built two worship centers so their people wouldn't have to WORSHIP in Jerusalem, in the southern Jewish nation of JUDAH. Israel's King JEROBOAM built two shrines, each with a GOLDEN CALF. He put one at the northern tip of his kingdom, in the city of DAN. He put the other near his southern border, in Bethel.

Today Bethel is a Palestinian West Bank village of about 2,000 people: Baytin. Jews have a nearby settlement of about 6,000 people: Bet El. Both names, Arabic and HEBREW, preserve the meaning of the name Jacob gave the place: House of God.

BETHLEHEM

Map 4 C6

(BETH le hem)

"The Savior—yes, the Messiah, the Lord— has been born today in Bethlehem, the city of David!" Luke 2:11

- Jesus' birthplace
- Shepherds visit baby Jesus
- King David's hometown
- Ruth meets future husband Boaz
- Rachel buried nearby
- King Herod ordered infant boys killed

BIG THINGS were bound to happen in the little burg of Bethlehem. A PROPHET predicted it 700 years before Jesus was born:

"Bethlehem, you might not be an important town in the nation of Judah. But out of you will come a ruler. . . ." His greatness will reach from one end of the earth to the other. And he will bring them peace (MICAH 5:2, 4–5 NIrV).

This prediction is why King HEROD's religion advisers pointed the WISE MEN to Bethlehem when they came looking for ISRAEL's future king (Matthew 2:4–6).

More than a thousand years before the birth of Jesus, King DAVID was born and raised there—working for his father as a SHEPHERD. It was David's home because that's where his great-grandfather BOAZ met and married RUTH, an Arab girl from what is now Jordan.

Jesus was born in Bethlehem because his legal father, JOSEPH, had to report to his FAMILY's hometown for a CENSUS. Joseph dangled on David's family tree.

Early Christian writers in the AD 100s said Jesus was born in a cave—one of many that honeycomb the area. Some caves served as BARNS, others as homes—even today. Christians built the Church of the Nativity over that cave in about AD 327, shortly after the ROMAN EMPIRE legalized CHRISTIANITY.

This CHURCH is one of the few that survived the Muslim invasion in the AD 600s. Invaders saw pictures of their Arab ANCESTORS inside: wise men from the east, in what is now Iraq or Iran.

Israelis captured the city from Jordan in the Six-Day War of 1967. It's now part of the occupied West

O LITTLE PRISON TOWN. That's what many say Bethlehem feels like today, with the protective wall Israel built around it. Israelis say they need the wall to protect citizens from attacks by Palestinians who live there. Palestinians have turned their side of the wall into protest murals.

Bank. Israel governed the city until 1995, when they returned control to the Palestinians as part of a peace plan.

Israelis have since built a 25-foot-high wall (8 m) around Bethlehem. They say it's to protect JEWS on Israeli land outside the city. Bethlehem residents call it the Apartheid Wall, a name reminiscent of the racism that once dominated South Africa. Residents and many tourists alike agree that it gives Bethlehem the feel of a prison town. Israelis argue that the wall is necessary to protect Jews from terrorists.

BETHLEHEM STATS

- Population: 22,000
- Religion: 72 percent Muslim, 28 percent Christian
- Location: West Bank, 5 miles (8 km) south of Jerusalem
- Elevation: Nearly half a mile high (about 1 km)
- Government: Palestinian Authority
- Main tourist attraction: Church of the Nativity
- Meaning of name: "House of Bread" (Hebrew), "House of Meat" (Arabic)

BETH-PEOR   Map 1 E6

(BETH PEE or)

Moses, the servant of the LORD, died. . . . His grave is in the valley across from Beth Peor. Deuteronomy 34:5–6 NIRV

- Moses lectured Jews on the Law
- Moses buried

WITH JUST 10 MILES (16 km) to go before crossing into the PROMISED LAND, MOSES and the Exodus JEWS pitched their tents at Beth-peor in what is now Jordan. There he gave his farewell speech—preserved in the book of DEUTERONOMY. He reviewed all the laws GOD gave the Jews and urged the people to obey them. Then he climbed nearby MOUNT NEBO to look across the JORDAN RIVER valley into what is now ISRAEL. He died there and was buried in a valley by Beth-peor.

BETHPHAGE   Location Uncertain

(BETH fayg) or (BETH fah gee)

As Jesus and the disciples approached Jerusalem, they came to the town of Bethphage on the Mount of Olives. Matthew 21:1

- Jesus began his Palm Sunday donkey ride here

JESUS CLIMBED up on a DONKEY near Bethphage and began his ride down the MOUNT OF OLIVES into JERUSALEM. Christians commemorate the day as Palm Sunday, when JEWS greeted him as the MESSIAH and waved palm branches like flags. His ride began somewhere on the eastern slopes of the Mount of Olives. BETHANY is there, just a couple miles (3 km) from Jerusalem. The location of Bethphage is unknown.

BETHSAIDA

Map 4 D3

(beth SAY uh duh)

"Sorrow awaits you. . .Bethsaida! For if the miracles I did in you had been done in wicked Tyre and Sidon, their people would have repented." Luke 10:13

- Jesus fed 5,000
- Fishing village condemned by Jesus for unbelief
- Hometown of disciples Philip, Andrew, Peter

JESUS was on his way to Bethsaida, a FISHING village on the north shore of ISRAEL's freshwater lake: the SEA OF GALILEE. Somewhere apparently outside the village, a crowd gathered—5,000 men, not counting women and children. Jesus divided the people into groups of 50 and fed them with "five loaves and two fish" (Luke 9:16). Later he condemned the people of Bethsaida for not believing him in spite of the MIRACLES they had seen him perform.

BETH-SHAN

Map 1 D4

(beth SHAN)

They cut off Saul's head. . .they hung his body up on the wall of Beth Shan.
1 Samuel 31:9–10 NIRV

- Bodies of Saul and sons hung on city wall

PHILISTINES OVERRAN the ARMY of King SAUL at the battle of MOUNT GILBOA, leaving Saul and three of his sons dead. Then they took the four bodies to the busy crossroads town of Beth-shan and hung them like war trophies on the city wall. It was a good location for getting the word out. One branch of the main ROAD through ISRAEL—the Way of the Sea—ran through Beth-shan. The city also sat at the intersection of Israel's two biggest valleys: the JORDAN RIVER valley running north and south, along with the JEZREEL VALLEY running east and west.

BETH-SHEMESH

Map 1 C6

(beth SHE mish)

The people of Beth-shemesh were harvesting wheat in the valley, and when they saw the Ark, they were overjoyed! 1 Samuel 6:13

- Philistines returned Ark of Covenant here
- Jewish border town near Philistines

A WAR TROPHY, the ARK OF THE COVENANT stayed in Philistine custody for seven months—until the PHILISTINES had all they could take of the plagues that trailed the Ark from town to town on its war trophy tour. This Ark, a GOLD-covered chest, held the 10 COMMANDMENTS. Philistines captured it after defeating the Jewish ARMY in a battle. They returned it to Beth-shemesh, a Jewish city about 16 miles (26 km) southwest of JERUSALEM.

BETROTHAL

(see WEDDING)

BIBLE

All Scripture is inspired by God and is useful for teaching, for showing people what is wrong in their lives, for correcting faults, and for teaching how to live right.
2 Timothy 3:16 NCV

- Holy book of Jews and Christians

THE BIBLE is not your typical book. It's a library.

Writers scattered across a millennium left their mark on Jewish and CHRISTIAN history—usually without signing their names.

They wrote in just about every style of writing possible: fiction and nonfiction, comedy and tragedy, love SONGS and war cries, POETRY and PARABLES, history and prophecy, laws and LETTERS, how-to and why bother.

How-to: "Resist the devil, and he will flee from you" (James 4:7).

Why bother: "What good is wealth. . . . The more you have, the more people come to help you spend it" (Ecclesiastes 5:11).

HOW WE GOT THE BIBLE

Short course: only the good Lord knows. Everybody else is guessing.

The process was gradual. Bible experts agree on that much.

First WRITING on record in the Bible came from GOD: 10 COMMANDMENTS. "The words on them were written by God himself" (Exodus 32:16).

Jewish tradition credits MOSES with the first five books in the Bible. And the Bible confirms that he wrote the laws at least: "Moses wrote this entire body of instruction in a book and gave it to the PRIESTS" (Deuteronomy 31:9).

Many Bible experts guess that stories about Jewish KINGS, heroes, and villains got passed along by word of mouth for many GENERATIONS, since most people didn't read or write. Then when DAVID came along and kick-started a sputtering Jewish nation, officials started to write down the history of their people.

It's unclear when writers of the OLD TESTAMENT finished—or when the JEWS settled on which books made the cut for their Bible. Some scholars say the Jews settled on their books a century or so before Jesus. Others say the debates continued after Jesus.

The NEW TESTAMENT had a shorter run in the writing—about half a century from start to finish.

Churches copied and passed around the stories of Jesus and the letters by PAUL, PETER, and others. In time, 27 writings gained special favor. These 27 showed up on a list for the first time in an AD 367 Easter letter from Bishop Athanasius to his churches. "These are fountains of SALVATION," he wrote. "In these alone is proclaimed the doctrine of godliness. Let no one add to them, or take from them."

BIBLE 1.0: OLD TESTAMENT

The Bible comes in three main sets:

- Old Testament, the Jewish holy book.
- New Testament, the Christian add-on, which Jews skip.
- Apocrypha, Catholic and Orthodox bonus books, which Protestants skip.

The OLD TESTAMENT is where folks find three-fourths of the Protestant Bible, if they're counting words—some three quarters of a million words in the Bible, depending on the translation.

Folks counting individual Bible books will find 39 in the Old Testament—and another 27 in the New Testament, for a total of 66 in the Protestant Bible. The Apocrypha, included in Catholic and Orthodox Bibles, adds still more—of varying numbers, depending on the church group.

Jews arrange their Bible differently than Christians. Here's a snapshot of the CHRISTIAN Bible, and a short description of each book.

SCRIBE AT WORK. A Jewish scribe from Yemen touches up an old copy of the Torah, the Jewish Law, which many Christians know as the first five books of the Bible.

LAWS, HISTORY

Genesis
Beginning of universe, humanity, Jewish race

Exodus
Moses frees Jews from Egyptian slavery

Leviticus
Jews organize as a nation

Numbers
Jews spend 40 years in the badlands

Deuteronomy
Moses reviews Jewish laws, and dies

HISTORY OF JEWS

Joshua
Jews invade and retake homeland

Judges
Heroes rescue Jews from oppressors

Ruth
Arab woman becomes mother of King David's family

1, 2 Samuel
Saul becomes Israel's first king, followed by David

1, 2 Kings
Israel splits in two; both nations fall within 400 years

1, 2 Chronicles
Jewish history, tailored to show God at work

Ezra
Jews return home from exile in Iraq

Nehemiah
Jews rebuild Jerusalem walls

Esther
Jew becomes Iranian queen, saves Jews from genocide

POETRY

Job
Loses his wealth, health, children; blames God

Psalms
Jewish songs of worship

Proverbs
Practical advice for young men

Ecclesiastes
One man's search for the meaning of life

Song of Songs
Intimate, erotic love song

PROPHECY ABOUT JEWS, ENEMIES

Isaiah
Warns Jews to stop sinning

Jeremiah
Lives to see predictions come true: Jewish nation falls

Lamentations
Eyewitness to Jerusalem's fall describes the horrors

Ezekiel
Predicts end of Jewish nation, followed by its rebirth

Daniel
Exiled Jew advises Babylonians (Iraq) and Persians (Iran)

Hosea
Marries a hooker to illustrate Jewish nation's unfaithfulness

Joel
Warns of a locust-like invasion of warriors

Amos
Defends the poor and accuses exploitive, rich Jews

Obadiah
Condemns nation of Edom for murdering Jewish refugees

Jonah
Reluctant prophet convinces people of Nineveh (in Iraq) to repent

Micah
Predicts the Messiah will come from Bethlehem

Nahum
Predicts the end of the Iraqi-based Assyrian Empire

Habakkuk
Vows to trust God no matter what

Zephaniah
Predicts the end of humanity, or Jewish nation

Haggai
Convinces Jews to rebuild their Temple

Zechariah
Predicts the coming of a savior

Malachi
Accuses rehab Jews suffering a spiritual relapse

72

BIBLE 1.0A: APOCRYPHA

Catholics and Orthodox Christians add extra books to their Old Testament—books that Jews and Protestants have skipped because they said the material was unreliable.

Many call this collection the *Apocrypha* (ah POC ruh fuh), a GREEK word meaning "hidden." Others call it *deuterocanonical*, meaning "added later" to the Bible.

The books showed up in the first known translation of the Jewish Bible combined with other revered Jewish writings: a Greek edition called the SEPTUAGINT, meaning 70. That's a reference to the number of translators working on the project. It was compiled during the 200s–100s BC. When a Christian scholar—Jerome (about AD 345–420)—translated the Old Testament into Latin, the language of the ROMAN EMPIRE, he worked from the Septuagint. So he included the Apocrypha. But he added a disclaimer, agreeing with Jewish scholars that these books in the Apocrypha, written mainly between 300 BC and AD 70, were less reliable than the books tagged as SCRIPTURE.

Protestants dropped the Apocrypha from their Bibles when they broke from the Catholic Church in the early 1500s. Catholics fired back at the Council of Trent (1545–1563), expressing even greater confidence in the Apocrypha, from which they drew some important teachings, such as the existence of purgatory.

Tobit
Jewish man in Nineveh gives executed Jews a proper burial

Judith
A Jewish widow, Judith saves her city from Assyrians

Esther additions
107 extra verses to Esther's story

Wisdom of Solomon
Wise sayings that point people to righteous living

Sirach
Like Psalms and Proverbs, features songs and wise advice

Baruch
Jeremiah's assistant confesses the Jewish nation's sins

Letter of Jeremiah
Jeremiah warns exiles in Babylon not to worship idols

The Prayer of Azariah and the Song of the Three Jews
Prayer of Daniel's friends in a furnace

Susanna
Daniel proves Susanna is wrongly accused of having an affair

Bel and the Dragon
Daniel uncovers hoaxes about two fake gods

1 Maccabees
Jewish priest leads a successful revolt against Syrian occupiers

2 Maccabees
More on the war of independence

1 Esdras*
Fall of Jerusalem, deportation of Jews, and their return home to rebuild Jerusalem

Prayer of Manasseh
King Manasseh confesses his sins

Psalm 151*
David's song after killing Goliath

3 Maccabees*
God protecting Jews in Egypt from elephants

2 Esdras**
Prophet Ezra's visions of end times

4 Maccabees**
Jews urged to observe Jewish laws even though Syrians are executing Jews who do.

* in Orthodox Bibles, not Catholic
** not in Orthodox or Catholic Bibles, but in some other Christian Bibles

CATHOLICS BACK THEIR BIBLE. When Protestants drop the Apocrypha from their Bible, Catholics convene the Council of Trent (1545) to reconfirm their confidence in those books written between the time of the Old and New Testaments. The artist shows in the foreground the Bride of Christ (aka the Church) trampling on Heresy, while the Holy Spirit descends on the Council.

BIBLE 2.0: NEW TESTAMENT

The Christian add-on to the Jewish Bible traces the story of the Christian movement from the birth of Jesus to the spread of his teachings during the first Christian century.

Most scholars say Paul was probably the first to write anything that ended up in the New Testament. He started writing LETTERS to churches perhaps as early as the late AD 40s—almost 20 years after Jesus.

The GOSPELS about Jesus didn't come earlier, perhaps because no one felt they needed his story in writing. They had the eyewitness DISCIPLES. And many Christians seemed to think Jesus was coming back soon. The four Gospels about Jesus weren't written for decades, after the disciples began dying off and people realized they needed to preserve the stories and teachings.

REVELATION, possibly written in the AD 90s, closed the book on the Bible. It's the last book in the Bible and probably the last one written.

WRITING A LETTER from prison, Paul tells Timothy that all Scripture "is given by inspiration of God" (2 Timothy 3:16 NKJV). Paul was talking about his Bible, the Old Testament. But in time, Christians came to think of this very letter as God's Word, too.

GOSPELS ABOUT JESUS

Matthew
Jesus' story, emphasizing prophecies he fulfills

Mark
Most action-packed account of Jesus' life

Luke
Possibly a doctor's take on Jesus' life and ministry

John
Jesus' story, emphasizing his teachings

HISTORY: BIRTH OF THE CHURCH

Acts
Jesus' disciples jump-start the Christian movement

PAUL'S LETTERS TO CHURCHES

Romans
What Christians believe about Jesus and eternal life

1, 2 Corinthians
Paul tries to solve problems in the Corinth church

Galatians
Christianity is about a bunch of grace, not a bunch of rules

Ephesians
Tips for how to live the Christian life

Philippians
Paul's thank-you letter to a generous congregation

Colossians
Dealing with heretics in the church

1, 2 Thessalonians
Jesus is coming back, but in the meantime don't get lazy

PAUL'S LETTERS TO PASTORS

1, 2 Timothy
Advice about how to pastor a church

Titus
Advice about how to pastor a tough congregation

Philemon
Letter of recommendation for a runaway slave turning himself in

LETTERS TO CHRISTIANS EVERYWHERE

Hebrews
Essay arguing that Jesus made the Jewish religion obsolete

James
Christian dos and don'ts

1, 2 Peter
Advice for persecuted Christians

1, 2, 3 John
Warning against "antichrists" who say Jesus only pretended to die

Jude
Fighting the heresy that it's okay to sin because God forgives

PROPHECY ABOUT END TIMES

Revelation
Visions of disaster on earth and of Jesus coming back for his followers

See also WORD OF GOD.

BILDAD

(BILL dad)

Perhaps before 2000 BC

Bildad the Shuhite replied to Job. . . "Does God twist justice? . . . Your children must have sinned against him." Job 8:1, 3–4

- One of Job's comforters

WHEN JOB LOST HIS CHILDREN, health, and herds in a series of tragedies, Bildad was one of four friends who came to comfort him. Instead, they all insisted that because GOD is just, he must have had good reason for dumping this mess on JOB. In a cruel dig at Job, whose kids died when a windstorm collapsed their HOUSE, Bildad said, "The home of the wicked will be destroyed" (Job 8:22).

BIRDS

Noah opened the window he had made in the boat and released a raven. Genesis 8:6–7

SCREAMERS AND TWEETERS are two categories of birds in the BIBLE.

"Screamers," from the HEBREW word *ayit*, described birds of prey: vultures, eagles, and ravens. They were nonKOSHER, off the menu for hungry JEWS. Some speculate they were forbidden because they fed on dead carcasses. If Jews came into contact with a dead person or ANIMAL, they had to go through cleansing rituals before worshiping GOD (Numbers 19:11–12).

"Tweeters," from the Hebrew word *tsippor* referred to vegetarian birds: QUAIL, pigeons, and partridge. All welcome entries on a kosher menu.

Birds played featured roles in several Bible stories:

- Noah's flood. Noah released a raven and a dove to see if the floodwaters had receded enough for them to find a landing place (Genesis 8:7–11).
- Quail for the Exodus. When Moses and his fellow Jews wanted meat during their march out of slavery in Egypt, "quail flew in and covered the camp" (Exodus 16:13).

- Peter's denial. Jesus predicted that before the morning rooster crowed, Peter would deny knowing him three times. It happened during Jesus' trial. "Just then, a rooster crowed" (Mark 14:68).

BIRTH

I hear a cry, like that of a woman in labor, the groans of a woman giving birth to her first child. Jeremiah 4:31

NO PAIN, NO GAIN. That's the BIBLE's take on childbirth, it seems.

Giving birth was a painful experience from the very beginning, when GOD decided to punish Eve for eating the FORBIDDEN FRUIT: "I will sharpen the pain of your pregnancy, and in pain you will give birth" (Genesis 3:16).

Yet, gaining a child was considered a great BLESSING. It was Job One for WOMEN. If they couldn't do that job, many considered themselves cursed of God. So did others, as HANNAH discovered: "Her rival WIFE taunted her cruelly, rubbing it in and never letting her forget that GOD had not given her CHILDREN" (1 Samuel 1:6 MSG).

Even in NEW TESTAMENT times, when male physicians took care of the sick, giving birth wasn't coed. Not typically. Women giving birth were helped by other women: a MIDWIFE or female family and friends.

MIDWIVES help a woman deliver her child, in this stone art from Roman times. One midwife holds the mom-to-be, who's seated on a birthing stool. Another prepares to catch the baby.

CHILDBIRTH—THE HOW-TO BOOK

Soranus, a Roman physician from the AD 100s, wrote about childbirth in his book *On Midwifery and the Diseases of Women*.

Birthing stool. The pregnant woman sat a birthing stool with someone holding on to her from behind. If the delivery looked like it might be difficult, the woman was placed on a hard bed.

Midwife. A midwife usually handled the delivery, even if a male doctor was available to direct. Women were better suited to it, many thought. And there was the modesty matter.

Lubricating oil. The midwife saturated the vagina with olive oil to help ease the delivery.

Stretching the birth canal. With fingernails clipped and hands lubricated, the midwife inserted a finger from her left hand into the vagina. Making circular motions, she would gently widen the birth canal with her left hand while lubricating it with oil in her right hand. She would continue to do this between contractions.

Pushing. The midwife would tell the woman to take a deep breath and push. The midwife would grab the child and pull it out when the muscles were relaxed, not contracted.

Cutting the cord. The umbilical cord was cut four finger widths from the baby's belly and then tied with wool yarn.

Evaluation of the child. The midwife would then check the child for deformity, strength in crying, and pain responses. This was to see if the child was "worth raising."

Cleaning. If the child was a keeper, the midwife sprinkled it with powered salt to protect against infection. Then she rinsed it in warm water and rubbed it with olive oil. Using her fingers, she cleaned out the openings of the child's body and added drops of oil to the eyes to wash away the thick residue from the uterus.

Wrapping. The midwife wrapped the baby tightly in strips of cloth—swaddling clothes—about 2 inches (5 cm) wide. They said this would help the child grow straight. It also protected the child from eye injury caused by its own fingernails. The child was kept swaddled for more than a month, though changed as necessary, washed, rubbed in oil, and dusted with dried, powdered myrtle leaves.

Placed in a feeding trough. Wrapped, the baby was placed on a pillow filled with soft hay. Soranus said feeding troughs made good cribs for babies because they were slightly inclined, which elevated the baby's head.

BIRTHRIGHT

Esau. . .traded his birthright as the firstborn son for a single meal. Hebrews 12:16

- Privileges of the oldest son

SON NUMBER ONE got special treatment in Bible times. Two main privileges:

Double share of the inheritance. If a FATHER had two sons—ISAAC had twins: ESAU and JACOB—the INHERITANCE would get split three ways. The oldest SON would get two-thirds. The younger son would get one-third. It wasn't just a custom. It was Jewish law: "When the man is near DEATH and is dividing up his property, he must give a double share to his firstborn son" (Deuteronomy 21:16–17 CEV).

Alpha male. When the father died, the oldest son became leader of the extended FAMILY.

BITTER HERBS

Eat the Passover lamb with thin bread and bitter herbs. Numbers 9:11 CEV

FOR MORE THAN 3,000 YEARS—ever since the night MOSES led the enslaved JEWS to freedom out of EGYPT—Jewish people have celebrated their deliverance with a springtime PASSOVER MEAL. Food on the menu symbolizes something about the story. Bitter herbs apparently symbolized that "the Egyptians. . .made their lives bitter" (Exodus 1:13–14). The BIBLE doesn't say what herbs. Contenders: a salad of green plants such as lettuce, endive, or chervil.

BITTER WATER

"He [the priest] will make the woman drink the bitter water that brings on the curse." Numbers 5:24

SUSPECTED OF ADULTERY, Jewish women could be forced to endure a strange trial by ordeal. Her HUSBAND took his suspicion to the PRIEST. The priest would mix an unholy cocktail for her to drink as a test of infidelity: HOLY water, dirt from the floor of the WORSHIP center, and INK from a CURSE the priest wrote to threaten her with bitter suffering if she was guilty. The priest would scrape the curse ink off the SCROLL into the bitter water. Beyond that, many scholars say, it appears that the JEWS left the judgment and punishment to GOD. Some say the test was intended to placate jealous men who might otherwise have resorted to violence.

BITUMEN

(BIH choo men)
or (buh CHOO men)
They had brick for stone, and bitumen for mortar. Genesis 11:3 NRSV

TARRY ASPHALT is what it was. People used bitumen as MORTAR to hold BRICKS together, or as waterproofing for boats. The TAR could occur naturally in tar pits. Boat-sized globs of it occasionally popped to the surface of the DEAD SEA. People would row out and chop off chunks to sell.

FISHING FOR BITUMEN. Globs of bitumen, or tar, used to pop up from the Dead Sea floor. Locals harvested it for sale.

BLASPHEMY

"Every sin and blasphemy can be forgiven— except blasphemy against the Holy Spirit, which will never be forgiven." Matthew 12:31

DISSING GOD by saying something bad about him or treating him disrespectfully is blasphemy. When some Jewish scholars said Jesus got his MIRACLE-working power from SATAN, Jesus warned them that blasphemy against the HOLY SPIRIT is unforgivable. Bible experts today debate what Jesus meant by that. Theories:

- giving the devil credit for GOD's work
- rejecting the work of the Holy Spirit
- refusing to believe in Jesus and to repent of sins

Scholars agree that anyone worried they've committed the UNFORGIVABLE SIN shouldn't worry. As one Jewish poet put it: "He forgives all my sins" (Psalm 103:3).

BLESSING

They gave Rebekah their blessing and said, "We pray that God will give you many children and grandchildren." Genesis 24:60 CEV

IT'S THE OPPOSITE OF A CURSE. In the BIBLE, a blessing was a wish for happiness. It was more than a PRAYER but less than a guarantee. It was a statement of hope, with the expectation that GOD would bring the words to life. Once spoken, the ancients seemed to believe, the words of a blessing—or a CURSE—couldn't be taken back. The power had been unleashed.

Typically, when Jewish men knew they were going to die soon, they called in their CHILDREN to bless them. Elderly, half-blind ISAAC intended to give his favorite son, ESAU, a great blessing. But Esau's shifty little brother, JACOB, pretended he was Esau and got the five-star blessing.

Esau's leftover blessing, by comparison, sounds like a one-star disappointment: "You will live by the power of your SWORD and be your brother's slave. But when you decide to be free, you will break loose" (Genesis 27:40 CEV).

BLINDNESS

> He [Jesus] spit on the ground, made mud with the saliva, and spread the mud over the blind man's eyes. John 9:6

BLINDNESS WAS COMMON in Bible times—as it still is in developing countries, and perhaps for the same reasons. The world's leading cause of preventable blindness is a highly contagious bacterial infection: trachoma. Risk factors: poverty, poor hygiene, crowded living conditions, few bathrooms, lots of flies, CHILDREN ages 3–5.

It spreads by direct contact: touching secretions from the eyes or nose or secretions wiped on clothing.

A Roman science writer, Pliny (AD 23–79), wrote a collection of books called *Natural History* that included two remedies similar to the SPIT and mud techniques Jesus occasionally used:

- Spitball treatment. "To cure inflammation of the eyes, wash the eyes each morning with spit from your overnight fast."
- Mud in your eye. "To protect your eyes from developing eye diseases including inflammation of the eyes, do this. . . . Each time you wash the dust off your feet, touch your eyes three times with the muddy water."

The BIBLE warns against mistreating the blind: "Cursed is anyone who leads a blind person astray on the road" (Deuteronomy 27:18).

BLOOD

> "You must not eat meat that still has blood in it." Leviticus 17:12 NIrV

- Used to atone for sin
- Forbidden to eat; no pink meat

IT'S THE PRICE OF SIN. The BIBLE says that in the eyes of a HOLY God, SIN is a capital offense. Someone has to die. But GOD set up a substitute plan:

> "I have given you the blood of animals to pay for your sin on the altar. Blood is life. That is why blood pays for your sin" (LEVITICUS 17:11 NIrV).

Because animal blood was sacred currency reserved for God, JEWS weren't allowed to consume it in any way—not even in a medium rare steak.

It was the law. But the PROPHETS said that one day God would set up a new system, a "NEW COVENANT" agreement with his people. Jesus presented his ministry as the beginning of that new covenant and his blood as the last necessary SACRIFICE: "This is my blood of the new covenant. It is poured out to forgive the sins of many" (Matthew 26:28 NIrV).

NEW TESTAMENT writers said this was the last blood sacrifice that was necessary: "God's will was for us to be made holy by the sacrifice of the body of JESUS CHRIST, once for all time. . . . There is no need to offer any more sacrifices" (Hebrews 10:10, 18).

BOAT   (see SHIP)

BOAZ

(BO as)

1100s BC

> *Naomi had a relative by marriage, a man prominent and rich. . . . Boaz.*" Ruth 2:1 MSG

- Husband of Ruth
- Great-grandfather of King David

BOAZ WAS STILL A BACHELOR—and fast asleep—when the WIDOW Ruth crawled under his covers. He was a rich landowner in BETHLEHEM, camping out to protect his BARLEY harvest.

With his permission, RUTH had been picking leftover GRAIN missed by the harvesters. She slipped under his covers on the advice of her mother-in-law, the widow NAOMI. Boaz, Naomi had discovered, was related to her late husband. By Jewish custom, that made him a "FAMILY REDEEMER." He could save the two widows from poverty by marrying Ruth.

Sneaking into his bed served as Ruth's warm proposal:

"You are my family protector. So take good care of me by making me your WIFE" (Ruth 3:9 NIRV).

Boaz said "I do."

The couple had a son: OBED, grandfather of DAVID.

BODY OF CHRIST

> *The bread that we break is a sharing in the body of Christ.* 1 Corinthians 10:16 NCV

DURING COMMUNION, also known as the LORD'S SUPPER or Mass, worshipers commemorate the SACRIFICE of Jesus by drinking juice that represents his BLOOD and eating BREAD that represents his body. Some Christians, such as Catholics, say the juice and bread become the actual blood and body of Jesus. Others say they are merely symbols.

"Body of Christ" is also a phrase the apostle PAUL used to describe the CHURCH and to plead for UNITY IN THE CHURCH: "Together you are the body of Christ. Each one of you is part of his body" (1 Corinthians 12:27 CEV).

THE LORD'S SUPPER, also called Mass, commemorates the sacrifice of Jesus. The bread represents his body, and the juice his blood.

BOOK OF LIFE

> *Only those whose names are written in the Lamb's Book of Life will enter the city [heaven].* Revelation 21:27 NIRV

LIKE AN INVITATION LIST, the Book of Life shows up in the BIBLE as a list of people GOD will welcome into PARADISE. Most Bible experts say it's a symbol, not an actual book with a copyright date and an ISBN number. The metaphor is an old one from at least several centuries before Christ: "Your people will be saved. Their names are written in the Book of Life. . . . [They] will be like the stars for ever and ever" (Daniel 12:1, 3 NIRV).

BORN AGAIN

> *"Unless you are born again, you cannot see the Kingdom of God."* John 3:3

WHEN JESUS told a Jewish scholar that anyone who wants to be a CITIZEN of GOD's kingdom has to be born again, the scholar took him literally: "How can an old man go back into his MOTHER's womb and be born again?"

Jesus said he was talking about a spiritual rebirth, not a physical one: "Human life comes from human parents, but spiritual life comes from the Spirit" (John 3:6 NCV).

BOTTLE

> *A few dead flies floating in a bottle of your best perfume can stink it all up.* Ecclesiastes 10:1 AUTHOR'S PARAPHRASE

GLASS BOTTLES were rare and pricey in Bible times—often reserved for expensive PERFUMES and ointments. Most of the containers that functioned like our bottles do today were made of POTTERY or of animal skins sewn waterproof-tight.

BOTTOMLESS PIT

The demons kept begging Jesus not to send them into the bottomless pit. Luke 8:31

OFTEN TRANSLATED *ABYSS,* it's a waffling word with some nasty associations. Bible writers used it to describe the sea, the place of the dead, home of DEMONS, destiny of the beast in REVELATION, and Satan's PRISON for a thousand years. Not a place most folks would put on their bucket list.

BOW AND ARROW

By chance, a soldier shot an arrow which hit Ahab king of Israel between the pieces of his armor. 2 Chronicles 18:33 NCV

OFTEN THE FIRST WEAPON FIRED in battle, bows in Bible times could launch an arrow several hundred yards (meters).

By about the time of ABRAHAM, around 2000 BC, hunters and warriors were making composite bows—reinforcing wood with animal horn or sinew, the tough tissue that binds muscle to bone. This gave the bow more firing power, but it was harder to master than the wooden bow.

Arrows were shafts of wood, sometimes hollowed to increase their range. Arrowheads were cut from stone or shaped from metal. Some men etched their names into the arrowheads, intending to reuse them.

BOWLS

Jesus answered, "The man who has dipped his hand with me into the bowl is the one who will turn against me." Matthew 26:23 NCV

BOWLS WERE CRAFTED from lots of different material: clay, wood, stone, LEATHER, and BASKET-like fibers. The most expensive were made of GLASS, ALABASTER stone, or metal. People used bowls for everything from kneading BREAD dough to drinking WINE, to carrying food to the TABLE.

See also BASIN.

BRANCH

Like a branch that sprouts from a stump, someone from David's family will someday be king. Isaiah 11:1 CEV

A BRANCH ISN'T JUST A BRANCH in the BIBLE. It's often a symbol. NEW TESTAMENT writers portrayed Jesus as the fulfillment of prophecies about a branch shooting up from the dead stump of King DAVID's long-gone dynasty. Jesus would become the promised king of an even more glorious kingdom.

Jesus also used the symbol, describing himself as the source of spiritual life for hungry souls: "I am the VINE. You are the branches. If anyone remains joined to me. . .he will bear a lot of fruit" (John 15:5 NIRV).

BOWS GOT STRONGER when they were layered. Composite bows typically had a wood core, a layer of horn on the side facing the archer, and a layer of sinew (such as animal tendons) on the outside, which stored most of the tension. Glue and string held the layers together.

STEPHEN M. MILLER'S ILLUSTRATED BIBLE DICTIONARY

BREAD

> Jesus said, "I am the bread of life. No one who comes to me will ever go hungry."
> John 6:35 NIrV

BREAD AND WATER: bottom-line basics on any menu in Bible times.

Most often, people made bread fresh every day from WHEAT or BARLEY flour. But they sometimes mixed in some ground-up beans, LENTILS, or other GRAINS and veggies. They would add SALT, water, and old dough as yeast. Then they would knead it all together, working it into a disk-shaped loaf up to a foot (0.3 m) across. They'd let it rise, and then they'd bake it or fry it.

They might bake it on a hot rock and cover it with hot ashes, fry it on a metal plate, or bake it like a pizza in a clay oven fired by wood or grass.

In his most famous PRAYER, Jesus spoke of bread as a minimum daily requirement: "Give us today our daily bread" (Matthew 6:11 NIrV). He also implied that, spiritually speaking, he was the minimum daily requirement: "GOD's bread. . .who comes down from HEAVEN and gives life to the world" (John 6:33 NCV).

IN A ROMAN BAKERY, grain is ground into flour by crushing it in a stone grinding mill. Bakers store the flour in sacks, until they mix it into bread dough and bake it in a stone oven. Customers buy the fresh bread at the bakery.

BREAD OF THE PRESENCE

> "Always keep fresh Bread of the Presence on the Table before me." Exodus 25:30 MSG

HOLY BREAD, a dozen loaves—one for each tribe of ISRAEL—was kept inside the Jewish WORSHIP center: the tent TABERNACLE, and later the Jerusalem TEMPLE.

Why is unclear. But to some it's as though GOD wanted to remind the JEWS that he was their provider, the source of their nourishment—both physical and spiritual.

PRIESTS baked a fresh dozen for each new SABBATH and then ate the week-old BREAD.

Once when DAVID and some of his men were on the run from King SAUL, the priest allowed them to eat the holy bread because "It had just been replaced that day with fresh bread" (1 Samuel 21:6).

Older Bible translations call this bread "showbread."

BREASTPIECE

(see CHESTPIECE)

BRIBE

> "A bribe makes wise folks act like fools and good folks act like the devil."
> Deuteronomy 16:19 AUTHOR'S PARAPHRASE

BRIBES WERE ILLEGAL under Jewish law. Yet they remained a constant complaint of the PROPHETS—especially those best known as advocates for the POOR and oppressed:

- "You cheat honest people and take bribes; you rob the poor of justice" (Amos 5:12 CEV).
- "Rulers and JUDGES use both hands to scoop up their bribes" (Micah 7:3 AUTHOR'S PARAPHRASE).

BRICK

A POOR MAN'S BRICK was made of mud and straw dried in the sun. Stubble of straw helped hold the bricks together, like metal rebar reinforces concrete today.

Workers would stomp in the mud, mixing the mud and stubble together. They'd shape the brick with a wooden MOLD and then carefully remove the mold and let the brick dry thoroughly.

JEWS enslaved in EGYPT before MOSES freed them were forced to make bricks. The Jews supplied bricks for entire cities, including "the cities of PITHOM and RAMESES as supply centers for the king" (Exodus 1:11).

For stronger, longer-lasting bricks, workers would fire the bricks in KILNS. Bricks like that have survived thousands of years.

BRIDE

IN A MAN'S WORLD—which describes Bible times—WOMEN passed from one male master to the next: FATHER to HUSBAND. Ladies had little to say in the matter, short of throwing a hissy fit.

The father of a SON would work out a deal with a father of a daughter. The BRIDEGROOM-hopeful had to pay the father of the bride a fee: compensation for the loss of a household SERVANT. The bride-to-be had to bring a DOWRY into the marriage to help kick-start the new household—though if the marriage failed, the woman got the equivalent of her dowry back.

The BIBLE doesn't say at what age women got married. Many historians speculate that it was often very soon after the young woman's menstrual cycle began—when she could start having CHILDREN. In EGYPT, girls often married between ages 12 and 14 to young men ages 14 to 20.

In perhaps the Bible's best-known tale of a bride,

the SONG OF SONGS reads like the love letters of two youngsters juiced up on hormones and eager for the honeymoon:

"My bride, you're my very own garden—loaded with delicious fruit"
(SONG OF SONGS 4:12–13 AUTHOR'S PARAPHRASE).

HUSBAND HUNTING. Single Bedouin women of the Beersheba area, where Abraham lived, traditionally wore this style of dress. The clue that they were single: blue embroidery at the bottom. Married women embroidered their skirts in red, orange, yellow, or green. Coins on the burqa—301 of them—represented part of her dowry. The message conveyed by this particular outfit: Sugar Momma. She's available and not broke.

New Testament writers used *bride* and *bridegroom* as metaphors describing the loving relationship between Jesus (bridegroom) and the CHURCH. "Let us be joyful. . . . It is time for the Lamb's WEDDING. His bride has made herself ready" (Revelation 19:7 NIRV).

BRIDEGROOM

God will rejoice over you as a bridegroom rejoices over his bride. Isaiah 62:5

IN A MARRIAGE, which was generally arranged by the fathers of the BRIDE and groom, it was the groom's responsibility to pay his future father-in-law a bride fee. The fee was compensation for the loss of a hardworking daughter who cooked, cleaned, and did other chores around the house. In the time of MOSES, the fee seemed set at 50 SILVER coins (Deuteronomy 22:29), weighing in at about 1.25 pounds (570 g). That's close to double the 30-coin price of a slave (Exodus 21:32).

TRADITIONAL BEDOUIN attire is what many herders wear at their weddings.

The bride fee King SAUL required of DAVID, however, was "100 Philistine foreskins" (1 Samuel 18:25). But Saul, jealous of the GIANT-killer's popularity, was hoping David would come back dead. He came back with 200 foreskins.

Many experts speculate that WOMEN often married young, soon after their menstrual cycles began. That marked the beginning of their ability to produce CHILDREN—Job One for women in Bible times. Men, many say, had to wait longer. They needed to develop the skills to survive as the breadwinning head of a house.

Jesus and JOHN THE BAPTIST both compared Jesus to a bridegroom who had come for his bride: believers (Matthew 25:1–13; John 3:29).

See also WEDDING.

BRIMSTONE   (see SULFUR)

BRONZE

"Do I have the strength of a stone? Is my body made of bronze?" Job 6:12

AN UPGRADE FROM COPPER, bronze was stronger. It was a combo metal, an alloy of COPPER and tin. Considered a precious metal in MOSES' day, it ranked alongside GOLD and SILVER as "sacred offerings" (Exodus 25:3) suitable for construction of the tent WORSHIP center. Bronze remained a metal of choice for just about anything, especially WEAPONS. That's until some Middle Eastern metalworkers figured out how to smelt IRON—a process that needed hotter FURNACES. That technology developed in the 1200s BC, when JEWS and PHILISTINES were both settling in what is now ISRAEL. Philistines treated iron as their secret weapon, which gave them a big advantage over the bronze-armed Jews.

BRONZE SEA

Babylonians broke up. . .the great bronze basin called the Sea, and they carried all the bronze away to Babylon. Jeremiah 52:17

A MASSIVE BOWL used at the Jewish WORSHIP center, the bronze Sea held about 11,000 gallons (42,000 l) of HOLY water. "PRIESTS washed themselves in the Sea" (2 Chronicles 4:6), perhaps because cutting up ANIMALS for SACRIFICE was messy work. The Sea stretched about 7 feet tall and 15 feet across (2 by 4 m).

BRONZE SERPENT

Moses made a bronze snake and put it on a pole. Then when a snake bit anyone, that person looked at the bronze snake and lived. Numbers 21:9 NCV

POISONOUS SNAKES ON A PLAIN began biting JEWS who were heading home during the EXODUS out of EGYPT. There are plenty of killer SNAKES in the region, including Egyptian cobras and the devilish-looking horned vipers. On GOD's command, MOSES had a bronze snake erected on a pole—perhaps an instrument to boost the people's FAITH. Snake-bit folks got well when they looked at the bronze snake. Jews kept the snake. Centuries later King HEZEKIAH "broke up the bronze serpent that Moses had made, because the people of ISRAEL had been offering sacrifices to it" (2 Kings 18:4).

BUCKET

To the LORD, all nations are merely a drop in a bucket. Isaiah 40:15 CEV

GOATSKIN BAGS and other LEATHER bags were often used as WATER buckets in Bible times. They were easier to pull up from a WELL and carry than heavy clay pots.

BULL

"Offer a bull to remove the sins of Aaron and his sons so they will be given for service to the LORD." Exodus 29:36 NCV

A TOP-GRADE SACRIFICE, bulls were used in Jewish rituals to atone for the sins of PRIESTS, for rich people who could afford a bull, and for the entire nation. No defective bulls allowed: blind, crippled, injured, oozing sores, scabs, damaged testicles, one leg shorter than the other (Leviticus 22:22–24). One PROPHET warned that this was exactly what the JEWS were offering GOD, adding: "Try giving GIFTS like that to your GOVERNOR, and see how pleased he is!" (Malachi 1:8).

See also OX.

BULRUSH (see REED)

BURIAL

Asa had his own tomb cut out of a rock hill in Jerusalem. So he was buried there, and the tomb was filled with spices and sweet-smelling oils. 2 Chronicles 16:14 CEV

SAME-DAY BURIAL. That was the general rule for Bible-time JEWS. Reasons:

- They didn't usually EMBALM the dead.
- The climate was usually warm, so decomposition started quickly.
- Corpses were considered ritually unclean.
- Jewish law seemed to require it, at least for executed criminals, if not for everyone: "You must bury the body that same day" (Deuteronomy 21:23).

FAMILY and friends would usually wash the body. If they could afford fragrant SPICES and ointments to mask the smell of decay, they would rub these on the body or into the clothes or shroud they used to wrap the body.

Loved ones would mourn the dead in a procession that might include hired mourners and musicians.

BURIAL ON THE MOUNT OF OLIVES overlooking Jerusalem is the world's best location, according to some Jews. Tradition says people there will be the first to rise from the dead when the Messiah comes. "On that day his feet will stand on the Mount of Olives, east of Jerusalem. And the Mount of Olives will split apart" (Zechariah 14:4). Each stone on a grave represents a visitor.

Often, mourners would linger with the family for a week.

People of modest income were usually buried in the ground. Construction crews building a road several years ago at Beit Safafa, an Arab community on the outskirts of JERUSALEM, came upon a graveyard with about 50 unmarked graves from Bible times. Bodies were buried 5–7 feet (about 2 m) deep. They were apparently lowered down a vertical shaft and laid to rest in a horizontal niche at the bottom. A limestone slab sealed the horizontal opening. That left some air between the corpse and the ground—as a casket would—perhaps to keep the corpse from ritually contaminating the ground above. People who walked on ground contaminated by a corpse were considered ritually unclean—unfit to WORSHIP in the TEMPLE until they purified themselves. Some graves were painted white to warn Jews not to walk on them.

Another set of Bible-era graves discovered outside of Jerusalem looks like a cemetery of poor-man TOMBS. Each tomb was chiseled only a foot deep (30 cm) into bedrock and then covered with a stone slab. Some graves included a few coins and GLASS vials.

Wealthier people created tombs from caves, or they hired workers to chisel room-size tombs into the rock face of a hill—sometimes in an abandoned rock QUARRY. ABRAHAM and his family were buried "in the cave of MACHPELAH" (Genesis 25:9). Jesus was buried "in a new tomb that had been carved out of rock" (Luke 23:53)—the tomb of JOSEPH OF ARIMATHEA, a rich man who donated it to Jesus.

A wheel-shaped stone sometimes sealed the entrance of these tombs. Some stones rolled in a grooved track chiseled on an incline—uphill to open, requiring two or more people—but downhill to close. That made it harder to vandalize the tomb but easier for a single mourner to linger alone and close the door when it was time to go.

Like cemeteries today, some of the ancient graveyards featured garden landscaping.

see photo, page 489

BURNING BUSH

The angel of the LORD appeared. . .inside a burning bush. Moses saw that the bush was on fire. But it didn't burn up. Exodus 3:2 NIRV

MINDING HIS OWN BUSINESS, 80-year-old MOSES was grazing SHEEP in a field near MOUNT SINAI.

He noticed a bush on fire. When he went to investigate, a voice from inside the bush called his NAME and said, "I am the GOD of your ANCESTORS" (Exodus 3:6 NCV).

God commissioned Moses to go to EGYPT and demand that the king free the enslaved Jewish people.

Reluctantly, Moses went. When he managed to lead the JEWS to freedom, he brought them back to Mount Sinai, where they camped for about a year. During that time, Moses got the 10 COMMANDMENTS from God, along with many other laws that helped Moses organize the tribes into a nation.

FROM A BURNING BUSH, God speaks to Moses, sending him on a mission to free the Jews enslaved in Egypt.

BURNT OFFERING (see SACRIFICES)

STEPHEN M. MILLER'S ILLUSTRATED BIBLE DICTIONARY

CAESAR

Map 4 B4

(SEE zur)

"Give to Caesar what belongs to Caesar, and give to God what belongs to God."
Mark 12:17

- Title of the Roman emperor

BEFORE THERE WAS A CAESAR, there was Julius Caesar (about 12–44 BC), emperor of the ROMAN EMPIRE.

After Julius's assassination—"Et tu, Brute?"—his adopted heir and successor took the last part of his name and added it to his own: Caesar AUGUSTUS (63 BC–AD 14).

Afterward, the name Caesar became a title that all Roman emperors adopted.

Scholarly rivals of Jesus once tried to trick him with a lose-lose question, asking if JEWS should pay taxes to Caesar. A "yes" would have angered freedom-loving Jews who wanted the Roman occupying force gone. "No" might have gotten him arrested by Romans. Holding up a coin with Caesar's picture on it, Jesus told them to give to Caesar what belonged to him—and to show GOD the same courtesy.

CAESAREA

(cess uh REE uh)

C

A man named Cornelius lived in Caesarea. He was a Roman commander. . . . He prayed to God regularly. Acts 10:1–2 NIrV

- Roman capital of the Middle East for 600 years
- Built by Herod the Great
- Paul imprisoned there for two years
- Peter baptized Cornelius, the first non-Jewish Christian

CLEOPATRA owned the seaside village—until Caesar AUGUSTUS defeated her and Mark Antony in a tug of war for control of the ROMAN EMPIRE. Augustus gave the land to King HEROD THE GREAT, who built it into a

ROME'S CAPITAL OF THE HOLY LAND was Caesarea by the Sea. It's a ruin now, and a tourist attraction. The amphitheater at the bottom right dates to New Testament times. The curved area of the shoreline (center) was part of the huge harbor that King Herod the Great built, extending out into the sea.

STEPHEN M. MILLER'S ILLUSTRATED BIBLE DICTIONARY

sprawling, Roman-style harbor town and named it after CAESAR.

Herod piped in fresh springWATER from the Carmel Mountains, with the help of an AQUEDUCT some 6 miles long (10 km). Showing a taste for Roman living and architecture, he built PALACES, theaters, a hippodrome for CHARIOT races, temples, a SYNAGOGUE, a fortress with a moat, and a huge harbor—ISRAEL's only port.

PAUL sailed into this harbor after two missionary trips. He also languished in PRISON there for two years before appealing for a trial before Caesar. Here, too, PETER baptized the first non-Jewish CHRISTIAN convert on record: a GOD-loving Roman commander. That act set out the welcome mat for non-JEWS to join the Christian movement.

CAESAREA PHILIPPI
Map 4 D3

(cess uh REE uh FILL uh pie)

When Jesus came to the region of Caesarea Philippi, he asked his disciples, "Who do people say that the Son of Man is?" Matthew 16:13

* Where Peter said Jesus is the Messiah
* Where Jesus said Peter would lead the church
* Where Jesus predicted his death

ON A ROAD TRIP north of the SEA OF GALILEE, at the foot of Mount Hermon, Jesus asked his DISCIPLES what people were saying about him—and then what his disciples believed about him. PETER said, "You are the MESSIAH, the Son of the living GOD" (Matthew 16:16).

In response, Jesus used a clever wordplay to declare that Peter—whose NAME means "rock"—would become the rock on which "I will build my CHURCH" (Matthew 16:18). Catholics say Jesus' intent was to appoint Peter the first church leader, as in pope. Protestants say "church leader"—period. Peter's sermon kick-started the CHRISTIAN movement with 3,000 converts (Acts 2:41).

CAIAPHAS

(KYE uh fuss) or (KAY uh fuss)
High priest about AD 18–37
The people who had arrested Jesus led him to the home of Caiaphas, the high priest. Matthew 26:57

* Jewish high priest
* Led Jesus' trial
* Found Jesus guilty of a death penalty offense: blasphemy

CAIAPHAS HAD A BRAINSTORM. After hearing that Jesus raised LAZARUS from the TOMB, Caiaphas—the HIGH PRIEST and religious leader of the JEWS—decided to kill the man who could raise the dead.

He said he feared people might mistake Jesus for the MESSIAH and start a WAR for independence, which ROME would crush. "It is better if one man dies for the people than if the whole nation is destroyed" (John 11:50 NIrV).

With the collaboration of one of Jesus' DISCIPLES—JUDAS ISCARIOT—Caiaphas arranged for Jesus to get arrested at night. That way, there was no admiring crowd to protect the popular RABBI. Caiaphas then led an overnight secret trial in which he condemned Jesus to death.

At the insistence of Caiaphas and other Jewish

CAIAPHAS WAS HERE, in this bone box. So say many archaeologists. The box has his name chiseled into it.

leaders, Roman governor PILATE reluctantly sentenced Jesus to death the next morning.

Caiaphas had married a daughter of the previous high priest, Annas. He became the high priest afterward—a position appointed by the Romans. He held the job until Pilate's successor, Vitellus, replaced him by appointing a new high priest.

Some Bible experts in recent centuries suggested that Caiaphas was a mythical figure. But a Jewish historian from Caiaphas's century, Josephus, referred to the high priest as "Joseph, who was called Caiaphas."

In 1990 many scholars say, Caiaphas's bones were discovered in a bone box dug up from a JERUSALEM cemetery. The stone box called an ossuary—one of a dozen found there—is decorated with ornate designs befitting a person of distinction. But here's the clincher: etched into the stone is the name "Joseph son of Caiaphas." Inside were the bones of four children, one woman, and a man about 60 years old.

CAIN KILLS ABEL, his brother, in the world's first reported murder.

CAIN

(CANE)

Before 4000 BC

Cain attacked his brother, Abel, and killed him. Genesis 4:8

- Oldest son of Adam and Eve
- Murdered his little brother, Abel

THE WORLD'S FIRST BABY, Cain grew up to become a murderer. His motive—with four people on the planet—jealousy.

Cain was a farmer. His little brother ABEL was a SHEPHERD. At harvesttime, both gave offerings of thanks to GOD. Abel brought "the best of the FIRSTBORN lambs from his flock," and Cain brought "some of his crops" (Genesis 4:3–4).

God "accepted Abel and his GIFT, but he did not accept Cain and his gift" (Genesis 3:4). Why not Cain? The BIBLE doesn't say. Some Bible students speculate it's because Cain didn't offer a BLOOD sacrifice. But in Moses' day, God set up a sacrificial system that included GRAIN offerings.

Angry, Cain took his brother for a walk and killed him in the field.

For this, God sentenced Cain to life as a nomad: "No longer will the ground yield good crops for you" (Genesis 4:12).

Cain told God he was afraid someone might kill him—as if he didn't deserve it. God graciously put some kind of mark on Cain to ward off anyone who might try to hurt him. The Bible offers no clue about what the mark was. Some have guessed black skin. Scholars say that's a shot in the dark.

CALEB

(KAY luhb)

1400s BC or 1200s BC (debated)

Caleb calmed down the crowd and said, "Let's go and take the land. I know we can do it!" Numbers 13:30 CEV

- Jewish spy who scouted Canaan

ON THE BORDER of the PROMISED LAND—now called ISRAEL—MOSES and the Jewish refugees he was leading on their EXODUS out of EGYPT sent a dozen SPIES to scout ahead. Ten spies warned of heavily defended, walled cities. GIANTS, too.

Caleb and JOSHUA said these were no problem for GOD.

Majority ruled. It was a no go. For their lack of trust in him in spite of the MIRACLES they had seen, God sentenced the people to 40 years in the badlands. Of the adults in that GENERATION, only Joshua and Caleb lived to set foot on the Promised Land (Numbers 14:30).

CALENDAR

This month [Nisan, from mid-March to mid-April] is to be the first month of the year for you. Exodus 12:2 CEV

WHEN TO PARTY IN THE NEW YEAR is a problem for anyone using the BIBLE as a guide. There seem to be two New Years. One in the spring. One in the fall.

Spring New Year. GOD told MOSES to start the year in Nisan, the March/April month when JEWS celebrate PASSOVER to commemorate their release from SLAVERY in Egypt: "Passover begins at sundown on the fourteenth day of the first month" (Leviticus 23:5).

Fall New Year. God seemed to tell Moses that the end of HARVEST season marked the end of the year—and presumably the beginning of another one: "Celebrate the FESTIVAL of Ingathering at the end of the year, when you gather in your crops from the field" (Exodus 23:16 TNIV).

The solution? Josephus, a Jewish historian in Jesus' century, simply said the Jews had two New Years—one for religion and one for business (FARMING, in this agricultural society).

Jews followed a lunar calendar. Each month started with the blossoming slender crescent of a new moon. At that point in the month, most of the moon is still hidden from view, obscured by the earth's shadow.

Trouble is that a lunar month averages only 29.5 days. Multiply that by 12 months, and the lunar year equals only 354 days long. That's 11 days short of a solar year: 365 days.

In just three years, the SEASONS were off by a month. September would have felt remarkably like August—because it was. To adjust for that, Babylonians in what is now Iraq created a formula for adding 7 months to the calendar over a 19-year stretch. Jews adopted a similar plan. As needed, they added a "Second Adar," which was their last month of the year. A bit like us getting an extra December shopping season.

JEWISH CALENDAR

HEBREW MONTH	ENGLISH MONTH
Nisan	March/April
Iyyar	April/May
Sivan	May/June
Tammuz	June/July
Ab	July/August
Elul	August/September
Tishri	September/October
Marchesvan	October/November
Chislev	November/December
Tebeth	December/January
Shebat	January/February
Adar	February/March

CALVARY

(CAL vuh ree)

When they were come to the place, which is called Calvary, there they crucified him. Luke 23:33 KJV

- Site of Jesus' crucifixion

THE SKULL. That's what *Calvary* means in Latin, the language of the Romans who crucified Jesus. JEWS spoke ARAMAIC. They called the site of Jesus' execution GOLGOTHA, meaning "Place of the Skull."

Calvary was a Roman execution site just outside the walls of JERUSALEM. Why locals called it Skull Place is anyone's guess. It may have been near a cemetery, some speculate.

ON FOOT, a badlands traveler might average 20 miles (32 km) a day. Riding a camel can double the distance.

CAMEL

Enemy horde. . . arrived on droves of camels too numerous to count. And they stayed until the land was stripped bare. Judges 6:5

TRAVELING FIRST-CLASS through vast DESERTS and parched fields of Bible lands, a person needed a camel.

Without a drink, the Arabian camel can carry a rider tipping the scales at over 200 pounds (about 100 kg) some 40 miles (64 km) a day. At a WATER hole, camels can rehydrate themselves quickly, gulping down about 25 gallons (95 l) of water in 5–10 minutes.

The story of ISRAEL's hero GIDEON is the first time on record that people used camels in battle. Raiders from MIDIAN, in what is now Saudi Arabia, rode them when they stormed into Israel each summer to steal the HARVEST. Gideon drove them out.

JEWS owned camels, too. ABRAHAM had at least 10 (Genesis 24:10). JOB fielded a herd of "6,000 camels" (Job 42:12). Jews milked their camels and made tents and other essentials from their hair and hide. But Jews couldn't eat the critters because Jewish law declared camels "ceremonially unclean" (Leviticus 11:4).

For the curious, anthropologist Lloyd Cabot Briggs (1909–1975) said camel meat "tastes just like rather ordinary beef. . .[with] a slightly sweetish aftertaste, like horse but not quite so much."

ON SKULL HILL, better known as Gordon's Calvary, the face of the cliff resembles a skull, with two eye sockets and the bridge of a nose. A British general named Charles Gordon (1833–1885) pitched this hilltop as the possible site of Jesus' crucifixion. Most scholars say the actual site is now preserved inside Jerusalem's Church of the Holy Sepulchre.

(KAY nuh)

In Cana of Galilee Jesus did his first miracle.
John 2:11 NCV

- Jesus turned water into wine

APPARENTLY ON THE GUEST LIST, Jesus attended a WEDDING in the small village of Cana, about a half day's walk north of his NAZARETH hometown—some 9 miles (14 km). When the groom hosting the party ran out of WINE, Jesus' mother convinced Jesus to fix the problem. In his first MIRACLE on record, he changed no less than 120 gallons (454 l) of water into the party's finest wine.

Archaeologists say that a mound of ruins called Khirbet Qana is considered the top contender for Cana. Khirbet is Arabic for "ruins." *Cana* means "REED." Reeds grow in the nearby valley.

TURNING WATER INTO WINE becomes Jesus' first reported miracle. He does this at a wedding in Cana, a village near his Nazareth hometown.

(KAY none)

Abram left, just as the LORD had told him. . . for the land of Canaan. Genesis 12:4–5 NIrV

- Land God promised to Abraham's descendants, the Jews
- Ancient name for Israel

IRAQI ABRAHAM, by today's map, traded his riverfront hometown of UR for a life in the fields of what is now ISRAEL—at GOD's command.

"I will give you the whole land of Canaan," God told ABRAHAM. "You will own it forever. So will your CHILDREN after you" (Genesis 17:8 NIrV).

Abraham's grandson JACOB later led the JEWS to EGYPT to escape a DROUGHT, where they ended up enslaved. But MOSES brought them home—with instructions to wipe out the Canaanites. Jews abhorred the Canaanite religion, which apparently involved SEX rituals, yet failed to kill all the Canaanites.

In time, many Jews started worshiping Canaanite GODS. For that, Bible writers say, God let invaders from what is now Iraq overrun the Jewish homeland and EXILE the Jews abroad. Jews started returning home about 50 years later, rebuilding their nation.

CANAAN

(KAY none)

When Noah woke up with his hangover. . .he said, "Cursed be Canaan! A slave of slaves." Genesis 9:25 MSG

- Grandson of Noah
- Ancestor of Canaanites

CANAAN DIDN'T DO ANYTHING WRONG, but his grandpa NOAH lowered the boom on him. Noah was angry that his son HAM—Canaan's dad—had seen him passed out drunk. Worse, Ham told his brothers to come have a look-see. Apparently wanting to hit Ham where it hurt most, Noah dropped a CURSE on Canaan. Noah condemned him to become a nation of slaves. That's how JOSHUA later treated the Canaanites he didn't kill: "May you be cursed! From now on you will always be servants who cut wood and carry WATER for the house of my GOD" (Joshua 9:23).

CANDACE

(CAN duh see)

The eunuch. . .was minister in charge of all the finances of Candace, queen of the Ethiopians. Acts 8:27 MSG

- Title of Ethiopian queen

LIKE "CAESAR," title of Roman emperors, *Candace* was the title of ETHIOPIAN queens. A CHURCH leader named PHILIP baptized the queen's minister of finance who had come to JERUSALEM on a PILGRIMAGE.

CAPERNAUM

Map 4 D4

(kuh PURR nay um)

Jesus went to Capernaum, a town in Galilee, and taught there in the synagogue every Sabbath day. Luke 4:31

- Jesus' ministry headquarters
- Peter's home

JESUS PICKED A POOR-MAN'S TOWN for his ministry headquarters.

Capernaum was a simple FISHING village of about 1,000 working-class folks, some archaeologists say. No clues of wealth have been found there. And that's after extensive digs that started around 1905. Local POTTERY only. No imports. No fancy fresco art. No painted plaster. No expensive ROOF tiles.

Memorial above ruins of Peter's house

Synagogue ruins

Capernaum

CAPERNAUM—once Jesus' ministry headquarters, now a ruin—is a popular tourist attraction by the Sea of Galilee. Visitors tour the ancient synagogue and are able to see remains of Peter's house below a memorial with a see-through floor.

Other Bible experts say that even if Capernaum were cash-strapped, it may have been a busier burg than previously thought. Two clues:

Customs station. Located just inside GALILEE's eastern border, on a branch of a major trade route called Way of the Sea, the city may have maintained a customs station that taxed products coming and going. This is where Jesus met and recruited TAX COLLECTOR Matthew as a DISCIPLE.

Roman garrison. A Roman CENTURION, it seems, commanded a small garrison of soldiers nearby. This was the soldier who asked Jesus to heal his SERVANT.

It's anyone's guess what drew Jesus to this particular town. Convenience is one possibility. It seemed to be home to nearly half of his disciples—tax collector MATTHEW and four fishermen: brothers JAMES and JOHN, along with brothers ANDREW and PETER. The city was also just a day's walk from his NAZARETH hometown, some 20 miles (32 km) away.

Capernaum lies in ruins today, destroyed by Arab invaders in the AD 600s.

NEIGHBORS: PETER AND THE SYNAGOGUE

Among the village ruins are the remains of an ancient SYNAGOGUE, alongside one of the oldest Christian sites ever discovered: ruins of an ancient CHURCH built on what many say was probably Peter's HOUSE.

The first-century house was large enough for Jesus and his disciples to stay with Peter, as the BIBLE says they did. There were several buildings arranged around three COURTYARDS. A church was built on the site in the AD 300s, after Romans legalized CHRISTIANITY. A pilgrim visiting the site in the AD 380s—Lady Egeria—said she saw the "House of SIMON, called Peter." She said it had been turned into a church. Today an octagon memorial building with a see-through floor rests above the ruins.

The synagogue was only about 30 yards (meters) away from Peter's house. The ruins that survive aren't from the synagogue in which Jesus ministered. The ruins are from one built in the AD 400s. But many say JEWS probably built this synagogue on the site of the earlier once, since the foundation seems earlier.

ANCIENT CAPERNAUM STATS

Size: a dozen football fields (about 300 by 200 yards/meters)

Population: about 1,000

Location: northwest shore Sea of Galilee

Elevation: 686 feet (209 m) below sea level

Abandoned: AD 600s, after Arab invasion

Excavation began: 1905

HEALING PETER'S MOTHER-IN-LAW is just one of many wonders Jesus performs in Capernaum.

JESUS' TO-DO LIST AT CAPERNAUM

- Healed a man lowered through roof
- Healed Peter's mother-in-law
- Healed servant of Roman soldier
- Healed son of city official
- Exorcized an evil spirit
- Taught in synagogue every Sabbath
- Told Peter to go fishing for tax money

STEPHEN M. MILLER'S ILLUSTRATED BIBLE DICTIONARY

CAPPADOCIA
Map 3 L3

(cap uh DOE see uh)

I [Peter] am writing to God's chosen people who are living as foreigners in the provinces of Pontus, Galatia, Cappadocia. 1 Peter 1:1

JEWISH PILGRIMS from this mountainous territory in central Turkey came to JERUSALEM a few weeks after the CRUCIFIXION of Jesus. They came for the PENTECOST harvest FESTIVAL—just in time to hear PETER preach the sermon that launched the CHRISTIAN movement. Miraculously, pilgrims heard about Jesus in their "native languages" (Acts 2:8).

CARAVAN

The queen of Sheba. . .arrived in Jerusalem with. . .a great caravan of camels loaded with spices, large quantities of gold, and precious jewels. 1 Kings 10:1–2

THE MORE THE MERRIER when it came to long-distance TRAVEL. Large caravans offered enhanced protection for travelers along with MERCHANTS loaded with trade goods. Robbers targeted smaller entourages, which had less muscle to fight back.

Caravans usually followed established trade routes, often alongside rivers or on desert stretches with known watering holes at an oasis, a WELL, or the ancient version of a truck stop: a caravansary.

JOSEPH's brothers sold him to a "caravan of. . .Ishmaelite traders" (Genesis 37:25). The traders sold him as a slave in EGYPT.

CARCHEMISH
Map 2 J6

(CAR kuh mish)

King Nebuchadnezzar of Babylonia defeated King Neco of Egypt in a battle at the city of Carchemish near the Euphrates River. Jeremiah 46:2 CEV

IN A BATTLE OF THE SUPERPOWERS fighting for control of the Middle East in 605 BC, King Nebuchadnezzar of Babylon crushed the allied armies of ASSYRIA and EGYPT. It happened at Carchemish, a river town in northern SYRIA. JUDAH's King JOSIAH died trying to stop the Egyptians from passing through his land.

CARPENTER

The carpenter measures with a line and makes an outline with a marker; he roughs it out with chisels. Isaiah 44:13 TNIV

SON OF A CARPENTER, Jesus probably grew up learning how to cut trees and carefully SAW the timber into boards before crafting them into farm TOOLS, doors, window frames, and household furniture such as TABLES.

The GREEK word describing Jesus as a "carpenter" (Mark 6:3) is actually a more general word: *builder*. He may have worked also with stone, mud, and plaster.

CARPENTER AT WORK with a bow-powered drill. The bow string is wrapped around the chunk of wood that holds a drill. As the carpenter moves the bow left and right, the drill spins. Circa 1919 in what is now Israel.

CART

> *"Build a new cart and get two cows. . . .*
> *Hitch the cows to the cart. . . . Put the Ark of*
> *the Lord on the cart. . .send the cart straight*
> *on its way."* 1 Samuel 6:7–8 NCV

MINI-WAGONS, carts were used to haul everything from mud BRICKS to the GOLD-covered ARK OF THE COVENANT—ISRAEL's most sacred relic, which held the 10 COMMANDMENTS. Carts could run on two wheels or four, pulled by one critter or more—often slow-moving muscle machines: oxen.

CATTLE

> *Solomon and the people dedicated the temple*
> *to the Lord by offering twenty-two thousand*
> *cattle. . .as sacrifices to ask the Lord's*
> *blessing.* 1 Kings 8:62–63 CEV

CATTLE PROVIDED MORE THAN STEAKS to JEWS in Bible times. In fact, most Jews could rarely afford to eat meat. Instead, cattle provided:

- MILK
- manure as fertilizer and as fuel to burn
- cow power for hauling, plowing, THRESHING
- sacrifices for the TEMPLE

CEDAR

> *Cedar paneling completely covered the stone*
> *walls throughout the Temple.* 1 Kings 6:18

KING OF THE TREES, cedar was a builder's go-to wood when a customer needed the best. Cedar is durable and beautiful, and it's rot and bug resistant.

Cedar trees, best known in the mountain forests of LEBANON, could grow huge over 2,000 years: up to 130 feet (40 m) tall and 8 feet (2.5 m) thick. Egyptians imported cedar for SHIP masts and caskets. King SOLOMON floated cedar logs down the MEDITERRANEAN SEA to use in the Jerusalem TEMPLE and PALACE. Cedar was a popular choice for musical instruments, ornamental chests, and household furnishings for the rich and showy.

CENCHREA
Map 3 B3

(SIN cree uh)

> *Paul stayed in Corinth. . .then said good-*
> *bye to the brothers and sisters and went to*
> *nearby Cenchrea.* Acts 18:18

A HARBOR TOWN just east of CORINTH, Cenchrea is where PAUL left GREECE to head back home to what is now ISRAEL. Corinth, located on a 4-mile-wide (6 km) finger of land, had a second harbor in the west, Lechaeum, for travelers headed to ROME.

CENSER

> *"Take your censer and fill it with incense,*
> *along with fire from the Altar. Get to the*
> *congregation as fast as you can: make*
> *atonement for them."* Numbers 16:46 MSG

ALL ABOUT SMELL, some offerings were simply scented fires: INCENSE burners filled with fire from the ALTAR, sprinkled with fragrant incense. It was a PRIEST-

WITH AN OFFERING OF INCENSE, an evening service called Solemn Vespers is celebrated in an Oxford chapel. The tradition of offering incense may date back to the Jewish incense offering at the evening sacrifice.

only job. When 250 priest wannabes rebelliously tried offering incense, a fire from heaven cremated them (Numbers 16:35).

CENSUS

Caesar Augustus ordered a census to be taken throughout the Empire. Luke 2:1 MSG

BAD NEWS for average folks, a census was usually taken before collecting taxes or drafting men into military service. It helped leaders get a handle on their inventory. GOD once punished King DAVID for taking a census, perhaps because David wanted to brag about the size of his kingdom (1 Chronicles 21:7).

CENTURION

"Cornelius the centurion. . .is a righteous and God-fearing man. . . . A holy angel told him to ask you to come to his house." Acts 10:22 TNIV

- Commander of 100 Roman soldiers
- Jesus healed a centurion's servant
- Peter baptized one—the first Gentile Christian

JESUS GAVE HIGH PRAISE to a centurion in CAPERNAUM: "I haven't seen FAITH like this in all ISRAEL!" (Matthew 8:10).

LUKE's version of the story says the soldier loved GOD and built the Capernaum SYNAGOGUE where Jesus often taught. The soldier asked Jesus to heal his sick SERVANT—by long distance: "Just say the word from where you are, and my servant will be healed" (Matthew 8:6). Jesus did.

PETER baptized another God-loving centurion: CORNELIUS, who lived in CAESAREA, Rome's capital in the region. By doing so, Peter sent a huge signal: GENTILES are welcome in the CHRISTIAN movement. Until then, CHRISTIANITY was Jewish—like Jesus and all the APOSTLES.

Yet another centurion, after seeing how Jesus died,

declared, "This man truly was the SON OF GOD!" (Mark 15:39).

A CENTURION commanded a unit of 100 Roman soldiers. This is a model of a Roman soldier on display in Museum Quintana in Germany.

CHAFF

You mix the grain you sell with chaff swept from the floor. Amos 8:6

LIKE A HUSK that holds an ear of corn, chaff wraps around each kernel of WHEAT or BARLEY. Farmers threw the chaff-wrapped GRAIN into the air on a windy day. The heavy kernels fell close by, while the lightweight chaff blew further downwind. Chaff was worthless. PROPHETS used the term to describe sinful ISRAEL. AMOS accused rich landowners of cheating the POOR by mixing chaff with grain.

CHALDEA

Map 2 M7

(cal DEE un)

Babylon, the most glorious of kingdoms, the flower of Chaldean pride, will be devastated like Sodom and Gomorrah. Isaiah 13:19

ANOTHER NAME FOR BABYLON in the BIBLE, Chaldea started out as a loose confederation of tribes in what is now southern Iraq. Men from Chaldea eventually became leaders of the Babylonian Empire—the most famous: NEBUCHADNEZZAR, the king who destroyed JERUSALEM.

BIG WHEELS keep on turning, as this Assyrian chariot powers its way through a pride of lions during a royal hunt. On the battlefield, a chariot brought the fear factor of a tank, with overwhelming speed, power, and the weaponry of two or more warriors.

CHARIOT

Philistines mustered a mighty army of 3,000 chariots, 6,000 charioteers. 1 Samuel 13:5

ARMORED VEHICLES, chariots were the ancient fear-factor equivalent of a modern-day tank to a foot soldier with nothing but a rifle.

Middle Eastern armies fielded two-wheel chariots built of wood and plated with metal: BRONZE or IRON. Two horses pulled at least two riders: a driver and an archer. Some armies later added a third rider who carried a SHIELD.

A chariot corps could plow through ground troops, or quickly outflank and surround them, trapping them beneath a shower of arrows.

CHARITY

"When you give to someone in need, don't do as the hypocrites do—blowing trumpets. . .to call attention to their acts of charity!" Matthew 6:2

IT'S A BIG DEAL in the BIBLE—and a consistent theme: help the needy.

Bible writers gave special attention to society's most vulnerable: widows, orphans, and immigrants. They were most at risk and most in need of help.

"Every third year, instead of using the ten percent of your HARVEST for a big celebration, bring it into town. . . . Give food to the POOR who live in your town, including orphans, widows, and FOREIGNERS" (Deuteronomy 14:28–29 CEV).

CHARM

"Now use your magical charms! . . . Maybe they can make someone afraid of you."
Isaiah 47:12

LOOKING LIKE HARMLESS JEWELRY—a necklace, earrings, or a bracelet—amulets were supposed to give a person power. To ward off evil. To cause trouble for enemies.

Bible writers said the charms were worthless.

Amulets were often made of decorated metal, a bit like charm bracelets today. Others were small stones engraved with pictures, incantations, and names.

One stone amulet shows the picture of a rooster-headed, snake-legged spirit holding a shield and cracking a whip to chase away evil spirits. Etched with the names of ANGELS GABRIEL, MICHAEL, and Raphael, the GREEK inscription reads: "Oh powerful angels, bless and prosper John and Georgia and this family while they live."

AN EGYPTIAN GOOD-LUCK CHARM features a scarab beetle pushing a dung ball. Egyptians saw in that a parallel to what they believed their top god did: Re, the sun god, pushed the sun across the sky.

CHEESE

"Give these ten cuts of cheese to their captain." 1 Samuel 17:18

MILK DIDN'T LAST LONG in the hot climate of Bible lands, so people often churned the MILK of GOATS, cows, and CAMELS into cheese. DAVID took some cheese to the captain of his brothers during a battlefield face-off with the PHILISTINES.

CHEMOSH
(KEE mahsh)

Solomon built shrines on a hill east of Jerusalem to worship Chemosh the disgusting god of Moab. 1 Kings 11:7 CEV

- God of Moabites in Jordan

HUMAN SACRIFICE may be why Bible writers called the worship of Chemosh disgusting. King MESHA of MOAB inspired his soldiers to fight off an invading Israelite ARMY by sacrificing his oldest son "as a burnt offering on the wall" (2 Kings 3:27). When Moabites saw their PRINCE die, they fought all the harder.

CHERUBIM
(CHAIR a bim)

Each of the four cherubim had four faces: the first was the face of an ox, the second was a human face, the third was the face of a lion, and the fourth was the face of an eagle.
Ezekiel 10:14

CELESTIAL BEINGS—perhaps a kind of ANGEL—cherubim seemed to serve as guards.

After GOD exiled ADAM AND EVE from the Garden of EDEN, he posted guards to keep them out: "mighty cherubim" (Genesis 3:24).

Figurines of winged cherubim sat on top of ISRAEL's most sacred relic: the ARK OF THE COVENANT, which held the 10 COMMANDMENTS.

In a book written in the genre of APOCALYPTIC literature—noted for its extreme symbolism—the prophet EZEKIEL described a convoy of cherubim in ways they weren't described elsewhere in the BIBLE. They each had two or four faces (it varied) and hands under their wings, and they were covered with eyes all over their bodies. The four faces: OX, human, lion, eagle.

CHESTPIECE

> *Moses placed the chestpiece on Aaron and put the Urim and the Thummim inside it.*
> Leviticus 8:8

▪ Part of high priest's uniform

HIGH PRIEST AARON wore a jewel-studded pouch on his chest over his ROBE. This chestpiece, sometimes called a breastpiece, held a dozen gems. "Each stone will represent one of the twelve sons of ISRAEL, and the name of that tribe will be engraved on it like a SEAL" (Exodus 28:21).

Inside the pouch, the PRIEST carried two stones—called URIM AND THUMMIM—which he used somehow to determine GOD's yes or no to a question.

CHILDREN

> *The LORD took Abram outside and said, "Look up at the sky. Count the stars, if you can. . . . That is how many children you will have."*
> Genesis 15:5 NIRV

ONE OF GOD'S GREATEST BLESSINGS, as far as the BIBLE is concerned—that's what kids are.

Couples who didn't have children often considered themselves cursed. When RACHEL remained infertile, she pleaded with her husband, JACOB, "Give me children, or I'll die!" (Genesis 30:1).

WOMEN considered baby-making their most important job. Children helped the FAMILY survive by doing chores as youngsters and by sticking together as grown-ups in an extended family—pooling resources, fighting off enemies, and taking care of their elderly parents.

Jewish law required children to "Respect your FATHER and MOTHER" (Exodus 20:12 CEV). Sages advised the kids to learn from them, too: "Pay close attention, friend, to what your father tells you; never forget what you learned at your mother's knee" (Proverbs 1:8 MSG)

Parents were responsible for teaching their children, especially about GOD's laws: "Make sure your children learn them. Talk about them when you are at home" (Deuteronomy 6:7 NIRV). Jewish schools didn't seem to develop until about the time of Jesus. Before then, Jewish kids were usually homeschooled.

JESUS BLESSES CHILDREN in the crowd of listeners, though his disciples had tried to shoo them off.

MAKING BABIES is Job One for women in Bible times. Preferably boys—as far as the dads are concerned. They are physically stronger and better able to help Dad do important man stuff.

CHOSEN PEOPLE

> "Of all the people on earth, the LORD your God has chosen you to be his own special treasure." Moses to the people of Israel, Deuteronomy 7:6

- Nickname for the Jewish people
- Later a nickname for Christians

GOD CHOSE ONE MAN, ABRAHAM, to become the father of a select race of people: JEWS.

GOD singled them out for a reason. By devoting themselves to God, as Abraham had done, "Everyone on earth will be blessed" (Genesis 12:3 CEV).

Jesus, a Jew, seemed to fulfill that promise, some say. NEW TESTAMENT writers portray non-Jewish followers of Jesus as God's chosen people, too: "God loves you and has chosen you to be his own people" (1 Thessalonians 1:4).

CHRIST

> "We have found the Messiah" (which means 'Christ')." Andrew to Peter, John 1:41

IT'S A TITLE, NOT A NAME. In HEBREW, the ancient language of the JEWS, the word is *MESSIAH*. In GREEK, the international language of JESUS' day, the word is *Christ*. In English, it's "ANOINTED one," a leader anointed by GOD. Bible writers used the title to describe KINGS, PRIESTS, and especially Jesus.

CHRISTIAN

> It was at Antioch that the believers were first called Christians. Acts 11:26

- Someone who tries to live by the teachings of Jesus

IN THE BEGINNING, CHRISTIANS WERE JEWS. They called themselves followers of "THE WAY" (Acts 19:9). They may have picked that up from something Jesus said: "I am the way, the truth, and the life. No one

can come to the FATHER except through me" (John 14:6).

In time, this movement got tagged with a new name: Christian. It happened at a mixed-race CHURCH in ANTIOCH, SYRIA. That's where non-JEWS started joining the church. Suddenly, "the Way" wasn't Jewish anymore. *Christian* may have been an attempt to make that point—a new name for a new movement.

Oddly, this word describing a group of mixed races comes from a mixed language. *CHRIST* is GREEK, the international language of the day. It means "MESSIAH," God's ANOINTED leader. *Ians* comes from Latin, the language of ROME. It means "belonging to."

A Christian is someone who belongs to Christ.

CHRISTIANITY

> If someone asks about your Christian hope, always be ready to explain it. . .in a gentle and respectful way. 1 Peter 3:15–16

- Religion based on the teachings of Jesus and his apostles

IT'S A RELIGION WITH LOTS OF ELBOW ROOM. Some Christians protest gay marriage; some go to CHURCH with gay ministers. Some picket abortion clinics; some work there. Some are spiritually allergic to wine; some own wineries.

Cheers. Christianity is that diverse.

Catholic. Protestant. Eastern Orthodox. Anglican. Those are the four main groups. And there's broad diversity in each one.

Yet there are several key beliefs that unite almost all Christians—and every one of those beliefs spins around one NAME.

Jesus is the Son of God

> This is the Good News about Jesus the Messiah, the Son of God (MARK 1:1).

Jesus is the source of salvation

> "I am the way, the truth, and the life. No one can come to the Father except through me" (JOHN 14:6).

Jesus rose from the dead

If Christ has not been raised, then our preaching is worth nothing, and your faith is worth nothing. . . . If our hope in Christ is for this life only, we should be pitied more than anyone else in the world (1 Corinthians 15:14, 19 NCV).

Christians often argue over what it takes to qualify as a Christian. Some insist that we join a particular church, get our feet wet (baptized—dunked, not sprinkled), or pay our tithes. In the first generation, many Jewish Christians lobbied for all Christians—Jews or not—to obey the Jewish laws: circumcision, kosher food restrictions, Sabbath rules, and hundreds more.

Yet there's just one qualification, as the New Testament writers tell it. Each writer phrases it a bit differently. But it comes across the same way: trust in Jesus.

- "Anyone who believes in him will not die but will have eternal life" (John 3:16 NIrv).
- "Say with your mouth, 'Jesus is Lord.' Believe in your heart that God raised him from the dead. Then you will be saved" (Romans 10:9 NIrv).

See also Way, The.

CHRONICLES, BOOKS OF 1–2

Famous sound bite: "If my people, who are called by my name, will humble themselves, if they will pray and seek me and stop their evil ways, I will hear them from heaven. I will forgive their sin, and I will heal their land." God's promise to King Solomon, 2 Chronicles 7:14 NCV

RETURNING HOME from a 50-year exile in what is now Iraq, Jews wonder if they're still God's Chosen People. The Chronicles writer says yes. To prove it, he pitches Jewish history into a positive spin with a reassuring message: God never gave up on them—and he never will.

- Writer: Unknown. Ancient Jewish tradition credits Ezra, a priest who lived in the 400s BC. He helped rebuild Jerusalem after the Jews returned from exile in Babylon, modern Iraq.
- Time: The stories cover about 500 years, starting with Israel's first king in the 1000s BC and ending with the Jews returning from Babylonian exile in the 500s BC.
- Location: Most stories take place in Israel.

BIG SCENES

Who's who in the Jewish family tree. The chronicler admits that the Jews busted their contract with God—and lost their country because of it. But then he uses something as boring as a genealogy of about 2,000 names, starting with Adam, to show that God never deserted his people. Even now, the exiles are headed home led by Zerubbabel, a descendant of King David. *1 Chronicles 1–9*

King David picks Jerusalem. Israel's most famous king, a former shepherd boy and Goliath-killer, David makes Jerusalem his capital. Then, unlike King Saul before him, he secures and then expands Israel's borders. The Jews are no longer a loose confederation of 12 tribes. They're one nation and a force worthy of international respect. *1 Chronicles 10–29*

King Solomon builds a temple. Jews have worshiped God in a tent for perhaps 500 years. Now God gives Solomon the go-ahead to build a Temple in Jerusalem. It takes seven years and nearly 200,000 drafted men to get the job done. But it's built to last: 400 years (Babylonian invaders tear it down). Until then, it serves as the only worship center where Jews can offer sacrifices to God. *2 Chronicles 1–7*

Good-Bye Promised Land. After Solomon dies, Israel splits into two countries: Judah in the south, Israel in the north. Out of 39 kings, only four are good and godly. Jews worship idols, exploit the poor, and sell justice to the highest bidder—breaking their ancient contract with God. Their penalty: eviction. Invaders from what is now Iraq wipe both Jewish nations off the map and exile the survivors: Israel in 722 BC, by Assyrians; Judah in 586 BC, by Babylonians. *2 Chronicles 10–36*

Coming home. Ending his Jewish history on the upbeat, the chronicler reports the obvious—for those who might miss it. Assyria is gone. Babylon is gone. Israel is still alive. Persia, the new superpower, has freed the Jewish exiles to go home and rebuild their homeland. *2 Chronicles 36:22–23*

CHURCH

> *Those who believed what Peter said were baptized and added to the church that day—about 3,000 in all.* Acts 2:41

> ▪ People gathered to worship Jesus

CHURCH WAS NEVER A BUILDING. Not in the Bible. *Church* comes from a Greek word: *ekklesia,* "gathering." That's what church was—a gathering of souls, not a dot on a map.

Christians didn't start building churches in earnest until the AD 300s, after Rome legalized Christianity. Before then, most church groups met in homes and at other gathering places.

During the first weeks and months of the Christian movement, "All of the Lord's followers often met in the part of the temple known as Solomon's Porch" (Acts 5:12 cev). At this point, most if not all Christians were Jews. Some believers met in synagogues (Acts 13:5).

Later, when Jews began taking a stand against Christianity, believers started to distance themselves from the Jewish faith by meeting separately.

When the apostle Paul wrote to local churches, he sometimes identified where they met:

- ▪ Corinth: house of Aquila and Priscilla (1 Corinthians 16:19)
- ▪ Colosse: house of Philemon (Philemon 1:2)
- ▪ Laodicea: house of Nympha (Colossians 4:15)

CILICIA

Map 3 K4

(suh LEE see uh)

> *Paul said. . . "I am a Jew from Tarsus in the country of Cilicia."* Acts 21:39 NCV

> ▪ Paul's hometown province in southern Turkey

C

PAUL GREW UP in this river-rich strip of land along the northeast banks of the Mediterranean Sea. Stretching about 200 miles (320 km) east to west, it was famous for its crops—grapes and grain—along with the Cilician Gates, a pass through the Taurus Mountains.

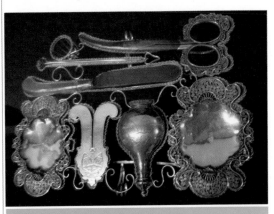

CIRCUMCISION tools include scissors, a knife, and a guide to hold the skin that needs cut, while protecting the head of the penis.

CIRCUMCISION

> *"From generation to generation, every male child must be circumcised on the eighth day after his birth."* Genesis 17:12

> ▪ Removal of penis foreskin
> ▪ Jewish ritual—a reminder they are God's people

IT WAS IN THE CONTRACT—the promises God and Abraham made to each other.

God's part of the deal

- ▪ "I will give you a lot of descendants."
- ▪ "I will give the whole land of Canaan to your family forever" (Genesis 17:6, 8 cev).

Abraham's part of the deal

- "You and all future members of your family must promise to obey me."
- "Circumcise every baby boy when he is eight days old" (Genesis 17:9, 12 CEV).

The penis, clipped of its foreskin, served as a daily reminder to every Jewish male. This mark of distinction was "to show that you are part of my agreement that lasts forever" (Genesis 17:13 NCV). God didn't make this CONTRACT with Abraham alone. He made it with every GENERATION of JEWS to come.

Non-Jews who converted as adults were expected to be circumcised as well, though some decided to WORSHIP God without observing this painful ritual.

Christians abandoned the practice. They said the ritual became obsolete because of God's new agreement, which makes SALVATION available to everyone through FAITH in Jesus. "It doesn't matter if you are circumcised or not. All that matters is that you are a new person" (Galatians 6:15 CEV).

A HOLE IN THE GROUND at Masada was plastered over and made to hold water. This cistern supplied the hilltop fortress built by Herod the Great.

CISTERN

They took him [Joseph] and threw him into the cistern. The cistern was empty; there was no water in it. Genesis 37:24 TNIV

- Pit to store water

WATER WAS PRECIOUS in the hot, parched Middle East of Bible times, as it is today. Some people chiseled pits into the native limestone rock, to store rainwater or WATER hauled in from streams and wells. They waterproofed the rock with plaster, and often covered the top to keep out debris and to reduce the evaporation.

Some cisterns got turned into temporary PRISONS. JOSEPH's brothers stowed him in a dry cistern, before selling him to slave traders. The prophet JEREMIAH got himself lowered "by ropes into an empty cistern in the prison yard" (Jeremiah 38:6)—punishment for urging JERUSALEM citizens to surrender to Babylonians who were laying SIEGE to the city.

CITIZEN

"Is it legal for you to whip a Roman citizen who hasn't even been tried?" Acts 22:25

OPPOSITE OF AN IMMIGRANT, a citizen in Old Testament times was native-born. Not a transplant, who was often called a "stranger," "FOREIGNER," or "alien."

In NEW TESTAMENT times, Roman citizens enjoyed special privileges, including the right to vote, exception from select taxes, the right to trial, the right to appeal to ROME's supreme COURT, the right to a quick execution instead of CRUCIFIXION.

Some Romans bought their citizenship: "And it cost me plenty!" (Acts 22:28).

Others, like PAUL, were citizens by luck of location.

He was born in TARSUS, a city that had warmly welcomed Roman officer Mark Antony (83 BC–30 BC). He responded by declaring Tarsus a Roman town.

SHAPED LIKE FLORIDA, the City of David—later called Jerusalem—crowned the ridge beside the Mount of Olives ridge (right).

CITY OF DAVID

See Jerusalem, Map 1 C5

The sacred chest had been kept on Mount Zion, also known as the city of David. . .in Jerusalem. 1 Kings 8:1 CEV

- Another name for Jerusalem

JERUSALEM BEFORE ITS GROWTH SPURT— that was the City of David, a site known by several names.

Canaanites called it Jebus before DAVID captured the town and named it after himself.

This WALLED CITY crowned a ridge known as Mount Zion, which spawned the nickname ZION. It was a small plug of ground about the size of 7 to 10 football fields.

See also JERUSALEM.

CITY OF REFUGE

"Designate cities of refuge to which people can flee if they have killed someone accidentally." Numbers 35:11

- Six Jewish cities of safe haven

IF JEWS KILLED SOMEONE ACCIDENTALLY, they could flee to one of six safe havens scattered among the 12 TRIBES OF ISRAEL: three towns west of the JORDAN RIVER, three east.

From nearly anywhere in Israel, a town was no more than a day's run away. Speed was essential in the early years of Israel's history. There was no legal system in most areas. By custom, justice fell to the dead victim's closest relative, the "AVENGER of blood" (Numbers 35:21 TNIV).

Bad custom.

At the city of refuge, a defendant would get a trial. If guilty of intentional MURDER, the defendant would get turned over to the avenger. If innocent, the defendant could stay in the city. Only when the HIGH PRIEST died could the defendant safely return home. Bible experts guess that the death of the high priest atoned for the accidental death of the victim. One DEATH cancels out the other.

Israel's 12 tribes, 6 cities of refuge

CLAUDIUS

(CLAW dee us)

10 BC–AD 54

Claudius Caesar deported all Jews from Rome. Acts 18:2

- Roman emperor (reigned AD 41–54)

ROMAN EMPEROR during the early years of PAUL's ministry, Claudius expelled all JEWS from ROME because

"they were continually making disturbances at the instigation of one Chrestus." Life of Claudius

Many Bible experts say "Chrestus" was probably a misspelling of Rome's Latin word *Christus*, for CHRIST. If so, the clash may have been between Jews who believed Jesus was the MESSIAH and Jews who didn't.

CLEAN AND UNCLEAN

"Learn the difference between what is holy and what isn't holy and between the clean and the unclean." Leviticus 10:10 CEV

JEWS WEREN'T ALLOWED to WORSHIP God in the TEMPLE—or even to touch another person—if they were ritually unclean. Unclean JEWS who touched another person would make that person unclean, too.

Laws of MOSES listed several ways a Jew might become unclean:

- contact with a dead person or an animal carcass
- discharge of body fluids such as menstruation or wet dreams
- skin DISEASES such as LEPROSY
- eating forbidden food (nonkosher) such as pork.

Getting rid of ritual impurity usually involved several steps, depending on the impurity. There was usually a waiting period—anywhere from a day to several months; seven days for touching a corpse. Jews usually

had to wash with WATER, too. For some impurities, they had to offer a SACRIFICE. With a skin disease, they had to get an all-clear from the PRIEST.

WELL-DRESSED, a Roman woman memorialized in a funeral statue from Pompeii shows one style of clothing women wore in the early years of the church.

CLOTHING

[Tamar] took off her widow's clothes. She covered her face with a veil so people wouldn't know who she was. Genesis 38:14 NIrV

REALIZING THEY WERE NAKED, ADAM AND EVE put on humanity's first clothes: FIG leaves. GOD outfitted them with something more durable: "clothing from animal skins" (Genesis 3:21).

Head-to-toe styles varied throughout the Middle

East during Bible times.

Headgear. Jews typically topped off with some kind of head covering—a hood-like cloth or a wrapped TURBAN. The fabric was light enough to let the breeze in during hot weather but heavy enough to provide shade. Wrapping it into a layered turban provide extra protection in cold weather, helping to retain the rising body heat.

Underwear. For underwear, men might wear a loincloth—a strip of wool or LINEN (woven from FLAX fibers)—wrapped several times around the hips and groin. Egyptian loincloths extended to the knees. Women might wear a shirt-like tunic to the knees or ankles. Many men wore this, too. But if ancient art is any clue, women seemed to prefer variety in fabric COLORS, while men didn't seem to care much about what color they wore. No surprise there.

Robe. As a second layer, Jews wore a neck-to-ankles ROBE, also known as a tunic. It was woven from coarse wool, for the POOR. Richer folks could afford smooth linen or imported SILK. Men and women each secured their tunics with a BELT wrapped around the waist.

Cloak. During cooler weather especially, people who could afford it wore an outer wrap—a bit like a poncho or a cape. They called it a cloak or a mantle. At night it doubled as a blanket. During the day, it doubled as a BAG: BOAZ told RUTH "to spread out her cape. And he filled it with a lot of GRAIN and placed it on her shoulder" (Ruth 3:15 CEV).

Footwear. PRIESTS probably went barefooted in the TEMPLE, out of respect for the sacred site. But along the stony trails and thistle-grown fields, leather SANDALS were a wonderful idea.

For little kids, especially on hot summer days, imagine Adam and Eve before the fig leaves. Kids wore little or nothing. Farewell to diaper rash.

For sad occasions, such as a funeral, people wore coarse clothing the way mourners today wear black.

For happy occasions, like a WEDDING, they decked out in their finest: colorful robes, fringed and embroidered, with the hems amped up with stylish designs such as stitched pictures of POMEGRANATES.

There was at least one big stylish no-no: cross-dressing: "The LORD your God is disgusted with people who do that" (Deuteronomy 22:5 CEV).

ON LAUNDRY DAY in Pompeii, ladies hang their clothes to dry. Many Roman clothing styles were preserved in Pompeii murals, buried in ash from the eruption of Mount Vesuvius in AD 79.

COINS (see MONEY)

COLOR

Lydia, who was from the city of Thyatira. . . sold expensive purple cloth. Acts 16:14 CEV

MOST JEWS in Bible times probably didn't worry about what color outfit to wear. They couldn't afford to. If the SHEEP gave them white wool, they wore white. If the FLAX fiber they harvested was tan, they wore tan LINEN; if it was off-white ivory, they wore ivory.

Jews who could afford to buy dyed threads and fabric, however, had a few delightful choices.

They could go top of the line: purple. That was the expensive color. It cost a bunch because in that world of desert-dwelling landlubbers, purple dye came from the MEDITERRANEAN SEA: the murex snail. Go fish. As far as the BIBLE tells it, PAUL accepted MONEY for himself from only one CHURCH: Philippi, the church he started in the home of LYDIA—a MERCHANT who sold expensive purple cloth.

Deep blue indigo wasn't cheap, either. It came from indigo plants imported from SYRIA, EGYPT, and India. Brownish red came from the crushed kermes insect on the leaves of an OAK tree. Yellow came from the rind of POMEGRANATE or from the pollen-producing nubs of a saffron crocus.

PURPLE DYE was expensive because it came from the sea: the murex snail.

COLOSSE   Map 3 G3

(coh LAH see)

We are writing to God's holy people in the city of Colosse, who are faithful brothers and sisters in Christ. Colossians 1:2

- Target city of two letters: Colossians, Philemon
- Home of runaway slave Onesimus

HOMETOWN OF A SLAVE-OWNING PASTOR

named PHILEMON, Colosse was a small burg off the beaten trail—headed to extinction. Its death blow came perhaps shortly after PAUL wrote his LETTER to the CHURCH: EARTHQUAKE in about AD 60.

There's no mention of Paul ever visiting Colosse, about a week's walk east of EPHESUS, some 120 miles (193 km). But he hoped to visit. That's what he told Philemon, in a letter asking him to welcome back the runaway slave ONESIMUS. The church met in Philemon's home.

Years before this, Romans built a main ROAD bypassing Colosse. The town was famous for its dark red, purplish wool cloth: *colossinum.*

Archaeologists are just beginning to explore the ancient ruins.

COLOSSIANS, LETTER OF

Famous sound bite: Whatever you do or say, do it as a representative of the Lord Jesus. Colossians 3:17

THE APOSTLE PAUL writes this letter of encouragement to a house CHURCH of Christians in COLOSSE, a city he had not visited.

- Writer: "This letter is from Paul" (Colossians 1:1).
- Time: Possibly AD 60–62.
- Location: Paul is writing "in prison," possibly under house arrest in Rome, awaiting trial in the emperor's supreme court. He is writing to Colosse, a city in what is now Turkey, about a week's walk east of Ephesus, some 120 miles (193 km).

BIG SCENES

Give Jesus his due—he's God. For Christians apparently confused about who Jesus is—GOD's son or an adopted human; divine/human combo or divine being who pretended to be human—PAUL clears the air:

- "Christ is the visible image of the invisible God."
- "He existed before anything was created."
- "Everything was created through him.
- "He holds all CREATION together" (Colossians 1).

Follow Jesus, not highfalutin philosophy. The teachings of Jesus weren't enough for some CHRISTIAN leaders. They urged Christians to do more. Observe Jewish rules about KOSHER FOOD, CIRCUMCISION, and HOLY holidays. Practice self-denial through FASTING and other hardships. Tap into the power of ANGELS in the spirit world. Paul calls it all hokum: "empty philosophies and high-sounding nonsense." His advice: "You accepted Christ Jesus. . .continue to follow him." *Colossians 2*

Think Christian, act Christian. Paul offers a few how-to tips for citizens of HEAVEN on earth.

- "Think about the things of heaven, not the things of earth."
- Run from sexual IMMORALITY, greed, anger, SLANDER.
- Work on your patience, HUMILITY, and kindness.
- Forgive others. God forgave you. Colossians 3

COLT

O people of Zion!. . . Look, your king is coming to you. . .he is humble. . .riding on a donkey's colt. Zechariah 9:9

YOUNG DONKEYS, like young horses, were called colts. The prophet ZECHARIAH predicted that a future KING of ISRAEL would ride into JERUSALEM on a DONKEY's colt and bring PEACE on earth. NEW TESTAMENT writers said Jesus fulfilled that prediction on Palm Sunday. That was just a few days before his sacrificial death paved the way for peace between sinful humans and their HOLY God. The DISCIPLES "brought the colt to Jesus and threw their garments over it for him to ride on" (Luke 19:35).

COMMUNION

The cup of blessing which we bless, is it not the communion of the blood of Christ? 1 Corinthians 10:16 NKJV

- Ritual honoring the death of Jesus
- Bread and wine represent the body and blood of Jesus

A RITUAL WITH MANY NAMES—Mass, Eucharist, LORD's SUPPER, Holy Communion—this act of WORSHIP comes from a single event: the LAST SUPPER. It has a single purpose, too: "Do this to remember me"

(Luke 22:19). That was Jesus talking to his DISCIPLES.

He met with them for one last MEAL, a few hours before his arrest. He gave them some BREAD and WINE. He said the bread "is my body" and the wine "is my BLOOD" (Matthew 26:26, 28).

Many Christians, including Catholics and Orthodox believers, teach that the bread and juice actually transform into the body and blood of Jesus during the ritual. Most Protestants say it only represents his body and blood.

CONCUBINE

[Solomon] had 700 wives of royal birth and 300 concubines. 1 Kings 11:3

- Second-class wife

A STATUS SYMBOL in some cases, WOMEN in Bible times were sometimes seen as trophies. The more a man had in his HAREM, the bigger his bragging rights. Some women were full-fledged wives. Others were secondary wives—or marital associates. Job description: please the man of the house, do chores, make babies. Many concubines were slaves given to a man as GIFTS or to seal peace treaties or trade deals.

CONFESSION

"As soon as you discover that you have committed any of these sins, you must confess what you have done." Leviticus 5:5 CEV

- Admission of sin

JEWS AND CHRISTIANS in Bible times were supposed to confess their sins to GOD—"and you will be forgiven" (Leviticus 5:6 CEV).

JEWS often had to offer an ANIMAL sacrifice, too. For some Jews, SACRIFICES became mindless rituals preformed out of habit—with no remorse for sins. Kill a GOAT, sin gone. Bible writers warned that confession doesn't work that way: "Offerings and sacrifices are not what you want. The way to please you is to feel sorrow

C

deep in our hearts" (Psalm 51:16–17 CEV).

For Christians, Jesus was the only sacrifice needed: "If we confess our sins to God, he can always be trusted to forgive us and take our sins away" (1 John 1:9 CEV).

CONSECRATION

"You must consecrate yourselves and be holy, because I am holy." Leviticus 11:44

- Devoting something or someone to God

JEWISH PRIESTS, the TEMPLE, along with WORSHIP furnishings and utensils were all devoted for sacred use only. The DEDICATION service usually involved rituals, such as ANOINTING with oil and offering ANIMAL sacrifices.

GOD told the JEWS—just as Jesus told his followers—that God's people should devote themselves to the LORD. It's that act of consecration, that commitment to serving GOD, that makes them HOLY in God's eyes.

CONTRACT

The LORD made a covenant with Abram that day and said, "I have given this land to your descendants." Genesis 15:18

OFTEN CALLED A *COVENANT* in the BIBLE, a contract is an agreement between two parties. The Bible's most famous contract is the agreement between GOD and ABRAHAM, father of the JEWS. God promised to give Abraham's descendants what is now roughly the land of Israel, in exchange for obedience.

God made a contract with the Jews of MOSES' day, too. God said if they obeyed the laws he had given them, he would bless them in their homeland. If they didn't, he'd evict them: "The LORD will scatter you among all the nations from one end of the earth to the other" (Deuteronomy 28:64). That happened in 586 BC when Babylonian invaders destroyed JERUSALEM and other Jewish cities.

CONVERSION

The number of believers greatly increased in Jerusalem, and many of the Jewish priests were converted, too. Acts 6:7

CONVERTS were people who changed their religious beliefs. Some converted to the Jewish faith. Jesus ripped up a group of Jewish scholars by charging that they "cross land and sea to make one convert, and then you turn that person into twice the child of HELL yourselves are!" (Matthew 23:15).

The CHRISTIAN movement fed on conversions—first from among JEWS who believed that Jesus was the MESSIAH that the PROPHETS had predicted, and later from among non-Jews who believed he was GOD's Son who offered them ETERNAL LIFE.

LAMB STEW boils over an open fire in the kitchen tent of Bedouin herders in Syria.

COOKING

"Any grain offering that has been baked in an oven, prepared in a pan, or cooked on a griddle belongs to the priest who presents it." Leviticus 7:9

MOST HOT FOOD in Bible times was either baked in a small oven or boiled or roasted over a fire.

When Jacob cooked LENTIL stew for his brother Esau—charging Esau his INHERITANCE rights as Isaac's oldest son—Jacob may have simmered the stew over a campfire. In the winter, some people cooked inside their tents and houses using charcoal-fired pots of metal or POTTERY—a bit like a small, indoor barbecue. It also provided some heat, along with toxins for the lungs.

A metal plate rested over some campfires and served as a mini-stovetop. The lady of the house could fry flat BREAD on the plate, roast kernels of GRAIN, or boil meat in a stew. Boiling meat was an easy way to make sure they followed the Jewish rule against eating meat with any BLOOD in it.

See also BAKING, KOSHER FOOD, MEALS.

COPPER

"People know where to mine silver. . .and how to smelt copper from rock." Job 28:1–2

BEFORE IRON AND BRONZE, copper was the most popular metal for everything from BOWLS to WEAPONS to working-class JEWELRY. By about the time of ABRAHAM, around 2000 BC, metalworkers started smelting copper with tin to form a stronger alloy: BRONZE. IRON—which takes a hotter FURNACE to melt it—came to the Middle East later, around the time the Jews and PHILISTINES were settling into what is now Israel in the 1200s BC.

CORBAN

(CORE ban)

"You allow people to say to their parents, 'Any help you might have received from us is Corban.' (Corban means 'a gift set apart for God.')" Mark 7:11 NIrV

- Loophole to weasel out of giving money to needy relatives, friends

A HEBREW WORD, *Corban* described an offering dedicated to GOD. In Jesus' day, Jewish scholars turned it into a loophole for JEWS who wanted to protect their assets—even from FAMILY members in need, Mom and Dad included.

Jesus wasn't pleased. He reminded the scholars that one of the 10 COMMANDMENTS was to "honor your FATHER and MOTHER" (Mark 7:10). Loopholes around that law—not KOSHER.

CORINTH

Map 3 B3

(COOR enth)

The reason I [Paul] didn't return to Corinth was to spare you from a severe rebuke. 2 Corinthians 1:23

- Greek hometown of Paul's pain-in-the-neck church
- Port city with harbor in two seas

NOTHING BUT TROUBLE is what PAUL seemed to get for the year and a half he spent planting a CHURCH in this working-class town.

In most other places he stopped during his missionary trips throughout Turkey and GREECE, he stayed just a few days or weeks. Why he stayed so long in Corinth is anyone's guess.

Two guesses: Lots of people. Great location.

Corinth was one busy trading hub smack in the middle of a land bridge connecting the Greek mainland in the north to the island-like plug of Greece in the south. Double-dipped in seaports, Corinth was a magnet city that drew travelers wanting a shortcut past the sometimes treacherous currents south of Greece.

Transporting cargo east to ROME, for example, a MERCHANT could unload his merchandise on Corinth's east port at the neighbor city of CENCHREA, in the Aegean Sea. Wagons could haul it some 4 miles (6 km) across the isthmus to Lechaeum, the port in the Adriatic Sea. Today a canal lets ships sail through.

After leaving Corinth, Paul wrote two LETTERS addressing their problems. Among them:

- Leadership. Squabbles over who should lead the church
- Sex. A church member sleeping with his stepmother
- Lawsuits. Church members suing each other

- Communion. Turning the COMMUNION service into a drunken potluck
- Jealousy. Arguing over whose spiritual gift is most important
- Mutiny. Rivals insisting Paul is not a real APOSTLE

CORINTHIANS, BOOKS OF 1–2

Famous sound bite: Three things will last forever—faith, hope, and love—and the greatest of these is love. 1 Corinthians 13:13

PAUL WROTE TWO LETTERS to this CHURCH he founded—a congregation that seemed to stir up more than its fair share of trouble.

- Writer: Paul wrote both letters.
- Time: Paul started the church in roughly AD 50, during his second missionary trip. He spent one and a half years in Corinth. He wrote 1 Corinthians in about AD 55 and 2 Corinthians a few months later.
- Location: Corinth, Greece, is southwest of Athens, on a finger-shaped isthmus connecting mainland Greece in the north to the near-island Peloponnese part of Greece in the south.

BIG SCENES

PASTOR WHO? With PAUL gone, the church seems divided over who's the boss. Members seem to split four ways, perhaps based on opinions about WORSHIP styles or what teachings are most important. Leadership contenders: Paul, PETER, Jesus, and APOLLOS, an eloquent TEACHER

A BUSY PORT CITY with harbors in two oceans, Corinth offered Paul a great location for spreading the story of Jesus. Today, a canal across the four-mile (6 km) isthmus lets ships bypass the city.

from EGYPT. Paul tells the people that he planted the seed and Apollos watered it, perhaps with his PREACHING. Paul's bottom line: "You belong to Christ." *1 Corinthians 1–4*

Sex sin. A church member is sleeping with his stepmother, and no one in the church has confronted him about it. Paul tells the church to call a meeting and excommunicate the man in the hopes that this stern action will jar him to his spiritual senses—so he can rejoin the church. *1 Corinthians 5*

Christians sue each other. Members of the same local church are taking each other to COURT, where non-Christian judges hear them tear each other down. "Isn't there anyone in all the church who is wise enough to decide these issues?" Paul asks. Lawsuits like that, he adds, undermine the ministry of the church and the message of love that it preaches. It would be better, Paul says, for the offended person to "accept the injustice and leave it at that." *1 Corinthians 6*

Christians doubt the Resurrection. Like good Greeks, some Corinthian Christians have no trouble believing in the ETERNAL LIFE of a disembodied SOUL. But the idea of a physical body rising from the dead—that sounds whacked. Paul reminds them that Jesus brought his body back with him—and 500 followers saw it. Paul adds that if all there is to CHRISTIANITY is what we get in this world, "we are more to be pitied than anyone in the world." *1 Corinthians 15*

Paul fights a mutiny. Accused of being a money-grubbing fraud and a fake apostle, Paul defends himself. He reminds the congregation that while he lived among them, starting the church, he didn't take their MONEY. He paid his own way, working as a bivocational PASTOR. He stayed with a couple named Aquila and Priscilla "and worked with them, for they were tentmakers just as he was" (Acts 18:3). Paul adds that he proved he was an APOSTLE by the MIRACLES he did among them. *2 Corinthians 1–2, 12*

CORNELIUS

(cor NEE lee us)

First century AD

"A man in dazzling clothes was standing in front of me. He told me, 'Cornelius, your prayer has been heard.'" Acts 10:30–31

- First-known Christian who wasn't a Jew
- Roman centurion

JEWS ONLY—that was CHRISTIANITY in the beginning. Even JEWS who followed Jesus thought non-Jews were ritually unclean and should be avoided. That changed after PETER and a Roman officer each had a VISION that brought them together. The HOLY SPIRIT filled Cornelius, allowing him to SPEAK IN TONGUES in front of Peter and other witnesses. Peter baptized the officer and his household—the first non-Jewish converts on record. Peter said, "GOD has shown me that I should no longer think of anyone as impure or unclean" (Acts 10:28).

CORNERSTONE

"Didn't you ever read this in the Scriptures? 'The stone that the builders rejected has now become the cornerstone.'" Matthew 21:42

- Stone linking two walls

A CRITICAL STONE in construction of a building, the cornerstone was one of the first that MASONS put down. It needed to be top quality. Jesus compared himself to a stone rejected by builders—referring to the Jewish leaders who opposed him. Jesus said GOD was taking that rejected stone and making it the foundation of God's entire kingdom.

COSMETICS

The young women were given beauty treatments for one whole year. . . . Their skin was rubbed with olive oil and myrrh, and. . . treated with perfumes and cosmetics. Esther 2:12 CEV

ESTHER GOT THE WORKS in a beauty makeover. It was in prep for meeting the Persian king. All the other queen contenders got the same treatment. King XERXES could afford the imported PERFUMES. Most average folks were limited to scented OLIVE OIL, which they rubbed on their skin and HAIR. It moisturized them in the dry Middle East. And it helped mask body odor at a time when bathing was rare.

STEPHEN M. MILLER'S ILLUSTRATED BIBLE DICTIONARY

Some women painted their eyelids, using sap mixed with crushed, colored minerals. They also colored their skin and lips with red ocher, a pigment from the soil. They dyed their hair and painted their nails red or black from colored powder of the HENNA plant.

FACE PAINTING. Cosmetics included red powder blush and molded tablets of white lead. These Greek cosmetic pots were found in a tomb from the 400s BC.

COUNCIL OF JERUSALEM

About AD 48

Apostles and church leaders met to discuss this problem about Gentiles. Acts 15:6 CEV

- First-known formal meeting of church leaders

CHRISTIANS COULDN'T AGREE on what to do about non-Jewish converts.

At the time, most Christians were JEWS. Many considered CHRISTIANITY a new branch of the Jewish religion—Jews who believed Jesus was the MESSIAH. They said every CHRISTIAN should be a good Jew, observing Jewish laws such as food restrictions and CIRCUMCISION for the men. A big ouch for GENTILES.

PETER and PAUL lobbied to let the Gentiles be Gentiles.

A council of leaders, led by a brother of Jesus—JAMES—settled on a compromise. Gentiles needed only to refrain from:

- eating meat left over from sacrifices to IDOLS
- eating meat with BLOOD in it
- practicing sexual IMMORALITY

The compromise didn't stick.

Hard-line Jewish Christians kept preaching their version of Christianity, which eventually died out. And Paul—the Gentile specialist—taught that it didn't matter what Christians ate, as long as they tried not to offend anyone eating with them (Romans 14:2–3; 1 Corinthians 8).

COURT

Some cases that come before you, such as murder. . .may be too difficult to judge. Take these. . .to the priests. . .and to the judge who is on duty at that time. Deuteronomy 17:8–9 NCV

FAMILY DISPUTES were usually settled by the man of the house or the head of the extended FAMILY if it involved different households in the family.

For other disputes, people took their case to city leaders—often at the city GATE, which was a busy meeting area for people coming and going. MOSES advised leaders to take the hardest cases to a group of PRIESTS and a JUDGE.

Later, Jewish KINGS appointed judges throughout the country. During the time of Jesus, a JERUSALEM council of Jewish leaders known as the SANHEDRIN served as a supreme court for Jewish matters. They interpreted Jewish laws and enforced them.

COURTYARD

Peter followed Jesus. He went right into the courtyard of the high priest. There he sat with the guards. He warmed himself at the fire. Mark 14:54 NIrV

LIKE A YARD WITH A FENCE, a courtyard was a plug of ground outside a HOUSE, surrounded by a wall. This is where many households kept some of the ANIMALS, stored their WATER in jugs, and cooked over an open fire. More practical than a luxury, courtyards were even popular among the poorer families.

COVENANT (see CONTRACT)

COVENANT, NEW

> "'The day is coming,' says the LORD, 'when I will make a new covenant with the people of Israel.'" Jeremiah 31:31

JEWS BUSTED their first agreement with GOD. They were supposed to obey the 10 COMMANDMENTS and the other laws MOSES gave them. They didn't. They worshiped IDOLS. They trashed justice. They exploited the POOR.

No more laws written on SCROLLS. "Here is the new agreement. . . . 'I will write my laws on their hearts and minds'" (Jeremiah 31:33 CEV).

The first covenant began with an ANIMAL sacrifice: "This is the BLOOD that puts the covenant into effect" (Exodus 24:8 NIrV). The replacement covenant began with the SACRIFICE of Jesus: "This new agreement begins with my blood which is poured out for you" (Luke 22:20 NCV).

That's why NEW TESTAMENT writers stopped teaching people to follow Jewish laws and TRADITIONS.

CREATION

> In the beginning God created the heavens and the earth. Genesis 1:1

IN SIX DAYS OR 14 BILLION YEARS, God created the universe. Those are the two main ways people of faith read the BIBLE's story of creation.

The Bible says GOD created everything in six days:

1. light
2. sea and sky
3. land with plants
4. sun and moon
5. sea life and BIRDS
6. land ANIMALS and humans.

Many Bible experts, however, say *day* doesn't necessarily mean 24-hour days.

Two reasons.

- God didn't create the tools for measuring 24-hour days until day four.
- "A day is like a thousand years to the LORD" (2 Peter 3:8).

Most astrophysicists say the universe began with a Big Bang about 14 billion years ago—and that it's still growing. Many people of faith who agree with the astrophysicists say God pulled the trigger.

The point of the Bible story, most scholars agree, was to credit God with creation—and to discredit myths about other GODS getting the job done. One ancient Babylonian story from what is now Iraq, *Enuma Elish*, said a battle of the gods created the world when one god got ripped in half. One half of the split god became the earth. The other half became the skies.

CRETE   Map 3 B5

(CREET)

> I left you in Crete to do what had been left undone and to appoint leaders for the churches in each town. Titus 1:5 CEV

- Mission field for Titus

"LIARS, CRUEL ANIMALS, AND LAZY GLUTTONS." Paul said that quote from a Cretan poet describes the people of Crete, a Mediterranean island south of GREECE. PAUL must have figured it was a great place to start churches, because he assigned his colleague TITUS the chore of finding a few good men to lead churches throughout the island.

Paul had hoped to winter there on his sea VOYAGE to ROME for trial. But just as the SHIP approached the harbor, a storm blew up. Winds pummeled the ship for 500 miles (800 km) over two weeks before running it aground off the coast of MALTA, an island south of Italy.

CRIME

"You must not convict anyone of a crime on the testimony of only one witness."
Deuteronomy 19:15

JEWISH LAWS WERE MORE CIVILIZED than Babylonian laws from what is now Iraq. That's what many history experts say after comparing the laws of MOSES to the CODE OF HAMMURABI, written a few centuries earlier.

For one thing, Babylonian law sometimes executed the innocent. If a HOUSE collapsed and killed a man's SON, for example, the builder's son would have to die. Both law codes had "an eye for an eye, a tooth for a tooth" (Exodus 21:24). But only the Babylonians tacked on what amounted to "a son for a son."

Also, Babylonian law gave lighter penalties for social heavyweights: NOBLES, rich, and free citizens. For example, if a free CITIZEN hit another, the fine was one GOLD coin paid to the victim. But if a slave hit a free citizen, the slave got an ear whacked off. Jewish law treated KINGS, herders, and slaves alike.

Sampler of Jewish crime and punishment, from Exodus 21–22; Leviticus 20:10:

- Murder, kidnapping, adultery: Execution.
- Stealing and killing one ox or sheep: Pay back five oxen or four SHEEP.
- Setting fire that accidentally spreads, burning a farmer's field: Pay for the crop.
- Lying about owning goods or property: Pay double its value.

BABYLON'S LAW known as the Code of Hammurabi stands on display in the Louvre Museum of Paris. Unlike Jewish law, Babylonian law allowed the innocent to suffer punishment for someone else's crime. An "eye for an eye" and a "son for a son."

CROSS

They nailed Jesus to a cross. . . . Soldiers also nailed two criminals on crosses, one to the right of Jesus and the other to his left.
Mark 15:24, 27–28 CEV

- Instrument of execution used on Jesus
- Symbol of Christianity

EXECUTION ON A CROSS was reserved for the worst offenses in Roman times: MURDER, treason, violent

ROBBERY. The victim was nailed or tied to the CROSS—feet to the vertical pole, arms to the horizontal crossbeam at the top.

"Each criminal who goes to execution must carry his own cross on his back," according to a first-century historian, Plutarch (about AD 46–120). Victims usually carried just the crossbeam. The vertical pole was often kept posted in the ground at an execution site.

Romans weren't the only ones to use crosses. ALEXANDER the Great hung 2,000 on crosses after he captured TYRE, in what is now LEBANON. One Jewish king, Alexander Jannaeus (reigned 103–76 BC), crucified 800 fellow JEWS who opposed him: PHARISEES.

Because the BIBLE says Jesus died on a cross as a SACRIFICE for HUMANITY's sins and then rose from the dead, the cross became a CHRISTIAN symbol of victory over SIN and DEATH. It also became a reminder of how much GOD loved the world: "so much that he gave his one and only Son, so that everyone who believes in him will not perish but have ETERNAL LIFE" (John 3:16).

See also CRUCIFIXION.

CROWN

David removed the crown from the king's head, and it was placed on his own head. The crown was made of gold and set with gems, and it weighed seventy-five pounds [34 kg].
2 Samuel 12:30

KINGS, QUEENS, AND HIGH PRIESTS wore crowns to symbolize their top-of-the-line status and authority. Archaeologists have uncovered many from Bible lands. One was fairly plain: a GOLD band etched with dots. ISRAEL's first high priest, AARON, wore a crownlike TURBAN that held a gold medallion inscribed with these words: "HOLY TO THE LORD" (Exodus 39:30).

CROWN OF THORNS

Soldiers twisted thorns together to make a crown. They put it on Jesus' head. Then they put a purple robe on him. John 19:2 NIrV

TO HUMILIATE JESUS, convicted of sedition for saying he was the MESSIAH—king of the JEWS—soldiers made him a crown of thorns.

One of several thorny plants growing in JERUSALEM is the Thorny burnet (*Sarcopoterium spinosum*). Its spikes grow to about an inch (3 cm).

THORNS STILL GROW in Jerusalem.

CRUCIFIXION

Pilate. . .ordered Jesus flogged with a lead-tipped whip, then turned him over to the Roman soldiers to be crucified. Matthew 27:26

- Method of execution used on Jesus
- Reserved for worst offenders
- Agonizing death; can take days

"MOST WRETCHED OF DEATHS," according to Roman writer Josephus (about AD 37–101), crucifixion could take several torturous days to kill a person.

Romans considered it the perfect form of capital punishment when they needed to send one particular message: NO ONE MESSES WITH ROME.

- Not cities. To intimidate defenders inside a besieged town, Romans would crucify many captives. To punish the conquered, they would crucify survivors.
- Not rebels. To deter rebellion, they would crucify insurgents by the hundreds. Remember Spartacus?

- Not hardcore criminals. Traitors, deserters, and violent offenders all risked death by crucifixion.

Crucifixion techniques varied, much like butchering an animal varies from butcher to butcher. Roman writer Plutarch (about AD 46–120) said, "Each criminal who goes to execution must carry his own CROSS on his back." Another writer, Seneca (about 4 BC–AD 65) said, "Some hang their victims upside down. Some impale them through the private parts. Others stretch out their arms onto forked poles."

Bible writers detailed how the Romans tortured Jesus.

Beaten. Romans often tied the victims to a pole and beat them with a whip studded with shards of metal or bone. Some considered this merciful because it produced a quicker death.

IN A HANGING OF A HANGING, a stained glass mosaic of the Crucifixion dangles from a wall. Artist Mia Tavonatti created the image.

Paraded. Victims typically carried their cross-beams to the execution site while wearing a sign advertising their crimes. The sign was then nailed to the cross. Jesus' sign said: "The King of the Jews" (Mark 15:26).

Nailed or tied. Romans secured the victims to the cross, either by tying or nailing their wrists and feet to the beams. Soldiers used NAILS on Jesus. So far, archaeologists have found the remains of just one crucified man from Jesus' century. Age: 20s. A nail pierced one heel bone. There's no evidence of injury to the hands or arms, suggesting those were tied.

Cause of death was usually a combo factor: blood loss, thirst, exhaustion. Many suffocated because the position of the body required them to push up on their feet to exhale. That's why Roman's broke the legs of the two criminals crucified with Jesus—so they'd die quickly, before SABBATH began at sundown. Jesus was already dead by then.

Jesus' crucifixion shows up in a Roman history book written during his own century:

"There was a wise man who was called Jesus, a good man. . . . Pilate condemned him to be crucified. . . . His disciples didn't abandon their loyalty to him. They reported that he appeared to them three days after his crucifixion, and that he was alive." Josephus, ANTIQUITIES OF THE JEWS

CUBIT

(CUE bit)

"Make a table of acacia wood—two cubits long, a cubit wide and a cubit and a half high." Exodus 25:23 TNIV

- Unit of measure

INCHES AND CENTIMETERS are standard units of measurement today, but cubits were the builder's standard in Bible times. It was roughly the distance from the tip of a man's middle finger to the end of his bent elbow—about 18–20 inches (46–51 cm).

See also MEASURES.

CUMIN

(COME un)

"You give God a tenth of the spices from your garden, such as mint, dill, and cumin. Yet you neglect the more important matters of the Law, such as justice, mercy, and faithfulness." Matthew 23:23 CEV

- Seeds used as spice and medicine

TINY SEEDS, cumin is big on flavor. People in Bible times used the strong flavor of cumin to season stew, BREAD, and other foods. They also crushed the seeds and mixed them into OLIVE OIL to use as PERFUME. Some ate the seeds as MEDICINE to soothe digestive problems.

CUMIN SEEDS used as flavoring and medicine. Strictly observant Jews tithed even a tenth of the seeds they owned.

CURSE

"If my father touches me and realizes I am trying to trick him, he will put a curse on me instead of giving me a blessing." Jacob to his mother. Genesis 27:12 CEV

A NASTY WISH for someone to get something they would never want. That's a curse, the opposite of a BLESSING.

People put curses on their enemies, their rivals, and even on FAMILY members who disappointed them.

JOSHUA invoked GOD's power after leveling JERICHO: "May the curse of the LORD fall on anyone who tries to rebuild the town of Jericho" (Joshua 6:26).

Many believed that a spoken word of blessing or curse unleashed power to make good or bad things happen. One king, trying to stop MOSES and the JEWS from invading his land, hired a seer to "curse these people" (Numbers 22:6). The seer blessed them instead—four times, predicting ISRAEL's victory.

CUSH
Map 2 I10

(KOOSH)

A river flows out of Eden. . .and from there divides into four rivers. . . . The second river is named Gihon; it flows through the land of Cush. Genesis 2:10, 13 MSG

THERE'S MORE CUSH THAN ONE, many Bible experts say. The Cush mentioned in the creation story seems to point to a region somewhere in the Persian Gulf area—the birthplace of civilization. But other references point to south of EGYPT, in what is now Sudan. In Bible times, that area was also known as ETHIOPIA.

CYMBALS

Praise God with cymbals, with clashing cymbals. Psalm 150:5 CEV

- Temple instruments

PUTTING POP IN THEIR MUSIC, TEMPLE musicians amped up the decibels with crashing cymbals. Crafted of BRONZE and measuring some 6 inches (15 cm) across—based on what archaeologists have found so far—these cymbals joined several other percussion instruments in the sacred Jewish band: TAMBOURINES, castanets, and BELLS.

C

(SI pruhs)

Barnabas took Mark and sailed to Cyprus, but Paul took Silas and. . .traveled through Syria and Cilicia." Acts 15:39–41 CEV

- First stop on Paul's first missionary trip
- Site of first known convert of Roman official
- Hometown of Barnabas

PAUL AND BARNABAS, the world's first CHRISTIAN missionaries on record, left the CHURCH they were copastoring in ANTIOCH, SYRIA. They were on a mission to take the story of Jesus abroad. First stop some 60 miles (96 km) west was the island nation of Cyprus—BARNABAS's home.

The men walked the hills from east to west, some 140 miles (225 km) across, starting up house churches in towns along the way. In the city of PAPHOS, they converted the governor, SERGIUS PAULUS—the first known Roman official to join the Christian movement.

Later PAUL and Barnabas were going to make a return trip but couldn't agree about taking JOHN MARK, Barnabas's cousin. He had joined them on the first trip but bailed halfway through the journey. Paul refused to take him again. So he chose SILAS to head off in a different direction while Barnabas and John Mark returned to Cyprus.

Today nearly 8 of 10 Cypriots (population one million) say they consider themselves Greek Orthodox Christians. Most others are Muslims.

CYRENE
Map 2 E7

(si REE nee)

There was a man walking by, coming from work, Simon from Cyrene, the father of Alexander and Rufus. They made him carry Jesus' cross. Mark 15:21 MSG

- City in what is now Libya

A LIBYAN carried the CROSS for Jesus. SIMON came from Cyrene, a city near the Mediterranean coast. It was home to a large community of JEWS. Simon may have been one of many Jewish pilgrims who made the nearly thousand-mile (1,600 km) trek to JERUSALEM for the PASSOVER festival.

CYRUS

(CY russ)

Ruled from 559–530 BC

"King Cyrus of Persia says: The LORD. . . has appointed me to build him a Temple at Jerusalem. . . . Any of you who are his people may go to Jerusalem in Judah to rebuild this Temple." Ezra 1:2–3

- Turned Persian kingdom into an empire
- Defeated Babylonian Empire
- Freed Jewish exiles to go home

AN IRANIAN PUT ISRAEL ON THE MAP.

King Cyrus freed Jewish political prisoners in what is now Iraq, allowing them to go home and rebuild JERUSALEM and the rest of their nation.

About 50 years earlier, Babylonians based in Iraq had conquered and dismantled the last Jewish nation: JUDAH. They deported most Jewish survivors to the BABYLON area, where they could keep an eye on them. Babylonians didn't want JEWS reviving their constantly rebellious nation.

Then along came Cyrus, ruler of the tiny kingdom of PERSIA in southern Iran. He gave the Middle East a makeover. Joining forces with MEDIA, a kingdom he had conquered in what is now northern Iran and eastern Turkey, he defeated the Babylonians.

One of his first acts as emperor was to free Babylon's political prisoners. His emancipation order appears not only in the BIBLE (2 Chronicles 36:22–23; Ezra 1:2–3), but a clay cylinder from his reign confirms that he freed the people captured from the west "and returned them to their homes."

CYRUS FREED Babylon's political prisoners, according to his own report preserved on this clay cylinder. That supports the Bible story, which says Cyrus freed the Jewish exiles to go home and rebuild their nation.

DAGGER

Ehud made a double-edged dagger that was about a foot long [30 cm]. . .and plunged it into the king's belly. Judges 3:16, 21

SHORT AS A KNIFE yet sharp on both edges like a SWORD, the dagger was a stealth weapon. Easy to hide. Quick on the draw.

Jewish insurgents trying to drive out Roman occupiers would carry daggers, stab Romans and Roman sympathizers in a crowd, and then walk off undetected. These guerrilla assassins earned their nickname: *Sicarii*, "dagger men."

One of ISRAEL's heroic JUDGES, EHUD, hid a dagger by strapping it to his thigh. He managed to get it past the security of a foreign king who oppressed the JEWS. During a private meeting with the king, Ehud stabbed him to death and then escaped through what some Bible translations call "the latrine" (Judges 3:23). Stinky way to become a hero.

DAGON

(DAY gon)

Philistine rulers held a great festival. . . praising their god, Dagon. They said, "Our god has given us victory over our enemy Samson!" Judges 16:23

- Top god of the Philistines

GOD HUMILIATED DAGON TWICE. Excellent timing. In each case the PHILISTINES were bragging about how great their chief god Dagon was.

First, Philistines paraded Israelite hero SAMSON into the temple of Dagon. Samson pushed out the support pillars, collapsing the temple.

Later the Philistines captured ISRAEL's most sacred relic, the ARK OF THE COVENANT, a chest that held the 10 COMMANDMENTS. When they put the Ark on display as a war trophy, at the foot of a statue of Dagon, the statue fell "face to the ground in front of the Ark" (1 Samuel 5:3).

ONE SYRIAN SOUL among 1.7 million living in Damascus today. In ages past, Damascus has been an occasional friend to neighboring Israel. But more often, not so much.

D

DAMASCUS

Map 4 F2

(duh MASS cuss)

"I [Paul] was blinded by the intense light and had to be led by the hand to Damascus by my companions." Acts 22:11

- Paul's destination during his conversion
- Main city of Syria
- Israel's sometimes ally, sometimes enemy

A WEEK'S WALK NORTH OF JERUSALEM, roughly 150 miles (241 km), Damascus was the oasis town where a PHARISEE named Saul hoped to arrest some JEWS and take them back to JERUSALEM for trial—and perhaps execution. Charge: BLASPHEMY. They were dissing GOD by saying he had a son named Jesus.

Instead, as Saul neared Damascus, he saw the light: a VISION of Jesus. He converted and became early CHRISTIANITY's most effective recruiter, the APOSTLE better known by the GREEK version of his HEBREW name: PAUL.

Damascus, capital of modern-day Syria, was at least 3,000 years old by that time. It was 1,000 years old when ABRAHAM passed through in about 2100 BC. Damascus was a natural meeting spot on the edge of the vast Syrian Desert. The reason: it had WATER—a large oasis fed by twin rivers that drained snowmelt from the Anti-Lebanon Mountains just west.

Damascus sometimes fought as Jewish allies. Sometimes as Jewish enemies.

Jewish allies: Damascus king BEN-HADAD joined forces with the southern Jewish nation of JUDAH and attacked the northern Jewish nation of ISRAEL (1 Kings 15:18–20). Damascus later joined forces with Israel and threatened Judah in the south (2 Kings 16:7).

Jewish enemies: King DAVID defeated their invasion force and captured their city (2 Samuel 8:5–6). King Ben-hadad attacked Jews led by King AHAB and lost (1 Kings 20:20–34).

Damascus today is home to about 1.7 million souls scattered over about 17 square miles (43 square km)—a plug of ground about 4 miles long and wide (6 km).

DAN

Map 1 B5, D3

> The tribe of Dan was trying to find a place where they could settle.
> Judges 18:1
> - Son of Jacob (1800s BC)
> - One of Israel's 12 tribes

SON OF JACOB and his wife RACHEL's surrogate, Bilhah, Dan produced a FAMILY that grew into the tribe of Dan. They were unlucky enough to get assigned the PROMISED LAND territory where the PHILISTINES lived—along the coast near today's Tel Aviv. Dan couldn't dislodge the mighty Philistines, so they moved north of the SEA OF GALILEE, settling at the scenic foot of MOUNT HERMON along what is now ISRAEL's border with Syria and LEBANON.

DANCING

> Aaron's sister Miriam. . .took a tambourine in her hand. All the women followed her. They played tambourines and danced.
> Exodus 15:20 NIrv

KING DAVID DANCED when he led the holy parade that brought ISRAEL's most sacred relic to JERUSALEM: the ARK OF THE COVENANT that held the 10 COMMANDMENTS. MIRIAM, sister of MOSES and AARON, danced

after the EXODUS JEWS escaped the Egyptians by crossing through a body of WATER. In Bible times, when there was reason to celebrate—WEDDING, military victory, homecoming—the Jews knew how to shake it up.

DANIEL

(DAN yull)

600s–500s BC

The king gave orders for Daniel to be arrested and thrown into the den of lions.
Daniel 6:16

- Jewish noble exiled to Babylon (Iraq)
- Appointed adviser to kings of Babylon then Persia (Iran)
- Survived a night in a pit with lions

PROBABLY JUST A TEENAGER, Daniel had the rotten luck of being a Jewish noble in JERUSALEM when Babylonian king NEBUCHADNEZZAR came to town. The king looted the TEMPLE and took 10,000 captives to what is now Iraq: Daniel along with "all Jerusalem's elite" (2 Kings 24:15).

Daniel got tapped to serve the king. It's because he met the criteria: he was either a noble or a member of the royal family, and he was "strong, healthy, and good-looking" (Daniel 1:4).

He earned a reputation as a DREAM interpreter. He interpreted Nebuchadnezzar's unsettling dreams, including one about a gigantic statue sculpted from various materials: GOLD head, SILVER chest, BRONZE belly, IRON legs, and feet of mixed iron and clay. Daniel said the gold head represented the king's empire. The other layers represented later, lesser kingdoms.

Daniel outlasted the Babylonian Empire. He became a royal adviser for the Persians when they emerged as the new Middle Eastern superpower. It was then, at perhaps age 80, some jealous rivals plotted to get rid of him. Playing off the king's vanity, they convinced him to sign an irrevocable law: for 30 days people could pray only to the king. Lawbreakers would get fed to the lions.

It was a setup. The officials knew Daniel prayed to GOD three times a day. The king had no choice but to send his most respected adviser to the lions. After a sleepless night of worrying about Daniel, the king rushed to the PIT to find his adviser still alive. The king then ordered the officials who had written the law to try their hand at spending some quality time with the lions—his way of saying, "You're fired."

DANIEL WAS OFF THE MENU in the lions' den. He spent the night there for getting caught praying to God instead of the king. Miraculously, he lived to tell the story. Not so for the politicians who set him up. The cats were really hungry by the time they arrived. Cat nipped.

DANIEL, BOOK OF

Famous sound bite: "My God sent his angel to shut the lions' mouths." Daniel 6:22

STORIES AND PROPHECIES about Daniel are featured in this book that stars the young Jewish noble taken captive to BABYLON. Daniel became an adviser to kings spanning two empires: Babylonian and Persian, based in what are now Iraq and Iran.

- Writer: Unknown. Daniel may have written the prophecies, since the writer uses "I" and "me." But the stories about Daniel, however, use "he" and "him," as though someone else wrote them.
- Time: Daniel's 60-year story started about 605 BC.
- Location: Daniel is taken captive from Jerusalem as a young man. He spends the rest of his life advising the kings of two foreign empires: first in Babylon (Iraq) and later in PERSIA (Iran).

BIG SCENES

Nebuchadnezzar's nightmare. In a jarring DREAM, the king sees a huge statue of a man: GOLD head, SILVER chest, BRONZE belly, iron legs, with feet of mixed iron and clay. The statue crumbles and blows away. Daniel interprets: The head is the king's golden empire of BABYLON. Each empire afterward will be increasingly inferior. Relieved, the king appoints Daniel top adviser in the ranks of the royal wise guys. *Daniel 2*

Fireproof Jews. Nebuchadnezzar builds a huge golden statue, perhaps inspired by his dream. He orders everyone to bow to it. Daniel seems gone, lucky for him. But three of his friends are on hand for the unveiling: SHADRACH, MESHACH, AND ABEDNEGO. They refuse to bow. The king orders them into a FURNACE, perhaps a BRICK-making KILN. When they fail to burn, the king orders them out, promotes them, and orders no one to diss their GOD. *Daniel 3*

Handwriting on the wall. Knees start knocking on Babylon's last king, BELSHAZZAR, when he sees a disembodied hand crash his palace party and start writing on the wall. It writes: "Numbered. Numbered. Weighed. Divided." Daniel gets the call to interpret. A paraphrase: "God has your number. Your number's up. You've been weighed, and you're a lightweight. Your kingdom has already been divided among the Medes and Persians." Belshazzar dies that night when invaders attack. *Daniel 5*

Lion tamer. Officials who covet Daniel's job as a top administrator in the new empire of Persia hatch a plan to get rid of him. Appealing to the king's ego, they manipulate him into signing a law ordering people to pray only to him for a month. Lawbreakers become cat food. They know Daniel prays to God three times a day. They catch him in the act, forcing the king to send him to the lions. Daniel survives, to the king's great relief. The king, recognizing he has been played, orders the lawmakers to meet their Maker by way of the lion's den. *Daniel 6*

Visions of the future. Daniel has several VI-SIONS. One vision comes after he's horrified by reading JEREMIAH's prediction that JERUSALEM will lie in ruins for 70 years. The ANGEL GABRIEL comes and assures him that the suffering of the JEWS will end after "a period of seventy sets of seven" (Daniel 9:24). Bible experts debate what to make of that cryptic timeline. Some say it points to end times, when Jesus returns to earth. Others say it refers to the Jews driving out Syrian invaders who desecrated the Jerusalem TEMPLE in 164 BC. *Daniel 9–12*

DARIUS

(duh RYE us) or (DARE ee us)

(522–486 BC)

King Darius sent this message. . . . "I hereby decree that you are to help these elders of the Jews as they rebuild this Temple of God."
Ezra 6:6, 8

DARIUS THE GREAT, king of the Persian Empire, gave permission for JEWS returning home from EXILE in BABYLON (Iraq) to rebuild their Jerusalem TEMPLE. Better yet, he ordered his GOVERNORS in the region to "pay the full construction costs. . .from my taxes collected" (Ezra 6:8).

DAVID

Ruled about 1010–970 BC

David said to Goliath, "You are coming to fight against me with a sword, a spear and a javelin. But I'm coming against you in the name of the LORD." 1 Samuel 17:45 NIRV

- Second king of Israel
- Killed Philistine champion, Goliath
- Chose Jerusalem as Israel's capital

KING OF MUSIC. Next to killing the Philistine giant Goliath, Israel's King David is perhaps most famous for his music. He soothed the troubled King Saul with his lyre. He wrote songs, including a funeral song for Saul. And he organized the music ministry for Jerusalem's future Temple.

LIKE CINDERELLA on the night of the ball, SHEP-HERD boy David got the order to miss the party. He had work to do.

His father JESSE and all of his seven brothers, on the other hand, would share a MEAL with a visiting dignitary: SAMUEL, a PROPHET.

Samuel brought a young cow with him to Jesse's home in BETHLEHEM. He said he came to offer a SAC-RIFICE and to invite Jesse's FAMILY to join him for some steak. That was just a cover story, only partly true. Samuel came to secretly ANOINT Israel's future KING who would one day replace King SAUL.

Jesse brought all of his sons except his youngest, David, who stayed in the field to guard the SHEEP.

When it came time for Samuel to pick out the next king, he knew something was wrong.

"Are these the only sons you have?" he asked Jesse.

"My youngest is taking care of the sheep," Jesse answered.

"Send for him. We won't sit down to eat until he arrives" (1 Samuel 16:11 NIrV).

As soon as Samuel laid eyes on David, GOD somehow got a message to the prophet: "Get up and anoint him. He is the one" (1 Samuel 16:12 NIrV).

Oddly, the boy destined to become ISRAEL's most celebrated king—founder of a dynasty that will survive half a millennium—was the great-grandson of an Arab and a Jew. BOAZ, a Jewish farmer from Bethlehem, married RUTH, from MOAB, in what is now the Arab country of Jordan.

GIANT KILLER

While the JEWS were resettling in Israel, after their four-century hiatus in EGYPT, Philistines were getting settled along the Mediterranean coast—on what the Jews considered their land. In one of many battles between the two nations, Saul's militia and the PHILISTINES were locked in a staring contest along their borders, about a half-day's walk from Bethlehem.

For 40 days, the Philistine champion warrior—GOLIATH—stepped forward and challenged any Israelite with chutzpah to fight him in mortal combat. Winner take all.

Tall order. Some ancient copies of the BIBLE say Goliath topped out at nearly 10 feet (3 m). Others say nearly 7 feet (2 m). Either way, most Jews figured they didn't measure up. Besides, the best weaponry they could field

D

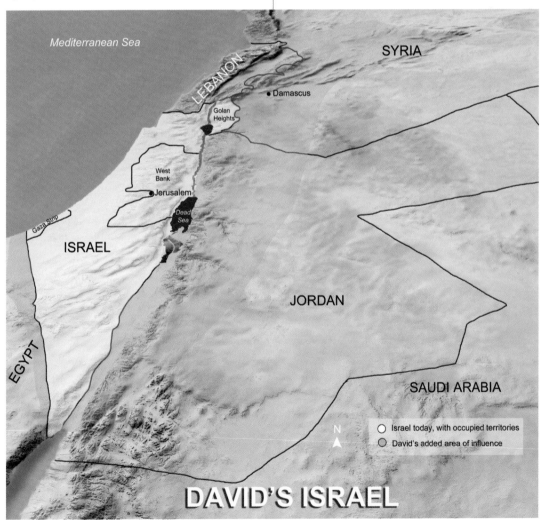

DAVID'S ISRAEL

○ Israel today, with occupied territories
○ David's added area of influence

was crafted of BRONZE. Philistines came into battle with a stronger metal—their secret weapon: IRON.

David arrived from Bethlehem as a delivery boy, bringing food to his three oldest brothers fighting in the militia. He arrived in time to see Goliath step forward and taunt Israel. David decided to shut him up. "I have done this to both lions and bears," David said, referring to how he protected his sheep. "And I'll do it to this pagan Philistine" (1 Samuel 17:36).

He did. One slingshot stone to Goliath's forehead was all it took.

Stone Age 1, Iron Age 0.

SAVVY KING

Jews went wild. Singing. DANCING. Irritating King Saul like crazy—to the point of crazy. He was not at all pleased with one SONG in particular:

"Saul has killed his thousands, and David his ten thousands!" (1 Samuel 18:7).

Jealousy eventually pushed Saul over the edge. While David tried to sooth him by playing HARP music, Saul threw a SPEAR at him—like a berserk music critic with lousy aim.

Later Saul sent David on military missions, hoping he'd come back dead. Instead, he'd come back with new bragging rights. In time, Saul ordered a team of his SOLDIERS to assassinate David. But David escaped.

Living the life of a fugitive constantly hunted by Saul, David gathered a small ARMY of about 400 men "who were in trouble or in DEBT or who were just discontented" (1 Samuel 22:2).

King Saul died in a battle with the Philistines. One of his sons became king: ISHBOSHETH. But a couple of years later, two of his own soldiers assassinated him.

By then, David was living in the south Israel town of HEBRON, where his own tribe of JUDAH had declared him king. Now Jews from all the other tribes did the same, declaring their long-time hero as king of all Israel.

"When Saul was our king," they said, "you were the one who really led the forces of Israel. And the LORD told you, 'You will be the shepherd of my people Israel. You will be Israel's leader' " (2 Samuel 5:2).

Under Saul, Israel had been a loose-linked confederation of tribes. They'd rally when threatened. But they

didn't look or act like the United Tribes of Israel, one nation under God. Not until David.

David turned Israel into a fighting machine. His warriors subdued the Philistines along with neighbors on all of Israel's borders—securing the boundaries of their nation.

He also found a suitable capital, JERUSALEM.

Great location: near the center of Israel, on the crest of a ridge, making it easy to defend. Another big plus, it was still unconquered and lying along the boundary of two tribes. That meant when David captured the city and declared it his capital, no tribe would have the legit complaint that he was playing favorites.

His army captured Jerusalem after a few men climbed up through a WELL shaft. People inside the city used the shaft like a well. They dropped their BUCKETS down the shaft to pull up WATER from a spring POOL in a cave below the city.

David turned the city not only into Israel's political capital—but into its religious center as well. He brought to town Israel's most sacred relic: the ARK OF THE COVENANT, a chest that held the 10 COMMANDMENTS.

HORRIBLE HUSBAND, PITIFUL PARENT

Brilliant on the battlefront, David stunk up the home front. A few of his most notable failures:

Adultery. Seven wives weren't enough. Walking on the ROOF—a spot people used like we use a balcony or a porch—David saw BATHSHEBA taking a BATH somewhere below, perhaps in the walled courtyard of her home. She was married to one of his soldiers, URIAH, away fighting a WAR for king and country. David ordered her to come up for a command performance. He had SEX with her. Next time he heard from her, it was a message: "I'm pregnant" (2 Samuel 11:5).

Murder. To cover up his affair, David arranged for Bathsheba's husband to die on the battlefield. Then "she became one of his wives" (2 Samuel 11:27).

Ignoring a rape. David did nothing when he found out that his oldest son, AMNON, raped his own half sister, TAMAR. She was David's daughter by another WIFE. That set in motion a chain of events that sparked a coup by another son, ABSALOM—Tamar's full brother. Absalom arranged payback for Amnon: assassination. In time, Absalom led a failed coup against David. That ended on the battlefield with "three DAGGERS. . .plunged. . . into Absalom's heart" (2 Samuel 18:14).

Anything but a saint, David had one redeeming characteristic. When confronted with his SIN, he was quick to admit his failures, to ask for God's FORGIVENESS, and to accept whatever punishment came his way. Revered as a great leader among his people—both in his day and in the centuries that followed—David seemed to know the Source of his greatness.

DAY OF ATONEMENT

"Do no work during. . .the Day of Atonement, when offerings of purification are made for you, making you right with the LORD your God." Leviticus 23:28

HOLIEST DAY OF THE YEAR, known today as *Yom Kippur*, it was a nationwide day of REPENTANCE. On the tenth day of the Jewish lunar month of Tishri (September/October), Jews everywhere were supposed to fast and repent of their sins.

This is the only day of the year that the HIGH PRIEST was allowed to go into the HOLY OF HOLIES, the most sacred room in the TEMPLE. That's where ISRAEL's most revered relic was kept: the Art of the Covenant, a chest containing the 10 COMMANDMENTS. There the priest sprinkled BLOOD on the chest—an offering to atone for his sins as well as the sins of the nation.

The priest also drove away a SCAPEGOAT that symbolically carried away the people's SIN. But not before laying both hands on the GOAT's head, to "transfer the people's sins to the head of the goat" (Leviticus 16:21).

See also FESTIVALS.

DAY OF THE LORD

The day of the LORD is near. . . . The Mighty One is coming to destroy you. Joel 1:15 NIrv

- Day of deliverance for the godly
- Doomsday for God's enemies

A FLIP-FLOPPER, the "day of the Lord" was good news in ISRAEL's early history, but horrible news later.

In the BIBLE's earliest stories, the "day of the Lord" meant help and deliverance—as it did during the EXODUS when GOD freed them: "On that day the LORD will come down on MOUNT SINAI" (Exodus 19:11).

Later, PROPHETS started warning sinful JEWS to stop hoping for the day of the Lord. "Why do you want that day to come? It will bring darkness for you, not light" (Amos 5:18 NCV). For their centuries of idolatry, injustice and other sins, God was coming to punish them by evicting them from their homeland.

NEW TESTAMENT writers flop the phrase again, back to good news for godly people: the return of Jesus. "The day of the Lord's return will come unexpectedly, like a thief in the night" (1 Thessalonians 5:2).

DEACONS

(DEE kun)

Deacons must be well respected and have integrity. 1 Timothy 3:8

- Church officers

MEN OR WOMEN could serve as deacons in the CHURCH. Paul commended "PHOEBE, who is a deacon" (Romans 16:1). The BIBLE doesn't say what deacons did in their churches. The GREEK term literally means "SERVANT."

PAUL described for his associate TIMOTHY what he wanted to see in deacons:

- respect for others
- integrity
- no heavy drinking
- honest with MONEY
- committed to the FAITH
- faithful in marriage
- ability to manage their children and household
- not prone to SLANDER
- self-controlled

"Fish will abound in the Dead Sea, for its waters will become fresh." Ezekiel 47:9

FISH UNLUCKY enough to land in the Dead Sea will—within moments—show why it's called the Dead Sea. They'll go belly up.

At least four times saltier than the ocean—higher by some recent measurements—Dead Sea water is one-quarter mineral. That's partly because it's a giant evaporation tank at the lowest spot on the face of the earth. That makes it the drainage pit of the Middle East. It stretches roughly 50 miles long and 10 miles wide (80 by 16 km). Its beachfront lies about a quarter of a mile below sea level (1,294 feet; 394 m).

DEAD SEA MUD, loaded with chemicals, is just what the doctor ordered for some skin ailments such as psoriasis and eczema. Israeli docs often prescribe a soak in the sea or a coat of mud.

In ancient times, people valued it for its SALT and for the occasional giant blobs of asphalt that popped to the top. People would row out in boats, hack the tarbergs into hunks, and sell them as waterproofing and MORTAR.

Today an Israeli mining company extracts minerals for sale—especially potassium compounds used in making fertilizer. Doctors also recommend the water and mud for treating certain skin disorders. That has spawned a health resort boom along the shores. Some guests cake themselves in the mineral-rich black mud. Others soak in the water—which is too buoyant to let them sink.

EZEKIEL predicted a day when a mysterious river flowing eastward from a Jerusalem TEMPLE would empty into the Dead Sea, turning it into a freshwater lake swarming with life. Some interpret that literally. Others read it as a metaphor for better days ahead, since Ezekiel was writing when the JEWS were EXILED from their homeland and living in what is now Iraq.

DEAD SEA SCROLLS ▷

"Write this down on a scroll as a permanent reminder." Exodus 17:14

▪ Jewish library of 2,000-year-old scrolls

A THOUSAND YEARS OLDER than the copies of the BIBLE that scholars used to translate the revered King James Version, the Dead Sea Scrolls aren't mentioned in the Bible. But many scholars say this stash of about 800 SCROLLS is among the most important archaeological discoveries related to the Bible. That's partly because the scrolls show how carefully JEWS preserved the words of their SCRIPTURE, which most Christians call the OLD TESTAMENT.

A community of monk-like isolationist Jews copied the scrolls and stored them in caves near their village of QUMRAN, along the banks of the DEAD SEA. The scrolls date from the 200s BC to AD 68. Some scrolls were found intact, others in fingernail-sized fragments that scholars pieced together like jigsaw puzzles.

The scrolls, discovered in 11 caves from 1947–1956, include many Jewish WRITINGS, along with at least a sampling of every Old Testament book except ESTHER.

THIS DEAD SEA SCROLL (inset) is a copy of the book of Isaiah. It was found in the winter of 1946–47, in this cave at Qumran alongside the Dead Sea. This copy of Isaiah, from more than a century before Jesus, is about 1,000 years older than the copy used to translate the King James Version of the Bible.

DEATH

None of us has the power to prevent the day of our death. There is no escaping that obligation, that dark battle. Ecclesiastes 8:8

BIBLE WRITERS SENT MIXED MESSAGES about death. Some said it's the end of the road for human beings. Others said it's not. Many Bible experts offer this theory: JEWS developed a gradual awareness of life after death.

Many of the oldest books in the BIBLE suggest that death is the end.

- Return to dust. "You were made from dust, and to dust you will return" (Genesis 3:19).
- Dead and dumb. "The living at least know they will die, but the dead know nothing. They have no further reward" (Ecclesiastes 9:5).

Yet, even in the OLD TESTAMENT there are glimmers of hope for something more, a home for spirits of the dead.

- Dead man talking. "Tomorrow. . .you and your sons will be here with me" (the spirit of dead SAMUEL talking to King SAUL, 1 Samuel 28:19).
- Living forever. "Many of those whose bodies lie dead and buried will rise up, some to everlasting life" (Daniel 12:2).

By the time of the NEW TESTAMENT, in the days of Jesus and the APOSTLES, ETERNAL LIFE had become popular among some Jewish groups such as the PHARISEES. It was a hallmark of CHRISTIANITY.

D

- Resurrection or bust. "If there is no RESURRECTION of the dead. . .then all our PREACHING is useless, and your FAITH is useless" (1 Corinthians 15:13–14).
- Death loses. "Our dying bodies have been transformed into bodies that will never die. . . . 'Death is swallowed up in victory. O death, where is your victory? O death, where is your sting?'" (1 Corinthians 15:54–55).

CHRISTIANS GATHER around the bedside of a dying saint. Paul told Christians that if resurrection is fiction, Christianity is tragedy.

STEPHEN M. MILLER'S ILLUSTRATED BIBLE DICTIONARY

DEBORAH, one of Israel's dozen heroic judges, normally worked as a prophetess and a trial judge. But once, she had to lead an army—thanks to a skittish general.

STEPHEN M. MILLER'S ILLUSTRATED BIBLE DICTIONARY

DEBORAH

(DEB or uh)

1100s BC

Deborah. . .was a prophet who was judging Israel at that time. Judges 4:4

- One of Israel's dozen heroic judges

PROPHET, JUDGE, HERO. Deborah was a military commander, too. Not to mention a WIFE. That's quite a resume for a woman at a time when men were men and everyone else was pitifully less.

Deborah—like SAMSON and GIDEON—was one of ISRAEL's dozen heroic leaders called JUDGES. This was before Israel had any KINGS. Most of these heroic leaders weren't literally judges who tried cases. Deborah was an exception. She was also a PROPHET—and for at least one battle, a commander.

The battle came after she told a Jewish general named BARAK that GOD wanted the JEWS to fight off some Canaanite forces who had been raiding them for 20 years. Barak refused to go to WAR without Deborah. She agreed but warned that he'd get no honor because God would give Jews the victory "at the hands of a woman" (Judges 4:9). And God did.

DEBT

If you have put up security for a friend's debt. . .swallow your pride; go and beg to have your name erased. Proverbs 6:1, 3

DEBTS WERE BAD NEWS in Bible times—a condition of the needy.

On the one hand, the BIBLE urges JEWS to help fellow Jews in need by freely lending them MONEY: "Do not charge interest as a money lender would" (Exodus 22:25).

On the other hand, the sages of PROVERBS repeatedly advised young men not to put up collateral for someone else's debt: "It's poor judgment" (Proverbs 17:18).

See also LOAN.

DECAPOLIS

Map 4 F4

(duh CAP oh liss)

The man went away into the region near the ten cities known as Decapolis and began telling everyone how much Jesus had done for him. Mark 5:20 CEV

- Where Jesus exorcised demons from a man

LOADED WITH DEMONS who called themselves *LEGION*, a man cried out to Jesus who healed him—sending the DEMONS into a herd of pigs. Jesus met the man while visiting Decapolis, a non-Jewish region whose name means "Ten Cities." It was located southeast of the SEA OF GALILEE, in what are now parts of Israel and Jordan.

DEDICATION

The king and all the people of Israel dedicated the Temple of the LORD. 1 Kings 8:63

- Devoting something to God

PEOPLE AND OBJECTS ALIKE were dedicated to GOD—for his use in any way he saw fit. JEWS held ritual dedications of their TEMPLE, the sacrificial ALTAR, and even the walls of JERUSALEM—in celebrations that featured SACRIFICES, MUSIC, and DANCING. Jews also dedicated their FIRSTBORN "of both humans and ANIMALS" (Exodus 13:2). The SABBATH, too, was considered a "day of rest dedicated to the LORD" (Exodus 20:10).

DELILAH

(duh LIE luh)

About 1075 BC

Delilah said to Samson, "Please tell me what makes you so strong and what it would take to tie you up." Judges 16:6

- Samson's Philistine girlfriend, betrayer

CHOOSING MONEY OVER LOVE, Philistine Delilah sold out her Jewish boyfriend SAMSON for a hefty reward: 28 pounds (12.5 kg) of SILVER from each Philistine ruler. There were probably five rulers, one for each major Philistine city. So Delilah may have gotten her weight in silver: 140 pounds (62.5 kg).

For that MONEY, she could have bought 183 slaves at the going rate MOSES posted: 12 ounces (342 g) of silver (Exodus 21:32).

Deal.

She kissed and coaxed from Samson the secret to his strength: his vow never to cut his HAIR. Then she arranged for a haircut while he napped. PHILISTINES arrested him, blinded him, and worked him like a MULE to power the grain-grinding wheel at their PRISON.

Samson's parents had told him to find a good Jewish girl (Judges 14:3).

SAMSON TAKES A NAP on Delilah's lap. When he wakes up, he'll have a haircut. Delilah will lose her boyfriend. But she'll likely gain her weight in silver as a reward.

DEMETRIUS

(duh MEE tree us)

First century AD

A silversmith named Demetrius had a business that made silver models of the temple of the goddess Artemis. Acts 19:24 CEV

▪ Sparked a riot to drive Paul out of Ephesus

PAUL DID SUCH A GOOD JOB evangelizing the city of EPHESUS that it hurt one particular business: sale of IDOLS. Ephesus was famous for its Temple of ARTEMIS, considered one of the Seven Wonders of the World.

Demetrius owned a business that manufactured idols of Artemis and her temple. Sales dwindling, he rallied the guild of silversmiths, charged PAUL with dissing the city's patron goddess, and managed to run Paul out of town.

Archaeologists found Demetrius' name on a list of men honored in Ephesus as protectors of the Temple of Artemis.

DEMONS

Jesus cast out the demon. . . . But the Pharisees said, "He can cast out demons because he is empowered by the prince of demons." Matthew 9:33–34

▪ Evil spirits

SATAN'S ARMY OF EVILDOERS is how NEW TESTAMENT writers portray demons. OLD TESTAMENT writers rarely mention them, leading Bible experts to conclude that belief in demons grew gradually and that perhaps the JEWS picked up some of their ideas during their EXILE in the 500s BC in what is now Iraq.

Many people throughout the ancient Middle East seemed to believe in spirit beings—good spirits and bad spirits. They said evil spirits could cause sickness, crop failure, and other disasters.

These spirits could even invade the body, Bible writers agreed, causing mental and physical illnesses— or granting unnatural powers: strength to break "chains from. . .wrists" (Mark 5:4) and the ability "to tell the future" (Acts 16:16 CEV).

DEMONS DIDN'T SHOW UP MUCH in Old Testament times. At least they didn't get much press by the Bible writers. That changed by the time of Jesus, when writers reported that demons were possessing people. Fortunately for many of the possessed souls, Jesus was an exorcist.

In some cases, many demons were said to have possessed a single person. One man had so many that the demons called themselves "LEGION" (Mark 5:9). MARY MAGDALENE, a devoted follower of Jesus, once hosted "seven demons" (Luke 8:2).

See also EXORCISM.

DENARIUS

(din AIR ee us)

"A landowner who went out early in the morning to hire workers. . .agreed to pay them a denarius for the day." Matthew 20:1–2 TNIV

- Roman coin

A DAY'S PAY for a working grunt in Jesus' world, a denarius was a Roman-issued SILVER coin.

See also MONEY, WAGES.

DERBE
Map 3 J3

(DUR bee)

They stoned Paul and dragged him out of town, thinking he was dead. . . . The next day he left with Barnabas for Derbe. Acts 14:19–20

- City that didn't run Paul out of town

ON HIS FIRST MISSIONARY TRIP, to what is now Turkey, PAUL visited four towns—three of which ran him off. Derbe was the exception. It was also Paul's last stop before heading home.

DESERT

The Holy Spirit led Jesus into the desert. There the devil tempted him. Matthew 4:1 NIrV

BIBLE-LAND DESERTS weren't hardcore deserts compared to the nearly rainless deserts of the Sahara and ARABIA.

Israel's Judean Desert, like the Sinai badlands, usually gets some RAIN—especially in the winter months. Sudden bursts can cause flash flooding in *wadis* (WAD ees), dry riverbeds that usually work nicely as walking trails.

These rains produce grazing fields, FLOWERS, and other vegetation in the spring. But they quickly burn off under the summer sun.

The desert was dangerous for humans. It was home to hungry critters, like jackals and LEOPARDS. And it was a haven for robbers preying on lone travelers—a fact Jesus used in his story of a "despised SAMARITAN" (Luke 10:33) who stopped to help a Jewish man who had gotten mugged.

DESTRUCTION, COMPLETE

"In those towns that the LORD your God is giving you as a special possession, destroy every living thing." Deuteronomy 20:16

THINK MEXICANS charging the Alamo while their buglers played "Èl Degüello," a signal meaning "show no mercy."

D

"Destruction" in the BIBLE was actually worse. Though the Mexicans killed all 183 defenders of the Alamo, they spared about 15 women and children. JOSHUA and the JEWS who invaded what is now ISRAEL were to spare no one and nothing. If it breathed, it died.

Men, women, children, pets, and livestock were all slaughtered.

Folks today might call it genocide, with the add-on crime of animal cruelty. Some Bible scholars call it a "ban." Jews were banned from taking anything from the destroyed city. No slaves. No GOLD. No food. All of these WAR treasures were banned from them and devoted to GOD—killed and burned like a SACRIFICE.

MOSES said God ordered the Jews to kill everyone in what is now Israel. Moses explained why: "If you don't destroy them, they'll teach you to follow all of the things the LORD hates. He hates the way they worship their GODS" (Deuteronomy 20:18 NIrv).

The warning Moses gave came true. Jews let some Canaanites live. Jews started worshiping IDOLS. And the Jews lost their homeland because of it; God sent Babylonian invaders from what is now Iraq to destroy the Jewish cities and deport the survivors.

Still, some Bible scholars struggle with the harsh command that Moses insisted came from God. They say they have trouble picturing God ordering the execution of children. Others argue that children grow up. And when they do, some want to return to their roots—and avenge their murdered parents.

DEUTERONOMY

(DO tuh RON uh me)

Famous sound bite: "The LORD our God is the only true God! So love the LORD your God with all your heart, soul, and strength."
Deuteronomy 6:4–5 CEV

IN HIS LAST SPEECH, Moses urged the second GENERATION of Exodus Jews to obey the laws GOD gave the

DEUTERONOMY preserves the last words of Moses. By book's end, he's allowed to see the Promised Land, depicted in this painting. Then he dies and is buried.

nation. Then Moses carefully reviewed the laws for them. The book's name means "Second Law," since this was the second time Moses delivered God's law to the Jews.

- Writer: "These are the words that Moses spoke to all the people of Israel. . . . Moses wrote this entire body of instruction in a book and gave it to the priests" (Deuteronomy 1:1; 31:9).
- Time: 1400s BC or 1200s BC (debated).
- Location: Near the Jordan River's east bank, in what is now the country of Jordan.

BIG SCENES

10 Commandments. Calling all the refugees together, Moses taught a review course on Jewish law. He started with the most important laws of all.

1. No GODS but God.
2. No IDOLS.
3. No irreverent use of God's NAME.
4. No work on the SABBATH.
5. Honor your parents.
6. No MURDER.
7. No adultery.
8. No stealing.
9. No lies about your NEIGHBOR.
10. No craving what belongs to someone else. *Deuteronomy 5*

Pass it on. Moses urged the people to memorize these 10 laws and the many others God had given them. He told them to teach these laws to their CHILDREN, talking about them day and night, at home or while traveling. *Deuteronomy 6*

How to worship God. Moses warned the Jews not to WORSHIP like the locals, the Canaanites, do. They had disgusting rituals, including SEX rites and HUMAN SACRIFICE. And they practiced these just about anywhere: in temples, under shade trees, and at hilltop shrines. But the Jews were to follow God's rules about ANIMAL sacrifices and crop offerings. They were to worship at just one central place: the TENT worship center, and later "at the place of worship he himself will choose from among all the tribes." That place would become the TEMPLE in JERUSALEM. *Deuteronomy 12*

Perks and penalties. After reviewing the laws, Moses reviewed the fine print of ISRAEL's CONTRACT with God. He made sure they knew about the BLESSINGS God promised them if they obeyed his laws: bumper crops, big families, protection from their enemies. And he warned them about the penalties for disobedience: crop failure, DISEASE, raiders, and eventually eviction from the PROMISED LAND. *Deuteronomy 18–30*

DEVIL (see SATAN)

D

DIANA (see ARTEMIS)

DILL

"You Pharisees. . .are show-offs. . . . You give God a tenth of the spices from your garden, such as mint, dill, and cumin. Yet you neglect the more important matters of the Law, such as justice." Matthew 23:23 CEV

A FRAGRANT SPICE from the parsley family, dill seasoned food, freshened breath, and treated intestinal gas.

DINAH

(DIE nah)

1800s BC

When the local prince, Shechem. . .saw Dinah, he seized her and raped her. Genesis 34:2

- Only daughter of Jacob
- Raped by Canaanite prince

JACOB'S DAUGHTER, Dinah, got raped when she left her FAMILY's camp and went to visit women in the nearby village of SHECHEM. The rapist was the village namesake: PRINCE Shechem.

Dinah had a dozen brothers. They killed every man in the village, looted the place, and enslaved the women and children.

When JACOB found out, he was livid. He broke camp and moved to BETHEL, a day's walk south, roughly 20 miles (32 km).

DIOTREPHES

(di OTT truh fees)

First century AD
Diotrephes likes to be the number-one leader. 3 John 1:9 CEV

- Control-freak church leader

FEARING COMPETITION, apparently, a CHURCH leader named Diotrephes ordered his congregation not to welcome CHRISTIAN travelers. He excommunicated members who disobeyed. The apostle JOHN accused him of slandering him and of ignoring his instructions.

DISCIPLE

Jesus. . .saw a man named Matthew sitting at his tax collector's booth. "Follow me and be my disciple," Jesus said. Matthew 9:9

A BIT LIKE GRAD STUDENTS under the wing of a prof, disciples in Jesus' day were often students under the instruction of a RABBI.

Disciples were generally either rabbi wannabes or serious students of Jewish teachings.

Usually disciples would pick a TEACHER much like grad students might pick a university—based on the credentials of the profs who would be teaching them.

Jesus did the opposite. He handpicked his dozen closest disciples—the men he wanted to spread his teachings abroad. NEW TESTAMENT writers also describe other followers as his disciples: "A large crowd of his disciples was there" (Luke 6:17 TNIV).

In time, *disciple* became a substitute word for any follower of Jesus—a CHRISTIAN (Acts 6:1).

DISEASE

"Suppose someone's skin has a swelling or a rash. . . . It could become a skin disease. Then he must be brought to the priest Aaron." Leviticus 13:2 NIrV

LEPROSY was one of the most feared diseases because it usually required permanent isolation from the public. PRIESTS had to examine JEWS suspected of any serious skin problem and order them quarantined until the symptoms disappeared.

Other common diseases: BLINDNESS, PARALYSIS, intestinal parasites, and dysentery.

People knew little about bacteria, viruses, and how the body worked. But they treated the symptoms as best they could—often with WINE for the stomach, along with herbs and salves.

Many Jews seemed to believe that sickness came from GOD as a punishment for SIN. Jesus refuted that when he said one particular man was born blind "so the power of God could be seen in him" (John 9:3). Jesus healed him.

See also HEALING, MEDICINE.

DIVINATION
(see SORCERY)

DIVORCE

"I hate divorce!" says the LORD. . . . "To divorce your wife is to overwhelm her with cruelty. . . . So guard your heart; do not be unfaithful to your wife." Malachi 2:16

DIVORCE WAS A GUY THING according to Jewish law. Only men could divorce; WOMEN could leave, but they couldn't initiate a divorce.

For Jewish men unhappily married, here's the how-to on getting a divorce:

"Suppose a man marries a woman but she does not please him. Having discovered something wrong with her, he writes her a letter of divorce, hands it to her, and sends her away from his house" (DEUTERONOMY 24:1).

With this letter of divorce, the woman was free to remarry. Without it, she couldn't—and still can't in some Jewish circles today.

By NEW TESTAMENT times, Jewish scholars disagreed over what the law meant by "something wrong with her." Some Jewish scholars insisted it meant ADULTERY.

Others said it could mean anything the man didn't like about her: looks or COOKING, to name a couple of the more popular.

Asked to take a position in this debate, Jesus said the Jewish law was written "only as a concession to your hard hearts, but it was not what GOD had originally intended" (Matthew 19:8).

DOCTOR   (see MEDICINE)

DONKEY

The donkey said to Balaam, "Am I not your trusty donkey on whom you've ridden for years right up until now?" **Numbers 22:30** MSG

AN ASS IF IT WAS WILD, the critter was called a donkey only when it was tamed. Wild, they roamed at will. Tamed, they became the preferred mode of transportation for many people in Bible times.

Standing about 3 feet (1 m) tall at the shoulders, the donkeys common in and around ancient Israel were sturdy, sure-footed ANIMALS that could maneuver rough landscape carrying heavy loads—about 20–30 percent of their own weight; and they could weigh in at about 500 pounds or more. They could move, too: up to about 40 miles per hour (64 km/h). And they lasted a lifetime for some owners: 30–50 years.

The most famous donkey was the one Jesus rode into JERUSALEM on Palm Sunday: "Look, your King is coming to you. He is humble, riding on a donkey" (Matthew 21:5). The most talented, however, was the talking donkey ridden by a seer named BALAAM.

DORCAS   (DOOR cuss)

First century AD
There was a believer in Joppa named Tabitha (which in Greek is Dorcas). . . . She became ill and died. **Acts 9:36–37**

- Raised from the dead by Peter

A CHRISTIAN KNOWN FOR HELPING THE POOR, Dorcas died and was washed for BURIAL in her hometown of JOPPA. But PETER showed up. He ordered everyone out of the room. Then he told Dorcas to get up. "She opened her eyes!" (Acts 9:40).

DOTHAN   Map 1 C4
(DOH than)

Joseph followed his brothers to Dothan and found them there. **Genesis 37:17**

- Where Joseph's brothers sold him to slave traders
- Where Elisha blinded Syrian soldiers

ON A MISSION FROM HIS FATHER, JACOB, 17-year-old JOSEPH left his home in HEBRON, south of JERUSALEM. He was to see how his brothers were doing shepherding the flocks. The mission took him on about a three-day walk some 60 miles (97 km) to Dothan in northern Israel. There his brothers sold him to slave traders headed to EGYPT.

Dothan was also where a Syrian patrol tried to capture ELISHA. Instead, he temporarily blinded and captured them.

DOVE

"If she cannot afford a lamb, she is to bring two doves." **Leviticus 12:8** NCV

SEVERAL KINDS OF PIGEONS were called *doves* in Bible times. Jewish law allowed poor WOMEN to offer doves as PURIFICATION sacrifices after delivering a baby. MARY the mother of Jesus offered doves—a clue that she and JOSEPH were POOR. NOAH released doves after the FLOOD to see if they would find a dry place to land.

> *Pharaoh king of Egypt. . .captured Gezer. . .*
> *and had given it as dowry to his daughter,*
> *Solomon's wife.* 1 Kings 9:16 NASB

* Bride's financial contribution to the marriage

GOLD, CATTLE, AND SHEEP might be among the assets a BRIDE brought into her marriage. This dowry provided not only seed currency for the start-up business of matrimony. It protected the bride if the marriage went belly-up.

The CODE OF HAMMURABI, a set of Middle Eastern laws written several centuries before MOSES, declares that the WIFE got to keep the value of her dowry if her HUSBAND died first or if he DIVORCED her.

If she died first, her kids inherited the value of her dowry—the husband didn't. It wasn't his in the beginning or the end. If the woman died first, without producing kids, the widower had to return the dowry to his wife's FAMILY. But he could deduct the value of the bride fee he had paid them for her. Usually, some scholars say, the man's bride fee was less than the value of the dowry.

See also WEDDING.

DREAMS

> *God came to Abimelech in a dream and told*
> *him, "You are a dead man."*
> Genesis 20:3

* How God communicated to people

A DREAM convinced Joseph to take Mary and young Jesus to Egypt before King Herod killed all the Bethlehem boys ages two and under.

IN VISIONS OF THE NIGHT is how GOD spoke to people, according to one of Job's friends (Job 33:15).

Throughout the ancient Middle East, people seemed to believe that their GODS spoke to them in dreams. Ancient books about how to interpret dreams suggest this belief was widespread. So do the many references in history to dream interpreters, some of whom served as royal advisers.

People seeking answers or direction from the gods would sleep in sacred places, such as a temple or a SHRINE.

JEWS and Christians alike told stories about God speaking in dreams—both to people of FAITH and to the faithless. The BIBLE is loaded with these stories.

- Canaanite King ABIMELECH got warned by God not to marry SARAH.
- JACOB on the run from ESAU dreamed of God promising Jacob a home for his FAMILY in what is now ISRAEL.
- Teenage JOSEPH dreamed that his family would one day bow before him.
- EGYPT's king was warned of a seven-year DROUGHT.
- King SOLOMON asked God in a dream for WISDOM, and God granted the request, tossing in a bonus: wealth and fame.
- Babylonian king NEBUCHADNEZZAR had dreams about the future, which the prophet DANIEL interpreted.
- WISE MEN who visited Jesus in BETHLEHEM were warned not to report back to King HEROD.
- MARY's husband JOSEPH was warned in a dream to leave the country before Herod killed the Bethlehem boys age two and under.
- Pilate's wife had a nightmare about Jesus and warned him to drop the trial.

See also VISION.

DROUGHT

"I have called for a drought. . .to wither the grain and grapes and olive trees. . .to starve you and your livestock." Haggai 1:11

IN SUN-BAKED BIBLE LANDS where WATER was likely as scarce in ancient times as it is today, RAIN could mean the difference between life and DEATH—between staying put and hitting the road for greener pastures.

It was a seven-year drought that forced JACOB to move his entire extended FAMILY to the drought-resistant NILE RIVER VALLEY in EGYPT. That's where the JEWS ended up enslaved until MOSES arrived to lead them home.

Moses warned the Jews that once they got back to what is now ISRAEL, if they didn't obey GOD they could expect disasters, including "scorching heat and drought" (Deuteronomy 28:22).

Centuries later the prophet HAGGAI warned the Jews that the terrible HARVEST they had just suffered was because God was punishing them with droughts until they rebuilt his TEMPLE, which had been torn down by invaders. They got started on the construction right away.

DRUNKENNESS

Asking an idiot for smart advice is like asking a drunk to toss you a knife.
Proverbs 26:9 AUTHOR'S PARAPHRASE

DRUNKS GET BAD PRESS in the BIBLE. As Bible writers tell it, bad things happen when GOD's people get plastered.

- NOAH passed out "naked inside his TENT" (Genesis 9:21). His sons saw him. Not a memory any son wants.
- LOT got his daughters pregnant; their idea for how to "preserve our FAMILY line" (Genesis 19:32). For the two sons born, daddy was their grandpa.

Jewish wise men of the OLD TESTAMENT and Christian writers of the NEW TESTAMENT agreed:

- "A staggering drunk is not much fun" (Proverbs 20:1 MSG).
- "Don't be stupid. . . . Don't destroy yourself by getting drunk" (Ephesians 5:17–18 CEV).

EARTHQUAKE

> *There was a powerful earthquake. An angel of the Lord came down from heaven. . .went to the tomb. . .rolled back the stone and sat on it.* Matthew 28:2 NIrV

EARTHQUAKES in the BIBLE shook up a lot of people. To name a few:

- The entire Philistine army. A timely quake while fighting the JEWS sent "the PHILISTINES running away" (1 Samuel 14:22).
- Roman soldiers crucifying Jesus. A quake at Jesus' CRUCIFIXION terrified Roman soldiers into declaring, "This man truly was the SON OF GOD!" (Matthew 27:54).
- Roman guards at Jesus' tomb. A quake at Jesus' RESURRECTION—followed by the appearance of a glowing ANGEL—dropped the Roman guards into a ladylike faint: "They shook and became like dead men" (Matthew 28:4 NIrV).

Fault lines scar the Middle East. One massive fault line trails the JORDAN RIVER valley and stretches all the way into Africa.

An earthquake in what is now Turkey popped open the doors of a PRISON where PAUL and SILAS were being held. They could have escaped but didn't. They ended up baptizing the jailer (Acts 16:33).

EBENEZER   Map 1 B5

(ebb uh NEE sur)

> *Samuel took a single rock and set it upright. . . . He named it "Ebenezer" (Rock of Help), saying, "This marks the place where GOD helped us."* 1 Samuel 7:12 MSG

- Where Philistines defeated the Jews

PHILISTINES BEAT THE JEWS at the battle of Ebenezer—location uncertain. Then they stole ISRAEL's most sacred relic: the ARK OF THE COVENANT, a chest that held the 10 COMMANDMENTS.

The prophet SAMUEL later commanded the JEWS in a successful counterattack. To commemorate the victory, he set up a stone monument and named it after the earlier lost battle—perhaps a bit like getting the last laugh.

ECCLESIASTES

> *Famous sound bite: To everything there is a season, a time for every purpose under heaven: a time to be born, and a time to die.* Ecclesiastes 3:1–2 NKJV

THE SMARTEST MAN who would ever live—as the BIBLE describes King SOLOMON—takes on HUMANITY's toughest question: Why on earth are we here?

- Writer: Solomon or someone claiming to be him. "These are the words of the Teacher, King David's son, who ruled in Jerusalem" (Ecclesiastes 1:1).
- Time: 900s BC if Solomon wrote it.
- Location: Israel.

BIG SCENES

Nothing makes sense. Solomon can't see the point of life. Everyone ends up the same: dead in the dust. It doesn't matter if they're good or bad, rich or poor, smart or dumb. In the end, the playing field is level—and they're buried in it. *Ecclesiastes 1*

Life goes on with or without us. Life rolls out in cycles we can't control any more than we can control the SEASONS of the year. A few of life's uncontrollable scenes:

- A time to be born. A time to die.
- A time to laugh. A time to cry.
- A time for peace. A time for war.
  Ecclesiastes 3

Money leads to worry, not happiness. MONEY is like whiskey to an alcoholic: there's never enough. Rich people end up worrying about how to get more without risking what they have. So they live under a cloud of dread. Solomon, rich himself, says money is good for two things:

- rounding up friends to help you spend it.
- watching it slip through your fingers
  Ecclesiastes 5

Wise advice: love God, love life. Solomon can't figure out the meaning of life. But he does manage to reach a conclusion: Enjoy life and obey the giver of life. Solomon says our perspective is too limited to figure out GOD: "People can never completely understand what he is doing" (Ecclesiastes 3:11 NCV). So Solomon's advice is to trust God and obey his commands. *Ecclesiastes 12*

ECLIPSE

"The sun will become dark, and the moon will turn blood red before that great and terrible day of the LORD arrives." Joel 2:31

UNUSUAL EVENTS IN THE SKY tended to frighten people in ancient times. We get a solar eclipse when the moon passes between the sun and Earth, blocking the sun. We get a lunar eclipse when Earth passes between the sun and moon; the moon falls into Earth's shadow. Something as dramatic as either eclipse would be seen as an ominous sign. Bible writers used eclipses as a metaphor to describe JUDGMENT DAY, when GOD would punish serial sinners.

EDEN   Location Uncertain

(EE den)

God planted a garden in Eden in the east, and there he placed the man he had made.
Genesis 2:8

- Home of Adam and Eve

A GARDEN PARADISE, Eden was home to the first humans. Its location, "in the east," may point toward the Persian Gulf areas of Iraq and Iran—east of where the writer probably lived, in what is now ISRAEL.

GOD evicted ADAM AND EVE from the Garden of Eden after they sinned.

The location of Eden remains a mystery with one intriguing clue: a river watered Eden and then broke

into four branches: TIGRIS, EUPHRATES, Pishon, GIHON. The first two rivers still flow through Iraq and empty into the Persian Gulf. The other two river names are lost to history.

One theory places Eden at the source of the Tigris and Euphrates: in the hills of Turkey. Another says the writer disguised the location by reversing directions—to hide Eden—and that the four rivers flowed into Eden. That would put Eden in what is now the Persian Gulf, which was once a river. Melting ice from the former Ice Age eventually filled the river valley with seawater, flooding Eden and turning it into a biblical version of the lost city of Atlantis.

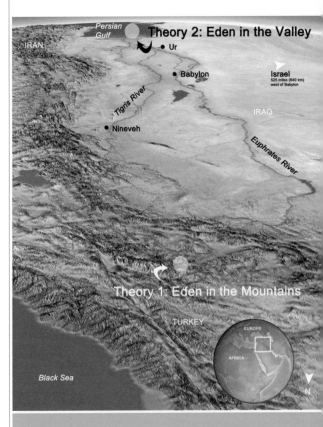

EDEN QUEST. One theory puts Eden in the mountains, near the source of the Tigris and Euphrates Rivers, the fertile region where civilization began. Another puts it in the Persian Gulf, once believed to have been a river valley until the ocean flooded it.

(EE dum)

"Every nook and cranny of Edom will be. . . looted. Every treasure will be found and taken." Obadiah 6

- Esau's nickname
- Esau's homeland in what is now Jordan

IT MEANS "RED." This nickname stuck to ESAU, because the dumbest thing he did was to trade his BIRTH-RIGHT as ISAAC's oldest son for a BOWL of red stew (Genesis 25:30). "Red" also describes the sandstone where he settled southeast of the DEAD SEA. The rock city of PETRA is a big tourist attraction there.

When Babylonians from what is now Iraq destroyed JERUSALEM in 586 BC, many Jewish WAR refugees fled to Edom. Sadly, folks of Edom arrested the Jews and turned them over to the Babylonians. For this, the Jewish prophet OBADIAH said GOD would wipe out Edom. Babylonians took care of that chore about 30 years after they leveled Jerusalem.

EDUCATION

Remember these commands I give you today. Teach them to your children.
Deuteronomy 6:6–7 NCV

SCHOOLS FOR JEWISH KIDS didn't seem to exist until Roman times, many scholars say. Though there's plenty of evidence that kids in what are now EGYPT and Iraq went to school—archaeologists found their homework—it seems Jewish kids got their smarts at home.

Fathers taught their CHILDREN the Jewish laws and TRADITIONS, as best they could. Some say "my child," written throughout PROVERBS, could be taken literally—as instructions to pass along to the kids. Men also taught their sons the family business or arranged an apprenticeship in another line of work. Mothers taught their daughters the way of the WOMEN.

By the time Romans started occupying the Jewish homeland, in about 63 BC, JEWS seem to have set up elementary schools in homes and synagogues—for boys only. They studied the Jewish Bible, but probably skipped non-religious topics such as math, world history, and GREEK literature.

Brainiac students had the option of going on to higher education—their version of grad school. The apostle PAUL apparently qualified. He said he was "brought up and educated here in JERUSALEM under GA-MALIEL" (Acts 5:34), who was described as "an expert in religious law" (Acts 22:3).

EGLON
Map 1 B6

(EGG lon)

About 1300 BC

Joshua and the Israelite army went on to Eglon . . .and killed everyone in it. Joshua 10:34–35

1. A JEWISH HERO named EHUD managed to sneak a DAGGER past security and into the PALACE of King Eglon of MOAB, in what is now Jordan. That king was working a protection racket on the JEWS, making them pay him. Ehud ended the racket by stabbing the king: "The dagger went so deep that the handle disappeared beneath the king's fat" (Judges 3:22).

2. Canaanite city Joshua destroyed. JOSHUA and the Jews defeated a coalition force of armies led by Canaanite kings of five cities, Eglon included. Then he went to each town and wiped out the population. Eglon, identified today as a ruin called Tell Aitun, was about 20 miles (32 km) southwest of JERUSALEM.

EGYPT
Map 2 H8

"I am sending you to Pharaoh. You must lead my people Israel out of Egypt." Exodus 3:10

- Jews spent 430 years there
- Jews freed from slavery there
- Birthplace of Moses
- Nile River provided safe haven in droughts

WITHOUT THE NILE RIVER, one of history's greatest civilizations would have remained a sandbox the combined size of Texas, Oklahoma, and Kansas.

That's a huge footprint for such a tiny foot. Egypt's livable area was only about the size of two of the tiniest states:

EGYPT AT NIGHT, as seen from Space Station.

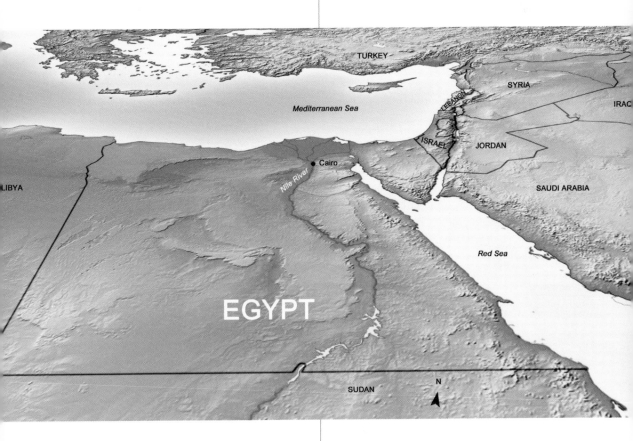

TURKEY

Mediterranean Sea

SYRIA

IRAC

LEBANON

ISRAEL

JORDAN

Cairo

Nile River

LIBYA

SAUDI ARABIA

Red Sea

EGYPT

SUDAN

N

STEPHEN M. MILLER'S ILLUSTRATED BIBLE DICTIONARY

New Jersey and New Hampshire. Egypt is a long and lanky oasis that snakes through a rainless DESERT alongside the NILE RIVER. Souls survive by living in the drought-resistant river valley that stretches only 6 to 9 miles (10–15 km) wide.

In Bible times, it was the go-to oasis in times of DROUGHT. Settlers went there from other regions of Africa and from throughout the Middle East.

ABRAHAM, father of the JEWS, migrated there to escape a drought. So did his grandson JACOB, who brought along his entire extended FAMILY—the founding ANCESTORS of ISRAEL's 12 tribes. One of Jacob's sons, JOSEPH, got sold to slave traders and ended up as a high official in Egypt. There Joseph convinced the king to let his family move down from Israel to weather out a seven-year drought.

The Jews ended up staying for 430 years, at least 80 of those as slaves. One of the kings after Joseph's time decided that the Jewish population explosion threatened national security. So he enslaved the Jews as a national workforce. It's unclear how long they worked as slaves. But they were slaves when MOSES was born. And Moses was 80 years old when he freed them (see EXODUS OF THE JEWS).

This pretty much describes the 2,000-year-old relationship between Egyptians and Jews, from the time of Abraham to Jesus: love, hate.

At times they fought as allies, trying to protect their hunk of the world from invaders such as Assyrians from what is now Iraq.

Other times, they were at each other's throats. In fact, history's first known reference to Israel comes from an Egyptian king's exaggerated brag about wiping them out. PHARAOH Merneptah (reigned about 1213–1204 BC) chiseled this note in stone apparently after decimating several cities in the Jewish homeland: "Israel is laid waste, his seed [people] no longer exists."

EHUD

(EE hud)

About 1300 BC

Ehud. . .pulled out the dagger strapped to his right thigh, and plunged it into the king's belly. . .so deep that the handle disappeared beneath the king's fat. Judges 3:21–22

Jewish hero

FAMOUS FOR STABBING A FAT KING, Ehud is listed among ISRAEL's dozen heroes—alongside SAMSON, GIDEON, and DEBORAH.

Ehud put a stop to King EGLON of MOAB, in what is now Jordan, who had been forcing the JEWS to pay him taxes.

EKRON

Map 1 B6

(ECK ron)

The men of Israel and Judah shouted and chased the Philistines all the way. . .to the gates of Ekron. 1 Samuel 17:52 NCV

Philistine city with walls

WHEN GOLIATH'S HEAD ROLLED, chopped off by SHEPHERD boy DAVID, the Philistine ARMY took off running. They ran as far as Ekron, one of their five strongholds, about 10 miles (16 km) west of the battleground. It's now a ruin called Tell Miqne, about 20 miles (32 km) west of JERUSALEM.

In its Philistine heyday, it covered about 50 acres—one of ancient Israel's largest cites. That's about the size of 50 football fields. Jerusalem in King David's day managed only about 10 acres.

ELAH VALLEY

Map 4 C6

(EE lah)

"I only have the sword of Goliath the Philistine, whom you killed in the valley of Elah." A priest to David, 1 Samuel 21:9

Battlefield where David killed Goliath

SAUL STAGED HIS MILITIA on a hillside overlooking the Valley of Elah, about 10 miles (16 km) west of JERUSALEM. PHILISTINES stood on the opposite hill, across the valley. Somewhere in between, SHEPHERD boy DAVID picked up five stones from a stream. It took just one to drop GOLIATH.

ELAM

(EE luhm)

Rebel kings of Sodom, Gomorrah. . .fought against King Kedorlaomer of Elam.
Genesis 14:8–9

- Nation in what is now Iran

LOT WAS UNLUCKY ENOUGH to live in Sodom when raiders arrived from Elam and BABYLON, in what are now Iran and Iraq. Sodom and its allies lost the battle. LOT got taken away as a slave. Fortunately, his uncle ABRAHAM gathered an ARMY of 318 men, chased down the raiders, and freed Lot along with the other captives.

ELDER

"If someone aspires to be an elder, he desires an honorable position. . . ." An elder must be a man whose life is above reproach.
1 Timothy 3:1–2

ELDERS IN ISRAEL or in the CHURCH were senior leaders. Their duties varied. In ISRAEL, each tribe seemed to have elders who made the decisions that affected the group. In the church, elders led local congregations like PASTORS and priests do today.

ELEAZAR

(EL ee A zur)

1400s or 1200s BC (debated)

"Go with Aaron and his son Eleazar to the top of the mountain. Then take Aaron's priestly robe from him and place it on Eleazar. Aaron will die there." Numbers 20:25–26 CEV

- Aaron's son and successor as high priest

AARON'S FIRST TWO SONS, both PRIESTS, died in a fire described as divine punishment for somehow using INCENSE burners improperly. That left Eleazar, AARON's third of four sons, to assume the duties of ISRAEL's top priest when Aaron died.

ELI

(EE lie)

1100s BC

Eli fell backward off his chair. . . . When he fell, he broke his neck and died. He was old [98] and fat. 1 Samuel 4:18 NIRV

- High priest who raised Samuel

A WEAK-WILLED DAD, Eli let his PRIEST sons get away with way too much. They had SEX with women who worked at the WORSHIP center. They even stole sacrificial meat reserved for GOD.

Yet Eli seemed to do a fine job raising SAMUEL, who replaced him as ISRAEL's spiritual leader. Eli's sons died in a battle. When Eli got the news, he fell out of his chair, breaking his neck.

ELIEZER

(EL ee ee zur)

1. 2100s BC
2. 1400s or 1200s BC (debated)

"Since you've given me no children, Eliezer of Damascus, a servant in my household, will inherit all my wealth." Abraham to God, Genesis 15:2

1. ABRAHAM'S TOP SERVANT, Eliezer may have been the one ABRAHAM entrusted to find a WIFE for his son ISAAC (Genesis 24).

2. Second son of Moses (Exodus 18:4).

ELIHU

(ee LIE hew)

Perhaps before 2000 BC

Elihu. . .was angry because Job refused to admit that he had sinned. Job 32:2

- One of Job's uncomfortable comforters

"YOU DESERVE THE MAXIMUM PENALTY" (Job 34:36). That's JOB's friend, Elihu, accusing Job of sinning. Like Job's other friends who came to comfort him, Elihu said Job must have sinned, otherwise GOD

E

STEPHEN M. MILLER'S ILLUSTRATED BIBLE DICTIONARY

wouldn't have let a storm kill his CHILDREN, raiders steal his herds, and a skin DISEASE wreck his health.

ELIJAH

(ee LIE jah)

Ministered about 865–850 BC

A chariot and horses of fire appeared and separated Elijah from Elisha. Then Elijah went up to heaven in a whirlwind. 2 Kings 2:11 NCV

- Escorted to heaven by a chariot of fire
- Prophet during reign of Ahab, Jezebel
- Called down fire from heaven
- Resurrected a dead boy near Beirut

FAMOUS FOR NOT DYING, Elijah was perhaps the only PROPHET who could have given MOSES a run for his money. His story is that spectacular.

Weatherman

The first time Elijah shows up in the BIBLE, he's forecasting the weather. "As surely as the LORD, the GOD of Israel, lives," he told King AHAB, "there will be no dew or RAIN during the next few years until I give the word!" (1 Kings 17:1).

The DROUGHT was God's punishment. Ahab and his queen from what is now LEBANON, Jezebel, were leading the northern Jewish nation of ISRAEL away from God. JEZEBEL was killing God's prophets and promoting her own religion: worship of Canaanite GODS BAAL and ASHERAH.

Helping the widow lady

Weathering out the drought, Elijah traveled to ZAREPHATH, a coastal city near what is now Beirut, Lebanon. There he met a starving widow COOKING one last MEAL for herself and her son. He convinced her to cook him the meal instead. In payment, he promised that as

ELIJAH accuses King Ahab and Queen Jezebel of forsaking God "by worshiping Baal" (1 Kings 18:18 CEV).

146

long as the drought lasted, she would have FLOUR and cooking oil.

Later the WIDOW's son died. Elijah climbed on the corpse and prayed: "O LORD my God, please let this child's life return to him" (1 Kings 17:21). Done.

Battle of the gods

Three years into the drought, Elijah went to see Ahab. Elijah challenged Jezebel's 850 pagan prophets to a spiritual duel. Team God versus Team Baal. One prophet against 850. Both teams would sacrifice a BULL. But to burn it, they had to call down fire from the sky.

Advantage, Baal. So it seemed. He was the storm god. Ancient pictures show him slinging lightning bolts.

Elijah gave Team Baal the first shot. They prayed, danced, and cut themselves all day, trying to get their god's attention. No fire. Elijah, not notably subtle, told them Baal might be on the toilet.

Elijah called down fire with a 20-second PRAYER. JEWS watching this arrested Jezebel's prophets and executed them.

The drought ended.

Oddly, instead of feeling emboldened by this victory, Elijah ran for his life. He was afraid of Jezebel, who vowed to kill him within 24 hours—royal punishment for slaughtering her 850 prophets and priests.

An ANGEL caught up with Elijah, fed him, and directed him to MOUNT SINAI—where God spoke to him as God had spoken to Moses several hundred years earlier. Encouraged, Elijah returned home.

Elijah's fiery finale

Somehow, Elijah knew it was time to leave the planet. Accompanied by his apprentice, ELISHA, he crossed the JORDAN RIVER into what is now the Arab country of Jordan.

Elisha asked if he could inherit Elijah's power.

"If you see me when I am taken from you," Elijah answered, "then you will get your request" (2 Kings 2:10).

"Suddenly a CHARIOT and horses appeared. Fire was all around them. The chariot and horses came between the two men. Then Elijah went up to HEAVEN in a strong wind. Elisha saw it" (2 Kings 2:11–12 NIRV).

A search party of 50 Jews later scoured the area looking for Elijah, in case the LORD returned him. They found nothing.

ELIPHAZ

(EL ee faz)

Perhaps before 2000 BC

Eliphaz the Temanite replied. . . "If you return to the Almighty, you will be restored— so clean up your life." Job 22:1, 23

- The first of Job's four comforters

ALL OF JOB'S COMFORTERS were most comforting when their mouths were shut. Once they started talking, they blamed JOB for his misery. They said he must have sinned. They said only SIN could explain why GOD allowed Job's CHILDREN to die in a windstorm, his herds to get stolen by raiders, and a skin DISEASE to shroud his body.

Many Bible experts say the point of the story is to prove the opposite—that bad things sometimes happen to good people.

ELISHA

(ee LIE sha)

Ministered about 850–800 BC

Elisha replied [to Elijah], "Please let me inherit a double share of your spirit and become your successor." 2 Kings 2:9

- Elijah's student and successor as a prophet
- Raised a couple's son from the dead

A WHIRLWIND escorted by chariots of fire carried off Elisha's mentor, the prophet ELIJAH. Suddenly, young Elisha was the lead PROPHET in the northern Jewish nation of ISRAEL. That's the Jewish nation that couldn't manage a single godly KING in its 200-year history.

Elisha's mission was to do what the kings were supposed to do but didn't. Point the JEWS to GOD. Remind them of God's power and promises. Urge them to obey him.

In his 50 years of ministry, spanning the reign of four kings—JORAM, JEHU, JEHOAHAZ, and Jehoash— Elisha ministered as the peoples' prophet.

Among his many MIRACLES:

- raising a boy who died of what may have been heatstroke.

- filling a WIDOW's jars with COOKING OIL so she could pay off her DEBTS without selling her sons into SLAVERY.
- HEALING a Syrian commander of LEPROSY.
- healing an infertile couple who later had a son.

ELIZABETH

(ee LIZ uh beth)

First century AD

"Elizabeth has become pregnant in her old age! People used to say she was barren."
Luke 1:36

- Mother of John the Baptist
- Relative of Jesus' mother, Mary

OLD AND INFERTILE, Elizabeth got pregnant shortly after her elderly husband ZECHARIAH returned from his week of TEMPLE duty as a PRIEST in JERUSALEM.

At the Temple, the ANGEL Gabriel told Zechariah

FAMILY REUNION. Elderly Elizabeth and her son, John the Baptist, visit with Mary and Jesus. Nearby is Elizabeth's husband, Zechariah. Elizabeth and Mary were related, though the Bible doesn't say how.

he would have a SON who would "prepare the people for the coming of the LORD" (Luke 1:17).

Six months into Elizabeth's pregnancy, GABRIEL appeared to MARY, too. He not only told her that she would become pregnant. He said her relative Elizabeth was already pregnant.

Mary hurried to be with Elizabeth, apparently staying until the delivery.

A few decades later, Elizabeth's son—JOHN THE BAPTIST—would baptize his relative, Jesus. That BAPTISM marked the beginning of Jesus' ministry, which would spark a worldwide movement that became known as CHRISTIANITY.

ELKANAH

(el KAY nuh)

1100s BC

"Why are you crying, Hannah?" Elkanah would ask. ". . .Why be downhearted just because you have no children? You have me."
1 Samuel 1:8

- Father of Samuel

HUSBAND TO TWO WIVES, Elkanah had CHILDREN by one WIFE but none by HANNAH, who was infertile. In a day when many saw INFERTILITY as punishment from GOD, Elkanah treated Hannah with compassion. In time, God answered Hannah's PRAYER. She gave BIRTH to SAMUEL, one of ISRAEL's most respected prophets.

EMBALMING

Jacob was embalmed. The embalming process took the usual forty days. Genesis 50:2–3

TURNING A CORPSE INTO A MUMMY wasn't especially Jewish. It was Egyptian; they invented the process more than 5,000 years ago.

Egyptians taught that people could be resurrected in an afterlife only after the SOUL was reunited with the body. And the body needed to be recognizable enough to lure back the soul.

Two JEWS in the BIBLE got embalmed: JACOB and

his son JOSEPH. They were mummified in EGYPT for transport back to Israel where they wanted to be buried.

The embalming process changed over the centuries. But it usually involved removing the organs, drying the corpse in a salty sandbox for a month or more, and then wrapping the corpse in LINEN.

Sometimes the organs were stored in four jars associated with GODS linked to the protection of each organ: LIVER, lungs, intestines, and stomach. The heart was the one organ that stayed inside the body.

As for the brain, Egyptians scooped it out with a spoon through a chiseled hole in the nose. They didn't seem to know what the brain did. So they trashed it.

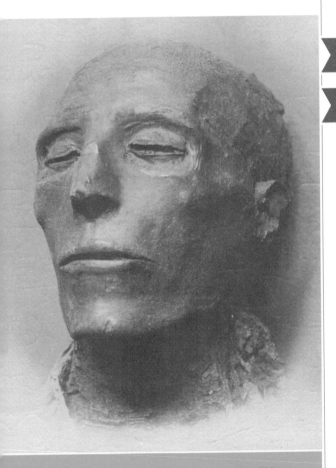

AGE 3330 YEARS, PLUS. And no wrinkles. This is a mummy of Egypt's king Seti I (reigned about 1290–1279 BC). He was the father of Rameses II, whom some say was the pharaoh Moses had to deal with while freeing the Jews from slavery.

EMERALD

The foundations of the city walls were decorated with every kind of jewel. . .jasper. . . sapphire. . .emerald." Revelation 21:19 NIrV

- Jewel used on high priest's chestpiece
- Foundation stone in New Jerusalem

MINED IN EGYPT during Bible times, emeralds were valued as gems. Greeks worked the mines in the time of ALEXANDER the Great. Egyptians mined the jewels for Cleopatra. Israel's HIGH PRIEST wore a CHESTPIECE with a dozen jewels, including an emerald. Each gem represented a tribe of ISRAEL (Exodus 28:21).

EMMANUEL (see IMMANUEL)

EMMAUS   Map 4 C5

(em MAY us)

The two from Emmaus told their story of how Jesus had appeared to them as they were walking along the road. Luke 24:35

- Where Jesus walked on Easter Sunday

ON THE DAY JESUS ROSE from the dead, he took a walk. Somehow hiding his identity, he joined two followers walking to Emmaus, a village 7 miles (11 km) from JERUSALEM. That's about a two-and-a-half-hour walk.

Jesus talked with the men, who were discouraged about the CRUCIFIXION. But Jesus reminded them about prophecies that showed the MESSIAH would suffer.

The men recognized him only when he prayed the BLESSING over BREAD they were about to eat. Then he disappeared. The men rushed back to Jerusalem to tell the DISCIPLES what happened. Jesus showed up, too.

It's uncertain where Emmaus was. Some ancient copies of the story say it was about 20 miles (32 km) from Jerusalem—a day's walk.

E

EMPEROR (see CAESAR)

END TIMES (see LAST DAYS)

ENDOR Map 1 D4

(en DOOR)

"There's a woman at Endor who can talk to spirits of the dead." 1 Samuel 28:7 CEV

- Where King Saul met a medium to consult dead Samuel

KING SAUL wanted to know if he was going to survive the next morning's battle against an overwhelming force of PHILISTINES. But he had no PROPHET to advise him; SAMUEL was dead.

So he slipped out of his camp on MOUNT GILBOA and made his way to Endor, a small village about 10 miles (16 km) away. There, he met with a woman who managed to call up the SPIRIT of Samuel—to the woman's horror. Samuel said that by tomorrow, SAUL and his sons would join him in the place of the dead.

Samuel was dead right.

ENGAGEMENT (see WEDDING)

EN-GEDI Map 1 D6

(en GED ee)

Saul. . .was told that David had gone into the wilderness of En-gedi. So Saul chose 3,000 elite troops. . .to search for David. 1 Samuel 24:1–2

- David's hideout from King Saul

ON THE LAM, David fled to the Spring of the Young Goat.

That's what En-Gedi means in the HEBREW language of the JEWS.

It's a perfect name for this hideout in Israel's badlands some 35 miles (56 km) south of JERUSALEM. You have to climb a steep, winding trail around massive boulders to reach this tiny oasis. It's hidden beneath towering cliffs about a mile (1.6 km) from the DEAD SEA and some 650 feet (198 m) above it.

There DAVID found protection in a honeycomb of caves, along with ample WATER from a spring-fed waterfall and POOL.

SAUL, insanely jealous of David's popularity, managed to track David and his men to En-Gedi. Unfortunately for Saul, he decided to relieve himself in the very cave where David and his men were hiding. David crept up behind Saul and quietly cut off part of the king's ROBE. When Saul left, from a distance David waved the cloth at Saul—proof that he could have killed the king. Humiliated, Saul went home.

HIDDEN OASIS. David's hideout, En-Gedi, was this tiny oasis hidden in a ravine near the Dead Sea.

ENOCH

(EE nuhk)

Before 4000 BC
Enoch lived 365 years. . . . Then one day he disappeared, because God took him.
Genesis 5:23–24

IF DEATH MARKS THE END OF LIFE, 969-year-old Methuselah wasn't the longest-living person. His father was: Enoch never died. Like Elijah, he was apparently airlifted to heaven.

EPAPHRODITUS

(ee PAFF row DIE tus)

I have all I need—and more! I am generously supplied with the gifts you sent me with Epaphroditus. **Philippians 4:18**

- Courier delivering gifts to Paul

IN JAIL somewhere, Paul got a care package from Christians in Philippi, in what is now Greece. Epaphroditus delivered it.

EPHESIANS, LETTER OF

Famous sound bite: Don't go to bed angry.
Ephesians 4:26 CEV

IN AN UPBEAT LETTER that reads like a pastor's sermon to a church he dearly loves, Paul offers practical advice about how to live as children of God.

- Writer: "This letter is from Paul" (Ephesians 1:1).
- Time: Paul probably wrote this during the last few years of his life, perhaps around AD 60–62.
- Location: Paul wrote "in chains" (Ephesians 6:20), possibly under the house arrest in Rome that's reported at the end of Acts. He wrote "to God's holy people in

Ephesus" (Ephesians 1:1), a city on what is now Turkey's west coast.

E

BIG SCENES

God's Chosen People, extended edition. As far as Jews were concerned, they were God's favorites: the chosen. Everyone else: "uncircumcised heathens" (Ephesians 2:11). No more, Paul says. Jews were just the first of God's chosen—not the last. In Old Testament times, God revealed himself through the laws of Moses. But in New Testament times, he revealed himself even more—through the life and teachings of his Son, Jesus. Paul says that anyone who believes this—Jews and non-Jews—"share equally in the riches inherited by God's children" (Ephesians 3:6). *Ephesians 1–3*

How to act like a Christian. Paul wants one thing from Christians. It's the same thing parents want of their kids. He wants them to get along with each other. Unity. He offers them a how-to list:

- Stay humble.
- Don't think of one person as more important than another.
- Work together with team spirit.
- Be patient and gentle with each other.
- Tell the truth, but in a spirit of love.
  Ephesians 4

How to live in peace on the home front. Before Paul orders wives to submit to their husbands, he paints a line down the middle of a two-way street: "Submit to one another" (Ephesians 5:21). Though he's a bachelor, Paul offers up some solid family counseling.

Husbands: "Love your wives, just as Christ loved the church" (Ephesians 5:25).

Children: "Obey your parents" (Ephesians 6:1).

Parents: "Don't exasperate your children by coming down hard on them. Take them by the hand and lead them" (Ephesians 6:4 MSG). *Ephesians 5–6*

How to dress for spiritual battle. Romans had occupied much of the Middle East for a century. Paul's readers knew what Roman soldiers looked like. Paul used that to help them picture the resources they'd need to fight spiritual battles. Paul was a scholar who knew his Bible, our Old Testament. And he seemed to link each piece of battle gear to a Bible verse.

Belt of truth: "He will wear RIGHTEOUSNESS like a BELT and truth" (Isaiah 11:5).

Body armor of righteousness: "He put on righteousness as his body ARMOR" (Isaiah 59:17).

Shoes of peace: "How beautiful. . .are the feet of the messenger who brings. . .good news of PEACE" (Isaiah 52:7).

Shield of faith: "God is my. . . SHIELD and my saving strength" (2 Samuel 22:3 NCV).

Helmet of salvation: "He. . .placed the HELMET of SALVATION on his head" (Isaiah 59:17).

Sword of God's Word: "The LORD. . .made my words like a sharp SWORD" (Isaiah 49:1–2 NIrv). *Ephesians 6:10–20*

EPHESUS

Map 3 E3

(EFF uh suhs)

"The whole world knows that the city of Ephesus guards the temple of the great Artemis." Acts 19:35 NIrv

- Home of Artemis's temple
- Where Paul spent about three years starting a church
- Rioters drove Paul out of town
- One of seven churches addressed in Revelation

MONEY TRUMPED RELIGIOUS TOLERANCE in Ephesus. PAUL learned that the hard way—when he got booted out of town nearly three years after he got there. His CRIME: He converted so many people to CHRISTIANITY that it hurt sales of silver IDOLS—figurines honoring ARTEMIS, the city's patron goddess.

Paul came to Ephesus during his third missionary trip. He must have thought it was the perfect place to start a CHURCH, for many reasons.

Lots of people. Many scholars rank it number three in the ROMAN EMPIRE, after ROME and ALEXANDRIA, EGYPT.

Great location. Ephesus was a port city on Turkey's west coast—the most popular port in the region for sailing to and from Rome.

Religious tolerance. Archaeologists digging through the Ephesus ruins have found over 100 inscriptions honoring various GODS.

Tourist attraction. Ephesus was home to what one ancient writer called the most wondrous of the Seven Wonders of the World: the Temple of Artemis, four times larger than the Parthenon of ATHENS. Writing in the 200s BC, Greek scientist Philon said he had seen all seven Wonders. "But when I saw the temple at Ephesus rising to the clouds, all these other Wonders were put in the shade."

When Paul first arrived in Ephesus, he taught for the first three months in the SYNAGOGUE. Some JEWS believed his message, that Jesus was the MESSIAH. Others didn't. Paul left the synagogue and started teaching at a lecture hall for the next two years. That's the most time Paul spent starting a church in any city on record.

He healed the sick, exorcised DEMONS, and won so many converts that the sales of Artemis idols plummeted. That got the attention of the manufacturer, DEMETRIUS. He called a meeting of his contractors and made a nice speech:

"Paul has persuaded many people that handmade gods aren't really gods at all. . . . Of course, I'm not just talking about the loss of public respect for our business. I'm also concerned that the temple of the great goddess Artemis will lose its influence and that Artemis—this magnificent goddess worshiped throughout the province of ASIA and all around the world—will be robbed of her great prestige!" (Acts 19:26–27).

As though Artemis was getting robbed instead of him.

A riot followed. Paul decided it was time to move on, and to entrust the church to the locals. In time, when the furor died down, he would send his closest associate back: TIMOTHY. "Stay right there on top of things so that the teaching stays on track" (1 Timothy 1:3 MSG).

Goth invaders from what is now Russia destroyed much of Ephesus and the Temple of Artemis in AD 262. The city rebuilt but never regained its glory.

Ephesus died by the 500s when the oceanfront river silted up, shutting down the city's riverfront harbor. Christian tourists visit the ruins today.

THEATER ON A HILL. The once-bustling city of Ephesus, now a ruin, featured an amphitheater that seated perhaps 20,000.

EPHOD
(EE fod)

"Make the ephod of finely woven linen and skillfully embroider it with gold and with blue, purple, and scarlet thread." Exodus 28:6

PART OF THE HIGH PRIEST'S UNIFORM, the ephod looked a bit like a flashy apron worn over a ROBE.

EPHRAIM
(EE fray im)

1800s BC
Joseph named his second son Ephraim, for he said, "God has made me fruitful in this land of my grief." Genesis 41:52

BORN IN EGYPT, JOSEPH's son became the father of one of ISRAEL's 12 tribes. Ephraim's grandfather, JACOB, blessed him and his brother MANASSEH. As a result, both had tribes named after them.

EPHRAIM, TRIBE OF
Map 1 C5
(EE fray im)

These were the clans of Ephraim. Their registered troops numbered 32,500. Numbers 26:37

AN EXTENDED FAMILY descended from JOSEPH's second son, Ephraim, settled in what is now central Israel. The territory covered rugged highlands stretching some 20 miles north and 30 miles west (32 by 48 km). That's where the JEWS pitched their tent WORSHIP center, in the city of SHILOH.

EPICUREAN

(ep uh CURE ee un)

Epicurean and Stoic thinkers began to argue with him [Paul]. Acts 17:18 NIrV

PHILOSOPHERS AGAINST FEAR AND PAIN, the Epicureans who argued with PAUL in ATHENS said people shouldn't be afraid of DEATH or GODS. Instead, they insisted, people should avoid negative people and sour experiences by seeking the company of pleasant souls and happy circumstances.

EPILEPSY

(EPP uh lepp see)

Whatever their sickness or disease, or if they were demon-possessed or epileptic or paralyzed—he healed them all. Matthew 4:24

OVERLOADED ELECTRICAL CHARGES in the brain cause seizures in epileptics—a DISEASE Jesus healed. Some problems described in the BIBLE as demon possession sound like epilepsy, some experts say. Example: a boy " 'has seizures and. . .often falls.' . . . Jesus rebuked the demon in the boy, and it left him" (Matthew 17:15, 18).

EPISTLE

(ee PISS el)

This letter [epistle] is from Paul. 1 Corinthians 1:1

IT'S GREEK for any kind of LETTER, whether it's to an individual or to a group of readers, such as a CHURCH. The NEW TESTAMENT contains both kinds of letters.

ESARHADDON

(EE shar HAD done)

Ruled 681–669 BC

As Sennacherib was worshiping. . .his sons Adrammelech and Sharezer killed him. . . . So Sennacherib's son Esarhaddon became king of Assyria. 2 Kings 19:37 NCV

HE BECAME KING of ASSYRIA in what is now Iraq after his brothers assassinated their father, SENNACHERIB, and then fled the country.

ESAU

(EE saw)

1900s BC

Esau said to Jacob, "Give me some of that red stew—I'm starved!" That's how he came to be called Edom (Red). Genesis 25:30 MSG

- Sold his inheritance rights for a bowl of stew
- Twin brother of Jacob
- Oldest son of Isaac

OVERPRICED BEANS. For a bowl of red lentil stew, Esau traded his inheritance rights as Jacob's oldest son. He would have gotten a double share of the estate. He was that hungry. Or dumber than a bag of beans.

NICKNAMED "RED," Esau earned that tag for being dumber than a BOWL of beans. Red beans—as in red LENTIL stew.

His NAME comes from the most famous scene in his story. Esau returned home from a hunt—empty-handed, empty stomach, empty head. JACOB, a homebody, had a pot of stew on to brew. Esau asked for a bowl. Jacob exploited all of Esau's emptiness. As the oldest son, Esau would inherit a double share of their FATHER's estate. And he would become the next leader of the extended FAMILY. At Jacob's insistence, he traded it all for an incredibly overpriced bowl of lentil beans.

Later, when their elderly and nearly blind father, ISAAC, incorrectly thought he was dying, he asked Esau to hunt some game and cook it up for him. Isaac planned to give him a final BLESSING—a FATHER's last wish and PRAYER for his favorite SON. While Esau was out HUNTING, Jacob stole the blessing—delivering a MEAL and dressing like Esau.

Livid when he got the news, Esau vowed to kill Jacob. But Jacob fled the country. By the time he came back, some 20 years later, Esau had cooled off enough to greet Jacob with a hug. Both men were wealthy. Jacob settled in what is now ISRAEL. Esau settled in EDOM, a territory south of the DEAD SEA in what is now Jordan.

ESCHATOLOGY   (see LAST DAYS)

ESTHER

(ES tur)

Husband ruled 486–465 BC

Queen Esther answered, "King Xerxes. . . Please spare my people." Esther 7:3 NIrV

- Jewish queen of Persia (Iran)
- Saved Jews from a holocaust

A HOT-LOOKING JEWISH ORPHAN, Esther won a Middle Eastern beauty contest that landed her a lifetime gig: queen of Iran, then known as PERSIA.

Palace officials dreamed up the empire-wide beauty contest as a way to find a queen for King XERXES. Lots of ladies got tapped for the contest. Each spent a year marinating in fragrant beauty oils at the HAREM before they auditioned overnight with the king.

A JEWISH ORPHAN, Esther wins a beauty contest to become queen of the Persian Empire based in what is now Iran.

Esther got the inside scoop on how to please the king, thanks to the harem's top EUNUCH. She pleased the king so well that he threw a party, gave his guests generous GIFTS, and declared Esther queen.

Persia's top official, a man named HAMAN, decided to wipe out all JEWS in the empire because one Jew refused to bow to him: Esther's cousin MORDECAI. Haman didn't know about the family connection.

Haman convinced the king to sign the decree. Neither seemed to realize Esther was a Jew—until Esther risked her life to tell the king.

It was dangerous to request an audience with the king. "Anyone who appears before the king in his inner court without being invited is doomed to die unless the king holds out his GOLD SCEPTER" (Esther 4:11). Fortunately, King Xerxes invited Esther in. She invited the king and Haman to two banquets. At the second one, she revealed that Haman's plot would kill her and all of her people.

Loyal to his queen, Xerxes executed Haman and gave Haman's job to Mordecai. The day Haman had set for the holocaust has become a springtime Jewish holiday: PURIM. Celebrated a bit like Mardi Gras, it's the happiest holiday on the Jewish CALENDAR.

ESTHER, BOOK OF

Famous sound bite: "Who knows if perhaps you were made queen for just such a time as this?" Mordecai to Esther, Esther 4:14

JEWISH QUEEN OF IRAN in what was then called PERSIA. Esther landed that gig after winning a beauty contest. The right person in the right place at the right time, she saved her fellow JEWS from an empire-wide holocaust.

- Writer: Unknown. The writing style is similar to Ezra and Nehemiah, stories set in about the same time.
- Time: King Xerxes reigned 21 years, from 486–465 BC.
- Location: Susa, capital of the Persian Empire. It's now Shush, Iran.

BIG SCENES

Firing Queen Vashti. Drunk at a royal bash for guys only, King XERXES decides to put his trophy WIFE on display. He orders in Queen VASHTI. She's hosting the ladies, and she refuses. What to do. Grant her wish. Forever. If she doesn't want to come, banish her from the king's presence. That's what the king's advisers suggest: "Then all the women will respect their HUSBANDS" (Esther 1:20 NCV). Sounds manly enough. The king agrees. *Esther 1*

Cue the beauty contestants. Missing his trophy wife, Xerxes is bummed. Advisers come to his rescue with another manly suggestion: hold a beauty contest. The king gets to keep the winner. Scouts travel from India to EGYPT, bringing back the prettiest VIRGINS. A local wins: Esther. She's a Jewish ORPHAN raised by her cousin MORDECAI. *Esther 2*

How to plan a holocaust. Mordecai refuses to bow when HAMAN, the king's top official, walks by. A proud man, Haman decides to kill Mordecai—and Mordecai's entire race: all Jews throughout the empire. By promising to donate to the royal treasury 375 tons of SILVER—apparently to be confiscated from the dead Jews—Haman convinces the king to sign off on the plan. Kill now, pay later. Neither seems to realize the queen is a Jew related to Mordecai. *Esther 3*

How to stop a holocaust. With the date set for the holocaust—March 7, 473 BC—Esther steps in. She tells the king she's a Jew. He's shocked. But the law he signed granting citizens the right to kill Jews and take their property is irrevocable. On the other hand, he's free to order troops to defend the Jews. And he's free to execute Haman. He does both. Jews celebrate the holocaust missed each spring during the FESTIVAL of PURIM. The name comes from a Persian word for "LOTS" (*pur*). A bit like dice, lots were what Haman used to pick the best date to kill the Jews. *Esther 4–9*

ETAM
Map 1 C6

(EE tum)

Then 3,000 men from Judah went to get Samson. They went down to the cave that was in the rock of Etam. Judges 15:11 NIRV

- Samson's hideout, location uncertain

SAMSON AGREED to let his fellow JEWS arrest him at Etam and turn him over to the PHILISTINES. He did that to keep the Philistines from retaliating against them for attacks SAMSON had carried out. Once in Philistine custody, though, Samson broke the ropes that held him. Then he grabbed a DONKEY's jawbone and pummeled to death 1,000 Philistines.

ETERNAL LIFE

"I tell you the truth, those who listen to my message and believe in God who sent me have eternal life." John 5:24

IT TOOK JEWS ABOUT 2,000 YEARS to warm up to the idea of an afterlife. So say many Bible experts. Even then, some JEWS couldn't work up the FAITH to believe in it.

Throughout much of the Jewish Bible, which Christians call the OLD TESTAMENT, the dead are considered dead. Period.

The BIBLE's first clear reference to life after DEATH shows up in a prophecy: "Huge numbers of people who

THE GRAVE isn't the end—if Christians got it right. If they got it wrong, Paul said Christians, "are more to be pitied than anyone in the world" (1 Corinthians 15:19).

lie dead in their graves will wake up. Some will rise up to life that will never end" (Daniel 12:2 NIrV).

Many scholars say DANIEL didn't write this. Instead, they say the history it describes points to a writer in about 175 BC promising hope to Jews martyred by Antiochus IV Epiphanes (ruled 175–164 BC), a Syrian invader who tried to wipe out the Jewish religion.

By the time of Jesus, one major Jewish group vouched for eternal life. According to Josephus, a Jewish history writer of that century, PHARISEES believed in "an immortal SOUL," but SADDUCEES didn't.

NEW TESTAMENT writers confirmed that: "The Sadducees say there is no RESURRECTION or ANGELS or spirits, but the Pharisees believe in all of these" (Acts 23:8).

Jesus said the Sadducees were wrong. "Your mistake is that you don't know the SCRIPTURES. . . . Long after ABRAHAM, ISAAC, and JACOB had died, GOD said to MOSES, 'I am the God of Abraham, the God of Isaac, and the God of Jacob.' So he is the God of the living, not the dead" (Mark 12:24, 26–27).

Beyond offering a lesson in grammar, Jesus made

his point with his resurrection. After that, his followers taught that all believers would rise from the dead. The apostle PAUL said if Christians are wrong about that, "Then people should pity us more than anyone else" (1 Corinthians 15:19 NIrV).

ETHIOPIA

Map 2 I10

(eeth ee OH pee uh)

An important Ethiopian official happened to be going along that road. . . . And Philip baptized him. Acts 8:27, 38 CEV

FURTHER NORTH than modern Ethiopia, the BIBLE version of Ethiopia was in what is now south EGYPT and Sudan. A CHRISTIAN named PHILIP met an Ethiopian official on the ROAD from JERUSALEM to GAZA, converted him, and baptized him. Then Philip disappeared.

See also CUSH.

157

EUCHARIST (see COMMUNION)

EUNICE

(YOU niss)

First century AD

I. . .remember the genuine faith of your mother Eunice. Paul to Timothy, 2 Timothy 1:5 cev

- Timothy's mother

WRITING FROM DEATH ROW, the apostle PAUL said he knew of TIMOTHY'S FAITH, passed down from Timothy's mother Eunice.

EUNUCH

(YOU nuhk)

Hegai, the king's eunuch in charge of the harem, will see that they are all given beauty treatments. Esther 2:3

- Castrated man, often a harem servant

TESTICLES were a deal breaker for men serving the king's wives in the royal HAREM. Testicles had to go.

On the bright side, some eunuchs became national leaders, perhaps because of their connections with the ladies. One CHRISTIAN eunuch "was in charge of all the wealth of CANDACE. She was the queen of ETHIOPIA" (Acts 8:27 NIrV).

EUPHRATES RIVER

Map 2 K6

(you FRAY tees)

"I have given this land to your descendants, all the way from the border of Egypt to the great Euphrates River." God to Abraham, Genesis 15:18

HUMAN CIVILIZATION began along the banks of two rivers, many historians say: the Euphrates and the TIGRIS. ABRAHAM'S hometown of UR sat alongside the Euphrates, a river that begins in the mountains of Turkey. It meanders through Syria and Iraq before draining into the Persian Gulf, a journey of about 1,700 miles (2,700 km).

GOD promised Abraham's descendants land extending to the river. King SOLOMON'S influence did seem to reach that far. But today the Euphrates lies more than 200 miles (320 km) north of modern Israel, in Arab territory. Many Arabs, however, also lay claim to Abraham—through his son ISHMAEL.

GONE FISHIN'. Iraqi fishermen cast a net into the Euphrates River near Al Qurna, in the southland where the river empties into the Persian Gulf.

EUTYCHUS

(U tuh cuss)

First century AD

As Paul spoke on and on, a young man named Eutychus, sitting on the windowsill. . .fell sound asleep and dropped three stories to his death. Acts 20:9

- Killed by a sermon
- Resurrected by the preacher

AFTER INDIRECTLY KILLING THIS BOY in Troas with what sounds like a long, boring sermon, Paul raised him from the dead then went back to preaching until dawn—in what might be described as chutzpah.

EVANGELISTS

These are the gifts Christ gave to the church: the apostles, the prophets, the evangelists, and the pastors and teachers. Ephesians 4:11

- Christian preachers

GIFTED PREACHERS, evangelists specialized in telling people about the story and teachings of Jesus. *Evangelist* comes from a Greek word that means "one who reports good news." Writers of the four Gospels about Jesus—Matthew, Mark, Luke, John—earned the nickname "Evangelists." Church leaders tagged them with that brand by the AD 200s.

EVE   (see Adam and Eve)

EVIL SPIRIT   (see Demons)

EXCOMMUNICATION

Call a meeting of the church. . . . Then you must throw this man out. 1 Corinthians 5:4–5

- Removing a church member from membership

IT'S A SANCTIFIED EVICTION of the unsanctified. In Old Testament times, Jewish law allowed Jews to expel fellow Jews from the community for flagrant sins such as incest. In New Testament times, Paul ordered the church in Corinth to expel a churchman who was sleeping with his stepmother. Paul said he hoped the excommunication would bring the man to his spiritual senses.

E

EXILE

722 BC for Israel
586 BC for Judah

"The Lord will exile you and your king to a nation unknown to you and your ancestors." Deuteronomy 28:36

- Eviction of the Jews from their homeland

MOSES WARNED that once the Jews reached the Promised Land, they weren't home free. He said if they disobeyed God by becoming serial sinners, God would exile them.

Centuries later, prophets began warning the Jews that if they didn't get their spiritual act together, God would send invaders to erase the Jewish nation from the political map and exile those lucky enough to survive.

Israel split into two nations in the mid-900s BC. First to fall was the northern Jewish nation of Israel. Assyrian invaders from what is now northern Iraq deported the survivors. As far as anyone knows, they never returned in any large group.

The southern Jewish nation of Judah fell in 586 BC to Babylonian invaders headquartered in what is now southern Iraq. Though deported to Babylon, these Jews were allowed to return about 50 years later, when Persians from what is now Iraq defeated Babylon to become the new superpower of the Middle East.

DEPORTED captives are led into exile by a soldier. After the Jewish homeland fell to invaders, Jews were exiled to what is now Iraq.

EXODUS OF THE JEWS

1400s or 1200s (debated)

"The Lord brought the people of Israel out of the land of Egypt like an army." Exodus 12:51

- Moses leads the Jews to freedom out of Egypt

A WEEK'S WALK turned into a 40-year marathon when MOSES led the JEWS out of EGYPT.

About a week is all it took a walker to TRAVEL the 150 miles (241 km) from the Nile Delta, where the Jews had been enslaved, to the border of what is now ISRAEL. They'd travel along a coastal ROAD that linked the two territories.

Moses took a road less traveled—the not particularly scenic route. He did this to avoid Egyptian forts and troops along the coastal road. "If the people are faced with a battle," GOD told Moses, "they might change their minds and return to Egypt" (Exodus 13:17).

Moses turned the crowd south, into the barren Sinai badlands. Egypt's CHARIOT corps chased them down and tried to herd them back to Egypt. But the Jews escaped through a wind-blown path through a body of WATER. When the Egyptians followed, the wind stopped, and the water rushed back into place, drowning them.

The Jews camped at the foot of MOUNT SINAI for about a year, while the BIBLE says God gave Moses the 10 COMMANDMENTS and many other laws. When the Jews arrived at KADESH oasis near Israel's southern border, Moses sent scouts ahead. They came back with shocking news. There were GIANTS in the land. And the cities had walls protecting them. The refugees panicked, refusing to go further.

For this vote of no confidence in God, he sentenced them to 40 years in the badlands. Scholars say they likely stayed at the oasis for most of that time.

Afterward, Moses took them into what is now Jordan, where he died. JOSHUA took over and led the invasion force to JERICHO—a border town on Israel's side of the JORDAN RIVER. It would become the first city to fall in the PROMISED LAND.

Bible experts don't agree on when the Exodus happened. They're working with theories two centuries apart.

1400s. Some say the Exodus began in 1440. Scholars get that number from a report that says SOLOMON started his TEMPLE in the fourth year of his reign (about 960 BC), "480 years after the people of ISRAEL were rescued from their SLAVERY in the land of Egypt" (1 Kings 6:1). Add 960 BC to 480 BC; it equals 1440 BC. Others say 480 years—which is a dozen 40-year GENERATIONS—could be a round-number symbolic way of saying "a long time." One generation for each of Israel's 12 tribes.

1200s. This later date is based partly on a report that says the Jewish slaves built the city of "RAMESES" (Exodus 1:11). That's the family name of a dynasty of 11 kings who ruled from 1293–1070 BC. Egypt's most famous builderking, RAMESES II, ruled from 1279–1212 BC.

EXODUS
Goodbye, Egypt, Hello Canaan

SCENIC ROUTE. Instead of leading the Jews along the shortest route out of Egypt, some 150 miles (241 km) to Canaan, Moses bypassed the Egyptian forts. His route is uncertain, but a traditional route shown here would have covered roughly 700 miles (1120 km).

EXODUS, BOOK OF

TRAPPED AS SLAVES IN EGYPT, JEWS find the exit. They cry out to GOD. He sends a deliverer—a fellow Jew who had been adopted by a former king of EGYPT and then raised as a PRINCE in Egypt: MOSES. Convincing the king to free this army of slave labor is a tough sell. But 10 plagues later, the king is okay with getting the Jews gone.

- Writer: Unknown. Jewish tradition credits Moses.
- Time: 1400s BC or 1200s BC. Scholars debate which.
- Location: Egypt.

BIG SCENES

Enslaving the guests. JACOB had moved his FAMILY to Egypt to weather out a DROUGHT in Israel. They stay 430 years—long enough to grow so large that Egypt's king considers them a security threat. He enslaves them. *Exodus 1*

Moses: Jewish prince of Egypt. To control the Jewish population, the king orders all newborn Jewish boys thrown into the NILE RIVER—fresh meat for crocodiles. The mother of baby Moses complies. But she makes sure her baby floats—in a waterproof BASKET. Also, she floats him where the PRINCESS bathes. The princess adopts Moses and raises him in the palace. *Exodus 2*

Fiery, talking bush. Grown up, Moses becomes a hunted fugitive after killing an Egyptian foreman for beating a Jewish slave. Moses ends up working as a SHEPHERD. While grazing SHEEP in the Sinai, he sees a BURNING BUSH. Out of the bush the voice of God orders him back to Egypt, to free the Jews. *Exodus 2–4*

"Let my people go." Accompanied by his older brother, AARON, 80-year-old Moses returns to Egypt and delivers God's message. The king isn't impressed. First, he's considered a god himself: son of Re, the powerful sun god in a DESERT nation. Second, he has never heard of the Jewish God. Third, if the Jewish God had any muscle, the Jews wouldn't be in this fix.

Ten plagues. Egypt's king is stubborn—so stubborn that his nation has to endure 10 plagues before he finally agrees to release the Jews. Each PLAGUE seems to target an Egyptian god, some scholars say, to show that God is stronger:

1. Nile River turns red
2. frogs
3. gnats
4. flies
5. livestock disease
6. boils
7. HAIL
8. LOCUSTS
9. three days of darkness
10. death of oldest child. *Exodus 7–11*

Passover, the meal. Jews eat one last MEAL in SLAVERY, while the ANGEL of death moves through the land killing the FIRSTBORN—but passing over the Jewish households. The king, who loses his own son, frees the Jews that night. To this day, Jews commemorate their deliverance by eating a springtime PASSOVER meal about the same time Christians celebrate Easter. *Exodus 11–12*

Crossing the sea. Egypt's stubborn king makes one last attempt to get his own way. Hoping to retrieve his slaves, he mobilizes his CHARIOT corps. They never return. They manage to trap the Jews against a body of WATER. But God sends an all-night wind to blow a path into the water. It becomes the Jewish exit but the Egyptian drowning tank. When the chariot corps tries to follow the Jews, the water pours back into place. That's the end of the Egyptian ARMY in the Exodus story. *Exodus 12–14*

10 Commandments. Moses leads the Jews to where he heard God speak at the burning bush. It's at MOUNT SINAI. They camp there for about a year. That's long enough for God to give Moses many of the laws that will establish the Jewish nation and guide the people—including the 10 most important laws:

1. WORSHIP only God
2. no IDOLS
3. no irreverent use of God's NAME
4. no work on the SABBATH
5. honor your parents
6. no MURDER
7. no adultery
8. no stealing

9. no lies about your NEIGHBOR

10. no coveting what others have. *Exodus 19–20*

Tent worship center. God wants to give the Jews tangible evidence that he's with them. So he has them build a TENT worship center in the middle of the camp. Here is where the Jews will bring their SACRIFICES to God. It's a portable version of what will later become the Jewish TEMPLE in JERUSALEM. *Exodus 25–26, 36–38*

"If I am empowered by Satan, what about your own exorcists? They cast out demons, too." Jesus to Pharisees, Luke 11:19

• Driving demons out of a possessed person

DEMONS ENTERED PEOPLE. That was a wide-spread belief throughout the ancient Middle East. These DEMONS caused a world of hurt: physical illnesses, destructive behavior, and lousy luck in general.

Pagans, JEWS, and Christians all conducted exorcism rituals. Many how-to records survive.

In one, the exorcist made a figurine of the possessed person, ordered the demon out, and then broke the figurine.

First-century Jewish historian, Josephus, said he watched an exorcist tie a RING to a small root and then put the ring next to the possessed man's nose. The exorcist pulled the ring as though pulling the demon out through the man's nose. The possessed man collapsed and the exorcist started reciting incantations, ordering the demon to never come back.

E

EXORCIST PRIEST. "Screams, writhing on the ground, insults, vomiting, physical assaults upon the priest, spewing thick sputum—these are what the exorcist sees habitually." So says Father Jose Antonio Fortea, a Spanish priest and exorcist who has written on the topic.

STEPHEN M. MILLER'S ILLUSTRATED BIBLE DICTIONARY

The BIBLE says some Jewish exorcists once tried invoking the NAME of Jesus and Paul. But the demon replied, "I know Jesus, and I know Paul, but who are you?" (Acts 19:15). The possessed man then attacked the would-be exorcists. What followed was a switcheroo as far as Bible exorcisms are concerned: the demon drove off the exorcists.

EZEKIEL

(ee ZEEK ee uhl)

Ministered from 593–571 BC

God's Word came to Ezekiel the priest. . .in the country of Babylon. Ezekiel 1:3 MSG

- Jewish priest, prophet living in Babylon (Iraq)

A PRIEST WITH NO TEMPLE, Ezekiel never got to follow his career path. PRIESTS ministered only at the Jerusalem TEMPLE, and only "between the ages of thirty and fifty" (Numbers 4:3). But when Ezekiel was 25, Babylonians from what is now Iraq took him captive to BABYLON.

GOD gave Ezekiel a second career: prophet in EXILE.

Speaking on behalf of God, Ezekiel condemned the Jews for their long list of sins: idolatry, corruption, exploitation. He warned that JUDGMENT DAY was coming. Ezekiel lived to see it. Babylon invaded JUDAH in 586 BC, leveled Jerusalem, and wiped the Jewish nation off the political map.

Afterward, he saw a remarkable VISION of bones in a valley coming to life. It was a metaphor: God would resurrect the Jewish nation. Ezekiel probably didn't live to see that happen. His ministry seemed to end about 30 years before Persians from what is now Iran defeated the Babylonians and freed the political prisoners, including the Jews.

EZEKIEL, BOOK OF

Famous sound bite: "Dry bones, hear the world of the LORD!" Ezekiel 37:4 TNIV

EXILED IN IRAQ—headquarters of the Middle Eastern superpower called the Babylonian Empire—a PROPHET named Ezekiel predicts the collapse of the Jewish nation. It's punishment for serial SIN. But Ezekiel's news isn't all bad. He says GOD will resurrect the Jewish nation, giving them a second chance and a fresh start.

- Writer: Ezekiel.
- Time: Ezekiel ministers for 22 years, from 593–571 BC.
- Location: Ezekiel writes from exile in Iraq, then known as Babylon.

BIG SCENES

On a mission from God. Ezekiel sees a bizarre VISION that scholars say sounds tailored for a priest like Ezekiel. He sees God arriving on a CHARIOT, accompanied by angelic beings. ISRAEL's most sacred relic—the ARK OF THE COVENANT that held the 10 COMMANDMENTS—is sometimes described as God's chariot. And it's topped with figures of angelic beings. God has Ezekiel eat a SCROLL—perhaps to symbolize that Ezekiel will begin speaking God's words to the people. *Ezekiel 1–3*

Ezekiel's haircut and shave. Ezekiel cuts his HAIR and BEARD—as a symbol of Jewish doom. He divides the hair into three piles:

- *Pile one, he burns.* The message: When BABYLON lays SIEGE to JERUSALEM, a third of the Jews will die of DISEASE and starvation.
- *Pile two, he chops with a sword.* After capturing Jerusalem, Babylonians will execute a third of the survivors.
- *Pile three, he throws to the wind.* A third of the Jews will survive, but they'll get deported to Babylon. *Ezekiel 5–7*

God leaves Jerusalem. In a vision tailored for Jews who can't imagine God letting pagan invaders desecrate his sacred TEMPLE, Ezekiel sees God leaving both the Temple and the town. *Ezekiel 8–10*

Bones. For centuries of sin—idolatry, corruption, exploitation—God sentences the Jewish political nation to death. Babylon will erase it from the map. But Ezekiel sees a vision of bones in a valley. God snaps the bones together, lashes them up with flesh, and breathes life into the corpses. RESURRECTION. That's what Ezekiel promises God will do to the Jewish nation. *Ezekiel 37*

EZRA

(EZ ruh)

Arrived in Jerusalem in 458 BC

Ezra was a scribe who was well versed in the Law of Moses. . . . He came up to Jerusalem from Babylon. Ezra 7:6

- Jewish scholar returned from exile
- Brought supplies to upgrade the Temple
- Condemned mixed marriages

HE'S FAMOUS for ordering Jewish men to run off their non-Jewish wives and CHILDREN.

Harsh and bigoted, some charge. They add that this Jewish scholar's demand lives on the flip side of RUTH's coin. She was an Arab from what is now Jordan. She married a Jew and gave BIRTH to King DAVID's grandfather. Ruth's mixed marriage produced ISRAEL's greatest dynasty of kings.

Ezra, however, said he was trying to stop a second EXILE. He said GOD evicted the JEWS from the PROMISED LAND because they married non-Jews and started worshiping IDOLS that the spouses brought into their marriages. Ezra didn't want an encore of JUDGMENT DAY.

EZRA, BOOK OF

Famous sound bite: "You have broken God's Law by marrying foreign women. . . . Confess your sins. . . . Divorce your foreign wives." Ezra 10:10–11 CEV

A DO-OVER is what GOD gives the JEWS. Ezra, an expert in Jewish law, wants to make sure they get it right this time. In the first go-round, Jews broke God's laws

and ended up EXILED in what is now Iraq and Iran. Back home now, they start rebuilding their homes and their lives. But when some marry non-Jews, Ezra orders DIVORCE—on a national scale.

- Writer: Unknown. Jewish tradition credits Ezra.
- Time: The story covers about 80 years. It starts when Persian king Cyrus frees the Jews to go home in about 538 BC. It ends with Ezra's return to Jerusalem in 458 BC.
- Location: Most of the story takes place in Jerusalem. But it starts with the Jews exiled in what is now Iraq and Iran.

BIG SCENES

Iranians help the Jews. Exiled from their homeland and scattered throughout the Middle East in 586 BC, Jews live as refugees for about 50 years. When Persians (Iran) conquer the Babylonians (Iraq), King CYRUS of PERSIA not only frees the Jews, but he sends them home in 538 BC with GOLD, SILVER, livestock, and other supplies they'll need to start rebuilding JERUSALEM and the TEMPLE. *Ezra 1–2*

Downsized: God's Temple. Even with Cyrus's generous contributions to the Jewish refugees, when it comes time to pony up the goods for rebuilding the Temple, the best the Jews can manage is half a ton of gold and three tons of silver. In gold, that's about the weight of a Harley Davidson Fat Boy mounted by a stout rider. In silver, it's about one and a half Volkswagen Beetles. Big downgrade from the first Temple. DAVID had stockpiled 4,000 tons of gold and 40,000 tons of silver—equal to a stadium's parking lot of about 8,000 Harley's and 13,000 Beetles. When some of the older Jews see how the Temple is shaping up, they cry. *Ezra 3–6*

Nixing mixed marriages. Ezra arrives in Jerusalem about 80 years after the first wave of Jews. An expert in the laws of MOSES, he begins teaching the people. When he finds out that 113 men have married non-Jews, he orders them to DIVORCE the WOMEN and to abandon their CHILDREN. He argues that mixed marriages are what led their ANCESTORS into idolatry—a SIN that got the Jews exiled. Ezra doesn't want his people heading down that road again. *Ezra 7–10*

FAIR HAVENS

Map 3 B5

Since Fair Havens was an exposed harbor—a poor place to spend the winter—most of the crew wanted to go on to Phoenix, farther up the coast of Crete. **Acts 27:12**

- Crete bay where ships anchored

AGAINST THE ADVICE OF PAUL, a seasoned traveler, the captain of a SHIP taking him to ROME left Fair Havens in south-central CRETE. It was risky sailing season: autumn. But the captain made a run for a better-protected harbor at nearby PHOENIX. A storm snatched the shipped and battered it for two weeks before running it aground near MALTA, an island south of Italy.

FAITH

Faith is being sure of what we hope for. It is being certain of what we do not see. **Hebrews 11:1** NIrV

- Trust

IN GOD WE TRUST. It's not just a phrase stamped on American money. Christians bank on it. Believers can't see GOD's face, hear his voice, or shake his hand. But they say they believe in him. And they're counting on spending eternity with him.

FALL OF HUMANITY

Adam sinned, and that sin brought death into the world. Now everyone has sinned. **Romans 5:12** CEV

- Caused by Adam and Eve eating forbidden fruit

THE ORIGINAL SIN, eating FORBIDDEN FRUIT, somehow shredded the relationship not only between GOD and humanity's first couple, but between God and all humanity. It was as though that first SIN broke the dam and unleashed a sin flood.

"Everyone was going to be punished because Adam sinned," PAUL wrote. "But because of the good thing that Christ has done, God accepts us and gives us the gift of life" (Romans 5:18 CEV).

The "good thing" Jesus did was to take the punishment for humanity's sin. In the eyes of God, sin is a capital offense. Jesus allowed himself to be executed.

FALSE PROPHETS

"I am against the false prophets," says the LORD. "They use their own words and pretend it is a message from me." **Jeremiah 23:31** NCV

- Religious frauds who say they speak for God

LIARS. That's how the BIBLE describes false prophets. They say GOD spoke to them in DREAMS and VISIONS. He didn't.

FAMILY

The LORD had said to Abram. . . "Leave your father's family. Go to the land I will show you." **Genesis 12:1** NIrV

NOTHING ON EARTH in Bible times was more important than family. It's where people found acceptance, security, and WISDOM for living.

Dad ruled. His job: provide food, shelter, and protection for the family; educate the kids in Jewish ways; teach the boys a trade; arrange marriages for the kids.

Mom's job: provide CHILDREN, make meals, and take care of other household matters.

In early Jewish times, men who could afford it and didn't know any better married more than one WIFE. They figured the bigger the family, the more workers they had—and the more protection if push came to shove. But extra wives meant extra baggage: jealousy, for one. In later times, one wife seemed adequate—and preferred.

Archaeologists say that typical houses seemed able to accommodate about half a dozen people: parents, children, and elderly grandparents.

Once the FATHER died, the oldest SON seemed to serve as head of the extended family. He made decisions that affected the entire group, including the families of his younger brothers. Several extended families—sometimes called clans—often lived in the same general area. Early in ISRAEL's history, JEWS divided their land among 12 tribes. Each tribe descended from one of JACOB's sons and was made up of many clans.

As important as the family was, Jesus said it takes second place to following him: "If you love your father or MOTHER or even your sons and daughters more than me, you are not fit to be my DISCIPLES" (Matthew 10:37 CEV).

FAMINE (see DROUGHT)

FARMING

> He named him Noah [a Hebrew word that sounds like "relief"], saying, "This one will give us a break from the hard work of farming the ground that GOD cursed."
> Genesis 5:29 MSG

- Most common job reported in the Bible

IT WAS AN AG WORLD in Bible times. Even shepherding took a backseat to farming, the sod-busting work mentioned more times in the BIBLE than any other occupation.

Most folks who wanted to eat had to grow their own crops, though city slickers without farmland could buy their FRUIT and veggies.

There are lots of ROCKS in Israel's soil. Plowing it was tough enough after IRON plows came along, in the 1200s BC—when JEWS were getting settled in the PROMISED LAND. Before that, with wooden plows it was anyone's guess what would break first—the ground, the PLOW, or the farmer's back.

Jews didn't usually have a nearby river they could use to irrigate their crops, as did farmers alongside the Nile and EUPHRATES Rivers. But it rains in Israel. Especially in the winter when farmers planted their most important GRAINS: WHEAT and BARLEY. Other popular crops: OLIVES, GRAPES, figs, dates, ALMONDS, FLAX (its stems provided fiber for LINEN), melons, cucumbers, onions, LENTILS, and chickpeas.

One reason Jesus told so many PARABLES about farming, scholars speculate, is because of his location: GALILEE, in northern Israel. First-century writers such as Josephus said it was fertile farmland. Historians estimate that in Jesus' hometown of NAZARETH, each household farmed about five acres—roughly five football fields. It would have taken about three hardworking weeks to plow.

F

SOWING SEEDS. A Roman farmer throws seeds in this engraving from early Christian times.

FASTING

> "When you practice some appetite-denying discipline to better concentrate on God, don't make a production out of it. It might turn you into a small-time celebrity but it won't make you a saint." Matthew 6:16 MSG

- Refusing to eat, for religious reasons

IT WAS LAW. JEWS had to fast one day a year. They couldn't eat anything from sunrise to sunset on the national day of REPENTANCE, *Yom Kippur,* also known as the DAY OF ATONEMENT.

Many fasted for other reasons, too:

- MOURNING
- repenting
- seeking GOD's help

Some people who fasted wore rough clothing and covered themselves in dust or ASHES to express their sorrow—much like people today wear black clothes at funerals.

In Jesus' time, Jewish scholars called PHARISEES also fasted on Mondays and Thursdays. They criticized Jesus' DISCIPLES for not fasting. Jesus defended his disciples. He said his followers should be celebrating their time with him; they could fast when he was gone (Mark 2:20). He also accused the scholars of fake fasting: "They try to look miserable and disheveled so people will admire them for their fasting" (Matthew 6:16).

FAT

> "The priest must present the fat of this peace offering as a special gift to the LORD. . . . All the fat belongs to the Lord." Leviticus 3:9, 16

- Part of sacrifice reserved for God

IN SOME ANIMAL SACRIFICES, the entire ANIMAL was burned as an offering to GOD. In others—such as the Peace Offering given to thank God for something, like the BIRTH of a child—worshipers got to eat much of the animal. What they couldn't eat was the fat.

"You must never eat any fat. . . . This is a permanent law for you" (Leviticus 3:17).

Fat was burned on the ALTAR as an offering to God.

FATHER

> My children, listen when your father corrects you. Proverbs 4:1

BOSS OF THE FAMILY in Bible times, Dad made the big decisions. These included who his CHILDREN would marry and what kind of work his sons would do when they grew up. Often the father taught his boys the family business—which was usually FARMING and shepherding. It was his job, too, to teach his children the Jewish laws and customs.

If the FAMILY got into DEBT, the father had the legal right to sell children into SLAVERY to other JEWS to cover the debt—a practice many Jews hated (Nehemiah 5:5).

Father, however, meant more than "Dad." In the BIBLE, it could refer to a respected leader: KING, prophet, PRIEST, or the head of a village.

DOING MAN STUFF—networking—a group of Bedouin herders pause to pose for what becomes a hand-painted portrait in the early 1900s. In Bible times, men ruled the family roost.

In the New Testament, the word often describes God—not just as the father of Jesus, but as the father of humanity: "Because we are his children, God has sent the Spirit of his Son into our hearts, prompting us to call out, 'Abba, Father' " (Galatians 4:6).

ARRESTED FOR DISTURBING THE PEACE in Jerusalem, the apostle Paul was taken to Rome's capital in the area: the seaport city of Caesarea. There, Roman governor Felix kept Paul in jail for two years. Festus replaced Felix, and sent Paul to Rome for trial in Caesar's court.

FELIX

(FEE licks)

Ruled about AD 52–59
Felix often sent for Paul and talked with him, because he hoped that Paul would offer him a bribe. Acts 24:26 CEV

- Roman governor of Judea

FESTIVALS

Remember this day and celebrate it each year as a festival in my honor. Exodus 12:14 CEV

- Jewish holidays

F

GOD PLANNED PARTIES for the Jews. Not just for their enjoyment—though most were a hoot: music,

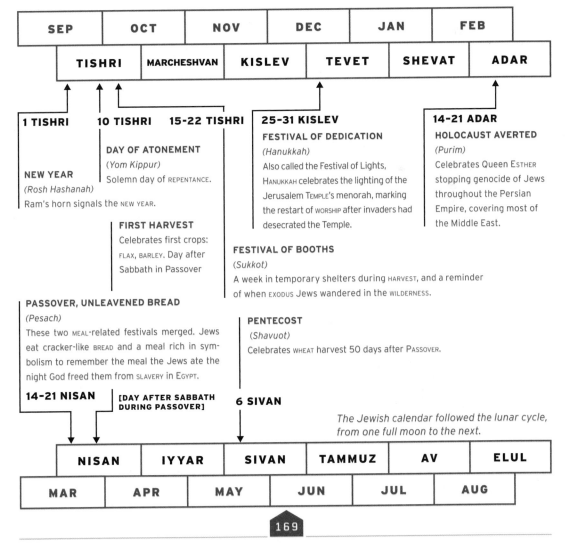

SEP	OCT	NOV	DEC	JAN	FEB
TISHRI	MARCHESHVAN	KISLEV	TEVET	SHEVAT	ADAR

1 TISHRI

NEW YEAR
(Rosh Hashanah)
Ram's horn signals the NEW YEAR.

10 TISHRI

DAY OF ATONEMENT
(Yom Kippur)
Solemn day of REPENTANCE.

15-22 TISHRI

FIRST HARVEST
Celebrates first crops:
FLAX, BARLEY. Day after
Sabbath in Passover

PASSOVER, UNLEAVENED BREAD
(Pesach)
These two MEAL-related festivals merged. Jews eat cracker-like BREAD and a meal rich in symbolism to remember the meal the Jews ate the night God freed them from SLAVERY in Egypt.

14-21 NISAN

[DAY AFTER SABBATH DURING PASSOVER]

25-31 KISLEV

FESTIVAL OF DEDICATION
(Hanukkah)
Also called the Festival of Lights, HANUKKAH celebrates the lighting of the Jerusalem TEMPLE's menorah, marking the restart of WORSHIP after invaders had desecrated the Temple.

FESTIVAL OF BOOTHS
(Sukkot)
A week in temporary shelters during HARVEST, and a reminder of when EXODUS Jews wandered in the WILDERNESS.

PENTECOST
(Shavuot)
Celebrates WHEAT harvest 50 days after PASSOVER.

6 SIVAN

14-21 ADAR

HOLOCAUST AVERTED
(Purim)
Celebrates Queen ESTHER stopping genocide of Jews throughout the Persian Empire, covering most of the Middle East.

The Jewish calendar followed the lunar cycle, from one full moon to the next.

NISAN	IYYAR	SIVAN	TAMMUZ	AV	ELUL
MAR	APR	MAY	JUN	JUL	AUG

169

DANCING, food. More importantly, GOD wanted these festivals, which were scattered throughout the year, to remind the Jews of their blessings and of their link to him.

FESTUS

(FESS tuss)

Ruled about AD 60–62

Festus shouted, "Paul, you are insane. Too much study has made you crazy!" Acts 26:24

- Roman governor of Judea

FESTUS WAS THE ROMAN who sent PAUL to ROME for trial in CAESAR's supreme COURT. Paul had lingered in jail at CAESAREA for two years while FELIX governed the Jewish territory. When Festus replaced Felix, Paul appealed for a trial in Caesar's court rather than risk a trial in JERUSALEM—in front of JEWS who were plotting to assassinate him.

FIG

Amos replied, "I'm not a professional prophet. . . . I'm just a shepherd, and I take care of sycamore-fig trees." Amos 7:14

- Sweet fruit common in the Middle East

FRUIT JERKY, figs could be eaten dried and pressed into chewy patties. Fresh, they're wonderfully sweet. They grow pear-shaped in both the wild and in orchards throughout Bible lands.

FRUITY SWEET, figs were a popular treat in Bible times. The prophet Amos owned a fig orchard.

FIRE AND BRIMSTONE

The LORD rained upon Sodom and upon Gomorrah brimstone and fire.
Genesis 19:24 KJV

- Burning sulfur

BRIMSTONE IS OLD ENGLISH LINGO for "SULFUR," a highly flammable chemical used today in gunpowder and matches. It's one of many chemicals found at the DEAD SEA, where many speculate the twin sin cities of SODOM AND GOMORRAH once stood.

Some also speculate that an EARTHQUAKE released underground pockets of natural gas common in the area. City LAMPS ignited the gas—as the theory goes—setting off an explosive rain of fire and flaming chemicals that destroyed the cities.

FIRSTBORN

The LORD said to Moses, "Dedicate to me every firstborn among the Israelites. . .of both humans and animals." Exodus 13:1–2

- First offspring—human or animal

THERE'S A REASON God asked the JEWS to dedicate the firstborn offspring to him: PASSOVER. On the night of the tenth PLAGUE OF EGYPT, GOD killed the oldest child in each Egyptian FAMILY and the firstborn among the livestock. But he passed over the Jews. This plague convinced the Egyptian king to free the Jews from their SLAVERY.

DEDICATION of the firstborn was intended to remind the Jews about how God helped them.

Jews sacrificed firstborn ANIMALS such as SHEEP or CATTLE. For animals they weren't allowed to sacrifice, they could substitute a sacrificial critter—or pay a fee: "its worth, plus 20 percent" (Leviticus 27:27).

As for humans: No SACRIFICE allowed. "You must buy back every firstborn son" (Exodus 13:13). The BIBLE doesn't say for how much.

FIRSTFRUITS

AS A THANK-YOU TO GOD, JEWS were to bring offerings of each of their crops to the WORSHIP center. They could do this during three HARVEST-related festivals scattered throughout the harvest SEASON. Spring: featuring BARLEY, which grows throughout the winter. Summer: WHEAT along with other crops. Fall: GRAPES, figs, OLIVES.

FISHING

JEWISH FISHERMEN worked mainly on a freshwater lake called the SEA OF GALILEE, along with the MEDITERRANEAN SEA, the JORDAN RIVER, and the Gulf of Aqaba tip of the RED SEA.

Commercial fishermen generally worked with NETS, hoping for a big haul. They would often row out on the lake at night. Night-cooled water lured fish up. TORCHES attracted the fish, too. In the dark, they couldn't see the nets.

Fishermen threw nets into the water. Sometimes they teamed up with another boat, stretching a long net between the two and rowing forward to trap fish.

JEWS, by law, were allowed to eat only fish with scales. No lobster, catfish, or eels. But they could eat the tasty tilapia that swam in the lake.

Fishermen sorted their daily catch and shipped it off to various markets. For distant markets, they dried or salted the fish.

At least four of Jesus' DISCIPLES were fishermen: brothers PETER and ANDREW, along with brothers JAMES and JOHN.

A fish became the early symbol of CHRISTIANITY—not just because Jesus promised to turn fishermen into "fishers of men." The GREEK word for fish—*ichthys*—worked as an acronym; it was a shorthand way of saying "JESUS CHRIST, GOD'S SON, SAVIOR." *I* is the first letter in Greek for "Jesus" (*Iesous*). *Ch* stands for "CHRIST," *Th* for "God," *Y* for "Son," and *S* for "Savior."

BIG HAUL. After a night of rotten luck, fishermen do as Jesus tells them: "Go out where it is deeper, and let down your nets to catch some fish" (Luke 5:4). Their luck changes.

Rahab had taken the men up to the flat roof of her house and had hidden them under some piles of flax plants that she had put there to dry. Joshua 2:3 CEV

- Plant used to make linseed oil, linen fabric

"I am about to cover the earth with a flood that will destroy every living thing that breathes." God to Noah, Genesis 6:17

- Flood that killed everyone but those in Noah's boat

ONE OF THE FIRST CROPS HARVESTED each spring, flax was a multitasker. Its seeds produced linseed oil used in MEDICINE, INK, and paint. Its stems produced one of the first known sources of fabric: LINEN.

Textile workers soaked the stems until the fibers separated. Then they beat them until they were soft and dried the fibers for weaving into just about anything: CLOTHING, sails, fishnets, sacks, ropes.

Jericho PROSTITUTE Rahab hid JOSHUA'S SPIES under drying piles of flax.

FLAX gives us linseed oil from the seeds and fabric from the fiber in the stems.

EARTH BECAME WATERWORLD, as the BIBLE tells it.

Anything that breathed got buried at sea—except those lucky enough to be sailing in NOAH's floodbuster:

- **Noah's extended FAMILY**
- **pairs of animals**

These humans and critters were intended to reboot life on earth.

Humanity's clock had run to 1,656 years. That's if Adam's family tree in Genesis 5 included all the men. Many scholars say it included just the notables. If so, humanity could have been eons old by the time GOD decided on a CREATION do-over.

The problem was SIN. "God saw that human evil was out of control. People thought evil, imagined evil. . . from morning to night" (Genesis 6:5 MSG).

The solution was Noah. "Noah was different. . .a good man, a man of integrity" (Genesis 6:8–9 MSG). God decided to wash the sin away. He'd kill everyone but Noah and his family of three married sons. They would survive on a huge boat they had to build. (See also ARK OF NOAH.)

Floodwater swallowed the land with pummeling rain and erupting groundwater. It lasted 40 days, a common Bible measurement that some scholars say simply means a long time.

By the time the rain stopped, "WATER covered even the highest mountains on the earth" (Genesis 7:19).

For five months Noah's floodbuster floated, until it came to a grinding halt "somewhere in the Ararat mountains" (Genesis 8:4 CEV). It took another seven months for the floodwater to recede enough that it was safe to disembark and begin rebuilding their lives. That means the Flood Cruise lasted a year.

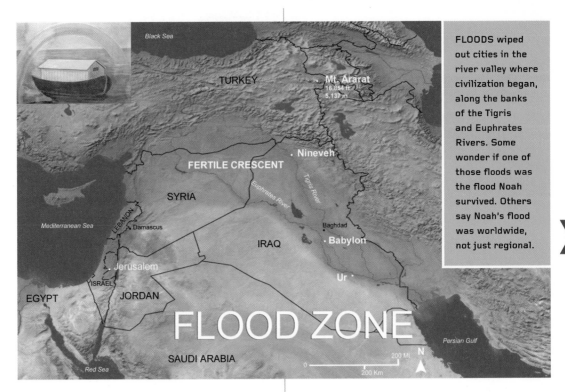

FLOODS wiped out cities in the river valley where civilization began, along the banks of the Tigris and Euphrates Rivers. Some wonder if one of those floods was the flood Noah survived. Others say Noah's flood was worldwide, not just regional.

Worldwide flood vs. regional flood

Many Christians who say the earth is just a few thousand years old insist that the flood:

- covered the world as we know it
- gave the earth a sudden facelift: mountains shoved up, valleys carved low

They argue that the Bible says God covered even the highest mountains.

Other Christians say the flood probably affected only the world as the ancients knew it: the Fertile Crescent, where civilization began along the TIGRIS and EUPHRATES Rivers in what is now Iraq.

Defending this position, scholars say archaeologists and geologists have found evidence of devastating regional floods in the Tigris and Euphrates valley but no evidence of a worldwide flood.

Other flood stories

Some 70 cultures around the world have ancient flood stories, from the Middle East to the South Pacific. Some sound remarkably close to the Bible flood.

Take the Epic of Gilgamesh, for example. It's an ancient Iraqi (Babylonian) story about a king named Gilgamesh, thought to have lived in the 2000s BC. That's many centuries before MOSES, whom Jewish tradition credits with writing the GENESIS flood story.

In the Iraqi flood story, a man survived a flood by building a boat for his family and for some ANIMALS. Like Noah, he released a DOVE after the flood to see if it would find a place to land. The dove didn't, and it came back to the boat just as the dove did in Noah's story.

Clearly, some Bible students say, there was once a whopper of a flood that made a whopper of an impression.

Good news from God. After the flood, he filled the sky with a rainbow and vowed, "Floods will never again destroy all life on the earth" (Genesis 9:15 NCV).

FLOUR

Gideon went home. . .opened a big sack of flour and made it into thin bread.
Judges 6:19 CEV

- Grain kernels crushed into a fine powder

KERNELS OF WHEAT or other GRAIN, such as BAR-LEY, were crushed into powdery flour. This was step one in making BREAD. JEWS crushed the kernels by rolling large MILLSTONES over them—often powered by an animal. Or, for flour on a smaller-scale, they crushed it by hand with a small rock.

See also BAKING.

FLOWERS

> *Rich people will disappear like wild flowers scorched by the burning heat of the sun.* James 1:10–11 CEV

ISRAEL PAINTS ITSELF IN FLOWERS almost year round. In the springtime, hillsides erupt with the reds and pinks of wildflowers: corn poppies, tulips, and mallows. Within a few weeks, they wither when the summer sun bears down. But a second wave splashes the fields in yellows and whites of chrysanthemums and chamomile. Into the fall, thorny bushes and flowering weeds add their sprinkle of tiny blooms in purple, white, yellow, and blue.

A MUSICIAN plays a double flute—art from a marble vase crafted about the time of Christ.

FLUTE

> *All the people followed Solomon into Jerusalem, playing flutes and shouting for joy.* 1 Kings 1:40

PERFECT FOR PARTIES yet suited to sadness, the BIBLE's main wind instrument pumped emotions at either extreme. Often made of reeds, IVORY, or metal, a flute might have anywhere from three to five finger holes. Musicians often played two flutes at a time. Some had REED mouthpieces, a bit like clarinets today.

FOOD (see MEALS)

FOOTWASHING

> *Jesus got up. . .and wrapped a towel around his waist. . . . Then he began washing his disciples' feet.* John 13:4–5 CEV

- Customary way of welcoming a guest

WALKING DUSTY TRAILS in SANDALS can dirty up a pair of feet within a few steps. Worse, walking the hot, dry turf of the Middle East can bake the feet and crack the skin.

Little wonder that common courtesy in Bible times included foot washing for houseguests. At the very least, hosts provided WATER and a towel for guests to wash their own feet. Hosts might even offer some OLIVE OIL to moisturize the skin.

If they wanted to crank up the HOSPITALITY, hosts might offer their guest a SERVANT to do the dirty work. But not a Jewish servant. Foot washing was considered too lowdown and dirty for a Jew—even for a Jewish slave. Foot washing was a job fit for no soul higher than the household's bottom-of-the-barrel slave.

That's why PETER didn't want Jesus washing Peter's feet at the LAST SUPPER.

Jesus washed them anyhow. He did it to teach his DISCIPLES a lesson: Serve others instead of expecting others to serve you. "I have given you an example to follow. Do as I have done to you" (John 13:15).

FORBIDDEN FRUIT

"You may freely eat the fruit of every tree in the garden—except the tree of the knowledge of good and evil. If you eat its fruit, you are sure to die." Genesis 2:16–17

- Fruit forbidden to Adam and Eve

THERE'S JUST ONE RULE God gave HUMANITY. It was one rule too many.

A SNAKE convinced Eve that if she ate fruit from the forbidden TREE OF KNOWLEDGE about good and evil, she'd be as smart as GOD. The last book in the BIBLE IDs "the ancient serpent. . . SATAN" (Revelation 12:9). But the Bible never identifies the fruit.

Eve convinced Adam to eat it, too. Suddenly, they realized they were naked—and that they disobeyed God.

God banished them from the Garden of EDEN and from access to fruit from the TREE OF LIFE—a hint, some scholars say, that if they had obeyed God, they would have lived forever.

FOREIGNER

Do not mistreat or abuse foreigners who live among you. Remember, you were foreigners in Egypt. Exodus 22:21 CEV

- Immigrants
- Travelers passing through

PEOPLE AT HIGH RISK—most likely to get exploited— were orphans and widows, along with foreigners living in the land or just passing through. By law, JEWS were to offer compassion and justice to these vulnerable souls (see Deuteronomy 24:17).

"Native-born Israelites and foreigners are equal before the LORD" (Numbers 15:15).

FORGIVENESS

If we confess our sins to God, he can always be trusted to forgive us and take our sins away. 1 John 1:9 CEV

- Pardon for the guilty

WHEN GOD FORGIVES, he does it to the max, as the PROPHETS tell it.

- "You will throw all of our sins into the bottom of the sea" (Micah 7:19 NIrV).
- "I [God] will not remember your sins anymore" (Isaiah 43:25 NIrV).

The apostle PAUL said GOD expects the same of his people: "Forgive each other, just as God forgave you" (Ephesians 4:32 NIrV).

FORNICATION

Sexual sins are sins against one's own body. Don't you know that your bodies are temples of the Holy Spirit? 1 Corinthians 6:18–19 NIrV

- Sex sin

THE DICTIONARY calls *fornication* SEX between two consenting, unmarried adults. But the word that Bible writers used is broader. It means any kind of sexual SIN, including sex with:

- "a close relative" (Leviticus 18:6)
- "an animal" (Exodus 22:19)
- "a man. . .with another man" (Leviticus 18:22 CEV).

FORTUNE-TELLING

"Do not let your people practice fortune-telling. . .witchcraft. . .or function as mediums or psychics." Deuteronomy 18:10–11

- Predicting the future

AGAINST JEWISH LAW, King Saul went to a psychic to find out if his army would win the next day's battle against the Philistines (see 1 Samuel 28). He got bad news.

The apostle Paul wrote that Christians fight "against evil spirits" in "the unseen world" (Ephesians 6:12). The only spirit worth trusting, as the Bible tells it, is God's Spirit—"the Spirit of truth" (John 15:26).

See also Sorcery.

FRANKINCENSE
(FRANK in cents)

The Wise Men. . .saw the child with his mother Mary. . . . They gave him gold, incense and myrrh. Matthew 2:11 NIRV

- Fragrant tree sap

A WOODY FRAGRANCE used in perfume and incense, frankincense is dried sap from Boswellia trees.

It was expensive for Jews in Israel because they had to import it from what is now Saudi Arabia and North African countries such as Ethiopia and Somalia. But Jewish priests needed it for their worship rituals. Frankincense was part of the recipe for the only incense Jews were allowed to burn in the Temple (Exodus 30:34).

FREE WILL

I am all too human, a slave to sin. . . . I want to do what is right, but I don't do it. . . . Who will free me. . . ? Thank God! The answer is in Jesus Christ our Lord. Romans 7:14–15, 24–25

- Freedom to accept or reject God's salvation

CHRISTIANS SPLIT OVER THIS IDEA. Those who follow in the tradition of theologians John Wesley (1703–1791) and Jacobus Arminius (1560–1609)—Methodists, for example—say God gives people the freedom to choose their own destiny. These Christians say that God in his grace reaches out to everyone, inviting them into a spiritual relationship with him.

One of their go-to verses: "Choose today whom you will serve. . . . But as for me and my family, we will serve the Lord" (Joshua 24:15).

Counterpoint: Joshua could choose only what God had already chosen for him.

Christians who lean toward the ideas of John Calvin (1509–1564)—such as Southern Baptists, Presbyterians—teach that God is sovereign. God decides who will and won't get saved.

One of their go-to verses: "God decided in advance to adopt us into his own family by bringing us to himself through Jesus Christ" (Ephesians 1:5).

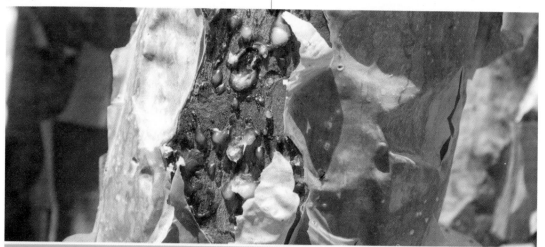

FRAGRANT SAP. Frankincense resin seeps from a cut in the bark of a Boswellia tree in the Middle Eastern country of Oman. The sap hardens and is sold for incense and perfume.

Counterpoint: God offers to adopt everyone, but not everyone agrees to the ADOPTION.

One add-on point that Calvin's theological kids argue is that God knows everything. Free Will kids essentially answer, "So what? Knowing what will happen isn't the same as making it happen."

See also PREDESTINATION.

FRUIT

> When you are attacking a town, don't chop down its fruit trees. . . . They produce food that you can eat. **Deuteronomy 20:19** CEV

ISRAEL and its neighboring countries produce many kinds of fruit: GRAPES, figs, POMEGRANATES, apricots, melons, and OLIVES, to name a few.

There's one law unique to Jewish fruit farmers.

If JEWS planted a fruit tree, they had to wait until the fifth HARVEST before eating any of it. "When you enter the land and plant fruit trees, leave the fruit unharvested for the first three years. . . . In the fourth year the entire crop must be consecrated to the LORD as a celebration of PRAISE. Finally, in the fifth year you may eat the fruit. If you follow this pattern, your harvest will increase" (Leviticus 19:23–25).

Bible experts say this law isn't about how to make trees produce more fruit, in the way that crop rotation might help a field. Instead, GOD was making a point: The land belongs to him, not to the Jews.

FRUIT OF THE SPIRIT

> The Holy Spirit produces this kind of fruit in our lives: love, joy, peace. **Galatians 5:22**
>
> ▪ Character traits of a Christian

REAL CHRISTIANS act like Christians, according to the apostle PAUL. He said that people guided by GOD'S Spirit produce nine wonderful character traits: love, joy, PEACE, patience, kindness, goodness, faithfulness, gentleness, and self-control.

FUNERAL   (see BURIAL)

FURNACE

> Soldiers tied up Shadrach, Meshach, and Abednego and threw them into the flaming furnace. **Daniel 3:21** CEV

FURNACES DIDN'T HEAT HOUSES in Bible times. Not usually, anyhow.

But they did bake POTTERY rock hard—in charcoal-fired KILNS that reached temps of 1800 degrees F (982 degrees C). That's the top end of a typical cremation chamber today.

These kilns could also melt COPPER and IRON in smelting crucibles that could top out over 2000 degrees F (1093 degrees C)—high enough to produce a low grade of iron called wrought iron.

When Babylonian King NEBUCHADNEZZAR, in what is now Iraq, ordered the prophet DANIEL's three Jewish friends tossed into a furnace, scholars say it was probably a kiln.

Ruins of some large kilns found in the area were shaped like railroad tunnels sealed at both ends. Kiln workers would put clay pottery or mud BRICKS on ledges inside. Then they'd set a fire on the ground below the ledges and seal the doors closed.

F

Gabriel may have delivered many of God's messages. But his NAME shows up just seven times in the BIBLE, visiting three people.

The prophet Daniel. After seeing a VISION about end times, the prophet DANIEL said he heard a voice say, "Gabriel, tell this man the meaning of his vision" (Daniel 8:16). Gabriel appeared, explained the vision, and left. Later Gabriel came back. This time he reassured Daniel that God took action on Daniel's PRAYER: "The moment you began praying, a command was given" (Daniel 9:23).

Zechariah, the father of John the Baptist. Gabriel made his first appearance in the NEW TESTAMENT by appearing to an elderly PRIEST in the Jerusalem TEMPLE: ZECHARIAH. There Gabriel said that Zechariah and his wife, ELIZABETH, would have a son who would "prepare the people for the coming of the LORD" (Luke 1:17).

Mary, the mother of Jesus. Six months later, Gabriel appeared to the VIRGIN MARY in NAZARETH: "You will conceive and give BIRTH to a son, and you will name him Jesus. He will be very great and will be called the Son of the Most High" (Luke 1:31–32).

GABRIEL delivered messages to at least three people in the Bible: the Virgin Mary, Daniel, and the father of John the Baptist. Jewish tradition says he was one of God's top angels.

GABRIEL

(GAY bree uhl)

"I am Gabriel! I stand in the very presence of God. It was he who sent me to bring you this good news!" Luke 1:19

- Angel messenger of God
- Announced the births of Jesus, John the Baptist

GABRIEL WASN'T JUST AN ANGEL. Not according to some ancient Jewish WRITINGS, which show up in Catholic and Eastern Orthodox Bibles. He was one of the elite—an ARCHANGEL, "one of the seven ANGELS who stand ready and enter before the GLORY of the Lord" (Tobit 12:15 NRSV).

GAD

1800s BC

The sons of Zilpah, Leah's servant, were Gad and Asher. Genesis 35:26

- One of Jacob's 12 sons

IN A BABY-MAKING CONTEST, rival sister wives LEAH and RACHEL tried to outdo each other by providing sons for their husband, JACOB. Each WIFE doubled her efforts by giving Jacob one of her SERVANTS as a surrogate wife. Gad was one of two sons by Leah's servant, Zilpah.

GAD, TRIBE OF

Map 1 E5

There were 40,500 men from the tribe of Gad. Numbers 26:18 CEV

- One of Israel's 12 tribes

DESCENDANTS OF JACOB'S SON Gad settled east of the JORDAN RIVER, in what is now the Arab country of Jordan. Assyrian invaders from what is now Iraq, led by King TIGLATH-PILESER III (reigned 745–727 BC), overran the tribe and deported the survivors "as prisoners to ASSYRIA" (1 Chronicles 5:26 CEV).

GADARENES

(GAD uh reens)

Jesus arrived at the other side of the lake in the area of the Gadarenes. Two men controlled by demons met him. Matthew 8:28 NIRV

- Territory east of Sea of Galilee
- Where Jesus sent demons into a herd of pigs

JESUS EXORCISED DEMONS, sending them into a herd of pigs that promptly charged into the SEA OF GALILEE and drowned. This happened in a mainly non-Jewish region in what is now Jordan.

GAIUS

(GAY us)

The whole city was in a riot, and some men grabbed Gaius. . .who had come from Macedonia with Paul. Acts 19:29 CEV

1. TRAVELING ASSOCIATE OF PAUL. Rioters in EPHESUS angry at the apostle PAUL lashed out at his traveling companions—Gaius among them. The associates were later released.

2. Church member who defied a control-freak pastor. JOHN addressed a short LETTER—3 John—to perhaps another Gaius. This Gaius welcomed visiting CHRISTIAN MINISTERS despite orders from his PASTOR to shoo them off. The pastor seemed threatened by outsiders who might challenge his authority.

GALATIA

Map 3 J3

(guh LAY shuh)

Paul and Silas traveled through the area of Phrygia and Galatia. Acts 16:6

- Roman province in central Turkey
- Location of churches Paul addressed in a letter: Galatians

ON HIS SECOND MISSIONARY TRIP, PAUL preached in cities throughout Galatia before crossing over to what is now Greece—introducing Europeans to the teachings of Jesus. Galatian cities: DERBE, ICONIUM, LYSTRA, Pisidian ANTIOCH.

G

GALATIANS, LETTER OF

Famous sound bite: You reap whatever you sow. Galatians 6:7 NRSV

JEWISH CHRISTIANS lobby hard for all other Christians to obey Jewish laws—including the tough ones: laws about CIRCUMCISION and KOSHER FOOD. Paul doesn't take it kindly. He gets screaming mad.

- Writer: Paul, perhaps dictating, but signing it "in my own handwriting" (Galatians 6:11).
- Time: Scholars guess Paul wrote this letter as early as AD 48 and as late as the mid-50s.
- Location: Paul wrote to Christians in Galatia, a Roman province in central Turkey.

BIG SCENES

Paul gives Peter a piece of his mind. PAUL tears into PETER for treating non-Jewish Christians like they're second-class citizens in GOD's kingdom. While visiting the predominantly non-Jewish CHURCH that PAUL pastored in ANTIOCH, Peter refused to eat with the GENTILES. That's how JEWS generally treated non-Jews. But Paul said it's no way for Christians to treat fellow Christians: "God has no favorites." *Galatians 2*

Paul on a rant against Jewish Christians.
Some Jewish Christians are trying to steer CHRISTIANITY back to the Jewish religion. They want all Christians to convert to the Jewish faith—and to observe all Jewish laws, including the most painful: circumcision for the men. Livid, Paul writes, "Why don't these agitators, obsessive as they are about circumcision, go all the way and castrate themselves!" (Galatians 5:12 MSG). Paul argues that the sacrificial death of Jesus has freed everyone from "SLAVERY to the law." *Galatians 5*

GALILEE   Map 4 C4

(GAL uh lee)

There will be a time in the future when Galilee. . .will be filled with glory.
Isaiah 9:1

- Northern Israel, where Jesus ministered

JESUS GREW UP in the rolling hills of Galilee, along the northern tip of what is now ISRAEL.

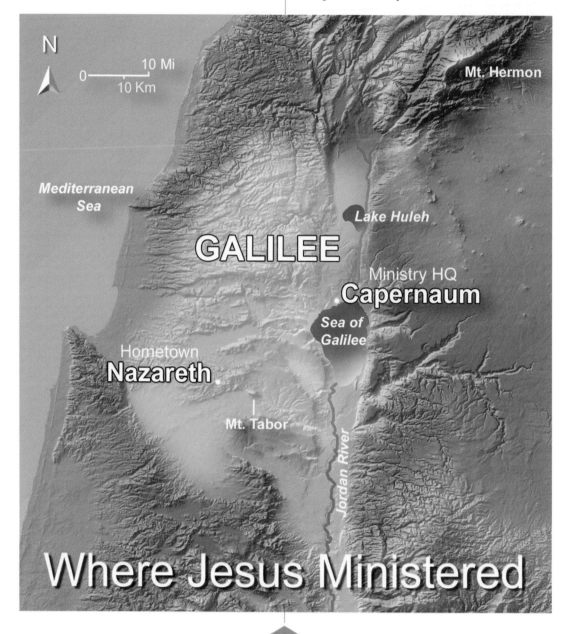

N

10 Mi
0
10 Km

Mt. Hermon

Mediterranean Sea

Lake Huleh

GALILEE

Ministry HQ
Capernaum

Sea of Galilee

Hometown
Nazareth

Mt. Tabor

Jordan River

Where Jesus Ministered

If a farmer couldn't grow crops in these fertile hills, he didn't deserve to call himself a farmer. That's pretty much how one first-century Jewish writer put it. "Every inch of soil has been cultivated," Josephus wrote. "Even the laziest people are tempted to take up a career in farming."

Galilee covered a swath of ground stretching some 30 miles (48 km) wide and 50 miles (80 km) north to south—home to 204 villages, according to Josephus. That included the tiny village of NAZARETH, where MARY and JOSEPH raised Jesus.

Besides FARMING crops such as WHEAT, BARLEY, GRAPES, and OLIVES, many folks fished for a living in the Sea of Galilee on Galilee's east border. Among the fishermen: at least four of Jesus' DISCIPLES—PETER, ANDREW, JAMES, and JOHN.

See also SEA OF GALILEE.

RAINY DAY IN GALILEE. The area generally gets plenty of rain—about 16 inches (40 cm) in a year. Almost what farms in western Kansas get, that's enough to keep the fields green and the farmers busy.

GALL

The soldiers gave Jesus [during the Crucifixion] wine mixed with gall to drink. He tasted the wine but refused to drink it. Matthew 27:34 NCV

- Some kind of drug added to Jesus' wine

AS JESUS HUNG ON THE CROSS, Roman soldiers may have tried to drug him with a painkiller—or

kill him with "POISON" (Psalm 69:21). They offered him WINE with gall, an unspecified substance.

Ancient Jewish writings said people sometimes gave condemned victims wine mixed with FRANKINCENSE as a painkiller. Other writings say that some JERUSALEM women provided a narcotic to the condemned. MARK called the substance "MYRRH" (Mark 15:23), though that may have been a drink offered at a different time.

GAMALIEL

(guh MAY lee uhl)

First century AD

Paul said, "I am a Jew. . . . I was brought up and educated here in Jerusalem under Gamaliel." Acts 22:3

- Paul's religious prof
- Member of Jewish high council

G

TOLERANT FOR A PHARISEE, Gamaliel served on what amounted to the Jewish supreme court. When some of Jesus' DISCIPLES showed up in COURT, arrested for refusing to stop teaching that Jesus rose from the dead, Gamaliel recommended the court release them. He said if the CHRISTIAN movement had GOD's backing, the court couldn't stop it. Otherwise, the movement would die.

Years later, when the apostle PAUL defended himself to a JERUSALEM mob, he invoked the NAME of his respected mentor, Gamaliel.

GAMES

"They are like children playing a game in the public square." Luke 7:32

FROM BOARD GAMES to Olympic marathons, kids and adults in Bible times found ways to have fun.

A few games mentioned in the BIBLE: a mind-stretching RIDDLE at SAMSON's WEDDING (Judges 14:12); Olympic-style foot races mentioned by PAUL (1 Corinthians 9:24); soldiers gambling for Jesus' clothes "by throwing dice" (Luke 23:34).

Some of the many other games discovered, shown in ancient art, or described in writings:

- swings
- team tag
- playing catch with nuts
- jacks, played with animal knucklebones
- chess-style board games

One of the most popular board games was a bit like checkers, but the players had to role dice to determine their next move.

A fully-preserved Egyptian board game called hounds and jackals (wild dogs) involved moving IVORY pieces around a board. Half the 10 pieces are carved in the shape of dog heads, the other half as jackal heads.

When Paul spent a year and a half starting the CHURCH in CORINTH, he may have seen the Olympic-style games held on the outskirts of town every two years: the Isthmian Games. Or he may have seen the actual Olympics held every four years at Olympia, southwest of Corinth about 75 miles (120 km).

See also ATHLETICS.

GARDEN OF EDEN (see EDEN)

GATE

"The father and mother must take the son to the elders as they hold court at the town gate." Deuteronomy 21:19

- Entrance into a walled city
- Popular meeting place

MASSIVE WOODEN DOORS, sometimes armored with sheets of BRONZE or IRON, served as gateways into walled cities. Many cities closed the gates at night to protect against attack.

Because gateways funneled everyone into town, gates became a natural meeting place—a town center of sorts—where vendors sold their products, city officials conducted business, and JUDGES held COURT.

BETHLEHEM's city gate is where BOAZ made the deal to marry RUTH (Ruth 4:1).

At the Philistine city of GAZA, an angry SAMSON tore off the city gate and lugged it some 40 miles (64 km) before tossing it on a hill near HEBRON (Judges 16:3).

DAMASCUS GATE in Jerusalem is often a busy place. It's where many folks enter the Old City of Jerusalem. And it's where vendors wait to hawk their souvenirs and other products.

STEPHEN M. MILLER'S ILLUSTRATED BIBLE DICTIONARY

GATH

Map 1 B6

David escaped from Saul and went to King Achish of Gath. 1 Samuel 21:10

- Goliath's hometown

ONE OF FIVE MAJOR CITIES of the PHILISTINES, Gath wasn't just the hometown of their champion warrior, GOLIATH. Strangely, it's where Goliath's killer—DAVID—sought asylum from King SAUL, who was insanely jealous of David's popularity. As it turned out, Gath's king liked having on his team the warrior who had killed his champion (1 Samuel 27).

GAZA

Map 1 A6

(GAH zuh)

Philistines grabbed Samson and poked out his eyes. They took him to the prison in Gaza. Judges 16:21 CEV

- Philistine city were Samson died

SWEET PAYBACK may have been why the PHILISTINES tossed SAMSON in the Gaza PRISON, forcing him to do an ANIMAL's work: pushing a millstone to grind GRAIN into FLOUR.

Earlier, Samson had humiliated the city by tearing off Gaza's city GATE and carrying it away.

Samson retaliated by dislodging the support pillars in a temple there, killing more than 3,000 Philistines "making fun of him" (Judges 16:27).

Today, Gaza, about 40 miles (64 km) south of Tel Aviv, is the main Palestinian city in the Gaza Strip. Population: about half a million—making it the largest city in the Palestinian territories.

GEDALIAH

(ged uh LIE uh)

Appointed 586 BC

King Nebuchadnezzar appointed Gedaliah son of Ahikam to rule the few people still living in Judah. 2 Kings 25:22 CEV

- Babylonian-appointed governor of the Jews

AFTER ERASING the Jewish nation from the world map—leveling JERUSALEM and deporting many survivors—Babylonian king NEBUCHADNEZZAR appointed a Jew named Gedaliah to rule the few left behind. Some of those JEWS assassinated Gedaliah seven months later.

GEHAZI

(guh HAZE eye)

About 850–800 BC

When Gehazi left the room, he was covered with leprosy; his skin was white as snow. 2 Kings 5:27

- Elisha's greedy servant

ELISHA HEALED a Syrian commander named NAAMAN of LEPROSY. ELISHA refused Naaman's offer of payment. Naaman left. But Elisha's SERVANT Gehazi caught up with the commander. Gehazi lied and said Elisha had changed his mind. Naaman gave Gehazi clothes and what may have been Gehazi's weight in SILVER, about 150 pounds (68 kg). When Elisha found out, he added leprosy to Gehazi's assets.

GEHENNA

See Jerusalem, Map 4 C5

(guh HEN uh)

"Every one who is angry at his brother. . . shall be in danger of the gehenna of the fire." Matthew 5:22 YLT

- Greek name for Hinnom Valley
- Jerusalem-area valley that became a symbol of God's judgment

HINNOM VALLEY, outside JERUSALEM's walls, became a symbol of GOD's judgment on the JEWS. HINNOM is where some Jews sacrificed to IDOLS—including HUMAN SACRIFICES. Sins like these, PROPHETS said, led God to allow invaders to evict the Jews from ISRAEL in 586 BC.

See also HELL.

G

GENEALOGY

Hobaiah, Hakkoz and Barzillai. . .priests looked for their family records. But they couldn't find them. So they weren't able to serve as priests. Nehemiah 7:63–64 NIrv

BORING TO MOST READERS TODAY, genealogies were to JEWS in Bible times what passports are to international travelers today: proof of identity.

- You weren't a Jew if you couldn't prove it.
- You weren't a Jewish PRIEST if you couldn't prove you descended from the tribe of LEVI.
- You weren't KING material if you couldn't prove you descended from the FAMILY of DAVID.

Good genealogies documented a person's identity. The BIBLE boasts about a dozen genealogies. Two trace the family tree of Jesus back to David to prove that he was MESSIAH-qualified.

Not all genealogies are complete, most scholars say. Some name only the notables. If the genealogy in Exodus 6 were complete, that would mean JACOB's son Levi (1800s BC) was the great-grandfather of MOSES (1400s BC or 1200s BC; scholars debate which). That's a span of 400–600 years.

Using the short number of 400 years, that's a bit like someone today saying his great-granddad was Rembrandt (1606–1669), his grandpa was President George Washington (1732–1799), and his dad was auto tycoon Henry Ford (1863–1947).

A few bodies have gone missing, some would argue.

A counterpoint is that the Bible says people lived longer in Moses' day. Moses: 120 years. His dad Amram: 137. His granddad Kohath: 133. His great-granddad Levi: 137 (Exodus 6:16–20; Deuteronomy 34:7). That totals 527 years.

GENERATION

Job lived 140 years after that, living to see four generations of his children and grandchildren. Job 42:16

- Time from birth of parents to birth of their children

IT COVERS ABOUT 35 TO 40 YEARS for most Bible writers. But it sometimes goes higher, up to 100 years. GOD warned ABRAHAM that his descendants would suffer in SLAVERY for "400 years. . .four generations" (Genesis 15:13, 16).

GENESIS

Famous sound bite: In the beginning God created the heavens and the earth. Genesis 1:1

A BOOK OF BEGINNINGS, Genesis tells about the beginning of the universe, HUMANITY, and the Jewish people.

- Writer: Unknown. Jewish tradition credits Moses.
- Time: The book starts with the creation of the universe and ends with Jacob moving his extended family to Egypt in about 1800 BC.
- Location: The stories take place throughout the Middle East but mainly in Israel and Egypt.

BIG SCENES

Creation. In six days—which some people of FAITH say were 24-hour days and others say were eons—GOD created the universe and life on earth. *Genesis 1*

Breaking God's one and only rule. God tells humanity's first couple, ADAM AND EVE, not to eat fruit from the TREE OF KNOWLEDGE—warning it will kill them. A SNAKE, identified in the last book of the BIBLE as "SATAN" (Revelation 12:9), convinces Eve that God lied and that she'll be as smart as God if she eats it. She and Adam chow down. God evicts them from the Garden of EDEN paradise. In time, they die. Some speculate the FORBIDDEN FRUIT robbed them of IMMORTALITY. *Genesis 3*

The world's first murder. With only four humans known to be alive—Adam and Eve along with their sons CAIN and ABEL—it seems odd that the motive for the first MURDER is jealousy. Cain kills his little brother, Abel, upset that God accepted Abel's SACRIFICE but rejected his. *Genesis 4*

Flood warning. God is fed up with humans after only 10 GENERATIONS. "Everything they thought and planned was evil" (Genesis 6:5 CEV). He decides to start over with the FAMILY of humanity's one good man: NOAH. God drowns humanity in a FLOOD. Only Noah's family survives, along with pairs of ANIMALS to reseed the planet. They weather the flood in a huge barge. *Genesis 6–8*

Abraham: Jew number one. God decides to choose a race of people who will provide the world with a living example of what it means to serve God—and to receive God's BLESSING for obedience. He chooses an Iraqi—ABRAHAM, from the city of UR in what is now southern Iraq. God sends him to what is now ISRAEL. Though Abraham is 75 years old when he arrives and married to 66-year-old SARAH who is infertile, God promises: "I will give this land to your descendants." *Genesis 11–12*

Abraham nearly kills his son. Abraham is 100 when his son ISAAC is born. Years later, on God's seemingly sadistic order, Abraham prepares to offer him as a HUMAN SACRIFICE—but God stops him at the last second. Many Bible experts say the story foreshadows the sacrificial death of Jesus. What Abraham was willing to do, God actually did. *Genesis 22*

Jacob cheats his brother and father. The father of ISRAEL's 12 tribes makes a horrible first impression to Bible readers. He exploits the hunger of his older brother, ESAU, by feeding him only in exchange for the INHERITANCE rights due the oldest SON: a double share of the estate. Later he tricks his old and nearly blind father, Isaac, into giving him the BLESSING intended for Esau. Still God sees something good in him. JACOB's dozen sons become the founding fathers of Israel's 12 tribes. *Genesis 25, 27, 35*

Jews move to Egypt. Jacob has a favorite son: JOSEPH, the first son of Jacob's favorite wife, RACHEL. Jealous of their little brother, Jacob's older sons sell 17-year-old Joseph to slave traders. They sell him in EGYPT. A good thing, as it turns out. Joseph rises to Egypt's number two position. When a seven-year DROUGHT hammers the Middle East, Joseph arranges for his extended family to weather out the drought in Egypt along the banks of the drought-resistant NILE RIVER. *Genesis 37–46*

G

SOUTHBOUND. The story of Genesis ends with Jacob moving his entire extended family to the Nile River in Egypt, to wait out a drought in what is now Israel. They stayed four centuries, ending up as a slave race. Cue Moses.

GENNESARET

Map 4 D4

(guh NESS uh ret)

Jesus and his disciples crossed the lake and came to shore near the town of Gennesaret.
Matthew 14:34 CEV

- Town in Galilee
- Sea of Gennesaret, also known as Sea of Galilee

AFTER WALKING ON WATER out to the DISCIPLES in a boat, Jesus had the men land at Gennesaret, a city on the west bank of the SEA OF GALILEE. There he healed crowds who came to greet him.

GENTILE

(GEN tile)

Peter told them, "You know it is against our laws for a Jewish man to enter a Gentile home like this or to associate with you."
Acts 10:28

- Anyone not a Jew

THE ONLY GOOD GENTILE was a dead Gentile. That was the Jewish take on non-JEWS when JOSHUA led his people into the PROMISED LAND—today's Israel. MOSES gave them stern marching orders that still trouble Bible experts: "You must completely destroy them" (Deuteronomy 7:2).

Later, however, PROPHETS predicted that the Jews "will be a light to guide the nations" (Isaiah 42:6).

Some leaders, such as EZRA, ordered Jewish men to DIVORCE their Gentile wives (Ezra 10:2–5). But scholars say there are counterpoints in the BIBLE. RUTH, a Gentile from what is now Jordan, produced ISRAEL's dynasty of KINGS; she was David's great-grandmother. ESTHER married a Gentile king and saved the Jews from a holocaust.

After Jesus left the planet, his DISCIPLES and CHURCH leaders—all Jews—agreed to allow Gentiles into the CHRISTIAN movement as full members (Acts 15).

GERAR

Map 1 A6

(GEE rahr)

King Abimelech of Gerar sent for Sarah and had her brought to him at his palace.
Genesis 20:2

- City in southern Israel

ABRAHAM LIED to King ABIMELECH of Gerar, a city about 45 miles (72 km) southwest of JERUSALEM. ABRAHAM said SARAH was his sister. He didn't want anyone killing him to marry the WIDOW. Years later, his son ISAAC did the same at Gerar for the same reason (Genesis 26:7). Like father like son.

GERASENES

(see GADARENES)

GERSHOM

(GUR shum)

1400s BC

Moses' first son was named Gershom.
Exodus 18:3

HIS NAME IS A PHRASE: "stranger there." *Ger* is "stranger" in HEBREW. *Shom* means "there." He was born in a land where MOSES was a FOREIGNER. Moses married ZIPPORAH, a shepherdess, near what is now the border of Jordan and Saudi Arabia.

GETHSEMANE

Map 4 D5

(geth SEM un nee)

They went to the olive grove called Gethsemane, and Jesus said, "Sit here while I go and pray." **Mark 14:32**

- Where Jesus prayed and was arrested

AFTER THE LAST SUPPER, Jesus and most of his DISCIPLES when to Gethsemane to pray. JUDAS ISCARIOT, however, went to get TEMPLE officers. He brought them to Gethsemane, where they arrested Jesus.

The BIBLE doesn't say where Gethsemane was. But early Christian pilgrims said it was an OLIVE grove on the

MOUNT OF OLIVES. The name means "olive press."

Archaeologists say a notch on the wall of a cave there is the kind farmers once used to press olives. They would slip a board in the notch and then hang stones on the other end of the board to crush baskets of olives pressed under the board.

Pilgrims today visit a nearby garden courtyard at the Church of All Nations. Old olive trees are the main attraction. Scholars say it's unlikely they date back to the time of Jesus, partly because a history writer from Jesus' century—Josephus—said Roman general Titus ordered all the JERUSALEM trees cut down. He needed them to make siege WEAPONS for the attack that demolished Jerusalem in AD 70.

A CUP OF PAIN. Praying at Gethsemane on the night of his arrest, Jesus says, "Please take this cup of suffering away from me. Yet I want your will to be done, not mine" (Mark 14:36).

GEZER
Map 1 B5

(GEEZ ur)

Horam, king of Gezer, arrived to help Lachish. Joshua attacked him and his army until there was nothing left of them.
Joshua 10:33 MSG

▪ Canaanite city captured by Joshua

JOSHUA'S MILITIA wiped out the ARMY of Gezer, a city about 20 miles (32 km) northwest of JERUSALEM. He assigned the city to the tribe of EPHRAIM, who "failed to drive out the Canaanites living in Gezer" (Judges 1:29). The ruin, a mound now called Tell el-Jazari, covers about 33 acres. (A football field is about an acre.) That makes it one of the largest ruins of JOSHUA's era.

GHOST

"Touch me and make sure that I am not a ghost, because ghosts don't have bodies, as you see that I do." Resurrected Jesus to his disciples, Luke 24:39

SAMUEL WAS A GHOST when he appeared to King SAUL at the home of "a medium at ENDOR" (1 Samuel 28:7). Saul wanted to know if he would lose the next day's battle with the PHILISTINES. Prophet SAMUEL said the king would lose the battle and his life, which he did.

GIANT

"We even saw giants there, the descendants of Anak. Next to them we felt like grasshoppers." Scouts reporting to Moses, Numbers 13:33

GOLIATH IS THE BEST-KNOWN GIANT in the BIBLE. Some ancient copies of the Bible stretch him up to 9 feet 9 inches (297 cm). The oldest copies lower his altitude: 6 feet 9 inches (206 cm). Either way, most Jewish warriors looked up to this Philistine champion.

During the Jewish EXODUS home from EGYPT, MOSES sent scouts into what is now ISRAEL. They reported seeing plenty of giants, apparently descended from a family of taller-than-normal folks—perhaps the height of many pro basketball players. NBA players average 6 feet 7 inches (200 cm).

There are several giant sightings in the Bible. A sampling:

▪ "Giant Nephilites lived on the earth" (Genesis 6:4).
▪ "A race of giants called the Emites had once lived in the area of Ar [a city, region, or perhaps both in the ancient country of

G

Moab, now part of Jordan]" (Deuteronomy 2:10).

- "King Og of BASHAN was the last survivor of the giant Rephaites. His BED was made of IRON and was more than thirteen feet long and six feet wide [4 by 2 m]" (Deuteronomy 3:11).

GIBEAH
Map 1 C5

(GIB ee uh)

"The men of Gibeah surrounded the house. They wanted to kill me, but instead they raped and killed my wife." Judges 20:5 CEV

- Capital of King Saul's Israel
- Civil war started here with rape, murder

KING SAUL'S BIRTHPLACE and capital, Gibeah was just 3 miles (5 km) north of what would become ISRAEL's eventual capital: JERUSALEM.

The city is perhaps most infamous for sparking Israel's first civil WAR. Some men raped to death the CONCUBINE—a lower-status WIFE—of a fellow Jew. The couple was passing through the area, controlled by the tribe of BENJAMIN. When tribal leaders refused to arrest the rapists, Israel's other tribes attacked and nearly wiped out the tribe of Benjamin.

Gibeah today is a dirt mound called Tell el Ful. Archaeologists dig there, looking for clues to the city's past.

GIBEON
Map 1 C5

(GIB ee un)

When the people of Gibeon heard how Joshua had defeated Jericho and Ai, they decided to trick the Israelites. Joshua 9:3–4 NCV

- Canaanite city
- Tricked Joshua into peace treaty

CANAANITES AT GIBEON knew JOSHUA wouldn't make peace with any Canaanites. So they sent men who convinced Joshua to make a peace treaty with Gibeon, lying that it was far away. It was only about 15 miles (24 km) west of JERICHO—less than a day's walk.

Angry at getting tricked, Joshua ordered them to haul WATER and wood for the JEWS. But he honored their treaty.

When a coalition ARMY of Canaanites attacked Gibeon for making the peace treaty with the Jews, Joshua came to Gibeon's rescue. The battle is famous because of Joshua's PRAYER: "Let the sun stand still over Gibeon" (Joshua 10:12).

FIT TO FIGHT. A gent shows how Gideon selected soldiers for his 300-man strike force. He picked those who drank water from a spring by cupping it in their hands. Those who lapped up water like dogs—face down—were sent home.

GIDEON

(GID ee un)

1100s BC

The LORD told Gideon, "With these 300 men I will rescue you and give you victory over the Midianites." Judges 7:7

- One of Israel's dozen heroes called "judges"
- He fought off Midianite raiders with only 300 men

IT READS LIKE A WISECRACK FROM AN ANGEL. Gideon was hiding in a hole in the ground. He was down there THRESHING wheat in a winepress because he didn't want raiders to see him from a distance.

"Mighty hero," said an ANGEL, suddenly appearing, "the LORD is with you!" (Judges 6:12).

GOD had a job for Gideon, the angel said. Raiders from MIDIAN—a country in what is now Saudi Arabia—had been stealing Jewish crops and livestock every HARVEST for seven years. Gideon was to put an end to their raids.

Gideon couldn't believe it. He made God prove it with two MIRACLES. First, God kept the ground dry overnight while saturating with dew a fleece Gideon set out. The second night, God did the opposite: wet ground, dry fleece.

Convinced of God's backing, Gideon gathered a militia of 32,000. But God had him pare it down to a strike force of 300. Their main battle tactic: trickery at night—a light and sound show.

There were more Midianites than Gideon could count, "settled in the valley like a swarm of LOCUSTS" (Judges 7:12). But when the tricks begin—JEWS blowing RAM'S HORNS and raising TORCHES—the panicked Midian raiders woke up and started killing each other in the dark. Survivors ran for home, though Gideon's men hunted them down and killed them.

GIFT

Giving a gift can open doors; it gives access to important people!
Proverbs 18:16

IT'S A WAFFLING WORD, as the BIBLE uses it.

Gift can mean a present offered as an expression of love or gratitude. Syrian commander NAAMAN brought MONEY and clothes to ELISHA—a thank you for curing his LEPROSY (2 Kings 5:5, 15).

But sometimes a gift was something else:

Bribe: "A secret gift. . .a BRIBE under the TABLE" (Proverbs 21:14).

Sacrifice: "CAIN presented some of his crops as a gift to the LORD" (Genesis 4:3).

Plunder: "A gift to the great king" (Hosea 10:6) from a defeated enemy.

GIHON
See Jerusalem Map 1 C5

(GUY hahn)

Hezekiah. . .built a tunnel that carried the water from Gihon Spring into the city of Jerusalem. **2 Chronicles 32:30** CEV

1. GIHON SPRING was JERUSALEM's main WATER source. It was in a cave outside the WALLED CITY—not a good location if invaders surrounded the city. That's why King HEZEKIAH built a TUNNEL to direct the water inside the city.

2. GIHON was also a river. It branched off from the main river that "flowed from the land of EDEN" (Genesis 2:10). Location unknown.

GILEAD
Map 1 E5

(GILL ee uhd)

They saw a group of Ishmaelites traveling from Gilead to Egypt. . .carrying spices, balm, and myrrh. **Genesis 37:25** NCV

- Fertile land in what is now Jordan
- Where Absalom died in coup

GILEAD'S CLAIM TO FAME was a BALM—an OINTMENT used to treat wounds: "Is there no balm in Gilead? Is there no physician there?" (Jeremiah 8:22 TNIV).

Fertile and heavily forested, this is where ABSALOM got yanked off his MULE when his HAIR snagged in "the thick branches of a great tree" (2 Samuel 18:9). He was leading a coup against his father, DAVID. Some of David's soldiers stabbed Absalom as he dangled there.

GILGAL
Map 1 C5

(GILL gal)

The people crossed the Jordan. . .and camped at Gilgal, east of Jericho. **Joshua 4:19** NCV

- Israel's first camp in the Promised Land

SOMEWHERE NEAR JERICHO, JOSHUA and the Jews pitched camp. They built a small monument from a dozen ROCKS taken from the JORDAN RIVER—one rock for each tribe GOD had finally brought into the PROMISED LAND of Israel.

G

GLASS

Wisdom . . . Nothing is its equal—not gold or costly glass. Job 28:12, 17 CEV

RARE AND EXPENSIVE until Roman times, glass showed up in Egyptian beads as early as 2500 BC—several centuries before ABRAHAM. Glass jars and other containers were made from MOLDS. Glass got cheaper in Roman times because some lucky soul in SYRIA discovered glassblowing.

GLEANING

"When you gather the grapes in your vineyard, don't glean the vines after they are picked. Leave the remaining grapes for the foreigners, orphans, and widows." Deuteronomy 24:21

- Picking harvest leftovers

BY LAW, Jewish HARVEST workers were allowed to make one pass through a harvest field, vineyard, or orchard. After that, leftovers were reserved for the POOR. Picking leftovers is how the WIDOW Ruth met her second husband, BOAZ, the farmer.

GLORY

The glory of the LORD settled down on Mount Sinai, and the cloud covered it for six days. Exodus 24:16

- Often a reference to someone's power or importance
- Can refer to God's presence or appearance

***GLORY* LINKS TO GOD** more often than not.

"All around him was a glowing halo, like a rainbow shining in the clouds on a rainy day. This is what the glory of the LORD looked like to me" (Ezekiel 1:28).

But in the BIBLE it can also refer to people. The prophet ISAIAH promised the Jewish nation that one day

"World leaders will be blinded by your glory" (Isaiah 62:2).

GLUTTON

"Our son. . .will not obey us. He eats too much, and he is always drunk." Deuteronomy 21:20 NCV

- Overachiever at the dinner table

GLUTTONY: NOT A GOOD THING. One of the seven "deadly sins," it could be lethal. Punishment for a gluttonous, rebellious SON: "throw stones at him until he dies" (Deuteronomy 21:21 NCV).

Jewish leaders weren't complimenting Jesus when they called him "a glutton and a drunkard, and a friend of TAX COLLECTORS" (Luke 7:34).

GNOSTIC

(NOSS tick)

Jesus Christ came to earth as a human. . . . Every spirit who refuses to say this about Jesus is not from God. 1 John 4:2–3 NCV

- Heresy that says anything physical is evil

GNOSTIC CHRISTIANITY, eventually branded a HERESY, seemed to get its start late in Jesus' century. Gnostics taught that SALVATION came through secret knowledge and that only the spiritual dimension was good; the physical world was evil. With a premise like that, many insisted that Jesus wasn't really human; he only appeared human. So he didn't really suffer on the CROSS or die. He faked it.

GOATS

Jacob became very wealthy, with large flocks of sheep and goats. Genesis 30:43

HARDY CRITTERS, goats can live off scant shrubs and scattered weeds that are fighting for their life on land a dirt farmer wouldn't buy with a plug shekel.

That made goats valuable assets in the badlands of the Middle East—for at least the past 9,000 years. With little investment, goats pay back in meat, MILK, goat hair woven into fabric, and goatskins sewn into tents, waterproof bags, and WINESKINS. JEWS also sacrificed them in WORSHIP.

GOD

In the beginning God created the heavens and the earth. Genesis 1:1

- Deity worshiped by Jews and Christians
- Worshiped as source of all creation

MOST FOLKS HAVE NEVER MET HIM. Yet people of FAITH say they love him.

For one, they say that anyone who could create such a wonderful universe must be some kind of wonderful.

For another, they figure they owe their life to this Creator—and that love is a fitting "Thank you very much."

What does God look like?

The BIBLE seems to give mixed messages about what God looks like—as though he's a shape shifter.

Human

- He made humans in his image, resembling him in some way—if not in looks, perhaps in attributes such as the capacity to love and create (Genesis 1:27).
- He took walks in the Garden of EDEN (Genesis 3:8).
- ABRAHAM saw him as a man traveling to Sodom (Genesis 18:1–2).
- Other times, he spoke to MOSES "face to face, as one speaks to a friend" (Exodus 33:11).

Fire

- He introduced himself to Moses from inside a BURNING BUSH (Exodus 3:2–4).
- He appeared to the JEWS from a fire on MOUNT SINAI (Exodus 19:18).

Cloud

- He came to Moses "in a cloud" (Exodus 34:5).
- Ditto for PRIESTS in the Jerusalem TEMPLE (2 Chronicles 5:14).

Jesus

- "Anyone who has seen me has seen the FATHER!" (John 14:9).

G

GOD THE FATHER, portrayed as King of Creation.

Yet, these may all be just manifestations of God, some say. When Moses asked to see God in all his GLORY, God gave him only a glancing look at his back, warning, "You may not look directly at my face, for no one may see me and live" (Exodus 33:20).

What is God like?

The Bible doesn't profile God. Not directly.

Bible experts do, however. They piece together a profile of his attributes. They draw from his own words and behavior, along with what Bible writers said about him.

Love. "God is love. God showed how much he loved us by sending his one and only Son into the world so that we might have ETERNAL LIFE through him" (1 John 4:8–9).

All-powerful. "Is anything too hard for the LORD?" (Genesis 18:14).

All-knowing. "He knows everything" (1 John 3:20).

All-present. " 'Am I not everywhere in all the heavens and earth?' says the LORD" (Jeremiah 23:24).

Eternal. "God lives forever!" (Deuteronomy 33:27 NIrV).

Just. "When God judges, he is fair" (2 Thessalonians 1:5 NIrV).

Spirit. "God is Spirit, so those who WORSHIP him must worship in SPIRIT" (John 4:24).

One-of-a-kind holy. "There isn't anyone HOLY like the Lord" (1 Samuel 2:2 NIrV). Many Bible experts say holiness doesn't merely describe God as the ultimate good guy—perfect in every way. Holiness is his unique, defining character trait.

Holy—as Bible writers use the word referring to God—means "unique" or "separate." In a good way. It describes someone in a class by himself. That's God.

What's his name?

Moses asked God his NAME.

God said, "I AM WHO I AM. . . . Say to the Israelites: 'I AM has sent me to you'" (Exodus 3:14 TNIV).

In ancient HEBREW, written in shorthand without vowels, "I AM" appears as YHWH.

Scholars can only guess what vowels to insert. Their guess at the full word: YAHWEH (YAH way). Many Bibles translate it "The LORD." Used nearly 7,000 times

in the Bible, it's the most common name for God.

Other names for God that show up in the Bible:

ABBA: It means "FATHER." Jesus addressed God this way.

Adonai: My Lord.

El: God.

El shaddai: God Almighty

Theos: God, in Greek

Yahweh jireh: The Lord will provide.

GODS (see IDOLS)

GOG

> *"Ezekiel, son of man, condemn Gog, that wicked ruler. . .in the land of Magog."*
> Ezekiel 38:2 CEV

A MYSTERY MAN, Gog may not be a man at all, some scholars say, but a symbol of evil that GOD will one day defeat.

EZEKIEL and REVELATION both talk about Gog's ARMY coming to attack God's people. But they predict that God will defeat Gog.

End-time specialists who say Gog will target Israel have offered guesses from all four directions. North: Russia. South: Arabs. East: Mongols. West: Goths from what is now Germany.

See also MAGOG.

GOLAN   Map 1 E4

(GO lawn)

> *"Anyone accused of murder can run to one of the Safe Towns. . .Golan in Bashan."*
> Joshua 20:4, 8 CEV

- City where accused killers could get a trial

IF JEWS KILLED SOMEONE by accident, they could run from the victim's AVENGER—fleeing to one of six cities scattered throughout ISRAEL. There they could get a trial. Golan was one of three cities of refuge on the east side of the JORDAN RIVER in what are now Syria and Jordan.

GOLD

> *"Cover the Ark [chest that held the 10 Commandments] inside and out with pure gold."* Exodus 25:11 NCV

- Bible's favorite precious metal

GOLD GETS TOP BILLING among precious metals in the BIBLE—mentioned first and most often.

Goldsmiths were working wonders with gold at least 5,000 years ago—a thousand years before ABRAHAM. In UR, Abraham's hometown in southern Iraq, archaeologists have turned up beautiful golden vases, BOWLS, and headdresses.

JEWS used gold in their TEMPLE. DAVID stockpiled 4,000 tons of gold for the project. His son, SOLOMON, built the Temple, overlaying the inside walls with "solid gold" (1 Kings 6:20).

A GOLDEN BOWL from Persia (now Iran). It was crafted about the time Persians freed the Jews (500s BC) and returned the golden objects Babylonians had looted from the Jerusalem Temple in 586 BC.

GOLDEN CALF

> *Aaron took the gold, melted it down, and molded it into the shape of a calf.* Exodus 32:4

- An idol Jews worshiped during the Exodus

IN FAIRNESS TO THE JEWS, they thought MOSES was a goner—dead or deserted.

He had climbed to MOUNT SINAI, where he got the 10 COMMANDMENTS, "written by the finger of GOD" (Exodus 31:18). He stayed "forty days" (Exodus 24:18), perhaps a round number that means many weeks.

The crowd grew worried. They badgered AARON, brother of Moses: "Make us some GODS who can lead us" (Exodus 32:1).

Apparently an easy touch, Aaron did as requested.

Moses came back livid. JEWS were already breaking the first two of the 10 commandments by worshiping an idol.

Aaron offered a laughable defense: "They gave me the gold, I threw it into the fire and out came this calf!" (Exodus 32:24 NCV).

Moses ordered the execution of those who engaged in the worship: some 3,000 souls. Aaron sided with his brother and survived. Moses then ordered the gold calf ground into powder and mixed with water, which the Jews had to drink.

Centuries later, King JEROBOAM of the northern Jewish nation of ISRAEL set up golden calves for people to worship in two cities: BETHEL and DAN (1 Kings 12:29).

GOLGOTHA

Map 4 D6

(gal GOTH uh)
or (GOAL goth uh)

> *Carrying his own cross, Jesus went out to a place called The Place of the Skull, which in the Hebrew language is called Golgotha.* John 19:17 NCV

- Location of Jesus' crucifixion

JESUS DIED on a hill just outside JERUSALEM, if Bible experts got their clues right.

Also known as CALVARY—ROME's Latin lingo for "The Skull"—the site was:

- visible "from a distance" (Matthew 27:55)
- "near the city" (John 19:20)
- alongside a ROAD with "people passing by" (Matthew 27:39)

G

Why the site was linked to a skull is up for grabs. Guesses: it got its name because it was an execution site, or it was near a cemetery, or the face of the hill was eroded to look like a skull.

One tradition dating back to the AD 300s, when Rome legalized CHRISTIANITY, says Jesus was crucified and buried on property now memorialized by Jerusalem's Church of the Holy Sepulchre. Though it's inside the walls of Jerusalem today, archaeological studies suggest the site was outside the walls in Jesus' day.

A competing theory surfaced in 1885, when British General Charles Gordon pointed out a hill now known as Gordon's Calvary. It sits above a cliff that's eroded to look a bit like a skull. There's a garden TOMB a short walk away, with a rolling stone like the one described in the BURIAL of Jesus. This tomb, however, was old in Jesus' day. And the BIBLE says Jesus was buried in a "new tomb" (Matthew 27:60).

If nothing else, this hilltop site with its nearby garden and tomb gives visitors a sense of the garden setting in which Jesus was buried (John 19:41).

THE BIGGER THEY COME, the harder they fall. Shepherd boy David proved the power of gravity when he dropped the Philistine champion, Goliath, with a single stone fired from a slingshot.

GOLIATH

(go LIE uhth)

1000s BC

Goliath stood and shouted. . . . "I am the Philistine champion. . . . Choose one man to come down here and fight me!"
1 Samuel 17:8

- Philistine champion warrior
- Killed by shepherd boy David

GOLIATH GOT NO TAKERS. He offered to settle the WAR between JEWS and PHILISTINES with a single battle between him and ISRAEL's best warrior—mortal combat.

But he was big. He was packing. And he may very well have been ugly.

Goliath specs:

- 9 feet 9 inches tall (nearly 3 m)—though older copies of the story found among the famous DEAD SEA SCROLLS put him at 6 feet 9 inches tall (over 2 m)

- protected by BRONZE coat of mail weighing 125 pounds (57 kg)
- bronze HELMET and leg ARMOR
- bronze javelin
- SPEAR as thick as a WEAVER's beam
- IRON spearhead as heavy as a 15-pound (6.8 kg) bowling ball
- SWORD, perhaps iron (Philistines guarded the secret of making iron)
- armor bearer holding his SHIELD.

No Jew wanted anywhere near this guy.

Until SHEPHERD boy DAVID came along—an expert in short-range artillery also known as the slingshot.

David dropped Goliath with a single stone that "hit him on the forehead and sank into it" (1 Samuel 17:49 NIRV). David grabbed Goliath's sword and decapitated him.

Horrified, the Philistine ARMY turned and ran. The Jewish army, suddenly courageous, charged after them.

GOMER

(GO mur)

700s BC

GOD spoke to Hosea. . . "Find a whore and marry her." . . . Hosea did it. He picked Gomer. Hosea 1:2–3 MSG

▪ Prostitute wife of prophet Hosea

IN A MARRIAGE MADE IN HEAVEN, God told HOSEA to hitch himself to a hooker. GOD explained why: "This will illustrate how ISRAEL has acted like a PROSTITUTE by turning against the LORD and worshiping other GODS" (Hosea 1:2).

GOMORRAH

(see SODOM AND GOMORRAH)

GOOD NEWS

(see GOSPEL)

GOPHERWOOD

God said to Noah. . . "Make yourself an ark of gopherwood." Genesis 6:13–14 NKJV

NO ONE KNOWS what kind of wood NOAH used to build the boat that saved him and his FAMILY in the FLOOD. "Gopherwood" doesn't translate to any wood we know today. Most Bible translators today offer a guess: cypress—top-grade wood that's rot-resistant and available in parts of the Middle East. It was the wood preferred by shipbuilders.

GOSHEN

Map 2 H8

(GO shun)

Pharaoh said to Joseph. . . "Give them the best land of Egypt. Let them live in the region of Goshen." Genesis 47:5–6

▪ Land in the Nile River's fertile delta

WHEN DROUGHT HIT, JACOB moved his entire extended FAMILY to the drought-resistant NILE RIVER in EGYPT. His son, JOSEPH, was a top official in Egypt at the time. Joseph had gotten the king's blessing to let the JEWS weather out the DROUGHT in Egypt's prime grazing fields of Goshen. That's in the delta, where the Nile fans out into many smaller streams that empty into the MEDITERRANEAN SEA.

G

Mediterranean Sea

Jerusalem

CANAAN
(Israel)

Dead Sea

Goshen
Nile River Delta

Rameses

Bitter Lake

Cairo

EGYPT

Nile River

Red Sea
Gulf of Suez

N

Land of Goshen
Livestock heaven

GOSPEL

(GOSS pell)

This is the Good News [Gospel] about Jesus the Messiah, the Son of God. Mark 1:1

- Means "Good News"

THERE'S SOME IRONY AT WORK in the history of this word. Bible writers described the birth of Jesus as Good News for the world. Romans said the same thing when celebrating the birthday of Caesar AUGUSTUS, the emperor reigning when Jesus was born.

The original GREEK word was *euangelion*, from which we get "EVANGELIST." Scholars translating the word into Old English centuries ago used the term *god-spell*, from which we got "gospel." Most Bibles today read, "Good News."

GOSPELS

(GOSS pells)

We wanted to preserve the truth of the gospel message. Galatians 2:5

- First four books of the New Testament

STORIES OF JESUS and his teachings are preserved in four books known as the Gospels: MATTHEW, MARK, LUKE, and JOHN.

The writers didn't identify themselves. But CHURCH leaders in the following century credited the men whose names now title the books: Matthew the TAX COLLECTOR disciple of Jesus; JOHN MARK who traveled with PAUL; the physician Luke who traveled with Paul; and John the disciple of Jesus and brother of JAMES.

The word *GOSPEL* means "Good News," one of the BIBLE's favorite ways of describing what the story of Jesus means to the world. As an ANGEL put it to SHEPHERDS in BETHLEHEM on the night Jesus was born: "I bring you good news that will bring great joy to all people" (Luke 2:10).

GOSSIP

A gossip tells everything, but a true friend will keep a secret. Proverbs 11:13 CEV

GOSSIPS DON'T GET GOOD PRESS in the BIBLE. They show up in bad company:

Evildoers. "Wrongdoers eagerly listen to gossip" (Proverbs 17:4).

Drunks. "I am the favorite topic of town gossip, and all the drunks sing about me" (Psalm 69:12).

GOVERNOR

Solomon placed twelve governors over the districts of Israel. 1 Kings 4:7 NCV

GOVERNORS RULED cities, territories, or provinces—usually on assignment from a king or emperor. PILATE was perhaps the most famous governor in the BIBLE. He ruled Rome's province of JUDEA in what is now southern Israel.

GRACE

"We believe that we are all saved the same way, by the undeserved grace of the Lord Jesus." Acts 15:11

GOD ACCEPTS PEOPLE just the way they are, no matter how messed up they are—as the BIBLE tells it. But GOD's not willing to leave them messed up. Grace is the acceptance and the help someone gets or gives—especially when it doesn't seem deserved.

GRAIN

With severe famine everywhere, Joseph opened up the storehouses and distributed grain to the Egyptians. Genesis 41:56

- Barley and wheat

THE MAIN FOOD in Bible lands came from grain, usually BARLEY and WHEAT. People used stones to crush the hard kernels into powdery FLOUR. Then they'd mix in some water, SALT, and OLIVE OIL to bake BREAD. They'd add old dough as yeast if they wanted the bread dough to rise.

Wheat was the most expensive grain. One NEW TESTAMENT writer suggested that for the price of one loaf of wheat a person could buy three loaves of barley. Poorer folks went for the barley, which tastes bland. If they could afford some wheat flour, they'd often mix it with barley to add some of wheat's delicious flavor.

GRAPES

Grapes were trampled in the winepress outside the city. Revelation 14:20

ISRAEL'S ROLLING HILLS and its hot, dry growing SEASON are perfect for vineyards. Their grapes—and the wines crushed from them—were sought throughout the ancient Middle East, from EGYPT to Iraq.

Wine was the favorite product made from grapes. But people ate the grapes fresh in season. They also dried them in the sun to make raisins—eating them as snacks, BAKING them into cakes, or giving them away as tasty gifts.

Some folks boiled the grapes down into thick, sweet syrup—a great place to dip a hunk of warm BREAD.

GREAT COMMISSION

Jesus came and told his disciples. . ."Go and make disciples of all the nations."
Matthew 28:18–19

▪ Job description Jesus gave his followers

THE LAST WORDS out of Jesus' mouth before he ascended into HEAVEN were a to-do list. The writers of MATTHEW and ACTS both preserve the message.

Jesus told his DISCIPLES to recruit more disciples "in JERUSALEM, throughout JUDEA, in SAMARIA, and to the ends of the earth" (Acts 1:8). He said they should teach these recruits to "obey all the commands I have given you" (Matthew 28:20).

The disciples didn't have to do this on their own, Jesus said. He promised that GOD would send the HOLY SPIRIT to give them the courage and power to do the work.

GREECE   Map 3 A3

Paul had a vision: A man from Macedonia in northern Greece was standing there, pleading with him, "Come over to Macedonia and help us!" Acts 16:9

▪ Country that once controlled the Middle East

G

SMALLER THAN FLORIDA, Greece once controlled most of the Middle East all the way to India—thanks to the land-grabbing military campaigns of ALEXANDER the Great (356–323 BC).

For all its glory, Greece is barely mentioned in the BIBLE. It's all about timing. Greece didn't rise to power until after the OLD TESTAMENT. By the time the NEW TESTAMENT rolled around, Greece had gotten itself conquered and carved up into two Roman provinces: MACEDONIA in the north, ACHAIA in the south.

The apostle PAUL started churches in both provinces, though his most famous Greek CHURCH was in CORINTH, in the southland.

GREEK

> Pilate posted a sign on the cross that read, "Jesus of Nazareth, the King of the Jews". . . written in Hebrew, Latin, and Greek.
> John 19:19–20

- International language of Jesus' day

EVERY BOOK IN THE NEW TESTAMENT was written in Greek—a language that dominated the Mediterranean world for about a thousand years. It started with ALEXANDER the Great's (356–323 BC) campaign to spread Greek culture at the tip of a sword.

NEW TESTAMENT writers used a particular dialect of Greek called *Koine* (COIN nee) meaning "common." It was street Greek, the simplified common lingo of the people—not the formal stuff that Greek highbrows loved.

GUEST

(see HOSPITALITY)

GUILT

> "Suppose someone in the community sins without meaning to. If he disobeys any of the Lord's commands, he is guilty."
> Leviticus 4:27 NIrV

IT'S NOT A FEELING. Not as Bible writers often used the word. Guilt is a spiritual condition caused by disobeying GOD.

As Jewish law teaches it, a person might be guilty without even knowing it. Or as a traffic cop might put it today, ignorance is no excuse.

Bible writers say the only remedy for guilt is God's gracious FORGIVENESS. JEWS sought God's forgiveness by offering SACRIFICES. Christians said that's no longer necessary because of Jesus' sacrifice: "Our guilty consciences have been sprinkled with Christ's BLOOD to make us clean" (Hebrews 10:22).

See also SIN.

Greek Empire

HABAKKUK

(huh BACK uhk)

Possibly 600s BC

This is the message that the prophet Habakkuk received in a vision. Habakkuk 1:1

- Prophet who complained about God

FED UP WITH GOD doing nothing about the Jewish nation's SIN, Habakkuk demanded to know when GOD was going to put a stop to it.

God answered. Habakkuk didn't like what he heard.

Apparently, the sin Habakkuk was talking about—violence and injustice—was taking place in the southern Jewish nation of JUDAH. Assyrians had already conquered and dismantled the northern Jewish nation of ISRAEL.

God said Judah was about to get wiped off the map, too. Babylonians from what is now Iraq would do the job.

Habakkuk said it didn't make sense to let the Babylonians punish the JEWS since Babylonians were even worse sinners than the Jews. God said the Babylonians would eventually get what was coming to them.

That was good enough for Habakkuk. He said he'd trust God even if the invaders decimated the Jewish homeland—which is exactly what they did in 586 BC.

HABAKKUK, BOOK OF

(huh BACK uhk)

Famous sound bite: Counting on God's Rule to prevail, I take heart and gain strength. I run like a deer. I feel like I'm king of the mountain! Habakkuk 3:19 MSG

A PROPHET COMPLAINS ABOUT GOD doing nothing to stop runaway SIN in the Jewish nation. Then when he finds out what GOD is going to do, he complains about that. In the end, though, his complaints evaporate and his FAITH shines as bright as anyone's in the entire Bible.

- Writer: Prophet Habakkuk or someone telling his story.
- Time: Uncertain. Many scholars guess it's shortly before Babylonians erased Judah from the world map in 586 BC.
- Location: The threat seems to come from the Babylonian Empire in what is now Iraq. Habakkuk lives in the southern Jewish nation of Judah.

BIG SCENES

A do-nothing God. In a VISION, Habakkuk asks GOD why he's doing nothing while the JEWS sin up a storm. "I see destruction and violence," the PROPHET complains. "There is no justice in the COURTS." Yet when Habakkuk calls on God to do something, he says God doesn't even listen. *Habakkuk 1*

God's bad decision. When God says not to worry—that he'll send Babylonian invaders to punish the Jews—Habakkuk can't believe it. The Babylonians are far worse than the Jews. It would be like putting a jaywalker on trial in front of a jury of convicted murderers. God says trust him—he'll make sure everyone gets what they deserve, Babylonians included. *Habakkuk 1–2*

In God he trusts. Habakkuk flashes back to God's past MIRACLES, such as parting the WATER for Jews during the EXODUS out of EGYPT. Given God's perfect track record, Habakkuk decides that no matter how bad life gets, God has earned his trust: "Even though the OLIVE crop fails, and the fields lie empty and barren. . . . I will rejoice in the LORD!" *Habakkuk 3*

HADAD

(HAY dad)

900s BC

Hadad, still only a boy, fled to Egypt with some Edomite officials who had served his father. 1 Kings 11:17 TNIV

- King of Edom and enemy of Solomon

WHEN KING DAVID INVADED EDOM, a neighboring kingdom in what is now Jordan, his SOLDIERS spent six months killing the enemy. But the king's son, Hadad,

H

escaped to EGYPT. After DAVID died, Hadad returned home to rebuild his country. The BIBLE says he proved a royal headache to David's son King SOLOMON.

HADES

(HAY dees)

"You will not leave my soul among the dead [Greek: in Hades]." Acts 2:27
- Place of the dead

HADES IS A WAITING ROOM for dead SOULS headed to HEAVEN or HELL. Or maybe it's more like Dead Town, with one great neighborhood—heaven—and one lousy neighborhood—hell.

Those are a couple ways Bible experts interpret what they read about Hades in the BIBLE.

Hades is the GREEK word used in the NEW TESTAMENT for a HEBREW term used in the OLD TESTAMENT: *SHEOL*.

A SLOW BOAT TO HADES is how Greeks in ancient times pictured the soul's journey to the underworld. In the Bible, Hades seems like a waiting room for souls of the dead, some say. Others say it's not a waiting room, but the destination of all the dead—some to a good neighborhood (heaven), some to a warmer climate.

In one Old Testament story, dead prophet SAMUEL appeared as a spirit to King SAUL, whom GOD had rejected. Samuel warned that "tomorrow. . .you and your sons will be here with me" (1 Samuel 28:19).

In a New Testament PARABLE by Jesus, a beggar named Lazarus ended up in the place of the dead with a miserly rich man. Though the beggar was comfortable, the rich man was tormented and thirsty. An impassible canyon separated the two, but they were well within shouting distance (Luke 16:26–27). Still, that's a parable. And students of the Bible are left wondering if they're supposed to take all the details literally.

The first Bible translators may have figured *Hades* was a fitting Greek translation for the Old Testament word because in Greek stories, Hades was the god of the dead. And in Greek mythology, Hades had a variety of living conditions—from comfortable to anything but.

HAGAR

(HAY gar)

2100s BC
Sarai, Abram's wife, took Hagar the Egyptian servant and gave her to Abram as a wife. Genesis 16:3
- Abraham's secondary wife
- Mother of Ishmael

MORE A SURROGATE MOTHER than a WIFE, Hagar was supposed to do what ABRAHAM's first wife SARAH couldn't do: make babies.

Hagar was Sarah's slave. Any CHILDREN she produced would, by custom, belong to her masters: Abraham and Sarah.

Hagar gave BIRTH to ISHMAEL. But 14 years later, Sarah gave birth to ISAAC. Afterward, Sarah convinced Abraham to drive off Hagar and Ishmael. Had she not done that, Ishmael as Abraham's oldest son would have inherited a double share of the estate and would have ruled over Isaac's FAMILY as head of the extended family.

HAGGAI

(Hag eye)

Prophesied 520 BC

Haggai. . .prophesied to the Jews in Judah and Jerusalem. Ezra 5:1

- Prophet who got Jerusalem's Temple rebuilt

IT TOOK A BUSTED HARVEST and some hard-sell preaching by the prophet Haggai to convince JEWS to rebuild the Jerusalem TEMPLE.

Babylonian invaders from what is now Iraq had demolished Jerusalem and EXILED the survivors about 70 years earlier. Persians from Iran freed the exiles to go home about 50 years after that, and the Jews immediately started rebuilding the Temple. But they stopped when some non-Jewish locals convinced the Persian king to halt the project.

Now, however, a new king was on the throne. Haggai said this was the perfect time to finish the Temple project they had started some 20 years earlier. He added that GOD agreed because he's the one who sent the bad HARVEST—as a motivator. Haggai said if the Jews got busy, God would give them great harvests as a reward.

HAGGAI, BOOK OF

Famous sound bite: "Is it right for you to be living in fancy houses while the Temple is still in ruins?" Haggai 1:4 NCV

A LOUSY HARVEST prods the JEWS to get busy rebuilding the Jerusalem TEMPLE, which has laid in ruins for about 70 years.

- Writer: Haggai, or someone telling his story.
- Time: Haggai prophesied from August 29–December 18, 520 BC. Dates are this exact because of dated Persian events Haggai mentions.
- Location: Jerusalem.

BIG SCENES

Low priority: God's house. JEWS have been rebuilding JERUSALEM for about 20 years. It's a job they had to do because Babylonian invaders leveled the city and EXILED the survivors some 70 years earlier. It has been only in the last 20 years that they were allowed to return and rebuild. A PROPHET named Haggai asks why they've built nice houses for themselves yet they haven't bothered to rebuild GOD's house, the Temple. Haggai says that God decided to punish them with a bad HARVEST. *Haggai 1*

Jews start rebuilding the Temple. Within three weeks, the Jews are busy rebuilding the Temple. It's nothing like SOLOMON's majestic Temple, paneled inside with golden walls. Some Jews who remember the earlier Temple are disappointed by the downsized WORSHIP center. But Haggai says God is not disappointed. The prophet promises a wonderful harvest ahead—and better days for the Temple. King HEROD will later double the size of the Temple grounds. And he'll give it such an extensive makeover that many will call it the Third Temple. *Haggai 2*

HAIL

The LORD sent thunder and hail. . . . It left all of Egypt in ruins. Exodus 9:23, 25

IN A WORLD OF OUTDOOR PEOPLE—farmers and herders—hail was a killer. Of humans, critters, crops. All of these died in the hailstorm PLAGUE God unleashed on EGYPT, to convince the king to free the Jewish slaves.

A hailstorm later helped JOSHUA win a battle: "The hail killed more of the enemy than the Israelites killed with the SWORD" (Joshua 10:11).

BIG ON BIG HAIR, Rome's elite set the trend for elaborate hairdos. Apostle Paul advised church ladies to skip over-the-top do's, and to work on their inner beauty.

HALLELUJAH

I heard what sounded like a great multitude. . . shouting, "Hallelujah! For the Lord God Almighty reigns." Revelation 19:6 TNIV

- Hebrew for "Praise the Lord"

IN A SHOCKER, this favorite word among people of FAITH is barely in the BIBLE. It shows up in just two books: PSALMS and REVELATION. In Psalms, a SONG book, the word may have been a congregational response. Later, JEWS started using it to express joy—perhaps in the way the invention of the delicious hot dog became "Hot dog!"

HAM

Before 2500 BC

Noah. . .got drunk and passed out, naked in his tent. Ham. . .saw that his father was naked and told his two brothers. Genesis 9:21–22 MSG

- Noah's second son

"HE'S THE ONE," Queen Esther says, pointing to Haman—her husband's top official. Haman had plotted the genocide of the Jews without realizing his queen was a Jew. Oops.

HAIR

Isn't it obvious that it's disgraceful for a man to have long hair? And isn't long hair a woman's pride and joy? 1 Corinthians 11:14–15

HAIRSTYLES CHANGED IN BIBLE TIMES. Stories and ancient pictures alike show that early in Jewish history, long hair was in—for both women and men. King DAVID's son, ABSALOM, died because his long hair got snagged in tree branches—yanking him off his MULE during battle.

By Roman times, though, short hair became the fashion for men. Some wore BEARDS. Others shaved.

Hairstyles for the ladies apparently went over the top, with designs requiring the fingers of a hair architect. PAUL advised CHRISTIAN women to skip the "fancy hairdos" (1 Timothy 2:9 CEV).

WHEN NOAH FOUND OUT that his son Ham saw him naked and called in the brothers to take a look, he was ticked. He put a CURSE on Ham's son, CANAAN, while BLESSING Ham's brothers who refused to look at him naked but respectfully covered him instead.

HAMAN

(HAY muhn)

400s BC

He [Haman] looked for a way to destroy all the Jews throughout the entire empire of Xerxes. Esther 3:6

- Persia's top official under the king
- Plotted to kill all Jews

ONE JEW DISSED HAMAN by refusing to bow when he walked by. So Haman hatched an ambitious plot to kill all JEWS in PERSIA—an empire spanning much of the Middle East, from India to EGYPT. He missed one detail: Queen ESTHER was a Jew. Her husband, King XERXES, ordered Haman executed.

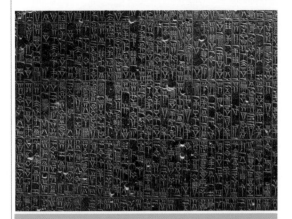

IT'S THE LAW in ancient Iraq: Babylon. This is a detail of words chiseled into a black stone over 7 feet (2 m) high. Some of the laws sound like ones in the Law of Moses. But these were written several centuries before Moses. See photo, page 116.

HAMMURABI, CODE OF

H

(HAM uh RAH bee)

1700s BC

"What other nation is great enough to have rules and laws that are as fair as these?" Deuteronomy 4:8 NIRV

- Laws by Babylonian King Hammurabi

KING HAMMURABI (ruled 1792–1750 BC) doesn't show up in the BIBLE. But some of his laws seem to.

Written at least 300 years before MOSES delivered the Jewish laws preserved in the Bible, Hammurabi's laws sometimes sound like Moses borrowed them.

"An eye for an eye" (Exodus 21:24) sounds pretty much like Hammurabi's law 196: "If a man puts out the eye of another, his eye should be put out."

Yet Moses sometimes seemed to amp up the fairness. While Hammurabi's law gave special treatment to NOBLES and other rich folks, sometimes letting them off with merely a fine instead of losing a body part, the laws of Moses treated rich and POOR alike.

Also, the laws of Moses didn't punish the innocent. But in Hammurabi's law, if a HOUSE collapsed and killed the homeowner's SON, the homebuilder's son could be executed—as in "an eye for an eye and a son for a son."

Paul went in and prayed for him, and laying his hands on him, he healed him. Acts 28:8

- Ritual for healing or conveying a blessing

CHRISTIANS RESTED THEIR HANDS on a person when they prayed to GOD for HEALING, as if channeling God's spiritual power to that person.

JEWS did much the same when they offered an ANIMAL sacrifice. But in that ritual, the transfer seemed more like a symbolic gesture of moving their sins into the animal. "He [High Priest AARON] will lay both of his hands on the GOAT's head and confess over it all the wickedness, rebellion, and sins of the people of ISRAEL. In this way, he will transfer the people's sins to the head of the goat" (Leviticus 16:21).

HANGING

Joshua killed each of the five kings and impaled them on five sharpened poles, where they hung until evening. Joshua 10:26

- Usually for display, not execution

LIVING PEOPLE DIDN'T GET HUNG in Bible times. Not usually, unless we count CRUCIFIXION.

Generally, people were executed first and hung later. Their bodies would get hung on a tree, a post, or a city wall—perhaps as a war trophy or as a warning for others not to make the same mistake that turned these people into corpses.

HANNAH

(HAN nuh)

1100s BC

Hannah. . .sobbed. She prayed to the LORD. . . "Please give me a son! If you do, I'll give him back to you." 1 Samuel 1:10–11 NIrV

- Mother of Samuel

HANNAH delivers her son Samuel to the high priest Eli, who will raise the boy. Hannah, previously infertile, had promised God that if he gave her a son, she would give him back—in a life of service to the Lord.

INFERTILE, Hannah prayed for a SON, promising to give the child back to GOD in service at Israel's WORSHIP center. God granted her request, and Hannah kept her promise. After young SAMUEL was able to eat solid food, Hannah took him to be raised by High Priest ELI.

HANUKKAH

(HAHN uh kuh)

It was now winter, and Jesus was in Jerusalem at the time of Hanukkah, the Festival of Dedication. John 10:22

- Also known as "Festival of Lights"
- Marks rededication of Jerusalem Temple

SYRIAN INVADERS captured JERUSALEM and in 167 BC offered pagan sacrifices on the Temple ALTAR. Three years later, Jewish rebels drove off the invaders and purified the TEMPLE. Then they spent eight days celebrating with MUSIC, DANCING, and SACRIFICES of thanks. JEWS today still commemorate the holiday, usually in December but sometimes starting in November.

See also FESTIVALS.

HARAN
Map 2 J5

(HAIR uhn)

Terah took his son Abram. . .to the land of Canaan, but when they reached the city of Haran, they settled there. Genesis 11:31 NCV

- Abraham's second hometown
- City in southern Turkey

ABRAHAM'S DAD GOT SIDETRACKED by this village. TERAH intended to move from UR in what is now southern Iraq to CANAAN (Israel). But apparently he liked what he saw in Haran, about two-thirds of the way to Canaan.

After Terah died, GOD told 75-year-old ABRAHAM to finish what his father started: Move to Canaan. Some of Terah's FAMILY stayed behind. Haran is where Abraham's son ISAAC and his grandson JACOB would later find their wives.

HAREM

Hegai [in charge of the king's harem] liked Esther and. . .put her and her maids in the best rooms in the harem. Esther 2:9 MSG

- A man's group of wives

MEN WITH MORE TESTOSTERONE than intelligence—the BIBLE implies—collected wives. The collection was called a harem. Often, the WOMEN stayed in what was also called a harem. It was a private section of the home or the PALACE.

If Bible stories about men with multiple wives are any clue, men who married multiple wives were clueless.

In JACOB'S TENT, jealousy ruled the roost (four wives). DAVID'S FAMILY came to blows: incestuous RAPE, MURDER, and a coup (at least eight wives). SOLOMON'S ladies led him into idolatry, which split ISRAEL into two countries (1,000 wives).

HAROD SPRING
See Jerusalem, Map 1 C5

(HAIR rod)

Gideon, and all of the people with him. . .set up camp beside the Harod spring. Judges 7:1 CEB

- Hillside spring

GIDEON WEEDED DOWN HIS ARMY from 32,000 to 300 at Harod spring, on the slopes of MOUNT GILBOA in northern Israel. He kept only the men who drank from the spring by cupping its WATER in their hands.

HARP

"They will be playing a harp, a tambourine, a flute, and a lyre." 1 Samuel 10:5

MANY BIBLES HAVE IT WRONG, according to some scholars. They say DAVID played a "harp." He actually played a miniature version: a LYRE. One other difference between a harp and a lyre is that harp strings ran different lengths. On a lyre, all the strings were about the same.

H

HARVEST

> *"Celebrate the Festival of Harvest, when you bring me the first crops of your harvest."*
> Exodus 23:16

- Payday for a farmer

FARMERS WORKED YEAR-ROUND, but in Bible times they generally got paid just once or twice—depending on what crops they grew.

Payday one: Farmers harvested GRAIN during spring and summer—first BARLEY then WHEAT.

Payday two. If they grew FRUIT and veggies, they harvested those later in the summer and into early fall.

See also FARMING.

HAZAEL

(HAY zay el)

Ruled about 842–800 BC

> *Hazael took a blanket, soaked it in water, and held it over the king's face until he died. Then Hazael became the next king.* 2 Kings 8:15

- King of Syria

SYRIA'S KING—deathly sick—sent Hazael to ask the prophet ELISHA if he'd get well. Elisha said no—adding that Hazael would become king. Hazael went home. He suffocated the king, became SYRIA's new ruler, and then named his son after the king he murdered: BEN-HADAD.

HAZOR

Map 1 D3

(HAY zor)

> *King Jabin of Hazor. . .had nine hundred iron chariots, and for twenty years he made life miserable for the Israelites.* Judges 4:2–3 CEV

- Canaanite city in northern Israel

JOSHUA'S MILITIA burned this Canaanite city, some 10 miles (16 km) north of the SEA OF GALILEE. Canaanites rebuilt it. A couple of centuries later the Canaanites started raiding the farms of Northland Jews.

DEBORAH put a stop to it when her militia crushed Hazor's CHARIOT corps at the battle of MOUNT TABOR.

HEALED by merely touching Jesus' robe, a woman with a bleeding problem—perhaps heavy menstrual periods— "had suffered a great deal from many doctors, and over the years she had spent everything she had to pay them, but she had gotten no better" (Mark 5:26).

HEALING

> *Do we all have the gift of healing? . . . Of course not!* 1 Corinthians 12:30

GOT A BOIL? Fig oil. Apply topically. Or maybe it was a FIG poultice; Bible translations vary. But figs in some form were ISAIAH's prescription for King HEZEKIAH's boil (2 Kings 20:7).

It worked.

Was that a home remedy, a widely used legit medical treatment, or just a FAITH-enhancing visual used by a MIRACLE-worker? The BIBLE doesn't say. It simply reports this and other healings and then usually leaves it to Bible experts to debate what category the healing fits.

A sampling of treatments:

- WINE for TIMOTHY's stomach (1 Timothy 5:23).
- soothing MUSIC therapy for King SAUL's depression (1 Samuel 16:23).
- mud and SPIT for BLINDNESS, a technique Jesus used (John 9:6).

One restriction some Jewish leaders imposed on healers—even on MIRACLE workers: no practicing MEDICINE on the SABBATH unless a person's life was at risk.

Jesus hated the absence of compassion in that law. He healed a man on the Sabbath right in front of the objecting JEWS (Mark 3:5). So there.

CHURCH leaders such as the apostle PAUL considered healing one of the many gifts GOD gave people—like the ability to teach, to show HOSPITALITY, or to speak in different languages.

See also DISEASE.

HEAVEN

> *"A great reward awaits you in heaven." Jesus in the Sermon on the Mount, Luke 6:23*

- Eternal home of God, angels, and God's people

ABRAHAM and other folks in early Bible times thought heaven was a dome above the earth, many Bible experts say.

Ancients figured that the sky was blue because of the water up there—and that RAIN fell when GOD opened heaven's windows.

By about the time of Jesus, JEWS had started writing about different levels of heaven. One of those writings, 2 Enoch, tells the story of one man's journey through seven heavens. That's where we got the phrase "seventh heaven."

The apostle PAUL seemed to agree: "I was caught up to the third heaven fourteen years ago. Whether I was in my body or out of my body, I don't know—only God knows. . . . But I do know that I was caught up to PARADISE and heard things so astounding that they cannot be expressed in words, things no human is allowed to tell" (2 Corinthians 12:2–4).

Some Bible writers did tell. The prophets EZEKIEL and DANIEL along with JOHN OF REVELATION all wrote about what they saw in their VISIONS of God's heavenly THRONE. But it's up for debate whether their descriptions—written in POETRY—should be read literally or figuratively.

John described NEW JERUSALEM—which many scholars say is another name for heaven—as though it's

EDEN without SIN. Streets of GOLD. Walls of jewels. No need for lights because "the GLORY of God illuminates the city" (Revelation 21:23). All of this in a cube 1,400 miles (2,220 km) in every direction. That's about the distance from New York City to Key West, Florida.

Many Bible experts see lots of metaphors in John's description.

They say John was using the most precious treasures from his world—jewels, gold, and light—to paint a symbolic picture of a breathtakingly wonderful spiritual world. As for the cube, that was the shape of the holiest spot on earth: the back room in Jerusalem's TEMPLE, where Jews kept their most sacred relic, the ARK OF THE COVENANT chest that held the 10 COMMANDMENTS. It was as though John was saying that the holiest spot on earth is just a tiny slice of heaven's holiness.

Whatever heaven is like, it's not just the place God calls home. Jesus made that much clear:

> *"There are many rooms in my Father's house. . . . I am going there to prepare a place for you. . . . Then you will also be where I am"* (JOHN 14:2–3 NIrV).

Paul seemed to be counting on it:

> *We know that when this earthly tent we live in is taken down (that is, when we die and leave this earthly body), we will have a house in heaven, an eternal body made for us by God himself* (2 CORINTHIANS 5:1).

HEBREW LANGUAGE

> *Five of Egypt's cities will follow the LORD. . . . They will even begin to speak Hebrew, the language of Canaan. Isaiah 19:18*

- Jewish language of the Old Testament

KISSING COUSIN of several Canaanite languages, the Hebrew lingo of JEWS sounds like a spinoff of languages people used in neighboring territories, such as Phoenician (in LEBANON) and Ugaritic (on SYRIA's coast). So say many linguists.

Most of the Jewish Bible, which Christians call the OLD TESTAMENT, was written in Hebrew. Without vowels. It was a shorthand technique that, sadly, makes it tough to figure out how the ancients pronounced certain words. Even the word for GOD, abbreviated YHWH. Scholars guess at the vowels: YAHWEH (YAH way).

HEBREWS, LETTER OF

Famous sound bite: Faith is being sure of what we hope for. It is being certain of what we do not see. Hebrews 11:1 NIrV

CHRISTIANS WERE GETTING DOUBLE-TEAMED with PERSECUTION. JEWS hammered them as heretics, arresting many and killing some. Then Roman Emperor NERO accused them of starting the fire that burned down much of ROME. Some Jews decided it was safer to quit CHRISTIANITY and go back to their old-time Jewish religion. But the writer of Hebrews warns them that there's nothing to go back to: the Jewish religion is obsolete.

- Writer: Unknown. Contenders: Paul, Barnabas, Apollos.
- Time: Possibly between AD 64 and 70. That's after Nero started persecuting Christians but before Rome destroyed Jerusalem's Temple.
- Location: Possibly written as an open letter to Jews everywhere.

BIG SCENES

Jesus trumps Moses. MOSES was GOD's top-of-the-line human, as far as many Jews were concerned. God spoke to Moses "face to face, as one speaks to a friend" (Exodus 33:11). But the Hebrews writer says Moses was just a SERVANT in God's house. Jesus, on the other hand, "is in charge of God's entire house." *Hebrews 3*

Jesus trumps the high priest. If Jews had a pope, he would have been the HIGH PRIEST. In matters of religion, nobody trumped the high priest. Until Jesus came. Though the priest ministered in a sacred WORSHIP center, Jesus ministers in God's presence. The priest sacrifices ANIMALS to cover his own sins, but Jesus never sinned. The priest dies, but Jesus rose from the dead. *Hebrews 4–9*

Jesus: the last sacrifice. The sacrificial system was a perpetual reminder that people were sinners. Every time they sinned, they had to offer a SACRIFICE. Each sacrifice was only a temporary fix. Then came Jesus. The Hebrews writer said Jesus made people HOLY by offering his body as the one and only sacrifice anyone would ever need—a sacrifice with no expiration date. *Hebrews 9–10*

Faith trumps ritual. Jews find comfort and spiritual security in rituals that extend back 4,000 years, to the time of ABRAHAM. Rituals like CIRCUMCISION and observing a SABBATH day of rest and worship. But the Hebrews writer says that ISRAEL's greatest leaders earned God's respect because of their FAITH. NOAH, Abraham, and Moses in the early years didn't even have any Jewish rituals to follow—the laws came later. Confidence in God is what these men had in common. *Hebrews 11*

HEBRON   Map 1 C6

(HE bron)

Abraham buried his wife, Sarah. . .in the cave of Machpelah, near Mamre (also called Hebron). Genesis 23:19

- Site of Abraham's family tomb
- Where David was crowned king

ABRAHAM CAMPED near Hebron, now a ridgetop city about 20 miles (32 km) south of JERUSALEM. Here is where ABRAHAM's wife SARAH died. Abraham bought a nearby cave and converted it into a family TOMB. Muslims and JEWS, both of whom revere Abraham, visit the Tomb of the PATRIARCHS built over what tradition says was the family's burial site.

"Don't be afraid of people. . . . They cannot harm your soul. . . . Fear God who can destroy both your body and your soul in hell."
Matthew 10:28 CEV

- Place of punishment in the afterlife

HELL IS AN ENGLISH INVENTION. It's an attempt to translate the symbol behind a location we can plot on a map: HINNOM Valley, just outside the walls of JERUSALEM.

Whenever Jesus used the word *hell*, he was saying the name of that valley. Replace *hell* with the HEBREW word "Hinnom" or with the GREEK version, "GEHENNA."

That doesn't mean hell is only a valley on the outskirts of Jerusalem. For JEWS, that valley came to symbolize GOD'S judgment. Jewish KINGS used to sacrifice humans to IDOLS in that valley. Sins like that, the PROPHETS explained, is why God let Babylonian invaders in 586 BC swarm in from what is now Iraq to destroy Jerusalem and deport the Jews—wiping the Jewish nation off the map.

Jews linked Hinnom Valley and God's judgment the way Americans link 9/11 to the terrorist attack on September 11, 2001.

Jesus painted graphic word pictures of hell:

- "unquenchable fires" (Mark 9:43)
- "prepared for the devil and his DEMONS" (Matthew 25:41)
- with plenty of room for sinners, religious HYPOCRITES and any other "Snakes! Sons of vipers!" (Matthew 23:33).

THE TROUBLE WITH HELL

Many scholars seem troubled by the traditional teaching about hell—that it's a place where sinners will be tortured forever. Here's why.

Torture isn't God's MO. These Bible experts say that when God punished someone in the BIBLE, he had a redemptive reason. Even the fall of Jerusalem in 586 BC was intended to eventually turn the Jews back to God. They say that eternal torture sounds more sadistic than redemptive.

Jesus often spoke in symbols. Some wonder if

BOOTED OUT OF HEAVEN, rebel angels end up in hell—a place Bible writers say was prepared for them. But as the Bible teaches it, hell has room enough for sinners. Scholars debate what hell is actually like.

STEPHEN M. MILLER'S ILLUSTRATED BIBLE DICTIONARY

the TEACHER who spoke of CAMELS trying to walk through the eye of a NEEDLE was using the same style of metaphor when he described hell.

A FEW CREATIVE THEORIES

Scholars offer theories like these about hell.

It's fiery hot. Sinners will burn, feeling the pain forever.

It's God's cold shoulder. The torment is being separated from God—the divine cold shoulder. Forever.

It's annihilation. Fire symbolizes DESTRUCTION. After the DEATH of the body comes "the SECOND DEATH" (Revelation 20:14). The death of the SOUL. It's the destruction that lasts forever, not the suffering.

It's temporary. Think parole. In time, everyone is reconciled with God. One go-to verse: "All the broken and dislocated pieces of the universe—people and things, animals and atoms—get properly fixed and fit together in vibrant harmonies, all because of his [Jesus'] death, his BLOOD that poured down from the CROSS" (Colossians 1:20 MSG).

See also HADES, LAKE OF FIRE.

HELMET

> *Saul gave David his own armor—a bronze helmet and a coat of mail.* 1 Samuel 17:38

SOLDIERS wore helmets in battle. Some helmets in Bible times were stitched together from LEATHER. Others were molded of BRONZE or IRON.

CIRCA ABRAHAM. A golden ceremonial helmet—vintage 2400s BC—from Abraham's hometown of Ur, a city in southern Iraq.

LENDING A HAND. A camel gets up close and personal with a hand tattooed in henna dye. The tattoo will last a week or more, depending on how often the camel comes calling.

HENNA

(HEN uh)

> *My lover is like a sachet of myrrh. . .a bouquet of sweet henna blossoms from the vineyards.* Song of Songs 1:13–14

A DESERT SHRUB, henna produces sweet-smelling white FLOWERS and orange-red dye. People in Bible times used the dye for temporary tattooing and to color HAIR, fingernails, and fabric.

HERESY

(HAIR uh see)

> *There will be false teachers among you. They will cleverly teach destructive heresies and even deny the Master.* 2 Peter 2:1

CHRISTIAN FRAUDS started roaming the church landscape in the early years, preaching a warped brand of CHRISTIANITY.

Based on warnings of NEW TESTAMENT writers, here are a couple of the heresies:

- Jesus was acting. "Many deceivers. . .deny that JESUS CHRIST came in a real body" (2 John 1:7). Instead, the heretics say Jesus was a spirit who only pretended to be human and to die.

- Sin is kosher. Only the spiritual world is good. The physical world is evil, so it doesn't matter if we commit sins, including what some would call "shameful IMMORALITY" (2 Peter 2:2).

HERMES

(HER meez)

They decided that Barnabas was the Greek god Zeus and that Paul was Hermes, since he was the chief speaker. Acts 14:12

- Greek messenger god
- Roman name: Mercury

IN GREEK MYTHOLOGY, Hermes delivered messages from the GODS to humans. When PAUL and BARNABAS went on their first mission trip to what is now Turkey, their healing MIRACLES and sermons led some locals to think they were gods. Paul and Barnabas cleared up that confusion pronto.

HEROD AGRIPPA I

(HAIR uhd uh GRIP uh)

AD 10–44, ruled AD 37–44

King Herod Agrippa began to persecute some believers. . . . He had the apostle James (John's brother) killed with a sword.
Acts 12:1–2

- King of Jewish homeland
- Executed James the disciple of Jesus

GRANDSON OF HEROD THE GREAT, he ended up ruling an area as large as Herod did—most of what is now ISRAEL. He's most famous in the BIBLE, though, for executing JAMES, one of Jesus' favorite DISCIPLES.

Roman historian Josephus (about AD 37–101) says Herod Agrippa died suddenly. The Bible says that after he let the people praise him as a god, "an ANGEL of the LORD struck Herod with a sickness. . . . He was consumed with worms and died" (Acts 12:23).

HEROD AGRIPPA II

(HAIR uhd uh GRIP uh)

AD 28–93, ruled about AD 50–93

Agrippa said to Paul, "You may speak in your defense." Acts 26:1

- Ruled parts of Israel, Syria, Lebanon

AT AGE 17 when his father, King HEROD AGRIPPA I, died, Agrippa II was too young to rule the region—most of what is now ISRAEL. That was Roman Emperor CLAUDIUS's decision. But six years later, Claudius gave him a slice of the northland, in LEBANON and SYRIA—followed later by still more, including GALILEE.

He and his sister BERNICE—engaged in an incestuous affair—visited CAESAREA while PAUL was in jail. In the BIBLE he's perhaps most famous for what he said while Paul, in chains, was talking to him: "Do you think you can persuade me to become a CHRISTIAN so quickly?" (Acts 26:28).

Agrippa remained loyal to ROME even when the JEWS revolted in AD 66. After Rome recaptured the Jewish homeland, Rome restored Agrippa to power.

H

HEROD ANTIPAS

(HAIR uhd AN tuh puhs)

Ruled 4 BC–AD 39

Herod had John's head cut off in the prison. His head was brought in on a big plate. Matthew 14:10–11 NIrV

- Ruled Galilee as governor
- Beheaded John the Baptist
- Mocked Jesus, putting him in a royal robe

"THAT FOX" is what Jesus called him. Perhaps thinking more of a violent chicken thief than a cunning critter. After all, Herod Antipas would get himself fired and deported to what is now France after asking ROME to promote him to king.

One of the sons of HEROD THE GREAT, Antipas inherited the northern territory, including Jesus' home region: GALILEE.

The BIBLE and Roman historian Josephus (about

AD 37–101) both report that Antipas executed JOHN THE BAPTIST. John had angered Antipas's wife, HERODIAS, by calling their marriage INCEST. Herodias was Antipas's niece and sister-in-law—ex-wife of Antipas's brother.

Herodias got even at Antipas's birthday party. Her daughter's dance so aroused Antipas that he promised her anything. She consulted her mom, who wanted John's head on a platter.

Antipas also got in on the harassment of Jesus. When Roman governor PILATE sent Jesus to him during Jesus' trial, Antipas sent him back to Pilate dressed in a royal ROBE—a joke Pilate enjoyed. The two GOVERNORS "became friends that day" (Luke 23:12).

HEROD PHILIP

(HAIR uhd)

Ruled 4 BC–AD 34

Herod had arrested and imprisoned John as a favor to his wife Herodias (the former wife of Herod's brother Philip). Matthew 14:3

- Son of Herod the Great
- His ex-wife got John the Baptist killed

ONE OF THREE SONS of HEROD THE GREAT, Philip inherited a third of the kingdom—territory east of the SEA OF GALILEE in parts of Israel and SYRIA. But he's more famous for what he lost: his wife, HERODIAS. She left him for a husband upgrade. She married his half brother HEROD ANTIPAS, who ruled GALILEE.

HEROD THE GREAT

(HAIR uhd)

Reigned 40–4 BC

Herod. . .sent soldiers to kill all the boys in and around Bethlehem who were two years old and under. Matthew 2:16

- King of the Jews
- Remodeled Jerusalem's Temple
- Tried to kill baby Jesus

HE WASN'T THAT GREAT.

A paranoid control freak, he executed his WIFE,

three sons, and several other assorted family members. He feared they were stirring up a coup.

He was, however, great at hanging on to power. When he was about 25 years old, Romans made him GOVERNOR of GALILEE in northern Israel. He crushed

'KILL HER." That's what Herod the Great decreed for Mariamne—and she was his favorite wife. Paranoid like crazy and fearing a coup, Herod also executed three of his sons. Bad daddy. Bad husband. Yet, Herod the Great.

the resistance movement there—a feat that so impressed the Romans that they declared him king of the JEWS. In spite of the fact that Herod wasn't a Jew. Not racially. He came from IDUMEA, where Jews had forced the people to convert or die. Herod's family converted.

Jews already had a king—Antigonus II—appointed by ROME's enemy empire: Parthians, in what is now Iran. But with Rome's help, Herod captured the throne, executed Antigonus, and ruled for a GENERATION.

When WISE MEN showed up hoping to honor the next king of the Jews, Herod tried to put the skids on that by sending all the BETHLEHEM boys into the ground.

He was also great at building—quite the visionary. He doubled the size of JERUSALEM's Temple COURTYARD. Then he spent the last 20 years of his life renovating Israel's second TEMPLE to such an extent that many historians call it the third Temple.

Yet the Temple was a Tinker Toy compared to some of his other projects—especially the seaside city of CAESAREA, complete with a state-of-the-art harbor, springwater piped in with an AQUEDUCT, PALACES, theaters, temples, and a SYNAGOGUE. This city wowed the Romans. They made it their Middle Eastern capital—for 600 years.

Herod built fortress cities throughout the country, including one on top of an artificial mountain near Bethlehem: the Herodium. He was buried there, perhaps just a year or two after he had tried to assassinate baby Jesus in Bethlehem. Jewish historian Josephus (about AD 37–101) said he died a miserable death, suffering from "gangrene of the genitals."

JOHN'S HEAD ON A PLATTER is what the First Lady of Galilee wanted. John the Baptist's mistake was to accuse her of incest. It didn't matter that he was right.

brother, who was also her uncle: HEROD ANTIPAS. John called that INCEST.

When her husband upgrade offered a GIFT to Herodias's daughter, the daughter asked her mom for advice. Herodias suggested John's head on a platter.

HESHBON

Map 1 E5

(HESH bonn)

Israel captured all the towns of the Amorites and settled in them, including the city of Heshbon. . .capital of King Sihon.
Numbers 21:25–26

RETURNING FROM THE EXODUS in EGYPT, JEWS passed through what is now Jordan. There they conquered the nations that rallied to repel them, including Heshbon, and assigned to the tribe of WORSHIP leaders: the LEVITES (Joshua 21:39).

HERODIAS

(huh ROW dee us)

Born about 8 BC

Herod had arrested and imprisoned John as a favor to his wife Herodias Matthew 14:3

- Got John the Baptist's head on a platter
- Wife of Herod Antipas
- Granddaughter of Herod the Great

JOHN THE BAPTIST made the first lady of GALILEE feel like anything but a lady. Herodias had DIVORCED her husband, HEROD PHILIP. Then she married his half

HEZEKIAH

(hez uh KIH uh)

Reigned 715–687 BC

Hezekiah trusted in the LORD, the God of Israel. There was no one like him among all the kings of Judah. 2 Kings 18:5

- One of Judah's few good kings
- Built Hezekiah's Tunnel to carry springwater

A SAINT OF A KING SANDWICHED between two sinners, Hezekiah was nothing like his father King AHAZ or his son King MANASSEH. Both of those losers toasted their sons—each sacrificing a son to a pagan god as a burnt offering.

Hezekiah, on the other hand, set the bar for godly KINGS. "He remained faithful to the LORD in everything, and he carefully obeyed all the commands the LORD had given MOSES" (2 Kings 18:6). He destroyed the pagan worship centers his father had allowed—along with the BRONZE SERPENT that Moses crafted during the EXODUS because people were worshiping it (2 Kings 18:4).

By the time he became king at age 25, the northern Jewish nation of ISRAEL was gone—erased from the political map in 722 BC by Assyrian invaders from what is now Iraq. Fourteen years into his reign, Assyrians threatened to do the same to JUDAH.

Likely, they would have captured JERUSALEM had it not been for a one-two punch.

One punch from Hezekiah: He had the foresight to build a TUNNEL that pulled WATER into Jerusalem from an underground spring—allowing the city to withstand ASSYRIA's siege.

One knockout punch from God: "The ANGEL of the LORD went out to the Assyrian camp and killed 185,000 Assyrian soldiers" (2 Kings 19:35). The rest ran for their lives. King SENNACHERIB's record of the campaign confirms that he captured 46 Jewish cities, but that he managed only to lay SIEGE to Jerusalem, trapping Hezekiah "like a bird in a cage."

Greek historian Herodotus, writing 250 years after that military campaign, suggested bubonic plague killed the Assyrians. He said Sennacherib's ARMY was stopped one night by a rat infestation that killed many soldiers.

HIERAPOLIS

Map 3 G4

(HI ur OP o liss)

Epaphras, a member of your own fellowship. . . prays hard for you and also for the believers in Laodicea and Hierapolis. Colossians 4:12–13

- City in Turkey Paul mentioned

WARPED CHRISTIAN TEACHING was on PAUL's mind when he wrote his LETTER to the COLOSSIANS. He addressed his warnings to Christians in the city of COLOSSE. But he also mentioned neighboring cities, including Hierapolis. That city is now a ruins, possibly destroyed by an EARTHQUAKE about the same time Paul wrote the letter: around AD 60.

HIGH PLACE

I said to them, "What is this high place where you are going?" (This kind of pagan shrine has been called Bamah—"high place"—ever since.) Ezekiel 20:29

- Hilltop site of pagan shrine

HILLTOPS were as close to the heavens as people could get. That's probably why many preferred to worship there. In the BIBLE, "high places" often refers to Canaanite religions with X-rated fertility rites intended to please the GODS.

HIGH PRIEST

"The high priest has the highest rank of all the priests." Leviticus 21:10

ISRAEL'S TOP SPIRITUAL LEADER enjoyed job security for a lifetime. The high priest served as CEO of Israel's WORSHIP center—directing the rituals and managing the priests and support staff.

There was just one high priest at a time. He had to come from the tribe of LEVI. In addition, he had to descend from AARON, ISRAEL's first high priest. After

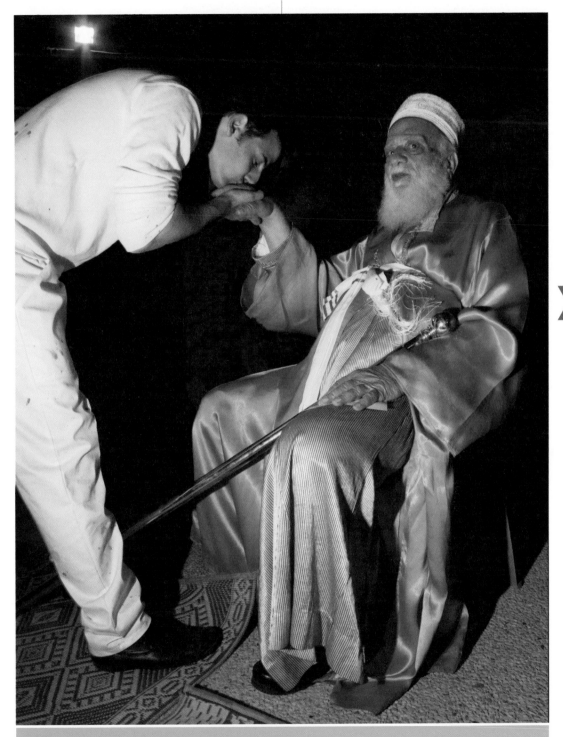

A KISS for the Samaritan high priest, from a worshiper speckled with blood from a Passover sacrifice. Jews no longer have priests or offer animal sacrifices. But a small community of Samaritans in central Israel observes both of those ancient Jewish traditions, with a Samaritan twist. Their worship center is Mount Gerizim, not Jerusalem.

SOLOMON built JERUSALEM's first TEMPLE, the field narrowed even further. He had to be a FIRSTBORN descendant of ZADOK, the high priest at the time.

Held to a higher standard than other priests, the high priest had a few extra rules to follow:

- Never dress for MOURNING (no torn clothes or uncombed HAIR).
- Never touch a corpse.
- Marry only a VIRGIN; no widows allowed.

The Aaron/Zadok dynasty lasted a thousand years, until Syrians invaded in the 100s BC. Jewish rebels drove them out, but then the rebel leader assumed the combo job of king/high priest.

When HEROD THE GREAT became king, he killed the high priest and appointed his own high priests whenever he wanted. Romans did the same after him. They appointed CAIAPHAS, the high priest who orchestrated Jesus' execution.

The priesthood ended in AD 70 when Romans crushed a Jewish revolt and destroyed the Temple. No Temple. No SACRIFICES. No need for a priest.

The Temple has never been rebuilt.

HILKIAH

(hill KI uh)

600s BC

Hilkiah the high priest said. . . "I have found the Book of the Law in the LORD's Temple!"
2 Kings 22:8

HILKIAH SPARKED A REVIVAL when he found a copy of the Jewish laws lost in the cobwebs of the Jerusalem TEMPLE. When King JOSIAH discovered all the rules the JEWS were breaking, he got rid of pagan shrines and led the people back to GOD.

HINNOM

See Jerusalem, Map 4 C5

(HEN nom)

Manasseh. . .sacrificed his own sons in Hinnom Valley. 2 Chronicles 33:6 CEV

- Jerusalem valley that became a symbol of hell

WHEN WE READ "HELL" in English Bibles, JEWS read the literal word in HEBREW: *Hinnom*. It's a valley just outside JERUSALEM's city walls, on the south side. *GEHENNA* is the version in GREEK, the international language of Jesus' day.

By the time Jesus starting teaching about the fires of Gehenna, the valley had come to symbolize GOD's judgment—his hellish eviction of Jews from their homeland in 586 BC.

PROPHETS said God allowed invaders from what is now Iraq to wipe the Jewish nation off the political map and to deport the surviving Jews because of their serial sinning. Of the sins they committed, none was more repulsive than sacrificing Jewish children to IDOLS—something King AHAZ and his grandson King MANASSEH both did in Hinnom Valley.

For this reason, when Jesus spoke of Hinnom, he wasn't usually talking geography. He was talking judgment. It's a bit like Americans talking about 9/11. They're not talking about a date. They're talking about a tragedy—a terrorist attack that killed thousands.

See also HELL.

HIRAM

(HI rum)

Reigned about 969–936 BC

Hiram supplied as much cedar and cypress timber as Solomon desired [for the Temple].
1 Kings 5:10

- King of Tyre, in Lebanon

NOT A JEW, Hiram helped build ISRAEL's holiest site, the Jerusalem TEMPLE. King of the leading city in PHOENICIA, he had access to the cedars of LEBANON—a rot-resistant, bug-repellant lumber preferred by builders.

He floated the timber down the sea to Israel. In exchange, SOLOMON gave Hiram some of Israel's northland. When Hiram saw the land, he renamed it: "Worthless" (1 Kings 9:13).

HITTITES

(HIT tight)

"Today you will know that the living God is among you. He will surely drive out the Canaanites, Hittites. . .ahead of you." Joshua 3:10

- A warrior race the Jews fought

A POWERFUL EMPIRE headquartered in what is now Turkey, Hittites migrated and raided south toward SYRIA and ISRAEL during OLD TESTAMENT times.

Their empire fizzled about the time the JEWS returned to Israel after their SLAVERY in EGYPT. The BIBLE says JOSHUA and his militia overpowered the locals in the area, Hittites included.

Later some Hittites assimilated into Jewish life and culture, it seems. BATHSHEBA's husband was "URIAH the Hittite" (2 Samuel 11:3). He was also a member of King DAVID's elite strike force.

HIVITES

(HI vites)

"I will lead you to a land flowing with milk and honey—the land where the Canaanites, Hittites. . .Hivites. . .now live." Exodus 3:17

HILL PEOPLE, the Hivites apparently lived in what are now the hills of LEBANON, near "the stronghold of TYRE" (2 Samuel 24:7 NKJV). Many Bible experts say the spelling of *Hivites* is an ancient typo that should have been spelled "Horites." Others say the Hivites were part of the larger group of Horites.

When one Hivite raped DINAH, daughter of JACOB, her brothers murdered all the men in the town (Genesis 34:2, 27).

HOLY

God's will was for us to be made holy by the sacrifice of the body of Jesus Christ, once for all time. Hebrews 10:10

- God's unique perfection
- People devoted to God
- Objects reserved for sacred use

THE WORD *HOLINESS* MULTITASKS in the BIBLE to the point that it baffles many readers.

Bible writers used the words *holy* and *holiness* to describe GOD, people, and even sacred objects like Temple LAMPSTANDS.

HOLY GOD

Holy means "unique" or "separate," someone in a class by himself. That's God.

"There isn't anyone holy like the LORD" (1 Samuel 2:2 NIRV). Many Bible experts say holiness doesn't merely describe God as the ultimate good guy—perfect in every way. Holiness is his unique, defining character trait.

HOLY PEOPLE

JEWS considered themselves God's holy people. They were unique; God chose them. They maintained that holiness by obeying his laws and by offering SACRIFICES when they sinned.

CHRISTIAN writers taught that followers of Jesus are holy because of Jesus' sacrifice. No more sacrifices were needed. But they also urged fellow Christians to remember who their FATHER was, and to act like it:

God has called us to live holy lives, not impure lives (1 THESSALONIANS 4:7).

But PAUL suggested that holiness is a work in progress:

It's not that I have already reached this goal or have already been perfected, but I pursue it (PHILIPPIANS 3:12 CEB).

H

HOLY OBJECTS

BOWLS, lampstands, and utensils used to butcher sacrificial meat at the Jewish WORSHIP center were all ritually ANOINTED with oil, "making them holy" (Leviticus 8:11).

They were holy because the Jews had set them aside from objects used for common, secular purposes. These and other objects in the worship center were reserved for sacred duty.

As objects devoted to God, they were considered holy.

OF ATONEMENT) to sprinkle BLOOD from a SACRIFICE. The blood atoned for the sins of the entire nation.

This room in the back of the Jerusalem TEMPLE was a cube measuring about 30 feet (9 m) in all directions and paneled in solid GOLD. Inside this room sat ISRAEL's most sacred relic: the ARK OF THE COVENANT, a chest that held the 10 COMMANDMENTS.

The room goes by various names, depending on the Bible translation. A sampling: Most Holy Place, Holy Place, Inner Room.

HOLY OF HOLIES

Solomon prepared the Most Holy Room inside the temple. That's where the ark of the covenant of the Lord would be placed.
1 Kings 6:19 NIrV

- Holiest room in the Temple

ONLY THE HIGH PRIEST was allowed inside the holiest room of the Jewish WORSHIP center. And then, only once a year. He went there on *Yom Kippur* (the DAY

HOLY SPIRIT

"Make disciples of all the nations, baptizing them in the name of the Father and the Son and the Holy Spirit." Matthew 28:19

- Third person of the divine Trinity
- Probably not a bird

CHRISTIANS WORSHIP two men and a bird, if classic artists got their paintings right.

In divine family portraits, GOD the FATHER and

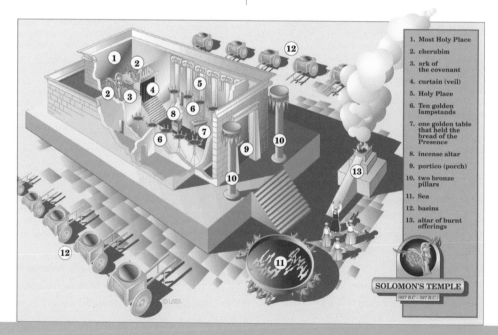

1. Most Holy Place
2. cherubim
3. ark of the covenant
4. curtain (veil)
5. Holy Place
6. Ten golden lampstands
7. one golden table that held the bread of the Presence
8. incense altar
9. portico (porch)
10. two bronze pillars
11. Sea
12. basins
13. altar of burnt offerings

SOLOMON'S TEMPLE
(957 B.C. – 587 B.C.)

THE MOST HOLY PLACE in the Jewish Temple was the back room, where Jews kept their most sacred relic: the Ark of the Covenant. It was a gold-covered chest that held the 10 Commandments.

God the Son are both painted as men. That's because the BIBLE says Jesus came to earth as a man—and that, from time to time, God the Father did, too.

But in all of the Bible stories the only time the Spirit shows up wearing anything close to a body, it's a body with feathers.

Many Bible translations seem to suggest the Spirit is, in fact, a DOVE. At Jesus' BAPTISM, "the Holy Spirit came down on him in the form of a dove" (Luke 3:22 NCV).

Other translations, however, reject the idea that the Holy Spirit could be taken out with birdshot.

They have the Spirit descending on Jesus "like a dove" (MSG).

WIND BENEATH THE WINGS

"Spirit" comes from a GREEK word: *pneuma*, which means wind or breath. Out of that stump word we get shoot words like: *pneumonia* (a disease in the lungs) and *pneumatic* (tools powered by air pressure).

When the Holy Spirit descended on Jesus' followers after he returned to HEAVEN, the room filled with "a sound from heaven like the roaring of a mighty windstorm." That wind, in a manner of speaking—pun intended—filled their lungs and came out as words: "Everyone present was filled with the Holy Spirit and began speaking in other languages, as the Holy Spirit gave them this ability" (Acts 2:2, 4).

Whatever the Holy Spirit looks like, Bible scholars agree that the Spirit is God's power and presence at work in people—giving them the courage, insight, and gifts to do things they'd never be able to do on their own.

ONE SPIRIT FOR ALL

The OLD TESTAMENT sometimes reads like the Holy Spirit had a part-time job, while the NEW TESTAMENT reads like he got hired on full-time.

As Old Testament writers tell it, the Holy Spirit wasn't available to just anyone. The Spirit came mainly to KINGS, PROPHETS, champion warriors, and other leaders in extraordinary circumstances:

> *The Spirit of the LORD entered Gideon, and he blew a trumpet to call the Abiezrites to follow him* (JUDGES 6:34 NCV).

THIS IS MY BELOVED SON

GOD'S SPIRIT DESCENDS LIKE A DOVE during the baptism of Jesus. Since then, artists have been portraying the Holy Spirit with feathers.

STEPHEN M. MILLER'S ILLUSTRATED BIBLE DICTIONARY

The Spirit of God came upon Saul's men, and they also began to prophesy (1 SAMUEL 19:20).

The Spirit of the LORD took control of David and stayed with him from then on (1 SAMUEL 16:13 CEV).

One prophet said there was coming a day when the Holy Spirit wouldn't be this limited: "I will pour out my Spirit upon all people" (Joel 2:28).

In PETER's first sermon after the ASCENSION OF JESUS—immediately after the Holy Spirit descended on him and the other DISCIPLES—Peter quoted that prophecy. He said God had just fulfilled it.

Some 3,000 JEWS believed him, and the CHRISTIAN movement was on its way.

Thanks to the Holy Spirit.

HOMOSEXUALITY

No one who is immoral. . .or behaves like a homosexual will share in God's kingdom.
1 Corinthians 6:9–10 CEV

- Having sex with a person of the same sex

THERE'S NOTHING GAY about the BIBLE's take on homosexuality.

Christians do, however, debate how to interpret the Bible's advice. And they argue over whether Bible writers were actually talking about homosexuals. Perhaps, some speculate, the Bible writers were talking about heterosexuals gone wild—far beyond the borders of their natural sexual orientation.

One go-to verse some use to support this comes from the apostle PAUL. He wrote about people who "exchanged natural sexual relations for unnatural ones" (Romans 1:26 TNIV). As in a straight person experimenting with gay SEX.

The counterpoint is that by "natural," Paul was thinking about guys with gals. Not guys with guys and gals with gals. Under ancient Jewish law, same-sex sex was about as kosher as eating pork off the belly of a dead man at Passover.

Some scholars argue that the idea of homosexuality as a unique sexual orientation began only in the 1800s. Because of this, they add, the Bible's original HEBREW and GREEK words translated *homosexual* don't mean the same thing to us as they did to folks in Bible times. To Bible-era folks, man-on-man, woman-on-woman sex got lumped into the broad category of sex SIN. That happened, some scholars say, in spite of the fact that folks didn't yet understand sexual orientation—that people may come wired with one set of desires or another, and that homosexuality is discovered, not chosen.

Yet if there's a difference between homosexuality and same-sex activity among heterosexuals, Bible writers don't seem to make that distinction. Consistently, they offer the identical advice to same-sex couples as they offer to heterosexual couples who aren't married: Don't be doing that thing.

"Do not practice homosexuality, having sex with another man as with a woman. It is a detestable sin" (LEVITICUS 18:22).

So detestable that in OLD TESTAMENT times it drew the death penalty.

Curiously, Jesus never mentioned the topic. Yet many say they read his teachings about love, FORGIVENESS, and tolerance—and see in them clues for addressing the controversy.

The topic remains so divisive that churches have split over whether it's okay to ORDAIN practicing homosexuals.

HOPHNI AND PHINEHAS

(HOFF nee) (FIN ee us)
1100s BC
The sons of Eli were scoundrels who had no respect for the LORD or for their duties as priests. 1 Samuel 2:12–13

- Sons of the high priest Eli
- Lousy priests

ROTTEN SONS and corrupt PRIESTS, they slept with the help—women who worked at the Jewish WORSHIP center. Ignoring their father's plea to shape up, they also stole whatever sacrificial meat they wanted—even meat reserved for GOD as a burnt offering.

They died in battle. They had carried to the battlefront ISRAEL's most sacred object—the ARK OF THE COVENANT. They hoped it would inspire the troops. But PHILISTINES won the battle, stole the Ark, and killed the priests.

HORN   (see RAM'S HORN)

HOSANNA

> They shouted, "Hosanna! Blessed is the one who comes in the name of the Lord!" John 12:13 NIrV

- Hebrew for "save us"

WHEN JESUS RODE INTO JERUSALEM on a DONKEY, the crowds shouted *Hosanna,* calling him the King of ISRAEL. They believed he was the promised MESSIAH, scholars say. They hoped he would save them from the Romans who had occupied their homeland for a century. It later came as a shock to his followers that his mission was, instead, to save them from SIN.

HOSEA

(ho ZAY uh)

About 750–722 BC

The LORD gave this message to Hosea. . . "Go and marry a prostitute." Hosea 1:1–2

- Prophet in northern Jewish nation of Israel
- Married a prostitute

IT'S A MATCH MADE IN HEAVEN that begs a question: Why on earth would GOD ask a HOLY man to marry a hooker?

He wouldn't. That was the consensus of many Jewish

scholars in ancient times. The story is a parable, they said. A fictional tale intended to make a point.

Many today disagree. They say it was a factual story intended to make a point: "This will illustrate how ISRAEL has acted like a PROSTITUTE by turning against the LORD and worshiping other GODS" (Hosea 1:2).

God's punishment for Israel: Assyrian invaders erased the nation from the political map in 722 BC and EXILED many of the survivors. The tribes that had once lived there are remembered as the Lost TRIBES OF ISRAEL.

HOSEA, BOOK OF

> *Famous sound bite: "They sow the wind, and reap the whirlwind." Hosea 8:7* NKJV

THE PROPHET HOSEA warns ISRAEL that the end is near. For two centuries of relentless sinning, the chosen ones are about to get unchosen—evicted from the PROMISED LAND.

- Writer: Unknown. Perhaps Hosea or someone reporting his story.
- Time: About 750–722 BC.
- Location: Northern Jewish nation of Israel.

BIG SCENES

Mrs. Floozy. GOD tells Hosea to marry a PROSTITUTE, GOMER, so she'll have kids by other men. God explains why: "This will illustrate how Israel has acted like a prostitute by turning against the LORD and worshiping other GODS" (Hosea 1:2). Gomer has three kids. Hosea doesn't get credit for being the father of any of them. But he does name them. Each name tracks with a complaint God has against Israel. Son Lo-Ammi, for example, means "Not my people." In other words, the JEWS are no longer God's people and the Lord is no longer their God. *Hosea 1*

The Good-Bye Girl. Gomer runs away. She ends up enslaved or perhaps working for a pimp; same thing. God tells Hosea to find her and buy her back. "This will illustrate that the LORD still loves Israel, even though the people have turned to other gods and love to worship them" (Hosea 3:1). In spite of that—perhaps

H

because of that—God warns that he will punish Israel. But in time, he promises, he'll bring them home to live under the shade of his protection. *Hosea 3, 9, 14*

HOSHEA

(ho SHE uh)
Ruled 732–724 BC

Hoshea son of Elah conspired against Pekah and assassinated him. He began to rule over Israel. (2 Kings 15:30)

- Last king of northern Jewish nation of Israel

KING BY ASSASSINATION, Hoshea snatched ISRAEL's throne by killing King PEKAH in 732 BC. Hoshea's reign ended when he stopped paying taxes to the Assyrian Empire—Middle Eastern superpower headquartered in Iraq. They came to collect. Everything. They destroyed Israel's capital, dismantled the political system, and imprisoned Hoshea.

See also TIGLATH-PILESER III.

HOSPITALITY

Don't forget to show hospitality to strangers, for some who have done this have entertained angels without realizing it! Hebrews 13:2

COMMON COURTESY could mean the difference between life and DEATH. That was the reality in the badlands of the ancient Middle East—a part of the planet sparsely populated, lightly watered, with almost no inns.

If travelers were lucky enough to make it to a city, they often waited at a public spot—like the city GATE—hoping someone would host them for the night. No shelter, no food, and no water could kill a vulnerable traveler.

Jesus told his DISCIPLES—circuit-walking MINISTERS—"Don't hesitate to accept hospitality, because those who work deserve to be fed" (Matthew 10:10).

Years later, one of Jesus' disciples—JOHN—chewed out a control-freak PASTOR named DIOTREPHES who ordered his congregation not to welcome Christian teachers traveling through. "Don't let this bad example influence you," John wrote. "You are being faithful to GOD when you care for the traveling teachers who pass through, even though they are strangers to you" (3 John 1:5, 11).

HOUR

(see TIME OF DAY)

HOUSE

"I will destroy the beautiful homes of the wealthy—their winter mansions and their summer houses, too." God to Israel, Amos 3:15

THERE WERE HOUSES. And there were mansions. Money made the difference. No surprise.

Once JOSHUA led the JEWS back to Israel, archaeologists say that the most common Jewish house had four rooms. There was one big room in the back; it ran the full width of the house. The front half got split up into three rooms.

Stones supported the bottom part of the house. Mud BRICK or wood finished off the top. The ROOF—supported by wood and plastered with mud and lime—was flat. Homeowners used it like we would use a balcony or a porch. On hot nights, they slept there. In the day, they might work there or dry clothes and crops. By law, they had to "build a railing around the edge of its flat roof. That way you will not be considered guilty of MURDER if someone falls from the roof" (Deuteronomy 22:8).

The rich lived in mansions (see painting, page 243). Excavations suggest that AMOS was right to complain about the inequality between the rich and the POOR. It was common for the rich to huddle together in an elite section of town. There they lived in sprawling houses, elegantly appointed with the kind of lavish murals on plastered walls found in the ruins of Pompeii.

A DECK ON THE ROOF was a feature of many houses in Bible times. By law, Jews were supposed to build a wall around the roof to protect people from falling off.

HULDAH

(HULL duh)

About 650–600 BC

The priest Hilkiah went to speak to the prophet Huldah. 2 Kings 22:14 NIrv

- Female prophet in Jerusalem

BAD NEWS from the prophet Huldah. She said GOD was going to destroy JUDAH, the last surviving Jewish nation. She dropped that bombshell after the JEWS found a lost copy of the laws of MOSES and realized how far they had strayed from God. That's when the HIGH PRIEST consulted Huldah for advice, got the word, and passed it on to King JOSIAH.

HUMAN SACRIFICE

"Never sacrifice your son or daughter as a burnt offering." Deuteronomy 18:10

FIRSTBORN SONS were a favorite human sacrifice in some religions during Bible times. That's because the GODS deserved the best, folks thought. And a FAMILY's first SON was the best they could ever hope to offer.

King MESHA of MOAB, in what is now Jordan, turned back a Jewish attack on his city by shocking the invaders: "He took his son, his FIRSTBORN who would succeed him as king, and sacrificed him on the city wall" (2 Kings 3:27 MSG). Mesha sacrificed the PRINCE to the god CHEMOSH.

Some JEWS picked up those bad habits of their

223

neighbors. At least two KINGS did it, too: AHAZ and MANASSEH, the father and son of godly King HEZEKIAH.

The prophet JEREMIAH warned that GOD would destroy the Jewish nation for this very reason: "They burn their children in the fire to BAAL" (Jeremiah 19:5 NCV).

HUMANITY

Who among men knows the thoughts of a man except the spirit of the man which is in him?
1 Corinthians 2:11 NASB

WHAT YOU SEE isn't what you get, as the BIBLE teaches it. There's more—at least if you're looking in the mirror.

Humans are more than flesh and blood that will one day dry up and blow away. As the Bible teaches it, they have an invisible quality, too. One that can last forever. It's a SOUL—a SPIRIT within the body.

Some Bible experts speculate that this is what the GENESIS writer described when he quoted GOD at the CREATION of Adam: "Let us make human beings in our image, to be like us" (Genesis 1:26).

HUMILITY

If you put yourself above others, you will be put down. But if you humble yourself, you will be honored. Matthew 23:12 CEV

- A top-of-the-line virtue

GOD WILL BRING DOWN the self-proclaimed high and mighty. And he'll lift up the lowly.

Bible writers beat that drum all the way through the BIBLE—Old Testament and New:

- "You [GOD] rescue the humble, but your eyes watch the proud and humiliate them" (2 Samuel 22:28).
- "Pride leads to destruction; humility leads to honor" (Proverbs 18:12 CEV).
- "Don't try to impress others. Be humble, thinking of others as better than yourselves" (Philippians 2:3).

HUNTING

"Take your bow and a quiver full of arrows, and go out into the open country to hunt some wild game for me." Genesis 27:3

- Rarely mentioned in the Bible

FARMERS AND HERDERS, the JEWS didn't seem to get into hunting as much as their neighbors did.

There's plenty of ancient art showing Egyptians on the hunt, as well as Assyrians from what is now Iraq. But when a Jew is killing a wild critter in some Bible story, it's usually because the critter is attacking a herder's flock.

For those Jews who did hunt, game on their KOSHER menu included deer, antelope, gazelle, and wild GOAT.

A SURROGATE HUNTER, this hawk is trained to hunt game birds and small mammals like rabbits, then bring the prey back to the trainer. Falconry, as it's known, has been around the Middle East for several thousand years. Assyrian art from the palace of Sargon II in the 700s BC shows hawks on what appears to be a royal hunt.

HUSBAND

As the church submits to Christ, so you wives should submit to your husbands in everything. Ephesians 5:24

▪ Family boss, in ancient culture

A SINGLE GUY giving marital advice, the apostle PAUL sounded like the product of his patriarchal culture when he told wives to submit to their husbands. For in that ancient day, men were men and everyone else was pitifully less.

Like cocky roosters, men ruled the roost.

Surprisingly, to some Bible readers, Paul added a twist that could choke a crowing rooster. He said what's good for the goose is good for the gander: "Submit to one another" (Ephesians 5:21).

HYPOCRITE

"Don't be like the hypocrites who love to pray publicly on street corners and in the synagogues where everyone can see them." Matthew 6:5

▪ Greek for "actor"

PUTTING ON A SHOW is what the world's first hypocrites did. Literally. *Hypokrite* is the GREEK word for an actor who performs behind a mask.

Jesus added a little extra color to that word picture. Describing religious leaders who weren't religious, he said: "You're like manicured grave plots, grass clipped and the FLOWERS bright, but six feet down it's all rotting bones and worm-eaten flesh. . . . You're total frauds" (Matthew 23:27–28 MSG).

HYSSOP

(HISS up)

"Take a branch of a hyssop plant, dip it into the bowl filled with blood, and then wipe the blood on the sides and tops of the doorframes." Exodus 12:22 NCV

▪ Flowering shrub

ENSLAVED JEWS IN EGYPT used hyssop branches to paint the BLOOD of a sacrificial lamb over their doorposts during the first PASSOVER. That blood clued the ANGEL of death to pass over Jewish homes on his mission to kill the FIRSTBORN of EGYPT. This became the last of 10 plagues that convinced Egypt to free the JEWS.

H

HOLLYWOOD HYPOCRITES. This mosaic from first-century Pompeii shows the masks that Romans used in the theater during New Testament times. In the international language of the day, Greek, *hypocrite* and *actor* were the same word.

I AM

God said to Moses, "I AM WHO I AM. When you go to the people of Israel, tell them, 'I AM sent me to you.'" Exodus 3:14 NCV

- God's name

WRITTEN IN HEBREW SHORTHAND, which has no vowels, "I AM" appears as YHWH.

Bible experts have to guess what vowels to insert. Their most popular guess: YAHWEH (YAH way). Many Bibles translate it "The LORD." Used nearly 7,000 times in the BIBLE, it's the most common NAME for GOD.

For cowboys curious if the vowels might possibly have spelled YAHWHO—not a chance.

So said ancient HEBREW language expert Dr. Joseph Coleson, a prof at Nazarene Theological Seminary in Kansas City.

"While it could be fun," he told me, "no Semitic language ever would allow all three root letters (here, the HWH) to occur in succession together, in any form of any root, without vowels to break them up."

IBLEAM   Map 1 C4

(IB lee uhm)

Jehu's troops shot and wounded him [King Ahaziah of Judah] in his chariot. . .near Ibleam. 2 Kings 9:27 MSG

- City in northern Israel

TWO JEWISH KINGS DIED in one coup when CHARIOT commander JEHU overthrew AHAB's son, JORAM, king of the northern Jewish nation of ISRAEL. In a case of terrible timing, King Ahaziah just happened to be visiting Joram from the southland Jewish nation of JUDAH. Shot near Ibleam, Ahaziah made it 15 miles (24 km) to MEGIDDO before he died.

ICHABOD

(ICK uh bod)

She named the boy Ichabod. . .because her father-in-law and her husband had died. 1 Samuel 4:21 NIrV

- Grandson of high priest Eli
- Hebrew for "no glory"

TRAGIC NEWS sent the wife of a PRIEST named Phinehas into labor. She got word that PHILISTINES had killed her husband and brother-in-law in a battle—and that her father-in-law ELI died when he found out about his sons. Depressed, she gave her son a depressing NAME.

ICONIUM   Map 3 I4

(i CONE ee uhm)

The people of Iconium. . .decided to make trouble for Paul and Barnabas and to stone them to death. Acts 14:4–5 CEV

- City Paul visited in Turkey

ON HIS FIRST MISSIONARY TRIP, Paul took the story of Jesus to several cities in what is now Turkey. He and his partner BARNABAS narrowly escaped getting stoned to death in Iconium.

Angry JEWS from Iconium followed him to the next town, LYSTRA, where they convinced the people to stone PAUL and leave him for dead. He recovered and moved on to the next town of DERBE.

IDOLS

"No carved gods of any size, shape, or form." Exodus 20:4 MSG

- Statues or figurines of gods

NOT ONE IMAGE OF GOD has ever been found in archaeological digs in Israel.

That might have something to do with commandment number 2 of 10, which says don't make an idol "of anything in the heavens or on the earth or in the sea" (Exodus 20:4).

Israel was odd that way. Middle Eastern ruins are littered with figurines and statues of other GODS—even among people who worshiped a single god.

Most ancient idols don't have their names engraved on them. So archaeologists have to guess which god an idol represents—based on the looks of the idol along with where it was found and how old it is:

- Canaan's god of rain, BAAL, shows up holding a lightning bolt like a SPEAR.
- Fertility gods such as ASHERAH are often holding their breasts.
- Artemis, patron goddess of the city of EPHESUS, showed up all over the ruins of Ephesus.

WHY JEWS WORSHIPED IDOLS

There are several popular guesses about why JEWS were attracted to other gods once they returned to their homeland.

God specialized in war. Given how GOD freed them from EGYPT and helped them retake their homeland, some Jews seemed to figure that WAR was God's specialty. So they worshiped him as one of many.

Canaanites were better farmers. The Jews weren't known for their expertise as farmers. They had been making BRICKS as slaves in Egypt for GENERATIONS. When they saw how well their idol-worshiping neighbors did at FARMING—compared to how poorly they did—they may have figured there was something to the gods the Canaanites worshiped. Especially BAAL, the top god who controlled fertility in family, field, and flock.

Worshiping with sex is fun. Some of the worship rituals seemed to include having SEX with Canaanite priests and priestesses. The sex was to entertain and stimulate the gods, who would then reward the worshipers with RAIN for the crops, lots of CHILDREN, and growing flocks.

WHY JEWS STOPPED WORSHIPING IDOLS

God tried firing warning shots over Israel's bow to steer Jews away from idols.

The warning shots came as PROPHETS, who for the most part got themselves ignored and dissed. God fired

again, with DISEASES, famines, and raiders.

But to get the people's attention, God had to sink their ship.

ISRAEL went under.

In 722 BC, God allowed Assyrian invaders from what is now northern Iraq to dismantle the northern Jewish nation of Israel and deport many of the survivors. In 586 BC, Babylonians from southern Iraq did the same to the southern Jewish nation of JUDAH.

EXILED in Iraq, Jewish survivors finally started paying attention to what the prophets had said, since their words were preserved in WRITING. From that, the Jews concluded that their idolatry was what most upset God. So when Persians from what is now Iran freed them to go home, they left with a determination never to make the same mistake again.

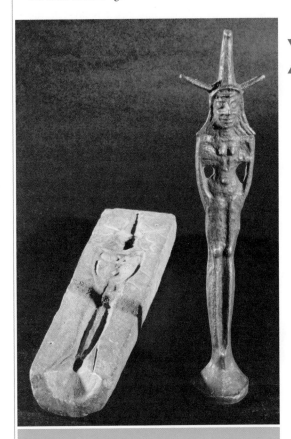

HOW TO MAKE A GOD. Some folks made their idols from molds like this Canaanite one from about the time of Moses. The mold was found in Nahariya, a northern Israeli city along the coast. The modern figurine cast from the mold is of a goddess.

IDUMEA

See Edom, Map 2 J8

(id you ME uh)

A large crowd followed him [Jesus]. They came from all over Galilee, Judea, Jerusalem, Idumea, from east of the Jordan River.
Mark 3:7–8

- Greek for "Edom"
- Homeland of Herod the Great

IN AN ARAB MIGRATION into Israel, displaced citizens of EDOM in what is now Jordan moved into southern Israel. They moved there several centuries before Christ. JEWS eventually forced them to convert to the Jewish faith—or die. That's how the Idumean family of HEROD THE GREAT became Jews. And that's why most Jews didn't consider him their king. Racially, he wasn't a Jew.

ILLYRICUM

Map 3 A2

(ill LEER ee cum)

I [Paul] have fully presented the Good News of Christ from Jerusalem all the way to Illyricum.
Romans 15:19

- Land northwest of Greece

THERE'S NO RECORD of PAUL going this deep into Europe—into what is now Albania and Serbia. But he said his ministry extended that far, perhaps in influence if not PREACHING.

IMAGE OF GOD

God said, "Let us make human beings in our image, to be like us." Genesis 1:26

GOD AND HUMANS have something in common. What it is, scholars can only guess. In a few of their educated guesses, scholars say we resemble GOD in:

- Physical appearance. God looks human. The writer used the same phrase to describe Adam's son SETH "who was just like him—in his very image" (Genesis 5:3).
- Ability to create life. God told humans, "Be fruitful and multiply" (Genesis 1:28).
- The value of our life. God warned NOAH, "If anyone takes a human life, that person's life will also be taken by human hands. For God made human beings in his own image" (Genesis 9:6).

Other guesses include the ability to reason or to love. In addition, the BIBLE teaches that people have a SOUL that's capable of lasting forever.

IMMANUEL

(em MAN u el)

"The virgin will conceive a child! She will give birth to a son and will call him Immanuel."
Isaiah 7:14

- Hebrew for "God is with us"
- Nickname for Jesus

JESUS WASN'T WHO ISAIAH HAD IN MIND when he predicted that a VIRGIN would have a son called Immanuel. ISAIAH was talking about a woman and son in his day, some 700 years before Jesus—perhaps his own WIFE and son. Or maybe the future wife and son of King AHAZ.

He was trying to convince the king of JUDAH that GOD would protect the nation from a coalition ARMY of Syrians and JEWS from the northern Jewish nation of ISRAEL. By the time the child was able to eat solid food, Isaiah promised, God would eliminate the threat.

MATTHEW saw the prophecy pulling a double shift. He applied it also to the Virgin MARY and her son (Matthew 1:23).

See also VIRGIN BIRTH.

IMMORALITY

I can hardly believe the report about the sexual immorality going on. . . . A man in your church is living in sin with his stepmother.
1 Corinthians 5:1

SEX SINS—among the worst sins on the planet. At least they show up in rotten company on the list Jesus put together—a don't-do list that includes "stealing and MURDER" (Mark 7:21 NIrV).

The apostle PAUL said SEX sin is different than most sins because it's "a sin against your own body." He offered this advice: "Run from sexual SIN!" (1 Corinthians 6:18).

IMMORTALITY   (*see* ETERNAL LIFE)

INCENSE

"Aaron must burn sweet-smelling incense on the altar every morning." **Exodus 30:7 NCV**

▪ Scented smoke

GOD GAVE JEWISH PRIESTS a recipe for the incense he wanted them to burn at the WORSHIP center.

"Gather fragrant SPICES—resin droplets [tree sap, perhaps MYRRH], mollusk shell, and galbanum [another tree sap]—and mix these fragrant spices with pure FRANKINCENSE, weighed out in equal amounts. . . . Blend the spices together and sprinkle them with SALT to produce a pure and HOLY incense" (Exodus 30:34–35).

JEWS weren't allowed to use this recipe anywhere else. The smell was unique to worship.

See also CENSER.

A PRIEST BURNS INCENSE during a worship service, much like Jewish priests once did in Bible times.

INCEST

"You must never have sexual relations with a close relative, for I am the LORD." **Leviticus 18:6**

NO SEX ALLOWED with any of the following WOMEN, according to Jewish law—written from a man's point of view: MOTHER, stepmother, daughter, sister, half sister, stepsister, granddaughter, aunt, daughter-in-law, sister-in-law, or any kind of mother-daughter combo. That means if a man has SEX with a woman, he can't have sex later with the woman's mother or daughter. Jumping generations isn't kosher.

INFERTILITY

Her rival wife taunted her cruelly, rubbing it in and never letting her forget that GOD had not given her children. **1 Samuel 1:6 MSG**

▪ Inability to have children
▪ Many Jews considered this a deserved curse from God

MAKE BABIES. That was Job One for WOMEN in Bible times.

I

The more the merrier. And the wealthier. That's because in the days before computer gaming, kids worked.

And when they grew up, they added security to the FAMILY—social security that took care of elderly parents, as well as private security to protect the family with muscle, when needed. When JACOB's daughter DINAH got raped, her brothers charged into the rapist's town and "slaughtered every male there" (Genesis 34:25). Overkill, several centuries before the law, "an eye for an eye."

Some of the BIBLE's most famous women were healed of infertility:

- ABRAHAM's wife SARAH gave BIRTH to ISAAC at age 90.
- Elderly ELIZABETH gave birth to JOHN THE BAPTIST.
- Jacob's wife RACHEL gave birth to JOSEPH and BENJAMIN.
- HANNAH gave birth to the prophet SAMUEL.
- Manoah's WIFE gave birth to SAMSON.

INHERITANCE

> "Get rid of that slave woman and her son. He is not going to share the inheritance with my son, Isaac." Sarah to Abraham, Genesis 21:10

A DOUBLE DIP OF INHERITANCE is what the oldest SON usually got—twice as much as any other son. That was the custom in Bible times.

Daughters got squat, unless they didn't have any brothers. Under Jewish law:

- No sons, daughters inherit the property.
- No daughters, brothers get it.
- No brothers, uncles get it.
- No uncles, nearest male relative gets it (Numbers 27:8–11).

After SARAH gave BIRTH to ISAAC, she talked ABRAHAM into shooing off HAGAR and her son, ISHMAEL. Ishmael was Abraham's oldest son. And even though he was born to Hagar—Sarah's SERVANT who acted as a surrogate mother when Sarah was infertile—by custom Ishmael would have gotten a double share of the inheritance.

It was probably a double share of inheritance that JACOB convinced his brother ESAU to trade him for a BOWL of stew (Genesis 25:33).

INK

> "I wrote them down in ink, word for word, on this scroll." Jeremiah 36:18

SCRIBES used ink made from soot mixed with tree sap—a combo that worked nicely for writing on paper-like PAPYRUS.

But for ink that would stick to the kind of LEATHER parchment used in the 2,000-year-old DEAD SEA SCROLLS, SCRIBES needed a mixture of IRON and crushed oak galls (tiny round insect-made balls that look like warts growing on the leaves).

Most ink was black. But scribes used other colors, too. For red: a mineral called cinnabar. For purple: secretions from sea snails like a murex.

GOOD SAMARITAN INN doesn't date to the time Jesus told the now-famous parable about a Samaritan helping a mugged Jew. But it commemorates the story. And it got the general location right: the barren stretch between Jericho and Jerusalem.

Herod. . .sent soldiers to kill all the boys in and around Bethlehem who were two years old and under. Matthew 2:16

KING HEROD WANTED BABY JESUS DEAD. The king considered Jesus a threat. That's because sages from an Eastern country—perhaps Iraq or Iran—told him a star had signaled the birth of a new Jewish king. HEROD's own scholars said ancient PROPHETS had predicted the MESSIAH would be born in BETHLEHEM.

Herod sent the sages to Bethlehem to check it out and report back to him. When they didn't return, he ordered the Bethlehem boys slaughtered. Jesus escaped because an ANGEL warned JOSEPH to get his FAMILY out of the country. They fled to EGYPT and stayed there until Herod died.

BABY KILLER King Herod the Not-So-Great ordered the execution of all Bethlehem boys ages two and under. After hearing from wise men who had come from abroad to worship the newborn king of the Jews, he was afraid the child would grow up to become the Messiah—leaving Herod with no job and no dynasty to pass on to his boys.

INSPIRATION OF THE BIBLE

I

All Scripture is inspired by God and is useful to teach us what is true and to make us realize what is wrong in our lives. 2 Timothy 3:16

HOW INSPIRED is the Bible? That's the question that gets some Christians riled up.

Many treat the BIBLE almost as though GOD dictated it. They describe SCRIPTURE with words like *infallible* and *inerrant*. And they insist that the original copies—called the "autographs"—had no mistakes. Not even in LETTERS Paul wrote to his friends.

Other Christians ask why we bother talking about the original copies when we don't have any. They say the question should be: How reliable are the Bibles we do have, since our Bibles are copies of copies of translations of translations?

Their answer: Reliable enough. Their tech word to describe that level of inspiration: *plenary*. It means "full" or "complete," as in the Bible has everything anyone needs to know about God and about what God expects of his people.

Either way—whether the Bible's inspiration is "perfect" or "good enough"—most Christians agree that it's

INN

She [Mary] dressed him [Jesus] in baby clothes and laid him on a bed of hay, because there was no room for them in the inn. Luke 2:7 CEV

TRAVELERS OFTEN AVOIDED INNS. For good reason, if ancient reviews are accurate: bedbugs and prostitutes. In Bible times, travelers seemed to prefer the HOSPITALITY of locals.

By Roman times, inns started showing up along popular trade routes. Many were little more than a wall around a WELL, where travelers could rest in the open air alongside their ANIMALS. Others provided shelter, a BED, and food.

In a PARABLE, Jesus said a good SAMARITAN took an injured man to an inn where he paid "the innkeeper two SILVER coins, telling him, 'Take care of this man'" (Luke 10:35).

a mistake to ignore this book. As Jesus told a group of scholars who seemed to know their manmade rules better than they knew their Bible, "Your mistake is that you don't know the Scriptures, and you don't know the power of God" (Matthew 22:29).

When PAUL wrote to TIMOTHY, saying that "All Scripture is inspired by God," Paul was talking about his Bible, the OLD TESTAMENT. The NEW TESTAMENT hadn't been written yet. But Christians came to apply the same confidence in the New Testament that Paul had for the Old Testament.

INTERCESSION

Pray for all people. Ask God to help them; intercede on their behalf. 1 Timothy 2:1

* Praying for someone else

MOSES INTERCEDED for the JEWS when they worshiped a GOLDEN CALF. God said he would kill them all and start over with the FAMILY of MOSES. But Moses convinced GOD to "forgive their SIN" (Exodus 32:32).

IRON

His [Goliath's] spear was like a fence rail—the spear tip alone weighed over fifteen pounds [6.8 kg]. 1 Samuel 17:7 MSG

A SECRET WEAPON is what PHILISTINES called it. Iron swords, SPEAR tips, and chariot ARMOR helped them manhandle the bronze-armed JEWS for at least a century or two.

Iron itself was no secret. It's the most abundant element on earth. The secret was how to stoke a FURNACE hot enough to melt it. Philistines managed to get the temp up over 2000 degrees F (1093 degrees C)—high enough to produce a low grade of the metal: wrought iron.

Philistines during the 1200s BC carefully guarded their secret: "There were no blacksmiths in the land of Israel in those days. The Philistines wouldn't allow them for fear they would make swords and spears for the

IRON: SECRET WEAPON. Philistines controlled the secret of making a fire hot enough to forge iron weapons during the 1200s BC. Jews were stuck with softer bronze until the secret eventually slipped out.

Hebrews. So whenever the Israelites needed to sharpen their plowshares, picks, axes, or sickles, they had to take them to a Philistine blacksmith" (1 Samuel 13:19–20).

It wasn't until around 1000 BC that King DAVID managed to overpower the Philistines. By then, he also had gotten his hands on iron. He stockpiled iron for future construction of the Jerusalem TEMPLE: "so much iron and BRONZE that it cannot be weighed" (1 Chronicles 22:14).

SPARED. Isaac is saved from becoming a human sacrifice when God calls a halt to Abraham's test of faith. God provides a ram, which got stuck in a nearby thicket.

ISAAC

(I zack)

2000s BC

"Your son Isaac will be born about this time next year, and the promise I am making to you and your family will be for him and his descendants forever." **Genesis 17:21** CEV

- Son of Abraham and Sarah
- Father of Jacob and Esau

A MIRACLE BABY, Isaac was born to a woman who had been infertile for about 90 years: SARAH, WIFE of 100-year-old ABRAHAM.

GOD had promised the elderly couple he would give their descendants what is now the land of Israel. Isaac's son, JACOB, would produce a dozen sons who would become the founding fathers of ISRAEL's 12 tribes.

Isaac was an unbuttered bagel kind of guy compared to his dad. Not much adventure in his life—pretty much the opposite of Abraham's story. That's why we have the old saying "An Abraham is usually followed by an Isaac."

Even the most exciting moment in his story was driven by his father. It's when God asked Abraham to SAC-RIFICE Isaac—and then stopped the execution at the last second. Many scholars say God did this to foreshadow his sacrifice of Jesus.

Jewish TRADITION says this near-sacrifice shocked Sarah to death. She died at age 127, which would have put Isaac at age 37.

Three years later, Abraham sent a SERVANT to his former home in HARAN to find a wife for Isaac. The servant came back with a distant relative: REBEKAH. Isaac "loved her and was comforted over the loss of his mother" (Genesis 24:67 CEV).

ISAIAH

(i ZAY uh)

About 740–700 BC

These are the visions that Isaiah son of Amoz saw concerning Judah and Jerusalem.
Isaiah 1:1

- Prophet of southern Jewish nation of Judah

ISAIAH NOT ONLY PREDICTED JESUS 700 years ahead of time. He wrote like he witnessed key events in Jesus' life—such as the VIRGIN BIRTH and CRUCIFIXION.

- "The virgin will conceive a child! . . . [She] will call him IMMANUEL (which means 'GOD is with us')" (Isaiah 7:14).
- "He was pierced for our rebellion. . . . He was buried like a criminal; he was put in a rich man's grave" (Isaiah 53:5, 9).

Details like these are so specific that some skeptics figured Isaiah's prophecies were written after Jesus. Then folks discovered the ancient library of DEAD SEA SCROLLS, which included a copy of Isaiah's prophecies written 100 years before Jesus.

NEW TESTAMENT writers quote Isaiah's prophecies about Jesus so much that some Bible experts call the book of Isaiah the Fifth GOSPEL.

Isaiah's ministry in JERUSALEM spanned four KINGS. He predicted the fall of both Jewish nations: ISRAEL in the north and JUDAH in the south. He lived to see Assyrians from what is now Iraq invade and dismantle Israel in 722 BC. Tradition says Judah's worst king, MANASSEH, ordered Isaiah cut in half with a wooden SAW.

ISAIAH, BOOK OF

(i ZAY uh)

Famous sound bite: For unto us a Child is born, unto us a Son is given; and the government will be upon His shoulder. And His name will be called Wonderful, Counselor, Mighty God, Everlasting Father, Prince of Peace. Isaiah 9:6 NKJV

THE PROMISED LAND IS TOAST. Isaiah says GOD is going to wipe both Jewish nations off the map, ISRAEL in the north and JUDAH in the south. The good news is that God will give the Jews a do-over. He'll send a MESSIAH from King DAVID'S FAMILY to build the best kingdom ever. NEW TESTAMENT writers say Jesus fulfilled that promise.

- Writer: Isaiah, though many experts say he wrote only the first 39 chapters, which are set in his time.
- Time: Chapters 1–39 are set in the 700s BC; 40–55 describe the exile in the 500s BC; 56–66 describe the return from exile

in the 500s and 400s BC.
- Location: Isaiah ministered in Jerusalem, capital of the southern Jewish nation of Judah. His predictions involved nations throughout the Middle East.

BIG SCENES

Isaiah up. In a VISION, Isaiah is transported to God's THRONE room filled with angelic beings. God asks who will deliver his messages to the people. Isaiah answers, "Here I am. Send me." God warns that the people will ignore the messages Isaiah delivers. For how long? Isaiah asks. Until the Jewish homeland lies deserted, God answers. *Isaiah 6*

Virgin Birth. A combo ARMY of Arabs from SYRIA and Jews from the northland nation of Israel threaten Judah. Isaiah tells the king not to worry because Syria and Israel will be eliminated by the time the child of a mysterious VIRGIN (perhaps the king's new WIFE) is able to eat solid food. New Testament writers say this prophecy pulls a double shift—pointing to the VIRGIN BIRTH of Jesus. *Isaiah 7*

Jewish nations fall. Isaiah predicts the fall of both Jewish nations. He'll live to see northland Israel fall to Assyrian invaders in 722 BC. In their 200-year history, Jews in Israel can't manage a single KING who gets a godly thumbs-up. Isaiah's own nation of Judah, which produces just a few godly kings such as HEZEKIAH and JOSIAH, will eventually fall to Babylonians in 586 BC. *Isaiah 9-10, 22, 28*

Enemy nations doomed. Isaiah warns neighboring nations of the Jews that God will soon get around to them. ASSYRIA: "When you are done destroying, you will be destroyed" (Isaiah 33:1). Ditto for BABYLON. Other nations doomed include EGYPT, Syria, and ARABIA. *Isaiah 13, 19, 33*

A suffering savior. Isaiah describes a mysterious suffering "SERVANT" whom many Jews say represents the Jewish people who have suffered throughout history. Many Christians say it's Jesus crucified. Isaiah's description of the servant: despised, innocent, whipped, pierced, treated like a criminal, slaughtered, buried in a rich man's TOMB—all of which seem to track with the story of Jesus' CRUCIFIXION. *Isaiah 53*

A do-over for the Jews. The end of the two

Jewish nations isn't the end of Israel. Like all Jewish PROPHETS who predict destruction for the Jews, Isaiah promises that God will give his people a fresh start. *Isaiah 60–61*

ISHBOSHETH

(ish BO sheth)

Ruled about 1010–1008 BC

Ishbosheth, Saul's son, was forty years old when he became king, and he ruled from Mahanaim for two years. 2 Samuel 2:10

- King Saul's son
- Second king of Israel

A WIMPY KING, Ishbosheth inherited what was left of the throne after his dad and three brothers died in battle against the PHILISTINES. The southland JEWS in the tribe of JUDAH defected to DAVID.

The wimp in him surfaced when he merely accused his general—ABNER—of sleeping with one of SAUL's wives. Any KING worthy of a CROWN would have stuck Abner with a sharp object.

Abner decided to defect to the rebel forces of David. But David's general, JOAB, killed Abner before he had a chance to arrange for his ARMY to join David's forces.

When Ishbosheth heard about Abner's death, "he lost all courage" (2 Samuel 4:1). Two of his SOLDIERS knew a lame duck with they saw one. They assassinated him. Duck soup.

David would become ISRAEL's next king.

ISHMAEL

(ISH mail)

2000s BC

"Name him Ishmael. . . . This son of yours will be a wild man. . . . He will live in open hostility against all his relatives."
Genesis 16:11–12

- Son of Abraham and Hagar
- Half brother of Isaac
- Considered father of Arab nations

ABRAHAM'S FIRST SON, Ishmael, was born to a surrogate mother: HAGAR, slave of ABRAHAM's wife, SARAH.

The plan was for Hagar to produce an heir for her masters. But after Sarah gave BIRTH to her own son, ISAAC, Sarah convinced Abraham to send Hagar and Ishmael away.

Abraham hated the idea because he loved his son. But GOD signed off on Sarah's plan: "Do whatever Sarah tells you, for Isaac is the son through whom your descendants will be counted. But I will also make a nation of the descendants of Hagar's son because he is your son, too" (Genesis 21:12–13).

Ishmael lived to age 137—long enough to father 12 sons who founded a dozen tribes scattered from EGYPT to ARABIA.

I

ABANDONED. When Abraham and Sarah told Hagar to take her son Ishmael and leave, Hagar feared they would die in the desert. But God promised to give Ishmael a nation of descendants. Many consider him the father of the Arab people.

(IS ray uhl)

"Your name will no longer be Jacob. . . . From now on you will be called Israel."
Genesis 32:28

▪ New name God gave Jacob

JACOB WRESTLED a mysterious man all night long. The man may have been GOD, some scholars guess, given what happened afterward. JACOB was heading home, hoping to make peace with ESAU, the brother he had robbed of his INHERITANCE. When the man showed up in Jacob's camp, Jacob grabbed him and wouldn't let go

until the man blessed him. At sunrise the man broke free. Then he gave Jacob the NAME that JEWS would adopt for their nation: Israel. In HEBREW, the word *yisra'el* means "he struggles" (*yisra*) with "God" (*el*).

ISRAEL, NATION OF

Map 3 L7

(IS ray uhl)

"Listen, O Israel! Today you are about to cross the Jordan River to take over the land."
Deuteronomy 9:1

▪ Jewish nation descended from Abraham

ISRAEL IS DEAD AND GONE. That news flash—by a bragging Egyptian king in about 1230 BC—is the first time Israel's name shows up outside the BIBLE. King Merneptah introduced Israel to the world by claiming he had wiped them off the planet.

The Jewish nation began nearly a thousand years earlier as a promise to ABRAHAM, a 99-year-old man with an 89-year-old infertile wife, SARAH:

> *"I will give you many children. . . . I will give you the whole land of Canaan. You will own it forever. So will your children after you."*
> GENESIS 17:6, 8 NIrv

Abraham's grandson JACOB later moved the entire extended FAMILY to EGYPT—at the king's invitation. The JEWS went there to weather out a DROUGHT. They ended up staying "430 years" (Exodus 12:40). The family grew so large that a later king considered them a threat to national security. So he enslaved them all. MOSES convinced the king to free the Jews—though Moses had to unleash 10 plagues on the country before the king took him seriously. JOSHUA led the invasion into CANAAN, now known as Israel and Palestinian territories.

Joshua divided the land among Israel's 12 tribes, each tribe an extended family descended from a son of

Mediterranean Sea

LEBANON

Beirut

Damascus

Mount Hermon

Golan Heights

SYRIA

Sea of Galilee

Nazareth

Tel Aviv

West Bank

Amman

Jerusalem

Gaza Strip

Dead Sea

ISRAEL

JORDAN

EGYPT

Gulf of Aqaba (Red Sea)

N

SURROUNDED BY ARABS and the deep blue sea, the predominately Jewish nation of Israel makes security a top priority. Many Palestinians accuse the Jews of apartheid. Many Jews say they have no choice but to isolate Palestinians in an attempt to protect themselves from terrorist attacks.

Jacob. It is unclear when this happened. Some scholars say in the 1400s. Others say in the 1200s.

GOD was their KING. Prophets such as SAMUEL spoke for God. But when elderly Samuel appointed his BRIBE-taking sons as leaders for the next generation, tribal elders objected. "Your sons are not like you," they said. "Give us a king" (1 Samuel 8:5).

Enter the DONKEY herder SAUL, Israel's first king.

Then a SHEPHERD, DAVID, Israel's most celebrated king. He did what Saul couldn't. He secured Israel's borders. David's son SOLOMON expanded Israel's reach north, all the way to the EUPHRATES RIVER, in what is now Syria.

Sadly, the people got fed up with Solomon's never-ending building projects—TEMPLE, PALACES, fortress cities. Solomon funded the projects with taxes. And he secured the workforce by drafting his people, as some countries today draft young adults for military service.

When Solomon's son REHOBOAM succeeded him, the people thought it was a perfect time to ask for a break. They thought wrong. King Rehoboam vowed higher taxes and harder work.

Northerners seceded from the union. The country split in two. Rehoboam's tribe stuck with him: JUDAH. That became the name of the southern Jewish nation. The tribe of BENJAMIN joined them. All the tribes up north started their own country: Israel.

Southerners WORSHIPED at the JERUSALEM Temple. Northerners worshiped calf IDOLS at the cities of BETHEL and DAN.

Northern kings were stinkers, spiritually speaking. In over 200 years of rule, not one of Israel's 19 kings got a godly thumbs-up. Assyrian invaders from what is now Iraq ended the nation in 722 BC, deporting the survivors who became known as the lost TRIBES OF ISRAEL. Southern kings weren't much better. Of Judah's 20 kings in about 350 years, only four got God's stamp of approval. Babylonian invaders ended that nation, leveled Jerusalem, and deported many survivors in 586 BC.

About 50 years later, Persians from what is now Iran defeated the Babylonians to become the world's new superpower. They freed the Jews, many of whom went home to start rebuilding Jerusalem and their homeland. But the Jews weren't able to regain their former glory. They had to bow to one master after another. Persians. Then the Greeks. And finally the Romans, who occupied

BEFORE ISRAEL'S rebirth as a nation in 1948, Jews like this man pictured at the turn of the 1900s began moving back to Palestine and buying up tracts of land. It started as a Zionist movement in 1897, when one Jew—Theodor Herzl—had a dream of creating a legally recognized homeland for the Jews.

their homeland for over a century before destroying Jerusalem and its Temple in AD 70. Jews haven't had a Temple since. That's when the Jewish sacrificial system died, along with the priesthood that conducted those rituals.

Arabs invaded Israel in the AD 600s and controlled the Jewish homeland for the next 1,300 years.

ISRAEL TODAY

Many Jews wanted their country back. In 1897 a Jewish Hungarian journalist named Theodor Herzl organized a Zionist movement. His goal: create for the Jews a home in Israel, recognized by law.

Jews started returning to Israel, buying property from Palestinians.

The genocide of six million Jews during World War II convinced the United Nations that the Jews needed a

DRAFTED. Once they reach the age of 18, Jewish men and women alike are required to serve in the Israel Defense Forces. Three years for the men. Two for the women.

safe haven—a homeland. They proposed dividing Israel among the Jews and the Arabs.

No deal. Arabs rejected it. The Jews responded by declaring Israel's independence in 1948. War broke out. And another in 1967. Jews won both. In the process, they captured the Sinai and the Gaza Strip from Egypt, the West Bank from Jordan, and the Golan Heights from Syria.

They gave the Sinai back to Egypt in 1979, in trade for peace. And they gave the Palestinian Authority control of the Gaza Strip and selected cities and rural areas inside the West Bank.

It's not enough for many Palestinians who don't recognize the nation of Israel at all. It's too much for some Jews who insist that God gave them the land—forever.

Moderates on both sides struggle to find a way to peace.

One nation, with Jews and Palestinians as equal citizens—not on the table at the moment.

Separate mini-nations, segregated by race—on the table. For decades.

The question isn't just how much land the Israelis should trade for peace—in a region the size of New Jersey and surrounded by Arab nations and the deep blue sea. The question is also what to do about Palestinians and Jews who each want it all.

Little wonder that Palestinians and Jews alike ask tourists visiting the Holy Land to "Pray for the PEACE of Jerusalem" (Psalm 122:6 KJV).

ISRAEL, THREE STATS

Size: New Jersey—about 250 miles long, 70 miles wide (400 by 113 km)

Population: 8 million—6 million Jews, 2 million Palestinians

Religion: 4.8 million Jews
1.3 million Muslims
1.2 million secular Jews
160,000 Christians

ISRAEL, ON THE CLOCK:
BIG EVENTS

2000 BC*	God promises the land to Abraham's descendants
1900	Jacob moves Jews to Egypt to escape drought
1440 or 1290	Moses leads Jews out of Egyptian slavery
1400 or 1250	Joshua leads invasion of Canaan
1044	Saul becomes Israel's first king
1000	King David makes Jerusalem his capital
956	King Solomon builds the first Temple
930	Israel splits in two: Judah, Israel
722	Assyria erases Israel from the map
586	Babylon erases Judah from the map
538	Jews return to Jerusalem to rebuild
63	Romans capture Jerusalem
AD 66	Jews revolt against Roman occupation
70	Romans destroy Jerusalem and Temple
614	Muslim Arabs invade, capture Israel
1099	Christian Crusaders fight to recapture Israel
1947	UN proposes division of land: Jews/Palestinians
1948	Israel declares independence; wins war
1967	Israel captures West Bank in Six-Day War

*Most dates approximate

ISSACHAR

(IS uh car)

1800s BC

The sons of Leah were Reuben (Jacob's oldest son), Simeon, Levi, Judah, Issachar, and Zebulun. **Genesis 35:23**

- Fifth son of Jacob and Leah

IN A BATTLE to see who could give Jacob the most sons, his wives, Rachel and Leah, made a trade. Rachel, who was infertile, bought from Leah a mandrake root thought to cure infertility. The price she paid: give Leah an extra night with Jacob. That's when Leah conceived Issachar. Sperm 1, Mandrake 0.

ISSACHAR, TRIBE OF

Map 1 D4

(IS uh car)

Issachar was the fourth tribe chosen to receive land. The northern border for its clans went from Mount Tabor east to the Jordan River. **Joshua 19:17 CEV**

MOSTLY RUGGED HILLS south of the Sea of Galilee is what the tribe of Issachar got when Joshua divided the Jewish homeland among the 12 tribes. The plug of ground stretched about 20 miles wide and 10 miles north to south (32 by 16 km).

IVORY

The king [Solomon] made a huge throne, decorated with ivory and overlaid with fine gold. **1 Kings 10:18**

A LUXURY ITEM, thanks to elephant tusks, ivory was used in jewelry, lavish furniture, inlaid panels, and other decorations. In early Bible times, during the days of King Solomon, elephants roamed throughout Syria—Israel's neighbor to the northeast.

JABBOK RIVER

Map 1 E5

(JAB bock)

During the night Jacob got up and took his two wives, his two servant wives, and his eleven sons and crossed the Jabbok River with them. Genesis 32:22

ISRAEL GOT ITS NAME along the banks of the Jabbok River in what is now the Arab country of Jordan. That's where JACOB, returning home for a tense reunion with his brother ESAU, spent the night wrestling a mysterious man that some scholars speculate was GOD—or at least an ANGEL. The man renamed Jacob "ISRAEL," the name JEWS would adopt for their nation.

JABIN

(JAY bin)

1400s BC or 1200s BC (debated)

On that day Israel saw God defeat Jabin, the Canaanite king. Judges 4:23

- two kings of Canaanite city of Hazor

JOSHUA'S MILITIA, invading what is now ISRAEL, launched a surprise attack on a coalition of perhaps a dozen armies in the northland led by King Jabin.

JOSHUA managed to neutralize Jabin's tactical advantage: "Joshua crippled the horses and burned all the chariots" (Joshua 11:9). Joshua's militia won the battle.

Several GENERATIONS later, Jewish SOLDIERS led by the prophet DEBORAH defeated another King Jabin of HAZOR. His CHARIOT corps invaded GALILEE but got stuck in mud during a rainstorm.

JACOB

(JAY cub)

1900s BC

Esau said to Jacob, "I'm starved! Give me some of that red stew!"... "All right," Jacob replied, "but trade me your rights as the firstborn son." Genesis 25:30–31

- Father of 12 sons/tribes of Israel
- Son of Isaac and Rebekah

A CROOK, at least in his early years, Jacob is perhaps most famous for cheating his twin brother.

That's saying something, because he's also well known as:

- one of the founding fathers of the Jewish nation
- father of 12 sons who produced ISRAEL's 12 tribes
- the man whose God-given NAME late in life—Israel—became the country's name.

Jacob cheated his older twin ESAU out of two important perks of being the oldest brother.

A double share of the family estate. He got that by exploiting Esau's hunger after a hunt. Jacob wouldn't give Esau any stew until Esau agreed to give Jacob this INHERITANCE right as the oldest SON.

The father's deathbed blessing. ISAAC loved Esau best and planned to give him the best BLESSING. Jacob exploited Isaac's near BLINDNESS and pretended to be Esau. So he stole the best blessing.

When Esau vowed to kill Jacob for this, Jacob fled 700 miles (1,100 km) north, to relatives in southern Turkey. But along the way he had a DREAM. It's a bit shocking to many readers because the dream suggests that GOD saw something good in this dirt bag of a human being. God promised to give the land to Jacob's descendants. This was a continuation of God's promise to do the same to Jacob's grandfather, ABRAHAM.

HOW TO CHEAT A CHEATER

Working in Turkey as a SHEPHERD for his Uncle LABAN, Jacob got what most readers would agree he deserved: cheated.

It happened after he fell in love with Laban's daughter RACHEL, and agreed to work as Laban's shepherd for seven years for the right to marry her. On the WEDDING night, Laban pulled a switcheroo.

Jacob woke up the next morning with the wrong woman: Rachel's older sister LEAH, who was apparently hard on the eyes.

Laban said it was customary to marry off the oldest daughter first. But apparently it wasn't customary to bother telling the groom what the custom was. Jacob got to marry Rachel a week later, but only after agreeing to work another seven years for Uncle Laban.

Wives had one main job in Bible times: make babies. Sisters Rachel and Leah launched into a baby-making competition. "The LORD knew that Jacob loved Rachel more than he did Leah, and so he gave CHILDREN to Leah, but not to Rachel" (Genesis 29:31 CEV).

When the score hit 4 to 0, Rachel told Jacob to use her SERVANT Bilhah as a surrogate mother. Leah offered Jacob her servant as well: Zilpah. Jacob ended up with a dozen boys (two by Rachel) and one daughter, DINAH.

After 14 years of serving Laban followed by six more of working for a share of the flocks, Jacob became wealthy with flocks of his own. He decided to go home—hoping Esau had cooled off but fearing he hadn't.

In one of the BIBLE's weirdest stories, Jacob on his way home spent the night wrestling a man who sounds like a celestial being. Bible experts guess that the man may have been an ANGEL or God himself—or perhaps the story is a metaphor about Jacob wrestling with his own troubles.

Jacob refused to release the man until he got a blessing. About daybreak, the man said, "Your NAME will no longer be Jacob. You have wrestled with God and with men, and you have won. That's why your name will be Israel" (Genesis 32:28 CEV).

A few hours later, Esau arrived, welcoming his brother with a hug.

Jacob settled in what is now south Israel, near HEBRON. He died in EGYPT after moving his FAMILY there during a DROUGHT. But his son JOSEPH EMBALMED his body and took him home for BURIAL in the cave TOMB where his father and grandfather were buried.

JACOB'S WELL   Map 4 C5

The well that Jacob had dug was still there, and Jesus sat down beside it. . . . A Samaritan woman came to draw water from the well.
John 4:6–8 CEV

JEWS AND SAMARITANS were about as friendly as today's Israelis and Palestinians. Yet Jesus asked a SAMARITAN woman to draw him some WATER from a well Jacob had dug—offering in return to give her spiritual "living water."

RUNAWAY JACOB, in a dream, sees a stairway to heaven. At the top is God, promising to give Jacob's descendants all the land in the region today called Israel.

J

241

Early CHRISTIAN tradition places the well in central Israel, beneath a CHURCH in the city of Balatah. Still a deep well, the water level fluctuates between about 75 and 100 feet (23–30 m).

JAEL

(JAY el)

1100s BC

Sisera. . .fell fast asleep. Jael took a hammer and drove a tent-peg through his head into the ground, and he died. Judges 4:21 CEV

- "Wife of Heber the Kenite" (Judges 5:24)
- Killed Canaanite commander Sisera

A HERDER'S WIFE with a hammer and a TENT peg managed to kill ISRAEL's most feared enemy.

That enemy—SISERA, a Canaanite commander of a CHARIOT corps—ran for his life after losing a battle with the JEWS. His ARMY had been raiding Jews in GALILEE for about 20 years.

Headed home, he stopped at Jael's tent for a drink of MILK and a power nap.

He never woke up.

The BIBLE doesn't say if Jael was a Jew. But she was married to a KENITE, people who had treated the Jews kindly (1 Samuel 15:6). So she may have been looking out for the Jews. Otherwise, she may have missed the lecture on

IF I HAD A HAMMER. A herder's wife named Jael hammers a tent peg into a napping Canaanite commander on the run from a lost battle.

HOSPITALITY. Or she could have been putting up another tent but was tragically nearsighted. As in, "Oops."

JAIRUS

(jay I russ)

First century AD

Jairus, a leader of the synagogue, came to Jesus. . . . Jairus' only daughter, about twelve years old, was dying. Luke 8:41–42 NCV

- Jesus raised his daughter from the dead

FAMILY AND FRIENDS were already MOURNING Jairus's daughter when he arrived with Jesus. The Capernaum SYNAGOGUE leader had hoped Jesus would heal the girl. Instead, Jesus raised her from the dead. But not before the mourners broke into laughter at Jesus' diagnosis: "She's only asleep" (Luke 8:52). He soon gave them another reason to laugh.

JAMES, BROTHER OF JESUS

Executed about AD 66

"He is just the son of a carpenter. His mother is Mary, and his brothers are James, Joseph, Simon, and Judas." Matthew 13:55 NCV

- Brother of Jesus
- Leader of Jerusalem church

JESUS WAS A FAKE MESSIAH as far as his brothers were concerned—James included: "Even his brothers didn't believe in him" (John 7:5).

There's no telling when brother James changed his mind. Perhaps at the RESURRECTION: "He [Jesus] appeared to James. Then he appeared to all the apostles" (1 Corinthians 15:7 NIRV).

James became leader of the CHURCH in JERUSALEM— and the bull's-eye target of JEWS who considered CHRISTIANITY a HERESY. First-century Jewish historian Josephus reported that Jews pushed James from a high spot at the TEMPLE and finished him off by STONING him.

Many Bible experts credit James with writing the short New Testament LETTER of James.

JAMES, DISCIPLE

Executed about AD 44

King Herod Agrippa began to persecute some believers. . . . He had the apostle James (John's brother) killed with a sword.

Acts 12:1-2

- Brother of John
- A favorite disciple of Jesus

ONE OF THE FIRST DISCIPLES to join Jesus, James was the first to die for it.

King HEROD AGRIPPA started persecuting Christians, apparently to boost his popularity among the JEWS. He ordered James executed about a decade after Jesus' CRUCIFIXION.

Before becoming Jesus' DISCIPLES, James and his brother, JOHN, were fishermen who worked on the SEA OF GALILEE with their dad, ZEBEDEE.

The brothers, along with PETER, became Jesus' three best friends. He took them with him when he left other disciples behind: at the TRANSFIGURATION when ELIJAH and MOSES appeared (Matthew 17:1), and during the PRAYER in GETHSEMANE on the night of his arrest (Mark 14:33).

Nicknamed the "SONS OF THUNDER," James and John seemed to have an extra helping of adrenaline. When a SAMARITAN village turned Jesus away, they asked permission from Jesus to "call down fire from heaven to burn them up" (Luke 9:54). Jesus declined.

Early CHRISTIAN writings report that during the decade after Jesus ascended into HEAVEN, James preached in SPAIN, where he is now the patron saint.

JAMES, LETTER OF

Famous sound bite: Faith in Jesus isn't enough. Unless it compels you to do kind things for others, your faith is worthless.

James 2:17 author's paraphrase

- Writer: James—likely the brother of Jesus and leader of the Jerusalem church, many Bible experts say.
- Time: Probably written during the first three decades after Jesus returned to heaven. Jews executed James in about AD 66.
- Location: James writes to "Jewish believers scattered abroad" (James 1:1).

J

HOME OF THE RICH. Excavations in Jerusalem's Jewish Quarter unearthed the ruins of a rich Jew's house, depicted here. James warned people who got rich by walking on the backs of the poor: "This treasure you have accumulated will stand as evidence against you" (James 5:3).

BIG SCENES

The bright side of suffering. Living in the city where JEWS orchestrated the execution of Jesus, James likely faces PERSECUTION every day. But James encourages all believers facing persecution: "Consider it an opportunity for great joy. For you know that when your FAITH is tested, your endurance has a chance to grow." *James 1*

Treat the poor like they're rich. There's a tendency to treat rich folks like they're better than poor folks, James says. They're not. POOR folks are better. In at least two ways, according to James. (1) They're not the ones oppressing and exploiting people. (2) They're the ones GOD favors: "Aren't they the ones who will inherit the Kingdom?" James is quoting Jesus' SERMON ON THE MOUNT, Matthew 5:3, "God blesses those who are poor . . .for the KINGDOM OF HEAVEN is theirs." *James 2:1–13*

Got religion? Act like it. "What good is it, dear brothers and sisters, if you say you have faith but don't show it by your actions. . . . Faith by itself isn't enough. Unless it produces good deeds, it is dead and useless." *James 2:14–26*

Watch your mouth. The tongue is tiny, but so is the spark that starts a forest fire. "The tongue is a flame," James warns. "It can set your whole life on fire." James doesn't suggest that people can perfectly master their mouths. People can't be perfect. But they can be careful. *James 3*

Pray. It makes a difference. "The PRAYER of a godly person is powerful," James says. "It makes things happen" (James 5:16 NIrV). James actually seems to add that if we pray for HEALING, we'll be healed. Period. But most Bible experts say he's presuming Christians will defer to God's will, as Jesus did when he prayed on the night of his arrest: "I want your will to be done, not mine" (Matthew 26:39). *James 5*

JAPHETH

(JAY fith)

Before 2500 BC

Noah was the father of three sons: Shem, Ham, and Japheth. Genesis 6:10

ONE OF NOAH'S GOOD SONS, Japheth refused to do what his brother HAM did: take a look at NOAH as

he lay passed out, drunk, and naked. SHEM and Japheth backed into Noah's TENT and covered him.

JASHAR, BOOK OF

(JAY shar)

The sun stood still and the moon stayed in place. . . . Is this event not recorded in The Book of Jashar? Joshua 10:13

HEROIC STORIES OF THE JEWS are probably what the lost *Book of Jashar* contained, Bible experts speculate.

One story: JOSHUA's battlefield victory after praying for the sun to stop moving or shining so intensely; scholars debate which. The book also contained a funeral SONG DAVID wrote to honor King SAUL and JONATHAN: "the Song of the Bow" (2 Samuel 1:18).

JEBUSITES

(JEB u sites)

David then led his men to Jerusalem to fight against the Jebusites, the original inhabitants of the land who were living there. 2 Samuel 5:6

JERUSALEM WAS JEBUS before King DAVID conquered it. Mounted on a ridgetop and protected by walls, Jebus was easy to defend and tough to attack. That's why the JEWS still didn't have control of it centuries after they invaded what is now ISRAEL.

David's men found a secret way into the city. They apparently climbed a shaft the Jebusites used like a WELL to dip their BUCKETS into a spring in a cave below the ridgetop.

JEHOAHAZ

(juh HO uh has)

Reigned about 815–802 BC

When Jehu died. . .his son Jehoahaz became the next king. 2 Kings 10:35

- King of northern Jewish nation of Israel

THE DYNASTY OF AHAB AND JEZEBEL died the day a CHARIOT commander named JEHU led a coup and assassinated AHAB's son, King JORAM. Jehu became king. Jehu's son, Jehoahaz, took over when Jehu died.

Constant battles with SYRIA left ISRAEL weak. "Jehoahaz's ARMY was reduced to 50 charioteers, 10 chariots, and 10,000 foot SOLDIERS" (2 Kings 13:7). Meanwhile, the Assyrian Empire in what is now Iraq was on the rise. Within about 80 years, in 722 BC, Assyrian invaders dismantled Israel and evicted Jewish survivors from their homeland.

JEHOIACHIN

(juh HOY uh kin)

Reigned in 597 BC

Jehoiachin was eighteen years old when he became king, and he reigned in Jerusalem three months. 2 Kings 24:8

- King of southern Jewish nation of Judah

SURRENDER became the first item of business for newly crowned, 18-year-old King Jehoiachin.

With three strikes of rotten luck against him, he was already out before he stepped up to the plate.

- Strike 1. His father, King Jehoiakim, had stopped paying taxes to the most powerful king in Babylonian history: Nebuchadnezzar.
- Strike 2. Nebuchadnezzar had come to collect, laying siege to Jerusalem.
- Strike 3. Jehoiachin's dad died, leaving him in charge.

Jehoiachin surrendered. Nebuchadnezzar took him and all of Jerusalem's top officials captive to Babylon, where he could keep an eye on them.

JEHOIAKIM

(juh HOY uh kim)

Reigned 609–598 BC

During Jehoiakim's reign, King Nebuchadnezzar of Babylon invaded. . . . Jehoiakim surrendered and paid him tribute for three years but then rebelled. 2 Kings 24:1

- King of south Jewish nation of Judah

DOUBLE-DIPPED IN DUMBNESS, King Jehoiakim is famous for two standout acts of stupidity.

Stupid, part one. He shredded the SCROLL of prophecies JEREMIAH dictated. Those prophecies warned the JEWS to stop sinning and not to resist BABYLON. Jeremiah dictated a second draft, adding criticism of the king.

Stupid, part two. He rebelled against the strongest king in Babylonian history. He did this by withholding TAX money to NEBUCHADNEZZAR's Babylonian Empire.

Nebuchadnezzar came to collect. He took more than taxes. Jehoiakim died, apparently of natural causes. His son JEHOIACHIN took over just in time to surrender. Nebuchadnezzar looted the city and took the king and all of JERUSALEM's social elite captive to Babylon.

J

JEHOSHAPHAT

(juh HAH suh fat)

Reigned 873–849 BC

When the Aramean chariot commanders saw Jehoshaphat in his royal robes, they went after him. 1 Kings 22:32

- King of the southern Jewish nation of Judah

MISTAKEN IDENTITY nearly got King Jehoshaphat killed in battle.

He and AHAB, king of the northern Jewish nation of ISRAEL, had joined forces to fight an ARMY from what is now Syria. The Syrian king told his men to target Ahab, a respected warrior-king who knew his way around a battlefield.

Jehoshaphat, not quite so savvy, wore a royal ROBE to battle. He might as well have worn a bull's-eye.

Once the enemy spotted him, they thought he was Ahab. They lit out after him. He screamed. The BIBLE doesn't say what. But it convinced the attackers he wasn't King Ahab of macho military fame. Jehoshaphat hitting high C might have done the trick.

Ahab died in the battle, killed by a stray arrow that pierced a joint in his ARMOR.

JEHOVAH

(juh HO vah)

God is my salvation. . .the LORD JEHOVAH is my strength and my song. Isaiah 12:2 KJV

- Means "the Lord"

"I AM" is God's NAME, as GOD explained to MOSES in their first meeting—at the BURNING BUSH.

Written in ancient HEBREW shorthand, without vowels, that translates into English as YHWH. Scholars guess at the vowels: YAHWEH (YAH way).

At the time scholars translated the King James Version of the BIBLE, they used different letters—JHVH—and filled them in with different vowels: JEHOVAH.

JEHU

(JAY hue)

Reigned 842–814 BC

"It must be Jehu son of Nimshi, for he's driving like a madman." 2 Kings 9:20

- Chariot commander who led a coup

AHAB AND JEZEBEL'S DYNASTY ended with a coup. AHAB was already dead, killed in battle. But his son, JORAM, was king of ISRAEL. JEZEBEL served as the queen mother.

Jehu killed them both. He shot Joram with an arrow. And he convinced Jezebel's SERVANTS to toss her sorry self out an upstairs window; it didn't take much convincing—with the king already dead and Jezebel deserving the title Queen of Mean.

Jehu got the idea for a coup from the prophet ELISHA. The prophet privately ANOINTED him as Israel's next KING. Jehu seemed to pass this off as the act of a nutcase.

But when he told his troops about it, they rallied like a charged political caucus waving sharp objects.

Suddenly wanting to be king, Jehu led his men on a wild ride some 40 miles (64 km) west, to the king's summer PALACE at JEZREEL. After killing the king, he ordered the heads of all 70 of Ahab's other sons.

ISRAEL'S KING JEHU BOWS before Assyrian king Shalmaneser III, while delivering tribute—taxes demanded by the empire. The art is a scene from the Black Obelisk of Shalmaneser, dated about 827 BC, during Jehu's lifetime.

JEPHTHAH

(JEFF thuh)

1100s BC

Jephthah was a strong soldier. . . . His father was named Gilead, and his mother was a prostitute. Judges 11:1 NCV

- Heroic Jewish warrior
- Made a dumb vow that killed his daughter

IT WASN'T HIS FAULT that he got booted out of his FAMILY.

It was his dad's fault.

Jephthah wasn't born to his dad's WIFE. He was born to his dad's hooker.

Jephthah's half brothers—born to his dad's wife—

shooed him off: "You're not family. We're not about to let you inherit any of the family estate" (Judges 11:2 AUTHOR'S PARAPHRASE).

Jephthah moved away and started an ARMY. Great timing. Ammonites in what is now Jordan had decided to take back the land that the JEWS had captured in the time of MOSES.

Panicked, Jewish leaders recruited Jephthah and his ready-made army. That's when Jephthah made a tragic promise. He said if he won the battle, he'd SACRIFICE the first thing that greeted him when he came home—as though it might be a GOAT instead of his daughter.

He won the battle. He lost his daughter. She's the one who greeted him. "Her father kept the vow" (Judges 11:39).

JEREMIAH

(jerr uh MY uh)

Prophesied 627–586 BC

Zedekiah, his servants, and the people of Judah did not listen to the words the LORD had spoken through Jeremiah the prophet.
Jeremiah 37:2 NCV

- Prophet who wrote the book of Jeremiah
- Saw Babylonians destroy Jerusalem

BARELY A TEENAGER—perhaps just 13—Jeremiah got GOD's call to deliver the worst news in Jewish history: Their nation was about to get erased from the world map.

It was a horrifying prophecy, which Jeremiah lived to see.

The son of a PRIEST, Jeremiah lived in ANATHOTH, a village about 3 miles (5 km) north of JERUSALEM. He could have been a priest, too—a lucrative, respected job. Instead, God gave him the thankless job of delivering news that no one wanted to hear—and that most people ignored.

He started off well, however. His 40-year ministry began the same year that King JOSIAH—the last good Jewish KING—launched a spiritual reform movement. The king destroyed pagan shrines. But when Josiah died about 20 years later, it was all downhill for JUDAH, the last surviving Jewish nation.

Jeremiah lived through four godless kings, warning them to turn the nation back to God. That's when he wrote the book of Jeremiah—twice. King JEHOIAKIM burned the first copy.

When Babylonian invaders arrived from what is now Iraq, Jeremiah advised surrender. For that, the Babylonians spared him. But they didn't spare Judah or its capital, Jerusalem. Once Babylonians broke through the walls, they leveled the city, slaughtered many of the Jews, and then took most of the others captive to BABYLON.

Remaining Jews fled to EGYPT, forcing elderly Jeremiah to go with them. That's the last mention of him in any documents that survive.

THE WEEPING PROPHET. That's the nickname of Jeremiah, shown here lamenting over the fall of Jerusalem. He predicted the fall. Then he witnessed it. Babylonian soldiers from what is now Iraq leveled the city and destroyed the Temple.

JEREMIAH, BOOK OF

Famous sound bite: Can a leopard change his spots? Jeremiah 13:23 NCV

IT'S LIGHTS OUT FOR JERUSALEM and the last surviving Jewish nation: JUDAH. GOD assigns a boy named Jeremiah to spend the next 40 years warning JEWS about the coming horror—the end of ISRAEL. Jeremiah lives to see his horrifying predictions come true.

- Writer: Jeremiah dictated it to a scribe named Baruch (Jeremiah 36:4).
- Time: Jeremiah ministered about 40 years: 627–586 BC.
- Location: Judah, the southern Jewish nation with its capital in Jerusalem.

BIG SCENES

Kid prophet. "I can't speak in public," Jeremiah objected when God told him to become a PROPHET; "I'm just a kid" (Jeremiah 1:6 AUTHOR'S PARAPHRASE). The HEBREW word for "kid," many Bible experts say, suggests about age 13. That's when Jewish boys today celebrate their coming-of-age Bar Mitzvah. *Jeremiah 1*

Sins of the Jews. Jeremiah lays out God's case against the Jews like he's the prosecuting attorney in COURT. He lists one SIN after another, including the worst sin of all: Idolatry. "One GENERATION after another has set up pagan altars. . .everywhere in your country" (Jeremiah 17:2 CEV). Jeremiah puts it this way—JUDAH's idolatry is to God what a WIFE's ADULTERY is to her HUSBAND. *Jeremiah 5, 17*

Jews in a pottery shop. God sends Jeremiah to a POTTERY shop for an object lesson. Jeremiah sees the potter mess up a pot-in-process. The potter smashes the clay back into a ball and starts over. God says that's exactly what he's going to do to the Jewish nation. *Jeremiah 18*

Sentence: 70 years. Time is up. It's too late for the Jews to repent. God is sending Babylonian invaders from what is now Iraq to punish the Jews. The PROMISED LAND will become a "desolate wasteland." Jews lucky enough to survive will get deported and will live as refugees "for seventy years." *Jeremiah 25*

Jerusalem is toast. BABYLON's ARMY surrounds JERUSALEM on January 15, 588 BC. The SIEGE drags on for two and a half years, starving many Jews to death. When Babylon finally breaks through the walls, they slaughter many of the civilians and take most of the survivors captive. As for the city, they burn it and level it—as they had already done to outlying Jewish cities. By the time they're done, the Jewish nation is done. No KING. No capital. No government. It's erased from the world's map. *Jeremiah 39, 52*

JERICHO

Map 1 D5

(JERR uh koh)

Priests blew their trumpets. . .and the soldiers shouted as loud as they could. The walls of Jericho fell flat. Joshua 6:20 CEV

- Canaanite border town destroyed by Jews
- Home of tax collector Zacchaeus
- Winter getaway for Herod the Great

WHEN JERICHO'S WALLS came tumbling down, it was more of an attention-getter than most folks realize.

Those weren't just any walls.

Jericho was the oldest WALLED CITY on the planet—as far as archaeologists have been able to tell. They estimate the city was 7,000 years old by the time JOSHUA and his Jewish militia arrived.

A border town on a sprawling oasis, Jericho perched itself on top of a 10-acre knoll—a mound about 75 feet (23 m) high, stretching about 350 yards long by 150 yards wide (320 by 137 m). Surrounded by double walls—one high and one low—Jericho must have looked impregnable.

Until the walls fell down.

Then it looked like a speed bump.

OASIS CITY

People loved this town because of its location about 6 miles (10 km) on CANAAN's side of the JORDAN RIVER—in what is now the West Bank. For two main reasons:

- mild, tropical climate for year-round FARMING
- plenty of spring WATER

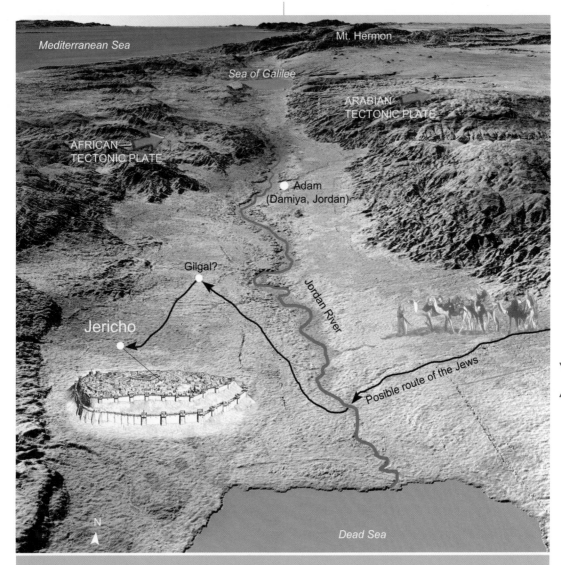

Mediterranean Sea

Mt. Hermon

Sea of Galilee

ARABIAN
TECTONIC PLATE

AFRICAN
TECTONIC PLATE

Adam
(Damiya, Jordan)

Gilgal?

Jericho

Jordan River

Posible route of the Jews

N

Dead Sea

QUAKE ZONE. One theory of how God dropped the walls of Jericho and dammed the Jordan River so Joshua and the Jews could cross into Canaan: earthquake and aftershocks. The Jordan River lies on a fault line, where two plates of land are shifting northeast at different speeds. In 1927 a quake dropped some cliffs into the Jordan, damming the river for 21 hours. It happened at the very site where the Bible says the water stopped for Joshua: near the Jordanian city of Adam, known today as Damiya.

The winters are so mild there—about 800 feet (244 m) below sea level—that King HEROD THE GREAT built a luxurious winter getaway with three PALACES and a near Olympic-size swimming pool.

BIBLE STORIES FROM JERICHO

Jericho is most famous for falling down. But other Bible stories played out there, too.

Spies. Joshua sent two SPIES to scout the town.

They talked too much and almost got arrested. But with the help of a PROSTITUTE named RAHAB, they escaped. In turn, the JEWS spared Rahab and her FAMILY.

Walls down. Archaeologists can't agree when the walls fell. Some have said in about 1400 BC. Some guess around 1200 BC. Erosion did a job on the evidence because Jericho lay dead until the time of ELIJAH and King AHAB, the 800s BC—that's four to six centuries.

Runaway king. After Babylonian invaders

destroyed JERUSALEM in 586 BC, Jewish King ZEDEKIAH made a run for it. He got as far as the Jericho plains, about 20 miles (32 km) away, before Babylonians caught him.

Jesus met tax man. New Testament Jericho grew up a couple miles (3 km) away. There is where Jesus noticed the tax man ZACCHAEUS up a tree, trying to catch a glimpse of him as he passed through on his way to Jerusalem. To everyone's shock, Jesus spent the night with Zacchaeus—who ended up vowing an over-the-top TAX refund to everyone he had cheated.

Jesus healed a blind man. Blind BARTIMAEUS told Jesus he wanted to see. "Go," Jesus answered, "for your FAITH has healed you" (Mark 10:52).

JERICHO TODAY

Israel released the city to Palestinian control after the 1993 Oslo Accords. Jericho was the first city transferred, probably because it was isolated from trouble spots like GAZA, where Israelis and Palestinians frequently clashed.

Some 20,000 live in the area. Some folks are herders. Many make their living by farming citrus FRUIT, dates, bananas, and winter vegetables.

JEROBOAM

(JERR uh BO uhm)

Jeroboam was a very capable young man, and when Solomon saw how industrious he was, he put him in charge of the labor force.
1 Kings 11:28

- Two kings of the northern Jewish nation of Israel

1. JEROBOAM I (reigned about 930–909 BC). The first Jewish KING named Jeroboam split the nation into a pair of competing countries. He started off as a project foreman on some of King SOLOMON's building projects. But after Solomon started worshiping IDOLS, a PROPHET predicted that Jeroboam would take 10 of ISRAEL's 12 tribes and start a new country.

That's what happened. When Solomon died, Jeroboam and leaders of the northern tribes asked Solomon's son King REHOBOAM for relief from the heavy taxes Solomon had imposed. When the king refused, the northerners seceded from the union. They named Jeroboam their king.

Not a good thing. He built two shrines: golden BULLS. He told his people to worship there instead of going to JERUSALEM, in the southern Jewish nation of JUDAH.

2. Jeroboam II (reigned about 793–753 BC). This king of Israel was the great-grandson of JEHU, the CHARIOT corps commander whose coup brought down King AHAB's family dynasty. Like all kings of the northern Jewish nation of Israel, he got a thumbs-down on the religion scale: "He did what was evil in the LORD's sight" (2 Kings 14:24).

JERUSALEM

Map 1 C5

(jah ROO sah lem)

"I'm going to Jerusalem, where prophets go to die. It wouldn't be right for me to be killed anywhere else." Jesus to his disciples,
Luke 13:33 AUTHOR'S PARAPHRASE

- Jewish capital established by King David
- Sacred to Jews, Christians, Muslims
- Where Jesus was executed and rose from the dead

THE HOLY CITY, Jerusalem—as painted from the Mount of Olives around 1881.

HOLY CITIES BLEED more than most cities. That's true of Jerusalem—conquered dozens of times and leveled into a rock pile no less than five times.

Part of the reason for this violence is because it's sacred. People fight over it.

- Jews want it. King DAVID made it the Jewish capital 3,000 years ago.
- Christians want it—or at least the right to worship there. Jesus died and rose from the dead in this city. His DISCIPLES started the CHRISTIAN movement there.
- Muslims want it. Their prophet Muhammad is said to have ascended to heaven from the rock inside the city's landmark: a 1,300-year-old Muslim shrine called the Dome of the Rock. Muslims controlled the city and the Holy Land now called Israel for most of the past 1,400 years.

Even in early Bible times, before Christians and Muslims, Jerusalem was a city to die for. That's because it was sacred to the JEWS and strategic for Middle Eastern neighbors coveting the only hospitable land bridge connecting EGYPT and other African countries to the northland world of the Middle East and Europe.

No wonder Bible PROPHETS—anticipating Jerusalem's brightest possible future—saw nothing better than the opposite of what they had experienced in WAR and destruction:

> *"I [God] will give Jerusalem a river of peace and prosperity"* (ISAIAH 66:12).

Yet in Bible times, as today, peace remained elusive enough that one prophet complained: "We hoped for peace, but no peace came. We hoped for a time of healing, but found only terror" (Jeremiah 14:19).

That prophet, JEREMIAH, lived to see Babylonian invaders from what is now Iraq tear Jerusalem to the ground, one stone at a time.

JEWISH JERUSALEM

JOSHUA led the Jews on their invasion of CANAAN, now Israel, in either the 1200s BC or the 1400s BC—scholars debate which. At the time, Jerusalem was called Jebus. It was the well-defended hometown of a group of Canaanites called JEBUSITES.

J

STEPHEN M. MILLER'S ILLUSTRATED BIBLE DICTIONARY

The BIBLE says Joshua's militia defeated Jebusite armies who fought alongside their Canaanite allies (Joshua 10). But they apparently never captured the city, which was well positioned on a ridgetop and surrounded by a wall.

Once the Jews conquered most of Canaan's highland city, Joshua assigned each tribe to mop up their assigned territory. "But the tribe of JUDAH could not drive out the Jebusites, who lived in the city of Jerusalem" (Joshua 15:63).

David handled that chore with the help of his ARMY.

"David made the fortress his home, and he called it the CITY OF DAVID. He extended the city, starting at the supporting terraces" (2 Samuel 5:9). David extended Jebus approximately 10 acres—equal to about two and a half Walmart Supercenter stores—to about 15 acres. David's son and successor, King SOLOMON, would more than double that to 32 acres.

Jerusalem became not only ISRAEL's political capital, but its spiritual capital as well. David built an ALTAR there for offering SACRIFICES to GOD. He also brought to town Israel's most sacred relic: the ARK OF THE COVENANT, the GOLD-plated chest that held the 10 COMMANDMENTS. He would have built the first Jewish TEMPLE, if God had let him. But God assigned that to Solomon.

Once built, the Temple became the only place on earth where God allowed Jews to offer sacrifices. MOSES had predicted as much: "You must seek the LORD your God at the place of WORSHIP he himself will choose from among all the tribes" (Deuteronomy 12:5).

That's why it was a big deal when Babylonian invaders from what is now Iraq leveled Jerusalem—and the Temple.

IRAQI JERUSALEM

Two Iraqi empires erased the Jewish homeland from the world map. Both empires—ASSYRIA and BABYLON— were based in what is now Iraq.

Israel had split in two after Solomon. They hadn't liked the high taxes Solomon charged. And they hated getting drafted to work on his never-ending building projects: Temple, PALACE, fortress cities. When his son

SHIMON Ze'vi is one of 800,000 souls living in Jerusalem today. Two out of three are Jews, Ze'vi among them.

and successor REHOBOAM promised more of the same, the northern tribes started their own country.

The northland Jewish nation of Israel fell to Assyria in 722 BC. Most Jewish survivors got deported to Iraq. The southern Jewish nation of JUDAH—with its Jerusalem capital—fell to Babylon in 586 BC. Again, most survivors got deported to Iraq.

Iranians—called Persians at the time—freed the Jews about 50 years later. PERSIA crushed Babylon and became the new superpower of the Middle East. CYRUS, king of Persia, freed Babylon's political prisoners and invited them to go home and rebuild their cities and worship centers.

Jews took him up on the offer.

ITALIAN JERUSALEM

Jews rebuilt Jerusalem and other cities in their homeland. But it took about 400 years for them to get back their independence. And once they got it, it didn't last.

At first, they lived under the thumb of Persia. Then along came ALEXANDER the Great. He defeated the Persians. And in 332 BC he claimed Jerusalem and the rest of the Jewish land.

Jews revolted in 168 BC after a Greek ruler named Antiochus IV Epiphanes tried to replace the Jewish religion with Greek religion.

Jews won. Free at last. For a century. Civil WAR broke out at the very time the ROMAN EMPIRE decided to expand into the Middle East.

Enter Roman general Pompey. He conquered DAMASCUS in 63 BC. Then he set up shop there. Each side of the warring Jews sent AMBASSADORS to Pompey, asking for his help. He chose a side—as though it mattered—and he conquered Jerusalem the same year.

That was the year freedom died, as far as Jews were concerned.

The Jewish nation would answer to ROME for most of the next 500 years. When the Jews rebelled in AD 66, Romans came back with a vengeance and in AD 70 tore Jerusalem to the ground—including the Temple, which has never been rebuilt.

Muslim Arabs captured the city and the region in the AD 600s. Then came the Christian Crusaders, battling the Arabs for centuries in a tug of war over the Holy Land.

From the time the Romans first arrived, Jews had to wait nearly 2,000 years before they got back their

HOLIEST PLACE ON EARTH for Jews is the Western Wall in Jerusalem. It's all that's left of their ancient Temple, destroyed by Romans in AD 70. A retaining wall, the huge stones held up the western side of the Temple hilltop.

homeland and control over at least part of Jerusalem. In 1948 the United Nations gave them part of PALESTINE, including part of Jerusalem. Palestinians fought the decision, and the Jews. They lost. Jews won control of the entire city after the Six-Day War of 1967.

INTERNATIONAL JERUSALEM

Today Israelis control Jerusalem. They seem to welcome just about anyone not threatening to blow it up. More than a million tourists a year.

From about 10 acres and an estimated 1,000 people when King David captured it, Jerusalem has sprawled its current population of about 800,000 souls onto more than 31,000 acres (49 square miles; 126 square km).

Jews. Two out of every three residents are Jewish. To Jews, Jerusalem is the holiest city on earth. And the holiest spot in the city is the Western Wall, sometimes called the Wailing Wall—a name many Jews consider insensitive. This wall is all that's left of the Jerusalem Temple. It was part of a retaining wall that held up the side of a hill. The Temple sat on top of the hill.

Muslims. Most of the rest of Jerusalem's citizens are Muslim Arabs. To Muslims, Jerusalem is the third holiest city on earth, after Mecca, where Muhammad was born and Medina, where Muhammad was exiled.

Christians. Only about two percent of Jerusalem's residents are Christians—most of them Arab. To many Christians, Jerusalem's Church of the Holy Sepulchre—built in AD 335 as the first CHURCH after Rome legalized CHRISTIANITY—marks the place where Jesus was crucified, buried, and rose from the dead.

See also ZION.

JERUSALEM, NEW

(jah ROO sah lem)

I saw the holy city, the new Jerusalem, coming down from God out of heaven.
Revelation 21:2

▪ Where God lives forever with his people

IT'S A NICKNAME FOR HEAVEN—a term of endearment, according to some students of the BIBLE.

Others disagree. They take a more literal read of what JOHN said he saw in an end-time VISION. These people of FAITH say they expect to see "a NEW HEAVEN and a new earth," along with a "NEW JERUSALEM" (Revelation 21:1, 2).

Specs from REVELATION, which some take literally and others read figuratively:

Natural lighting. "The city has no need of sun or moon, for the GLORY of GOD illuminates the city, and the Lamb is its light" (21:23).

Cube-shaped. "Its length and width and height were each 1,400 miles [2,220 km]" (21:16). For JEWS, the holiest place on earth was a cube: the room in the TEMPLE where they kept their most sacred relic, the ARK OF THE COVENANT that held the 10 COMMANDMENTS.

Gemstone walls. In New Jerusalem, jasper, sapphire, EMERALD, and other jewels—earth's greatest treasures—are merely mundane, good for nothing more than building the city walls.

Main Street river walk. A river flows down the center of Main Street. Trees of life grow beside it. "The leaves were used for MEDICINE to heal the nations" (22:2).

A place to call home. Most importantly, many say, God is there with his people. Forever. "God's home is now among his people! . . . And there will be no more DEATH or sorrow or crying or pain. All these things are gone forever" (21:3–4)

See also HEAVEN.

JESSE

(JESS ee)

1000s BC

"Go to Bethlehem. Find a man named Jesse who lives there, for I have selected one of his sons to be my king." God to Samuel,
1 Samuel 16:1

▪ Father of King David

JESSE'S GRANDMA WAS AN ARAB—RUTH—but his son DAVID became the most celebrated KING of the JEWS.

SON OF GOD. It's an idea that most Jews couldn't latch onto—regardless of the miracles they saw Jesus do. Their Bible said there was only one God. And it didn't say anything about him having a son.

JESUS CHRIST

(GEEZ us)

Born about 6 BC; died about AD 33
"You [Mary] will have a son. His name will
be Jesus. He. . .will be called the Son of God
Most High. . . . His kingdom will never end."
Luke 1:31–33 CEV

- Son of God
- Messiah predicted by Jewish prophets
- Circuit-walking rabbi, preacher, healer
- Father of Christianity

NO WONDER JEWS HAD TROUBLE warming up to Jesus.

He wasn't anything like the hero they expected—the MESSIAH king whom PROPHETS said would save ISRAEL.

He looked like the opposite of royalty.

- Illegit. Harshly put, from a human's point of view, he was a bastard—an illegitimate SON conceived outside of marriage. NEW TESTAMENT writers, however, said he was conceived through the power of the HOLY SPIRIT, literally "the SON OF GOD" (Luke 1:35).

255

- Born in a barn. More likely a cave that served as a BARN. Either way, his first bed was "a feeding trough" (Luke 2:7 NCV).
- Peasant. When it came time for MARY's ritual cleansing after delivering Jesus, she qualified for the poor person's SACRIFICE: "two young pigeons" (Luke 2:24; Leviticus 12:8).
- Pacifist. JEWS expected a hero like the warrior king DAVID—a Messiah who would (1) defeat the Romans who had been occupying their homeland for a century and (2) restore Israel's independence. Instead, they got a pacifist RABBI who advised Jews to turn the other cheek (Matthew 5:39).

BORN IN A BARN. Jewish scholars expected the Messiah to be born in Bethlehem. They said the prophet Micah had predicted it. The surprise was where in Bethlehem: a stable—perhaps a cave used as a barn. Bethlehem's Church of the Nativity marks the location of a cave said to have been the birthplace of Jesus.

BIGGEST OBJECTION TO JESUS

As far as observant Jews are concerned, there's only one God. And God never said anything about having a son.

Jews don't have creed statements of belief like Christians do. But if they did, this would be at the top of the list because it's their most basic belief:

"Listen, O Israel! The LORD is our God, the LORD alone" (DEUTERONOMY 6:4).

Here's the closest Jesus came to explaining how he could be divine without trashing that pivotal verse: "Anyone who has seen me has seen the FATHER!" (John 14:9).

That abstract statement alone wouldn't have convinced many Jews. What did convince many, however, were the MIRACLES—one in particular. Crowds saw him heal the sick and even raise the dead. But when he rose from the dead himself, that clinched it. After that, his DISCIPLES were no longer afraid to put their lives on the line by passing along his story and teachings. Most would die as MARTYRS, according to early Christian reports.

HIS EARLY YEARS

Birth. He was born in BETHLEHEM, thanks to a Roman-ordered CENSUS. Jews had to register in their ancestral hometown. Jesus' legal father, JOSEPH, was a descendant of King David, who grew up as a SHEPHERD in Bethlehem.

Jewish scholars of Jesus' day taught that the prophet MICAH predicted that the MESSIAH would be born there: "Bethlehem. . .out of you will come a ruler over Israel. . . . His greatness will reach from one end of the earth to the other. And he will bring them PEACE" (Micah 5:2, 4–5 NIrv).

That's why King HEROD's Jewish advisers pointed the "WISE MEN" to Bethlehem after they arrived in the capital of JERUSALEM, hoping to honor the newborn king of the Jews.

Growing up. Jesus grew up in NAZARETH, in the home of a construction worker. The GREEK word describing Joseph is *tekton* (TECK tone). That's a multitasking word. It can mean CARPENTER or builder. Many Bible experts speculate that Jesus and his father helped

STONE HER? That's the question Jews ask Jesus, after presenting him with a woman caught in adultery. Jewish law says stoning her is kosher. Jesus invites the person who has never sinned to throw the first stone. And the defense rests.

rebuild Nazareth's neighboring Jewish city of SEPPHO-RIS, a short 3-mile (5 km) walk away. Invaders had destroyed it when Jesus was a child. But HEROD ANTIPAS, ruler of GALILEE, ordered it rebuilt.

The BIBLE says Jesus had several brothers and sisters: "He's just the carpenter's son, and we know Mary, his mother, and his brothers—JAMES, Joseph, Simon, and Judas. All his sisters live right here among us" (Matthew 13:55–56). Some Christians, including many Catholics, say Jesus was Mary's only child. Guesses about the other kids: They were Joseph's CHILDREN from a previous marriage, or they were cousins of Jesus.

Scholars can only speculate about what kind of kid Jesus was. The Bible skips his childhood, except for a brief mention of him as a 12-year-old. After a visit to Jerusalem, he missed the CARAVAN home to Nazareth, a four-day walk. He got distracted by talking with Jewish scholars at the Jerusalem TEMPLE. Even so, the story describes him as an obedient son who "became wise. . . grew strong. God was pleased with him and so were the people" (Luke 2:52 CEV).

ROAMING RABBI

"Jesus was about thirty years old when he began his public ministry" (Luke 3:23).

That's a round number, most scholars say. It tracks with the age of adults mature enough to become WORSHIP leaders. Age 30 was when Jewish PRIESTS could begin their ministry.

Jesus was possibly in his mid-30s. He was born before King Herod died in AD 4. And Jesus launched his ministry after JOHN THE BAPTIST, who started his ministry sometime between AD 27 and AD 29. That's a guess based on Roman rulers mentioned in the GOSPEL of LUKE.

Jesus quickly gained fame for his HEALING miracles. He cured BLINDNESS, LEPROSY, PARALYSIS—and he exorcised DEMONS. In time, he introduced himself as the Messiah who came to save Israel. He did that by quoting a prophecy many Jews linked to the Messiah:

> *"The Spirit of the LORD is upon me, for he has anointed me to bring Good News to the poor. He has sent me to proclaim that captives will be released, that the blind will see, that the oppressed will be set free"* (LUKE 4:18).

Jews in his hometown of Nazareth were not impressed. They tried to throw him from a cliff. He escaped, walking through the crowd.

HIS BIG IDEA

The "KINGDOM OF GOD" is the one idea Jesus taught more than any other.

This wasn't another name for HEAVEN. It was another name for God's kingdom—in heaven and on earth. Wherever souls serve him. That's God's kingdom. Yet it's not just a place. It's also a way of doing business. God's business.

Jesus wanted people to know the laws of the land in God's kingdom—how God operates and what God expects of citizens in his kingdom.

Jesus often told fictional stories called PARABLES to teach people about this. In the famous parable of the Good SAMARITAN, Jesus drove home the point that when the Bible says God's people should help their NEIGHBORS, it doesn't mean just fellow Jews. It means anyone we come in contact with who's in need.

HIS CHUTZPAH

Jesus bet his entire ministry on a dozen working grunts. Not a brainiac among them.

Four fishermen, perhaps more. One taxman. Possibly one freedom fighter called a ZEALOT. And the good Lord knows what else. When Jewish scholars interrogated the brightest among them, PETER and JOHN, they judged them as "ordinary men with no special training

in the SCRIPTURES" (Acts 4:13).

It's anyone's guess how long Jesus taught the disciples before he got the Jews so riled up that they orchestrated his execution. That fact doesn't get reported in any of the four GOSPELS: MATTHEW, MARK, Luke, JOHN. Guesses range from one year to several.

HIS DEATH

In the end, Jewish leaders in Jerusalem arrested Jesus on charges of HERESY—teaching non-Jewish ideas that dissed God. The clincher for High Priest CAIAPHAS running the trial came with this exchange.

Caiaphas: "Are you the Messiah, the SON OF GOD?"

Jesus: "Soon you will see the SON OF MAN sitting at the right side of God All-Powerful and coming on the clouds of heaven."

Caiaphas: "This man claims to be God! We don't need any more WITNESSES!" (Matthew 26:63–65 CEV)

Religion wasn't enough to convince Roman governor PILATE to sentence Jesus to death. He needed politics. The Jews accommodated, charging Jesus with sedition. They warned Pilate: "If you release this man, you are no 'friend of CAESAR.' Anyone who declares himself a KING is a rebel against Caesar" (John 19:12).

Depending on exactly when this happened, that may have been quite a threat. By AD 31, Pilate was already on shaky ground with Caesar TIBERIUS. That's the year that the Roman official who had recommended Pilate for the job, Sejanus, was executed—charged with plotting a coup. Birds of a feather.

Pilate ordered Jesus executed that day, Friday morning. Jesus was nailed to a CROSS and dead before sundown.

ALIVE AGAIN

Jesus rose from the dead on Sunday morning. Even a Roman history book from that century reported the news:

> *"There was a wise man who was called Jesus, a good man. . . . Pilate condemned him to be crucified. . . . His disciples didn't abandon their loyalty to him. They reported that he appeared to them three days after his crucifixion, and that he was alive."* JOSEPHUS (ABOUT AD 37–101), *ANTIQUITIES OF THE JEWS*

New Testament writers say Jesus spent 40 days appearing periodically to his followers. "He appeared to the Twelve," PAUL wrote, "After that, he appeared to more than 500 believers at the same time. Most of them are still living" (1 Corinthians 15:5–6 NIrV).

When it came time for Jesus to leave the planet—in an event called the ASCENSION—he gave his disciples a mission that launched the CHRISTIAN movement: "Tell everyone about me in Jerusalem, in all JUDEA, in SAMARIA, and everywhere in the world" (Acts 1:8 CEV).

They started in Jerusalem—PREACHING within earshot of the very Jewish leaders who had arranged Jesus' execution. Bold.

A ROMAN NECKLACE from about 400 years before Christ shows detailed craftsmanship.

During the EXODUS out of EGYPT, Jews melted gold jewelry to make a calf god. MOSES "ground it into powder, threw it into the WATER, and forced the people to drink it" (Exodus 32:20).

First-generation CHURCH leaders urged Christians not to worry about "outward beauty of fancy hairstyles, expensive jewelry, or beautiful clothes. You should clothe yourselves instead with the beauty that comes from within. . .a gentle and quiet spirit" (1 Peter 3:3–4).

JETHRO

(JETH row)

1400s BC

Moses' father-in-law, Jethro, the priest of Midian, heard about everything God had done for Moses and his people, the Israelites.
Exodus 18:1

MOSES WORKED AS A SHEPHERD for his father-in-law Jethro for 40 years before returning to EGYPT to free the JEWS. Jethro probably lived near the east bank of the RED SEA in what is now Saudi Arabia.

JEWELRY

"I [God] gave you [Jerusalem] lovely jewelry, bracelets, beautiful necklaces, a ring for your nose, earrings for your ears. . . . You were adorned with gold and silver."
EZEKIEL 16:11–13

MEN AND WOMEN both wore earrings, bracelets, necklaces, and other jewelry.

The POOR couldn't generally afford much more than BRONZE or beads, if anything.

The rich, however, were budgeted for GOLD, SILVER, IVORY, and gems: "red carnelian, pale-green peridot, white moonstone, blue-green beryl, onyx, green jasper, blue lapis lazuli, turquoise, and EMERALD" (Ezekiel 28:13).

JEWS

Haman. . .looked for a way to eliminate not just Mordecai but all Jews throughout the whole kingdom of Xerxes. ESTHER 3:5–6 MSG

- Descendants of Abraham, Isaac, and Jacob
- Converts to the Jewish faith

ABRAHAM WASN'T A JEW. Not technically. Neither was MOSES. Nor DAVID.

There was no such thing as a Jew until after the Jewish nation died, many historians say. That nation was called JUDAH. Babylonian invaders from what is now Iraq erased it from the map in 586 BC.

Judah is where the similar-sounding term *Jew* came from. It's a bit like calling a person from Great Britain a "Brit."

Survivors of Babylon's attack on Judah were deported to Iraq. There, people started referring to them as Jews. The tag stuck. It came to distinguish anyone descended from the original people of Israel, as well as converts to the FAITH.

Jews were also the first Christians. Racially, Jesus and all of his DISCIPLES were Jews.

RABBI Seymour Weller instructs children in the Torah (Jewish Scripture) at the Jewish day school of the Ati'Day Yisroel Orthodox synagogue in Little Rock, Arkansas. Technically, two of the world's most famous Jews—Abraham and Moses—weren't Jews. The name "Jews" didn't seem to show up until nearly a thousand years after Moses, in the 500s BC.

JEZEBEL

(JEZZ uh bell)

Reigned about 875–854 BC

As for Jezebel, dogs will eat her body there in Jezreel. Elijah to King Ahab,
1 Kings 21:23 CEV

- Wife of Israel's King Ahab
- Former princess from Lebanon
- Killed prophets of God

QUEEN OF MEAN, Jezebel was—oddly enough—part of a Jewish peace plan. But that was before she tried to kill all of God's PROPHETS.

She had been a PRINCESS in the city kingdom of SIDON, about 25 miles (40 km) south of Beirut, LEBANON. Israel's King OMRI arranged for his son AHAB to marry her, to strengthen ties between the two nations.

It nearly killed ISRAEL—at least the Jewish religion there.

Jezebel worshiped the Canaanite GODS of BAAL and ASHERAH. Fiercely evangelical, she promoted her religion by supporting 850 of her prophets and priests with MONEY from the Jewish treasury.

As for Jewish religion, "Jezebel had tried to kill all the LORD's prophets" (1 Kings 18:4). One hundred survived by hiding in caves.

ELIJAH boldly challenged Jezebel's 850 prophets and priests to a battle of the gods. The challenge: Call down fire from the sky to burn up a sacrifice.

Advantage, Baal—it would seem. He was the god of weather. In pictures, he holds a bolt of lightning as his SPEAR.

Baal lost.

It was Elijah who called down fire. Jewish crowds rallied to Elijah's cause and slaughtered Jezebel's religioous leaders.

Jezebel sent this message to Elijah: "May the gods strike me and even kill me if by this time tomorrow I have not killed you just as you killed them" (1 Kings 19:2).

QUEEN JEZEBEL, knowing she's about to die in a coup, puts on her makeup.

Elijah ran for his life—for nearly 300 miles (480 km). At MOUNT SINAI God asked him where he was going and then managed to turn him around by giving him a job: ANOINT Israel's future KING, JEHU.

Jehu wouldn't become king for more than a dozen years, after Ahab's son JORAM became king—with Jezebel the queen mother.

Jehu, a CHARIOT corps commander, led his men to the king's summer PALACE at Jezreel. He shot King Joram with an arrow as the king rode out to greet him.

When Jezebel got the news Jehu was coming for her, "She painted her eyelids and fixed her HAIR and sat at a window" (2 Kings 9:30).

Some might give her points for boldness, but HAREM EUNUCHS gave her a shove.

"Throw her down!" Jehu yelled. "So they threw her out the window, and her blood spattered against the wall and on the horses. And Jehu trampled her body under his horses' hooves" (2 Kings 9:32).

Dogs ate her corpse. Elijah had predicted it years before—after Jezebel arranged the MURDER of a local man so she could confiscate his property and plant a vegetable garden.

When it came time to plant her, there wasn't quite enough left to put in the ground: skull, feet, and hands.

JEZREEL

Map 1 C4

(JEZ reel)

King Ahab wanted a certain vineyard. It belonged to Naboth from Jezreel. . . . [Ahab said,] "I want to use it for a vegetable garden." 1 KINGS 21:1–2 NIRV

- Vacation town for King Ahab

KILLER VEGGIES and a pile of 70 heads at the front gate didn't do much for the reputation of Jezreel—a ridgetop city with a great view of Jezreel Valley below.

It was a wonderful location in northern Israel. King AHAB used it as a summer getaway, where his PALACE could catch cool afternoon breezes from the MEDITERRANEAN SEA 25 miles (40 km) west.

His wife JEZEBEL arranged the MURDER of a palace NEIGHBOR, NABOTH, after he refused to sell his land to Ahab. The king wanted a vegetable garden. And he got it.

Years later, a CHARIOT commander launched a coup at Jezreel—ending Ahab's dynasty. He killed King JORAM, Ahab's son, along with Queen Mother Jezebel. Then he ordered the heads of all 70 of Ahab's sons, which were delivered "in baskets" (2 Kings 10:7).

JEZREEL, SON OF HOSEA

(JEZ reel)

"Name the child Jezreel, for I am about to punish King Jehu's dynasty to avenge the murders he committed at Jezreel." Hosea 1:4

- Son of prophet Hosea

A NASTY NAME FOR A KID, "Jezreel" became the symbolic NAME of HOSEA's first son, born to his wife GOMER, a former PROSTITUTE. Hosea's three CHILDREN all got names symbolizing how GOD was going to punish ISRAEL for its sins.

J

JEZREEL VALLEY

Map 1 B4

(JEZ reel)

The Israelites in the Jezreel Valley saw that their army had fled and that Saul and his sons were dead. 1 Chronicles 10:7

- Also known as Valley of Armageddon

THE PERFECT BATTLEFIELD, as Napoleon once described it, Jezreel Valley in northern Israel isn't just the site of dozens of famous battles—including one that killed King SAUL and his sons. It's also the most fertile farmland in the country, today specializing in WHEAT, cotton, and sunflowers.

Some Bible students say it's probably where the end-time Battle of ARMAGEDDON will be fought, though many others say they doubt there will be such a battle. *Armageddon* isn't a legit word, most scholars agree. Best guess: it's a combo word JOHN minted for the book of REVELATION: *Har Megiddo*, meaning "hill of MEGIDDO." Megiddo was a hilltop fortress overlooking the valley.

Today the valley is home to a patchwork quilt of

Sea of Galilee

Jordan River

Jezreel

Mt. Tabor

Nazareth

JEZREEL VALLEY

Megiddo

Carmel Mountains

De
Se

Mediterranean Sea

Haifa

N

JEZREEL VALLEY: Israel's breadbasket

JEZREEL VALLEY in northern Israel is the country's breadbasket—the largest stretch of fertile farmland.

farms, cities, and the Ramat David Israeli Air Force Base.

JOAB

(JOE ab)

1000s BC

Joab took three spears and stuck them through Absalom's chest. 2 Samuel 18:14 CEV

- King David's general and nephew

THE MILITARY MAN behind ISRAEL's greatest warrior king didn't end well. Clinging to Israel's sacred AL-TAR, hoping to escape execution, he got no love (1 Kings 2:28).

It was DAVID's fault. Dying, David told his son King SOLOMON, "Don't let him grow old and go to his

grave in peace" (1 Kings 2:6).

David said he wanted Joab punished for murdering two commanders: ABNER and Amasa. David didn't mention that Joab had also executed David's son ABSALOM—against David's orders. But he was likely thinking it.

JOASH

(JOE ash)

Reigned about 832–803 BC

Joash remained hidden in the Temple of the LORD for six years while Athaliah ruled over the land. 2 Kings 11:3

- King of south Jewish nation of Judah

ORDERED EXECUTED at age one by his grandmother, Joash was saved by an aunt. Grandmother ATHALIAH declared herself JUDAH's queen after her son, King Aha-ziah died. She ordered all heirs executed to eliminate her competition. Six years later a PRIEST who supported the boy and helped hide him orchestrated a coup. Killer grandma got a taste of her own medicine: assassination. When Joash grew older, he ordered an extensive repair of the TEMPLE—a welcome thank you to the priests who had hidden him.

JOB

(JOHB)

Perhaps before 2000 BC

The LORD asked Satan, "Have you noticed my servant Job? He is the finest man in all the earth." Job 1:8

- Loyal to God during suffering

NOT ALL THAT PATIENT, Job did some serious complaining to GOD after his kids died, his herds got stolen, and his health failed: "God rips me apart, up-roots my hopes" (Job 19:10 CEV).

It's unclear when and where Job lived. Uz was home, but no one knows where Uz was. The writer of the story mentions the Sabeans and adds other clues suggesting he lived in the era of the Jewish founder, ABRAHAM.

Some Bible experts say they wonder if the story is more fiction than fact—more like a parable intended to disprove a common Jewish misconception: that bad things happen to people because they sinned and God is punishing them.

Job's troubles started after God bragged about him to a spirit being called SATAN. In HEBREW, *satan* sim-ply means "ACCUSER." Satan said Job would crack under pressure. A pressure test followed, along with a debate between Job and some friends who accused him of sin-ning up this storm—provoking God.

By story's end, God gave Job more CHILDREN, larger herds, and restored health.

JOB, BOOK OF

Famous sound bite: "Naked I came from my mother's womb, and naked shall I return." Job 1:21 NRSV

BLESSED WITH A BIG FAMILY, huge herds, and good health, Job loses it all. It's a test: GOD allows an AC-CUSER to test Job's faithfulness. Job's friends arrive to com-fort him, but they end up trying to convince him to repent. They say Job must have done something terrible to deserve all this misery. Job insists he's innocent. God confirms it.

- Writer: Unknown.
- Time: Perhaps around Abraham's time, about 2000 BC.
- Location: Uz, an unknown region.

BIG SCENES

God's deal with Satan. In what sounds like a meeting in HEAVEN, God brags about Job's faithfulness. God is talking to a spirit being identified as the ACCUSER (*SATAN* in HEBREW). SATAN replies, "Take away every-thing he has, and he will surely curse you to your face!" God takes that bet. The test is on. *Job 1*

Job's disasters. A firestorm burns up Job's SHEEP and SHEPHERDS. Raiders steel his other herds: DONKEYS, oxen, and CAMELS. A windstorm blows down the HOUSE, killing all 10 of his CHILDREN. That's day one. Day two: Boils erupt all over his body. *Job 1–2*

Job's comfortless comforters. Four friends come calling, silent at first. When they start talking, they accuse Job of SIN. Their rationale: God wouldn't dump this misery on Job unless he deserved it. For most of this long book, Job debates the men, insisting he's innocent. He also complains about God treating him unfairly. *Job 2–37*

God gets the last word. God speaks from a WHIRLWIND. Instead of explaining why Job is suffering, God asks questions no human could answer. First one: "Where were you when I laid the foundations of the earth?" Job falls silent, except to repent for doubting his Creator. God restores Job's health and herds and gives him 10 more children. As for the comforters, God gives them what for: "I am angry with you." Then he orders Job to pray for them. *Job 38–42*

J

Jochebed complied. But she made sure her son floated: "She got a BASKET made of PAPYRUS reeds and waterproofed it with TAR" (Exodus 2:3).

She put Moses among reeds where the PRINCESS bathed, and posted daughter MIRIAM nearby. The princess saved Moses and accepted Miriam's offer to find a nurse to care for him: Jochebed, who drew a salary for mothering her son. The princess named Moses and raised him as a PRINCE in EGYPT.

JOEL

> "What you see was predicted long ago by the prophet Joel: 'In the last days,' God says, 'I will pour out my Spirit upon all people.'"
> Peter, Acts 2:16–17

- Prophet

LIKE LOCUSTS, an invading ARMY will swarm over the Jewish homeland. That's the message of a mysterious PROPHET named Joel. Scholars can only guess when he lived and which invasion he was talking about.

JOEL, BOOK OF

> Famous sound bite: Hammer your plows into swords. Joel 3:10 NIRV

COMPARING AN INVASION FORCE to a nation-decimating swarm of LOCUSTS, the prophet Joel warns that an ARMY is headed to the Jewish homeland. It's JUDGMENT DAY for the JEWS: punishment for centuries of SIN. But afterward, a fresh start.

- Writer: Joel, son of Pethuel. The Bible reveals nothing more about him.
- Time: Unknown. Guesses span 500 years, from about 800 BC to 300 BC.
- Location: Unknown. There's no mention of where Joel lived or who he was addressing. He mentions both Jewish nations: Israel in the north and Judah in the south.

MOTHER OF MOSES, Jochebed prepares to put baby Moses in a basket and float him in the Nile River, where the princess bathes. Savvy strategy.

JOCHEBED

(JOCK uh bed)

1500s BC
Amram and Jochebed became the parents of Aaron, Moses, and their sister, Miriam.
Numbers 26:59

- Mother of Moses

SMARTER THAN EGYPT'S KING, Jochebed managed to save her baby son, MOSES, while obeying the king's order intended to kill newborn JEWS.

The king ordered all newborn Jewish boys thrown in the NILE RIVER.

BIG SCENES

Swarm. "Sound the alarm," Joel writes. "The DAY OF THE LORD is upon us." Not a good day. GOD's not coming to rescue the Jews this time. He's sending invaders to devour the land like a swarm of 100 million hungry locusts. *Joel 1–2*

After the swarm. Judgment Day isn't the last day. There's a new day coming, Joel promises. Whether it's in this life or the next, a metaphor or a literal read, it's hard to tell. But it sounds great: "Mountains will drip with sweet WINE." "WATER will fill the streambeds of JUDAH." "I, the LORD, will make my home in JERUSALEM with my people." *Joel 3*

JOHN THE BAPTIST

About 6 BC–AD 29

"Of all who have ever lived, none is greater than John the Baptist." Jesus, Matthew 11:11

- Prophet who baptized Jesus
- Relative of Jesus
- Beheaded by King Herod Antipas

LIKE THE ANNOUNCER for a starring act, John wasn't on stage long. His ministry may have lasted just a year or so. But it was long enough to draw a crowd—and then to point the people to Jesus.

LUKE implies that John got his first message from GOD "in the fifteenth year of the reign of Emperor TIBERIUS" (Luke 3:1 NRSV). That's about AD 28 or 29. John died before Jesus, whose CRUCIFIXION is estimated anywhere from AD 30 to 33.

Yet in that short time, John managed to draw enough attention that he got himself executed and written up in a Roman history book published during his own century:

"Herod [Antipas, ruler of Galilee] killed John. . .who was called the Baptist. . .a good man who commanded the Jews to exercise virtue, both in righteousness to one another and in faithfulness to God." JOSEPHUS (ABOUT AD 37–101), ANTIQUITIES OF THE JEWS

JOHN THE BAPTIST, as the son of a priest, could probably have lived a life of relative luxury as a priest himself. He chose poverty, as a prophet—dressing in spartan clothes and eating cheap food: locusts (desert grasshoppers) and wild honey.

MIRACLE BABY

Like Jesus, John got an angelic introduction. GABRIEL appeared to John's father, ZECHARIAH, a JERUSALEM Temple PRIEST.

Gabriel told Zechariah, "Your WIFE, ELIZABETH, will give you a son, and you are to name him John. . . . And he will turn many Israelites to the LORD their God" (Luke 1:13, 16).

Six months into Elizabeth's pregnancy, Gabriel appeared to a Nazareth woman named Mary. He told her she would give BIRTH to Jesus—and that her relative Elizabeth was already pregnant. Mary traveled to the home of Zechariah and Elizabeth, near Jerusalem. She stayed with them for about three months—apparently long enough to see John's birth and DEDICATION.

PROPHET INSTEAD OF A PRIEST

Born into a priest's FAMILY, John probably could have served as a TEMPLE priest. Well paid. Well respected.

Instead, he became a PROPHET and a preacher. Instead of dressing for success, he dressed cheaply and ate cheaper: "John wore clothes made out of CAMEL's hair. He had a leather BELT around his waist. And he ate LOCUSTS and wild honey" (Mark 1:6 NIrV).

He looked and sounded like a prophet in a day when prophets were little more than nostalgic characters from Jewish history. People seemed to love that retro in him.

His message resonated, too. After a century of Roman occupation, JEWS were looking for God's MESSIAH to finally come. John said it was about to happen. Quoting ancient prophecies such as "Prepare the way for the LORD's coming!" (Luke 3:4), John urged people to repent and be ready when the Lord arrives.

John initiated the ritual of BAPTISM, apparently as a vivid symbol of spiritual cleansing.

Jesus launched his own ministry by having John baptize him, though John resisted: "I am the one who needs to be baptized by you" (Matthew 3:14).

JOHN BEHEADED

Calling the first lady of GALILEE a pervert is pretty much what did John in.

He had criticized the marriage of HEROD ANTIPAS, Galilee's ruler, calling it INCEST. By Jewish law, it was. Herod's wife, HERODIAS, had DIVORCED his brother to marry him. The broken law: "Do not have sexual relations with your brother's wife" (Leviticus 18:16).

Herodias's daughter danced for Herod at his birthday party. Delighted at what he saw, Herod offered her anything she wanted. She consulted her mother, who requested John's head on a platter (Matthew 14:1–12).

JOHN, DISCIPLE

First century AD

Jesus. . .saw James and John, the sons of Zebedee. They were in a boat, mending their nets. . . . Jesus asked them to come with him.
MARK 1:19–20 CEV

- A favorite disciple of Jesus
- Brother of James, another disciple
- Son of fisherman Zebedee

ONE OF THE "SONS OF THUNDER," the apostle John and his brother got that nickname from Jesus.

One guess about why: They weren't subtle.

Once, they asked Jesus if they could have the seats of honor beside him when he ruled his kingdom. That irked the other 10 DISCIPLES. Another time, they acted like thunder was their daddy. When SAMARITANS refused to welcome Jesus and his entourage into town, they said, "Should we call down fire from heaven to burn them up?" (Luke 9:54).

Jesus, not particularly fond of violence, scolded them.

Jesus was, however, fond of John, along with JAMES and PETER. They were his best friends. He took them places he didn't take the others. They were the only ones who saw him transfigured into a celestial form when he met the spirits of MOSES and ELIJAH (Luke 9:28).

Early CHURCH leaders said John wrote the GOSPEL of John. A clue: He mentions all the disciples but himself. Also, he calls himself "the disciple he [Jesus] loved" (John 19:26).

Church leaders said John moved to EPHESUS and wrote the three LETTERS of John along with REVELATION.

JOHN MARK

First century AD

Barnabas and Saul. . .sailed to the island of Cyprus. . . . John Mark was with them to help.
Acts 13:4–5 NCV

- Possible author of Gospel of Mark
- Paul's traveling associate

HE DIDN'T FINISH WHAT HE STARTED, and that made the apostle PAUL angry. John Mark accompanied Paul and BARNABAS on the first known missionary trip. After PREACHING in CYPRUS, they sailed to what is now Turkey. John Mark deserted them after reaching the swampy coast.

When it came time for a second trip, Paul and Barnabas argued about taking John Mark. Barnabas took John Mark. Paul went in a different direction, taking SILAS (Acts 15:36–41).

If John Mark is the same person later called simply

Mark, then he made up with Paul because they worked together again. Mark would have been his Roman NAME, John his HEBREW name—just as Paul had two names: Paul (Roman) and Saul (Hebrew).

Early CHURCH leaders said Mark wrote the GOSPEL of MARK.

JOHN OF REVELATION

First century AD

I, John, am your brother and your partner in suffering. . . . I was exiled to the island of Patmos for preaching. . .about Jesus.
Revelation 1:9

- Author of Revelation

THE MAN BEHIND THE MOST MYSTERIOUS BOOK in the BIBLE remains a mystery himself.

Early CHURCH leaders said he was the apostle John, one of Jesus' three closest DISCIPLES, with PETER and JAMES.

Many Bible experts today say they doubt it. For two main reasons:

- His writing style doesn't track with the other writings of the apostle John: the GOSPEL of John and LETTERS 1, 2, 3 John.
- He referred to "the twelve APOSTLES" (Revelation 21:14) in the third person, as though he wasn't one of them.

Other scholars, however, say they see some similarities in word choices. And they add that the writer of the Gospel of John seemed humble; he mentioned all the other apostles by name, but not himself. Instead, he seemed to refer to himself as "the disciple Jesus loved" (John 13:23).

JOHN, GOSPEL OF

Famous sound bite: "God loved the world so much that he gave his one and only Son, so that everyone who believes in him will not perish but have eternal life." John 3:16

ONE OF FOUR BOOKS ABOUT JESUS, John's Gospel is perhaps the most cerebral—for the deep thinkers. It spotlights the teachings of Jesus, barely mentions the MIRACLES, and skips the PARABLES. The writer says he wrote the book "so that you will put your FAITH in Jesus as the MESSIAH and the SON OF GOD" (John 20:31 CEV).

- Writer: One of Jesus' 12 disciples (John 21:24). Early church leaders said John.
- Time: Lifetime of Jesus, about 6 BC–AD 33.
- Location: Israel, mainly in the northland region: Galilee.

WHICH JOHN and which end of the world? That's what many Bible experts want to know about the author of the last book in the Bible: Revelation. Was he John the disciple of Jesus or another John? And was he talking about the future or the past—Roman persecution of Christians?

BIG SCENES

JESUS, IN THE BEGINNING. John wants to prove Jesus is divine. He starts at the beginning—before CREATION. He calls Jesus the Word. To Greek philosophers, Word (*Logos*) was a tech term they used to describe the source of everything created. John adds that this Word:

- "was God"
- "existed in the beginning with God"
- "became human"
- "came into the very world he created."
  JOHN 1:1–18

Lamb of God, headed to sacrifice. Jesus begins his ministry by having his relative—John the Baptist—baptize him. John introduces Jesus as the Messiah the JEWS have been waiting for: "Look! The LAMB OF GOD who takes away the SIN of the world!" Somehow, John the Baptist seems aware of what's going to happen to Jesus. Just as Jews sacrificed lambs to atone for sin, God would offer the life of Jesus as the last sacrifice anyone would ever need. *John 1:19–34*

Seven miracles of Jesus. John reports the first miracle of Jesus: turning water into WINE at a WEDDING in CANA. It's the first of SEVEN miracles, each intended to show the divinity of Jesus: healings, walking on water, feeding thousands with almost nothing, raising LAZARUS from the dead. *John 2, 4, 5, 6, 9, 11*

"You have to be born again." Jesus tells a Jewish leader named NICODEMUS that it's not enough to believe that God sent him. Nicodemus needs a spiritual rebirth. *John 3*

"I am the way [to God]." When Jesus describes himself, he seems to invoke God's NAME: I AM. Centuries earlier, when MOSES asked for God's name, God said "I AM" (Exodus 3:14). Jesus used that same phrase seven times. I AM: Bread of Life; Light of the World; Gate for the sheep; Good SHEPHERD; RESURRECTION and the Life; the Way, Truth, and Life; true Vine. *John 6, 8, 10, 11, 14, 15*

Jesus stoops to wash feet. John skips the LAST SUPPER, perhaps because he knows the earlier GOSPELS had already covered it. He adds something new that took place there: Jesus washing the feet of the DISCIPLES—

as though he's a slave. John reports Jesus telling the disciples that if he's not too high and mighty to take on the role of a SERVANT, they shouldn't be either. *John 13*

Temporarily dead. Romans crucify Jesus. Jewish leaders insisted. They said Jesus spoke disrespectfully about God, claiming to be his Son. And they said he claimed to be King of the Jews, which could sound like insurrection against ROME had Jesus not added, "My Kingdom is not of this world." Dead by sundown on Friday, Jesus is up and walking by sunrise on Sunday—risen from the dead. *John 18–20*

JOHN, LETTERS OF 1–3

Famous sound bite: If we confess our sins to God, he can always be trusted to forgive us and take our sins away. 1 John 1:9 CEV

HERETICS IN CHURCH are reinventing Jesus and preaching a warped version of CHRISTIANITY. The writer warns churches not to get sucked into it.

- Writer: Unidentified. Early church leaders credited the apostle John.
- Time: Perhaps as late as the AD 90s, 60 years after Jesus.
- Location: Church leaders said John lived in Ephesus, in what is now Turkey. If so, he may have written to churches in the area.

BIG SCENES

Distorting Jesus. Creative thinkers in the CHURCH get away with SIN. They argue that only spiritual things are good; everything physical is bad. That means: (1) Jesus wasn't physical; he only pretended to die. (2) Since people are physical, they can't help but sin; but because of GOD's spirit in them, they remain HOLY while sinning. John says God's people don't live like the devil. *1 John 1–2:17*

Antichrists 2,000 years ago. In the entire Bible, there are just four verses that mention the ANTICHRIST. All four are in these short letters. The writer describes the antichrists as groups of people:

- They're everywhere.
- They deny the deity of Jesus.
- They deny Jesus came in a human body.
- They live in Jesus' century. 1 John 2:18–29; 4:1–6

Let your love shine. Love one another, the writer says, repeating a teaching Jesus made famous. Then do something about that love: "Let's not merely say that we love each other; let us show the truth by our actions." *1 John 3, 2 John*

JONAH

(JOE nuh)

700s BC

The Lord sent a huge fish to swallow Jonah. Jonah 1:17 NIrV

- Jewish prophet sent to Nineveh

A SUICIDE MISSION is what God's orders must have sounded like to Jonah. He was a PROPHET living in the northern Jewish nation of ISRAEL just a few decades before Assyrian invaders from what is now Iraq wiped Israel off the political map.

God told Jonah to go to ASSYRIA's capital, NINEVEH, and tell its people the city was about to be destroyed. Jonah booked passage on a boat headed in the opposite

UNDER THE SEA is on display at Kuroshio Sea, an aquarium in Okinawa. The Bible doesn't say what kind of fish swallowed Jonah. That may be because no one saw it in the storm. Or perhaps the landlubber Jews couldn't tell a whale from a Loch Ness monster.

direction. Sailors threw him overboard during a storm to appease God. A fish swallowed him and spit him ashore three days later.

He delivered the message. Nineveh repented. God spared the city.

JONAH, BOOK OF

> Famous sound bite: The LORD sent a big fish to swallow Jonah, and Jonah was inside the fish for three days and three nights.
> Jonah 1:17 CEV

GOD ORDERS JONAH to go to the capital of the brutal Assyrian Empire, in what is now Iraq, and tell its people that GOD is going to destroy the city. Jonah sails in the opposite direction. Getting swallowed by a fish convinces him to do as he was told. The Assyrians repent. God spares the city.

- Writer: Jonah, or someone reporting his story.
- Time: During reign of King Jeroboam II (about 793–753 BC).
- Location: Jonah lives in north Jewish nation of Israel, but travels to Nineveh in what is now northern Iraq.

BIG SCENES

Man overboard. NINEVEH is east of Israel. Jonah boards a SHIP headed somewhere west. God stirs up one fine storm, which the sailors blame on Jonah. They toss him overboard. A fish swallows him and three days later spits him up on the shore. *Jonah 1–2*

A city in mourning. Jonah goes to Nineveh. There, he delivers God's message: Nineveh will fall in 40 days. The king believes him and orders everyone to repent and stop sinning. God spares the city. *Jonah 3*

A prophet bummed. Jonah could have been proud to have been among the few PROPHETS who actually got someone to take him seriously, and whose message produced the effect God intended. Instead, he's embarrassed that his prophecy didn't come true. He pouts: "I'm better off dead!" *Jonah 4 MSG*

JONATHAN

(JOHN uh thun)

Died about 1004 BC
David and Jonathan became best friends.
1 Samuel 18:1 CEV

- Oldest son of King Saul

JONATHAN IS MOST FAMOUS for betraying his father to protect his best friend, DAVID.

King SAUL churned crazy green with envy after David killed GOLIATH. Suddenly, every Jew and his sister were singing ballads about David instead of Saul. That's also when Jonathan and David became best friends.

Once Saul went off the deep end and decided to kill David no matter what, Jonathan sent David a warning to run for his life.

Jonathan died with his father and two brothers in a battle with the PHILISTINES.

JOPPA

Map 4 B5

(JOP uh)

Jonah ran from the LORD. He went to the seaport of Joppa and bought a ticket on a ship. **Jonah 1:3** CEV

- Jonah's port of debarkation
- Site of Peter's vision of nonkosher animals
- Where Peter raised Tabitha from the dead

CEDARS OF LEBANON got floated down the sea to Joppa, headed overland to JERUSALEM for Solomon's TEMPLE. This port city is now the southern half of the Israeli twin cities of Tel Aviv-Yafo, Israel's second-largest metro area after Jerusalem.

JORAM

(JOE ram)

Reigned 850–843 BC
Jehu drew his bow and shot Joram between the shoulders. The arrow pierced his heart.
2 Kings 9:24

- Son of Ahab, Jezebel
- King of Israel

KING AHAB'S FAMILY DYNASTY ended the day his son and successor died—assassinated in a coup led by a CHARIOT corps commander: JEHU.

JORDAN RIVER

Map 4 D4

When the priests carrying the Ark came to the edge of the [Jordan] river. . .the water upstream stopped flowing. Joshua 3:15–16 NCV

■ Where Jesus was baptized

COMPARED TO WORLD-CLASS RIVERS like the Nile, Mississippi, or Rhine, the Jordan is a runt of a river.

Meandering along Israel's eastern border with Jordan, it stretches between the SEA OF GALILEE and the DEAD SEA for about 65 miles (105 km) as a dove flies or 135 miles (217 km) as a fish swims.

It was likely a more formidable river in Bible times, before farmers started pumping up the WATER to irrigate their crops. It averages only about 30 yards (27 m) across and 2–10 feet (1–3 m) deep. But when JOSHUA and the JEWS planned to cross it during the springtime flood

THE JORDAN RIVER flows from the Sea of Galilee through a quake-prone valley some 65 miles (105 km) before emptying into the Dead Sea—the lowest spot on the face of the earth and the drainage pit of the Middle East.

ESCAPE TO EGYPT. Joseph takes Mary and baby Jesus to Egypt after learning in a dream that King Herod wants to kill the child. The family stays there until Herod dies in 4 BC.

season, it would have been impassable—until GOD stopped the water upstream at the city of ADAM.

The Jordan River runs along a huge fault line. EARTHQUAKES have dropped the dirt cliffs into the river and dammed it up many times, including at the ruins of Adam in 1927, when the river stopped for 21 hours.

see map, page 249

JOSEPH OF ARIMATHEA

(JOE zuhf of AIR uh muh THEE uh)

First century AD

Joseph of Arimathea took a risk and went to Pilate and asked for Jesus' body. Mark 15:43

- Buried Jesus in his tomb

A TOP JEW, and a member of the Jewish ruling council known as the SANHEDRIN, Joseph risked his reputation and career by coming out of the closet as a follower of Jesus. He got permission to remove Jesus' body from the CROSS and bury it in his family TOMB.

JOSEPH, HUSBAND OF MARY

(JOE zuhf)

First century AD

Joseph was a good man and did not want to embarrass Mary in front of everyone. So he decided to quietly call off the wedding. Matthew 1:19 CEV

- Father of Jesus
- Carpenter or general contractor

SOME CHRISTIANS SQUIRM at the idea that Jesus was the son of Joseph, since the BIBLE says Jesus was the SON OF GOD, conceived through the HOLY SPIRIT. Bible writers didn't have a problem with it: "His NAME is Jesus, the son of Joseph from NAZARETH" (John 1:45). Joseph was Jesus' legal father.

Joseph lived in the small ridgetop village of Nazareth. He worked as a builder or CARPENTER—the GREEK word describing him can go either way. He may have worked with stone and plaster, perhaps helping reconstruct the neighboring city of SEPPHORIS, capital of GALILEE. Working with wood, he may have built household items such as wooden plows, doors, and TABLES.

When he learned of MARY's pregnancy, he planned to quietly DIVORCE her—until an ANGEL appeared to him in a DREAM and convinced him the pregnancy was of God. After Jesus was born, Joseph took his FAMILY to EGYPT. He went there to save Jesus from King HEROD, who saw him as a threat after WISE MEN came to WORSHIP the "newborn king of the JEWS" (Matthew 2:2).

Joseph didn't seem to be around when Jesus started his ministry. Some speculate that he was an older man with CHILDREN from a previous marriage, later identified as Jesus' four brothers and his sisters (Mark 6:3). Others say those were Mary's children after Jesus.

JOSEPH, SON OF JACOB

(JOE zuhf)

1800s BC

Jacob loved Joseph more than any of his other children because Joseph had been born to him in his old age. Genesis 37:3

- Jewish administrator of grain in Egypt
- Father of Manasseh and Ephraim

SPOILED ROTTEN as the favorite son of JACOB, he

- wore a special ROBE that marked him as Daddy's pet
- bragged about DREAMS that predicted he'd be more important that anyone else in his FAMILY
- tattled on his 10 big brothers whenever he got the chance.

By age 17, he ended up getting sold to slave traders headed to EGYPT. His brothers sold him out. REVENGE.

In Egypt, Joseph managed the household affairs of POTIPHAR, a palace official. Potiphar's WIFE, however, wanted the handsome young Joseph to take on a more intimate affair: her.

When he refused, she accused him of RAPE. He

J

spent at least two years in PRISON, perhaps much longer.

His ability to interpret dreams won him a parole. A fellow prisoner who got released passed that info along to the king, who had been troubled by bizarre dreams: seven skinny cows eating seven fat ones; seven withered heads of GRAIN eating seven healthy heads.

Joseph said that meant seven years of bumper crops would dissolve into seven years of DROUGHT.

Impressed, the king put Joseph in charge of stockpiling grain during the bumper-crop years. During the drought, Joseph got the king's permission to invite his FAMILY to move down and weather out the drought along the green banks of the drought-resistant NILE RIVER.

JOSHUA

(JOSH oo uh)

1400s BC or 1200s BC, debated

Joshua took control of the entire land. . . dividing the land among the tribes.
Joshua 11:23

- Jewish commander during the Exodus
- One of 12 scouts sent to Canaan (Israel)
- Successor to Moses

OVER 600,000 JEWISH MEN left EGYPT during the EXODUS, as the CENSUS reported it. Only two made it into the PROMISED LAND of CANAAN, now called Israel: Joshua and CALEB.

All other adults died during their 40 years in the WILDERNESS badlands south of Israel. Joshua and his buddy were two of the dozen SPIES Moses sent to scout Canaan. And they were the only two with enough FAITH in GOD to recommend the invasion, in spite of the GIANTS and the fortified cities they would have to fight.

Joshua was a warrior who, on orders from MOSES, had already led the Jewish refugees into battle against armies that tried to block their path home to what is now ISRAEL.

Forty years later, when it came time for Moses to die and for Generation Next to invade Canaan, God chose Joshua to lead them: "The LORD told Joshua, 'Be brave and strong! I will help you lead the people of Israel into the land that I have promised them' " (Deuteronomy 31:23 CEV).

Starting with JERICHO, on Canaan's eastern border,

Joshua led his lightly armed militia throughout the central hill country. That's where their hit-and-run mobility gave them an advantage over the more heavily armored Canaanites with their war chariots.

Joshua took out the southland armies first, then the northland coalition forces.

Afterward, he divided the land among the dozen tribes and told them each to mop up their own territory—a chore they never managed to finish.

Near the end of his life, Joshua called the leaders together and warned, "If you abandon the LORD and serve other GODS, he will turn against you and destroy you, even though he has been so good to you" (Joshua 24:20).

That's exactly what happened. "After that GENERATION died, another generation grew up who did not acknowledge the LORD or remember the mighty things he had done for ISRAEL" (Judges 2:10).

Joshua died at age 110. The JEWS buried him in the hills where he had fought, settled, and lived.

JOSHUA, BOOK OF

Famous sound bite: "Choose today whom you will serve. . . . But as for me and my family, we will serve the LORD." Joshua's farewell,
Joshua 24:15

ACTING ON THE PROMISE God made to ABRAHAM perhaps 700 years earlier, Joshua leads Abraham's descendants on the invasion of CANAAN, which will become known as Israel.

- Writer: Unknown. Jewish tradition says Joshua wrote most of it.
- Time: Bible experts debate whether the stories took place in the 1400s BC or the 1200s BC.
- Location: Most of the story takes place in Canaan, in what is now Israel and Palestinian territories.

BIG SCENES

Two spies, one hooker. Camped on what is now Jordan's western front, Joshua and the JEWS send a pair of SPIES into Canaan. Mission: check out the defenses of JERICHO, the border town. They check into the HOUSE of a PROSTITUTE, RAHAB. Rookie spies, they spill the beans on the invasion and nearly get caught. Rahab helps them escape in exchange for sparing her and her FAMILY later. *Joshua 2–3*

Crossing a river in flood stage. During springtime flooding, the JORDAN RIVER has topped its banks, making it impassable for the Jews in this era before bridges. GOD somehow stops the water upstream near the city of ADAM. An EARTHQUAKE did the same in 1927, dropping cliffs that dammed up the Jordan for 21 hours near the ruins of Adam. *Joshua 3–4*

Jericho speed bump. Protected on a hill and surrounded by double walls—one at the bottom of the hill and another at the top—Jericho looks impregnable. Until the walls collapse. Some wonder if an earthquake aftershock may have helped, in a miracle of perfect timing. *Joshua 5–8*

Freezing the sun to fight in the shade. After an all-night march from the Jordan River valley up into the Judean hills, it's time for the Jews to fight a daybreak battle. Joshua prays for the sun and moon to stop, and they do. Some read this as POETRY, or as Joshua praying for the sun to stop shining so intensely, which would further weaken his troops. A hailstorm kills most of the enemy. *Joshua 9–10*

Twelve tribes carve up the land. Jews capture most of Canaan's hill country, where their lightly

AND THE WALLS come tumblin' down. Joshua leads the Jews into the Promised Land, where they destroy the border town of Jericho after the walls miraculously collapse.

armed militia has the advantage over more heavily armed locals. Joshua then divides the land among the tribes, ordering each one to mop up any resistance in its own territory. *Joshua 10–11, 13–21*

JOSIAH

(joe SIGH uh)

Reigned 640–609 BC

Josiah was eight years old when he became king. . . . He did what was pleasing in the LORD's sight. 2 Kings 22:1–2

- King of Judah
- Last good king of Jews

WITH HIS DADDY MURDERED, eight-year-old Josiah was suddenly KING of the southern Jewish nation of JUDAH, ruling in JERUSALEM. By age 20, he launched a religious reform movement, destroying pagan shrines throughout the country.

Ten years later, he renovated the TEMPLE. When, in the process, the HIGH PRIEST found the sacred Jewish law book—perhaps the book of DEUTERONOMY—Josiah was shocked at what the book said. The shocker wasn't just how many of GOD's laws the people were breaking. The big shocker was the punishment God promised for disobedience: banishment from the land.

HULDAH, a prophetess, confirmed it would happen. But she said God would delay it until after Josiah's time.

Josiah died in battle, trying to stop Egyptians from marching through his land. The Egyptians were rushing to reinforce the Assyrians in a hopeless battle against the Babylonians.

A couple of decades later, the Babylonians erased Judah from the world map and deported most of the Jewish survivors.

JUBAL

(JEW buhl)

Jubal was the first to play harps and flutes. Genesis 4:21 CEV

FOUNDING FATHER of MUSIC.

JUBILEE YEAR

"Make the fiftieth year a special year, and announce freedom for all the people living in your country. This time will be called Jubilee." Leviticus 25:10 NCV

- Debts forgiven
- Slaves freed
- Farmland not planted

TWICE A CENTURY—once a GENERATION—JEWS got a reminder that GOD owns everything. In the year of Jubilee, there was no planting, no harvesting, no collecting DEBTS, and no keeping slaves. Land rented or sold to anyone outside the ancestral FAMILY returned to the original family.

Bible experts say it's unclear to what extent the Jews practiced this law that could seem impractical for many reasons—such as the need to eat. God did, however, promise bumper crops during the year before the land holiday. "The land will produce enough crops for three years" (Leviticus 25:21).

JUDAH, NATION OF

Map 1 D6

(JEW duh)

Rehoboam son of Solomon was king in Judah. . . . He reigned seventeen years in Jerusalem. 1 Kings 14:21

ISRAEL SPLIT into two nations when King SOLOMON's son and successor, REHOBOAM, refused to lower the taxes. Ten tribes in the northland seceded from the union and took the name of ISRAEL. The southland tribes of Judah and tiny BENJAMIN took the name of the larger tribe.

The only GOD-approved WORSHIP center was the Jerusalem TEMPLE in Judah. But Israel's King JEROBOAM built pagan shrines for northland JEWS. That's because he didn't want his people going back to Jerusalem in Judah. If they did, they might link back up with Israel's legit KINGS, "the dynasty of DAVID" (1 Kings 12:26).

In the BIBLE's list of kings after the split, the only ones identified as godly were kings of Judah—four of them: ASA, JEHOSHAPHAT, HEZEKIAH, and JOSIAH.

JUDAH, SON OF JACOB

(JEW duh)

1800s BC

Judah noticed her [Tamar, his daughter-in-law] and thought she was a prostitute. . . . So he stopped and propositioned her.
Genesis 38:15–16

- Founder of Israel's strongest tribe
- Fathered children with his daughter-in-law
- Saved his little brother Joseph from murder

AS A WIDOWER, Judah fathered twin boys with a VEIL-covered woman he thought was a PROSTITUTE. She was his disgruntled, widowed daughter-in-law—disgruntled because Judah had promised to give her a replacement husband but didn't. Without one, she was destitute.

Once Judah found out who she was, he protected her from the execution that Jewish law allowed.

As a young man, Judah had also saved the life of his 17-year-old brother, JOSEPH. Judah talked his other nine brothers out of killing Joseph, who was one spoiled kid as well as Daddy's pet (Genesis 37:26).

JUDAH, TRIBE OF

Map 1 D6

(JEW duh)

*"Kings will come from Judah's family; someone from Judah will always be on the throne." **Genesis 49:10 NCV***

- Tribal family of David, Jesus

JOSHUA DIVIDED the Jewish homeland among 12 tribes—extended families descended from JACOB's dozen sons. The tribe of Judah descended from Jacob's fourth son, Judah. After the tribes split into two nations, the southland nation took the name of this dominant tribe.

When Jacob blessed his son Judah, he said, "All your relatives will bow before you" (Genesis 49:8). JEWS from all over the country did just that when they came to JERUSALEM, in Judah, to WORSHIP at the TEMPLE.

JUDAISM

(see JEWS)

JUDAS, SON OF JAMES

(JEW duhs)

First century AD

*The other Judas, not Judas Iscariot, then spoke up. **John 14:22** CEV*

- Disciple, the "other Judas"

JESUS HAD TWO JUDAS DISCIPLES. Judas Iscariot sold him out to Jewish leaders. The other Judas, also identified as the "son of James" (Luke 6:16), is mentioned only briefly.

JUDAS ISCARIOT

(JEW duhs is CARE ee uht)

Died about AD 33

*Jesus said, "Judas, would you betray the Son of Man with a kiss?" **Luke 22:48***

- Helped Jews arrest Jesus
- Disciple of Jesus
- Treasurer of the disciples

HE BETRAYED JESUS. That's the infamous highlight of what many consider a lowlife: Judas Iscariot, "son of Simon Iscariot" (John 6:71).

One of Jesus' 12 DISCIPLES, Judas was also the group's treasurer—who treated himself to the MONEY. That could be why he complained when Mary, at BETHANY, poured expensive PERFUME on Jesus. Judas said it should have been sold to help the POOR, perhaps thinking he could have been put in charge of the money.

"Not that he cared for the poor—he was a thief, and since he was in charge of the disciples' money, he often stole some for himself" (John 12:6).

Money was one possible motive for betraying Jesus. Bible writers said Judas got a reward: "thirty pieces of SILVER" (Matthew 26:15).

Another possible motive: "SATAN entered into Judas Iscariot" (Luke 22:3).

Some wonder if Judas was trying to force Jesus into

JUDAS ISCARIOT, the disciple who led the Temple police to Jesus, doesn't usually get the flattering treatment on canvas. Many artists painted him as a redhead—as though redheads are to godliness what some say blondes are to intelligence.

declaring himself the MESSIAH so Jesus would launch a revolt to drive out the Romans and free Israel.

Whatever his motive, when Judas discovered that the JEWS planned to execute Jesus, he returned the money and "went out and hanged himself" (Matthew 27:5).

JUDE

First century AD

This letter is from Jude, a slave of Jesus Christ and a brother of James. Jude 1:1

- Possibly a brother of Jesus
- Nickname for Judas
- Author of the Letter of Jude

JUDAS WAS HIS REAL NAME, but he also went by Jude. Jude was one of Jesus' four brothers: "JAMES, Joseph, Simon, and Judas" (Matthew 13:55). Early in Jesus' ministry, "even his brothers didn't believe in him" (John 7:5).

Early CHURCH leaders say this Jude was the same Jude who wrote the New Testament LETTER of Jude.

JUDE, LETTER OF

Famous sound bite: Now to Him who is able to keep you from stumbling. . . . To God our Savior, who alone is wise, be glory and majesty, dominion and power, both now and forever. Amen. Jude 24–25 NKJV

JUDE WRITES this one-chapter letter of encouragement to Christians everywhere.

- Writer: Jude, brother of James, and possibly of Jesus.
- Time: Perhaps in the AD 60s, given the heresies Jude addresses.
- Location: Roman Empire.

BIG SCENES

Heresy alert. Jude warns his readers about fraudulent Christians who "live immoral lives, defy authority, and scoff at supernatural beings. . . . These people are grumblers and complainers, living only to satisfy their desires. They brag loudly about themselves, and they flatter others to get what they want." *Jude 8, 16*

God's sentence for sinners: death. Fake Christians slip into the CHURCH and start preaching that it's okay to SIN because GOD forgives us. To that, Jude offers a history lesson. He reminds his readers about how God handled some notable sinners, including the people of SODOM AND GOMORRAH (toasted), and the JEWS of what is now ISRAEL (wiped off the map in 586 BC).

JUDEA
Map 4 D5

(jew DEE uh)

Jesus was born in Bethlehem in Judea, during the reign of King Herod. Matthew 2:1

- Roman name for Jewish homeland

A WAFFLING WORD, *Judea* could refer to a small plug of turf in and around JERUSALEM. Or it could refer to territory larger than modern Israel. HEROD THE GREAT, called "king of Judea" (Luke 1:5), ruled parts of what are now ISRAEL, Jordan, and Syria.

Judea is the word Greeks and Romans used for "Judah." JUDAH was the name of Israel's largest tribe. And after ISRAEL split in two, "Judah" became the name of the southern Jewish nation.

JUDGE

Joshua called the tribes of Israel together. . . including the old men, the judges, and the officials. Joshua 24:1 CEV

- Leader who settled disputes
- Hero such as Samson, Gideon

SOME JUDGES BANGED HEADS to get justice.

SAMSON, for example. He was one of a dozen heroes called "judges" in the days before Israel had a KING. "The LORD raised up judges to rescue the Israelites from their attackers" (Judges 2:16).

Samson didn't debate points of law with the PHILISTINES. He hit them over the head with the jawbone of a donkey (Judges 15:15). Justice was served. At least as far as he was concerned.

Other judges in the BIBLE settled disputes in a more traditional manner. The PROPHET SAMUEL doubled as a circuit-riding judge working three cities: "Each year he traveled around, setting up his COURT first at BETHEL, then at GILGAL, and then at MIZPAH" (1 Samuel 7:16).

FAMILY leaders and city elders also served as local judges, often deciding cases at the city GATE—a popular gathering place.

JUDGES, BOOK OF

Famous sound bite: In those days Israel had no king; all the people did whatever seemed right in their own eyes. Judges 21:25

ISRAEL RIDES SIN LIKE A CYCLE. They ride it until they crash. Then they scream for help. Someone comes to their rescue. And they're off again, freewheeling. It works like this: The JEWS commit a SIN, such as worshiping IDOLS. GOD sends something to punish them—usually raiders. The Jews repent and ask God to save them. God sends a hero to their rescue. But then the Jews go back to sinning. This happens a dozen times.

- Writer: Unknown. Some guess the prophet Samuel.
- Time: After Joshua who died around 1375 BC or 1200 BC (scholars debate which), but before Saul became king in about 1065 BC.
- Location: Mainly in what are now Israel and Jordan.

BIG SCENES

The general is a lady. Northland Jews "did evil in the LORD's sight." So he lets a Canaanite king, JABIN, steal from them for 20 years. When they repent, God tells a prophetess named DEBORAH to declare WAR. She stages 10,000 warriors on the steep slopes of MOUNT TABOR. Jabin's CHARIOT corps arrives but gets stuck in a deluge. Jews charge down the hill while the Canaanites run for their lives. *Judges 4–5*

J

IN A SURPRISE ATTACK, Gideon's tiny strike force of 300 catches 135,000 invaders sleeping. Odds are against Gideon's Jews. But God is for them, as the Bible tells it. God wins.

STEPHEN M. MILLER'S ILLUSTRATED BIBLE DICTIONARY

Gideon's strike force. For seven years, Midianite raiders from what is now Saudi Arabia have been storming into Israel's farmland of GALILEE to steal the HARVEST. The Jews call on God for help. He sends GIDEON to the rescue—reinforced by 300 Jews. Their mission: drive off 135,000 Arabs. That's 450 Arabs per Jew. Gideon's militia surrounds the camp at night. They blow horns, smash jars, light TORCHES, and scream. Suddenly awake but confused, the Midianites fight each other and then run for home. *Judges 6–8*

Samson's haircut. He can level a field of 1,000 Philistine warriors with nothing but the jawbone of a DONKEY. Yet all it takes to bring him down is one Philistine girlfriend, DELILAH, with a soft lap and sharp scissors. She nags him into revealing the secret of his strength: his vow never to cut his HAIR. Then she arranges his first haircut—while he's napping with his head on her lap. Afterward he's arrested, blinded, and enslaved. Delilah collects a nice reward. *Judges 13–16*

Gang rape. By the book's end, anarchy rules ISRAEL. A Jewish man walking home with his CONCUBINE (a secondary WIFE) gets attacked by fellow Jews. They RAPE the woman to death. The husband chops her into 12 pieces and then sends the parts to Israel's 12 tribes, demanding justice. Eleven tribes attack the unrepentant tribe of BENJAMIN, nearly wiping it out. The story ends with chaos: "People did whatever they felt like doing." *Judges 19–21 MSG*

JUDGMENT DAY

> *"On judgment day, people will have to account for every careless word they have spoken."* Jesus, Matthew 12:36 NIrV

GOD ISN'T WAITING for the world to end before he passes judgment on people, punishing the wicked and rewarding the godly. Not as the BIBLE tells it. Judgment Day, as Bible writers use the phrase, works the timeline of human history—and then some.

End-time judgment. Jesus and NEW TESTAMENT writers both talked about Judgment Day at the end of world when GOD will separate all the saved from the unsaved—not good from the bad. In an end-time VISION, JOHN said he saw the dead raised for judgment. Those whose deeds in life didn't measure up were thrown into fire: "the SECOND DEATH" (Revelation 20:14). Some say this is the DEATH of the SOUL. Others say it's the soul suffering for eternity.

Judgment days in the past. Jewish PROPHETS talked about plenty of judgment days that have already taken place.

EZEKIEL envisioned the fall of JERUSALEM in 586 BC, when Babylonian invaders from what is now Iraq would level the city: "The day of judgment is here," he warned. "Your destruction awaits!" (Ezekiel 7:10).

JUSTIFICATION

> (JUS tuh fuh KAY shun)
>
> *Since we have been justified through faith, we have peace with God through our Lord Jesus Christ.* Romans 5:1 TNIV

• God's forgiveness

TO SOFTEN A TECH TERM, some theologians use this phrase to help explain what it means for GOD to justify us: It's "just as if I" had never sinned.

Once people repent and believe the BIBLE's teaching that the SACRIFICE of Jesus paid the price for their sins, they're justified. As the apostle PAUL put it, "We have now been justified by his BLOOD. . .reconciled to him [God] through the death of his Son" (Romans 5:9–10 TNIV).

The idea behind the word is that God is just. And justice requires a penalty for SIN, which is a capital offense in the eyes of a HOLY God. Jesus paid the price for everyone.

J

KADESH

Map 1 A8

(KAY dish)

All the people of Israel arrived at the Desert of Zin, and they stayed at Kadesh. Numbers 20:1 NCV

- Oasis where Jewish refugees of the Exodus stayed
- Miriam died here

MOSES AND EXODUS JEWS may have spent most of their 40 years in the badlands at Kadesh oasis.

Scholars guess it was the same spot today called Ain-Gedeirat—the largest oasis in the northern Sinai of EGYPT. It lies about 5 miles (8 km) past Israel's southern border. A spring there produces enough WATER per day to fill a quarter of a million gallons (nearly a million liters).

From this oasis, MOSES sent JOSHUA and 11 other SPIES to scout CANAAN. It's also where Moses and AARON somehow offended GOD when they struck a rock to provide water for the complaining JEWS.

KEBAR RIVER

Map 2 K6

(KEE bar)

The LORD gave this message to Ezekiel. . . beside the Kebar River in the land of the Babylonians. Ezekiel 1:3

AN IRRIGATION DITCH might be a better description of the Kebar. It's located near the city of Nippur in what is now southern Iraq. Near the Kebar is where EZEKIEL saw his first VISION of BABYLON's invasion that would erase the Jewish nation from the world map.

KENITES

(KEN nites)

Saul said to the Kenites, "You were kind to all of the people of Israel when they came up out of Egypt." 1 Samuel 15:6 NIrV

- Tribe of herders

WANDERING HERDERS, the Kenites treated JEWS kindly. JAEL, married to Heber the Kenite, showed her loyalty to the Jews by killing one of their enemies—SISERA—when he stopped to rest in her TENT. "Jael took a hammer and drove a tent-peg through his head" (Judges 4:21 CEV).

KIDRON VALLEY

See Jerusalem, Map 4 C5

(KID run)

Jesus crossed the Kidron Valley with his disciples and entered a grove of olive trees. John 18:1

- Between Jerusalem and Mount of Olives

TO SEE THE SUNRISE FROM JERUSALEM, people look east across the narrow Kidron Valley. On the other side of the valley sits a ridge of hills called the MOUNT OF OLIVES, where Jesus was arrested.

When it rains hard, the valley floor turns into a stream that drains into the DEAD SEA, east about 15 miles (24 km).

KILN

"Take handfuls of soot from a brick kiln, and have Moses toss it into the air while Pharaoh watches." God, Exodus 9:8

- Furnace to harden clay

ROCK-HARD BRICKS and ceramic POTTERY were baked in kilns—some of which reached temps of over 1800 degrees F (982 degrees C). That's the top end of cremation chambers today: 1400–1800 degrees F (760–982 degrees C).

Clay bakers put the objects on shelves, built a fire on the kiln floor, and sealed it shut, allowing just enough air to feed the fire.

DANIEL's fireproof friends—SHADRACH, MESHACH, AND ABEDNEGO—were probably put in such a kiln as punishment for not bowing to the king's idol (Daniel 3).

K

FIRING THE KILN in the 1930s, workers feed the fire with brush. Inside, most likely, are clay pots or bricks baking rock-hard and waterproof.

STEPHEN M. MILLER'S ILLUSTRATED BIBLE DICTIONARY

KING

"We want a king to be our leader." Jews to Samuel 1 Samuel 8:5 CEV

GOD WAS ISRAEL'S KING. He ruled through PROPHETS and other leaders, including MOSES, JOSHUA, and SAMUEL. When Samuel grew old and the JEWS feared they'd be stuck with his corrupt sons, they asked Samuel to select a king for them.

That depressed Samuel. But GOD said, "It is me they are rejecting, not you. They don't want me to be their king any longer" (1 Samuel 8:7).

Samuel warned the Jews what to expect of a king. Examples:

- a tenth of their possessions as a TAX
- a never-ending draft to get workers for the king's building projects, household chores, and farms.

The Jews persisted. God chose SAUL as ISRAEL's first king. And Samuel's warnings proved true, especially under the reign of King SOLOMON who drafted nearly 200,000 men just to build the Jerusalem TEMPLE.

Generally, a king passed his reign over to a SON—although there were exceptions, compliments of coups and kings without sons. DAVID's FAMILY dynasty lasted for some 400 years, until 586 BC, when Babylonian invaders from what is now Iraq wiped the Jewish nation off the map.

KINGDOM OF GOD

"What is God's kingdom like? . . .the smallest seed in all the world. But once it is planted, it grows larger than any garden plant." Mark 4:30–33 CEV

IT'S NOT ANOTHER NAME FOR HEAVEN. That's too limiting.

The Kingdom of God is wherever souls serve him—in HEAVEN and on earth. When Jesus stood among the crowds, he sometimes said, "the Kingdom of God is near" (Mark 1:15) or "the Kingdom of God has arrived among you" (Matthew 12:28).

The Kingdom of God was the main thing Jesus wanted to talk about. The reason he told many of his PARABLES was to help people understand:

- what it takes to become a CITIZEN of God's Kingdom: repent, for one (Mark 1:15).
- what GOD expects of citizens in his Kingdom: HUMILITY "like a child" (Mark 10:15).
- how the kingdom grows: by spreading Jesus' teachings like you're planting seeds (Mark 4:30–33).

Jews in Bible times often called it the Kingdom of Heaven instead of the Kingdom of God. They did that out of respect for God—not wanting to use his HOLY name.

KINGDOM OF HEAVEN

(see KINGDOM OF GOD)

KING'S HIGHWAY

"Please let us pass through your country. . . . We'll travel along the king's highway." Moses to King of Edom, Numbers 20:17 NIrV

AN ANCIENT CARAVAN ROUTE, the King's Highway stretched roughly 300 miles (483 km), from what is now DAMASCUS through Jordan to the Gulf of Aqabah at the RED SEA. Moses probably led the EXODUS out of EGYPT along this route.

See also ROAD.

KINGS, BOOKS OF 1–2

Famous sound bite: "Cut the living child in two, and give half to one woman and half to the other!" 1 Kings 3:25

THE RISE AND FALL OF ISRAEL is what this story is about. It begins with King DAVID dying and his son SOLOMON building a world-class nation—the envy of the Middle East. It ends 400 years later with ISRAEL getting wiped off the world map. Israel splits into two nations: Israel in the north and JUDAH in the south. Out of nearly four dozen kings in both nations, only half a dozen get a godly thumbs-up. The others lead the JEWS into idolatry, which GOD doesn't tolerate. Cue the Assyrian and Babylonian invaders from what is now Iraq.

- Writer: Unknown.
- Time: The stories cover about 400 years, from the final days of King David's reign to the fall of the Jewish nation in 586 BC.
- Location: Israel.

BIG SCENES

Hookers in King Solomon's family court. King David's son and successor, Solomon, asks God for just one thing: WISDOM to rule the nation. God's answer is nowhere more apparent than in Solomon's first reported COURT case. Acting as JUDGE, Solomon has to decide between two PROSTITUTES, each of whom lay claim to a baby boy. When Solomon offers to cut the baby in half so the women can share, one woman objects and the other doesn't. Case solved. *1 Kings 3*

Israel's first Temple. God gives Solomon the go-ahead to build Israel's first permanent WORSHIP center: a TEMPLE in JERUSALEM, which will survive for 400 years. Solomon drafts an army of nearly 200,000 workers, including 30,000 loggers to cut CEDAR in LEBANON and 80,000 QUARRY workers to cut huge limestone blocks. Taking seven years to finish, the Temple stretches about 30 yards long, 10 yards wide, and 15 yards high (27 by 9 by 14 m). *1 Kings 5–9*

Sheba goes shopping in Israel. The QUEEN OF SHEBA comes calling on Solomon, possibly from Yemen in the Arabian Peninsula, 1,500 miles (2,400 km) south. She's towing a massive CARAVAN loaded with rare SPICES, jewels, and 9,000 pounds (4,000 kg) of GOLD. It's a trading expedition, many scholars say. She leaves Israel with "whatever she asked for" (1 Kings 10:13). The writer then reports Solomon's annual revenue from traders, as though the stories are linked. *1 Kings 10*

KING'S HIGHWAY in Jordan—a caravan route in Bible times—is now a paved road that winds its way from the hills around Mount Nebo, dropping some 600 meters (nearly half a mile) into Jordan's mini Grand Canyon: Wadi Mujib. The highway ends near the red rock city of Petra, which is now a ruins and a tourist site.

STEPHEN M. MILLER'S ILLUSTRATED BIBLE DICTIONARY

Wise Solomon's dumb decision. Solomon marries 1,000 women, breaking two laws:

- Jews couldn't marry non-Jews because non-Jews would lead them "to worship other GODS" (Deuteronomy 7:4).
- "The king must not take many wives for himself, because they will turn his heart away from the LORD" (Deuteronomy 17:17).

Solomon does both and ends up worshiping IDOLS of his wives. For this, God vows to take most of the kingdom away from Solomon's FAMILY. *1 Kings 11*

Israel splits in two. Solomon's son and successor, REHOBOAM, refuses to reduce his father's heavy taxes. So the 10 northern tribes secede from the union in about 930 BC. Suddenly there are two kingdoms with two kings: Israel in the north, led by JEROBOAM, and Rehoboam's Judah in the south. *1 Kings 12*

Elijah vs. prophets of Baal. Israel's King AHAB marries a BAAL-loving JEZEBEL. Passionate about her religion, she executes the competition: PROPHETS of God. ELIJAH, however, challenges her 850 prophets and priests to a contest to see who can call down fire from the sky—seemingly a no-brainer for Baal, the storm god pictured with lightning bolts. But they lose. And Elijah has them all executed. *1 Kings 18*

Elijah's chariot of fire. Elijah tutors his replacement, ELISHA. When it's time for Elijah to leave the world, he and Elisha cross the JORDAN RIVER into what is now Jordan. There, "a strong wind took Elijah up into HEAVEN," accompanied by "a flaming CHARIOT pulled by fiery horses" (2 Kings 2:11 CEV). Some might say this sounds like a poetic description of a tornado and lightning storm. But most Christians throughout the ages seem to have taken the story literally. *2 Kings 2*

Israel erased. The northern Jewish nation dies first, about 200 years after seceding from the union. Of the 19 kings they had, not one worshiped God. Assyrian invaders from what is now northern Iraq invade and conquer Israel in 722 BC, destroying the cities and deporting many of the survivors. Those Jews become known as the Lost TRIBES OF ISRAEL. *2 Kings 17*

Judah erased. The southern Jewish nation survives almost 140 years longer, thanks in part to four godly kings out of 20 rulers. But the people's addiction to idolatry eventually earns them the consequences MOSES warned them about: "The LORD will scatter you among all the nations from one end of the earth to the other" (Deuteronomy 28:64). Judah stops paying taxes to the current Middle Eastern superpower: BABYLON, in southern Iraq. In 586 BC, Babylon comes to collect: everything. Most Jewish survivors are deported. The last Jewish nation is dead. *2 Kings 24–25*

NOT A HAPPY KING, Israel's first ruler was a troubled soul. King Saul's advisers called in David to soothe him with harp music, not realizing that David's popularity after killing Goliath is what depressed Saul.

KIRIATH-JEARIM   Map 1 C5

(KEER ee ath JEE uh rim)
The Ark remained in Kiriath-jearim for a long time—twenty years. 1 Samuel 7:2

ISRAEL'S MOST SACRED RELIC, the chest that held the 10 COMMANDMENTS, was stored in this village about 10 miles (16 km) north of JERUSALEM. PHILISTINES had captured it in battle but gave it back when a PLAGUE seemed to accompany it.

KISHON RIVER

Map 1 C4

(KISH on)

The Kishon River swept Sisera's men away.
Judges 5:21 NCV

MORE LIKE A STREAM—or a dry riverbed in the heat of summer—the Kishon flows westward through the JEZREEL VALLEY. But a flood there once helped the JEWS defeat an invading CHARIOT corps.

A Jewish PROPHET named DEBORAH positioned her militia on the slopes of MOUNT TABOR. When a Canaanite general named SISERA approached along the stream, a downpour apparently turned the Kishon into a chariot-killing river—washing some away and trapping others in mud. The Jews charged down the hill and routed their enemy.

KISS

Greet one another with a holy kiss.
1 Corinthians 16:20 NIrV

A KISS WAS A HANDSHAKE in Bible times, as in many cultures today. That peck on the cheek wasn't sexual; it was simply a warm welcome—glad to see you.

Nearly blind ISAAC told his adult son, "Please come a little closer and kiss me, my son" (Genesis 27:26).

The BIBLE's most famous kiss is the one JUDAS ISCARIOT used as a signal, to ID Jesus to arresting officers—to which Jesus replied, "Judas, would you betray the SON OF MAN with a kiss?" (Luke 22:48).

But there's romantic kissing in the Bible, too: "Kiss me—full on the mouth! Yes! For your love is better than WINE" (Song of Songs 1:2 MSG).

KNIFE

Moses' wife, Zipporah, took a flint knife and circumcised her son. Exodus 4:25

TOOLS INSTEAD OF WEAPONS, most knives uncovered from Bible times seem best suited for chores such as cutting food, skinning ANIMALS, and pruning branches. Made of flint, COPPER, BRONZE, and IRON, they typically measured about 6 to 10 inches (15–25 cm).

KORAH

(KOR uh)

Korah. . .along with a few Reubenites. . .
rebelled against Moses. Numbers 16:1–2 MSG

IN A TURF BATTLE OVER RELIGION, Korah led 250 LEVITES in a revolt against MOSES and AARON.

Levites were assistants to the PRIESTS. Aaron and his sons were the only priests. But Korah seemed to think Levites should get to serve as priests, too. A promotion.

Moses decided to let GOD decide. He told Korah and his discontented Levite buddies to report to the WORSHIP center with censers, containers for burning INCENSE offerings—a sacred chore reserved for priests.

The ground cracked open and swallowed Korah and his lieutenants. Fire from the LORD—perhaps lightning—killed the rest of the 250. A demotion.

KORAZIN

Map 4 D3

(KOH ray zin)

"What sorrow awaits you, Korazin. . . . If the miracles I did in you had been done in wicked Tyre and Sidon, their people would have repented." Jesus, Matthew 11:21

A RUIN TODAY, Korazin was a village about 2 miles (3 km) north of Jesus' ministry headquarters in CAPERNAUM.

KOSHER FOOD

(KOH sure)

"Of all the land animals, these are the ones you may use for food." Leviticus 11:2

ON THE MENU for observant JEWS: beef, lamb, and any fish with scales.

Off the menu—forbidden as nonkosher: pork, rabbit, and any shellfish such as crab and lobster.

The BIBLE doesn't explain the reason for the laws. Some experts guess that GOD was simply taking the first steps in teaching Jews to obey him—and in creating customs that set the Jews apart as his unique people.

K

LABAN

(LAY bun)

1900s BC

Jacob said to Laban, "Give me Rachel so that I may marry her." . . . *He brought his daughter Leah to Jacob, and they had sexual relations.*
Genesis 29:21, 23 NCV

- Jacob's uncle and father-in-law
- Father of Rachel and Leah
- Tricked Jacob into marrying Leah
- Rebekah's brother

SNEAKY AND GREEDY, Laban not only tricked his nephew JACOB into marrying both of his daughters; he made Jacob pay the BRIDE fees due to the bride's FAMILY by working for him for 14 years.

Jacob had agreed to work seven years as a herder, for the privilege of marrying RACHEL. But on the WEDDING night, Laban switched brides. He gave Jacob the oldest daughter, LEAH—who was apparently not a looker. Jacob didn't realize he had married Leah until daylight. Too late.

When he complained, Laban said it was the custom to marry off the oldest daughter first—though apparently not the custom to tell the groom the custom.

Laban said Jacob could marry Rachel in a week if he agreed to work another seven years for her.

Laban lived in HARAN, a community in what is now Turkey. Jacob stayed there long enough to work off his 14 years of bride fees and then grow rich in herds. After 20 years, he moved his family back to his home in what is now ISRAEL.

LACHISH

Map 1 B6

(LAY kish)

Sennacherib, the king of Assyria, and all of his forces surrounded Lachish. They got ready to attack it. 2 Chronicles 32:9 NIrV

- Jewish city destroyed by invaders

A FORTRESS CITY protecting JERUSALEM's southern exposure to Egyptians and PHILISTINES, Lachish

perched on a hilltop about 25 miles (40 km) south of ISRAEL's capital.

Double walls surrounded the hill, enclosing 18 acres on the hilltop—roughly the size of 18 football fields.

JOSHUA and the JEWS captured the city from the Canaanites.

Invaders from what is now Iraq destroyed the city twice. First came the Assyrians in 701 BC, then the Babylonians in 586 BC.

Today the ruin is known as Tell ed-Duweir, also known as Tell Lachish. *Tell* means "mound of ruins."

THE LAKE OF FIRE is a Bible description of hellish judgment that many Christians take literally. They say it'll be hot, like the lava from this volcano eruption at Kilauea in Hawaii. Others say the fire symbolizes destruction of evil souls, not eternal torment.

LAKE OF FIRE

Death and Hell gave up their dead. . . . *Then Death and Hell were thrown into the lake of fire. The lake of fire is the second death.*
Revelation 20:13–14 NIrV

AFTER JUDGMENT DAY, the lake of fire becomes the destiny of SATAN, his DEMONS, and "anyone whose name was not found recorded in the BOOK OF LIFE" (Revelation 20:15).

Some scholars say the lake of fire, like HELL, is one of several names for the place of eternal punishment. Some wonder if the Bible writer's reference to "SECOND DEATH" refers to the DEATH of the SOUL—that after the dead are raised for JUDGMENT DAY, those found sinful are annihilated rather than tormented. If so, it's the DESTRUCTION that lasts forever, not the suffering.

LAMB OF GOD

John saw Jesus coming toward him and said, "Look! The Lamb of God who takes away the sin of the world!" John 1:29

- A phrase describing Jesus' mission

JEWS SACRIFICED LAMBS to atone for their sins. JOHN THE BAPTIST seemed to understand that Jesus came to offer himself as a SACRIFICE for the sins of HUMANITY.

Perhaps John—a PROPHET himself—was thinking of a prophecy written 700 years earlier: "He was led like a lamb to the slaughter. . . . My righteous SERVANT will make it possible for many to be counted righteous, for he will bear all their sins" (Isaiah 53:7, 11).

LAME

Jonathan had a son named Mephibosheth, who was crippled in both feet. He was five years old when. . .she [his nurse] dropped him. 2 Samuel 4:4 NCV

IN A DAY WHEN WALKING was often the only means of transportation—especially for the POOR—lame folks were pitied.

Lame people, like the blind, were disqualified from serving as PRIESTS. Yet the BIBLE paints GOD as caring for the lame and promising a time when the blind will see and "the lame will leap like a deer" (Isaiah 35:6).

Jesus healed both. And when JOHN THE BAPTIST sent messengers to ask Jesus if he was the MESSIAH promised by ISAIAH, Jesus offered this answer. "Tell him what you have heard and seen—the blind see, the lame walk. . .the deaf hear" (Matthew 11:4–5).

LAMENTATIONS, BOOK OF

Famous sound bite: Great is his faithfulness. Lamentations 3:23

SADDEST BOOK IN THE BIBLE, Lamentations is an eyewitness report of the fall of JERUSALEM—and the end of the Jewish nation. Babylonian invaders from what is now Iraq level the capital along with other major cities, and then deport most of the survivors so they can't revive the Jewish nation.

- Writer: Unknown. Jewish tradition credits the prophet Jeremiah, who wrote "The Book of Laments" (2 Chronicles 35:25), perhaps another name for this book.
- Time: 588 BC–586 BC, marking the beginning and end of Babylon's siege of Jerusalem.
- Location: Jerusalem.

BIG SCENES
Dead Jerusalem. "Jerusalem, once so full of people, is now deserted," the writer weeps (Lamentations 1:1). Then he describes what he saw during BABYLON's two-and-a-half-year SIEGE of the city:

- Babies "dying in the streets."
- Nobles' "skin sticks to their bones."
- Mothers "cooked their own children. They have eaten them to survive" (Lamentations 2:11, 4:8, 10).

Hope anyhow. EXILED into what is now Iraq, the writer clings to hope by reminding himself that GOD's "mercies begin afresh each morning." Then, in his final words, the writer asks for some fresh MERCY: "Restore us, O LORD, and bring us back to you again! Give us back the joys we once had! Or have you utterly rejected us? Are you angry with us still?" *Lamentations 3, 5*

L

STEPHEN M. MILLER'S ILLUSTRATED BIBLE DICTIONARY

LAMPS in Jesus' day were often clay pots filled with olive oil. A rope wick fed through the spout burned as long as the oil lasted.

LAMP

"No one lights a lamp and then covers it with a bowl. . . . A lamp is placed on a stand, where its light can be seen by all who enter the house." Luke 8:16

FILL A SMALL CLAY POT with OLIVE OIL. Add a wick, light a fire. That's how folks in Bible times lit up the dark.

The lamps looked a bit like a short, squat pitcher with a spout where the wick came out. Some had multiple spouts and wicks for extra light.

In the BIBLE, lamps often symbolized good things such as insight and guidance from GOD: "The light from his lamp showed me the way through the dark" (Job 29:3 CEV).

LAMPSTAND

"Make a lampstand out of pure gold. . . . Six branches must come out from the sides. . . three on one side and three on the other." Exodus 25:31–32 NIrv

THINK MENORAH, the Jewish candelabrum that holds SEVEN lights. Crafted of GOLD and decorated with golden ALMOND FLOWERS, this is the lampstand that MOSES said GOD designed for ISRAEL's tent WORSHIP center. Lampstands for everyday use were usually made of stone, POTTERY, or wood and were built to hold one or more lamps.

LAODICEA   Map 3 F3

(lay ODD uh SEE uh)

To the church in Laodicea. . . "I am going to spit you out of my mouth." Revelation 3:14, 16 NIrv

- One of seven churches in Revelation

JESUS CHEWED OUT the CHURCH in Laodicea, a city in what is now western Turkey. A PROPHET named JOHN said Jesus' stern words came to him in a VISION.

Jesus said the church was like lukewarm WATER, neither hot nor cold—perhaps a reference to the water piped into the city from nearby hot springs. Jesus said he was going to spit it out.

He also said they needed to buy some eye salve from him, to treat their spiritual blindness. Laodicea was famous for its eye salve.

LAST DAYS

ALSO KNOWNS AS "END TIMES," it's *eschatology* to Bible scholars. That's from the GREEK word *eschatos*, meaning "last."

It's a shifty phrase in the BIBLE.

Sometimes it describes life at the moment:

- "This is the last hour. You heard that the enemy of Christ would appear at this time, and many of Christ's enemies have already appeared. So we know that the last hour is here" (1 John 2:18 CEV).
- "Christ was chosen even before the world was created, but because of you, he did not come until these last days" (1 Peter 1:20 CEV).
- "What you see was predicted long ago by the prophet Joel: 'In the last days,' God says, 'I will pour out my Spirit upon all people'" (Acts 2:16–17).

Sometimes it points to a distant future:

- "In the last days the mountain on which the LORD's Temple stands will become the most important of all mountains" (Isaiah 2:2 NCV).

What this wide-ranging use of the phrase means, many scholars say, is that "last days" refers to the last stage in God's plan to save people—the stage that began when Jesus opened the door to SALVATION for everyone.

Other scholars say "last days" can also refer to when Jesus comes again, bringing "a NEW HEAVEN and a new earth, for the old heaven and the old earth had disappeared" (Revelation 21:1).

LAST SUPPER

JESUS' LAST MEAL, which he ate with his DISCIPLES a few hours before his arrest, became one of CHRISTIANITY's

L

JESUS'S LAST MEAL with his disciples took place in a Jerusalem house the night of his arrest. Christians commemorate the meal with a sacred ritual: eating bread and drinking wine or grape juice. The rite is known by many names, including communion and the Eucharist.

most revered sacraments—a ritual known by several names: the LORD'S SUPPER, COMMUNION, MASS.

Apparently knowing he would be in the grave when most JEWS would be eating the PASSOVER meal the next night, on Friday, Jesus seems to have arranged for an early Passover MEAL on Thursday. He gathered his disciples in an upstairs room in a JERUSALEM HOUSE. There he gave them BREAD, saying it was his body that was about to be broken for them. And he gave them WINE, saying "This is my BLOOD. . .poured out as a SACRIFICE for many" (Mark 14:24).

Jesus asked that whenever they shared bread and wine together in the future they would remember him. Christians have been doing that ever since.

Some Christians, especially Roman Catholics, teach that the bread and wine transform into the actual body and blood of Jesus. Others, such as most Protestants, say the bread and juice simply represent Jesus' body and blood.

A RABBI carries into worship the synagogue's scroll containing the Law of Moses, known in Hebrew as the Torah.

LAVER

(see BASIN)

LAW OF MOSES

> "Teacher, which is the most important commandment in the law of Moses?"
> Matthew 22:36

A FLEXIBLE PHRASE, "Law of Moses" can refer to the first five books in the BIBLE: GENESIS, EXODUS, LEVITICUS, NUMBERS, and DEUTERONOMY. Ancient Jewish tradition credits Moses as the writer of those books.

But "Law of Moses" can also refer to the hundreds of laws preserved in the four books starting with Exodus. The Bible says GOD gave Moses these laws during the Jewish exodus out of EGYPT. Moses got the 10 COMMANDMENTS at MOUNT SINAI. The other laws came later, during the year the JEWS camped at Sinai and perhaps later, while they served their 40-year sentence in the badlands.

These laws covered a wide territory of topics, from rules about how to properly sacrifice ANIMALS to about what to do in cases of ROBBERY, RAPE, and manslaughter.

When a scholar asked Jesus to ID the most important

law, Jesus said, "You must love the LORD your God with all your heart, all your SOUL, and all your mind.' This is the first and greatest commandment. A second is equally important: 'Love your NEIGHBOR as yourself.' The entire law and all the demands of the PROPHETS are based on these two commandments" (Matthew 22:37–40).

LAYING ON OF HANDS

(see HANDS, LAYING ON OF)

LAZARUS

(LAZ uh russ)

First century AD

> ***Jesus shouted, "Lazarus, come out!" And the dead man came out, his hands and feet bound in graveclothes. John 11:43–44***

- Raised from the dead by Jesus
- Brother of Mary and Martha

JESUS WAITED UNTIL LAZARUS WAS DEAD before coming to his rescue.

The two were friends. LAZARUS lived with his sisters Mary and MARTHA in BETHANY, a village on the outskirts of JERUSALEM. All three were followers of Jesus, and they had hosted him in their home.

Yet when Jesus got word that Lazarus was sick, he waited two days before going to him. By then, Lazarus was four days dead. That's one day longer than many Jews said the SOUL would linger by the body, hoping for resuscitation.

When Jesus arrived and saw the family and friends MOURNING, he wept. The writer didn't say why. Perhaps the emotional pain of his friends moved him.

In perhaps Jesus' most dramatic MIRACLE of all, so far, he called Lazarus out of the grave.

The reaction of Jewish leaders seems more than ironic—even funny. They decided that the only way to stop this man who could raise the dead was to kill him (John 11:53). And Lazarus, too (John 12:10). Again.

They were afraid Jesus would draw a following as ISRAEL'S promised MESSIAH and that he'd lead a revolt against ROME. "Then the Roman ARMY will come and destroy both our TEMPLE and our nation" (John 11:48).

LAZINESS

Having a lazy person on the job is like a mouth full of vinegar or smoke in your eyes.
Proverbs 10:26 CEV

LAZY IS CRAZY as far as Bible writers tell it. A sampling of their criticism:

- "Lazy people want much but get little" (Proverbs 13:4).
- "As a door swings back and forth on its hinges, so the lazy person turns over in BED" (Proverbs 26:14).
- "Some people are too lazy to fix a leaky ROOF—then the HOUSE falls in" (Ecclesiastes 10:18 CEV).

L

LAZARUS rises from the grave, four days dead and walking. It's Jesus' most remarkable miracle—until he rises from the dead himself.

SKINNED. A tanner scrapes the soft tissue and blood off the inside of an animal hide. If he doesn't want the fur, he'll scrape that side, too. Then he'll dry the skin on a stretching frame (right) and finish it with smoke, which gives leather its brown color. Unsmoked hides get stiff when wet.

LEAH

(LEE uh)

1900s BC

Laban had two daughters. Leah, the oldest, had nice eyes. But Rachel had a nice everything else. Genesis 29:16–17 AUTHOR'S PARAPHRASE

- Jacob's first wife, married by trickery
- Mother of six sons

JACOB DIDN'T LOVE LEAH. He arranged to marry RACHEL. But the father of these two sisters pulled a switcheroo, substituting Leah in the dark.

The writer of the ancient story compared the sisters, but it's unclear what he was saying about Leah. Some Bible translations say she had "no sparkle" in her eyes, "weak eyes," "soft eyes," or "nice eyes." Whatever the case, the context suggests it was the flip side of the shekel from Rachel, who had "a beautiful figure and a lovely face" (Genesis 29:17).

Half of the 12 TRIBES OF ISRAEL came from Leah, mother of six of JACOB'S dozen sons. Leah's sons became the founding fathers of the tribes of REUBEN, SIMEON, LEVI, JUDAH, ISSACHAR, and ZEBULUN.

LEATHER

"Complete the tent [Tabernacle] covering with a protective layer of tanned ram skins and a layer of fine goatskin leather."
Exodus 26:14

ANIMAL HIDES provided the raw material for lots of things people needed in Bible times—from the home front to the battlefront.

Soldiers wore leather helmets, BELTS, SANDALS, and SWORD sheaths, and they carried well-oiled leather SHIELDS to deflect arrows and artillery ROCKS of slingers.

At home, leather became tents, BUCKETS, WINE-SKINS, and even SCROLLS on which to write. Many of the famous DEAD SEA SCROLLS were written on leather. Most scrolls had broken into tiny pieces, producing a pile of what would have been like dozens of jigsaw puzzles dumped into a trash bin. Scientists used DNA testing to separate the puzzles by determining which pieces went together on the same strip of leather.

See also TANNER.

LEBANON

Map 1 D2

(LEB uh none)

"Cut down cedar trees in Lebanon for me."
1 Kings 5:6 NIrV

CEDARS OF LEBANON, from Israel's neighbor nation to the north, were the top-grade lumber that King SOLOMON ordered for his TEMPLE and PALACE in JERUSALEM. Most of Lebanon's forests disappeared in the 1500s under Islamic rule of the Turkey-based Ottoman Empire. Little remains today.

ISRAEL had a notorious QUEEN from SIDON, Lebanon, about 25 miles (40 km) south of Beirut: JEZEBEL.

LEEKS

"We remember the fish we used to eat for free in Egypt. And we had all the cucumbers, melons, leeks, onions, and garlic we wanted."
Numbers 11:5

FOOD FOR A FIRST DATE probably shouldn't include leeks, a member of the onion family—with a similar taste and kick in the nose. Egyptians ate the leaves raw in salads and cooked them in soups and stews.

LEGION

Jesus demanded, "What is your name?" "Legion," he replied, for he was filled with many demons. **Luke 8:30**

THE ROMAN EMPIRE fielded 25 legions of soldiers during Jesus' ministry years, scattering them throughout Europe, Africa, and the Middle East—including two in EGYPT and four in SYRIA. A legion numbered anywhere from 5,400 to 6,000 men.

LEHI

Map 1 C6

(LEE hi)

Samson approached Lehi. . . . He found a fresh jawbone of a donkey. He grabbed hold of it and struck down 1,000 men.
Judges 15:14–15 NIrV

NEAR THIS JEWISH VILLAGE, probably somewhere along the Philistine border, SAMSON broke free of the ropes that held him for the PHILISTINES who arrested him. They had hunted him down and arrested him for crimes against their nation. Suddenly free, Samson grabbed a DONKEY's jawbone and killed 1,000 Philistines.

LENTILS

Jacob gave Esau some bread and lentil stew.
Genesis 25:34

COUSIN OF PEAS, lentil seeds are rich in protein. It's also one of the oldest plants cultivated. People in Bible times used it in soups and stews, and they ground the dry beans into FLOUR for BREAD.

LEOPARD

My bride, together we will leave Lebanon! We will say good-by to the peaks. . .where lions and leopards live in the caves.
Song of Songs 4:8 CEV

NOW NEARLY EXTINCT in Bible lands, leopards were once very much at home there—and a threat to herders and travelers.

LEPROSY

There stood Miriam, her skin as white as snow from leprosy. **Numbers 12:10**

NOT ALL LEPERS in the Bible had leprosy, most Bible experts agree. Some probably had eczema, psoriasis, or a temporary rash—not what doctors today call Hansen's disease, an infection caused by bacteria that produces lesions on the skin, including light patches that numb the nerves so the patient doesn't feel pain.

Numb to pain, lepers sometimes fail to get an injury treated. Infection sets in, and the body part needs amputated.

L

There was plenty of room for misdiagnosis because PRIESTS did the diagnosing. Anyone suspected of having leprosy was quarantined for a week. If the symptoms persisted, they got another week. After that, it was *hasta la vista*—leave the community.

Those who were healed were restored to the community during eight days of cleansing rituals (Leviticus 14:1–32).

Leprosy was one of the many DISEASES Jesus healed, including "a man with an advanced case of leprosy" (Luke 5:12).

LETTERS

Jezebel wrote some letters, signed Ahab's name to them, and used his own seal to seal them. 1 Kings 21:8 NCV

TO KEEP A LETTER PRIVATE, people in Bible times would write on an animal skin or a PAPYRUS sheet. Then they would roll or fold the sheet, tie string around it, push a plug of wax or clay into the string, and press their personalized stamp into the plug. Kings had signet rings to make their mark. Anyone who wanted to read the letter had to break it open. (See also SEALS.)

People also wrote messages on clay tablets and even pieces of broken POTTERY—like we write on scraps of paper.

Some folks wrote their own notes. Others—perhaps illiterate or simply needing help writing a formal document—hired professional writers: SCRIBES.

Most of the books in the NEW TESTAMENT were originally letters. PAUL dictated his letter to Christians in ROME: "I, Tertius, the one writing this letter for Paul, send my greetings, too" (Romans 16:22).

SCRATCH PADS. That's what folks did with broken pieces of pottery. They would etch short messages into the hard clay or write notes in ink if they had any handy.

LEVI

1800s

Simeon and Levi are two of a kind, ready to fight at the drop of a hat. Genesis 49:5 MSG

- Son of Jacob and Leah

ODDLY ENOUGH, for a son JACOB criticized as too violent, Levi became the ancestral father of the LEVITES: the tribe in charge of WORSHIP. PRIESTS came from this tribe. So did all of their assistants who helped them at the worship center.

LEVIATHAN

The LORD will. . .punish Leviathan, the swiftly moving serpent, the coiling, writhing serpent. He will kill the dragon of the sea. Isaiah 27:1

- Sea monster in ancient legends

IN A MYTHOLOGICAL STORY from SYRIA, Leviathan is a sea monster who joins forces with Mot, the Canaanite god of the underworld. Together they fight CANAAN's chief god: BAAL. Bible writers refer to the story as a way to PRAISE God, who is strong enough to defeat the most vicious power of evil.

LEVIRATE MARRIAGE

(LEV uh rite)

"His widow must not marry anyone outside the family. Instead, she must marry her late husband's brother." Deuteronomy 25:5 CEV

SOCIAL SECURITY for Jewish widows without CHILDREN involved remarriage—to the nearest relative of her dead HUSBAND.

WOMEN had few rights apart from men. A woman without a husband or a SON could end up destitute. Jewish law protected widows by requiring the nearest relative to marry the WIDOW and give her a son to inherit the FAMILY estate of the dead husband.

RUTH proposed to BOAZ, declaring him "my FAMILY

REDEEMER" (Ruth 3:9), meaning a relative eligible to marry her. He accepted.

LEVITES

(LEE vites)

"Put the Levites in charge of the holy tent." Numbers 1:50 NIrV

- Jewish priests and other worship leaders

LEVITES WERE ISRAEL'S WORSHIP LEADERS. They were also members of the tribe of LEVI—an extended FAMILY of Jews descended from Levi, one of JACOB's 12 sons.

They took care of the TENT worship center and later the TEMPLE in JERUSALEM. They maintained the facility, provided security, and helped in worship services by providing MUSIC and assisting the PRIESTS with SACRIFICES and other rituals.

Priests were Levites, too. But they had to descend from one particular Levite: AARON, the brother of MOSES. Aaron served as ISRAEL's first HIGH PRIEST. His sons assisted him as priests.

Levites didn't inherit any major section of Israel. Instead, they were spread throughout the country into 48 LEVITICAL CITIES, so Jews in all the scattered tribes had easy access to knowledgeable worship leaders.

In addition to getting these cities, the Levites got to keep meat "from the offerings burned on the ALTAR" (Joshua 13:14). In most sacrifices, only part of the meat was burned. The rest went to the worship leaders as salary. They could eat it or trade it for other necessities.

LEVITICAL CITIES

(luh VIT te cul)

The people of the Levi tribe had a total of forty-eight towns within Israel, and they had pastures around each one of their towns. Joshua 21:41–42 CEV

JEWS FROM THE TRIBE OF LEVI didn't get a slice of ISRAEL's pie—a wedge of land like the other tribes got.

L

Instead, the BIBLE says each tribe donated selected cities to the LEVITES: 48 scattered throughout the country. This gave each tribe easy access to knowledgeable WORSHIP leaders.

LEVITICUS

A RULE BOOK, Leviticus is GOD's how-to guide for the JEWS, teaching them how to live as God's people.

- Writer: Unknown. Jewish tradition says Moses wrote it.
- Time: 1440s BC according to some Bible experts, and around 1290 BC according to others.
- Location: Camped at the base of Mount Sinai, somewhere in the Sinai Peninsula in what is now Egypt. Location of the mountain is uncertain. One tradition puts it near the southern tip of the peninsula.

BIG SCENES

How to get forgiven: give blood. In the eyes of a HOLY God, SIN is a capital offense. Any sin. But God sets up a sacrificial system, accepting ANIMALS as a substitute for sinners. "Life is in the BLOOD, and I have given you the blood of animals to SACRIFICE in place of your own" (Leviticus 17:11 CEV). Sacrifices include BULLS, SHEEP, GOATS, and BIRDS (usually for the POOR). *Leviticus 1–7*

A priest for the Jews. God has the Jews build a tent WORSHIP center according to his specifications. Then he arranges for the tribe of LEVI—Jews known as LEVITES—to maintain the facility. He sets up a priesthood. AARON becomes the HIGH PRIEST, with his sons serving under this authority as PRIESTS. In the future, only descendants of Aaron may serve as priests. *Leviticus 8*

Kosher menu. Jews are what they eat, according to Jewish law—KOSHER or nonkosher. God sets up a menu unique to the Jews. People will be able to tell a Jew from a non-Jew by what is eaten or not eaten. Off the menu as nonkosher, any meat with blood still in it (blood belongs to God in sacrifices). No pork. No

LEVITICUS, a book of Jewish rules, includes a detailed how-to on offering animal sacrifices to God—one of the main ways Jews worshiped.

shellfish. No rabbit. Many Bible experts speculate that the food restrictions had nothing to do with health concerns but everything to do with (1) helping distinguish the Jews as God's unique people and (2) teaching them Obedience 101. *Leviticus 11, 17*

Holy holidays. God sets up a CALENDAR of religious holidays. *Yom Kippur*, or the DAY OF ATONEMENT, is a day for all Jews to fast and repent of sins from the past year. PASSOVER, held near Easter each spring, reminds them of God freeing them from SLAVERY in EGYPT. Several holidays are HARVEST festivals of thanks to God: PENTECOST (WHEAT), First Fruits (FLAX, BARLEY), FESTIVAL of Booths (fall crops such as GRAPES, OLIVES). *Leviticus 23, 25*

LILY

LILIES AREN'T USUALLY LILIES in the BIBLE, many scholars say. Not lilies as we define them today. That's why several modern Bible translations simply call the lilies Jesus referred to as "FLOWERS" (TNIV) or "wild flowers" (NIrv). GALILEE's springtime fields light up in a rainbow of color—especially red from the poppylike crown anemone. Lilies grow there, too.

LINEN

> "There was a rich man who was dressed in purple and fine linen and lived in luxury every day." Luke 16:19 TNIV

- Fabric from flax fibers

RICH JEWS IN ISRAEL could afford "fine linen," which Bible experts say probably refers to a SILKlike fabric imported from EGYPT. It came from dried fibers in the stalks of a vegetable called FLAX. It grew in Israel. But Egypt's soil along the NILE RIVER is perfectly suited for flax.

People in Bible times used linen for clothes, BURIAL shrouds, tents, and SHIP sails.

LIVER

> The king of Babylon. . .decides by divination which of the two roads to take. . . . He examines a goat liver. Ezekiel 21:21 MSG

JEWS BURNED AN ANIMAL'S LIVER along with both kidneys in one of many prescribed SACRIFICES to atone for SIN (Leviticus 4:9). People of other nations used animal livers to tell the future. They would sacrifice an ANIMAL and then examine the liver. Nodules or marks in certain areas were seen as signs.

LOAN

> "You may charge interest to foreigners, but you may not charge interest to Israelites." Deuteronomy 23:20

LENDING TO PEOPLE IN NEED is a good thing, the BIBLE teaches. "If you help the POOR, you are lending

LINEN starts with stalks of flax that look a bit like hay. Workers shred the stalks into fiber then weave the fiber into thread.

to the LORD—and he will repay you!" (Proverbs 19:17).

Lending MONEY wasn't supposed to be a money-making venture for JEWS—at least not when the debtor was a fellow Jew. So read the laws of MOSES.

Evidence from the Bible and from other history suggests not all Jews obeyed that law. PROPHETS accused Jews of giving the green light to "loan racketeers" (Ezekiel 22:12). Jews in the Egyptian city of Elephantine went on record, charging fellow Jews 12 percent interest in the 400s BC. (See also BANKING.)

Jews were allowed, however, to accept collateral as a promise that the borrower would repay the loan. But the lender couldn't take collateral that would produce a hardship for the debtor:

- Clothes. "Never accept a WIDOW's garment as security for her DEBT" (Deuteronomy 24:17).
- Tools needed to make a living. "If someone owes you something, do not take his two stones for grinding GRAIN. . .in place of what he owes, because this is how the person makes a living" (Deuteronomy 24:6 NCV).

LOCUST

"I will bring a swarm of locusts on your country. They will cover the land so that you won't be able to see the ground."
Exodus 10:4–5

MIGRATORY GRASSHOPPERS with wings. That's the desert locust (*Schistocerca gregaria*) that plagued Bible lands. They were born in African and Arabian DESERTS, where predators were few.

Egg pods hatch in the warm ground and can grow into massive swarms of millions of locusts per square mile (1.6 square km). Each egg pod packs 80 to 150 eggs. Up to 1,000 egg pods have been found under a square yard (meter) of soil. That's 80,000 to 150,000 baby locusts.

A PLAGUE of locusts was one of 10 plagues the BIBLE says MOSES used to convince EGYPT's king to free the JEWS from SLAVERY.

One PROPHET compared an ARMY of invaders to "a vast army of locusts" (Joel 1:6), warning that this invasion force would decimate the Jewish homeland on a much larger scale.

LOIS

(LOW us)

First century AD

I remember your genuine faith, for you share the faith that first filled your grandmother Lois and your mother, Eunice. 2 Timothy 1:5

- Timothy's grandmother

IN PAUL'S LAST KNOWN LETTER, written while he was awaiting execution in ROME, he commended the FAITH of his closest associate, TIMOTHY, along with Timothy's mother and grandmother.

THINK GRASSHOPPER, more gregarious than normal. That's why the scientific name for the desert locust seems fitting: *Schistocerca gregaria*.

LORD

The king of Israel [Ahab] accepted the terms [of King Ben-Hadad]: "As you say, distinguished lord; I and everything I have is yours." 1 Kings 20:4 MSG

- Term of respect
- Title often applied to God

LIKE "SIR," *Lord* was a go-to word folks used to address someone whose authority they recognized and respected. It's how a SERVANT might have addressed a master, a WIFE her HUSBAND, or a young man an ELDER in the community.

LORD'S DAY

It was the Lord's Day, and I was worshiping in the Spirit. Revelation 1:10

- Sunday, first day of Jewish week
- The day Jesus rose from the dead

THE FIRST CHRISTIANS WERE JEWS who worshiped on Saturday, the Jewish SABBATH. But Christians also met on Sunday, marking the day of Jesus' RESURRECTION. "On the first day of the week, we gathered with the local believers to share in the LORD'S SUPPER. PAUL was PREACHING to them" (Acts 20:7).

Meetings like this may have started as just a short time of WORSHIP and COMMUNION, followed by the people returning to their chores of the day. By the end of the first century, most church historians say, Christians had made the transition from worshiping on the Jewish Sabbath to the Lord's Day. JEWS no longer welcomed them into the synagogues on the Sabbath. Jews considered them heretics.

LORD'S PRAYER

When Jesus had finished praying, one of his disciples said to him, "Lord, teach us to pray." Luke 11:1 CEV

JESUS WASN'T A FAN of showy, long-winded public prayers.

Two GOSPEL writers reported a prayer Jesus gave his DISCIPLES as an example of the short, to-the-point style he recommended. Luke 11:2–4 offers the condensed version. MATTHEW reports a slightly longer version in Jesus' famous SERMON ON THE MOUNT:

"Our Father in heaven, may your name be kept holy. May your Kingdom come soon. May your will be done on earth, as it is in heaven. Give us today the food we need, and forgive us our sins, as we have forgiven those who sin against us. And don't let us yield to temptation, but rescue us from the evil one" (MATTHEW 6:9–13).

LORD'S SUPPER

(see COMMUNION, LAST SUPPER)

LOT

2100s BC

Angels took Lot, his wife, and his two daughters. . .and led them out of the city [Sodom]. . . . One of the angels said, "Run for your lives!" Genesis 19:16–17 CEV

- Abraham's nephew
- Escaped Sodom's fire

ORPHANED, Lot migrated with his uncle ABRAHAM from what is now Iraq to Israel. When their herds grew too large to graze together, the men parted company. Lot moved to what became known as sin city: Sodom. It was somewhere in a fertile plain in the area.

Raiders stormed Sodom and kidnapped Lot, along with other citizens. Abraham rescued them all.

When GOD decided to burn Sodom off the planet, he sent ANGELS to get Lot and his FAMILY out of town. Lot's WIFE died, when pausing to look back, "she turned into a pillar of SALT" (Genesis 19:26)—perhaps caught in the superheated spray of exploding minerals.

L

"When direction from the LORD is needed. . . Eleazar the priest. . .will use the Urim—one of the sacred lots." Numbers 27:21

- Tool to help make decisions

A BIT LIKE FLIPPING A COIN, throwing lots was one way people in ancient times made tough decisions. Lots may have been as simple as a stone with a mark on one side.

The Jewish HIGH PRIEST carried "Thummim and Urim—the sacred lots" (Deuteronomy 33:8), which they used to determine GOD's will.

When sailors wanted to find out who on board caused the storm that engulfed their SHIP, "lots identified JONAH as the culprit" (Jonah 1:7). When Jesus' DISCIPLES decided to replace JUDAS ISCARIOT, they used lots "and MATTHIAS was selected to become an APOSTLE with the other eleven" (Acts 1:26).

LUCIFER (see SATAN)

LUKE

First century AD

Luke, the beloved doctor, sends his greetings.
Colossians 4:14

- Associate of Paul
- Possible writer of Gospel of Luke, Acts

ONE BIBLE WRITER WASN'T A JEW. If early CHURCH leaders got it right, a GENTILE physician named Luke wrote a two-part history of the church.

Early church leaders credit this traveling associate of PAUL with writing the story of Jesus, known as the GOSPEL of Luke, along with its sequel, the story of how the church got started: ACTS.

LEAVE IT TO LUKE, a physician, to give us the Bible's most beloved story of Jesus' birth—including the doctorly detail of Mary wrapping her baby in swaddling clothes.

LUKE, GOSPEL OF

Famous sound bite: Our Father which art in heaven, hallowed be thy name. Thy kingdom come. Thy will be done. Luke 11:2 KJV

LONGEST BOOK IN THE NEW TESTAMENT, the Gospel of Luke presents "a careful account" of Jesus' life and ministry compiled from "eyewitness reports circulating among us from the early DISCIPLES" (Luke 1:2, 3).

- Writer: Uncertain. Early church leaders credit one of Paul's associates: "Luke, the beloved doctor" (Colossians 4:14).
- Time: Lifetime of Jesus, from about 6 BC–AD 33.
- Location: Israel.

BIG SCENES

World's most famous birth announcement. The ANGEL Gabriel appears to MARY, fiancée of JOSEPH. Gabriel's news shocks Mary, a VIRGIN: "You will conceive and give BIRTH to a son, and you will name him Jesus." When Mary asks how, GABRIEL says, "The HOLY SPIRIT will come upon you. . . . Nothing is impossible with GOD." *Luke 1*

God born in a barn. Very pregnant, Mary travels with Joseph to BETHLEHEM to register for a CENSUS. No vacancies. They end up finding shelter in a stable, perhaps one of the many caves in the area. Jesus is born there. Mary wraps him in strips of cloth—a detail ignored by other GOSPEL writers, but one that would seem appropriate coming from a physician. *Luke 2*

Jesus, the child prodigy. Jesus is 12 years old when he and his FAMILY make the four-day PILGRIMAGE to JERUSALEM for the annual PASSOVER holiday. There Jesus wows the Jewish scholars at the TEMPLE. He asks insightful questions. And he offers amazing answers. *Luke 2:41–52*

Jesus' unneighborly neighbors. Grown up, Jesus launches his ministry of teaching and HEALING. But when he returns home to NAZARETH, he gets no love. A riot breaks out in the SYNAGOGUE after he implies that he's the promised MESSIAH. The mob takes him to the edge of town, hoping to pitch him off a cliff. But in all the confusion, he walks away. *Luke 4*

Doing something about the weather. MATTHEW, MARK, and Luke all report the story of Jesus stopping a storm. Jesus and the disciples are sailing across Israel's huge lake, the SEA OF GALILEE. A storm erupts, which the weary Jesus seems capable of sleeping through. But the disciples wake him because they think the boat is about to go down. Jesus tells the wind and the waves to stop, and the Sea of Galilee becomes Lake Placid—stunning the disciples. *Luke 8:22–25*

One good Gentile, a Samaritan. A Jewish scholar knows that his Bible says JEWS should "love your NEIGHBOR as yourself" (Leviticus 19:18). But he asks Jesus who qualifies as a neighbor. Many Jews teach that only fellow Jews qualify. Jesus answers the question with a story about a Jew who gets mugged on the barren stretch of road between JERICHO and Jerusalem. The man is left for dead. Two Jewish worship leaders walk by, ignoring him. But a SAMARITAN—from a race of people many Jews hated—stops and helps the injured man. Jesus asked the scholar who acted neighborly. The answer was obvious: not the Jews. *Luke 10:25–37*

One dumb son, a prodigal. When Jewish leaders criticize Jesus for hanging out with lowlifes—implying that birds of a feather flock together—Jesus responds with a story about a young man who wastes his share of the family INHERITANCE on wild living. When the man comes home, broken and humiliated, his FATHER welcomes him by throwing a party. Jesus says that's how HEAVEN reacts when a sinner repents. Jesus says RABBIS are spiritual guides who should surround themselves with lost souls looking for God. *Luke 15*

Jesus, a dead man walking. Jewish leaders orchestrate the execution of Jesus on grounds of insurrection, saying he claims to be the king of the Jews. Jesus is dead by sundown on Friday, but alive and walking by Sunday morning. *Luke 22–24*

LYDIA

(LID ee uh)

First century AD

Lydia. . .a merchant of expensive purple cloth. . .was baptized. . . . She said [to Paul], "Come and stay at my home." Acts 16:14–15

PAUL'S FIRST CONVERT IN EUROPE, Lydia was a businesswoman living in PHILIPPI, a Greek town near the Aegean Sea.

Apparently rich, Lydia invited PAUL and his associate, SILAS, to hold WORSHIP services in her home. Throughout Paul's ministry, this CHURCH sent him MONEY to support his mission trips. The NEW TESTAMENT book of PHILIPPIANS is a thank-you LETTER he wrote for just such a gift.

LYRE

Praise the LORD with melodies on the lyre;
make music for him on the ten-stringed harp.
Psalm 33:2

- David's preferred instrument
- Smaller version of a harp

LIKE A BANJO AND A UKULELE, a HARP and
a lyre had strings in common. Sometimes they were
played together in Jewish WORSHIP. But they were different instruments. The lyre (HEBREW: *kinnor*) was DAVID's
favorite. It was small enough for a SHEPHERD to carry—
and a pleasant way to pass the day.

LYSTRA   Map 3 I3

(LIE struh)

You know all about how I [Paul] was
persecuted in Antioch, Iconium, and Lystra—
but the Lord rescued me. 2 Timothy 3:11

- Where a mob stoned Paul
- Timothy's hometown

AFTER CALLING PAUL A GOD for HEALING a crippled man, the people of Lystra in what is now Turkey,
became convinced by some JEWS that PAUL was just another heretic. They stoned him and dragged him out of
town, where they left him for dead. He lived. He got up
and continued his missionary travels, eventually returning
to the city and meeting TIMOTHY, who would become his
most trusted associate.

ROAD TRIP. David's instrument of choice, the lyre
was soothing enough to play around livestock and
portable enough to take on the road.

MACEDONIA

Map 3 C3

(MASS uh DOE nee yuh)

Paul had a dream: A Macedonian stood on the far shore and called across the sea, "Come over to Macedonia and help us!"
Acts 16:9 MSG

- Roman province in north Greece

CHRISTIANITY CAME TO EUROPE because PAUL had a VISION while he was in Turkey. He saw a man in Macedonia calling for help.

MACHPELAH

Map 1 C6

(mack PEE luh)

Abraham buried his wife, Sarah, there in Canaan, in the cave of Machpelah, near Mamre (also called Hebron). Genesis 23:19

- Grave of Abraham and family

JEWS, CHRISTIANS, AND MUSLIMS alike show their respect for ABRAHAM by visiting the traditional site of his grave in HEBRON, about 20 miles (32 km) south of JERUSALEM. Buried with him: wife SARAH, son ISAAC, Isaac's wife REBEKAH, grandson Jacob, JACOB's wife LEAH.

MAGDALA

Map 4 D4

(MAG duh luh)

When the Sabbath was over, Mary of Magdala. . .bought spices, in order to come and anoint His body. Mark 16:1 NTMS

- Hometown of Mary Magdalene

A FISHING VILLAGE about 5 miles (8 km) from Jesus' ministry headquarters in CAPERNAUM, Magdala is today the Israeli city of Migdal.

MAGI

(see WISE MEN)

MAGIC

(see SORCERY)

MAGOG

(MAY gog)

When the 1,000 years are over, Satan will be set free from his prison. . . . He will bring Gog and Magog together for battle.
Revelation 20:7–8 NIrV

IN VISIONS ABOUT END TIMES, two prophets—EZEKIEL and JOHN OF REVELATION—wrote of GOG and Magog as enemies of ISRAEL. Ezekiel wrote about Gog of Magog "from the distant north" (Ezekiel 39:2), while John wrote about the nations of Gog and Magog "from every corner of the earth" (Revelation 20:8).

Some Bible experts say Magog probably comes from the ancient Akkadian language (Iraq): *mat Gog*, which simply means "land of Gog." Some also speculate Gog refers to Gyges, king of Lydia (west Turkey) in the 600s BC.

MAHER-SHALAL-HASH-BAZ

(MAY ur SHALL uhl HASH bahs)
700s BC

I slept with my wife, and she became pregnant and gave birth to a son. And the LORD said, "Call him Maher-shalal-hash-baz."
Isaiah 8:3

- Isaiah's son
- Longest name in the Bible
- Rotten name for a kid to spell

LET'S NICKNAME HIM "SWIFTY." The boy's NAME means something close to "swiftly raided, swiftly robbed." It's a symbol of what ISAIAH said Assyrian invaders from what is now Iraq would do to ISRAEL. They did it in 722 BC.

M

MALACHI

(MAL uh kih)

400s BC

This is the message that the LORD gave to Israel through the prophet Malachi.
Malachi 1:1

- Jewish prophet

WAS THIS HIS NAME, or just a description of the prophet? That's what Bible experts want to know about the man who wrote the last book in the OLD TESTAMENT. *Malachi* means "my messenger." About the only safe conclusion scholars say they can make about him is that he wrote sometime after 450 BC, roughly a century after the JEWS returned from EXILE in what is now Iraq.

MALACHI, BOOK OF

Famous sound bite: "'You sacrifice disabled or sick animals. Isn't that wrong? Try offering them to your governor!'"
Malachi 1:8 NIrV

JEWS ARE SINNING AGAIN, a century after GOD brought them home from EXILE in what is now Iraq. Though they're not worshiping IDOLS—the main SIN that got them deported—they're breaking other laws: offering defective SACRIFICES, failing to TITHE, and exploiting the POOR. Malachi warns them that JUDGMENT DAY is coming "like a red-hot FURNACE" (Malachi 4:1 CEV).

- Writer: Malachi, which means "my messenger" and might be a title instead of a personal name.
- Time: Clues in the content suggest Malachi wrote in the 400s BC.
- Location: Israel, perhaps when it was still the tiny Persian province of Judah, about 20 by 30 miles (32 by 48 km) centered around Jerusalem.

WHERE'S THE BEEF? One of Malachi's beefs with the Jews is that they're offering diseased and crippled critters to God in sacrifice. That's not only against Jewish law. It's in bad taste.

BIG SCENES

Jewish sin—an encore performance. Malachi levels charges against descendants of the JEWS who were exiled for past sins:

- They skip paying the 10 percent tithe that funds the TEMPLE ministry.
- They sacrifice defective animals when Jewish law requires healthy animals.
- PRIESTS make up their own rules.
- Married men sleep around.
- They exploit society's most helpless: widows, orphans, immigrants, and people seeking justice in court. *Malachi 1–3*

Elijah rides again. The prophet ELIJAH left earth in a WHIRLWIND, escorted by a CHARIOT of fire. Malachi says Elijah is coming back "before the DAY OF THE LORD arrives." Since then, many Jews have anticipated the return of Elijah as the MESSIAH's advance man. Jesus said JOHN THE BAPTIST fulfilled Malachi's prediction: "John is the Elijah who was supposed to come" (Matthew 11:14 NIrV). *Malachi 4*

MALCHUS
(MAL cuss)

First century AD

Simon Peter drew a sword and slashed off the right ear of Malchus, the high priest's slave. John 18:10

WHILE HELPING ARREST JESUS, Malchus lost an ear. Compliments of PETER'S SWORD. It's a story reported in all four GOSPELS, though only JOHN names the victim. Jesus "touched the man's ear and healed him" (Luke 22:51).

MALTA
Map 2 D6
(MALL tuh)

They decided to run the ship onto the beach if they could. . . . Safe on shore, we found out that the island was called Malta.
Acts 27:39; 28:1 NIrV

- Island where Paul's ship ran aground

FOR TWO WEEKS, A TYPHOON pummeled the ship PAUL was sailing in to ROME. The SHIP ran aground at the island of Malta, south of Italy. Paul wintered there and then continued on to Rome, where he stood trial in CAESAR'S supreme COURT.

MAMMON
(MAM mun)

"You cannot serve God and mammon." Jesus, Matthew 6:24 NKJV

- Aramaic word for "wealth"

JESUS SAID IT'S IMPOSSIBLE for people to devote themselves to building the KINGDOM OF GOD when they're zoned in on building their own. Bible scholars translate *mammon* various ways, all pointing toward wealth: MONEY, riches, or material possessions.

MAMRE
Map 1 C6
(MAM ree)

Abram moved his tents and went to live near the great trees of Mamre at the city of Hebron. Genesis 13:18 NCV

- Abraham's camp

AFTER PARTING COMPANY with his nephew LOT, who moved to Sodom, ABRAHAM camped at an OAK grove near HEBRON. That's about 20 miles (32 km) south of JERUSALEM. Mamre apparently got its name from its owner, a king who was an ally of Abraham

M

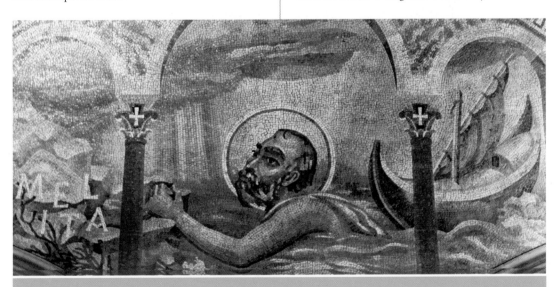

PAUL SWIMS FOR HIS LIFE after the ship he's sailing to Rome gets caught in a storm and runs aground near the island of Malta.

(Genesis 14:13). Abraham and some of his FAMILY were buried nearby.

MANASSEH, KING

Map 1 B5, E4

(muh NASS uh)

Reigned 696–642 BC

Manasseh practiced magic and witchcraft. . . and sacrificed his own son. 2 Kings 21:6 CEV

- Possibly the worst Jewish king ever
- Son of the most godly king, Hezekiah

AN UNLUCKY NUMBER FOR THE JEWS, Manasseh was the thirteenth KING of the southern Jewish nation of JUDAH.

Unlucky for two reasons. He wasn't just a bottom-of-the-barrel rotten apple. He stunk up the place longer than any other Jewish king: about 55 years.

He was only 12 when his father, saintly King HEZEKIAH, died. When Manasseh grew up, he decided to follow in the footsteps of his unsaintly grandfather, King AHAZ. He built pagan shrines, offered HUMAN SACRIFICE, practiced SORCERY, and consulted psychics.

Jewish TRADITION says he ordered the prophet ISAIAH cut in half with a wooden SAW.

One Bible story says he repented after he "finally realized that the LORD alone is GOD!" (2 Chronicles 33:13).

MANASSEH, SON OF JOSEPH

(muh NASS uh)

1800s BC

"Manasseh will also become a great people, but his younger brother will become even greater." Genesis 48:19

- Joseph's oldest son
- Ancestral father of Israel's Manasseh tribe

JACOB'S FAVORITE SON, JOSEPH, didn't get a tribe named in his honor. He got two: one named after each of his sons. Manasseh was his oldest. EPHRAIM his youngest.

MANASSEH, TRIBE OF

(muh NASS uh)

"The divisions of Ephraim, Manasseh, and Benjamin are to camp on the west side of the Tabernacle, beneath their family banners." Numbers 2:18

NAMED AFTER JOSEPH'S OLDEST SON, this extended Jewish FAMILY descended from Manasseh settled in two locations. Half the tribe settled in central Israel, below the SEA OF GALILEE in a stretch of land from the JORDAN RIVER to the MEDITERRANEAN SEA. The other half settled east of the Sea of Galilee, in what are now parts of Jordan and Syria.

MANDRAKE

(MAN drake)

"I will let Jacob sleep with you tonight if you give me some of the mandrakes." Rachel to Leah, Genesis 30:15

- Ancients considered it an aphrodisiac, fertility drug

HOPING TO GET PREGNANT, JACOB's favorite wife, RACHEL, made a swap with her sister, Jacob's other wife. Rachel got some mandrake roots, which are shaped a bit like a human torso and were thought to help women get pregnant. LEAH got an extra night with Jacob. And she got pregnant that night. Sperm 1. Mandrake 0.

MANGER

She [Mary] wrapped him [baby Jesus] snugly in strips of cloth and laid him in a manger. Luke 2:7

- Feeding trough for livestock
- Jesus' first bed

WITH BETHLEHEM CROWDED during registration for a CENSUS, MARY ended up giving BIRTH to Jesus in a stable, perhaps in one of the many caves in the area. She placed Jesus in a feeding trough, which may have been a box crafted from wood or a ledge carved into the rock.

A FEEDING TROUGH called a manger became Jesus' first baby bed.

MANKIND (see HUMANITY)

MANNA

(MAN uh)

Israelites named it manna (What is it?). It looked like coriander seed, whitish. And it tasted like a cracker with honey.
Exodus 16:31 MSG

- Mysterious food God provided during the Exodus

TREE SAP or hardened bug juice. Those are the two most popular guesses for identifying *manna,* HEBREW for "What is it?"

The BIBLE says that while the JEWS were traveling home to Israel after SLAVERY in EGYPT, GOD sent them food each morning except on the SABBATH: "When the dew evaporated, a flaky substance as fine as frost blanketed the ground" (Exodus 16:14). The people crushed the flakes to FLOUR and made flat cakes of sweet BREAD.

Some gourmet chefs today cook with sweet tree sap that's marketed as manna. It comes from a variety of trees and bushes in the Middle East, including the

IT'S RAINING BREAD CRUMBS. Or something white. Jews called in manna, Hebrew for "What is it?" Whatever it was—and scholars are still guessing—it was honey sweet.

M

309

TAMARISK, camel thorn, and flowering ash.

Middle Eastern herders sweeten their tea with the secretions of an aphid-like insect called the manna mealy bug or the tamarisk manna scale.

MARAH
Location Uncertain

(MARR uh)

When they came to the oasis of Marah, the water was too bitter to drink. So they called the place Marah (which means "bitter"). Exodus 15:23

ESCAPED SLAVES on the run from EGYPT, MOSES and JEWS of the EXODUS traveled three days to an oasis in the Sinai badlands. They named the oasis Marah (HE-BREW for "bitter") because the WATER was too bitter to drink. At GOD's instruction, Moses threw some wood into the water, which neutralized the bitterness.

The region, laced in SALT and alkaline, is known for its metallic-tasting water. Botanists say they don't know of any wood that would neutralize the taste.

MARK
(see JOHN MARK)

MARK, GOSPEL OF

Famous sound bite: "Follow Me, and I will make you become fishers of men." Jesus to fishermen Peter and Andrew, Mark 1:17 NKJV

SHORTEST AND MOST ACTION-PACKED of the four GOSPELS about Jesus, the Gospel of Mark skips the VIRGIN BIRTH and all the other stories leading up to Jesus' ministry. Instead, it jumps feet first into the JORDAN RIVER, where Jesus gets baptized and then begins his ministry of teaching and HEALING. Mark, loving action, emphasizes what Jesus did more than what Jesus said.

- Writer: Uncertain. Early church leaders credit John Mark, a minister who traveled with Paul.
- Time: The stories cover the ministry of Jesus, which may have spanned two or three years, possibly ending in AD 33. Experts are left guessing about the timeline.
- Location: Israel.

BIG SCENES

Jesus launches his ministry with a splash. A PROPHET named JOHN THE BAPTIST says he's preparing the way "for the LORD's coming." Then, in the next scene, he's baptizing Jesus. Suddenly, the ministry of Jesus is up and running. He starts selecting his DISCIPLES, healing the sick, and PREACHING in towns throughout GALILEE, in what is now northern Israel. *Mark 1*

Jesus is bad when he does good on the Sabbath. Jewish law says not to work on the SABBATH. But it doesn't define work. So one group of JEWS—PHARISEES—take on that job. For them, work includes healing people. MIRACLE or not, it's practicing MEDICINE as far as they're concerned. Jesus disagrees. He heals a man right inside the SYNAGOGUE, arguing that the Sabbath is a day for doing good. *Mark 3*

Jesus, the storyteller. Jesus doesn't seem interested in preaching boring, philosophical sermons. Instead, he tells fictional stories with spiritual meanings. They're called PARABLES. They help people understand the ideas he's trying to get into their heads. To explain why some people will embrace his teachings and others won't, he talks about a farmer sowing seeds. Some seeds land on good soil, representing those who take his words to heart. Other seeds fall on less hospitable ground, such as among thorns, which represent people whose FAITH gets crowded out by life's worries and TEMPTATIONS. *Mark 4*

Jesus, the exorcist. Jesus not only heals people with physical DISEASES he also exorcizes DEMONS. Perhaps his most dramatic EXORCISM is of a man possessed with an army of demons who call themselves Legion. A LEGION of soldiers in the Roman ARMY numbered from 5,400 to 6,000 men. With Jesus' permission, the demons are allowed to escape into a herd of pigs. But the pigs fall down a steep hillside into the lake, where they drown. *Mark 5*

John the Baptist gets decapitated. John essentially calls the First Couple of Galilee perverts. HEROD ANTIPAS, Galilee's ruler, has married his brother's ex-wife. Jewish law considers that INCEST. When Herod promises his stepdaughter anything she wants, she consults her mother. An obedient daughter if nothing else, she requests the head of John. *Mark 6*

A widow with small change and a big heart. At the Jerusalem TEMPLE, Jesus watches Jews drop off their cash donations. Some donate a lot. Then along comes a poor WIDOW. She donates the two smallest coins in circulation. Jesus says that as far as he's concerned, she "has given more than all the others." *Mark 12*

Arresting Jesus. JUDAS ISCARIOT, one of Jesus' disciples, betrays him for a reward. Judas leads a detachment of Temple guards and Roman soldiers to arrest Jesus while Jesus is praying on the MOUNT OF OLIVES one night. Matthew 27:5 adds the report that when Judas realizes the Jews are sentencing Jesus to death, he returns the MONEY and hangs himself. *Mark 14*

Jesus: crucified, dead, alive again. Romans crucify Jesus the next morning on grounds of insurrection, for claiming to be king of the Jews. He's dead by late afternoon and rushed into a TOMB before sundown. Reason for the rush: it was Friday. Sundown marked the beginning of the Sabbath, when Jews have to stop all work—including funeral preparations. Women plan to return on Sunday morning to wash his body and give him a proper BURIAL. When they arrive, an ANGEL greets them: "He is risen from the dead!" *Mark 15–16*

EMPEROR 666. That's what many Bible experts say about Nero, the first Roman emperor to persecute the Christians. The letters in his name as it appeared on Roman coins had number equivalents that added up to 666.

MARK OF THE BEAST

"If you can, figure out what the beast's number means. It is man's number. His number is 666." Revelation 13:18 NIrV

SOME ANCIENT BIBLE TRANSLATIONS report the number as 616. Many Bible experts say both numbers are code names for NERO, the first Roman emperor to persecute Christians.

Letters had numerical equivalents in ancient times. Letters in the name and title of Nero that appeared on Roman coins—Nero CAESAR—add up to 666. That's if you translate the words from GREEK, the international language of the day, into HEBREW. The numbers add up to 616 if you translate from Latin, the official language of Rome, into Hebrew, the language of JEWS.

Scholars who read the future into REVELATION say the number points to a ruler that JOHN called the beast—an end-time tyrant and kindred spirit of Nero. Some identify this beast as the ANTICHRIST.

MARKETPLACE

Jewish leaders were jealous [of Paul] and got some worthless bums who hung around the marketplace to start a riot in the city. Acts 17:5 CEV

IN MANY TOWNS, the main city GATE served as a shopping mall. Farmers, potters, and other vendors set up displays just outside the gate or just inside. This became a popular meeting spot, too.

MARRIAGE   (see WEDDING)

MARS HILL   (see AREOPAGUS)

MARTHA

First century AD

Martha. . .said, "Lord, don't you care that my sister has left me alone to do all the work? Tell her to help me." Luke 10:40 NCV

* Sister of Mary and Lazarus

MARTHA COMPLAINED TO JESUS twice. She lived in BETHANY with her sister, Mary, and her brother, LAZARUS, and her complaints had to do with them.

Mary first. The ladies were hosting Jesus for a MEAL, but Mary was spending her time talking with Jesus while Martha cooked. Martha asked Jesus to have Mary help her. Instead, he said Mary was spending her time wisely.

Martha later complained that Jesus hadn't come in time to heal Lazarus. But he came in time to raise him from the dead.

MARTYRED. Roman Catholic tradition says Saint Valentine was a priest in Rome who was beheaded on February 14 in about AD 270. That was 43 years before Rome legalized Christianity, in AD 313.

MARTYR

(MAR tur)

As Stephen was being stoned to death, he called out, "Lord Jesus, please welcome me!". . .Then he died. Acts 7:59–60 CEV

▪ Victim killed because of religious beliefs

JESUS WARNED his followers, "Some of you will be killed. There's no telling who will hate you because of me" (Luke 21:16–17 MSG).

Most of Jesus' 12 DISCIPLES died as martyrs, according to early CHURCH leaders. But the BIBLE reports only the execution of JAMES, "killed with a SWORD" (Acts 12:2).

The Bible also says that before PAUL converted to CHRISTIANITY he "was eager to kill the LORD's followers" (Acts 9:1). Jewish PERSECUTION of believers in JERUSALEM scattered Christians abroad, as they ran for their lives. But they took their FAITH with them.

Romans began joining in on the persecution of Christians in AD 64, after Roman Emperor NERO blamed Christians for starting a fire that destroyed much of ROME. Branded as illegal, Christianity wasn't legalized until AD 313.

MARY, MOTHER OF JESUS

First century AD

This is how Jesus the Messiah was born. His mother, Mary. . .while she was still a virgin. . .became pregnant through the power of the Holy Spirit. Matthew 1:18

▪ Wife of Joseph

MARY DOESN'T GET MUCH ATTENTION in the BIBLE. That's a bit surprising to many, given her role: VIRGIN mother of the SON OF GOD.

She shows up mainly in the stories of Jesus' BIRTH reported in the books of MATTHEW and LUKE. MARK's book mentions her NAME only once. JOHN's book doesn't mention her name at all.

If Mary followed ancient Jewish TRADITION, she was just a young teenager when she got engaged to JOSEPH, a builder. Young WOMEN typically got engaged shortly after they became able to have CHILDREN, when their monthly periods started.

Mary and Joseph lived in the hilltop village of NAZARETH, in what is now northern Israel.

The Bible says Mary once scolded 12-year-old Jesus for staying at the Jerusalem TEMPLE when he was supposed to have left with the rest of the CARAVAN headed home: "Why have you done this to us? Your father and I have been frantic, searching for you everywhere" (Luke 2:48).

Christians debate whether or not Mary gave birth to Jesus' sisters and four brothers (Matthew 13:55). Many Catholics say Mary remained a virgin and that these children were Joseph's by a previous marriage, or perhaps were cousins of Jesus. Most Protestants say they were Mary's children. It's partly because of verses that suggest her virginity eventually ended: "While she was still a virgin, she became pregnant" (Matthew 1:18). Catholics translate the phrase differently, "Before they lived together, she was found with child" (NAB).

As Jesus hung on the CROSS, he entrusted the care of his mother to one of his DISCIPLES: John, according to early CHURCH leaders. Several church writers say John and Mary moved to EPHESUS, in what is now Turkey, where Mary spent her final years.

MARY MAGDELENE became a devoted follower of Jesus after he exorcized her, casting out seven demons. She got the honor of becoming the first person on record to see him resurrected.

MARY MAGDALENE

(MAG duh lin)

First century AD

Mary Magdalene found the disciples and told them, "I have seen the Lord!" John 20:18

- First to see resurrected Jesus
- Financial contributor to Jesus
- Exorcised of seven demons

ONE OF JESUS' MOST DEVOTED FOLLOWERS, Mary Magdalene was "the woman from whom he had cast out seven DEMONS" (Mark 16:9).

Mary owed Jesus her life.

It's a debt she paid with loyalty as well as cash: "Mary Magdalene. . .and many others. . .were helping to support Jesus and the Twelve with their own MONEY" (Luke 8:2–3 NIRV).

Mary came from the FISHING village of MAGDALA, near Jesus' ministry headquarters in CAPERNAUM.

Contrary to popular opinion, she wasn't the unidentified "immoral woman" who washed Jesus' feet with her tears and HAIR, many scholars insist (see Luke 7:37). If she had been, scholars argue, that would have been the perfect opportunity to introduce her. Instead, Luke waited to introduce her in the very next story.

Mary had a starring role in the RESURRECTION. "After Jesus rose from the dead early on Sunday morning, the first person who saw him was Mary Magdalene" (Mark 16:9). And her NAME was the first name he spoke: "Mary!" (John 20:16).

MASADA Map 4 D6

(muh SAH duh)

M

- Hilltop fortress of Herod the Great

JEWS REVERE THIS FLAT-TOP MESA towering 1,424 feet (434 m) above the DEAD SEA. Masada isn't mentioned in the BIBLE, but JEWS treat it with reverence because of what happened there in NEW TESTAMENT times.

More than 900 Jews committed suicide rather than surrender to Romans. It happened in AD 73, seven years after the Jews rebelled against ROME in AD 66. Masada, a seemingly impregnable fortress built by HEROD THE GREAT, became the last Jewish holdout in their doomed revolt.

Romans broke into the fortress after spending nearly two years building a huge ramp up the side of the cliffs—only to find the defenders dead.

Israeli soldiers now pledge their allegiance at the Masada ruin, vowing, "Masada shall not fall again!"

STONE MASONS shape the blocks then send them on their way in the early 1900s. Jews in Bible times imported expert masons from what is now Lebanon to help build the Jerusalem Temple.

MASONS

"Hire carpenters, builders, and masons. . . buy the timber and the finished stone needed to repair the Temple." 2 Kings 22:6

- Builders who work with stone

JEWS IMPORTED THEIR MASONS from LEBA-NON when they wanted topnotch craftsmanship. That's where DAVID got his stone workers when he needed a PALACE; they came from the coastal city of TYRE. That's also where David's son SOLOMON got the masons who built the first Jerusalem TEMPLE.

MATTHEW

(MATH you)

First century AD

Jesus. . .saw a man named Matthew sitting at his tax collector's booth. "Follow me and be my disciple," Jesus said to him. Matthew 9:9

- Tax collector
- Disciple of Jesus

A TOLLBOOTH OPERATOR at the FISHING village of CAPERNAUM, Matthew left his job to become a DIS-CIPLE of Jesus. Early CHURCH leaders said he wrote the GOSPEL of Matthew.

MATTHEW, GOSPEL OF

Famous sound bite:" Treat others as you want them to treat you." Matthew 7:12 CEV

MORE THAN ANY OTHER GOSPEL, Matthew ze-roes in on one goal: Convince readers Jesus is the MESSIAH Jewish PROPHETS have been predicting for centuries. In telling the story of Jesus, from birth to death to RESUR-RECTION, Matthew reports about 60 OLD TESTAMENT prophecies that he says Jesus fulfilled.

- Writer: Uncertain. Early church leaders credit Matthew, one of Jesus' 12 disciples.
- Time: Lifetime of Jesus, from about 6 BC–AD 33.
- Location: Israel.

BIG SCENES

Jesus' odd family tree. Since ISRAEL's proph-ets said the Messiah would come from King DAVID's FAMILY, Matthew starts his story by tracing Jesus' ances-try back to David. He mentions several WOMEN, which is surprising enough; in that day, women don't rate. Even more oddly, he skips the notable women, such as SARAH and REBEKAH, founding mothers of Israel. In-stead, he plucks seemingly rotten apples from the family tree, including several connected with SEX sins: TAMAR, RAHAB, and BATHSHEBA. Some scholars guess it's to in-troduce MARY's VIRGIN BIRTH—to show that GOD works wonders through unlikely people. *Matthew 1:1–17*

Joseph and the pregnant fiancée. JOSEPH plans to break off the engagement after he finds out Mary is pregnant. But an ANGEL in a DREAM convinces him that the child is of God. *Matthew 1:18–25*

Wise men following a star. Sages who study the stars see a SIGN in the sky that suggests a future Jew-ish KING has been born. They TRAVEL to the Jewish capi-tal in JERUSALEM from their home in the East, perhaps Iraq or Iran. Jewish scholars point them to BETHLEHEM because the prophet MICAH said the Messiah would be born there. The sages find young Jesus and give his par-ents GOLD, FRANKINCENSE, and MYRRH. *Matthew 2*

Satan tempts Jesus. Grown and ready to start his ministry, Jesus is baptized by JOHN THE BAPTIST. Then Jesus retreats for a time of PRAYER and FASTING in the Judean badlands. There SATAN tempts him with food and power—apparently in an attempt to lure him away from his mission. Jesus doesn't take the bait. He resists each TEMPTATION by quoting from the BIBLE. Tempted with BREAD, Jesus says, "People do not live by bread alone, but by every word that comes from the mouth of God." *Matthew 3–4*

Jesus' most famous sermon. It's called the SERMON ON THE MOUNT. And it's packed with some of Jesus' most notable sound bites:

- "Do to others whatever you would like them to do to you."
- "Love your enemies!"
- "Don't score up treasures here on earth. . . . Store your treasures in HEAVEN." *Matthew 5–7*

Feeding a crowd with a snack pack. Following Jesus is a crowd of 5,000 men—not counting women and children. Moved by their devotion, Jesus heals the sick. As evening approaches, he feeds them all with nothing but the MEAL of a boy: five loaves of bread and two fish. All four GOSPEL writers report this MIRACLE. *Matthew 14*

Jesus transforms into a celestial being. Shortly before his CRUCIFIXION, Jesus retreats to a hilltop for a time of prayer. He takes his three closest DISCIPLES: PETER and the brothers JAMES and JOHN. There, in an event called the TRANSFIGURATION, Jesus "was transformed so that his face shone like the sun, and his clothes became as white as light." MOSES and ELIJAH appear and talk with him. *Matthew 17*

The Palm Sunday donkey ride. Jewish pilgrims in Jerusalem for the PASSOVER holiday cheer Jesus on Sunday as he rides a DONKEY into Jerusalem. They treat him like a king, paving his path with palm branches and cloaks—and quoting Bible verses that many JEWS say refers to the Messiah: "Blessings on the one who comes in the name of the LORD!" *Matthew 21*

Last supper and a prayer. On the following Thursday night, Jesus celebrates what seems like an early Passover meal with his disciples. Passover is Friday evening. But he'll be dead by then. After the meal, which Christians commemorate in a ritual sometimes called Holy COMMUNION or Mass, Jesus leads his disciples to a nearby OLIVE grove where he prays. JUDAS ISCARIOT betrays Jesus by leading TEMPLE officers there to arrest him. *Matthew 26:1–56*

Executed and reanimated. Jewish leaders convince Roman governor PILATE to crucify Jesus early Friday morning on grounds of insurrection—for claiming he's king of the Jews. By sundown, Jesus is dead and lying in a TOMB. Sunday morning, it's rise and shine. Resurrected, he gives his disciples a job: "Go and make disciples of all the nations." No longer afraid of dying, they will launch what becomes the CHRISTIAN movement (see ACTS). *Matthew 26:57–28*

MATTHIAS

(muh THI us)

First century AD

Matthias was selected to become an apostle with the other eleven. **Acts 1:26**

- Judas' replacement as disciple

AFTER JESUS ASCENDED TO HEAVEN, his 11 DISCIPLES decided to replace JUDAS ISCARIOT, who had committed suicide. "They nominated two men. . .'who were with us the entire time we were traveling with the LORD Jesus—from the time he was baptized by JOHN until the day he was taken from us' " (Acts 1:21–23). They drew LOTS, leaving the decision to GOD. Matthias got the job.

MEALS

At the lunch break, Boaz said to her [Ruth], "Come over here; eat some bread. Dip it in the wine." **Ruth 2:14 MSG**

TWO MEALS A DAY. Sometimes three. That's what Bible experts say most JEWS ate.

Breakfast was often a light meal after the morning chores—in midmorning or around noon. This may have been the lunchtime break RUTH took during BARLEY harvest. Or perhaps it was an extra snack between breakfast and supper. She and the harvesters ate BREAD, WINE, and roasted GRAIN.

Supper, eaten around sunset, was a heavier meal. The menu could have included veggie stew, CHEESE, goat

M

BIBLE UNIT	NATURE'S UNIT	TODAY'S UNIT
Cubit	Elbow to fingertip	18–20 inches (46–51 cm)
Handbreadth	Width of four fingers	3 inches (8 cm)
Homer	Load of grain a donkey could carry	6.5 bushels (229 l)
Span	Thumb to pinky on extended hand	9 inches (23 cm)
Yoke	Land a team of oxen could plow in a day	1 acre, about the size of a football field

RABBIT STEW. A nomadic Bedouin in Syria shows off a wild rabbit someone caught. Near the tent hangs the partly butchered carcass of a sheep. In Bible times, meat was a rare treat, too expensive for most folks.

curds, OLIVES, and desserts of sweet FIG cakes, melon, and dates—to mention a few of the more affordable foods.

Meat was a no-go for most people. Too expensive. The rich might eat it anytime. But most other folks ate meat only as a special treat, during festivals and while hosting guests.

See also BAKING, COOKING, KOSHER FOOD.

MEASURES

"Make a table of acacia wood—two cubits long, a cubit wide and a cubit and a half high." Exodus 25:23 TNIV

NATURE HELPED SIZE UP THE WORLD in Bible times—before tape measures, liter bottles, and measuring cups.

see chart above

MEDIA   Map 2 M6

King Xerxes gave a big dinner. It was for all of his nobles and officials. The military leaders of Persia and Media were there. Esther 1:3 NIrV

- Iran-based Middle Eastern kingdom
- Defeated by Persians

MEDES AND PERSIANS—a pair of Iran-based kingdoms—teamed up to dethrone the Middle Eastern superpower of the moment: BABYLON, in what is now Iraq.

Media's sprawling kingdom swallowed up northern Iran, eastern Iraq, and half of Turkey. PERSIA initially seemed content with only south Iran. But in time Persia turned on Media, conquering it in 549 BC and later forcing the Medians to help them defeat Babylon.

Suddenly, the Middle East had a new superpower: the Persian Empire.

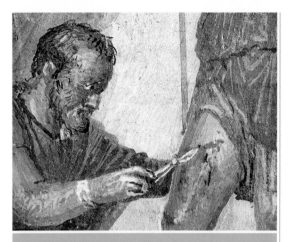

ROMAN SURGERY. A physician removes an arrowhead from a man's thigh, in a painting from first-century Pompeii, Italy.

MEDICINE

(see Disease, Healing)

Is there no medicine in Gilead? Is there no physician there? Jeremiah 8:22

EAR WAX, MUDDY WATER, AND BEAR GREASE were among the many folk remedies for what ailed people in Bible times.

Some ingredients were known to help:

- soothing ointment from Gilead in what is now Jordan
- eye salve from Laodicea in what is now Turkey
- wine to clean a wound, calm a stomach, or settle the nerves.

But reliable medicine was the exception, not the rule. Many prescriptions preserved in a science book by a Roman writer named Pliny (AD 23–79) seem worse than a folk remedy—more of a joke remedy.

- Snake bite: apply ear wax.
- Inflamed joints: Apply dirt mixed with sweat from a wrestler.
- Itching: Apply mud mixed with donkey urine.
- Inflamed eyes: Rinse dust from feet, apply muddy drops into eyes.

When Jesus showed up and actually started HEALING people, he drew a crowd.

MEDITERRANEAN SEA

Map 2 F7

(MED uh tur RAIN ee uhn)

"I will make your borders secure from the Red Sea to the Mediterranean Sea. They will go from the desert to the Euphrates River." Exodus 23:31 NIrV

M

THE MEDITERRANEAN SEA is about as wide as the United States.

STEPHEN M. MILLER'S ILLUSTRATED BIBLE DICTIONARY

JEWS DIDN'T GO DEEP-SEA FISHING much. More sea-fearing than seafaring, they worked as herders and farmers, avoiding the Mediterranean Sea on their nearly 200-mile-long (320 km) western border.

ISRAEL didn't have a natural harbor. That may be why the JEWS remained landlubbers for so long. That began to change when King HEROD THE GREAT (reigned 40–4 BC) built a huge, Roman-style harbor at CAESAREA—large enough to accommodate 300 ships. It's one reason Rome made Caesarea their capital of the Middle East.

From there, Jews could sail to the far end of the sea—SPAIN, some 2,200 miles (3,540 km) west, about the distance from New York City to Spokane.

MEGIDDO
Map 1 C4

(muh GIDD oh)

King Solomon forced people to work hard for him. . . . They rebuilt the wall of Jerusalem. They built up Hazor, Megiddo and Gezer.
1 Kings 9:15 NIrv

- Fortress city in northern Israel

A WALLED FORTRESS, the hilltop city of Megiddo guarded the best pass through Israel's Carmel Mountains. Armies and caravans using Israel as a bridge to and from EGYPT preferred this route.

Perched above the south edge of Israel's largest and most fertile valley—JEZREEL VALLEY—Megiddo defenders could see enemies coming from miles away. More than 30 major battles have been fought in this valley—as early as the 1400s BC when Egyptian invaders defeated Canaanites there, and as late as 1973 when Israelis repelled a Syrian artillery attack on Ramat David Airbase there.

Today Megiddo is a ruin and a tourist attraction.

MELCHIZEDEK

(mel KIZ uh deck)

2100s BC

Melchizedek, the king of Salem [Jerusalem] and a priest of God Most High, brought Abram some bread and wine. **Genesis 14:18**

ODDLY, the BIBLE describes this mysterious king as a

PRIEST several centuries before GOD set up the priestly system with AARON as the first HIGH PRIEST. Since Melchizedek came first, JEWS revered him above all other priests. That's why one NEW TESTAMENT writer described Jesus as "our eternal High Priest in the order of Melchizedek" (Hebrews 6:20).

ABRAHAM gave Melchizedek a tenth of all the booty he recovered from raiders who had attacked Sodom and kidnapped Abraham's nephew, LOT.

MYSTERIOUS MELCHIZEDEK gets a tithe offering from Abraham—which must have come as a pleasant surprise, since God was still several centuries from setting up rules about tithing.

MEMPHIS
Map 2 H8

(MEM fuss)

"Get ready to leave for exile, you citizens of Egypt! The city of Memphis will be destroyed." **Jeremiah 46:19**

- Ancient Egypt's capital

OLDER THAN ABRAHAM by about 1,000 years, EGYPT's capital city of Memphis rested along the banks of the NILE RIVER about 15 miles (24 km) south of Egypt's modern capital, Cairo.

Fragments of colossal statues along with scattered ruins are all that's left testifying to the city's former glory.

MEPHIBOSHETH

(muh FIB uh sheth)

1000s BC

*Jonathan had a son named Mephibosheth. . . .
He was five years old when. . .the child's
nurse. . .dropped him, and he became
crippled.* 2 Samuel 4:4

▪ Crippled son of Jonathan

AS KING SAUL'S GRANDSON, Mephibosheth
feared that the new king—DAVID—would kill him so he
couldn't claim his right to rule. Instead, David treated
him kindly out of respect for the boy's father, who had
been David's best friend: JONATHAN. SAUL and Jonathan
had died in battle.

MERCHANTS

*She makes belted linen garments and sashes
to sell to the merchants.* Proverbs 31:24

▪ Shop owners and traveling traders

SOME MERCHANTS took their goods on the road,
risking ROBBERY for a big payoff in hard-to-get trade
goods: "SILVER and GOLD, CLOTHING, WEAPONS, SPICES,
horses, and MULES" (1 Kings 10:25). Other merchants
set up shop at home, buying from locals and traveling
traders, and then reselling the goods at a profit.

MERCY

*You, O Lord, are a God of compassion and
mercy.* Psalm 86:15

GOD AND GOD'S PEOPLE help folks who can't
help themselves. That's *mercy*—one English word for
various HEBREW words sometimes translated as kindness
and steadfast love.

MERCY SEAT

*"Put the mercy seat on the top of the ark. . . .
There I will meet with you, and from above
the mercy seat."* Exodus 25:21–22 NRSV

▪ Lid on the Ark of the Covenant

ISRAEL'S MOST SACRED OBJECT was the
GOLD-plated chest called the ARK OF THE COVENANT. It
held the 10 COMMANDMENTS. The lid covering the chest
was called the mercy seat. JEWS considered this seat the
earthly THRONE OF GOD—the place where they could
find mercy and FORGIVENESS. It was there that the HIGH
PRIEST, once a year on *Yom Kippur* (DAY OF ATONE-
MENT), sprinkled sacrificial BLOOD to atone for the sins
of the nation, including his own sins.

MERIBAH

Location Uncertain

(MARE uh buh)

*Moses struck the rock. . .and water gushed
out. . . . Moses named the place. . .Meribah
(which means "arguing") because the people
of Israel argued with Moses.* Exodus 17:6–7

THIRSTY IN THE BADLANDS south of what is now
ISRAEL, JEWS on the EXODUS out of EGYPT demanded
MOSES find them WATER. At GOD's command, he hit a
rock with his walking staff and water came out.

MESHA

(ME shuh)

800s BC

*King Mesha of Moab raised sheep. He was
forced to give the king of Israel 100,000
lambs and another 100,000 rams.*
2 Kings 3:4 MSG

▪ Defeated Jews by sacrificing his son

KING MESHA, in what is now Jordan, rebelled against
the JEWS. He stopped paying the annual taxes ISRAEL
had demanded. Israel sent the ARMY to collect. When
Mesha saw his army losing, he took his son—the crown

M

STEPHEN M. MILLER'S ILLUSTRATED BIBLE DICTIONARY

PRINCE—and sacrificed him on the city wall for everyone to see. The Jews retreated, perhaps driven off by an enemy suddenly enraged at the loss of their future king.

MESHACH (see SHADRACH)

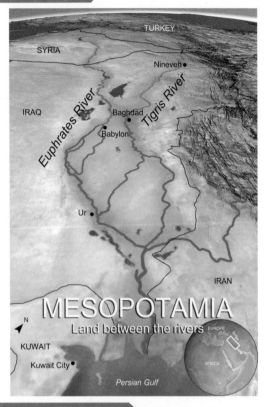

SYRIA
TURKEY
Nineveh
Euphrates River
Tigris River
IRAQ
Baghdad
Babylon
Ur
IRAN

MESOPOTAMIA
Land between the rivers

EUROPE

N

KUWAIT
Kuwait City

AFRICA

Persian Gulf

MESOPOTAMIA   Map 2 L7

(MESS uh puh TAY me uh)

"God appeared to our ancestor Abraham in Mesopotamia." Acts 7:2

■ Fertile part of Iraq

"BETWEEN THE RIVERS." That's what the word means. The rivers: TIGRIS and EUPHRATES, which flow south through Iraq, emptying into the Persian Gulf.

Civilization seems to have gotten its start along this slice of land in what became known as the Fertile Crescent. This is where the first-known empires grew up: SUMER, ASSYRIA, and BABYLON. It was also home to ABRAHAM, who came from UR, a city in what is now southern Iraq.

MESSIAH

(muh SIGH uh)

"I know the Messiah is coming—the one who is called Christ. When he comes, he will explain everything to us." Samaritan woman to Jesus, John 4:25

JESUS WASN'T THE ONLY MESSIAH. Just the most famous.

Messiah is a HEBREW word. It means the same thing as the GREEK word *CHRIST*. Both words mean "ANOINTED one"—a leader chosen by GOD for special duty, usually as a KING or a PRIEST. Both leaders were anointed with oil in a ritual of coronation or ordination.

God's anointed leaders were held in high esteem by people devoted to God. Young DAVID refused to kill King SAUL even though Saul, jealous of David's popularity, was trying to kill him. David's simple explanation: "The LORD forbid that I should kill the one he has anointed!" (1 Samuel 26:11).

Centuries later, PROPHETS started talking about a unique Messiah who would come to save ISRAEL:

"The time is coming. . .when I will raise up a righteous descendant from King David's line" (JEREMIAH 23:5).

"He will be called: Wonderful Counselor, Mighty God, Everlasting Father, Prince of Peace. His government and its peace will never end" (ISAIAH 9:6–7).

The Messiah's God-anointed job:

■ bring GOOD NEWS to the POOR
■ comfort the brokenhearted
■ free the prisoners
■ repair the destroyed cities
■ restore the honor of Israel (Isaiah 61:1–7).

By the time JESUS launched his ministry, Romans had been occupying Israel for about a century. JEWS were desperate for freedom. Messiah fever was spiking.

Many Jews were expecting a warrior messiah like King David—someone who would burst into history at any moment and free them from ROME. What they got was a pacifist RABBI offering to free them from SIN.

Curve ball.

Jesus read the Isaiah 61 prophecy to a group of NAZARETH Jews. It was a prophecy many Jews said referred to the Messiah. Jesus proclaimed himself the fulfillment: "The SCRIPTURE you've just heard has been fulfilled this very day!" (Luke 4:21).

Jesus told a SAMARITAN woman anxiously waiting for the Messiah, "I AM the Messiah!" (John 4:26).

For most Jews, though, Jesus didn't measure up to their expectations. For others—especially those who saw him come back from the dead—he more than measured up.

JESUS ARMED. Jews in Bible times hoped for a warrior king like David to come as their Messiah and free them from the Romans. Jesus came as a pacific rabbi, to free them from sin. Many Christians say the prophecies about a warrior Messiah will be fulfilled with Jesus returns in the Second Coming.

METALWORKING

A silversmith named Demetrius had a business that made silver models of the temple of the goddess Artemis. Acts 19:24 CEV

IDOLS, WEAPONS, AND TOOLS such as PLOW blades were crafted from metal—usually COPPER, BRONZE, and IRON, though sometimes SILVER and GOLD for more decorative objects.

Metalworkers often melted and refined the metal in a small pit FURNACE: a hole dug in the ground, fired with charcoal because it burned hotter than wood. Bellows puffing air kept the fire hot.

By the time of King DAVID, PHILISTINES discovered how to make the toughest metal of Bible times: iron. They would heat it, hammer it, dip it in water, and repeat the cycle.

METHUSELAH

(muh THOO suh luh)

Before 2500 BC

Methuselah lived 969 years, and then he died. Genesis 5:27

- Oldest man in the Bible

NOAH'S GRANDAD Methuselah outlived NOAH (950 years) by 19 years and Adam (930 years) by 39 years.

MICAH

(MY kuh)

Prophesied 742–686 BC

The word of the LORD came to Micah, who was from Moresheth. He saw these visions about Samaria and Jerusalem. Micah 1:1 NCV

- Jewish prophet
- Predicted birth of Jewish king in Bethlehem

A SMALL-TOWN PROPHET, Micah lived in a village about 20 miles (32 km) south of JERUSALEM. He predicted the fall of both Jewish nations: ISRAEL, with its capital in SAMARIA; JUDAH, with its capital in Jerusalem.

Micah is best known for predicting the BETHLEHEM birth of the MESSIAH—"Peacemaker of the world!" (Micah 5:4 MSG).

M

MICAH, BOOK OF

Famous sound bite: You, Bethlehem. . . from you will come the leader who will shepherd-rule Israel. . . . Peacemaker of the world!
Micah 5:2, 4 MSG

A SMALL-TOWN PROPHET, Micah is most famous for predicting a small-town MESSIAH. He warned that both Jewish nations would fall to invaders, but that in the years ahead GOD would raise up a SAVIOR from the tiny village of BETHLEHEM.

- Writer: Micah or someone reporting his story.
- Time: Micah ministers about 65 years during the reigns of three kings of Judah: Jotham, Ahaz, Hezekiah; roughly 742–686 BC.
- Location: Micah comes from Moresheth, a village about a day's walk southwest of Jerusalem. He predicts the collapse of both Jewish nations: Israel in the north and his own nation of Judah in the south.

BIG SCENES

Jews: Time to pay for your sins. For non-stop injustice, the capital cities of both Jewish nations "will be plowed" (Micah 1:6; 3:12). That's a graphic picture of DESTRUCTION—bustling cities turned into farmland. A sampling of the injustice that warrants this punishment:

Greedy rich: "When you want a piece of land, you find a way to seize it."

Exploitive rulers: "You skin my people alive."

Profiteering prophets: PROPHETS and PRIESTS alike minister for what they can get out of it: food and MONEY. *Micah 1–3*

Not all the news is bad. JEWS will lose their homeland. Survivors will get deported. But in time, Micah says God will bring the Jews home. JERUSALEM will become important again, and people from all over the world will come to visit. Leading the nation will be a ruler from the tiny village of Bethlehem. "He will be the source of PEACE." Centuries later, Jews said this prediction pointed to the coming Messiah. NEW TESTAMENT writers said it pointed to Jesus, as well, born in Bethlehem. *Micah 4–7*

WARRIOR ANGEL Michael slays "the dragon—that old serpent, who is the devil, Satan" (Revelation 20:2).

MICHAEL

"Michael, the chief of the angels, is the protector of your people." Daniel 12:1 CEV

- Archangel

NOT AN ANGEL TO MESS WITH, Michael sounds like the general of HEAVEN's army. Several Bible writers described him as a fighter.

- He guarded the Jewish nation and fought off "the spirit prince of. . .PERSIA" (Daniel 10:13).
- He was "one of the mightiest of the ANGELS" (Jude 1:9).
- When WAR broke out in heaven, "Michael and his angels fought against the dragon and his angels" (Revelation 12:7), forcing them out of heaven.

MICHAL

1000s BC

Michal, David's wife, warned him, "If you don't escape tonight, you will be dead by morning." 1 Samuel 19:11

- David's first wife
- Saul's daughter

HOPING IT WOULD KILL DAVID, King SAUL ordered him to collect the foreskins of 100 PHILISTINES—for the privilege of marrying his daughter, PRINCESS Michal.

DAVID delivered 200.

Later, when Saul sent assassins to kill David, Michal stalled the killers while David fled and became a fugitive.

Furious, Saul married Michal to another man. After Saul died and David became KING of JUDAH, he ordered Michal back—against her will. She later expressed disgust with David for DANCING in public "like any vulgar person might do!" (2 Samuel 6:20).

She died childless.

MICHMASH
Map 1 D5

(MICK mash)

Philistines moved their camp to the pass at Michmash. 1 Samuel 13:23 CEV

IN STRIKE-FORCE STYLE, Prince JONATHAN and his ARMOR bearer killed about 20 PHILISTINES guarding the pass at Michmash, some 7 miles (11 km) north of JERUSALEM. That and a well-timed EARTHQUAKE sent the Philistine ARMY running, though they greatly outnumbered King SAUL's militia.

MIDIAN
Map 2 J9

(MID ee un)

Moses escaped from Pharaoh and went to live in Midian. Exodus 2:15 NIrV

- Where Moses lived for 40 years

AFTER MOSES MURDERED an Egyptian slave driver for beating a Jewish slave, MOSES fled east to Midian.

There, somewhere near the border of Jordan and Saudi Arabia, he met a herder with seven daughters. Good odds. Moses married one of them, ZIPPORAH. He worked for his father-in-law for 40 years, until GOD ordered him back to EGYPT to lead the enslaved JEWS home.

MIDWIFE

While she [Tamar] was in labor, one of the babies reached out his hand. The midwife grabbed it and tied a scarlet string around the child's wrist, announcing, "This one came out first." Genesis 38:28

- Delivery nurse

EVEN WHEN DOCTORS WERE AVAILABLE, most women in Bible times seemed to prefer a midwife to help deliver their babies. That addressed modesty concerns. In addition, most midwives had "been there, done that." Most doctors had not.

See also BIRTH.

MILETUS
Map 3 E3

(my LEE tus)

From Miletus, Paul sent for the elders of the church at Ephesus. Acts 20:17 NIrV

PAUL SAID GOOD-BYE in the port city of Miletus, on Turkey's west coast. He was addressing leaders at the CHURCH he founded in neighboring EPHESUS. PAUL was sailing back to JERUSALEM, where he would be arrested. He told his colleagues, "None of you will ever see me again" (Acts 20:25 NIrV).

MILK

Abraham took some yogurt and milk and the roasted meat, and he served it to the men. Genesis 18:8

MILK FROM GOATS, SHEEP, cows, and CAMELS were a main source of food in Bible times. Because it soured

M

quickly in the heat, the people made much of it into butter, CHEESE, and yogurt.

MILLENNIUM

> I saw an angel. . .with the key to the bottomless pit and a heavy chain. . . . He seized the dragon. . . Satan—and bound him in chains for a thousand years. Revelation 20:1–2

- 1,000 years

TO GOD, 1,000 years are like "a passing day" (Psalm 90:4). The last book in the BIBLE says GOD will defeat evil on earth and toss SATAN into a PIT for 1,000 years. Some Christians take that literally and look for a 1,000-year reign of PEACE on earth. Others take it as a symbol of what life will be like after ROME falls.

MILLSTONES for crushing grain, olives, and other produce came in different sizes. Some were small enough for one person to roll. Others took an ox or some other heavyweight.

MILLSTONES

> A woman on the roof dropped a millstone that landed on Abimelech's head and crushed his skull. Judges 9:53

- Stone to grind grain into powder, press olives into oil

GRINDING STONES—some of which were shaped a bit like a wheel—were rolled in a stone trough to grind GRAIN kernels into FLOUR or to crush OLIVES into OLIVE OIL. The millstones came in different shapes and sizes.

MINING

> They sink a mine shaft into the earth far from where anyone lives. They descend on ropes, swinging back and forth. Job 28:4

"DIGGERS." That's what the BIBLE writers called miners. They dug TUNNELS, pits, and channels along the ground in and around Israel, including neighboring Jordan.

COPPER was a popular mineral in the region.

Mining it or any other mineral was dangerous work. The miners, mostly slaves and prisoners, risked getting crushed by falling rocks or getting poisoned by toxic air. Roman emperor TIBERIUS (ruled from AD 14–37) sent 4,000 Jewish captives to mine SILVER and IRON in Sicily.

MINISTER

> Aaron's sons. . .were anointed and ordained to minister as priests. Numbers 3:2–3

A MINISTER IS A SERVANT. At least the English word *minister* translates GREEK words that mean SERVANT. But in the BIBLE, most ministers were servants of GOD.

In the OLD TESTAMENT, Jewish PRIESTS served God when they conducted their WORSHIP rituals such as burning INCENSE and sacrificing ANIMALS. In the NEW TESTAMENT, PAUL and other CHURCH leaders served God by teaching, feeding the hungry, and treating the sick.

CALMING A STORM is a miracle that gets the attention of Jesus' disciples. They begin to realize that he's more than a wonderworking prophet. But Jesus doesn't seem to get their full attention until he comes back from the dead. At that point, he has them at hello.

MIRACLES

"I have a greater witness. . .my teachings and my miracles. The Father gave me these works to accomplish, and they prove that he sent me." John 5:36

MIRACLES WEREN'T SUPERNATURAL—
defying the laws of physics. Not as far as folks were concerned in Bible times. Laws of physics weren't a factor then. Instead, many people seemed to believe that anything was possible because spiritual or magical forces had the power to make it happen.

When the amazing did happen—MOSES parting the WATER for Jewish refugees on the EXODUS out of EGYPT or Jesus HEALING the sick—people saw it as proof that the miracleworker had GOD's backing and should be taken seriously.

After Jesus' CRUCIFIXION, RESURRECTION, and ASCENSION back to HEAVEN, the miracles his DISCIPLES performed helped jump-start the CHRISTIAN movement. Their words alone—that Jesus didn't stay dead—would have been hard to believe if it hadn't been that "the APOSTLES performed many miraculous signs and wonders" (Acts 2:43).

MIRIAM

(MEAR ee uhm)

1400s BC or 1200s BC (debated)

Miriam the prophet, Aaron's sister, took a tambourine and led all the women as they played their tambourines and danced.
Exodus 15:20

- Sister of Moses, Aaron
- prophet

AS A LITTLE GIRL, Miriam was probably the unidentified sister of MOSES who watched over him when he was a baby, floating in a BASKET in the NILE RIVER until the PRINCESS found him and adopted him.

When Moses led the JEWS out of SLAVERY in EGYPT, Miriam got jealous of him and argued that she was a PROPHET of equal stature. GOD disagreed. He said he spoke to her and other prophets only in VISIONS. But with Moses, "I speak to him face to face" (Numbers 12:8).

God then turned Miriam's skin DISEASE-white. At Moses' request, God healed her. But God ordered Miriam to stay outside the camp for a week: spiritual timeout.

MIRRORS

M

Bezalel made a large bowl and a stand out of bronze from the mirrors of the women.
Exodus 38:8 CEV

MIRRORS WERE METAL in Bible times—polished BRONZE, COPPER, SILVER, or GOLD. Distortion in those mirrors prodded PAUL to compare HUMANITY's limited view of GOD to "a dim reflection. . .looking into a mirror" (1 Corinthians 13:12 NCV).

MITE, WIDOW'S

People put money into the treasury. . . .
Then one poor widow came and threw in two mites. **Mark 12:41–42 NKJV**

SMALLEST COIN IN CIRCULATION, the "widow's mite" was a Roman lepton. A day's WAGES for the average working man was a DENARIUS. It took 80 lepta to make a denarius. For an eight-hour day, a lepton would have paid for six minutes.

MIZPAH
Map 1 C5

(MIZ puh)

The Benjaminites got wind that the Israelites were meeting at Mizpah. Judges 20:3 MSG

FOR ALLOWING THE GANG RAPE of a Jewish woman traveling through their tribal land, and then for refusing to punish the rapists, the tribe of BENJAMIN got decimated—only 600 survivors. As a staging ground for that battle, the other tribes assembled their armies of 400,000 men at the city of Mizpah, a few miles north of JERUSALEM.

MOAB
Map 2 J7

(MO ab)

The barley harvest was just beginning when Naomi and Ruth, her Moabite daughter-in-law, arrived in Bethlehem. Ruth 1:22 CEV

- Land settled by Lot's descendants
- Homeland of Ruth

EAST OF THE DEAD SEA in what is now the Arab country of Jordan, people called Moabites lived on a fertile plug of ground surrounded by badlands. Moabites were frequent enemies of the JEWS. King MESHA of Moab once fought off a Jewish ARMY that had come to collect taxes.

MOAB, SON OF LOT

(MO ab)

2100s BC

Lot's daughters became pregnant by their own father. When the older daughter gave birth to a son, she named him Moab. Genesis 19:36–37

WITH SODOM DESTROYED by a catastrophic fire, LOT's two daughters thought they and their father were the last three people on earth. They got their father drunk enough to get them pregnant. One son, Moab, became the father of the Moabites. The other, Ben-ammi, founded the Ammonites. Both races fought the JEWS.

MOLD

To whom can you compare God?. . . Can he be compared to an idol formed in a mold? Isaiah 40:18–19

MOLDS CARVED FROM STONE or shaped from clay allowed people in Bible times to mass-produce metal IDOLS, ornate BOWLS, and TOOLS.

They melted the metal—GOLD, SILVER, BRONZE, COPPER—and poured it into the mold.

Artisans whom King SOLOMON hired to build the first Jewish TEMPLE used molds to make huge objects, such as two bronze pillars and the massive bronze BASIN more than 7 feet (2 m) deep.

see photo, page 227

MOLECH

(MOLE lack)

Josiah destroyed the high places. . . . He didn't want anyone to use them to sacrifice his son or daughter in the fire to the god Molech. 2 Kings 23:10 NIrV

BURNING CHILDREN in sacrifice is apparently one way some people in Bible times worshiped Molech, a Canaanite god.

Even some JEWS got caught up in this—including at least two KINGS: AHAZ and his grandson MANASSEH both sacrificed sons to Molech.

Jews sacrificed children in the Valley of HINNOM, just outside the walls of JERUSALEM. Centuries later they linked this valley to GOD's judgment. They said that because of what happened there, God allowed invaders to destroy the Jewish cities and EXILE the survivors.

Most Bible references to "HELL" are literally a reference to this valley. Whenever Jesus used the word *hell*, he was saying the name of that valley, "Hinnom" in HEBREW or "GEHENNA" in GREEK.

MONEY

> *The love of money is the root of all kinds of evil.* 1 Timothy 6:10

BEFORE COINS—during most of OLD TESTAMENT times—people measured their wealth by the size of their herds, their property, along with their gems, GOLD, and SILVER. They used each of these as currency, alongside the option of trading services and goods. JACOB agreed to work seven years to cover the BRIDE fee for marrying RACHEL.

Persians in what is now Iran starting producing coins about 500 years before Christ. In NEW TESTAMENT times, JEWS dealt in coins from several sources: local currency along with coins from ROME, GREECE, and PERSIA.

Craftsmen "struck" coins—literally. They shaped blank coins using MOLDS. Then they put the coins between two flat dies etched with designs, heated them, and struck the dies with a heavy hammer blow. This pressed the die images into the soft, heated metal coin.

Counterfeiters working in Roman currency put cheap COPPER inside silver and gold coins. To fight back, Rome started striking coins with notched edges, which showed that their coins contained solid gold or silver.

See also DENARIUS, SHEKEL.

MONEY CHANGERS

> *Jesus. . .scattered the money changers' coins over the floor. . . . He told them . . . "Stop turning my Father's house into a marketplace!"* John 2:15–16

- Currency exchangers

TRAVELERS IN BIBLE TIMES, like today, needed a way to exchange the currency of their homeland for the local currency. Money changers provided this service, often for a fee of 4 to 8 percent.

Money changers were in greatest demand in cities like JERUSALEM, which attracted pilgrims and other travelers from all over the Mediterranean World.

JEWS had a unique need for this service. When Jewish men paid their annual half-SHEKEL Temple TAX, worship leaders required payment in one particular SILVER coin. So money changers set up booths on the TEMPLE property, with permission of the worship leaders—who possibly charged rent for the space.

Jesus drove out the money changers during his last week of ministry. Jewish worship leaders arrested him on Thursday and orchestrated his execution on Friday.

MONTH

(see CALENDAR)

MORDECAI

(MORE duh khi)

400s BC

> *Mordecai had a very beautiful cousin named Esther. . . . He had raised her as his own daughter, after her father and mother died.* Esther 2:7 CEV

- Queen Esther's cousin who raised her
- Provoked a near-miss of a holocaust of Jews

A JEW IN WHAT IS NOW IRAN, Mordecai refused to bow before the Persian king's top official. Big mistake. That's because the official, HAMAN, had a big ego.

In retaliation, Haman plotted the genocide of Mordecai's race—throughout the entire Middle East.

Mordecai convinced ESTHER to appeal to the king by revealing that she, too, was a Jew.

The king ordered Haman executed, creating a job opening for Mordecai.

MOREH

Map 1 D4

(MORE uh)

> *Abram traveled through the land as far as Shechem. There he set up camp beside the oak of Moreh.* Genesis 12:6

WHEN ABRAHAM ARRIVED in the heartland of what is now ISRAEL, he camped at Moreh. There, GOD told him, "I will give this land to your descendants" (Genesis 12:7).

M

(mo RYE uh)

Solomon began to build the Temple of the
Lord in Jerusalem on Mount Moriah.
2 Chronicles 3:1 NCV

▪ Hill of Jerusalem

ABRAHAM NEARLY SACRIFICED his son Isaac
in "the land of Moriah" (Genesis 22:2). Jewish TRADI-
TION says this Moriah was the same as Mount Moriah,
where SOLOMON built the Jerusalem TEMPLE. Could be.
The BIBLE says ABRAHAM's walk from his home in BEER-
SHEBA took three days. That's about how long it would
take to walk to Jerusalem, north some 45 miles (72 km).

MORTAR

You cannot separate fools from their
foolishness, even though you grind them like
grain with mortar and pestle. **Proverbs 27:22**

1. SEALANT FOR STONE BUILDINGS. Construction workers used asphalt-like TAR as an ancient
version of cement mortar. Sometimes called BITUMEN, it
held BRICKS and stones together. When tar wasn't available, they mixed up their own mortar from clay, lime,
sand, and water.

    2. Bowl for grinding grain, herbs. Cooks
used small stone BOWLS called mortars to crush GRAIN
into FLOUR or to crush herbs and SPICES to mix into
stews and BREAD dough.

MOSES

(MO zuhs)

1400s BC or 1200s BC (debated)

Moses was Israel's greatest prophet. God
talked to him face-to-face, and gave him
power to do incredible miracles.
Deuteronomy 34:10–11 AUTHOR'S PARAPHRASE

▪ Israel's most revered prophet
▪ Led Jews out of slavery in Egypt
▪ Delivered God's laws to the Jews

LAWGIVER MOSES delivers the 10 Commandments
to the Jewish refugees. It seems appropriate that
the laws are inscribed in stone since they form the
bedrock foundation on which all of Israel's other
laws are built.

ISRAEL'S FIRST LEADER—and perhaps the most
beloved—was an 80-year-old man who didn't want the job.

    Yet Moses ended up freeing the JEWS from SLAVERY
in EGYPT and leading them to the border of what is now
their homeland, ISRAEL.

    In the process, he divided them into a dozen tribes,
organized them into a nation, and gave them hundreds
of laws to live by—including the most revered of all: the
10 COMMANDMENTS.

BABY IN A BASKET, TO GO

By the time Moses was born, the Jews had been in Egypt
for about 350 years. JACOB had led them there to escape a DROUGHT. They stayed. They grew large enough
to threaten Egypt's national security. They ended up enslaved, as a worker race building cities for the king.

    To control the Jewish population, Egypt's king or-
dered newborn Jewish boys tossed into the NILE RIVER.

    Technically, the mother of Moses—JOCHEBED—
complied. But she put him in a mini-lifeboat: a waterproof BASKET. Location: where the PRINCESS bathed. The
princess found baby Moses, adopted him, and raised
him as a prince in Egypt. Bonus: She hired Jochebed as
the nanny. Mom got a paycheck.

FUGITIVE PRINCE ON THE RUN

Somewhere along the way, Moses found out he was a Jew. He went to visit his people and was appalled by how the Egyptians were treating them. He killed one slave driver for beating a Jew.

The king wouldn't tolerate an adopted Jew killing a full-blooded Egyptian. He wanted Moses dead. Suddenly a fugitive, Moses fled east across the SINAI PENINSULA. He found a home in MIDIAN, a nation on the eastern side of the RED SEA, along what is now the border of Jordan and Saudi Arabia.

Moses married a herder's daughter, ZIPPORAH. For 40 years he worked as a SHEPHERD for her father.

DEBATE AT THE BURNING BUSH

While grazing SHEEP in near MOUNT SINAI, Moses walked over to a fiery bush that wasn't burning up.

"GOD called to him from the middle of the bush, 'Moses! Moses!'" (Exodus 3:4).

God told Moses to go back to Egypt and free the Jews. A debate followed. It went something like this.

Moses: I'm a nobody.

God: I'll go with you. I'm a somebody.

Moses: The Jews will want to know who sent me, and I don't know your NAME.

God: I am I AM.

Moses: Nobody's going to believe this.

God: They'll believe the MIRACLES I'll do.

Moses: I get tongue-tied.

God: I made your tongue. I can unravel it.

Moses: Come on, please send somebody else.

God: For heaven's sake, Moses! Do this. You can take your big brother along. He likes to talk.

TEN PLAGUES TO FREEDOM

There's a new king in Egypt, which may explain why Moses didn't get executed on the spot when he showed up as an 80-year-old runaway fugitive.

Moses asked the king to let the Jews take a three-day walk into the DESERT to hold a religious FESTIVAL to worship God.

God who?

That was pretty much the reply of Egypt's king, himself considered a god: son of Re, Egypt's top god. Re was the sun god in a desert land. Powerful.

It took 10 plagues for Moses to convince the king to let the Jews go.

The plagues:

- Nile River turned blood red
- frogs
- gnats
- flies
- livestock disease
- boils
- HAIL
- LOCUSTS
- three days of darkness
- death of firstborn

EXODUS ROAD TRIP

Moses led the Jews toward Mount Sinai, which an ancient tradition locates about 200 miles (322 km) southeast, near the southern tip of the SINAI PENINSULA.

When it dawned on Egypt's king that the Jews weren't coming back, he mustered his ARMY and went after them. He caught up with them and trapped them beside a body of WATER described as a sea of reeds—perhaps a lake or the tip of the Red Sea.

In one of the BIBLE's most famous miracles, Moses raised his staff, cuing an east wind that plowed an escape route through the water. When the Egyptians tried to follow, the water crashed in on them. That ended the Egyptian threat. They didn't show up again in the 40-

M

END OF THE LINE. Moses gets to see the Promised Land, but he doesn't get to set foot on it. He dies in what is now the Arab country of Jordan.

year story that followed.

The Jews reached Mount Sinai and camped there for about a year. Moses met with God on the mountain. That's where he got the two stone tablets etched with the 10 Commandments, the bedrock foundation for the hundreds of Jewish laws to come: domestic, civil, criminal, and religious.

These laws worked a bit like a national Constitution, a Bill of Rights, and a worship manual all rolled into one. The LAW OF MOSES, as it became known, directed Jews about how to live in PEACE with each other and with God. It told them what SACRIFICES to offer God in worship and how to offer them. It even provided the blueprint for the first Jewish worship center, with a tent SANCTUARY, a portable ALTAR, and a COURTYARD surrounded by a curtain wall.

FORTY YEARS IN THE BADLANDS

After organizing the Jews into a dozen tribes, Moses led this nation north, out of the Sinai badlands. The Jews camped at KADESH, an oasis on Egypt's side of the modern border with Israel.

A dozen scouts, one from each tribe, traveled into CANAAN, now known as Israel. The majority report—10 out of the 12 scouts—recommended against invasion. Too many walled cities to conquer. GIANTS lived there, too.

Terrified, the Jews refused to go any further.

Moses must have been dumbfounded. For in the past year, God had always come through for the Jews: parting the water, defeating the Egyptians, along with providing MANNA, QUAIL, and even drinkable water from ROCKS and mineral-tainted pools.

For their lack of FAITH, God sentenced the Jews to 40 years in the badlands.

Almost the entire adult GENERATION would die there. The only two adults who would step foot onto the PROMISED LAND would be the two scouts who had advised the Jews to press the invasion: JOSHUA and CALEB.

Forty years later, at age 120, Moses led the Jews to the east side of the JORDAN RIVER, into what is now Jordan. His brother and sister—AARON and MIRIAM—were already dead: he would die soon, too.

In one last assembly, he called together Generation Next. He gave them a history lesson, to make sure they knew what God had done for them and the previous generation. He also reviewed the laws. His speech is preserved in the book of DEUTERONOMY.

Afterward, Moses climbed MOUNT NEBO. There he looked across the Jordan River valley into the Promised Land. He died and was buried.

More than a thousand years later he returned, the Bible says—this time inside the Promised Land. As three of Jesus' DISCIPLES watched, "Jesus was completely changed. His face was shining like the sun, and his clothes became white as light. All at once Moses and ELIJAH were there talking with Jesus" (Matthew 17:2–3 CEV).

Moses, more than any other Jewish leader, forged Israel into a nation of souls who pledged their allegiance to no GODS but God.

MOTHER

"Honor your father and mother."
Exodus 20:12

JOB ONE FOR A WOMAN in Bible times was to make babies—preferably males, because it was a man's world.

They made the rules. They ruled the roost. They owned the roost.

WOMEN couldn't usually own property any more than a minor today can sign a CONTRACT on a house without an adult cosigner.

Women who couldn't have babies often got lousy treatment. JEWS figured GOD controlled everything. So if a woman couldn't have a baby, many Jews figured it was because God was punishing her for some terrible SIN—such as ADULTERY.

Mom was boss of the kids, though—second in command after Dad. She took care of them and taught them while they were young. The FATHER took over the training of the boys when they grew old enough to work in the FAMILY business—often herding or FARMING. The mother continued teaching her daughters household jobs such as COOKING, cleaning, and sewing.

One of the top 10 Jewish laws reminds CHILDREN of all ages that mothers—just like fathers—deserve respect and honor. (See TEN COMMANDMENTS.)

MOUNT ARARAT is the highest of many mountains in the Ararat mountain range. The Bible says Noah's ark came to rest in the Ararat mountains, not on Mount Ararat.

The ark came to rest on the mountains of Ararat. Genesis 8:4 TNIV

- Highest mountain in Ararat range
- Elevation: 16,854 feet (5,137 m)

NOAH'S ARK didn't necessarily land on Mount Ararat, an extinct volcano in eastern Turkey.

The BIBLE says NOAH's barge landed in the "mountains of Ararat," a range large enough to cover Kansas.

For the past 200 years, however, explorers have targeted Mount Ararat partly because it's the highest mountain in the range.

Some claim to have seen the ARK.

One French explorer, Fernand Navarra, carried home a 5-foot (2 m) log of hand-cut timber he said he found 13,000 feet (about 4,000 m) up the mountain. Carbon tests dated the wood to a max of 1,200 years ago. Some speculate the wood may have been part of a monument built by Crusader-era monks intended for visiting pilgrims.

In the third century BC, a Babylonian priest named Berossos said some people in the area claimed to know where Noah's ark was. He said some even wore CHARMS made from the ship's waterproofing material, asphalt-like TAR found in tar pits.

(CAR muhl)

"Summon all Israel to join me [Elijah] at Mount Carmel, along with the 450 prophets of Baal and the 400 prophets of Asherah." 1 Kings 18:19

- Where Elijah executed pagan prophets
- Elevation: 1,791 feet (546 m)

MORE LIKE HILLS, Carmel is a forested mountain range in northern ISRAEL. Stretching about 15 miles (25 km) long, the hills are blanketed in orchards, vineyards, and grain fields.

These hills overlook Israel's largest and most fertile valley: the JEZREEL VALLEY. That made Carmel a strategic site—especially because of one particular pass through the mountains: MEGIDDO. JEWS built a fortress city there to protect the pass from invaders.

Soldiers fought many battles in the area. But the most famous battle didn't involve a single soldier. The prophet ELIJAH challenged 850 pagan prophets and priests of BAAL and ASHERAH to a spiritual battle, to see which god could send fire from the sky to burn up a sacrifice.

GOD won. Elijah ordered the 850 pagan prophets and priests executed.

see map, page 262

M

TURKEY · Mt. Ararat · Little Ararat · Aras River (national boundary) · ARMENIA · N

Mediterranean Sea

Mt. Tabor
Possible site:
Jesus transforms
into glowing presence

LEBANON

Damascus

Mt. Hermon

SYRIA

Sea of Galilee

Mt. of Beatitudes
Jesus preaches
Sermon on the Mount

Mt. Ebal

Mt. Gerizim

West Bank

Mt. Gilboa
King Saul and sons
die in battle

JORDAN

Mt. Carmel
Elijah executes
Baal prophets

Jerusalem

Gaza Strip

Dead Sea

ISRAEL

Mt. of Olives
Jesus arrested
while praying

Mt. Nebo
Moses dies

N

MOUNTAINS OF FAME

MOUNT EBAL

Map 1 D5

(E bull)

"After the LORD your God helps you take the land, you must have a ceremony where you announce his. . .curses from Mount Ebal."
Deuteronomy 11:29 CEV

- Curse Mountain
- Elevation: 3,084 feet (940 m)

ONE OF TWO mountain sentinels, Mount Ebal teams up with MOUNT GERIZIM to guard a pass through a narrow valley in central ISRAEL.

The mountains are famous because of JOSHUA. When he led the JEWS on the conquest of the land after the EXODUS out of Egypt, he gathered the Jews in the valley between these hills. Leaders standing on the slopes of Mount Ebal read from the laws of MOSES the CURSES they would experience if they disobeyed GOD. Leaders standing on Mount Gerizim read the BLESSINGS for obedience.

MOUNT GERIZIM

Map 1 D5

(GARE uh zim)

"After the LORD your God helps you take the land, you must have a ceremony where you announce his blessings from Mount Gerizim."
Deuteronomy 11:29 CEV

- Blessing Mountain
- Elevation: 2,890 feet (881 m)

MOUNT EBAL'S TWIN, Mount Gerizim is located near ancient SHECHEM and the modern-day West Bank city of Nablus. The 130,000 people who live there are governed by the Palestinian National Authority.

MOUNT GILBOA

Map 1 D4

(gill BOW uh)

Saul gathered all the army of Israel and camped at Gilboa. When Saul saw the vast Philistine army, he became frantic with fear.
1 Samuel 28:4–5

- King Saul died here
- Elevation: 1696 feet (517 m)

PHILISTINES from the southland coast made a move on ISRAEL's most fertile land: the massive JEZREEL VALLEY in the north. Israel's first KING, Saul, gathered his ARMY on Mount Gilboa, overlooking the Philistine camp in the valley below. When he saw the overwhelming force of PHILISTINES, he knew he was a goner. He and three of his sons died in the doomed battle.

MOUNT HERMON

Map 1 D2

My bride, together we will leave Lebanon! We will say good-by to the peaks of. . .Hermon, where lions and leopards live in the caves.
Song of Songs 4:8 CEV

- Highest mountain in Israel, Lebanon, Syria
- Elevation: 9,232 feet (2,814 m)

AT NEARLY TWO MILES HIGH (3 km), Mount

Hermon is a snow magnet—and a major source of water for ISRAEL, LEBANON, and SYRIA.

Hermon's triple peaks collect more than a meter of snow each winter (3 feet), which isn't bad for a DESERT region. The snow melts into the porous limestone to feed underground oasis springs and the JORDAN RIVER.

MOUNT HOREB   (see MOUNT SINAI)

MOUNT NEBO

Map 1 E5

(NEE bow)

Moses climbed Mount Nebo. . . . The LORD showed him the whole land of Judah all the way to the Mediterranean Sea.
Deuteronomy 34:1–2 NIrV

- Moses died here
- Elevation: 2,631 feet (802 m)

BEFORE HE DIED, MOSES got a panoramic view of the PROMISED LAND from Mount Nebo. He was standing in what is now the Arab country of Jordan, about 10 miles (16 km) away and about a mile (1.6 km) above the JORDAN RIVER valley—ISRAEL's eastern border. Jordanians today call the mountain Jebel en-Neba.

MOUNT OF BEATITUDES

Map 4 D3

(be AT uh toods)

When Jesus saw the crowds, he went up on a hill. . .and he began to teach them.
Matthew 5:1–2 NCV

- Where Jesus preached the Sermon on the Mount
- Elevation: about 1,100 feet (335 m)

ON THE SLOPES OF THIS HILL beside the SEA OF GALILEE, Jesus preached his most famous sermon. The sermon began with a prescription for developing a happy attitude toward life—it's a list of advice from Jesus: the BEATITUDES. That's where the hill gets its name.

The hill's location is uncertain. But the best guess

M

is a gently rolling hillside about a mile's walk (1.6 km) from Jesus' ministry headquarters in the FISHING village of CAPERNAUM. That guess is based on an ancient tradition that goes back to at least the AD 300s, when ROME legalized CHRISTIANITY and pilgrims started visiting the area. Early Christians built several churches on the hill, though Muslim invaders tore them down in the AD 600s.

Today a group of Catholic nuns maintains the Chapel of the Beatitudes there. It's a popular tourist attraction built in the 1930s by money raised, oddly enough, by World War II Italian dictator Benito Mussolini.

At the foot of this hill lies the Plain of GENNESARET. That might explain why LUKE's version of the sermon says Jesus preached "on a large, level area" Luke (6:17), while MATTHEW described it as a hill. The audience may have sat on the slopes, in nature's amphitheater, while Jesus spoke from the plain below.

RISING ABOVE JERUSALEM is a ridge of hills known as the Mount of Olives. On the slopes of that ridge Temple police arrested Jesus while he was praying. The gray area on the right side of the ridge is a cemetery for souls who wanted to be buried near Jerusalem.

MOUNT OF OLIVES
See Jerusalem, Map 4 C5

Jesus taught in the temple each day, and he spent each night on the Mount of Olives. Luke 21:37 CEV

- Where Jesus was arrested, and later ascended
- Elevation: 2,694 feet (820 m)

ISRAEL'S MOST FAMOUS HILL isn't a hill. It's a three-peak ridge of hills—and the best place to get a great view of JERUSALEM. That may be why Jesus seemed drawn to the Mount of Olives.

Jerusalem was built on a ridge, too. But the Mount of Olives, just across the narrow KIDRON VALLEY, rises higher and stretches about 2 miles (3 km) long, north to south. Travelers coming from JERICHO and other cities in the north would cross the Mount of Olives to get to Jerusalem.

On the Mount of Olives is where Jesus:

- "began to weep" (Luke 19:41) a few days before the CRUCIFIXION, when he saw the city ahead
- prayed before his arrest, at an "olive grove called GETHSEMANE" (Mark 14:32)
- ascended "into a cloud. . .rising into HEAVEN" (Acts 1:9–10)

MOUNT SINAI
Map 2 I8

(SI ni)

All of Mount Sinai was covered with smoke because the LORD had descended on it in the form of fire. Exodus 19:18

- Where Moses got the 10 Commandments
- Elevation: 7,497 feet (2,285 m)

ISRAEL WAS BORN IN EGYPT at the foot of Mount Sinai, some 250 miles (402 km) south of JERUSALEM.

That's where an ancient Jewish TRADITION says MOSES received GOD's laws and where he organized the Jewish refugees escaping from Egyptian SLAVERY into a nation of 12 tribes.

Locals today call the craggy mountain in the SINAI badlands by its Arabic name, Jebel Musa: "Mountain of Moses." A monastery was built at the foot of the mountain in AD 530: St. Catherine's Greek Orthodox Monastery, a popular tourist attraction. One of the oldest surviving copies of the BIBLE was found in this monastery: the *Codex Sinaiticus*, copied about 300 years after Jesus.

Bible experts don't agree which route Moses took during the EXODUS. So there are about a dozen contenders for Mount Sinai, which the Bible also refers to as Mount Horeb.

Wherever the mountain was, it was there that:

- Moses heard God speaking from a BURNING BUSH
- Moses received the 10 COMMANDMENTS and hundreds of other laws
- Moses and the Exodus JEWS camped for over a year
- ELIJAH fled after Queen JEZEBEL threatened to kill him.

MOUNT TABOR sits like a lonely, lost hill in the middle of the Jezreel Valley.

MOUNT TABOR

Map 1 D4

(TAY boor)

Deborah said to Barak, "Go!" . . . So Barak went down Mount Tabor. His 10,000 men followed him. Judges 4:14 NIRV

- Staging area for Deborah's attack on invaders
- Possible site of Jesus' transfiguration
- Elevation: 1,929 feet (588 m)

A LONE DOME on a flat plain, Mount Tabor was the perfect spot for an ARMY of foot soldiers to wait for an invasion force of charioteers. Chariots couldn't make the climb up the hill. But foot soldiers could certainly charge down the hill—especially in a rainstorm that trapped the chariots in mud.

That's what happened when a PROPHET named DEBORAH rallied northland JEWS to fight off an invading CHARIOT corps.

Tabor sits in the JEZREEL VALLEY, only about 5

miles (8 km) east of Jesus' hometown, NAZARETH. That's one reason it's a top contender for the unidentified mountain where the BIBLE says Jesus transformed into what sounds like a celestial being of light: "His face shone like the sun, and his clothes became as white as light" (Matthew 17:2).

MOURNING

Jacob tore his clothes in grief, dressed in rough burlap, and mourned his son a long, long time. Genesis 37:34 MSG

GRIEF WAS HARD ON THE CLOTHES and on the skin. People in Bible times often expressed their sorrow by tearing their clothes and putting on scratchy, burlap-like clothes made from GOAT or CAMEL hair—fabric better suited for grain sacks. That's why it was sometimes called SACKCLOTH.

Other expressions of grief:

- sprinkling dust on the head
- shaving the head
- beating the chest
- sobbing
- singing sad SONGS
- hiring mourners

Jewish law restricted how far JEWS could take the mourning: "Do not cut your bodies for the dead, and do not mark your skin with TATTOOS" (Leviticus 19:28).

MULE

"King David has just declared Solomon king!" . . . They had him ride on the king's own mule. 1 Kings 1:43–44

- Ancient hybrid transportation

A MULE IS WHAT YOU GET when you cross a lady horse with a gentlemen DONKEY—or for the critter savvy, that's a mare with a jackass.

JEWS weren't allowed to crossbreed their livestock: "Do not mate two different kinds of animals" (Leviticus 19:19). But they were apparently allowed to buy them.

M

King David and his sons rode mules: "Sons of the king jumped on their mules and fled" (2 Samuel 13:29). Solomon was introduced as king while riding a mule. Absalom died in battle after falling off his mule.

Mules were valued for their strength, stamina, and gentle spirit. They could handle hardships and terrain too tough for most other pack animals.

MURDER

"All murderers must be put to death, but only if evidence is presented by more than one witness." Numbers 35:30

DON'T MURDER. It's one of Israel's most basic laws—one of the 10 Commandments.

In early Jewish history, trials were held by local elders. Conviction required at least two witnesses confirming the murder. The penalty was execution—conducted by one of the victim's relatives.

In one notable exception to execution—history's first reported murder—God didn't take Cain's life after Cain murdered his brother Abel. Instead, God banished him from the land.

When outsiders ruled Israel—empires such as Persia and Rome—trials and executions were handled by government authorities. That's why the Jews couldn't execute Jesus but had to convince the Roman governor, Pilate, to order the execution.

MUSIC

"Let us look for someone who can play the harp. When the black mood from God moves in, he'll play his music and you'll feel better." 1 Samuel 16:16 MSG

MUSIC THERAPY is nothing new. Jews used it 3,000 years ago to treat King Saul's depression.

They used music like we do, too: in worship service, singing to pass the time at work and on the road, lamenting the death of a friend. David "composed a funeral song for Saul and Jonathan" (2 Samuel 1:17). It's called "Song of the Bow," and the lyrics are preserved in the Bible.

The book of Psalms is a collection of song lyrics. The tunes are lost to time. There's no indication that the notes were written in any form. Historians speculate they were simply passed along by one generation singing or performing for the next one.

Instruments mentioned in the Bible include harp, lyre, ram's horn, tambourine, cymbals, flute, gong, and a rattle-like sistrum.

David organized a music ministry for the Jerusalem worship center. He had it up and running long before his son Solomon built the Temple. "The men used their music to serve in front of the holy tent, the Tent of Meeting" (1 Chronicles 6:32 NIrV).

See also Jubal.

ONE PIPER PIPING, two men a-lounging. Double-barreled flutes like this were common in Bible times. Psalm 5 was a song intended for flute accompaniment.

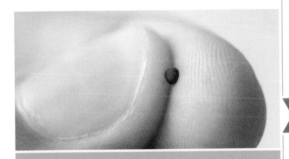

BLACK MUSTARD grew throughout Galilee, where Jesus taught about having faith no larger than a tiny mustard seed.

MUSTARD

"The Kingdom of Heaven is like a mustard seed. . .the smallest of all seeds, but it becomes the largest of garden plants."
Matthew 13:31–32

- Used for cooking oil, medicine

A BALL no thicker than the edge of a quarter or a euro, mustard seeds are tiny. But they grow into plants nearly 2 to 5 feet high (less than 2 m). People in Bible times crushed the seeds to make COOKING oil and strong-smelling mustard poultices to place over aching or injured parts of the body.

Jesus once told his DISCIPLES, "If you had FAITH no larger than a mustard seed, you could tell this mountain to move from here to there. And it would" (Matthew 17:20 CEV).

MYRRH

The Wise Men went to the house. There they saw the child with his mother Mary. . . . They gave him gold, incense and myrrh. Matthew 2:11 NIRV

- A wise man's gift for baby Jesus

LIKE FRANKINCENSE, myrrh is a fragrant, dried sap used to scent PERFUME and to burn as sweet-smelling INCENSE. It was also used as a painkiller—offered to Jesus on the CROSS: "WINE drugged with myrrh, but he refused it" (Mark 15:23).

The sap comes from an evergreen shrub—*Commiphora abyssinica*—native to parts of EGYPT's side of Africa and to what many believe was the QUEEN OF SHEBA's part of ARABIA, in the southland nation of Yemen.

MYRTLE

"Go out into the mountains, and bring back branches from. . .myrtle trees, palms, and shade trees. Make shelters with them."
Nehemiah 8:15 NCV

A SHRUB that grows alongside streams, myrtle was one of the plants JEWS used to build temporary shelters to celebrate the FESTIVAL of Booths. That's a holiday to celebrate the HARVEST and to remember GOD's protection of MOSES and the Jews during the EXODUS out of EGYPT.

MYSTERY RELIGIONS

Don't let anyone capture you with. . .high-sounding nonsense that come[s] from human thinking and from the spiritual powers of this world. Colossians 2:8

- Popular in Roman times

SECRET WORSHIP RITUALS are the reason many religions in the ROMAN EMPIRE were called "the mysteries."

The apostle PAUL probably encountered several of these religions—one in particular during his three-year stay in EPHESUS: worship of ARTEMIS, patron goddess of Ephesus.

Many of these mysterious cults seemed clustered around what is now Turkey. Several seemed to have mutated into mystery religions after contact with Greek religions. For example, cults devoted to Isis (a magical healer), Mithra (god of light), and Cybele (a Mother Nature goddess of earth, wild plants, and animals).

Some of the secret rituals apparently included ecstatic dancing and self-mutilation such as castration.

Bible experts say some mystery religions were a bit like CHRISTIANITY. Some of these religions, like Christianity, promised union with a god, along with ETERNAL LIFE.

M

NAAMAN

(NAY uh muhn)

800s BC

Naaman was the commander of the Syrian army. . .a brave soldier, but he had leprosy.
2 Kings 5:1 CEV

- Elisha cured this Syrian general of leprosy

A JEWISH SLAVE GIRL captured in a raid on ISRAEL pointed her master—SYRIA's top general, Naaman—to a cure for his skin DISEASE. Bible experts say the disease may or may not have been LEPROSY. The ancients painted leprosy with a broader brush than docs do today.

Prophet ELISHA could heal him, the slave said. Naaman paid the prophet a visit. After reluctantly doing as Elisha told him—taking a BATH in the muddy JORDAN RIVER—his skin cleared up.

See also GEHAZI.

NABAL

(NAY bull)

About 1000 BC

Nabal was a very rich man. . . . His wife Abigail was sensible and beautiful, but he was. . .rough and mean. 1 Samuel 25:2–3 CEV

- First husband of Abigail, who later married David
- Died of shock at shocking news

A HERDER with 4,000 SHEEP and GOATS, he was so stingy that he refused to give any supplies to DAVID's men who had helped protect his livestock.

When David found out about Nabal's refusal, he led his men to kill the herder and take the supplies. But Nabal's WIFE heard about the refusal, too. She took supplies to David while her husband lay drunk. When her husband sobered up and she told him what had almost happened, Nabal died of what sounds like a heart attack or a stroke.

See also ABIGAIL.

NABOTH

(NAY both)

800s BC

Ahab said to Naboth, "Since your vineyard is so convenient to my palace, I would like to buy it to use as a vegetable garden." 1 Kings 21:2

- Murdered over vegetables

UNLUCKY ENOUGH to own a nice plot of ground beside King AHAB's summer getaway in JEZREEL, Naboth died for refusing to sell it to him. Depressed, Ahab slipped into a funk. His WIFE, Queen JEZEBEL, told him not to worry; she'd get the land. She arranged for Naboth to get stoned to death for a CRIME he didn't commit: cursing GOD. Then she confiscated his land.

BEARDED LADIES is pretty much what the prophet Nahum calls the fierce Assyrians who erased Israel from the political map. He says God's going to lift their skirts, humiliating them in front of the world.

NAHUM

(NAY hum)

600s BC

I am Nahum from Elkosh. And this is the message that I wrote down about Nineveh.
Nahum 1:1 CEV

- Prophet who doomed Assyria

SCHOLARS DON'T KNOW MUCH about this prophet. Not when he lived. Not where he lived—at least not beyond knowing the city's name.

Nahum predicted the fall of ASSYRIA, the empire that destroyed the northern Jewish nation of ISRAEL in 722 BC. Assyria was based in NINEVEH, in what is now northern Iraq. Babylonians from what is now southern Iraq destroyed Nineveh in 612 BC.

NAHUM, BOOK OF

Famous sound bite: "I will lift your skirts and show all the earth your nakedness." Nahum delivering God's message to the Assyrian Empire, Nahum 3:5

IT SOUNDS LIKE "DITTO" to the message JONAH gave the Assyrians earlier: GOD is going to let your enemies destroy you. Perhaps about a century earlier—if the scholars' timeline guesses are right—ASSYRIA had erased the northern Jewish nation of ISRAEL from the world map. Those EXILED Jews became famous as the Lost TRIBES OF ISRAEL.

- Writer: A prophet named Nahum or someone reporting his story.
- Time: Clues in the prophecy suggest Nahum wrote during a 50-year span: after Assyrians destroyed the Egyptian capital of Thebes in 663 BC but before Babylonians destroyed the Assyrian capital of Nineveh in 612 BC.
- Location: Nahum lived in Elkosh, a site unknown. He targeted Nineveh, capital of the Assyrian Empire, in what is now northern Iraq.

BIG SCENE

Girlie men in skirts. In what sounds a bit like calling the toughest convict in the prison yard a sissy, the prophet Nahum calls the vicious Assyrian Empire a girl. This is an empire that considered pictures of their soldiers skinning victims alive and impaling them on fence posts as suitable for the palace wall. But Nahum paints a different picture for them: God lifting their skirts for the world to see them exposed. *Nahum 2–3*

IRON NAILS like this, from Roman times, may have been the kind carpenters like Joseph and his sons used. Nails like this may have also held Jesus to the cross.

NAILS

When the soldiers came to the place called "The Skull," they nailed Jesus to a cross. Luke 23:33 CEV

ABOUT A THOUSAND YEARS before ABRAHAM, COPPER and BRONZE nails replaced wooden pegs. And about 1,000 years after Abraham—sometime around 1200 BC—IRON nails replaced the softer metals. That made it possible for folks to build wooden houses and PALACES two or more stories high.

Romans sometimes nailed CRUCIFIXION victims to the CROSS rather than tying them.

NAIN   Map 4 D4

(NAYN)

Jesus went to a town called Nain. . . . Just then, a dead person was being carried out. He was the only son of his mother. . .a widow. Luke 7:11–12 NIrV

- Jesus raised a widow's son from the dead

ABOUT A TWO-HOUR WALK from his hometown in NAZARETH, 6 miles (10 km) away in Nain, Jesus stopped the funeral procession of a WIDOW's only SON. Jesus told the dead boy to get up. The boy did just that.

N

NAME

"Name him Jesus—'God saves'—because he will save his people from their sins."
Matthew 1:21 MSG

MANY NAMES OF PEOPLE in the BIBLE offer clues about them.

JACOB means "heel grabber." He was born immediately after his twin brother, ESAU, and he came out clutching his brother's heel.

MOSES means "pulled out." The PRINCESS of EGYPT gave him that name after pulling him out of the NILE RIVER, where he was floating in a BASKET.

ISAIAH's son, MAHER-SHALAL-HASH-BAZ, has the longest name in the Bible. It symbolizes what Isaiah said the Assyrians would do to ISRAEL: "swiftly raid, swiftly rob."

NAOMI

(nay OH me)

1100s BC

Naomi took the baby and cuddled him to her breast. And she cared for him as if he were her own. Ruth 4:16

- Ruth's mother-in-law
- Great-great grandmother of King David

NOT YOUR TYPICAL SITCOM MOTHER-IN-LAW, Naomi so endeared herself to her daughter-in-law, RUTH that Ruth refused to abandon her after both became widows. Ruth didn't have to stay with the elderly Naomi. Ruth was young enough for her father to find her another husband.

Years earlier, Naomi, her husband, and their two sons had moved from BETHLEHEM to MOAB (today's Jordan) to escape a DROUGHT. The sons married but died about 10 years after their father. Ruth decided to return to Bethlehem with Naomi. There Ruth remarried a Jew, gave BIRTH to OBED, who would become King DAVID's grandfather, and apparently took care of Naomi.

NAPHTALI

(NAF tuh lie)

1800s BC

The sons of Bilhah, Rachel's servant, were Dan and Naphtali. Genesis 35:25

- Son of Jacob
- Ancestral father of one of Israel's 12 tribes

ONE OF JACOB'S DOZEN SONS, Naphtali was born to a surrogate mother: the slave of Jacob's wife, RACHEL. Each of JACOB's wives—LEAH and Rachel—used a slave to help provide Jacob with a large FAMILY. WOMEN in Bible times considered baby-making their most important contribution to the family. The more kids, especially boys, the more workers in the family and the more security in old age.

WIDOWED and with both sons dead, Naomi found herself destitute. But her daughter-in-law Ruth refused to abandon her. With Naomi's help, Ruth remarried, giving Naomi a grandson—who grew up to become the grandfather of King David.

NAPHTALI, TRIBE OF

Map 1 C3

(NAF tuh lie)

There were 45,400 men from the tribe of Naphtali. Numbers 26:48 CEV

- One of Israel's 12 tribes

NORTHERN JEWS, this tribe settled in ISRAEL's far northland area—above the SEA OF GALILEE, and below the mountains of LEBANON.

NARD

Mary took a very expensive bottle of perfume [nard] and poured it on Jesus' feet. She wiped them with her hair, and the sweet smell of the perfume filled the house. John 12:3 CEV

- Perfume imported from the Himalayas

NARD HAD AN EARTHY, CYPRESS-LIKE SMELL with a sky-high price. Premium nard was made of oil extracted from roots and stems of the spikenard plant native to India's Himalayan Mountains. MERCHANTS importing it to ISRAEL by CARAVAN traveled nearly two years each way, some 2,500 miles (4,000 km). The delivery fee was enormous: almost a year's salary for a 16-ounce (0.5 l) flask.

NATHAN

(NAY thun)

Ministered about 1010–970 BC

Nathan told David. . . "You murdered Uriah the Hittite by having the Ammonites kill him, so you could take his wife [Bathsheba]." 2 Samuel 12:7, 9 CEV

- Prophet during David's reign

CALLING KING DAVID AN ADULTERER and a murderer was something the prophet Nathan managed to do with flair. To confront DAVID about his affair with BATHSHEBA and his MURDER of her husband, Nathan told David a story: a nasty rich man stole a poor man's pet lamb, which he killed and ate.

Livid, David said the rich jerk deserved to die. Nathan replied, "You are that rich man!" (2 Samuel 12:7 CEV). David confessed and repented.

Decades later, while David lay old and dying, Nathan helped convince him to appoint the next KING: SOLOMON, the son David had with Bathsheba.

NATHANAEL

(nuh THAN uhl)

First century AD

"Nazareth!" exclaimed Nathanael. "Can anything good come from Nazareth?" John 1:46

- Disciple of Jesus

NOT FOND OF HIS NEIGHBOR CITY— NAZARETH—Nathanael couldn't believe it when PHILIP told him the MESSIAH came from there. Nathanael was from CANA, about a half-day walk to the north.

Yet Nathanael became convinced Jesus was the genuine article. It took a MIRACLE. Jesus said he saw him—apparently in the SPIRIT—while Nathanael stood under a FIG tree before Philip approached him.

NATIVITY

(see JESUS CHRIST)

NAZARETH

Map 4 C4

(NAZ are uth)

Joseph took the child and his mother. . .to a town called Nazareth, and lived there. Matthew 2:21, 23 NCV

- Jesus' hometown

JESUS GREW UP in a dip of a town that many travelers would walk right past without noticing. Nazareth was nestled in the dip of a ridge above the sprawling JEZREEL VALLEY—ISRAEL's most fertile farmland.

The tiny farming village couldn't have had more than a few hundred residents, scholars say. They base

N

that guess on scant archaeological discoveries found there.

Nearby was the capital of Israel's northern region of GALILEE: SEPPHORIS, about 4 miles (6 km) north. Jesus' father, JOSEPH, was a builder who may have worked in Sepphoris since Romans were rebuilding it during Jesus' growing-up years.

When Jesus returned to Nazareth as an adult, the locals got upset when he hinted that he was the MESSIAH.

"They mobbed him and forced him to the edge of the hill on which the town was built. They intended to push him over the cliff, but he passed right through the crowd and went on his way" (Luke 4:29–30).

NAZARETH was a tiny farming town nestled in the dip of hills. Vintners chiseled square holes cut into the rock hills, where they pressed grapes into wine. Olive trees laced the slopes, while small plugs of plowed fields in the valley grew barley, wheat, and other crops.

NAZIRITES

(NAZ uh rite)

"As long as they are Nazirites, they must not eat anything grapevines produce."
Numbers 6:4 NIrV

- Jews who took a unique vow of devotion to God

JUST AS MONKS TAKE A VOW of celibacy or silence, some JEWS took a vow of special devotion to

GOD—usually for a short time, but some for a lifetime. Those Jews were called Nazirites.

Nazirites couldn't drink WINE or even eat GRAPES or raisins. They couldn't cut their HAIR. And they couldn't go near a dead body—even if it was a close relative. If they did, they had to perform elaborate PURIFICATION rituals before resuming their vow.

SAMSON was "dedicated to God as a Nazirite from BIRTH" (Judges 13:5). That's why he didn't cut his hair. Until DELILAH arranged a haircut for him.

NEAPOLIS   Map 3 D3

(NEE ah poh liss)

We boarded a boat at Troas. . .and the next day we landed at Neapolis. From there we reached Philippi. Acts 16:11–12

- Greek port where Paul started his mission to Europe

STILL IN TURKEY, Paul had a VISION of a man from what is now northern Greece pleading with him to come and help the people there. PAUL took that as a SIGN from GOD to take his PREACHING to the next continent. After landing at the port town of Neapolis (Kevalla today), he walked about 10 miles (16 km) inland to PHILIPPI. There he started the first CHRISTIAN congregation in Europe.

NEBUCHADNEZZAR

(neb uh cud NEZ ur)

Reigned 605–562 BC

King Nebuchadnezzar of Babylon led his entire army against Jerusalem. . . . He burned down the Temple. . .the royal palace, and all the houses. 2 Kings 25:1, 9

- King of Babylonian Empire
- Destroyed Jerusalem
- Dismantled the Jewish nation
- Deported the Jews

AN IRAQI KING, Nebuchadnezzar erased the Jewish nation off the map.

342

In the process, he leveled JERUSALEM and he EXILED most survivors, taking them captive to Iraq, home of the Babylonian Empire he ruled.

Nebuchadnezzar wasn't just the king of BABYLON and son of the dynasty founder. He was Babylon's most powerful, longest reigning king: 43 years. During that time, he led Babylon into its Golden Age of prosperity.

WAR was the route he took.

First, he defeated the world's first known super-power: the Assyrian Empire, based in what is now northern Iraq. He destroyed their capital of NINEVEH, too. When the Assyrian ARMY tried to regroup and the Egyptians rushed up to reinforce them, Nebuchadnezzar's army defeated both forces at the Battle of CARCHEMISH in SYRIA.

Then he turned his army south, pillaging through Syria, LEBANON, and into what is now ISRAEL. The northern Jewish nation of Israel was already long gone—wiped out by Assyrians in 722 BC. But Nebuchadnezzar marched into the southern Jewish nation of JUDAH and ordered the JEWS to start paying him taxes.

They did for a few years. When they stopped, in 597 BC, Nebuchadnezzar came back to collect his taxes—and then some. He took all the GOLD objects that King SOLOMON of Israel had placed in the TEMPLE (2 Kings 14:14)—perhaps stealing the gold-plated ARK OF THE COVENANT, the most sacred Jewish relic. That chest held the 10 COMMANDMENTS of MOSES.

He also took 10,000 hostages, including the cream of society's crop—likely the prophet DANIEL as well. Nebuchadnezzar handpicked a new Jewish king, too.

The Jews did as they were told. For a few years.

When they stopped sending TAX money yet again, Nebuchadnezzar had all he could take of this tiny rebel kingdom.

He came back. And in one of the worst years in Jewish history—586 BC—he wiped the last surviving Jewish nation off the map. His men burned and leveled Jerusalem, including Solomon's 400-year-old Temple. Most Jews lucky enough to survive the slaughter ended up taking a long walk to Iraq as captives exiled from their now-dead nation.

Twice, the BIBLE says Nebuchadnezzar praised GOD.

First time: After watching Daniel's friends, SHADRACH, MESHACH, AND ABEDNEGO survive execution in a FUR-NACE, he warned that if anyone spoke "a word against the God of Shadrach, Meshach, and Abednego, they will be torn limb from limb, and their houses will be turned into heaps of rubble. There is no other god who can rescue like this!" (Daniel 3:29).

Second time: After returning from a bout of insan-ity, living in the wild, and eating grass like a cow, he praised "the King of heaven" for restoring him "as head of my kingdom" (Daniel 4:36–37).

IN A SWEET DREAM, Babylon's king Nebuchadnezzar sees a huge statue with a gold head, silver chest, bronze belly, iron legs, and clay feet. The prophet Daniel explains that the gold head represents Nebuchadnezzar's kingdom. The diminishing minerals represent the lesser kingdoms to come.

NECO

(NEE koh)

Reigned 610–595 BC

While Josiah was king, Pharaoh Neco, king of Egypt, went to the Euphrates River to help the king of Assyria. 2 Kings 23:29

- King of Egypt

EGYPTIAN KING NECO rushed north to reinforce his Assyrian allies who were trying to fight off the rising star of the Middle East: the Babylonian Empire, destined to become the world's next superpower. He and the Assyrians lost at the Battle of CARCHEMISH, in what is now Syria. Earlier, however, Neco's troops did manage to break through the Jewish blockade at MEGIDDO, killing JUDAH's King JOSIAH.

BONE NEEDLE, from Roman times. Someone carved this sometime between the first and third centuries, while the Christian church was getting stitched together.

NEEDLE

"It is easier for a camel to go through the eye of a needle than for a rich person to enter the Kingdom of God!" Mark 10:25

FOLKS SEWED clothes with tiny needles crafted from bone, IVORY, COPPER, and BRONZE.

Most Bible experts agree that when Jesus said it was harder for a rich person to squeeze through the eye of a needle than to get into HEAVEN, he meant a legit needle—though he was exaggerating. Some have suggested he referred to a small door into a city—perhaps small enough that a person needs to bow down to get inside. Most scholars call that a wild guess with no evidence to back it up.

NEGEV   Map 1 C8

(NEG ev)

Moses sent them to check out Canaan. He said, "Go up through the Negev Desert. Go on into the central hill country. See what the land is like." Numbers 13:17–18 NIrv

- Israel's southland: hot and dry

THE NAME SAYS IT. In HEBREW, *negev* means "dry" or "parched." It's not a DESERT with sand dunes. It's more like barren badlands. Lots of ROCKS and dirt. Few plants, except after the springtime rains. And it makes up roughly half of ISRAEL. Settlements and irrigation are adding some color to the landscape.

NEHEMIAH

(nee uh MY uh)

In Jerusalem 445–433 BC

These are the words of Nehemiah. . .the king's wine taster. Nehemiah 1:1, 11 NIrv

- Jewish wine steward in Persia (Iran)
- Led rebuilding of Jerusalem's walls
- Governor of Jewish province for 12 years

A JEW IN IRAN, Nehemiah worked as a WINE STEWARD in PERSIA's palace—until he heard that the walls of JERUSALEM lay in ruins.

He got permission from Persian king ARTAXERXES to lead an expedition to rebuild the walls. He also got at least a temporary promotion: GOVERNOR of the tiny Persian province of JUDEA, which was Jerusalem and the surrounding countryside and villages.

Nehemiah's team of local builders managed to repair the walls in a mere 52 days. But the work was possibly just a quick patch job to secure the city while more permanent repairs could be made.

Famous sound bite: "The joy of the LORD is your strength!" Nehemiah 8:10

A JEWISH WINE STEWARD in what is now Iran gets the Persian king's permission to go and rebuild the city walls of JERUSALEM. The initial repair takes only 52 days, but he stays and governs the province for a dozen years. His name is Nehemiah.

- Writer: Unknown. Ancient Jewish tradition credits a priest named Ezra.
- Time: Nehemiah remained in Jerusalem for a dozen years: 445–433 BC.
- Location: The story starts in Susa, capital of Persia, in what is now Iran. It continues in Jerusalem.

BIG SCENES

A wine taster's wish. It's springtime, and the WINE taster for Persian king ARTAXERXES has been bummed since autumn. That's when he got word that the city walls of his homeland capital, Jerusalem, remain busted. That's about a century and a half after Babylonian invaders tore them down. And about a century after the first wave of Jewish refugees returned home to rebuild their country. Nehemiah not only gets the king's permission to go and rebuild the walls, he gets an armed escort and free timber for the project. *Nehemiah 1–2*

Men at work. Jerusalem leaders back Nehemiah's project. Non-Jewish locals, however, don't want to see the JEWS back in control of their homeland. They try to lure Nehemiah into a meeting so they can kill him. They plan a preemptive strike on the construction workers. Nehemiah squashes that plan by posting armed guards. Builders finish the repairs in 52 days. That speed terrifies the enemies because they figure GOD helped the Jews. *Nehemiah 2–6*

NEIGHBOR

"Love your neighbor as yourself." Leviticus 19:18

SHOWING COMPASSION toward a neighbor was Jewish law. But it wasn't clear who qualified as a neighbor. Some RABBIS taught that only fellow JEWS qualified.

One Jewish scholar asked Jesus "Who is my neighbor?" (Luke 10:29).

Jesus answered with the PARABLE of the Good SAMARITAN. It's the story of a Jew who got mugged and left for dead. Two fellow Jewish worship leaders walked past him. But a Samaritan stopped to help. Samaritans and Jews had a Palestinian-Israeli kind of dislike for each other.

Jesus asked the scholar which person acted like a neighbor to the injured man.

Obvious answer: the Samaritan.

NEPHILIM

(NEFF uh lim)

The children of the supernatural beings who had married these women became famous heroes and warriors. They were called Nephilim. Genesis 6:4 CEV

- "Sons of God" who married human women

N

"SONS OF GOD," as some Bibles describe them, married beautiful women—producing a race of people called Nephilim.

This was before the FLOOD that NOAH's family survived—and that the Nephilim presumably didn't, though they resurfaced in a scouting report to MOSES (Numbers 13:33).

Bible experts are left guessing who these sons of God were:

Spirit beings, such as angels. But Jesus said ANGELS don't marry (Matthew 22:30).

Nobles. Bible writers sometimes called KINGS and other leaders "gods. . .children of the Most High" (Psalm 82:6).

Righteous men. Bible writers called the JEWS GOD's children: "The LORD says: ISRAEL is my FIRSTBORN son" (Exodus 4:22).

NERO

(NE row)

37–68 BC, ruled 54–68 BC

Paul replied. . . "I am not guilty of any of these crimes. . . . I now ask to be tried by the Emperor himself." Acts 25:10–11 CEV

▪ Roman emperor

NERO ORDERED PETER AND PAUL EXECUTED, according to early CHURCH leaders.

Nero's name isn't mentioned in the BIBLE, but he was the emperor when the apostle PAUL appealed to the Roman supreme COURT and then sailed to ROME for trial—as reported in the book of ACTS.

Nero was the first known Roman ruler to systematically persecute Christians. He is said to have blamed them for setting the fire that destroyed much of Rome in AD 64. PETER and Paul were likely executed during that wave of PERSECUTION, many Bible experts say.

Some Bible scholars say Nero is the beast of REVELATION: "Let the one with understanding solve the meaning of the number of the beast, for it is the number of a man. His number is 666" (Revelation 13:18). Some ancient Bibles put the number at 616.

Either number works for Nero. Letters had number values.

666. Start with a Roman coin that says "Nero CAESAR." Translate the letters from GREEK (the international language) to HEBREW (the Jewish language). Add the Jewish letters. They equal 666.

616. Next, translate "Nero Caesar" from Latin (the Roman language) to Hebrew. Add the letters. They equal 616.

See also MARK OF THE BEAST, ROMAN EMPIRE.

NERO was the first Roman emperor to put a hurt on the Christian movement. He reportedly blamed them for setting fire to Rome.

FISHING GALILEE. With Holy Land tourists watching, a man shows the technique for tossing a fishing net into the water. Lead weights lining the outside of the net cause it to sink, trapping fish unlucky enough to be swimming directly below.

NETS

When Jesus was walking by Lake Galilee, he saw Simon and his brother Andrew throwing a net into the lake because they were fishermen. Mark 1:16 NCV

FISHERMEN on the SEA OF GALILEE used several kinds of nets.

Cast net. Fishermen could throw a round net into the water, from shore or from the boat. This net, loaded with weights on the edge, fell like a parachute, trapping fish inside.

Drop net. A bit like a long volleyball net with weights at the bottom, it was dropped over the side of the boat and used to surround a school of fish.

Tow net. This long net—often stretching a couple hundred yards (meters)—got towed behind two boats.

Hunters also used nets to catch BIRDS and other prey.

NEW COVENANT

"I will make a new covenant with the people of Israel. . . . I will put my law in their minds. I will write it on their hearts." Jeremiah 31:31, 33 NIrV

▪ Replacement for the laws Moses gave

SOME 600 YEARS BEFORE JESUS, the prophet JEREMIAH made a bold prediction: GOD would replace his covenant agreement with ISRAEL. The JEWS would no longer have to debate how to observe the hundreds of laws MOSES gave them—the laws that helped define them as God's people. Instead, God would put his laws inside the human conscience.

Jesus said his sacrificial death marked the launch of the new covenant. Holding a cup of WINE that he said represented the BLOOD he would shed the next morning, he told his DISCIPLES at the LAST SUPPER: "This cup is the new covenant between God and his people" (Luke 22:20).

Years later, a Bible writer declared the first covenant dead: "When God speaks of a 'new' covenant, it means he has made the first one obsolete. It is now out of date and will soon disappear" (Hebrews 8:13).

NEW HEAVEN

> I saw a new heaven and a new earth, for the old heaven and the old earth had disappeared. Revelation 21:1

QUOTING GOD, a prophet named ISAIAH spoke of a radically changed world. No sadness there—only joy. "Look! I am creating new heavens and a new earth, and no one will even think about the old ones anymore" (Isaiah 65:17).

Many JEWS as well as some Christians today have taken this literally. They say they expect that one day GOD will eradicate SIN and create a new and perfect universe: the Garden of EDEN 2.0.

Others read the words as POETRY—and as a symbol of the wonderful life ahead in eternity, wherever it is and whatever it looks like.

NEW JERUSALEM (see JERUSALEM, NEW)

NEW TESTAMENT

> Only God can write such a letter. His letter authorizes us to help carry out this new plan of action. 2 Corinthians 3:5–6 MSG

- 27 books and letters of Christian teachings

A TESTAMENT is an agreement—a CONTRACT, or a plan of action. It's also known in the BIBLE as a covenant. The New Testament is a collection of WRITINGS from the first Christian century about GOD's "new agreement" with HUMANITY.

This collection of books, essays, and LETTERS tells

about God fulfilling his earlier promise to the Jews:

" 'The day is coming,' says the LORD, 'when I will make a NEW COVENANT with the people of ISRAEL and JUDAH. This covenant will not be like the one I made with their ANCESTORS when I took them by the hand and brought them out of the land of EGYPT. They broke that covenant' " (Jeremiah 31:31–32).

Jesus said his sacrificial death marked the launch of this new agreement. At the LAST SUPPER, the night before his CRUCIFIXION, he held up a cup of WINE that represented the BLOOD he would shed. He told his DISCIPLES: "This cup is the new covenant between God and his people" (Luke 22:20).

The New Testament presents the teachings of this new agreement.

NEW YEAR

> "Celebrate the Festival of Trumpets each year on the first day of the appointed month in early autumn." Numbers 29:1

- Autumn holiday for Jews

NEW YEAR'S DAY FOR JEWS is in autumn. It falls sometime between September and October. It's the first day of the ancient Jewish month of Tishri, based on the lunar CALENDAR.

In Bible times it was both a day of rest and a day for offering SACRIFICES to GOD on behalf of the entire nation: one BULL along with SHEEP and GOATS. JEWS call the holiday *Rosh Hashanah* (rosh hah SHAWN uh), HEBREW for "the beginning" or "first of the year."

See also FESTIVALS.

NICODEMUS

(nick uh DEE muhs)

First century AD

> A Pharisee named Nicodemus. . .one of the Jewish rulers. . .came to Jesus at night and said, "Rabbi, we know you are a teacher who has come from God." John 3:1–2 NIRV

- A top Jewish leader who believed Jesus

A **JEWISH SCHOLAR** who advised the HIGH PRIEST and other Jewish leaders, Nicodemus was a secret follower of Jesus.

He went to talk with Jesus under cover of night. That conversation produced the most quoted verse in the BIBLE. Jesus told Nicodemus, "GOD loved the world so much that he gave his one and only Son, so that everyone who believes in him will not perish but have ETERNAL LIFE" (John 3:16).

Nicodemus later defended Jesus publicly, at a meeting with the PHARISEES: "Is it legal to convict a man before he is given a hearing?" (John 7:51).

When Jesus died, Nicodemus brought to the TOMB burial supplies, "perfumed OINTMENT made from MYRRH and aloes" (John 19:39).

NICODEMUS was a closet Christian—a secret follower of Jesus—and a top Jewish leader. Coming out of the closet, Nicodemus buried Jesus in his own family tomb.

NICOLAITANS

(nick uh LAY uh tons)

"There is one thing you are doing right. You hate what the Nicolaitans are doing, and so do I." Revelation 2:6 CEV

- Christian cult of heretics

JOHN OF REVELATION said Jesus hated the behavior of this mysterious group of supposed Christians. They had apparently wormed their way into the churches at EPHESUS and PERGAMUM, in what is now Turkey. They committed SEX sins and ate food offered to IDOLS.

NILE RIVER

Map 2 H9

Pharaoh gave this order to all his people: "Throw every newborn Hebrew boy into the Nile River." Exodus 1:22

LONGEST RIVER IN THE WORLD, stretching over 4,000 miles (about 6,600 km), the Nile could reach from New York City to Los Angeles and most of the way back again.

Even in the worst DROUGHT, the Nile was a reliable source of WATER. That's why JEWS such as ABRAHAM and JACOB moved there from time to time to weather out the weather in ISRAEL.

Oddly, as far as many ancients were concerned, it flowed north and it usually flooded at the most convenient time: during the hottest part of the year—late summer or early autumn. That's because its water sources were so far away, deep in the central African highlands.

The Nile River was the attraction that got the Jews enslaved in EGYPT. Jacob moved his FAMILY there during a seven-year drought. They settled in the fertile delta called GOSHEN, where the river fans out into streams that drain into the MEDITERRANEAN SEA. In time, the Jews grew into such a large group that Egypt's king labeled them a threat to national security. So he enslaved them. They spent over 400 years in Egypt before MOSES managed to free them, with help from Above. (See PLAGUES OF EGYPT.)

see photo, page 350

N

EGYPT'S LIFELINE is the drought-resistant Nile River Valley. That's where most Egyptians live. Outside the narrow valley, Egypt is a desert. See "Nile River," page 349.

NIMROD

(NIM rod)

Before 2500 BC

Nimrod. . .was the first heroic warrior on earth. . .the greatest hunter in the world. Genesis 10:8–9

- Noah's great-grandson

A LEGENDARY HUNTER AND WARRIOR, Nimrod is credited with launching a kingdom in what is now Iraq and building landmark cities such as BABYLON and NINEVEH.

NINEVEH   Map 2 K6

(NIN uh vuh)

"Nineveh has more than 120,000 people living in spiritual darkness. . . . Shouldn't I feel sorry for such a great city?" God to Jonah, Jonah 4:11

- Capital of Assyrian Empire (northern Iraq)

CAPITAL OF THE WORLD'S FIRST SUPER-POWER, Nineveh was the home base from which Assyrians ruled the Middle East with terrorist-style ferocity. They not only skinned victims and impaled them on fence posts. They preserved those scenes in art, which they hung on the palace walls.

That helps explain why the prophet JONAH didn't want to go there and deliver GOD's message: "Forty days from now Nineveh will be destroyed!" (Jonah 3:4). Imagine a rabbi delivering a message like that to Hitler in Berlin in 1945. But in Nineveh's case, the BIBLE says the Assyrians believed Jonah and repented. God spared them—a temporary reprieve for a REPENTANCE that wouldn't last.

Assyrians erased the northern Jewish nation of ISRAEL from the map in 722 BC, deporting most of the survivors. They also destroyed many cities in the southern Jewish nation of JUDAH, but while laying SIEGE to JERUSALEM, they couldn't manage to outlast the defenders led by King HEZEKIAH.

Babylonians from what is now southern Iraq attacked the Assyrians and destroyed Nineveh in 612 BC.

N

STEPHEN M. MILLER'S ILLUSTRATED BIBLE DICTIONARY

The once-great city remains a ruin just east of Mosul, Iraq, across the TIGRIS RIVER. Archaeologists found Assyrian King ASHURBANIPAL's ancient library of 20,000 tablets loaded with information about the Assyrians.

NOAH

(NO uh)

Before 2500 BC

God said to Noah, "I have decided to destroy all living creatures. . . . Build a large boat."
Genesis 6:13–14

INSIDE OF A MEASLY 10 GENERATIONS, human beings had morally trashed the world. Fed up with them, GOD decided on a do-over.

NOAH releases a dove to see if the floodwater has dried up enough for the bird to find a landing spot. It comes back. The same thing happened in a Babylonian flood story, the Epic of Gilgamesh. The earliest version of that story dates to several centuries before Moses, whom many credit with writing the Genesis flood story.

He'd make a fresh start with the FAMILY of Noah, "the only blameless person living on earth at the time" (Genesis 6:9).

God told Noah he was going to cover the earth with a FLOOD, and that Noah needed to build a barge big enough to hold his family and pairs of ANIMALS that would reseed the world. The barge was longer than a football field and half as wide: 150 yards long, 25 yards wide, and 15 yards high (138 by 23 by 14 m). (See also ARK OF NOAH.)

If Noah lived where scholars say civilization began, he probably would have been an Iraqi by today's map. Scholars call the cradle of civilization the Fertile Crescent, a crescent-shaped stretch of land between the TIGRIS and EUPHRATES Rivers. It's an area that archaeologists say suffered from devastating floods that wiped out major riverfront cities.

After the flood, Noah became a farmer. Vineyards he planted led him to become the first person on record to get drunk. Passed out, naked, and over 600 years old, he could not have been a pretty sight. One of his sons, HAM, called the others to take a gross-out look. Instead, they covered their father. When Noah sobered up and found out what Ham had done, he put a CURSE on Ham's family by way of Ham's son, Canaan. (For the effects of the curse, see CANAAN.)

Noah lived another 350 years, the BIBLE says, dying at age 950. That makes him the third-longest-living human in the Bible, after his grandfather METHUSELAH (969 years) and his great-great-grandfather Jared (962 years).

NOB

Map 1 C5

(nahb)

Doeg killed eighty-five priests. Then he attacked the town of Nob, where the priests had lived, and he killed everyone there.
1 Samuel 22:18–19 CEV

▪ City destroyed for helping David

KING SAUL, INSANELY JEALOUS of David's popularity after DAVID killed GOLIATH, wanted nothing more than David dead. SAUL found out that David—now a fugitive—had gotten some food from a PRIEST named Ahimelech, in the city of Nob, near JERUSALEM.

Saul ordered all 85 priests in the city executed—along with everyone else, including the ANIMALS.

NOBLES

> *The king of Babylon killed all the sons of Zedekiah. . .and then killed all the nobles of Judah.* Jeremiah 39:6 MSG

JEWISH NOBLES were the cream of society's crop: community leaders or rulers, such as elders in charge of a tribe or of a city.

NOD
Location Uncertain

> *Cain went away from the Lord. He lived in the land of Nod. It was east of Eden.* Genesis 4:16 NIrV

- Land where Cain went after killing his brother

AFTER MURDERING HIS BROTHER ABEL, CAIN was condemned by GOD to become "a homeless wanderer" (Genesis 4:12). He moved east of EDEN to Nod, a word that means "wandering."

NOMADS
(NO mads)

> *"I will allow nomads from the eastern deserts to overrun your country. They will. . . pitch their tents on your land."* Ezekiel 25:4

- People without a permanent home

MANY HERDERS in Bible times were nomads who followed the good weather, pitching their tents wherever they could find grazing pasture and WATER for their livestock.

In some cases, they were able to settle into one area for years, sometimes on the outskirts of a town where they could trade for supplies they needed. ABRAHAM

camped at SHECHEM in central ISRAEL when he first arrived in the region. But when a famine hit, he migrated south to the DROUGHT-proof NILE RIVER in EGYPT (Genesis 12:6, 10).

NUMBERS

> *Let the one with understanding solve the meaning of the number of the beast, for it is the number of a man. His number is 666.* Revelation 13:18

- Often used symbolically in the Bible

LETTERS IN THE JEWISH ALPHABET could multitask. They spelled. They counted. They could do both because letters had number equivalents.

The MARK OF THE BEAST—666—points to the first Roman emperor to persecute Christians, many Bible experts say: NERO. That's because the letters in his name as it appeared on Roman coins—Nero CAESAR—added up to 666.

Some numbers carried symbolic baggage, which Bible writers packed into their stories. Three of these numbers symbolized "completion."

Seven. It represented completion because GOD rested on Day SEVEN after making the universe. REVELATION is addressed to seven churches perhaps, scholars say, because they represent all churches.

Three. It represented completion, too, because the ancients believed CREATION had three parts: heaven, earth, and the underworld. JEWS, such as the prophet DANIEL, prayed three times a day. The Jewish TEMPLE had three rooms.

Four. There were four directions, four corners of the earth, and four winds: north, south, east, west. Forty, a multiple of four that shows up a lot in the BIBLE, represented a long time. Jesus was tempted in the DESERT for 40 days. EXODUS Jews spent 40 years in the badlands. In at least some cases, many scholars say, the numbers may simply have indicated the full extent of time God determined, whatever it was: 40 years in the desert, or 20, or 10. The Jews had served their full sentence—whatever God determined was full.

NUMBERS, BOOK OF

Famous sound bite: *"The LORD bless you and keep you; the LORD make His face shine upon you, and be gracious to you. . .and give you peace."* Numbers 6:24–26 NKJV

AFTER A YEAR CAMPED at MOUNT SINAI, MOSES and the Jewish refugees continue their EXODUS out of EGYPT, toward CANAAN (now called ISRAEL). Their scouts bring back terrifying news: Canaan is defended by walled cities and GIANTS. The JEWS refuse to go any further. GOD sentences them to lifetime in the badlands—40 years. That's long enough for the GENERATION to die. God waits to lead Generation Next into the PROMISED LAND.

- Writer: Unknown. Jewish tradition credits Moses.
- Time: The story covers 40 years, in either the 1400s BC or 1200s BC; scholars debate which.
- Location: The story starts in Egypt's Sinai Peninsula at the foot of Mount Sinai. It ends in Moab, a kingdom in what is now the Arab country of Jordan, just east of Israel.

BIG SCENES

Leaving Mount Sinai. During their year camped at the foot of Mount Sinai, Moses has organized the refugees into a 12-tribe nation. He has given them the 10 COMMANDMENTS and hundreds of other laws to govern them. Now it's time to move on and reclaim their homeland. There will be blood, Moses knows. So he takes a CENSUS of the fighting men, which is where the book gets its name: Numbers. *Numbers 1*

Fast food for the road. Three weeks into their march through the desolate badlands, the refugees complain that they have no meat. They do have MANNA, mystery food that covers the ground each morning, and that they can grind into FLOUR for BREAD. God sends a flock of migrating QUAIL into the camp, lumbering low and slow enough from their long flight that the Jews can pluck them from the air. *Numbers 10–11*

Intel: mission impossible. JOSHUA is part of a scouting expedition of 12 that Moses sends into Canaan—one scout from each tribe. Their intel report of fortified cities and supersized warriors paralyzes the Jews. They refuse to go any further. God grants their wish by punishing their lack of FAITH in him. He sentences them to 40 years in the badlands. *Numbers 13–15*

Attempted coup against Moses. The tribe of Moses and his brother, AARON, the HIGH PRIEST, is devoted to maintaining the tent WORSHIP center. They're LEVITES, from the tribe of Levi. Some are PRIESTS. Most are assistants. A group of 250 assistants decide they deserve to be priests. Moses tells them to bring censers of burning INCENSE—a ritual reserved for priests. God sends fire from the sky to burn up most of the rebels. The leaders get swallowed up in an EARTHQUAKE crevice. *Numbers 16*

Water in the rock dooms Moses. When the Jews complain that they need WATER, Moses provides it from solid rock. But in the process, Moses does something wrong—it's not clear what. God tells Moses to use his walking stick to hit a rock. Moses hits the rock twice instead of once. And he seems to take credit for the MIRACLE by saying, "Must we bring water for you out of this rock?" For whatever he did wrong, he is forbidden by God from entering the Promised Land. *Numbers 20 NKJV*

Snakebit. After the 40 years are up, Moses leads Generation Next through more badlands, toward what is now the Arab country of Jordan. When the Jews complain about the rough journey, God sends poisonous SNAKES to remind them that he's in charge. The cure for a snake bite: Look at a BRONZE snake God has Moses make. *Numbers 21*

Donkey talk. A king in what is now Jordan hires a seer named BALAAM to come and put a CURSE on the approaching Jews. Along the way, Balaam's DONKEY stops. When Balaam hits it, the donkey talks, saying he had good reason to stop. Suddenly the seer can see what his donkey had seen all along: an ANGEL in front of them, SWORD drawn. The angel tells Balaam to bless the Jews instead of cursing them. Balaam is smart enough not to argue with an armed celestial being. He blesses the Jews— four times—predicting their victory in the battles ahead. *Numbers 22–25*

The war begins. Moses and the Jews want to pass peacefully through Jordan. But the locals don't seem to believe it. So they attack. The Jews win. They claim their first land in the region: much of what is now western Jordan and part of Syria. *Numbers 21, 25, 31–32*

OAKS

"They carved your oars from the oaks of Bashan." Ezekiel 27:6

HARDWOOD TREES so strong that they not only symbolized strength, but oaks were considered sacred by many people. Some folks built shrines beneath them.

"You will be ashamed of your idol worship in groves of sacred oaks" (Isaiah 1:29).

OATH

Esau swore an oath, thereby selling all his rights as the firstborn to his brother, Jacob. Genesis 25:33

- A spoken contract

IN A DAY WHEN FEW COULD READ OR WRITE, a verbal promise was as close as many could get to the written CONTRACT we have today.

ABRAHAM made his SERVANT take an oath to follow his explicit instructions for finding a WIFE for Abraham's son ISAAC.

Some invoked GOD in their oaths. Jesus advised against it: "I tell you not to swear by anything when you make a promise! HEAVEN is God's THRONE, so don't swear by heaven. . . . When you make a promise, say only 'Yes' or 'No'" (Matthew 5:34, 37 CEV).

OBADIAH

(oh buh DIE uh)

After 586 BC
The LORD God gave Obadiah a message about Edom. Obadiah 1 CEV

IN THE JEWISH BIBLE'S SHORTEST BOOK— 21 verses—a PROPHET named Obadiah condemned the kingdom of EDOM in what is now Jordan. But he didn't say a thing about himself. He appears to have condemned Edom for their cruelty toward Jewish refugees fleeing BABYLON's destruction of JERUSALEM in 586 BC.

OBADIAH, BOOK OF

(oh buh DIE uh)

Famous sound bite: "As you have done, it will be done to you." Obadiah 15 TNIV

JEWISH WAR REFUGEES run for their lives, trying to escape invaders—possibly Babylonians who erased their nation from the world's political map in 586 BC. The JEWS run to EDOM, in what is now ISRAEL's Arab neighbor to the east: Jordan. Edom turns out to be a bad choice for a safe haven.

- Writer: Obadiah. Because the word means "servant of God," some scholars say it's not a name of the writer, but a description.
- Time: Perhaps sometime during the 33-year stretch between the time when Babylonians conquered Judah in 586 BC and when they followed up by conquering Edom in 553 BC.
- Location: Edom, a kingdom in what is now Jordan.

BIG SCENE

Killer cousins. As the BIBLE tells it, Jews descended from JACOB. The people of Edom descended from Jacob's brother, ESAU. But when Jewish WAR refugees fled to Edom, the people of Edom murdered many of them and arrested others, turning them over to the invaders who had attacked the Jewish homeland. Obadiah warned that the people of Edom would get a dose of their own medicine. *Obadiah 1*

OBED

(OH bed)

1100s BC
Obed was the father of Jesse. Jesse was the father of David. Ruth 4:22

- Son of Ruth and Boaz

SON OF A JEWISH FATHER from BETHLEHEM and an Arab mother from what is now Jordan, Obed became the grandfather of ISRAEL's most revered dynasty of KINGS. Obed's grandson, DAVID, launched a dynasty

O

that endured more than 400 years—until invaders destroyed Jerusalem in 586 BC.

OFFERINGS (see Sacrifices)

OG

(AHG)

1400s or 1200s, debated

King Og of Bashan was the last survivor of the giant Rephaites. His bed was. . .more than thirteen feet long and six feet wide [4 by 2 m]. Deuteronomy 3:11

- Giant and king of a Canaanite region

TALLER THAN NORMAL, King Og was one of the reasons most Jewish refugees with Moses didn't want to invade the land in and around what is now Israel. Og was one of the giants that the scouts said left them feeling "like grasshoppers" (Numbers 13:33).

He ruled Bashan, a kingdom in what is now southern Syria, bordering Israel. His army attacked the Jews but lost the battle. The Jews killed him and his sons and then took his land. And apparently his bed.

OINTMENT

Isaiah had said to Hezekiah's servants, "Make an ointment from figs and spread it over the boil, and Hezekiah will recover." Isaiah 38:21

- Salve used as medicine or perfume

STARTING WITH OLIVE OIL as a base, people added spices or other plants to produce an ointment. They would put ointment in a poultice bag or rub it into the skin to treat illness. Other times they used it as a fragrant perfume.

Scents added to the base often included the woodsy smell of frankincense or myrrh, the zingy smell of cinnamon, or the flowery scent of saffron.

See also Anoint.

OLD TESTAMENT

All Scripture is inspired by God and is useful to teach us what is true and to make us realize what is wrong in our lives. Paul describing the Jewish Bible to Timothy, 2 Timothy 3:16

- Jewish Bible
- Two-thirds of the Protestant Bible

THE BIBLE HAS 66 BOOKS in the Old and New Testaments. Thirty-nine in the Jewish Bible, which Christians call the Old Testament. Twenty-seven in the New Testament writings that grow out of the life and teachings of Jesus.

Tally up the words and, depending on the translation, both testaments add up to roughly 770,000 words—some 590,000 in the Old Testament and about 180,000 in the New.

That comes as a bit of a shock to many Christians, given how little time they spend with the Old Testament—reading it and listening to sermons from it.

Jews and Christians arrange the books in different order. Jews organize it into three categories: Law (first five books of the Bible), Prophets, and Writings (about a dozen books such as Psalms, Proverbs, Ruth, and Esther).

When Paul wrote a letter to his associate, Timothy, saying "all Scripture is inspired," he was talking about the only Bible they knew at the time—their Bible, the Old Testament. Many Christians say that description also applies to the very letter Paul wrote, and to the rest of the New Testament, though Paul may not have realized it at the time.

OLIVES

Jesus went with them [his disciples] to the olive grove called Gethsemane, and he said, "Sit here while I go over there to pray." Matthew 26:36

PERFECT FRUIT for the Middle East's inhospitable soil, olives can grow for centuries on a single tree planted in a rocky plug of ground that would qualify as a farmer's nightmare.

A tree's peak production, though, took place during a single decade: about age 40–50. That means farmers who planted a grove were planning ahead, for the next GENERATION. And when SAMSON burned Philistine olive orchards (Judges 15:5), the PHILISTINES had good reason to hunt him down.

People ate the FRUIT and used the oil for LAMPS and COOKING and as a base for MEDICINE and PERFUME.

HARVEST season began in September, with green olives for the meals. Harvest continued through November, when the mature, dark olives were collected.

- Sacrifices: added to GRAIN offerings brought to the TEMPLE
- Anointing: poured onto PRIESTS and KINGS, commissioning them for GOD's work
- Cooking: added to the frying pan
- Light: poured into oil LAMPS
- Medicine: mixed with herbs and SPICES to treat the sick
- Perfume: mixed with spices and other fragrant plants

Olive farmers produced two grades of oil from two pressings. The best oil came from the first crushing of the olives. That virgin oil often got used in PERFUMES, ritual ANOINTING, and lamps. A second crushing got out the leftover oil, often used in COOKING.

OMEGA (see ALPHA AND OMEGA)

OMRI

(OHM rye)

Ruled about 886–875 BC

Omri. . .sinned more than all of the kings who had ruled before him. . . . His son Ahab became the next king. 1 Kings 16:25, 28 NIRV

- King of north Jewish nation: Israel
- Father of Ahab

KING OMRI started a FAMILY dynasty that ruled the northern Jewish nation of ISRAEL for 40 years.

He's most famous because of his son, AHAB. Omri arranged for Ahab to marry a PRINCESS from LEBANON: Jezebel. Oddly, the marriage was to promote peace. Sadly, when JEZEBEL became QUEEN of Israel she promoted anything but peace. She tried to wipe out the Jewish religion by killing the PROPHETS.

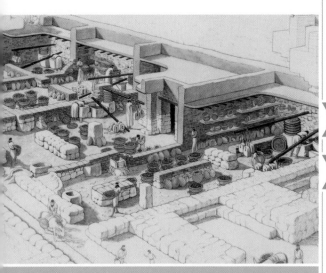

IN AN OLIVE OIL FACTORY at Ekron, along ancient Israel's coast, workers put olives in porous baskets then crush the baskets under logs weighed down by stones. The oil drains into a vat and is bottled for sale.

OLIVE OIL

"Command the people of Israel to bring you pure oil of pressed olives for the light, to keep the lamps burning continually." Exodus 27:20

ON THE ANCIENT GROCERY LIST, olive oil was a must-have—right up there with BREAD and water. In fact, people used it to make bread, mixing it into the dough and then using it like butter for dipping the bread later.

People used olive oil for everything from religious rituals to health care:

(OH nan)

1800s BC

The Lord considered it evil for Onan to deny a child to his dead brother. So the Lord took Onan's life. Genesis 38:10

- Died for refusing to let his wife get pregnant
- Grandson of Jacob

CHILDLESS WIDOWS married a close relative, if they could, in hopes of producing a SON to inherit the dead man's estate. It was Jewish law—a form of social security, to provide for the WIDOW. When TAMAR's husband died, she married his brother Onan. But whenever Onan had SEX with Tamar, he refused to release his semen inside her because he knew the child wouldn't be his heir. For this, the BIBLE says, GOD killed him.

See also LEVIRATE MARRIAGE.

ONESIMUS

(oh NESS uh muhs)

First century AD

It seems you lost Onesimus for a little while so that you could have him back forever. He is no longer like a slave to you. . .he is a beloved brother. Philemon 15–16

- Runaway slave converted by Paul

A RUNAWAY SLAVE from COLOSSE in western Turkey, Onesimus somehow met PAUL and converted to CHRISTIANITY. Paul was a prisoner at the time, perhaps under house arrest in ROME, waiting for trial.

Paul convinced Onesimus to return to his slave owner, PHILEMON, who happened to be a CHRISTIAN. The Colosse congregation met in Philemon's HOUSE. Paul sent Onesimus back with a LETTER that seemed to ask Philemon to free Onesimus so he could help in Paul's ministry.

Decades later, a man named Onesimus became bishop of the CHURCH in Colosse's neighboring city of EPHESUS. Scholars wonder if the bishop was the one-time slave.

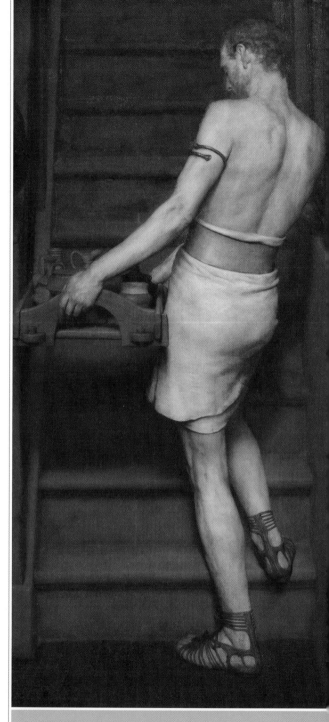

ONESIMUS wasn't just a runaway slave. He was the slave of a Christian who hosted church meetings in his home. Paul sent Onesimus back to his slave master.

OPHIR
Location Uncertain

(OH fur)

> They sailed to Ophir and brought back to Solomon some sixteen tons [14 metric tons] of gold. 1 Kings 9:28

- Mysterious region famed for gold

SOMEWHERE ALONG THE COAST of the RED SEA, perhaps in Africa, SOLOMON's fleet of merchant ships came to a land called Ophir. There they apparently traded Jewish products such as OLIVE OIL and WINE for GOLD.

OPHRAH
Location Uncertain

(OFF ruh)

> An angel from the LORD went to the town of Ophrah. . . . Gideon was nearby, threshing grain in a shallow pit. Judges 6:11 CEV

- Gideon's hometown

JEWISH HERO GIDEON was doing his farmwork in a hiding spot so raiders wouldn't see him. That's when an ANGEL appeared and addressed him as "strong warrior" (Judges 6:12).

That description could sound sarcastic. But as the story unfolded, it proved true. GIDEON would assemble a militia that would drive off raiders that had been harassing the JEWS. Gideon lived in the village of Ophrah, somewhere in what is now central ISRAEL, in land assigned to the tribe of MANASSEH.

ORACLE

> "Say to them, 'Thus says the Lord GOD: This oracle concerns the prince in Jerusalem.'" Ezekiel 12:10 NRSV

- A prophet's message from God

OUTSIDE THE BIBLE, oracles were either messages from the GODS or places to go to get those messages. The Oracle at Delphi, in GREECE, is perhaps the most famous. It's where Greeks sought answers from their gods.

HEAVEN SCENT. At the Oracle of Delphi, a priestess sits above vapor released from a break in the earth's crust. When she speaks unintelligible words in ecstasy, prophets interpret them.

O

But in the BIBLE, an oracle is a message that a PROPHET delivers from GOD.

Oracle comes from a HEBREW word that means "burden." That implies the prophet is a bit like a truck driver hauling heavy cargo he has to unload.

ORDAIN

"Dress Aaron and his sons in these clothes, pour olive oil on their heads, and ordain them as my priests." Exodus 28:41 CEV

- Appointing someone to serve God

JEWISH PRIESTS were ANOINTED with oil in an ordination ceremony that marked the beginning of their ministry.

Ordain literally means "fill the hands." That might be another way of saying, "Get busy." Or perhaps it referred to the sacrificial offerings that would be entrusted into the hands of the PRIESTS.

Christians ordained their CHURCH leaders as well, in a ritual that involved laying hands on the person and praying for them. PAUL advised TIMOTHY, "Do not ordain anyone hastily" (1 Timothy 5:22 NRSV).

ORPAH

(OR puh)

1100s BC

Orpah kissed her mother-in-law good-by. But Ruth held on to her. Ruth 1:14 NIrv

- Naomi's daughter-in-law

ORPAH MISSED HER SHOT at becoming the mother of ISRAEL's greatest dynasty of KINGS. That honor went instead to her sister-in-law, RUTH.

Both Moabite women from what is now Jordan became widowed, along with their Jewish mother-in-law, NAOMI. Orpah went home to her father, as Naomi advised. But Ruth followed Naomi to BETHLEHEM. There, Ruth married BOAZ and became the mother of OBED, who would grow up to become the grandfather of King DAVID.

ORPHANS

"Be fair-minded and just. . . . Do not mistreat foreigners, orphans, and widows." Jeremiah 22:3

WITHOUT SOCIAL SECURITY or government programs to protect the helpless, the people at greatest risk were orphans, widows, and people new to the area. They were the easiest to exploit.

Jewish law required the JEWS to treat them and other needy people with fairness and compassion. Yet some of the PROPHETS complained that Jewish leaders "deprive the POOR of justice. . .prey on widows and take advantage of orphans" (Isaiah 10:2).

OTHNIEL

(AHTH nee el)

Perhaps 1300s BC

When the people of Israel cried out to the LORD for help, the LORD raised up a rescuer to save them. His name was Othniel. Judges 3:9

- Jewish hero
- Nephew of Caleb

BEFORE THE JEWS HAD A KING, they had a dozen heroic leaders that Bible writers called JUDGES. SAMSON, GIDEON, and DEBORAH were three of the most famous. But the first was Othniel. He raised a militia and drove off Syrian raiders who had harassed the JEWS for eight years.

OVEN

(see BAKING)

OX

If you steal an ox. . .you must pay the owner double. Exodus 22:4 CEV

LARGE, CASTRATED BULLS were easygoing work critters widely used in hauling and plowing. Bible writers, however, seem to have used the term *ox* more generally. In the BIBLE, it can refer to any kind of large CATTLE.

See also BULL.

PADDAN-ARAM

Map 2 J6

(PAY done AIR um)

Esau knew that his father, Isaac, had blessed Jacob and sent him to Paddan-aram to find a wife. Genesis 28:6

- Where Jacob married Leah, Rachel

AFTER STEALING THE DEATHBED BLESS-ING that his father, ISAAC, had intended for ESAU, JACOB left town, the village of BEERSHEBA. Wise decision, since his brother Esau vowed to kill him once their father died. Jacob moved about 700 miles (1,100 km) north to live with his uncle LABAN.

Laban lived in HARAN, a village in the region of Paddan-aram, a stretch of land covering parts of Turkey and SYRIA.

PALACE

It took Solomon 13 years to finish constructing his palace and the other buildings that were related to it.
1 Kings 7:1 NIrV

ISRAEL'S FIRST KING, Saul, didn't bother with a palace. He lived at home. King DAVID, however, built a palace in his new capital city of JERUSALEM. David imported from LEBANON "CEDAR timber and carpenters and stonemasons" (2 Samuel 5:11).

David's son SOLOMON upped the ante. He, too, imported supplies and artisans—more than David. And he spent nearly twice as much time building his palace complex as he did the TEMPLE: 13 years for the palace and 7 years for the Temple. His complex included: living areas for him and his wives, the Hall of Justice for settling disputes, and the Palace of the Forest of Lebanon with 45 rooms perhaps for royal guests, and the Hall of Pillars perhaps for royal functions.

King AHAB reportedly had an "IVORY palace" (1 Kings 22:39). At the very least, it was accessorized with ivory. Archaeologists found in the ruins of his palace in SAMARIA pieces of furniture inlaid with ivory.

By the time Jesus was born, King HEROD THE GREAT had built palaces throughout his kingdom—an elegant, main palace in Jerusalem and getaway palaces such as his winter estate in JERICHO, with swimming pools, gardens, and a Roman-style bathhouse with a steam room.

PALESTINE

Map 3 L7

(PAL uh stine)

- Roman name for Jewish homeland

ISRAEL WASN'T PALESTINE in Bible times. Romans didn't start using that name until after they crushed a Jewish revolt in AD 135. That's when they retired the Jewish-friendly name *JUDEA* and substituted it with *Palestine.*

The name comes from the PHILISTINES, the race of people who lived on ISRAEL's seacoast—including along the Gaza Strip area where Palestinians live today. Greek historian Herodotus (400s BC) gave the name of Palestine to the entire region—parts of what are now Israel, Jordan, and Syria.

PALM TREE

You are slender like a palm tree, and your breasts are like its clusters of fruit.
Song of Songs 7:7

- Fruit tree that produces dates

PALM TREES are wonderfully suited to the dry, rocky Middle Eastern soil. They have a deep root system for hunting moisture and storing it.

Date palm trees start producing high-energy, nutritious FRUIT after about five years—and the trees can continue producing for 200 years. The fruit grows in bunches, a bit like bananas. A single tree can produce 4 to 12 bunches a year—up to roughly 200 pounds (90 kg) of fruit, harvested in the late summer and early fall.

see photo, page 362

P

PAMPHYLIA

Map 3 H4

(pam FILL ee uh)

Barnabas wanted to take John Mark with them. But Paul didn't think it was wise to take him. Mark had deserted them in Pamphylia. Acts 15:37–38 NIrV

- Malaria-prone coastal region of Turkey

ON HIS FIRST MISSIONARY TRIP, Paul sailed from Cyprus to Turkey, landing in the hot and swampy area of Pamphylia. That's where John Mark, one of his traveling associates, bailed. He went home. When it came time for a follow-up trip, Paul refused to take John Mark with him. Paul took Silas instead.

PAPHOS

Map 3 I5

(PAY fuss)

They [Paul, Barnabas] traveled all across the island [Cyprus] until they came to Paphos. Acts 13:6 NIrV

- Capital of Cyprus

THE FIRST ROMAN OFFICIAL on record to convert to Christianity was Sergius Paulus, governor of the island of Cyprus, who lived in Paphos. It was the capital, located on the island's west coast.

PAPYRUS

(pup PIE russ)

"Can papyrus reeds grow tall without a marsh?" Job 8:11

- Native Egyptian plant used to make paper

PAPYRUS REEDS grew along the banks of the Nile River. Egyptians used reed in many ways—for everything from boat sails to chewing gum.

Papyrus is most famous for Egyptian paper, made from the spongy core inside the tall stalks. Paper manufacturers would slice the core into long strips, lay them flat in a crisscross pattern like tic-tac-toe grids with no space between them. Then they would press the strips together and let them dry into thin sheets.

The basket Jochebed made for her baby son Moses was "made of papyrus reeds and waterproofed. . . with tar" (Exodus 2:3).

CHEAP DATES. Nutritious, abundant, and inexpensive, dates were a popular menu item in Bible times. See "Palm Tree," page 361.

PAPYRUS paper was made from the spongy core inside the stems of papyrus reeds, which grew along the banks of the Nile River and nearby lakes.

STEPHEN M. MILLER'S ILLUSTRATED BIBLE DICTIONARY

P

JESUS TOLD SHORT STORIES and one-liners to create mental pictures for people that helped them better understand GOD and what God expected of them.

Example: The laws of MOSES required JEWS to "love your NEIGHBOR as yourself" (Leviticus 19:18). But some Jews taught that only fellow Jews qualified as neighbors. When a Jewish scholar asked Jesus about that, Jesus answered with the parable of the Good SAMARITAN. It's the story of a Jew who got mugged. Two Jewish worship leaders walked by and saw him lying there injured, but they ignored him. Along came a Samaritan, from a race of people who typically didn't get along well with the Jews. He helped the man.

Jesus asked the scholar which of the three acted neighborly. Obvious answer: "The one who showed him MERCY." Jesus' point: "Now go and do the same" (Luke 10:37). That's how God's people are supposed to act.

Bible experts today don't agree on what qualifies as a parable.

The short list has Jesus telling only about 40. Other experts stretch the list to about 65 by including some messages that sound like mere comparisons: "I am the true grapevine, and my FATHER is the gardener" (John 15:1).

PARADISE IS CROWDED with saints in this painting by Carlo Saraceni, an Italian artist from the 1600s. The Trinity hovers above, along with the Virgin Mary and John the Baptist. Jesus said "Of all who have ever lived, none is greater than John the Baptist" (Matthew 11:11).

DYING ON THE CROSS, Jesus promised a fellow victim hanging beside him, "I assure you, today you will be with me in paradise" (Luke 23:43).

Paradise was a Jewish nickname for HEAVEN—eternal home of the righteous dead.

The word seems to come from an ancient reference to the Garden of EDEN. JEWS in Roman times who translated their HEBREW Bible into GREEK, the international language of the day, called the Garden of Eden "Paradise." Since this garden paradise was originally a sinless place of perfect PEACE, Jews who believed in an afterlife decided "Paradise" was a good name for the place they hoped to spend eternity, resting in peace.

See also ABRAHAM'S BOSOM.

PARALYSIS

> Jesus turned to the paralyzed man and said, "Stand up, pick up your mat, and go home!" Matthew 9:6

JESUS HEALED at least three paralyzed people.

Roof guy. Friends of one paralyzed man couldn't get through a crowd to reach Jesus, who was teaching from inside a HOUSE. So they ripped a hole in the ROOF and "lowered the man on his mat, right down in front of Jesus" (Mark 2:4).

Pool guy. One paralyzed man sat beside a Jerusalem POOL, hoping someone would push him into the WATER when—as rumor had it—an ANGEL touched the water and "the water bubbles up" (John 5:7).

Servant guy. The SERVANT of a Roman soldier "lies in BED, paralyzed and in terrible pain" (Matthew 8:6). Jesus healed him by long-distance.

The BIBLE doesn't say what caused the paralysis in any of the victims. It could have been from the trauma of a fall, from a stroke, or from a DISEASE that produced nerve damage.

PARAN   Map 1 D8

(PAY run)

> The Israelites broke camp and left the Sinai Desert. And some time later. . .stopped in the Paran Desert. Numbers 10:12 CEV

AFTER CAMPING A YEAR at the foot of MOUNT SINAI, MOSES and the JEWS of the Exodus moved north out of EGYPT and toward what is now ISRAEL. They camped at KADESH oasis in the Martian-like badlands of Paran, just south of Israel. They may have spent much of the next 40 years there.

PASSION OF CHRIST

> He [Jesus] shewed himself alive after his passion by many infallible proofs. Acts 1:3 KJV

- Jesus' suffering during his execution

BACK IN SHAKESPEARE'S DAY, when the King James Version of the BIBLE was translated, *passion* meant "suffering." It comes from the GREEK word *pathos*; the NEW TESTAMENT was written in Greek.

"Passion" came to refer to the suffering Jesus faced during his final hours: arrest, trials, BEATING, and CRUCIFIXION.

Though many Bible experts still use the "passion of Christ" as a technical way of referring to Jesus' suffering, hardly anyone else does. Modern Bibles translate *passion* as "suffering."

PASSOVER

> "It is the Passover sacrifice to the LORD, for he passed over the houses of the Israelites in Egypt. And though he struck the Egyptians, he spared our families." Exodus 12:27

- Major Jewish holiday commemorating the Exodus

ONCE A YEAR in the spring, about the time of Easter, observant JEWS eat a sacred MEAL rich in symbolism. It's the Passover meal, called *Pesach* in HEBREW. The word means "to pass over." The point of the meal is to remind the Jews that GOD freed their ANCESTORS from Egyptian SLAVERY some 3,000 years ago—and he's still on the job looking out for his CHOSEN PEOPLE.

The BIBLE says God himself set up the holiday. He did it the very night he freed them.

God was about to unleash the tenth PLAGUE, sending a death ANGEL to kill the FIRSTBORN of EGYPT but to pass over the Jewish households. Since they'd be freed immediately afterward, God had them eat a meal for the road. Roast lamb, bitter salad, and no-rise BREAD; there wouldn't be time for the yeast to raise the dough.

"This is a day to remember," God told MOSES. "Each year, from GENERATION to generation, you must celebrate it as a special FESTIVAL to the LORD. This is a law for all time" (Exodus 12:14).

This symbolic meal was the LAST SUPPER Jesus had with his DISCIPLES.

Jews today serve the meal at home as part of a scripted WORSHIP service. Added to the ancient menu

P

are mixed nuts and FRUIT to symbolize the MORTAR the slaves used to build Egypt's cities. A saltwater dip represents tears of the slaves. Boiled eggs represent SACRIFICES Jews made once they reached ISRAEL and built the TEMPLE. WINE celebrates God's promise fulfilled: "I will free you" (Exodus 6:6).

DESTINED TO DIE, a sheep is prepared as a Passover sacrifice. Jews no longer offer animal sacrifices. But this community of Samaritans in Israel does.

PASTOR

Christ chose some of us to be apostles, prophets, missionaries, pastors, and teachers. Ephesians 4:11 CEV

- Leader of a local church

"PASTOR" wasn't yet a formal title for the leader of a local congregation. It was more of a description. The original word, written in GREEK, is the same word other NEW TESTAMENT writers used for "SHEPHERD." In a sense, the pastor was a shepherd of the flock entrusted to his care.

PASTORAL LETTERS

(pass TOR al)

If anyone wants to provide leadership in the church, good! But there are preconditions: A leader must be well-thought-of. . .cool and collected, accessible, and hospitable. 1 Timothy 3:1–2 MSG

- Three letters Paul wrote: 1, 2 Timothy, Titus

TWO PASTORS—TIMOTHY and TITUS—got some pastoring advice from their mentor, PAUL. Tips like how pastors should behave and how to deal with problem people in the CHURCH. That is why these particular letters earned the nickname "Pastoral Letters."

Paul's advice came by mail:

- two letters to Timothy, pastoring the church in EPHESUS, in what is now Turkey
- one letter to Titus, recruiting pastors to serve congregations on the island of Crete.

PATMOS

Map 3 D4

(PAT muhs)

I, John. . .was exiled to the island of Patmos for preaching the word of God and for my testimony about Jesus. Revelation 1:9

- Island where John wrote Revelation

A TINY ISLAND some 40 miles (64 km) off Turkey's west coast, Patmos stretched only about 10 miles long and 6 miles at its widest (16 by 10 km). Romans apparently exiled JOHN there for teaching CHRISTIANITY, which by then (probably AD 90s) was an outlawed religion. It was there that John received a series of VISIONS preserved in the last book of the BIBLE, REVELATION.

PATRIARCH

(PAY tree ark)

"You will be called Abraham, for you will be the father of many nations." **Genesis 17:5**

- Term for three Jewish founding fathers

ABRAHAM, ISAAC, AND JACOB are the patriarchs of Israel—the three founding fathers. God promised to build a nation of descendants through these three. In time, the nation became known as Israel. The word *patriarch* comes from the Greek word for "FATHER/FATHERS," *pater/patrois.* Bible experts today seem to prefer "ancestor," because it allows them to include the wives of these men.

PAUL

About AD 6–64

Paul had a vision: A man from Macedonia in northern Greece was standing there, pleading with him, "Come over to Macedonia and help us!" **Acts 16:9**

- Converted after seeing a vision of Jesus
- Started churches throughout Roman world
- Wrote almost half the New Testament books

NOT PARTICULARLY HUMBLE, Paul described himself as a Jew's Jew:

> I was a much better Jew than anyone else my own age, and I obeyed every law that our ancestors had given us.
> GALATIANS 1:14 CEV

And then some.

That's because he was a PHARISEE. This brand of Jew, now extinct, was famous for

(1) taking single laws in the BIBLE—such as "don't work on the SABBATH"—and turning each one into dozens of manmade laws, sometimes hundreds of laws; and
(2) bullying others into obeying those laws.

Paul wasn't just a Pharisee. He was a Pharisee's Pharisee: "I was a student of GAMALIEL," "a highly respected TEACHER" (Acts 22:3; 5:34 CEV).

This background helps explain Paul's first scene in the Bible: He guarded the ROBES of Jews STONING Stephen to death for PREACHING about Jesus. A Jewish Jew wouldn't tolerate a fellow Jew who said GOD had a Son.

Paul got his hands dirty, too. Like a bounty hunter sent from God on a holy quest, he hunted down Jewish followers of Jesus:

"I threw these believers. . .into the JERUSALEM jail right and left, and whenever it came to a vote, I voted for their execution. I stormed through their meeting places, bullying them into cursing Jesus, a one-man terror obsessed with obliterating these people. And then I started on the towns outside Jerusalem" (Acts 26:10–11 MSG).

ARMED APOSTLE. A statue of the apostle Paul stands outside a church in Rome marking the spot where tradition says he was buried. His sword commemorates the weapon Romans reportedly used to behead him.

STEPHEN M. MILLER'S ILLUSTRATED BIBLE DICTIONARY

HELLO, JESUS

Headed to DAMASCUS to arrest Jesus-loving JEWS there, Paul was suddenly blinded by an explosion of light in the sky.

He dropped to the dirt. A disembodied voice spoke: "I am Jesus the Nazarene, the one you are persecuting" (Acts 22:8).

Paul, also known by his HEBREW name of Saul, didn't argue. He simply asked what Jesus wanted him to do.

Go to Damascus.

Funny. Paul was going there to arrest followers of Jesus, but he ended up getting arrested by Jesus. And converted.

Still blind, Paul had to be led into the city by his traveling associates. There a local CHRISTIAN named ANANIAS healed him. Jesus told Ananias to do that because Paul "is my chosen instrument to take my message to the GENTILES and to kings, as well as to the people of ISRAEL" (Acts 9:15).

Jesus apparently knew that the Christian movement would face its stiffest resistance from intolerant Jewish traditionalists. So he recruited an intolerant Jewish traditionalist.

PAUL UPGRADES HIS RELIGION AND REBOOTS

Jesus gave Paul something to think about. For more than a decade. That's how long Paul went underground.

He decided not to go back to Jerusalem, where his colleagues might stone him as a heretic and a traitor. Instead, he spent those years in SYRIA and Saudi Arabia—probably processing the teachings of Jesus and linking them to the Jewish faith. Paul also needed to study Jewish prophecies and discover how Jesus fulfilled many of them.

He came out of his study convinced that CHRISTIANITY wasn't just another branch of the Jewish religion. He said anyone could follow Jesus—Jew or not. And they didn't have to convert to the Jewish faith to do it.

Radical idea. It split the CHURCH.

The controversy started because Christianity was originally a Jewish movement. All the DISCIPLES were Jews. So were the first Christians. Because of that, when non-Jews wanted to join the movement many Jewish Christians said they needed to follow all the Jewish laws, including those about CIRCUMCISION and food restrictions.

The trouble with that argument was that non-Jews were getting filled with the HOLY SPIRIT after doing nothing more than expressing their belief in Jesus. PETER saw it (Acts 10:45). So did Paul and BARNABAS, in the church they started co-pastoring in ANTIOCH, Syria.

Church leaders debated the matter in the first-known church leadership meeting, led in Jerusalem by the brother of Jesus: JAMES. His decision: Non-Jews didn't have to become Jews.

Not everyone signed on. Jewish Christians who disagreed would argue their position for decades, until Jewish leaders near the end of the first century ordered Jewish Christians to make up their minds: Are they Jews? Or are they Christians? They can't be both. That's when Christianity started to become mainly a non-Jewish movement.

Paul helped. Big time.

TRAVELING SALESMAN—SELLING JESUS

Paul jump-started the Christian movement by traveling roughly 10,000 miles (16,000 km), starting house churches throughout the Roman world—mainly in what are now Turkey and Greece.

He and a man named Barnabas had been copastoring a mainly non-Jewish church in Antioch, Syria. But during a prayer meeting one day, they felt compelled to take the story of Jesus abroad.

With their local church's encouragement, and likely with their financial support, the two men sailed to Barnabas's homeland: the island of CYPRUS. They preached their way from one end of the island to the other, ending in PAPHOS, where they managed to convert the Roman governor, SERGIUS PAULUS.

From there, they sailed north to Turkey. They preached in several towns: Antioch in PISIDIA, ICONIUM, LYSTRA, and DERBE. But it was a roller coaster ride. Big ups and big downs. One day, in Lystra, they were mistaken for GODS because they healed a crippled man. Later in that same town some Jews tracking them convinced the locals that the two were heretics. Up next: riot. The fickle crowd stoned Paul and left him for dead.

He got up, and the following day he was off to the next town: Derbe.

In three missionary trips spanning about a decade, Paul experienced plenty of trouble—fulfilling a prediction Jesus made when Paul converted: "I will show him how much he must suffer for my NAME's sake" (Acts 9:16).

Paul reported a sampling of his sufferings:

- Whipped. "Five times the Jews gave me 39 strokes with a whip."
- Clubbed. "Three times I was beaten with sticks."
- Stoned. "Once they tried to kill me by throwing stones at me."
- Shipwrecked. "Three times I was shipwrecked. I spent a night and a day in the open sea."

2 CORINTHIANS 11:24–25 NIrv

Normally, Paul didn't stay long in any town. Two exceptions: CORINTH (a year and a half) and EPHESUS (about three years). Both were busy hubs of activity and international trade. Corinth was a crossroads town in GREECE, with nearby ports in two seas. Ephesus was a seaside town on Turkey's west coast and a major port for ships going to and from EGYPT in the south and ROME in the west. These were perfect spots to spread the word about Jesus not only among a massive crowd of locals,

but to travelers who would carry the word away with them to the far ends of the ROMAN EMPIRE.

In the course of his travels, Paul wrote LETTERS. Some were addressed to churches, often to answer their questions or to settle disputes. Some were addressed to his colleagues. His most influential work was a letter he wrote to Christians in Rome, introducing himself and his beliefs. That letter—ROMANS—is Christianity's first theology book, outlining what Christians believe.

THE END OF PAUL

By the time Paul returned to Jerusalem after his third missionary trip—and at the end of a decade of missionary travels—Jews throughout the empire wanted him dead. None more than Jewish leaders in Jerusalem.

When he showed up at the TEMPLE to WORSHIP, Jews arrested him and a mob tried to kill him. Roman troops nearby rescued him and took him into custody. The commander got word that a band of more than 40 Jews planned to attack his soldiers and MURDER Paul. So he mustered a force of 200 armed men and 70 cavalry, and then he escorted Paul to the seaport of CAESAREA, Rome's capital in the Middle East.

Paul's Last Mission Trip
2,800 miles (4,500 km), 4 years

A TRAVELING MAN, Paul covered an estimated 10,000 miles (16,000 km) spreading the news about Jesus.

Paul lingered in PRISON for two years before appealing to CAESAR's supreme COURT in Rome.

ACTS, the Bible book about the early church, ends with Paul awaiting trial. Snippets of writing from early Christian leaders suggest that Paul was released, ministered in SPAIN, and only later was executed in Rome, perhaps during the emperor Nero's PERSECUTION of Christians. NERO accused them of setting the fire that burned much of Rome in AD 64.

Paul had told Christians in Rome that he hoped to see them "on my way to Spain" (Romans 15:28). And a bishop named Clement, writing about 30 years after Paul's time, confirmed that the APOSTLE "went to the limit of the West." Spain marked the western limit of the Roman Empire.

DATING PAUL

AD

6	Born in Tarsus
20	Studies as a Pharisee
33	Converts to Christianity
44	Co-pastors in Antioch, Syria
46	First missionary trip
48	Second missionary trip
49	Starts church in Corinth
52	Third missionary trip
57	Arrested in Jerusalem
60	Sails to Rome for trial
64	Executed in Rome

Dates approximate

PEACE

"I am leaving you with a gift—peace of mind and heart. And the peace I give is a gift the world cannot give. So don't be troubled or afraid." John 14:27

- A sense of happiness, well-being

"PEACE BE WITH YOU," was a common greeting in Bible times—just as "Go in peace," was a common way of saying good-bye.

The HEBREW word for it is *shalom* (shuh LOHM). It's sort of like saying, "I hope everything is going well for you—that you feel fulfilled and comfortable in GOD's care."

In fact, Bible writers say that the way to find peace is to find God and follow his advice. "Doing what is right will bring peace and rest. When my people do that, they will stay calm and trust in the LORD forever" (Isaiah 32:17 NIRV).

Or as one Jewish songwriter put it, goodness and peace are kissing cousins: "RIGHTEOUSNESS and peace have kissed!" (Psalm 85:10).

PEKAH

(PEE kuh)

Reigned about 740–732 BC

In a single day Pekah. . .Israel's king, killed 120,000 of Judah's troops, all of them experienced warriors. 2 Chronicles 28:6

- King of north Jewish nation of Israel

KING PEKAH got his job by murdering the king before him. And he lost his job by getting murdered by the king after him.

In between, Pekah joined a coalition of small nations trying to break free of the Middle Eastern superpower, ASSYRIA, based in what is now Iraq. He attacked the southern Jewish nation of JUDAH because they refused to join the allies. Judah called on the Assyrians, who defeated the coalition forces. Later, in 722 BC, Assyrians conquered the nation of ISRAEL and EXILED most of the survivors.

PEKAHIAH

(PECK uh HI uh)

Reigned about 742–740 BC

Pekahiah became king of Israel. . . . Pekah killed Pekahiah. He became the next king after him. 2 Kings 15:23, 25 NIRV

- King of northern Jewish nation of Israel

AN EVIL KING, as the BIBLE reports it, Pekahiah survived as ISRAEL's ruler for only two years. The next king assassinated him in a coup.

PENIEL

Map 1 E5

(pen NI el)

Jacob named the place Peniel (which means "face of God"), for he said, "I have seen God face to face." Genesis 32:30

TWENTY YEARS after cheating his brother Esau out of their father's BLESSING, Jacob was headed home for a tense reunion. The night before the reunion, JACOB wrestled a mysterious man whom he apparently thought was GOD. Jacob wouldn't let go until he got the man's blessing—which is odd since insisting on a blessing is what got him in trouble in the first place. But with this blessing, he got a new NAME: ISRAEL. In time, the JEWS adopted it as the name of their nation.

PENTATEUCH

(PEN tuh tuke)

▪ First five books of the Bible

ALSO KNOWN AS "LAW OF MOSES," *Pentateuch* is scholar-jargon for the five books that ancient Jewish tradition credits to MOSES: GENESIS, EXODUS, LEVITICUS, NUMBERS, DEUTERONOMY. The BIBLE doesn't use the word.

PENTECOST

(PEN tah cost)

Paul had decided to sail on past Ephesus. . . . He was hurrying to get to Jerusalem, if possible, in time for the Festival of Pentecost. Acts 20:16

▪ Jewish springtime harvest festival

IT MEANS ONE THING TO JEWS, and another to Christians.

To Jews, Pentecost is a harvest FESTIVAL called *Shavuot*, "Festival of Weeks." That's because they celebrated this HARVEST festival several weeks after PASSOVER—about 50 days. And "50" is why it's also called Pentecost,

P

AT PENTECOST the Holy Spirit fills the followers of Jesus with courage and miracle-working power—enough to jump-start the Christian movement in the very city that executed Jesus less than two months earlier.

371

from the GREEK word for "50."

To Christians, it's the day the HOLY SPIRIT arrived, filling the followers of Jesus with the boldness and MIRACLE-working power that helped them launch the CHRISTIAN movement.

Jesus had ascended, and his followers were waiting in JERUSALEM for the Spirit that he had promised would come. The city was crowded with Jewish pilgrims who had come from all over the ROMAN EMPIRE to celebrate the first harvested crops of the SEASON.

After the Spirit arrived and gave Jesus' followers the ability to speak in languages they had never studied, they used their ability to preach to the international crowd. Thousands were convinced that Jesus' DISCIPLES had GOD's backing. So they joined the movement: "about 3,000 in all" (Acts 2:41).

PERFECTION

"Be perfect, even as your Father in heaven is perfect." Jesus, in Sermon on the Mount, Matthew 5:48

CAN DO. That's what some Christians say about Jesus' call to be perfect—especially Christians in holiness denominations such as the Church of the Nazarene.

To back up their belief, holiness Christians quote Bible verses such as 1 Thessalonians 4:3—"GOD's will is for you to be HOLY." And they argue that it's possible for Christians to mature to a point that they no longer commit SIN.

Critics say these Christians typically define sin more narrowly than the BIBLE does, which makes it easier not to sin. For many holiness Christians, it's sin only if they know it's wrong but they do it anyhow. In the OLD TESTAMENT, however, God set up a system of sacrificial rituals including "for those who sin unintentionally" (Leviticus 4:2).

In other words, ignorance of God's law was no excuse.

For most other Christians, Jesus' call to perfection is just another example of how he used exaggeration to get people's attention and to try nudging them in the right direction. For example, he also warned the rich that it's harder for them to get into HEAVEN than it is for a CAMEL to squeeze through the eye of a NEEDLE.

Most Christians see moral perfection as the bulls-eye that people should shoot for.

As PAUL put it in one of his LETTERS, "I am not perfect. But Christ has taken hold of me. So I keep on running and struggling to take hold of the prize" (Philippians 3:12 CEV).

PERFUME

Myrrh, aloes, and cassia [cinnamon] perfume your robes. Psalm 45:8

BEFORE SOAP AND DEODERANT—in a hot and dry part of the world where WATER was often in short supply and baths were few and far between—perfume was a nose saver.

To make perfume, people usually started with an OLIVE OIL base. Then they added various fragrant SPICES, tree sap, and oils pressed from FLOWERS, plant roots, and bark.

Two favorites were FRANKINCENSE and MYRRH, imported from what is now the Arabian Peninsula, North Africa, and India. Expensive perfumes like this were often stored in prized flasks. White-stone ALABASTER was a top-of-the-line model. The perfume was sealed inside, preserved for special occasions—such as anointing a body for BURIAL.

Mary of BETHANY broke open a jar of cypress-smelling spikenard perfume—about 16 ounces [0.5 l]. Then she poured it on Jesus' feet. Imported from India, the BIBLE says this perfume was worth a year's salary for a working grunt.

See also ANOINT, OINTMENT.

PERGA
Map 3 H4

(PURR guh)

Paul and his companions sailed to Perga in Pamphylia. Acts 13:13 NIrv

- Port town in southern Turkey
- Where John Mark abandoned Paul

ON HIS FIRST MISSIONARY TRIP, PAUL traveled with BARNABAS and JOHN MARK across CYPRUS and then sailed to southern Turkey. Once they landed at Perga, a sweltering and swampy coastal town perfect for catching malaria, John Mark quit. He sailed home.

PERGAMUM
Map 3 E3

(PURR guh mum)

"Write this to Pergamum. . . . Why do you indulge that Balaam crowd. . .throwing unholy parties?" Revelation 2:12, 14 MSG

- City in western Turkey
- One of seven churches critiqued in Revelation

JESUS HAD COMPLIMENTS AND CRITICISM for the CHURCH in Pergamum, a beautiful Greek-style city near Turkey's west coast:

Stroke: They never once denied they were followers of Jesus.

Poke: They tolerated false teachers who seduced church members into SEX sins and eating food sacrificed to IDOLS.

PERSECUTION

"God blesses you when people mock you and persecute you and lie about you and say all sorts of evil things against you because you are my followers." Matthew 5:11

IT'S ABUSE: emotional, verbal, and physical—sometimes execution.

In the BIBLE, people targeted for persecution included individuals, groups such as JEWS or CHRISTIANS,

and entire nations such as ISRAEL.

The most common reason for persecution reported in the Bible: religious beliefs.

Folks most likely to get persecuted:

- **Prophets.** People didn't like what they said, since it was usually news of doom.
- **Jews.** People didn't like the Israelites' unique laws and customs that implied they were GOD's favorites.
- **Jesus.** Jewish leaders orchestrated his execution for saying he was the Messiah. They figured if Jews believed him, they would rally to support him in a revolution that the Romans would surely crush.
- **Christians.** Jews considered them heretics who dissed God by saying he had a son. That's a key reason Jews persecuted Paul with stoning, beatings, imprisonment, and attempted assassination.

See also ROMAN EMPIRE.

PERSEVERANCE

Pursue righteousness and a godly life, along with faith, love, perseverance, and gentleness. Fight the good fight for the true faith. 1 Timothy 6:11–12

- Christian response to persecution, temptation

IN THE FACE OF OPPOSITION, Christians are to hold on to their FAITH.

That was the advice of PAUL, who endured fierce PERSECUTION that eventually killed him. Writing to Christians in ROME, the city where CHURCH leaders said he was tried and executed, Paul said: "Be patient in suffering, persevere in PRAYER" (Romans 12:12 NRSV).

Another writer reminded Christians that Jesus suffered: "Think of all the hostility he endured from sinful people; then you won't become weary and give up" (Hebrews 12:3).

P

STEPHEN M. MILLER'S ILLUSTRATED BIBLE DICTIONARY

PERSIA, in just a few decades, morphed from a kingdom about the size of Tennessee to an empire about double the width of the United States.

PERSIA
Map 2 M6

(PURR zhuh)

King Cyrus of Persia says: "The LORD. . . has appointed me to build him a Temple at Jerusalem. . . . Any of you who are the LORD's people may go there for this task."
2 Chronicles 36:23

- Iran-based empire
- Conquered Babylonian Empire
- Freed exiled Jews to go home

PERSIA STARTED SMALL: A 300-mile-long (483 km) plug of ground in Iran along the Persian Gulf's east shore.

But by the time Jewish Queen ESTHER ruled there with her husband, XERXES (ruled 486–465 BC), Persia had bumped off the Babylonian Empire to become the new superpower of the Middle East—an empire stretching 5,000 miles (8,046 km) wide, from GREECE to India.

Persia's big dreamer—the king who made the jump from kingdom to empire: CYRUS (reigned from 559–530 BC).

Nine years into his reign, he conquered the Medes in what is now north Iran and eastern Turkey. He assimilated their resources into his kingdom. Then, 11 years later in 539 BC—with the extra Mede muscle and

wealth—he conquered BABYLON.

Jewish Queen Esther lived in Persia about half a century later, with her husband King Xerxes. Esther prevented an empirewide holocaust of the JEWS by alerting her husband to the plans of his top official, HAMAN.

Persia's 15 minutes of fame lasted about two centuries. That's when ALEXANDER the Great left Greece to begin his campaign to conquer the civilized world. He defeated the Persians in a series of battles between 334 and 331 BC.

PETER

Died about AD 64

"You are Peter (which means 'rock'), and upon this rock I will build my church."
Matthew 16:18

- Originally a fisherman
- Top disciple of Jesus
- One of Jesus' three best friends
- First top leader of Christian movement

DESPITE EVERY GOOD THING the BIBLE says about Peter—and it says plenty—he's best known for his most embarrassing moment.

STEPHEN M. MILLER'S ILLUSTRATED BIBLE DICTIONARY

It happened at night. Jesus was on trial inside the home of the Jewish HIGH PRIEST, CAIAPHAS. Outside in the COURTYARD, Peter awaited the outcome with a group of others.

Some in the group recognized him as a follower of Jesus, and they called him on it. He denied it. Three times. Immediately, a rooster crowed. Suddenly, Peter remembered what Jesus had predicted a few hours earlier: "Before the rooster crows twice, you will deny three times that you even know me" (Mark 14:30). Peter ran off weeping and apparently went into hiding—resurfacing only after Jesus' RESURRECTION.

STAINED REPUTATION. A stained glass window balances Peter's high and low moments. The rooster commemorates the night he three times denied knowing Jesus before the rooster crowed. The keys commemorate Jesus' promise to give him the keys to the kingdom of heaven, declaring him a leader in the future Christian movement, some say.

Before this humbling moment—and afterward—Peter was top dog among the DISCIPLES. Every time the list of disciples shows up in the Bible, Peter's NAME comes first. Whenever the disciples had a delicate question for Jesus, they got Peter to ask it for them.

Jesus recruited Peter and his brother ANDREW while the two were FISHING. "Come, follow me," Jesus said, "and I will show you how to fish for people!" (Matthew 4:19).

HEADLINES IN PETER'S MINISTRY

Walked on water. Sailing in a boat at night, Peter and the other disciples saw Jesus walking toward them—on the water. Peter stepped out of the boat and started walking to Jesus, though he "began to sink" (Matthew 14:30).

Jesus' best friend. Peter seems to have been one of Jesus' three best friends, along with JAMES and his brother JOHN. Jesus took them places he didn't take the others. They alone saw his celestial form at the TRANSFIGURATION (Matthew 17:1). They alone saw him raise a little girl from the dead (Luke 8:51). And on the night of Jesus' arrest, the other disciples slipped away some distance while the three stayed close to Jesus (Mark 14:33).

Got keys to heaven. After Peter declared Jesus the SON OF GOD, Jesus seemed to put him in charge. The statement is so strong that Catholics call Peter the first pope: "You are Peter. . .and upon this rock I will build my CHURCH. . . . I will give you the keys of the KINGDOM OF HEAVEN. Whatever you forbid on earth will be forbidden in heaven, and whatever you permit on earth will be permitted in heaven" (Matthew 16:18–19).

Tried to stop arrest of Jesus. Peter defended Jesus from arresting officers, hacking off the ear of "MALCHUS, the high priest's slave" (John 18:10).

Rushed to Jesus' empty tomb. On Sunday morning, women went to Jesus' TOMB to prep his body for BURIAL. When they reported back to the disciples that Jesus was gone, "Peter jumped up and ran to the tomb" (Luke 24:12).

Preached the sermon that launched the church. After Jesus ascended to HEAVEN and the HOLY SPIRIT filled the disciples while they prayed in JERUSALEM, Peter preached a sermon to the Jewish pilgrims in town for the PENTECOST FESTIVAL. "About three thousand believed his message and were baptized" (Acts 2:41 CEV).

Opened the church to non-Jews. He baptized

P

a Roman officer after a VISION convinced him that "God shows no favoritism. In every nation he accepts those who fear him and do what is right" (Acts 10:34–35).

PETER'S DEATH

Early church writers said Peter was executed as part of Emperor NERO's PERSECUTION of Christians. Origen, a church leader in the AD 200s, wrote that "Peter was crucified at ROME with his head downward." Apparently this was at his request, because he didn't feel worthy to suffer as Jesus had.

Some say Jesus had predicted as much. In what sounds like a reference to CRUCIFIXION, Jesus once told Peter, "When you are old, you will stretch out your hands" (John 21:18).

PETER, LETTERS OF 1–2

Famous sound bite: Give all your worries and cares to God, for he cares about you.
1 Peter 5:7

PETER HEARS THAT CHRISTIANS are suffering in Turkey. He doesn't ID the suffering. Perhaps JEWS are upset that Christians say GOD has a son. Or maybe locals are angry that they've stopped worshiping the local GODS. Whatever the source of suffering, Peter reminds the Christians that Jesus suffered all the way to the grave—and that they may have to do the same.

- Writer: "This letter is from Peter, an apostle of Jesus Christ" (1 Peter 1:1).
- Time: Perhaps shortly before Peter's execution in about AD 64.
- Location: Peter addresses Christians in what is now Turkey.

BIG SCENES

Suffer now, enjoy eternity later. Peter says many Christians are going to have to suffer, just as Jesus did. Some may suffer to death, as MARTYRS. But here's the good news: Peter says they'll rise again just as Jesus did. Christians have "a future in HEAVEN—and the future starts now!" *1 Peter 1:1–12; 3:13–4:19 MSG*

Obey the boss. Peter advises CHRISTIANS to treat their leaders with respect—even those who aren't respectable, including corrupt politicians and cruel slave masters. Apparently, many at the time felt threatened by the Christian movement. "By doing good, you might cure the ignorance of the fools who think you're a danger to society." *1 Peter 2:13–25 MSG*

Watch out for fake Christians. Peter warns Christians to watch out for frauds and heretics who mix fact with fiction. Hungry for MONEY, they'll say God wants us all to be rich. Hungry for SEX, they'll say that nothing that gives us pleasure is wrong. Hungry for attention, they'll brag themselves up one street and down the next. *2 Peter 2*

Jesus is coming, someday. Nearly a GENERATION after Jesus left the planet, some wonder if he's ever coming back. Peter says Jesus will come when the time is right. He says that with God, a thousand years is like a day. So until Jesus comes, Peter says, Christians should try to live peaceful and godly lives. *2 Peter 3*

PETRA

Map 1 E8

(PET ruh)

Amaziah also killed 10,000 Edomites in the Valley of Salt. He also conquered Sela [Petra]. 2 Kings 14:7

- Fortified rock city in Edom (in modern Jordan)
- *Petra* is Greek for "rock" or "cliff"
- *Sela* is Hebrew for "rock" or "cliff"

PETRA WAS A ROCK CITY no army in its right mind wanted to attack.

Soldiers had to funnel through a narrow crack in a rock mountain. That mile-long (1.6 km) path stretched only a few yards (meters) wide, but the cliffs on both sides rose to about 250 feet (76 m)—almost as high as a football field is long. Great place for an ambush.

Inside the natural fortress, many homes and public buildings were carved out of solid rock cliffs.

One PROPHET warned Petra's citizens not to get too comfy. Delivering a message from GOD, the prophet said, "You thought you were so great, perched high among the rocks, king of the mountain, thinking to yourself, 'Nobody can get to me!' . . . Think again. . .I'll bring you down to earth" (Obadiah 3–4 MSG).

Babylonians from what is now Iraq conquered EDOM in 553 BC.

Today, Petra is a tourist attraction some 50 miles (80 km) south of the DEAD SEA in the Arab country of Jordan.

PETRA'S ENTRANCE. Invaders wanting to reach the rock city of Petra had to travel through this narrow crack in the cliff— photographed from inside a massive room chiseled into a nearby cliff.

PHARAOH

(FARE oh)

It was Moses and Aaron who spoke to Pharaoh, the king of Egypt, about leading the people of Israel out of Egypt. Exodus 6:27

- Title for Egypt's king

IT'S NOT THE NAME of an Egyptian king. *Pharaoh* was his title. But in the beginning, it was just the name of his palace: *Pharaoh* means "great house."

Time changed that. Just as "White House" came to mean more than the place where the president lives—

and can mean the president himself—Pharaoh came to mean the king of EGYPT.

The BIBLE's most famous pharaoh was the stubborn king MOSES had to deal with. That king put his nation through 10 plagues before he agreed to free the Jewish slaves.

Bible experts don't agree on which king it was because they can't agree on which century Moses lived. Some point to Thutmose III (reigned 1470–1426 BC). Others put their money on Ramses II (reigned 1279–1212 BC).

PHARISEES

(FARE uh sees)

I [Paul] was a member of the Pharisees, who demand the strictest obedience to the Jewish law. Philippians 3:5

- One ancient branch of the Jewish religion
- Famous as rule lovers
- Opponents of Jesus

NOT A FAN OF PHARISEES, Jesus called them HYPOCRITES: "You are careful to TITHE even the tiniest income from your herb gardens, but you ignore the more important aspects of the law—justice, MERCY, and FAITH" (Matthew 23:23).

Pharisees were influential members of a religious party that prided itself in following all the Jewish laws— and then some. They not only observed the hundreds of laws MOSES gave the JEWS, they developed extra laws about how to carry out the laws of Moses.

For example, "Don't work on the SABBATH" begged the question: What qualifies as work? Pharisees defined work. They said Jesus shouldn't heal people on the Sabbath because he was practicing MEDICINE. And they said his DISCIPLES shouldn't pick a snack of GRAIN while walking through a field on the Sabbath because that was harvesting.

Jesus actually got angry when they opposed him HEALING a man with a deformed hand. His response: "The law permits a person to do good on the Sabbath" (Matthew 12:12).

Pharisees also wrote loopholes around laws (see CORBAN).

P

PAUL was educated as a Pharisee before he converted to CHRISTIANITY. His insights into the most rigid, legalistic branch of the Jewish religion made him an ideal debater in the synagogues and an effective defender of the CHRISTIAN faith.

Pharisees faded from history after Rome destroyed the Jewish TEMPLE in AD 70. That's when the Jewish sacrificial system of WORSHIP died, along with most of the laws related to how to worship GOD at the Temple.

PHILADELPHIA

Map 3 F3

(fill uh DELL fee uh)

"Write this to Philadelphia. . . . You didn't deny me [Jesus] when times were rough." Revelation 3:7–8 MSG

- City in western Turkey
- One of seven churches critiqued in Revelation

JESUS HAD NOTHING BUT COMPLIMENTS for the CHURCH in Philadelphia, an agricultural town on Turkey's west coast. At least that's what JOHN OF REVELATION reported.

Philadelphia was famous for its vineyards. Half the vineyards in the region were destroyed at the order of Roman emperor Domitian in AD 92—perhaps to boost profits for Italian grape farmers. That's about the time many scholars say John of Revelation wrote the church, passing on Jesus' compliments and his promise to protect the believers there.

PHILEMON

(fi LEE muhn)

First century AD

Philemon. . .I hear about your faith in our Lord Jesus and about your love for all of God's people. Philemon 4–5 CEV

- Christian slave owner
- Leader of church in Colosse

PLEADING FOR A RUNAWAY SLAVE, Paul wrote a LETTER to the slave owner. That letter survives

in the BIBLE. It's named after the slave owner: Philemon. The slave himself, ONESIMUS, delivered the letter. PAUL asked Philemon to welcome Onesimus home. And then Paul hinted that he would like Onesimus sent back to help him as an assistant.

PHILEMON, LETTER OF

Famous sound bite: He is no longer like a slave to you. He is more than a slave, for he is a beloved brother. Philemon 16

PAUL SENDS A RUNAWAY SLAVE HOME to the slave owner, a CHURCH leader named Philemon. The slave, ONESIMUS, carries this letter. It's a plea for Philemon to welcome the slave home as a brother.

- Writer: Paul.
- Time: Possibly AD 60–62.
- Location: Paul is a prisoner somewhere, possibly under house arrest in Rome while waiting for his trial in Caesar's supreme COURT.

BIG SCENE

Show some Christian mercy. PAUL not only asks Philemon to welcome Onesimus back as a brother, he hints that he'd like Philemon to free the slave: "I wanted to keep him here with me while I am in these chains for PREACHING the GOOD NEWS, and he would have helped me on your behalf. But I didn't want to do anything without your consent. I wanted you to help because you were willing, not because you were forced." *Philemon 1*

PHILIP

First century AD

Philip went to look for Nathanael and told him, "We have found the very person Moses and the prophets wrote about! His name is Jesus." John 1:45

1. DISCIPLE OF JESUS. The most famous Philip in the BIBLE was one of Jesus' 12 DISCIPLES. He recruited another disciple: NATHANAEL.

2. FOOD PANTRY MINISTER. After Jesus returned to HEAVEN, the disciples brought on some associates to help them administer a charitable food distribution program in JERUSALEM. Philip was one of them, along with STEPHEN.

Philip did evangelistic work, too. While traveling throughout the region, he converted a sorcerer named SIMON and he baptized an ETHIOPIAN official who was headed home after worshiping in Jerusalem.

PHILIPPI
Map 3 D3

(FILL a pie)

You know how badly we had been treated at Philippi. 1 Thessalonians 2:2

- Greek city where Paul started Europe's first known church

IN A VISION, Paul saw a man from what is now northern Greece asking him to come and help the people there. PAUL was in neighboring Turkey at the time. He set sail for the Greek area, a Roman province called MACEDONIA.

Philippi was a large town there, near the coast of the Aegean Sea.

Paul started a small CHURCH there, in the home of a Jewish businesswoman, LYDIA.

He also got in trouble for HEALING a demon-possessed slave girl who made MONEY for her owners by working as a fortune-teller. That provoked a riot. Paul and his associate, SILAS, got beaten and put in jail overnight. The next morning they were asked to leave town.

But Christians in Philippi maintained close ties with Paul, helping support his ministry by sending contributions.

PHILIPPIANS, LETTER OF

Famous sound bite: At the name of Jesus everyone will bow. Philippians 2:10 CEV

IN PRISON, Paul gets a care package from the CHURCH in PHILIPPI—possibly food, clothing, MONEY, and reading material. He writes this letter of thanks, warning that there may come a time when they'll have to suffer like he's doing. But he reminds them that ETERNAL LIFE with Christ is worth the price.

- Writer: Paul.
- Time: Uncertain. Possibly during Paul's two-year arrest in Rome, from about AD 60–62.
- Location: Paul offers two hints. He's "in chains" (Philippians 1:13), and he doesn't know whether he'll "live or die" (Philippians 1:20). Guesses: Rome, Ephesus, Caesarea. Top contender: Rome because of the threat of execution.

BIG SCENES

The perks of prison. Writing like an optimist, PAUL says GOD is using his PRISON experience to spread the GOOD NEWS. Palace guards are getting acquainted with the teachings of Jesus. Local Christians are growing a spiritual backbone and telling their stories. Even fraudulent preachers motivated by greed and ego are teaching about Jesus. "So I rejoice." *Philippians 1*

Life is a marathon. Paul cheers the Christians on, pointing them toward the goal of spiritual maturity. He admits that he's not perfect. "I press on to reach the end of the RACE and receive the heavenly prize." And he urges the Philippians to do the same. *Philippians 3:12–21*

PHILISTIA
Map 1 A6

(fill IS tee uh)

Uzziah declared war on the Philistines. . . . Then he built new towns in. . .Philistia." 2 Chronicles 26:6

- Philistine homeland in Israel

WHEN JOSHUA AND THE JEWS invaded and settled in what is now ISRAEL, so did the PHILISTINES.

Jews settled mainly in the central highlands at first.

Philistines—a seafaring people—settled on the Mediterranean coast in what became known as Philistia. The region stretched from what is now the Palestinian Gaza Strip to Tel Aviv. Philistines built five key cities: ASHDOD, ASHKELON, EKRON, GATH, and GAZA.

P

UNDER ARREST, captured Philistines show up in war trophy art preserved in the mortuary temple of Egypt's king Rameses III.

PHILISTINES

(FILL is teens)

One day when Samson was in Timnah, one of the Philistine women caught his eye.
Judges 14:1

- Warlike people who migrated to Israel

JEWS OF THE EXODUS weren't the only people trying to conquer CANAAN (today's ISRAEL) and turn it into their homeland. They had competition: Philistines, a hard-fighting group of seafaring people probably from islands and coastal lands in the Mediterranean.

Philistines settled along Israel's coast in a region known as PHILISTIA.

At first they seemed stronger than the JEWS and may have come close to assimilating the Jews into their culture. SAMSON, however, turned the nations into enemies and steered the Jews toward freedom, as predicted: "He will begin to rescue Israel from the Philistines" (Judges 13:5).

Angry at the Philistines for murdering his Philistine WIFE, Samson began killing Philistines and destroying their crops and herds.

In wars that followed, Philistines killed Israel's first KING, SAUL. They also controlled the secret of making IRON—giving them the hard edge over Israel's BRONZE WEAPONS.

King DAVID, however, broke the back of Philistine power. In time, Philistines became assimilated into Middle Eastern cultures.

The GREEK word for Philistine people—*Palaistine*—evolved into what is now a familiar name in the region: PALESTINE.

PHINEHAS

(FIN ee huhs)

1400s or 1200s (debated)

Phinehas thrust the spear all the way through the man's body and into the woman's stomach. **Numbers 25:8**

- Aaron's grandson
- Killer priest

PRIEST PHINEHAS knew how to stop a Jewish man from having SEX with a foreign woman. The couple was engaging in a fertility ritual honoring the woman's god.

Phinehas stabbed them both with a SPEAR while they were having sex.

The JEWS were camped east of the JORDAN RIVER at the time. The local women of MOAB had lured many Jews into the sex ritual. MOSES ordered the Jewish ringleaders executed, since the rituals had provoked GOD to unleash a PLAGUE on the Jews. One man boldly defied Moses and walked his pagan woman right past Moses and into a TENT. Phinehas followed. With a spear. That ended the plague, which had killed 24,000 people.

PHOEBE

(FEE bee)

First century AD

I [Paul] have good things to say about Phoebe, who is a leader in the church at Cenchreae. Romans 16:1 CEV

▪ Church leader or minister

THOUGH PAUL ordered WOMEN in some churches not to take leadership roles, perhaps because of local problems, he commended Phoebe—a leader in a CHURCH near CORINTH.

PHOENICIA

Map 1 D2

(foe NEE she uh)

We [Paul and soldier escorts] boarded a ship sailing for Phoenicia. We. . .landed at the harbor of Tyre. Acts 21:2–3

▪ Coastland in what is now Lebanon

THERE ARE TWO GREAT REASONS why the Phoenicians in what is now LEBANON became famous sailors.

They lived on a strip of land beside the MEDITERRANEAN SEA.

Their backyard was a forest where they harvested the cedars of Lebanon—a shipbuilder's preferred wood: rot-resistant and bug unfriendly.

King SOLOMON imported Phoenician CEDAR and recruited Phoenician builders for construction of his Jerusalem TEMPLE and PALACE. Phoenicia's King HIRAM in TYRE also provided Solomon with crews for the Jewish fleet of trading ships.

PHOENIX

Map 3 A4

(FEE nix)

Phoenix was a good harbor with only a southwest and northwest exposure. Acts 27:12

▪ Well-protected harbor on island of Crete

SAILING TO ROME for trial, PAUL—a seasoned traveler—urged the captain to pull in to the nearest harbor: FAIR HAVENS, CRETE. The weather was turning bad. But the captain decided to push on toward the better-protected harbour of Phoenix, on the island's western tip. They never made it. A storm ran them aground some 500 miles (about 800 km) further west, off the coast of MALTA.

PHRYGIA

Map 3 I3

(FRIDGE ee uh)

Paul and Silas traveled through the area of Phrygia and Galatia. Acts 16:6

PAUL TRAVELED THROUGH Phrygia twice, probably starting churches along the way. Phrygia was a Roman territory in what is now central Turkey. Cities with churches in the area included COLOSSE, LAODICEA, and ICONIUM. Jewish pilgrims visiting JERUSALEM from Phrygia heard PETER's sermon that launched the CHRISTIAN movement (Acts 2:10).

P

PHYLACTERIES

(fi LACK tuh rees)

"They do all their deeds to be seen by others; for they make their phylacteries broad."
Matthew 23:5 NRSV

- Tiny prayer boxes with Bible verses inside
- Also known by Hebrew name, *Tefillin*

SOME JEWISH MEN in Bible times, like some JEWS today, wore small, black LEATHER boxes tied to their forehead and left arm. Inside the boxes were some of the most important Bible verses.

One favorite: "The LORD is our GOD, the LORD alone. And you must love the LORD your God with all your heart, all your SOUL, and all your strength" (Deuteronomy 6:4–5).

The practice seems to come from a literal read of how to treat God's commandments: "Tie them to your hands and wear them on your forehead as reminders" (Deuteronomy 6:8).

Jesus condemned Jews who wore supersized prayer boxes and long prayer shawls as a way to show off how religious they were.

PHYSICIAN

(see MEDICINE)

PILATE, PONTIUS

(PIE luht, PON shuhs)

Governed Judea AD 26–36

Pontius Pilate was governor over Judea.
Luke 3:1

- Roman governor who sentenced Jesus to death

THERE'S A REASON PILATE sentenced Jesus to death even though Pilate didn't believe Jesus was guilty of any CRIME.

Survival.

That's what some historians speculate.

As GOVERNOR of the Roman province of JUDEA—the area around JERUSALEM—Pilate found himself in a

ISRAELI SOLDIER Lieutenant Asael Lubotzky straps on his prayer warrior uniform—phylacteries: pouches with Bible verses inside, worn on the forehead and arm. The term literally means to guard or protect—suited to a soldier.

tough spot. JEWS wanted Jesus dead, but they needed Pilate to pass sentence because only Roman leaders could condemn a person to death. When the Jews realized Pilate wouldn't execute Jesus on the religious grounds of dissing GOD by claiming to be God's Son, they accused Jesus of insurrection.

When Pilate refused to execute Jesus, the Jews pitched him what may have been a compelling threat: "If you release this man, you are no 'friend of CAESAR.' Anyone who declares himself a king is a rebel against Caesar" (John 19:12).

By this time, Pilate may have already been on shaky grounds with Caesar. That's because the man who had recommended him for the job, Sejanus, was executed in AD 31 during an attempted coup against Caesar.

Pilate lost his job several years later after ordering a bloody attack on a crowd of unarmed SAMARITANS. He was called back to ROME and was never heard from again.

Some CHRISTIAN groups say he died a Christian MARTYR. Other Christian writers from early times say he committed suicide after being exiled to France.

Philo, a Jewish writer who grew up in Pilate's generation, described Pilate as "rigid and stubbornly harsh. . . of spiteful disposition and an incredibly vengeful man" with a tendency for "BRIBES, acts of pride, acts of violence. . .constant murders without trial."

PILGRIMAGE

What joy for those whose strength comes from the LORD, who have set their minds on a pilgrimage to Jerusalem. Psalm 84:5

- Journey to a holy place

JEWISH MEN HEALTHY ENOUGH TO TRAVEL were expected to make the trek to the Jerusalem TEMPLE three times a year to observe religious festivals: PASSOVER in the spring, PENTECOST 50 days later, and the FESTIVAL of Shelters in the fall.

PILLAR OF CLOUD/FIRE

The LORD went ahead of them in a pillar of cloud. It guided them on their way.
Exodus 13:21 NIrV

- How God led the Exodus Jews home

WHEN THE JEWS ESCAPED EGYPT, freed from SLAVERY by a reluctant PHARAOH, the BIBLE says GOD led them by using a glowing pillar of light.

It looked like a cloud pillar in the day and fire at night. When the Egyptian ARMY came to arrest them and bring them back, the cloud moved behind the JEWS to block the army until the Jews could escape via a path God created through a body of WATER in front of them.

PISGAH   See Mount Nebo, Map 1 E5

(PIZZ guh)

Moses went up to Mount Nebo. . .and climbed Pisgah Peak. . . . And the LORD showed him the whole land [Canaan/Israel]. Deuteronomy 34:1

- Mountain peak where Moses saw Promised Land

JUST BEFORE MOSES DIED, he climbed Pisgah mountain peak on or near MOUNT NEBO. From there, about 10 miles (16 km) east of the JORDAN RIVER, in what is now the Arab country of Jordan, he saw the future Jewish homeland. Earlier, a seer named BALAAM—hired to CURSE the invading JEWS—blessed them instead from Pisgah (Numbers 23:13–26).

P

PISIDIA   Map 3 H3

(puh SID ee uh)

Paul and Barnabas traveled inland to Antioch of Pisidia. On the Sabbath they went to the synagogue for the services. Acts 13:14

- Region in Turkey where Paul converted Jews

ON HIS FIRST MISSIONARY TRIP, PAUL traveled through this mountainous territory in south-central

Turkey. He and Barnabas stopped in the main city, Antioch, where they met with a large Jewish community. The Jews welcomed them at first—and some believed their story about Jesus being the Messiah and rising from the dead. But a week later Jewish leaders ran them out of town when the Jews gathered for worship. That didn't stop the missionaries from going back on their return trip home.

PIT

> "Suppose someone's ox or donkey is killed by falling into an open pit that you dug. . . . You must pay for the dead animal, and it becomes yours." Exodus 21:33–34 CEV

A HOLE IN THE GROUND—either natural or dug—was often a storage space. Lined with plaster, it could hold water as a cistern. Covered, it could help keep wine cool. It also worked as a trap for animals or as a prison for criminals.

PITHOM
Map 2 I8

(PIE thom)

> Egyptians made the Israelites their slaves. . . . They forced them to build the cities of Pithom and Rameses as supply centers for the king. Exodus 1:11

- Egyptian city built by Jewish slaves

JEWS ENSLAVED in Egypt, much like Africans once enslaved in America, were exploited as forced labor. Jews made mud bricks for the king's building projects. Those bricks built the storage cities of Pithom and Rameses, probably somewhere in Egypt's fertile northland: the Nile Delta. Jews had settled there in a prime grazing area called Goshen.

PLAGUE

> "If you refuse to obey. . .the Lord will overwhelm you and your children with indescribable plagues." Deuteronomy 28:58–59

MANY DISASTERS IN THE BIBLE were God's doing, the writers said—punishment for sin. Catastrophes include disease, famine, crop failure, and locust infestation.

In one mystifying report, God sent a plague that killed 70,000 Jews (2 Samuel 24:15). The reason: David took a census. The writer didn't explain what was wrong with taking a census. Guesses include that David was on an ego trip, trying to brag about what a great king he was. Or David didn't collect the required half-shekel tax (Exodus 30:12).

PLAGUES OF EGYPT

> "If you refuse to let them go, I [God] will plague your whole country with frogs." Exodus 8:2 NIrV

- 10 disasters that convinced Egypt to free the Jews

WHEN EGYPT'S KING REFUSED God's demand to free the Jewish slaves, Moses unleashed 10 arm-twisting, nation-busting disasters that changed Pharaoh's mind.

Some Bible experts theorize that the plagues followed a seasonal cycle of natural disasters, beginning with annual autumn flooding of the Nile and ending with springtime harvest. Other scholars add that the plagues may have targeted Egyptian gods—to show that the Lord God is the real deal.

THE PLAGUE that broke the will of Egypt's king was the tenth plague Moses unleashed on the Egyptians: the death of their firstborn children—the king's included. That very night, the king freed all the Jewish slaves.

PLAGUE 1:
Nile River turns blood red
GOD OVERPOWERED:
Hapi, god of annual Nile flood
NATURAL DISASTER:
Toxic bacteria from decaying algae
washed into the river from upstream
swamplands during autumn flood season

PLAGUE 2:
Frogs
GOD OVERPOWERED:
Heqet (Heket), goddess of childbirth,
pictured with frog head
NATURAL DISASTER:
Frogs flee the poisoned water

PLAGUE 3:
Flying gnats
GOD OVERPOWERED:
Thoth, god of magic, can't
help Egypt's magicians
NATURAL DISASTER:
Mosquitoes, midges, and other insects
breed in pools of receding floodwater

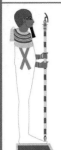

PLAGUE 4:
Flies
GOD OVERPOWERED:
Ptah (Peth, Peteh), creator god,
can't control the flies
NATURAL DISASTER:
Stable flies lay eggs in
decaying frogs, wet straw

PLAGUE 5:
Livestock disease
GOD OVERPOWERED:
Hathor, mother goddess,
pictured with cow ears, horns
NATURAL DISASTER:
Anthrax can be transmitted
through toxic drinking water

PLAGUE 6:
Boils
GODS OVERPOWERED:
Isis and other health gods such as Ptah
NATURAL DISASTER:
Stable flies carry diseases
that produce blisters

PLAGUE 7:
Hail
GOD OVERPOWERED:
Shu, god of dry air
NATURAL DISASTER:
Harvest begins in February,
and hail can wipe out a crop

PLAGUE 8:
Locusts
GOD OVERPOWERED:
Min, god of fertile crops
NATURAL DISASTER:
Even with pesticides today,
locusts are still a problem

PLAGUE 9:
Three-day darkness
GOD OVERPOWERED:
Re, sun god
NATURAL DISASTER:
A lingering, springtime sandstorm
called *Khamsin* (Arabic: "50 days"),
blowing in from Sahara Desert

PLAGUE 10:
Death of firstborn
GOD OVERPOWERED:
Pharaoh, son of Re
NATURAL DISASTER:
Pampered oldest children get
extra food from crops contaminated
with locust droppings

PLOW

Elisha left and took his oxen with him. He killed them and boiled them over a fire he had made with the wood from his plow.
1 Kings 19:21 CEV

THE SIMPLEST PLOW was a forked tree branch. The farmer held on to the two ends, and used the sharp point of the V to cut a path in the dirt.

Other wooden plows, pieced together from boards or tree limbs, included a triangle-shaped plowshare— some plated with metal, to better withstand the ROCKS it had to push aside. Favorite critters for pulling the plows: OXEN, DONKEYS, and CAMELS.

See also YOKE.

PLOWSHARE (see PLOW)

PLUMB LINE

The Lord said, "Look at what I am doing. I am hanging a plumb line next to my people Israel. It will show how crooked they are."
Amos 7:8 NIrV

▪ String tool for building a straight wall

CONSTRUCTION WORKERS who built walls used a plumb line to make sure the wall was going up straight and not leaning off at an angle. The plumb line was a string with a weight tied on the end. The weight was often made of lead, which is *plumbum* in Latin—the Roman language. That's how plumb line got its name.

PLOWING EGYPT, a farmer guides a wooden plow drawn by oxen. An upgrade came when farmers added metal tips called plowshares. Some of these fit over the wood a bit like a glove fits on a hand.

POETRY

Beautiful words stir my heart. I will recite a lovely poem about the king, for my tongue is like the pen of a skillful poet. Psalm 45:1

IT'S A SURPRISE TO MANY, but prophecies in the BIBLE were often written as poems. So were the PSALMS, a collection of ancient SONG lyrics. PROVERBS, too. Many PRAYERS as well.

The poems didn't seem to rhyme—a guess, since scholars can't be sure how the ancients pronounced their words; the OLD TESTAMENT was written in shorthand, without vowels.

Instead of using parallel pronunciation, the writers used parallel ideas. The first line said something. Then the second line said it again another way, or perhaps continued the idea.

When King HEZEKIAH recovered from what he thought would be a fatal illness, he wrote a poem of thanks to GOD. The first line raises the question he asked when he thought he would die. The second line asks much the same thing—adding force to the king's question. It feels like a one-two punch.

"I said, 'In the prime of my life, must I now enter the place of the dead? Am I to be robbed of the rest of my years?'" (Isaiah 38:10).

POISON

One of the young men. . .came back with a pocketful of wild gourds. He shredded them and put them into the pot without realizing they were poisonous. 2 Kings 4:39

POISON MEANS "HEAT" in the HEBREW lingo of OLD TESTAMENT Jews. That might come from the fact that some poison feels hot—including the bite of a snake or the sting of a bee.

Bible lands were full of poisonous plants along with venomous SNAKES such as cobras and horned vipers.

Bible writers also used "poison" as a metaphor of something that packed a wallop. Harsh words, for example: "No one can tame the tongue. It is restless and evil, full of deadly poison" (James 3:8).

POLYGAMY

"The king must not take many wives for himself, because they will turn his heart away from the LORD." Deuteronomy 17:17

- Having more than one wife

ISRAEL WAS BORN OF POLYGAMY. Jacob had CHILDREN by four women: two wives and their two co-operative slaves who functioned as surrogate mothers. Those four gave JACOB a dozen sons who became the founding fathers of ISRAEL's 12 tribes.

Polygamy was common in Bible times and still is in many countries. It was especially common among rulers and other rich folks. The bigger a man's HAREM of wives, the bigger his bragging rights—a bit like a man today bragging about his Harley in the garage, parked beside his Mercedes and his Lexus.

MOSES told JEWS not to let their future KINGS marry a lot of wives. He warned that foreign wives would lead the kings into idolatry. This is exactly what happened to SOLOMON, who built a harem of 1,000 WOMEN.

Most men in the BIBLE who had multiple wives—King DAVID among them—seemed to have more than their share of family problems. The ideal marriage as the Bible presents it, many scholars say, is the one man/one woman approach reported in the CREATION story.

POMEGRANATE

"The Lord your God is bringing you into a good land. . . . It has wheat, barley, vines, fig trees, pomegranates, olive oil and honey." Deuteronomy 8:7–8 NIRV

- Tree fruit

POMEGRANATE TREES produce bright red FRUIT that look like apples. But don't bite into them. The sweet spot is inside. The hard rind on the outside protects juicy seeds, each one wrapped in a tiny ball of Jell-O-like sweetness. JEWS used art of pomegranate fruit to

P

decorate the ROBES of their PRIESTS, as well as the walls of their TEMPLE.

POMEGRANATES, native to the Middle East, show up on ancient Jewish art. Jews preferred pictures of fruit. Pictures of people weren't kosher. "Graven images" not allowed: number two of the 10 Commandments.

PONTIUS PILATE   (see PILATE, PONTIUS)

POOL

"This dry valley will be filled with pools of water!" 2 Kings 3:16

IN THE DRY BIBLE LANDS, winter rains produced natural pools that people used as temporary wells. They would use it to WATER the livestock or carry the water home for COOKING or for storage in a CISTERN—a plaster-coated rock PIT used to store rainwater and water hauled from other sources.

Jesus told a blind man to wash his eyes in the "pool of Siloam" (John 9:7, see also SILOAM POOL), a reservoir in JERUSALEM that stored water from a nearby spring outside the city walls. King HEZEKIAH built a TUNNEL through solid rock, connecting the spring to the pool.

POOR

"There should be no poor people among you. . . . If there are. . .give freely to them, and freely lend them whatever they need."
Deuteronomy 15:4, 7–8 NCV

THERE'S BLAME TO GO AROUND, as the BIBLE tells it—plenty of reasons poor folks are poor:

Laziness. "LAZINESS leads to poverty" (Proverbs 10:4 CEV).

Exploitation by the rich. "They oppressed the poor and left them destitute. They foreclosed on their homes. They were always greedy and never satisfied" (Job 20:19–20).

Injustice of a money-loving court system. "You oppress good people by taking BRIBES and deprive the poor of justice in the COURTS" (Amos 5:12).

Disease and injury. "A blind man was sitting by the side of the road BEGGING" (Mark 10:46 NIrv).

Death of a loved one. "You must not exploit a WIDOW or an ORPHAN" (Exodus 22:22).

The Bible's remedy for poverty through laziness is work. For everything else, the Bible's remedy is compassion: "If you help the poor, you are lending to the LORD—and he will repay you!" (Proverbs 19:17).

POTIPHAR   (POT uh fur)

1800s BC
Midianite traders arrived in Egypt, where they sold Joseph to Potiphar, an officer of Pharaoh, the king of Egypt. Genesis 37:36

- Captain of Egypt's palace guard
- Owner of Joseph, sold as a slave

JACOB'S FAVORITE SON, 17-year-old JOSEPH, managed to get himself sold to slave traders. His older brothers did the selling. Their motive: jealousy.

They sold him to slave traders headed to EGYPT. Lucky for Joseph, the slavers sold him to Potiphar, a wealthy palace official who took a liking to him and put him in charge of the entire household. Unlucky for Joseph, Potiphar's WIFE took a liking to him as well. A lusting, actually. She tried to seduce him. When Joseph ran from the cougar attack, Potiphar's wife screamed RAPE.

Potiphar probably didn't believe her, some scholars guess, because he didn't execute Joseph. Instead, he put him in jail, perhaps to preserve his wife's reputation without killing an innocent man.

POTTER'S FIELD

See Jerusalem, Map 4 C5

> *They decided to get rid of it [coins returned by Judas] by buying the "Potter's Field" and use it as a burial place for the homeless.* Matthew 27:7 MSG

- Jerusalem cemetery paid for by Judas

AFTER JUDAS BETRAYED JESUS for a reward of 30 pieces of SILVER, he had second thoughts. He returned the MONEY to the Jewish PRIESTS.

But the priests didn't want to use it for anything HOLY because it was "payment for MURDER" (Matthew 27:6). So they bought a piece of ground from a potter and turned it into a cemetery.

POTTERY

> *"Take these documents—both the sealed and the open deeds—and put them for safekeeping in a pottery jar."* Jeremiah 32:14 MSG

PEOPLE USED POTTERY in lots of ways during Bible times:

- Dishes. They served food in pottery.
- Lamps. They used pots to burn OLIVE OIL.
- Storage. They stored everything from WATER, to GRAIN, to important documents. Many of the famous DEAD SEA SCROLLS— 2,000-year-old copies of the OLD TESTAMENT

POTTERY STYLES help archaeologists date digs. These two-handled jars with their geometric designs were common in Cyprus beginning about the time of King David. When jars like these show up in the ruins of a house in Israel, it suggests the homeowner was rich enough to afford imports.

and other Jewish WRITINGS—were found in pottery jars stashed in caves.

- Letters. They used broken pieces of pottery like we use notepads.

Archaeologists use pottery to date ruins. They can do that because pottery styles changed over the centuries, much like cars change from one decade to the next.

Potters often worked their clay on a turntable. Early on, potters turned the clay with one hand and worked it with another. Later someone invented a table they could turn with their feet, which freed up both hands to shape the clay.

PRAISE

> *I will praise you, LORD, with all my heart; I will tell of all the marvelous things you have done.* Psalm 9:1

- Gratitude to God

MOST PRAISE in the BIBLE is directed at GOD—in SONGS, POETRY, and PRAYERS.

After God parted a body of WATER for the Jewish refugees fleeing EGYPT, MIRIAM broke out her TAMBOURINE and led the ladies in a song and dance:

"Sing to the LORD,

    for he has triumphed gloriously;

he has hurled both horse and rider

    into the sea" (Exodus 15:21).

CALLING GOD. With cell phone in hand, a Jew takes his prayer to Jerusalem's Western Wall—the holiest site on earth for Jews. This wall is all that's left of their ancient Temple. Many people write prayers on slips of paper and stuff them into the cracks.

PRAYER

Don't worry about anything; instead, pray about everything. Tell God what you need, and thank him for all he has done. Philippians 4:6

▪ Talking to God

HUMANS TALK TO GOD. We ask for help. We ask FORGIVENESS. And from time to time, we thank GOD—though many MINISTERS would say not often enough.

There's no special trick to praying. No religious lingo required. No position preferred. People in the BIBLE prayed standing, sitting, kneeling, lying in BED, and even lying face down on the ground. Some prayed with their arms raised, as though reaching up to God.

Jesus told people not to pray show-off prayers—long, loud, flowery words in front of folks they want to impress.

When Jesus' DISCIPLES asked him how to pray, he prayed the LORD's PRAYER—a 30-second masterpiece of simplicity.

Other prayer tips from Jesus:

▪ **"Don't be like the** HYPOCRITES **who love to pray publicly."**
▪ **"Pray to your** FATHER **in private."**
▪ **"Don't babble on."** (Matthew 6:5–7)

As for his personal example, "Jesus often withdrew to the WILDERNESS for prayer" (Luke 5:16). He prayed for himself. And he prayed for his disciples and his followers to come: "I pray that you will keep them safe from the evil one" (John 17:15 NIrV).

PRAYER BOX (see PHYLACTERIES)

PREACHING

PROPHETS AND MINISTERS preached, though they went about it in different ways.

PROPHETS in OLD TESTAMENT times delivered messages from GOD, often from VISIONS or DREAMS they experienced.

MINISTERS in NEW TESTAMENT times typically told people about Jesus and his teachings, drawing from the life and teachings of Jesus himself.

In time, these teachings were written down in what became the New Testament GOSPELS about Jesus and the LETTERS from APOSTLES such as PAUL and PETER. These WRITINGS are the main source of information for preachers today.

Paul said that CHURCH leaders such as preachers should be well-respected and "able to encourage others with wholesome teaching and show those who oppose it where they are wrong" (Titus 1:9).

Paul wrote that anyone wanting to become a PASTOR should also not be money-hungry or quarrelsome. Those tips and more show up in letters of advice he wrote to colleagues TIMOTHY and TITUS (see 1 Timothy 3; Titus 1).

PREDESTINATION

DOES GOD CONTROL the eternal destiny of people? Or do people seal their own fate by the decisions they make in life? Christians don't agree.

Many people of FAITH, including lots of Baptists and Presbyterians, say GOD has it all figured out. He's working his plan. And that plan includes who will and won't be saved.

One of their go-to verses: "God chose us to belong to Christ before the world was created" (Ephesians 1:4 NIRV).

Other Christians, including Methodists and Nazarenes, argue that God chooses to save everyone—but that not everyone wants saved. SALVATION is a two-way street. God sends the invitation. We return the RSVP with a yes or a no.

One of their go-to verses: "God is being patient with you. He does not want anyone to be lost, but he wants all people to change their hearts and lives" (2 Peter 3:9 NCV).

See also FREE WILL.

PREFECT

THE MAN WHO SENTENCED JESUS TO DEATH was a Roman GOVERNOR, as most English Bibles report it. Romans called him "prefect," according to a Latin inscription found at Rome's Holy Land capital, in CAESAREA on what is now ISRAEL's coast. Prefects were appointed by the emperor to govern a region, and they reported to him.

Some early Christian writers called PILATE a procurator. It's unclear what the difference was between the two titles.

PRIESTS

P

ISRAEL'S PRIESTS traced their FAMILY tree back to AARON, big brother of MOSES. GOD picked Aaron as the nation's first HIGH PRIEST and his sons as the first priests to serve under his authority.

Not just any descendant of Aaron qualified as a priest. Excluded were men with certain physical problems: blind, LAME, skin DISEASES.

Their job description included:

- offering SACRIFICES
- teaching Jewish laws to the people
- maintaining the WORSHIP center
- collecting TITHES and offerings
- diagnosing skin diseases that left people ritually unfit to worship (Leviticus 13–14)
- administering PURIFICATION rituals for those healed of skin diseases
- conducting the test for women suspected of ADULTERY (Numbers 5:11–31).

Assisting the priests were LEVITES, members of Aaron's tribal family. They were descendants of JACOB'S son LEVI. They couldn't serve as priests unless they descended from Aaron's family, too. But they served as assistants to the priests, helping with upkeep and security at the worship center.

PRINCE

> The Hittites replied to Abraham, "Listen, my lord, you are an honored prince among us." Genesis 23:5–6

- Royalty or leader

THINK "NOBLE." In the BIBLE, a prince wasn't necessarily a king's son. A prince could also be a tribal leader, a local GOVERNOR, or simply a well-respected man in the community.

Locals considered ABRAHAM a prince. King DAVID praised SAUL's murdered general, ABNER, as "a prince and hero" (2 Samuel 3:38 MSG).

PRINCESS

> Pharaoh's daughter. . .saw the basket among the reeds. . . . When the princess opened it, she saw the baby [Moses]. Exodus 2:5–6

- Woman of royalty

A PRINCESS in the BIBLE usually refers to the daughter of a king, such as the Egyptian king's daughter who adopted baby MOSES. Some Bible translations also use the word to describe a QUEEN, including King SOLOMON's HAREM of 1,000 wives.

PRISCILLA AND AQUILA

(pruh SILL uh) (uh QUILL uh)
> Aquila had recently come from Italy with his wife Priscilla. The emperor Claudius had ordered all the Jews to leave Rome. Acts 18:2 NIrV

- Jewish couple expelled from Rome
- Worked with Paul as tentmakers

PAUL COVERED HIS OWN EXPENSES during the year and a half he stayed in CORINTH, starting the CHURCH there. He made and repaired tents, working with a couple named Priscilla and Aquila. They had moved to Corinth after the emperor expelled all JEWS from ROME for some reason—possibly over clashes about Jesus. Some Jews accepted him as MESSIAH, but most didn't.

Priscilla and Aquila later sailed with PAUL to SYRIA. They apparently learned a lot about Jesus during their time with Paul. They learned enough to offer some continuing EDUCATION to a respected preacher: APOLLOS. "They gave him a better understanding of the way of GOD" (Acts 18:26 NIrV).

PRISON

> *Praise the LORD. . . . For he broke down their prison gates of bronze; he cut apart their bars of iron.* Psalm 107:15–16

PRISON WASN'T FOR PUNISHMENT. Not usually. In Bible times, prison was just a holding tank. It's where suspects were kept until trial. If found guilty, they might be executed, beaten, or banished. But they weren't usually sentenced to more time in prison. One exception was young JOSEPH, kept in an Egyptian prison for at least two years (Genesis 40:22–41:1).

When the prophet JEREMIAH was arrested for treason, he was held in a HOUSE "converted into a prison" (Jeremiah 37:15). Later they "lowered him by ropes into an empty CISTERN in the prison yard" (Jeremiah 38:6).

PAUL spent years in various prisons. He and SILAS were freed from a prison in PHILIPPI after a "massive EARTHQUAKE" (Acts 16:26) broke open the doors. Later Paul spent two years locked up in a CAESAREA prison before appealing to Caesar's supreme COURT. In ROME he spent another two years at his own expense waiting for his trial. He lived under house arrest, guarded by Roman soldiers, but he was free to preach to visitors.

PROCOUNSUL

> *Proconsul, Sergius Paulus, an intelligent man. . .summoned Barnabas and Saul.* Acts 13:7 NRSV

- Roman governor

REPORTING TO THE SENATE in ROME, proconsuls were appointed for one-year terms to govern an area. SERGIUS PAULUS, the first known Roman official to convert to CHRISTIANITY, governed the island of CYPRUS. Gallio governed ACHAIA in what is now Greece. When JEWS brought charges against PAUL, Gallio dismissed the case, apparently not interested in trying a religious dispute (Acts 18:16).

PROCURATOR   (see PREFECT)

PRODIGAL SON

> *"The younger son. . .wasted his possessions with prodigal living."* Luke 15:13 NKJV

IN ONE OF JESUS' MOST FAMOUS STORIES, he told about a wild-child son who cashed out his share of the FAMILY estate and blew the wad on wild-child living.

It's known as the PARABLE of the prodigal son.

THE PRODIGAL SON is welcomed home by his father—even though the boy took his share of the family estate and blew it on wild parties and wild women. It's a fictional story Jesus told to illustrate God's love for sinners. The dad in the story represents God, most scholars agree.

Prodigal essentially means "spends money like the asteroid is going to hit tomorrow."

The day after tomorrow, so to speak, the Jewish kid was busted—and working on a pig farm. Not kosher.

He decided to go home and plead with his dad for a job on the farm. To the son's surprise, his dad welcomed him home, arms wide open. Threw him a party, too.

This wasn't a story about the wild child, many scholars say. It was about the FATHER—about his love for the son. The story, scholars add, illustrates GOD's love for sinful people who need to find their way home.

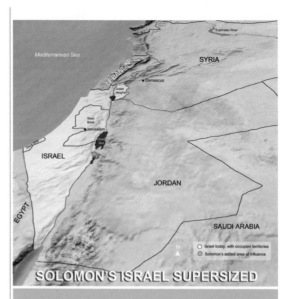

SOLOMON'S ISRAEL SUPERSIZED

ISRAEL was biggest in its heyday, when Solomon reigned as king. It was all of modern Israel, and then some.

PROFANE

"Do not profane my holy name, for I must be acknowledged as holy by the Israelites."
Leviticus 22:32 TNIV

- Treating a holy object as nothing special

DISSING GOD'S NAME—as in using it to cuss someone out—qualifies as profanity, as Bible writers used the term *profane*. Most Bible translations today, however, skip the word *profane* because it's old school. They get the point across another way: "Do not treat my NAME as if it were not HOLY" (Leviticus 22:32 NIrV).

It was also considered profane to use TEMPLE furnishings for everyday use. And the same goes for human beings: "Do not profane your daughter by making her a PROSTITUTE" (Leviticus 19:29 NRSV).

PROMISED LAND

See Canaan, Map 1 B6

He [God] chose the Promised Land as our inheritance, the proud possession of Jacob's descendants, whom he loves. Psalm 47:4

- Jewish homeland
- Roughly, modern Israel

TODAY'S ISRAEL is smaller than the land GOD promised to the JEWS.

God led ABRAHAM, father of the Jews, to what is now ISRAEL. Then God told him, "I am giving all this

land, as far as you can see, to you and your descendants" (Genesis 13:15).

MOSES quoted God to the Jewish refugees headed home during the EXODUS out of EGYPT: "I will fix your boundaries from the RED SEA to the MEDITERRANEAN SEA, and from the eastern WILDERNESS to the EUPHRATES RIVER" (Exodus 23:31).

That version and similar descriptions by Moses and later by JOSHUA would extend Israel to what are now parts of Syria and Jordan. In King SOLOMON's day—Israel's golden age of prosperity—Israel's controlling influence did extend that far.

PROPHET

"God will give you a prophet like me [Moses], who is one of your own people. Listen to him." Deuteronomy 18:15 NCV

- Delivered God's messages
- Not a fortune-teller

A BIT LIKE PRESS SECRETARIES, prophets spoke on behalf of someone else.

Jewish prophets delivered GOD's messages. They

usually got those messages from VISIONS, DREAMS, and voices they heard—such as the sound of God speaking to MOSES from a BURNING BUSH.

Often the messages were a mixed bag: bad news/good news.

Bad news: You JEWS have broken your agreement with God to obey his laws. You worship IDOLS, exploit the POOR, and ignore God. If you don't shape up, God's going to invoke the penalty clauses in the agreement: disaster, DISEASE, and eviction from your homeland.

Good news: It doesn't have to be this way. Honor your agreement and you'll get the perks God promised: bumper crops, big families, and protection from enemies. But even if you refuse and you lose your homeland, God will bring your descendants home for a fresh start. God is not giving up on you, even if you give up on him.

Prophecy wasn't a job most sane people would want. Several high-profile prophets tried to convince God to pick someone else.

Moses: "I cannot speak well" (Exodus 4:10 NCV).

Isaiah: "I am not pure" (Isaiah 6:5 NCV).

Jeremiah: "I am only a boy" (Jeremiah 1:6 NCV).

Jonah: He didn't argue. He ran. He booked passage on a SHIP sailing in the opposite direction from where God told him to go (Jonah 1:1–3).

LEGIT PROPHETS VS. FRAUDS

It was hard to tell a true prophet from a fraud. Anyone could say they had a message from God.

Some did: "I have heard the prophets who prophesy lies in my NAME. They say, 'I have had a DREAM!' . . . They prophesy from their own wishful thinking. They are trying to make the people of JUDAH forget me" (Jeremiah 23:25–27 NCV).

Moses offered this advice about how to spot a fraud: "If the prophet speaks in the LORD's name but his prediction does not happen or come true, you will know that the LORD did not give that message" (Deuteronomy 18:22).

Yet there were exceptions to that general rule. JONAH told the Assyrian citizens of NINEVEH in what is now Iraq: "Forty days from now Nineveh will be destroyed!" (Jonah 3:4).

But the people repented. So God didn't destroy the city. Many Bible experts chalk that up to Jonah's success. He got God's message across in a way that convinced the people to shape up—something most other Bible prophets couldn't accomplish with the stubborn Jews.

Prophecy seemed to fade from ISRAEL's scene after God dropped the hammer, allowing Babylonian invaders from what is now Iraq to destroy the Jewish cities and EXILE the survivors. But prophecy made a comeback in Jesus' day. Most prophecy in the NEW TESTAMENT pointed to Jesus and the CHRISTIAN movement that grew up out of his teachings.

JOHN THE BAPTIST, like prophets in earlier centuries, told the Jews to repent. But this time it was to

PROPHETS came in both genders. Miriam, big sis of Moses, was a prophet. When she lobbied for status equal to Moses, God struck her skin "white as snow from leprosy" (Numbers 12:10). Just temporary. Isolated for a week. Long enough to convince her not to do it again.

prepare for the coming of the MESSIAH, Jesus.

PAUL included prophets among the CHURCH leaders, along with "APOSTLES. . .EVANGELISTS, and the PASTORS and teachers" (Ephesians 4:11).

Like Jews in OLD TESTAMENT times, Christian leaders offered a litmus test for telling a genuine prophet from a fraud: "If someone claims to be a prophet and does not acknowledge the truth about Jesus, that person is not from God" (1 John 4:3).

With the writing of the BIBLE, which is said to contain the heart of God's messages to people, prophecy seemed to fade from the scene. Still, from time to time, people today claim to have a message from God. But as in ancient times, it's often hard to tell fact from fiction.

PROSTITUTE

Judah saw her [his daughter-in-law Tamar]. He thought she was a prostitute because she had covered her face with a veil. . . . He said, "Come. Let me make love to you."
Genesis 38:15–16 NIrv

- Trades sex for money
- Occupation of Rahab in Jericho
- Occupation of mother of Israel's hero Jephthah

THE FIRST STOP FOR TWO SPIES JOSHUA sent to scout JERICHO's defenses: "the HOUSE of a prostitute named RAHAB" (Joshua 2:1). They spent the night.

The BIBLE doesn't say if the sleepover was business or pleasure. But some historians say it would have been a good place for strangers to blend in without drawing attention to themselves. Locals may have avoided the area, while traveling salesmen and other strangers passing through might have been drawn there by the TEMPTATION, free of witnesses who knew them.

Prostitution was legal in most places—no crime, no punishment. But it was a job of last resort, typically for WOMEN in financial crisis or in SLAVERY.

GOD told the Jews, "Do not defile your daughter by making her a prostitute, or the land will be filled with prostitution and wickedness" (Leviticus 19:29).

He told PRIESTS not to marry a prostitute, adding

that any priest's daughter who became a prostitute "must be burned to death" (Leviticus 21:9).

A Jewish WIDOW named TAMAR resorted to prostitution to get pregnant by her father-in-law. She needed a son to inherit her late husband's estate, but her father-in-law, JUDAH, had refused to provide her with the replacement husband that Jewish law allowed. As it turned out, he became the biological father of his legal grandsons; Tamar had twins. Daddy was their grandpa.

Little is known about how prostitutes marketed themselves. Tamar waited for Judah at the side of a ROAD near the entrance to a city. In Roman times, cities hosted brothels. Some inns doubled as brothels, for customers willing to pay extra for the room service.

Some prostitutes worked in temples and shrines. For them, SEX was an act of worship to honor and invoke the power of a fertility god. A worshiper who wanted a good HARVEST, a large flock, or a big family would have SEX with the SHRINE prostitute. During the Jewish EXODUS out of EGYPT, some Jewish men had sex with women of MOAB (in Jordan) and then ate ANIMALS sacrificed to their GODS (Numbers 25:1–2).

PROVERBS, BOOK OF

Famous sound bite: Those who spare the rod hate their children. **Proverbs 13:24** NRSV

WISE ADVICE from grandfatherly types, targeting their sons and grandsons. That's how many Bible experts describe the book of Proverbs. Most of the sayings are short—easy to remember and quick to digest.

- Writer: Most of the sayings are attributed to King Solomon, though some are credited to a group of wise men.
- Time: Solomon reigned from about 970–930 BC.
- Location: Israel.

BIG SCENES

Trust God. You can't always trust your gut, especially on a full stomach. But you can trust GOD. *Proverbs 3*

The sex talk. Have SEX with your own WIFE, not some other guy's wife. ADULTERY will destroy your marriage and your reputation. And if the woman's HUSBAND finds out about it, you could wake up dead. *Proverbs 5–7*

Lazy is crazy. Forget the get-rich-quick schemes. MONEY that comes quickly tends to leave quickly. Earn your money the old-fashioned way: Work hard. *Proverbs 6:6–10; 12:24; 13:11*

When in doubt, shut up. Words can be hazardous to your health and the health of those you love. So watch what you say. *Proverbs 11:9; 18:21; 21:23*

How to raise kids. You don't have to beat the kids with a club; good SHEPHERDS don't beat their SHEEP with a ROD. But you do have to nudge them in the right direction from time to time. That's what discipline does. And that's what shepherds do with their rods. *Proverbs 13:24; 19:18; 22:6*

PSALM

> *God is the King over all the earth. Praise him with a psalm. Psalm 47:7*

- Song of worship

PSALMOS IS GREEK for "SONG." But in the BIBLE, psalms aren't just any songs. They're songs of WORSHIP usually directed at GOD: PRAISES, requests, and even complaints.

PSALMS, BOOK OF

> *Famous sound bite: Though I walk through the valley of the shadow of death, I will fear no evil. Psalm 23:4 NKJV*

AN ANCIENT JEWISH HYMNBOOK, Psalms is a collection of lyrics JEWS sang in WORSHIP. Not all of them are PRAISES. In fact, about half would fall under the category of downers—SONGS to sing at the Complaint Desk: requests and grievances.

- Writer: King David is credited with 73 of the 150 psalms, though his byline "of David" could mean he wrote them or merely inspired them.
- Time: The songs span about a thousand years, from the time of Moses (1400s BC or 1200s BC) to the Jewish exile in Babylon (Iraq) in the 500s BC.
- Location: Israel.

BIG SCENES

Blues. Writers unload their sharpest criticisms on GOD, almost as though he's to blame for their troubles: "My God! Why did you dump me miles from nowhere?" Yet in each song sung blue, the writer ends on an upbeat note, expressing hope that God will turn his situation around. *Psalms 22, 42, 130, 142 MSG*

The Lord is my shepherd. In perhaps the most famous ancient song of all, a writer praises God as a reliable and loving SHEPHERD: "He lets me rest in green meadows; he leads me beside peaceful streams." Even in the face of certain death, the writer says he feels protected and comforted by the hope that "I will live in the house of the LORD forever." *Psalm 23*

Road trip. More than a dozen songs seem intended for pilgrims traveling to JERUSALEM. Called "songs of ascent," they refer to climbing the hills to Jerusalem: "I look up to the mountains—does my help come from there? My help comes from the LORD" (Psalm 121:1–2). *Psalms 120–134*

God save the king. Some songs praise ISRAEL'S KING or ask God to help him: "Long live the king! May the GOLD of SHEBA be given to him. May the people always pray for him." *Psalm 72*

PTOLEMAIS   (see Acco)

P

PTOLEMY

(TOLL uh me)

When Ptolemy entered the towns he stationed forces as a garrison.
1 Maccabees 11:3 NRSV

- Dynasty of Greek kings in Egypt

AFTER ALEXANDER THE GREAT DIED, his generals divided up the empire. Ptolemy I (died about 283 BC) got EGYPT. He's not mentioned in the Protestant Bible, but he shows up in Catholic and Eastern Orthodox Bibles, in the Apocrypha, a collection of books written between the Old and New Testaments. Ptolemy's descendants ruled for about 275 years, until Romans took over in 51 BC.

PURIFICATION

"After waiting thirty-three days, she will be purified from the bleeding of childbirth."
Leviticus 12:4

- Ritual cleansing that allows a person to worship

JEWS BECAME UNFIT TO WORSHIP their HOLY God when they became ritually unclean.

Touching a corpse would make them unclean, according to the laws MOSES gave them. So could touching certain dead ANIMALS, suffering from a skin DISEASE, or even experiencing a flow of body fluids, such as wet dreams for men or a menstrual period for WOMEN.

Getting rid of the impurity usually involved a waiting period—often sometime between a day and a week. Some impurities required a BATH and a SACRIFICE.

Women who delivered a boy had to wait 40 days after the BIRTH—double that for a girl. When it came time for the purification, she had to sacrifice a year-old lamb—or a pair of BIRDS if she was POOR. Birds are what Jesus' mother, MARY, brought (Luke 2:22–24).

PURIM

(PEW rim)

The enemy of the Jews. . .plotted to crush and destroy them on the date determined by casting lots (the lots were called purim).
Esther 9:24

- Festival of a holocaust averted

THE WILDEST PARTY DAY on the Jewish CALENDAR is Purim. A bit like a kosher Mardi Gras, it comes with costumes, gift exchanges, and rich food.

The day-long FESTIVAL commemorates Queen ESTHER saving the JEWS from a holocaust plotted by the Persian king's top adviser, HAMAN. Neither Haman nor the king, XERXES, realized Esther was a Jew. She eventually worked up the courage to tell the king—in front of a shocked Haman. The king executed Haman.

Jews celebrate Purim on the 14th or 15th of their ancient month of Adar, which falls in February. The day got its name from *pur*, which means "LOTS." Haman used lots to pick the day of the genocide. Lots somehow worked like dice or the flip of a coin to help people make random choices.

PURPLE DYE

(see COLOR)

QUAIL

The LORD sent a wind that brought quail. . . . For miles in every direction there were quail flying about three feet above the ground.
Numbers 11:31

- Migrating quarter-pounder game bird

GOD FLEW IN FAST FOOD to the Jewish refugees MOSES led out of EGYPT. A wind blew a massive flock of migrating quail into their camp.

Each spring, *Coturnix coturnix* quail migrate from Africa to Europe. They weigh it at about a quarter pound (113 g) and stretch half the length of a foot-long hot dog (15 cm).

Exhausted from their marathon flight, the quail sometimes fly low and slow by the time they reach Egypt, especially when they're flying into a headwind. Ancient Egyptian art shows hunters catching them by hand and with NETS—just as the BIBLE says the JEWS did.

WITH A BIRD IN THE HAND, an Egyptian seems able to scoop up birds at will. That's what the Bible says Jews on the exodus out of Egypt were able to do when a flock of exhausted, migratory quail came along, flying low and slow.

QUARRY

Solomon did not want the noise of hammers. . . where the temple was being built. So he had the workers shape the blocks of stone at the quarry. 1 Kings 6:7 CEV

- Source of construction blocks

HUGE BLOCKS OF STONE used in projects such as the pyramids and the Jerusalem TEMPLE were cut from rock quarries and hauled to the construction sites.

In EGYPT, many of blocks of granite and other stones came from quarries in the southland. They were floated along the NILE RIVER on barges, to where workers erected the pyramids.

In Jerusalem, nearby limestone quarries provided stone for the Temple, the PALACE, and other buildings.

To cut a block, stonemasons drew a line on the bedrock. Then they drilled holes along that line. Next they hammered wooden wedges into the holes and poured water on the wood. As the wood soaked up the water and expanded, the block split free of the quarry.

QUEEN

As soon as Athaliah heard that her son King Ahaziah was dead, she decided to kill any relative who could possibly become king. . . . Athaliah ruled as queen of Judah. 2 Kings 11:1, 3 CEV

- Female ruler or wife of king

JEWS NEVER HAD A LEGIT QUEEN who ruled the nation. All the Jewish queens were wives of KINGS. There was, however, one illegit queen who ruled the southland Jewish country of JUDAH for six years: ATHALIAH.

She was the daughter of ISRAEL's King AHAB and possibly his most famous WIFE, the Queen of Mean: JEZEBEL. Athaliah had been the queen mother of Judah. But then her son, King Ahaziah, died.

A nasty granny, Athaliah killed her grandkids and took over the country. Sadly for her, she missed one grandson: JOASH. An aunt took him in the TEMPLE where the PRIESTS

Q

STEPHEN M. MILLER'S ILLUSTRATED BIBLE DICTIONARY

hid him for several years. When the HIGH PRIEST eventually unveiled the boy, the JEWS executed their fraud queen.

SHEBA'S HOMELAND was Yemen, many Bible scholars say. That's where this lady hails from—an Arab nation on the southern tip of the Arabian Peninsula, south of Saudi Arabia.

QUEEN OF SHEBA

(SHE buh)

Ruled 900s BC

King Solomon gave the queen of Sheba whatever she asked for, besides all the customary gifts he had so generously given. 1 Kings 10:13

- Queen who traded with Solomon

NO ONE KNOWS where Sheba was. One persistent and plausible theory points to the southwest corner of ARABIA in what is now Yemen.

If that's where the queen of Sheba came from, she traveled some 1,500 miles (2,400 km) up the coast of the RED SEA to meet King SOLOMON. The BIBLE says she came to check out his WISDOM. But because she brought a massive CARAVAN loaded with rare SPICES, jewels, and 9,000 pounds (4,000 kg) of GOLD, many scholars guess she came to shop.

A recently discovered BRONZE inscription says the kingdom of Sabaea (possibly Sheba) sent a trade expedition to the "towns of JUDAH." The text, written in South

Arabian letters, dates to about 300 years after Solomon and the queen of Sheba.

QUIRINIUS

(kwi RINN ee us)

50s BC–AD 21

The Roman emperor, Augustus, decreed that a census should be taken. . .when Quirinius was governor of Syria. Luke 2:1–2

- Rome's governor of Syria

THE BIBLE CLASHES with Roman history, some say, because the BIBLE reports that Quirinius was GOVERNOR of SYRIA at the birth of Jesus (about 6 BC, perhaps two years before HEROD THE GREAT died in 4 BC). Several sources in Roman history agree that Publius Sulpicius Quirinius didn't govern Syria until a decade later, in AD 6. Josephus, a Jewish historian of that century, added that a CENSUS was carried out under Quirinius in AD 6 or 7.

Some Bible scholars speculate that Quirinius may have held the job more than once.

QUMRAN

Map 4 D6

(KOOM ron)

- Ancient Jewish settlement
- Home of the Dead Sea Scrolls

QUMRAN isn't mentioned in the Bible. But this isolated community near the DEAD SEA is where archaeologists in the 1940s and 50s found copies of the Bible 1,000 years older than the copies used to translate the King James Version.

Monk-like isolationist JEWS lived in Qumran, along the banks of the Dead Sea some 15 miles (24 km) east of JERUSALEM. They settled there about 130 years before Jesus was born. They preserved sacred Jewish WRITINGS.

Romans wiped them out in AD 68, while crushing a nationwide Jewish revolt. But the Qumran Jews managed to stash their SCROLLS—about 800 of them—in caves throughout the area.

See also DEAD SEA SCROLLS.

RABBI

(RAB i)

"Teachers of the law and the Pharisees. . . love it when people call them 'Rabbi.'"
Matthew 23:2, 7 NIrV

- Respectful title of Jewish leaders
- Means "my teacher"

JESUS WASN'T A FAN OF THE TITLE "Rabbi," though he's one of the few actually addressed that way by Bible writers. JOHN THE BAPTIST was another (John 3:26).

Jesus told his DISCIPLES, "Don't let anyone call you 'Rabbi,' for you have only one TEACHER, and all of you are equal as brothers and sisters" (Matthew 23:8).

Rabbis weren't like scholars today who have gone through a course of study to earn a doctorate. Instead, they earned a reputation—as scholars and leaders who knew their way around Jewish laws and traditions.

People called Jesus a rabbi because the words he spoke showed that he knew SCRIPTURE and Jewish customs much better than most folks did.

RACA

(ROCK uh)

"Anyone who says to his brother, 'Raca,' must stand trial in the Sanhedrin."
Matthew 5:22 NIrV

- An idiot

RACA is a name-calling insult. It's a bit like calling someone an idiot—or worse, since using the word in public could lead to charges of SLANDER in the Jewish high COURT known as the SANHEDRIN.

RACE

I have fought the good fight, I have finished the race, and I have remained faithful.
2 Timothy 4:7

- Athletic competition

PAUL USED ATHLETIC COMPETITIONS such as footraces to compare the Christian life to a long journey with a prize at the end.

He seemed to have picked up this metaphor, scholars say, after spending a year and a half in CORINTH. Every two years an Olympic-style competition called the Isthmian GAMES was held on the outskirts of town.

RACHEL

(RAY chuhl)

1900s BC

Rachel was beautiful. She had a nice figure. Jacob was in love with Rachel.
Genesis 29:17–18 NIrV

- Jacob's favorite wife, and cousin
- Mother of Joseph, Benjamin

KISSING COUSINS, Rachel and JACOB produced the only romantic KISS reported in the BIBLE. Lovers in the SONG OF SONGS talked a good kiss, but the Bible actually reports Jacob puckering up: "Jacob kissed Rachel, and he wept aloud" (Genesis 29:11).

Jacob worked seven years for Rachel's father, LABAN, as a BRIDE fee—the price he had to pay to marry Rachel. Laban switched brides on the WEDDING night, with the help of a VEIL. And Jacob woke up with Rachel's older and apparently homelier sister, LEAH. But he got to marry Rachel a week later, after promising to

PUCKERING UP, Jacob kisses his cousin and future wife, Rachel.

work for Laban another seven years.

Rachel and Leah, along with their two slave maids acting as surrogate mothers, produced 12 sons whose descendants became the 12 TRIBES OF ISRAEL. Rachel died giving BIRTH to Jacob's twelfth son, BENJAMIN.

RAHAB

(RAY hab)

1400s or 1200s BC

Two spies left the Israelite camp. . .and went to Jericho, where they decided to spend the night at the house of a prostitute named Rahab. Joshua 2:1 CEV

- Jericho prostitute

SCOUTING THEIR FIRST TARGET in the PROM-ISED LAND—the border town of JERICHO—two Jewish SPIES spent the night with a hooker named Rahab.

The BIBLE doesn't answer the obvious question of why a hooker. Scholars tossing the gents the benefit of the doubt suggest it was a good place for them to blend in as strangers passing through. Others wonder if it was under the covers that they blew their cover. Someone found out they were Jewish spies and then reported them to the king.

By this time the JEWS were legendary for their military prowess. Rahab bet on them. She hid the spies on her ROOF, under piles of drying FLAX stalks. Then she helped them escape over the walls and pointed the king's men in the wrong direction.

For this, the Jews spared her and her FAMILY when Jericho fell.

She's listed in the family tree of Jesus as the mother of BOAZ, the BETHLEHEM farmer who married RUTH. If it's the same Rahab, that would have made her King DAVID's great-great-grandmother.

RAIN

You drench the plowed ground with rain, melting the clods and leveling the ridges. You soften the earth with showers and bless its abundant crops. Psalm 65:10

FOR FARMERS AND HERDERS in what is now ISRAEL, rain could mean the difference between life and DEATH.

During long DROUGHTS, JEWS sometimes moved to the drought-resistant NILE RIVER Valley in EGYPT. That's how they ended up enslaved there; JACOB had moved his entire extended FAMILY to the Nile Delta in Egypt's northland.

Israel gets most of its rain during the winter months: November through February—7 drops of every 10.

Rainfall amounts vary remarkably from one area of the country to the next because the landscape varies that much. Israel's Martian-like badlands in the south can get just an inch (25 mm) a year, while the fertile northland of GALILEE soaks itself in about 44 inches (1,120 mm). That's about what Kansans get in the fertile southeast part of the state, where WHEAT reigns.

RAINBOW

"I have placed my rainbow in the clouds. It is the sign of my covenant with you. . . . Never again will the floodwaters destroy all life." Genesis 9:13, 15

AFTER GOD SENT A FLOOD to wipe out civilization, he promised NOAH that he'd never do that again—at least not with WATER.

GOD signed the CONTRACT with a rainbow in the sky.

Thousands of years later, PROPHETS and preachers of doom began warning of an opposite approach to humanity's annihilation: "Fire will destroy everything. . . . God will judge the earth and everything in it" (2 Peter 3:10 NIrv).

RAISIN CAKES

"The people of Israel. . .love to offer raisin cakes to Baal and eat them." Hosea 3:1 NIRV

- Dried grapes pressed into patties

RAISINS squeezed into patties were a tasty, nourishing snack. They traveled well, too. That may be why people sometimes took them to pagan shrines and offered them as food to the GODS. PROPHETS condemned the JEWS for doing that.

RAM

Abraham looked up and saw a ram caught by its horns in a thicket. So he took the ram and sacrificed it as a burnt offering in place of his son. Genesis 22:13

- Male sheep

JEWS SACRIFICED RAMS, along with GOATS and CATTLE. Jewish refugees on the EXODUS out of EGYPT used rams' skin for the tent WORSHIP center. The JEWS also used ram horns, called shofars, like TRUMPETS to call the people to worship or to signal SOLDIERS on the battlefield.

RAMAH
Map 1 C5

(RAY mah)

Samuel went home to Ramah. 1 Samuel 15:34

- Samuel's hometown
- Where Rachel died in childbirth

HALF A DOZEN TOWNS in the BIBLE are called Ramah. The one that shows up most was a border town often caught in a tug of war between the northern Jewish nation of ISRAEL and the southern Jewish nation of JUDAH. Now called er-Ram, Ramah was in the tribal area of BENJAMIN near Judah's border. It was about five miles (8 km) north of JERUSALEM.

RAMESES II

(RAM uh sees)

Ruled 1279–1212 BC

Moses was eighty years old, and Aaron was eighty-three when they made their demands to Pharaoh. Exodus 7:7

- King of Egypt
- Possible pharaoh Moses argued with

THE BIBLE DOESN'T NAME the stubborn Egyptian king MOSES had to hammer with 10 plagues before the king would free the Jews. It just calls him by his title: PHARAOH. But some Bible scholars point to Rameses "the Great," a nickname he would have loved. He not only built monuments to himself throughout EGYPT, he had artisans chisel his name on monuments built for previous kings.

He was also famous for his building projects—a reputation especially suited to the kind of slave labor that the Jews provided. The BIBLE says they built "the

BIGGER THAN A GOD, the statue of Rameses II dwarfs the statue of Re, the sun god. Actually, both are spoken of as gods: Re the top god in this desert land, Rameses the son of Re.

R

cities of PITHOM and Rameses as supply centers for the king" (Exodus 1:11).

RAMESES, CITY OF

Map 2 H8

(RAM uh sees)

Egyptians made the Israelites their slaves. . . . They forced them to build the cities of Pithom and Rameses as supply centers for the king. Exodus 1:11

- Egyptian city built by Jewish slaves

NAMED AFTER A PHARAOH famed for his building projects, Rameses II (reigned 1279–1212 BC), the city of Rameses was built by Jewish slaves in the NILE RIVER Delta. That's where the Nile fans out into smaller streams that drain into the MEDITERRANEAN SEA.

The Delta, called GOSHEN in the BIBLE, was the fertile pastureland where the JEWS had settled. An earlier PHARAOH had invited JACOB to move his FAMILY down there to weather out the DROUGHT beside the river that never runs dry. But a later pharaoh enslaved the Jews.

Guesses about where the city of Rameses was include what are now the cities of Khatana-Qantir and San el-Hagar.

RAMOTH-GILEAD

Map 1 F4

(RAY moth GILL ee uhd)

The LORD said, "Who can entice Ahab to go into battle against Ramoth-gilead so he can be killed?" 1 Kings 22:20

- Jewish city of refuge
- Ahab died trying to recapture it
- Where Elisha anointed Jehu king

ACCUSED MURDERERS could flee to Ramoth-Gilead for protection from vengeful relatives of the victim. There, in a CITY OF REFUGE of Israel, they would get a trial.

The city was east of the JORDAN RIVER, somewhere near the border of SYRIA and Jordan. But in Bible times, the territory belonged to Israel—the tribe of GAD.

It was a bad news town for King AHAB's FAMILY. He died trying to take it back from Syria. It also marked the end of his family dynasty, because there is where ELISHA ANOINTED JEHU as Israel's next KING. Jehu, a military leader, then launched a coup and murdered Ahab's son, King JORAM.

RAM'S HORN

"When you hear the priests give one long blast on the rams' horns, have all the people shout as loud as they can. Then the walls of the town [Jericho] will collapse." Joshua 6:5

- Used as a trumpet

HORNS OF A MALE SHEEP were used as containers to hold OLIVE OIL or to reinforce wood bows, giving them more power. But they're best known for making noise.

Shofars—their HEBREW name—were used to call JEWS to WORSHIP or to give SOLDIERS direction in battle. They usually project a high-pitched sound, like a squeak amplified by a microphone.

The blast of a ram's horn announcing the arrival of GOD at MOUNT SINAI terrified the Jews during the EXODUS. The sound of ram horns at JERICHO is said to have helped bring down the city walls. Jews also used the horns in their religious rituals, calling the people to worship and praising God with MUSIC.

RAPE

If an engaged woman is raped out in the country, only the man will be put to death. Deuteronomy 22:25 CEV

SURPRISINGLY, BIBLE WRITERS said very little about punishment for rape. Jewish law condemned it as a capital offense, but only if the woman was engaged. It was also a death-penalty offense to have SEX with another man's WIFE, whether or not it was rape.

If a man had sex with an unengaged or unmarried woman, Jewish law said he had to pay her father

50 pieces of SILVER, marry her, and "never DIVORCE her" (Deuteronomy 22:29).

Crown prince AMNON, son of King DAVID, raped his own half sister, Tamar. No consequences for him. At least not until Tamar's full brother, ABSALOM, retaliated by orchestrating Amnon's MURDER. Tamar, considered damaged goods in her day, moved in with Absalom. There's no indication she ever got married.

RAZOR

> "Son of man, take a sharp sword and use it as a razor to shave your head and beard."
> Ezekiel 5:1

PEOPLE SHAVED with razors made of sharp metal such as IRON. They also used ROCKS that would sharpen to a fine edge, such as flint or volcanic glass known as obsidian.

JEWS who took a temporary or lifelong NAZIRITE vow of devotion to GOD were not allowed to cut their HAIR for the duration.

PAUL "shaved his head according to Jewish custom, marking the end of a vow" (Acts 18:18).

REBEKAH

(ruh BEC uh)

> 2000s BC
> *Isaac brought Rebekah into his mother Sarah's tent, and she became his wife. He loved her deeply, and she was a special comfort to him after the death of his mother.*
> Genesis 24:67

- Wife of Isaac
- Mother of Jacob, Esau

WHAT 40-YEAR-OLD ISAAC NEEDED after his mother died was a WIFE.

That's what ISAAC's father, ABRAHAM, decided. Abraham sent one of his most trusted SERVANTS on a wife-hunting expedition some 500 miles (800 km) north into what is now Turkey. That's where some of Abraham's relatives lived.

There the servant found Rebekah, "very beautiful and old enough to be married. . .still a VIRGIN" (Genesis 24:16). She was a second cousin of Isaac. Her father was Isaac's first cousin.

Rebekah agreed to marry the man she had never met. She gave BIRTH to twin sons, ESAU and JACOB. Esau

BLIND DATE FOR LIFE. On a matchmaker mission to find a wife for 40-year-old Isaac, a servant travels some 500 miles (800 km) north. There, in what is now Turkey, he finds Rebecca, greets her with gifts, and makes her an offer she can't refuse.

became Isaac's favorite son; Esau was an outdoorsman and hunter. Jacob stayed closer to camp, becoming his mother's favorite.

Rebekah convinced Jacob to trick elderly, nearly blind Isaac into giving him the BLESSING intended for Esau. When Esau found out about this, he vowed to kill Jacob. Rebekah sent Jacob off to her home, where he would meet his future wives: LEAH and RACHEL.

Rebekah never saw Jacob again.

RECONCILIATION

God was in Christ, reconciling the world to himself, no longer counting people's sins against them. 2 Corinthians 5:19

- Repairing a busted relationship

SIN BUILDS A WALL between GOD and people, the BIBLE teaches.

In OLD TESTAMENT times, God created the sacrificial system as a path to FORGIVENESS—a way to tear down the wall and restore the relationship.

Each ANIMAL sacrifice worked a bit like a heartfelt apology, repairing the damaged relationship—though on a spiritual level.

In addition to SACRIFICES offered throughout the year as needed, every autumn on the DAY OF ATONEMENT (*Yom Kippur*) observant JEWS spent the day FASTING—in repentance for sins they had committed during the year.

NEW TESTAMENT writers said the sacrificial death of Jesus replaced the need for animal sacrifices. His REPENTANCE reconciled repentant humans with a HOLY God. Writers also urged Christians to work hard at reconciliation with one another: "Do all that you can to live in PEACE with everyone" (Romans 12:18).

RED HEIFER

"Tell the people of Israel to bring you a red heifer, a perfect animal that has no defects. . . . The heifer must be burned."
Numbers 19:2, 5

- Ashes used for ritual cleansing

WHEN JEWS BECAME RITUALLY UNCLEAN— by touching a corpse, for example—they were no longer fit for WORSHIP. Before they could worship GOD again, they had to be ritually cleaned. The recipe for HOLY water to cleanse them included ASHES from a red cow.

RED SEA   Map 2 J9

God led them in a roundabout way through the wilderness toward the Red Sea.
Exodus 13:18

- Sea on Israel's southern border
- Made famous as water God parted for Jews

IT'S A SEA WITH AN ASTERISK in the BIBLE. When we read "Red Sea," the asterisk usually says it's *yam suf* in HEBREW, "sea of reeds."

That leaves many Bible experts wondering if MOSES led the Jewish refugees across a path through the Red Sea or through one of the REED-framed lakes north of there, such as Lake Timseh, Great Bitter Lake, or Little Bitter Lake.

On a map, the sea looks a bit like the long, skinny head of a bunny with two ears: the Gulf of Suez as the left ear and the Gulf of Aqaba on the right. Aqaba marks the southern tip of ISRAEL's boundary.

SOLOMON owned a fleet of trading ships that sailed out of a couple of port cities along the Gulf of Aqaba. The Bible simply calls the body of WATER we know as the Red Sea "sea." That's why most Bibles translate the word as "Red Sea." Every three years, Solomon's merchant sailors brought back exotic ANIMALS, GOLD, SILVER, and gems from African and Arabian countries. It was quite a chore, given the strong winds that sometime drove ships into the sharp coral reefs.

The Red Sea stretches about 1,450 miles (2,334 km) southward and averages about 150 miles (241 km) across.

WAS IT THE RED SEA Moses and the Exodus Jews crossed or one of the reed-laced lakes to the north? The Bible says God parted a body of water that most scholars translate "Sea of Reeds." Others translate it "Faraway Sea."

Parting which sea?
Guessing the route of Moses

Mediterranean Sea

Suez Canal

Rameses

EGYPT

Succoth
(Tel el Maskhuta)

Lake Timsah

Great Bitter Lake

Little Bitter Lake

Suez Canal

Red Sea

Gulf of Suez
(RED SEA)

N

R

REDEEMER, FAMILY

"I am your servant Ruth. . . . Spread the corner of your covering over me, for you are my family redeemer." Ruth 3:9

▪ Dead man's relative who married the widow

WIDOWS WERE IN BIG TROUBLE if they didn't have a man in their life—a FATHER, a HUSBAND, a son, or some other close relative who would take care of them.

A dead man's property didn't go to the WIFE. It went to his closest male relative, if he had one.

As a means of social security for widows, Jewish law said the dead man's brother should marry the WIDOW and give her a SON who could inherit her former husband's property. This was known as a LEVIRATE MARRIAGE.

It seems like JEWS extended that law to include other relatives. In the story of RUTH, her dead husband's brother had died, too. But she found another distant relative, a farmer named BOAZ. He married her. Their son, OBED, became the grandfather of King DAVID.

REDEMPTION

With his own blood—not the blood of goats and calves—he. . .secured our redemption forever. Hebrews 9:12

- Saving someone from injury or punishment

GOD IS A REDEEMER, as the BIBLE tells it. He redeemed—saved—his people many times, most notably by freeing them from Egyptian SLAVERY, with the cooperation of MOSES and the display of 10 plagues.

He also saved them from punishment for their sins. In the eyes of a HOLY God, SIN was a capital offense. GOD saved the JEWS from death by setting up a sacrificial system. This system allowed the Jews to sacrifice ANIMALS as substitutes for themselves. The animals died for the sins of people, so the people didn't have to die.

NEW TESTAMENT writers said the SACRIFICE of Jesus replaced animal sacrifices: "Christ made us right with God; he made us pure and holy, and he freed us from sin" (1 Corinthians 1:30).

REED

She got a basket made of papyrus reeds and waterproofed it with tar. . . . She put the baby [Moses] in the basket and laid it among the reeds along the bank of the Nile River. Exodus 2:3

GROWING ON THE BANKS of the NILE RIVER, these grassy reeds can reach 15 feet (5 m) high. Some reeds are PAPYRUS. People used the stems to weave baskets, to chop into ink pens, and to carve into FLUTES.

Inside the stem is a spongy tube of pith. Papermakers would slice the pith into long strips, crisscross them, and press them flat until they dried. This created papyrus sheets on which SCRIBES wrote.

ISRAEL's scribes often wrote on LEATHER: parchment made from skins of SHEEP and GOATS. There weren't many papyrus reeds in Israel.

REHOBOAM

(REE huh BOH uhm)

Ruled about 930–913 BC

Rehoboam spoke harshly to the people. . . . "My father [King Solomon] laid heavy burdens on you, but I'm going to make them even heavier!" 1 Kings 12:13–14

- Son of King Solomon
- King who caused Israel to split into two nations
- King of southern Jewish nation of Judah

JEWS NEEDED A BREAK after King SOLOMON died. They were fed up with Solomon's high taxes and his drafting of their young men to work on his massive building projects: the TEMPLE, PALACES, and fortified cities. So they asked for Solomon's son and successor to lighten up.

The new king's senior advisers suggested he grant the request. But instead, he took the advice of his young peers: Get tough.

In response, most of his country got gone.

The 10 northern tribes seceded from the union and formed their own country: ISRAEL, led by King JEROBOAM.

Down south, King Rehoboam was left with only the tribes of JUDAH and BENJAMIN, which united to become the country of Judah.

A few years later, EGYPT's King SHISHAK took advantage of the Jewish power struggle by invading and pillaging both nations. The story shows up in the BIBLE as well as in hieroglyphics from Shishak's reign, which decorated a temple wall at Karnak.

REHOBOTH

See Beersheba, Map 1 B7

(ree HOH both)

*He [Isaac] moved on. . .and dug another well.
. . . He named it Rehoboth. Genesis 26:22 TNIV*

- A well that Isaac dug

NOT A FIGHTER, ISAAC decided not to defend the first two wells his SERVANTS dug to provide water for his flocks. When intruders came and took them, he simply moved on, naming the first two wells Esek (Argument) and Sitnah (Hostility). No one claimed his third WELL, so he named it Rehoboth, which means "open space." The well was near BEERSHEBA, some 45 miles (72 km) south of JERUSALEM.

REPENTANCE

*"You were sorry and humbled yourself before
the LORD. . . . You tore your clothing in despair
and wept before me in repentance."*
2 Kings 22:19

- Expressing sorrow for doing something
wrong

REPENTANCE IS A CHANGING OF MIND that changes a person's behavior for the better.

In the BIBLE, it's not just an apology for doing something wrong. It's a promise to get it right the next time.

When people repent of SIN, they decide to start treating sin like a land mine: They walk away from it.

Instead, they walk toward GOD.

A soldier might think of it as an about-face: turn and march in the opposite direction.

RESTITUTION

*Zacchaeus stood before the Lord and said. . .
"If I have cheated people on their taxes, I
will give them back four times as much!"*
Luke 19:8

- Restoring something taken

STEALING AND CHEATING was against Jewish law. There was a price to pay for anyone caught doing it.

TAX collector ZACCHAEUS told Jesus he was sorry for overcharging his fellow JEWS. To prove that his REPENTANCE was real, he promised to give half his MONEY to the POOR—and to repay those he cheated with a tax refund four times what he overcharged them.

That quadruple refund tracks with one Jewish law. Penalty for stealing SHEEP: "four sheep for each sheep stolen" (Exodus 22:1). The rate was five to one for CATTLE.

The penalty for other kinds of stealing or cheating: "You must return what doesn't belong to you and pay the owner a fine of twenty percent" (Leviticus 6:4–5 CEV).

RESURRECTION

*If Christ wasn't raised from the dead, your
faith is a waste of time. . .and we Christians
are the most pitiful people on the planet.*
1 Corinthians 15:17, 19 AUTHOR'S PARAPHRASE

- Coming back from the dead

NO RESURRECTION, NO CHRISTIANITY.

That's how important the resurrection is to the CHRISTIAN religion, most Bible experts agree.

The apostle PAUL said if Jesus didn't rise from the dead and "all we get out of Christ is a little inspiration for a few short years, we're a pretty sorry lot" (1 Corinthians 15:19 MSG).

In the BIBLE, at least half a dozen people were raised from the dead. Prophets ELIJAH and ELISHA each raised a boy from the dead. Jesus raised three people.

Some of these folks may have been resuscitated from near-death: JAIRUS's daughter, for example. "The child isn't dead," Jesus said, "she's only asleep" (Mark 5:39).

Others were stone-cold dead. One was stinking dead: LAZARUS, four days ripe. "By this time there is a bad smell," his sister warned Jesus as he prepared to open the TOMB. "Lazarus has been in the tomb for four days" (John 11:39 NIRV).

Jesus was stone-cold dead, too, as the Bible tells it. Crucified on Friday and speared in the chest to confirm his death, he was placed in a tomb before sunset. Roman

R

guards protected his body from thieves through Sunday morning, when something terrified them—possibly the sight of a dead man walking. They ran away.

Later, when the DISCIPLES saw the resurrected Jesus, he had the opposite effect on them. They suddenly grew enough courage to overwhelm their common sense. Most of them had abandoned Jesus when he was arrested. They hid themselves in a locked HOUSE, fearing that the JEWS might arrest and crucify them, too. Common sense.

But after seeing Jesus alive again, they launched the Christian movement a few weeks later. They actually preached about Jesus in the very town that had crucified him—and in front of the same Jewish leaders who had orchestrated his death. Courage.

The resurrection that Jesus experienced is the same resurrection all believers can expect, according to Bible writers such as Paul.

"Just as Christ was raised from the dead by the glorious power of the FATHER. . .we will also be raised to life as he was" (Romans 6:4–5).

UP is the direction for this Christian martyr, executed by the sword. Paul wrote that if people aren't raised from the dead, there's no point to Christianity.

(ROO ben)

1800s BC

Leah became pregnant and gave birth to a son. She named him Reuben, for she said, "The LORD has noticed my misery."
Genesis 29:32

- Jacob's oldest son
- Talked brothers out of killing young Joseph
- Founder of Israel's tribe of Reuben

REUBEN WAS A PITY CHILD. God saw that JACOB didn't love LEAH, the woman he got tricked into marrying. So the BIBLE says GOD enabled Leah to give BIRTH to Jacob's first son.

Leah named her boy Reuben. That's HEBREW for "Look, a son!" It also sounds like the Hebrew for "He has seen my misery."

When Jacob's sons decided to kill their young brother JOSEPH out of jealousy, Reuben talked them out of it (Genesis 37:21).

Reuben also made the mistake of having SEX with one of his father's CONCUBINES, a lower-status WIFE. His father, Jacob, never forgave him of that. On his deathbed, Jacob said so: "You slept with my wife and disgraced my BED. And so you no longer deserve the place of honor [as oldest son and family leader]" (Genesis 49:4 CEV).

REUBEN, TRIBE OF

Map 1 F6

(ROO ben)

Moses gave the tribes of Gad, Reuben, and half of Manasseh the territory and towns that King Sihon the Amorite had ruled, as well as the territory and towns that King Og of Bashan had ruled. Numbers 32:33 CEV

TWO AND A HALF TRIBES of Israel's dozen never settled in what is now ISRAEL. GAD, Reuben, and half the tribe of MANASSEH settled in what is now western Jordan and southern Syria. The reason: location. The tribes had lots of livestock. And the land east of the JORDAN RIVER was "ideally suited for their flocks and herds" (Numbers 32:1).

REVELATION

I received my message from no human source, and no one taught me. Instead, I received it by direct revelation from Jesus Christ. Galatians 1:12

- Revealing a secret

GOD REVEALED his message to people in Bible times through PROPHETS and other leaders, such as APOSTLES like PAUL.

REVELATION, the last book in the Bible, reports a series of startling visions a man named John says he saw. Some students of the Bible say John saw the end of time and the beginning of eternity. Others say most of his visions describe persecutions during his own turbulent century.

411

Famous sound bite: "I am the Alpha and the Omega—the beginning and the end," says the Lord God. Revelation 1:8

LIFTED TO HEAVEN IN A VISION, a man named JOHN finds himself in GOD's THRONE room. He watches as someone whose description matches Jesus breaks seven SEALS on a SCROLL. Each snapping seal unleashes tragedy on earth. It's just the beginning of the horrors John will witness. But in the end, John says he sees God's people living happily in HEAVEN—forever.

- Writer: "This letter is from John" (Revelation 1:4). But which John? Most early church writers said it was Jesus' disciple. Others said it was another John, partly because he mentions "the twelve apostles of the Lamb" (Revelation 21:14) as though he's not one of them.
- Time: Possibly about AD 95.
- Location: John writes "exiled to the island of Patmos for preaching the word of God" (Revelation 1:9). That's about 40 miles (64 km) off Turkey's west coast.

BIG SCENES

Seven letters from Jesus. Like a secretary taking dictation, John transcribes Jesus' short notes to seven churches on Turkey's west coast. Jesus commends most for their FAITH, but he criticizes most for various lapses in judgment, such as tolerating HERESY and IMMORALITY within the CHURCH. Some scholars say the LETTERS are intended as an evaluation tool for all churches. In the BIBLE, "SEVEN" often symbolizes completion—as in the complete CHRISTIAN movement. God rested on the seventh day after completing CREATION. *Revelation 1–3*

Seven seals of doom. Jesus prepares to open a scroll, perhaps a symbol of God's message to humans. The scroll is sealed with seven plugs of hardened clay or wax. As Jesus breaks each seal, disasters strike the earth. Four horsemen of the apocalypse bring WAR, famine, and DEATH. Christians are martyred. EARTHQUAKES and other disasters devastate the planet. Some scholars read

the future into these terrors. Others say it's a history report: Rome's decimation of the Jewish homeland and JERUSALEM in AD 70. *Revelation 4–7*

Seven trumpets of doom. As God's scroll is rolled open, seven ANGELS blow horns. Each horn introduces a disaster, including HAIL, fire, and pollution. A third of all life on the planet dies. That "third," many scholars say, represents just "partial DESTRUCTION" instead of a literal third of all life. *Revelation 8–11*

Tag team beasts. A sea beast and a land beast—possibly symbols of nasty rulers—take control of the world. (See BEASTS OF REVELATION, MARK OF THE BEAST.) *Revelation 13*

Seven final horrors. John watches as seven angels dump seven BOWLS of God's punishment on the earth: fatal skin sores, a bloody sea, bloody rivers, solar blast, darkness, DROUGHT, earthquakes. *Revelation 15–16*

Judgment Day. With SATAN's forces in control of the earth, Jesus rides to HUMANITY's rescue. The tag team beasts get pitched into a LAKE OF FIRE, along with Satan and all his followers. *Revelation 19*

Heaven at last. John sees NEW JERUSALEM, perhaps his name for heaven—for it certainly sounds like PARADISE. John says there are no more tears in New Jerusalem. No death, either. God's people are living with God in this city laced in golden streets and framed by walls and gates of gemstones. Many Bible experts say these probably aren't literal descriptions but merely John's attempt to describe the indescribable in a way that would get his main point across: Heaven is wow wonderful. *Revelation 21–22*

REVENGE

Dear friends, don't try to get even. Let God take revenge. In the Scriptures the Lord says, "I am the one to take revenge and pay them back." Romans 12:19 CEV

PAYBACK was an itch. People in Bible times tended to scratch it with too much gusto. That's why the LAW OF MOSES and the Babylonian CODE OF HAMMURABI, a king in what is now Iraq, both agreed that payment should be limited.

Moses: "Punishment must match the injury: a life for a life, an eye for an eye, a tooth for a tooth" (Exodus 21:23–24).

Hammurabi: "If a man put out the eye of another man, his eye shall be put out" (Law 196).

Elsewhere, however, Bible writers such as MOSES and PAUL advised people not to take the law into their own hands. Revenge, they argued, is best left to GOD. Justice is a line item in his job description.

RHODA

(ROH duh)

First century AD

Peter knocked on the gate, and a servant named Rhoda came to answer. When she heard Peter's voice, she was too excited to open the gate. Acts 12:13–14 CEV

▪ Household servant in Jerusalem

WHEN AN ANGEL freed PETER from a Jerusalem PRISON, he knocked at the home of JOHN MARK's mother, where Christians were praying for his release. Rhoda answered the door. But when she saw the group's answer to PRAYER standing in front of her, she was so excited that she left him standing there; she ran to tell the others he was free. They didn't believe it until they saw Peter for themselves.

RIDDLE

Samson said to them, "Let me tell you a riddle. . . . Out of the one who eats came something to eat; out of the strong came something sweet." Judges 14:12, 14

▪ A saying with a hidden meaning

A PARTY GAME that tested a person's wit, riddles were a popular form of entertainment in Bible times. SAMSON bet his Philistine WEDDING guests they couldn't solve his riddle. But they threatened his BRIDE into nagging the answer out of him. He had crafted his riddle "out of the eater comes something to eat" after seeing a

honeycomb in the carcass of a lion.

"What is sweeter than honey?" the guests asked Samson. "What is stronger than a lion?" (Judges 14:18).

Their answer managed to put the skids on Samson's marriage and launched his one-man WAR against the PHILISTINES. He didn't appreciate his WIFE betraying him by revealing the secret.

RIGHTEOUSNESS

Abram believed the LORD, and the LORD counted him as righteous because of his faith. Genesis 15:6

▪ In a right relationship with God

RIGHTEOUS PEOPLE are GOD's kind of people, as the BIBLE tells it.

They'll make mistakes from time to time, but for the most part they look and act like citizens of THE KINGDOM OF GOD. They trust him. And they do what they believe he would want them to do: treat others with respect, seek justice for those who have been exploited, and help those who can't help themselves.

RING

"I saw Rebekah coming out with her water jug. . . . I put the ring on her nose." Genesis 24:45, 47

▪ Jewelry worn on fingers, ears, and nose

WIFE-HUNTING FOR 40-YEAR-OLD ISAAC, a household SERVANT sent by Isaac's father ABRAHAM found what he believed would be a wonderful match: a hardworking woman named REBEKAH.

The servant proposed marriage on behalf of Isaac, offering Rebekah and her father GOLD and jewels, including a nose ring. People in Bible times wore rings much like people do today.

Kings and many other people wore signet rings that worked like a stamp. They would press the unique design of the ring into a plug of soft clay or wax that

R

sealed closed a LETTER. The design on the plug let the person getting the letter know who the letter came from.

ESTHER's husband, King XERXES, gave his signet ring to his top official to act on his behalf (Esther 3:10).

RIVER OF LIFE

The angel showed me a river with the water of life, clear as crystal, flowing from the throne of God and of the Lamb.
Revelation 22:1

- Celestial river in John's vision of New Jerusalem

TOURING NEW JERUSALEM in a VISION, JOHN said he saw a crystal-clear river flowing from God's THRONE and then down the city's main street. It watered trees of life, which grew leaves "used for MEDICINE to heal the nations" (Revelation 22:2). Some Christians say this is a literal river that will flow from a NEW JERUSALEM God creates for earth. Others say the river is a symbol that GOD is the source of all life, in HEAVEN and on earth.

ROAD

"Let us pass through your country. We'll stay on the main road." Moses to king of Heshbon, in what is now Jordan. Deuteronomy 2:27 NIrV

ROMANS BUILT A STONE-PAVED highway system throughout the empire—an estimated 50,000 miles (80,000 km) of paved roads from SPAIN in the west to Iraq in the east.

They did it for one main reason: so their armies could get to where they needed to go as quickly as possible. They didn't need their wagons and war machines getting stuck in the mud somewhere in the middle of a WAR.

Before then, most roads were little more than dirt paths or dry riverbeds called *wadis* (WAH dees). Flash

THE RIVER OF LIFE flows from the throne of God, in John's vision of New Jerusalem—a place many say is another name for heaven.

floods were a danger in dry riverbeds. A storm upstream could unleash a gully washer, surprising travelers walking in the sunshine miles downstream.

See also KING'S HIGHWAY.

ROMANS BUILT ROADS TO LAST. Some are 2,000 years old and counting. They built the roads partly so their army could move throughout the empire as needed—even when rain churns dirt trails into mud bogs that swallow wagons.

ROBBERY

Don't rob the poor just because you can.
Proverbs 22:22

ONE OF THE 10 COMMANDMENTS—the bedrock fundamentals of Jewish law—prohibits robbery: "You must not steal" (Exodus 20:15).

Perhaps the most famous robbery in the BIBLE shows up in the PARABLE Jesus told about a Jew getting mugged on a daylong walk through the badlands between JERICHO and JERUSALEM. A good SAMARITAN helped him.

Highway robbery was all-too-common in the thinly populated Middle East. For that reason, many people preferred to TRAVEL in caravans or with other large groups. JEWS often traveled that way when they made PILGRIMAGES to Jerusalem to celebrate religious festivals such as PASSOVER.

Not all robbery that Bible writers condemned was of the illegal kind. Some thieves were simply the rich and powerful taking advantage of laws they wrote, which allowed them to exploit the not-so-rich.

ROBE

Jacob loved Joseph more than any of his other children. . . . So one day Jacob had a special gift made for Joseph—a beautiful robe. Genesis 37:3

MEN AND WOMEN wore long-sleeved, ankle-length robes as outer CLOTHING. Robes covered their undergarments, such as a shirt-like tunic and a cloth wrapped around their hips and thighs.

LINEN was the preferred fabric: strong, dirt resistant, quick-drying. It was also lightweight and cool in the hot Middle East. Linen was woven from the fibers of FLAX, the plant whose seeds produce linseed oil.

Others wore robes woven from wool, cotton, and animal hair such as CAMEL—a tad scratchy: "John's clothes were woven from coarse camel hair, and he wore a leather BELT around his waist" (Matthew 3:4).

The BIBLE's most famous robe was the one soldiers put on Jesus to humiliate him: "They dressed him in a purple robe, and they wove thorn branches into a CROWN and put it on his head. Then they saluted him and taunted, 'Hail! King of the Jews!' " (Mark 15:17–18).

ROCKS

"A man or woman who is a medium or a fortune-teller must be put to death. You must stone them to death." Leviticus 20:27 NCV

R

STONING SOMEONE TO DEATH was a popular form of execution in Bible times for one good reason: There are lots of rocks in the Middle East.

That's also why rocks show up so often in Bible stories:

Moses struck a rock "and WATER gushed out" (Exodus 17:6).

Jesus gave one of his DISCIPLES—SIMON—a new NAME: PETER. It means "rock." Jesus explained: "Upon this rock I will build my CHURCH" (Matthew 16:18). Later, Peter preached a sermon in JERUSALEM that launched the CHRISTIAN movement, converting 3,000 JEWS.

ROD, SHEPHERD'S

Even when I walk through the darkest valley, I will not be afraid, for you are close beside me. Your rod and your staff protect and comfort me. Psalm 23:4

- A walking stick

LIKE MANY PEOPLE WHO WALKED A LOT, shepherds often carried walking sticks they sometimes called a rod.

The rod doubled as a weapon, a bit like a baseball bat someone might keep in the house, just in case a varmint comes calling—four-legged or two-legged.

Shepherds used the rod to beat off predators or to gently nudge their straying SHEEP back toward the safety of the flock.

ROMANS, LETTER OF

Famous sound bite: All have sinned and fall short of the glory of God. Romans 3:23 TNIV

PAUL HOPED TO PASS THROUGH ROME on his way to SPAIN—the Roman Empire's western frontier. He also hoped the Christians in ROME would help fund the mission trip. So he wrote this letter to them to introduce himself and his beliefs. What he produced

MORE FOR TAPPING than clubbing, the rod of this Syrian shepherd seems like the right size for gently nudging sheep. That's what shepherds do when sheep are in danger of nibbling their way into trouble.

was CHRISTIANITY's oldest surviving statement of beliefs, which reads a bit like Christianity 101.

- Writer: Paul, dictating to "Tertius, who wrote down this letter" (Romans 16:22 TNIV).
- Time: About AD 57, near the end of his last missionary trip.
- Location: Paul is somewhere on the road to Jerusalem—perhaps in Turkey or Greece. He addresses the letter to Christians in Rome.

BIG SCENES

Debating atheists. PAUL implies that CREATION is the strongest argument for the existence of GOD: "Ever since the world was created, people have seen the earth and sky. Through everything God made, they can clearly see his invisible qualities—his eternal power and divine nature. So they have no excuse for not knowing God" (Romans 1:20). *Romans 1*

416

Why Jesus died. SIN is a capital offense in the eyes of a HOLY God. It's such a serious matter and so damaging to people that it requires the death penalty. In OLD TESTAMENT times, God allowed JEWS to substitute ANIMALS for themselves—to SACRIFICE animals to atone for sin. But when he introduced SALVATION to the rest of the world, he sent Jesus as a once-and-for-all sacrifice. "God presented Jesus as the sacrifice for sin. People are made right with God when they believe that Jesus sacrificed his life, shedding his BLOOD" (Romans 3:25). *Romans 3*

How to beat sin. "I am all too human, a slave to sin," Paul writes, perhaps talking about his life before becoming a CHRISTIAN. "I want to do what is right, but I don't do it. Instead, I do what I hate. . . . Who will free me from this life that is dominated by sin and DEATH? Thank God! The answer is in JESUS CHRIST our LORD." *Romans 6–7*

How to act like a Christian. Let God bring out the best in you, Paul writes. "The best," he says, looks like this:

- love each other
- work hard
- be patient
- help people in need
- don't take REVENGE
- submit to government officials
- accept new Christians the way they are, just as Christ accepted you. *Romans 12–15*

ROMAN EMPIRE

Roman emperor, Augustus, decreed that a census should be taken throughout the Roman Empire. Luke 2:1

- Land around the Mediterranean Sea
- Setting for the New Testament

STARTING SMALL—as seven villages on seven hills in what is now ROME—the Roman Empire eventually pushed out of Italy and swallowed up most of the Mediterranean coastland, from SPAIN in the west to Israel in the east.

Oddly enough, JEWS invited the Romans to ISRAEL.

Two brothers fighting for INHERITANCE rights to the Jewish throne each appealed to Rome for support, sending delegations to General Pompey in DAMASCUS in 63 BC.

Mistake.

Romans came. But they wouldn't leave.

They took over. In time, they named an Arab man king of the Jews: HEROD THE GREAT. His family had converted to the Jewish religion, threatened with the alternative: execution. So he was at least token Jewish by faith. But racially, he was an Arab. His family heritage tracked back to EDOM, in what is now Jordan.

In NEW TESTAMENT times, Rome was ruled by dictators called emperors. The empire had started as a republic, a bit like the United States—led by senators who supposedly represented the citizens. But by the time Jesus was born, roughly 6 BC, the senate had relinquished most of its power to Caesar AUGUSTUS. That launched almost 500 years of Roman rule by dictators.

Romans portrayed themselves as legit rulers. They won their territories only through "just wars," according to Roman politician Cicero (106 BC–43 BC), who lived during Rome's expansion into Israel.

Jews begged to differ. In AD 66, they rebelled against a century of Roman occupation, driving out the token Roman forces stationed there. Rome came back with a vengeance, overwhelming the Jewish defenders, and in AD 70 destroying JERUSALEM and leveling the TEMPLE—which has never been rebuilt.

Jews weren't the only ones on the outs with Rome. So were Christians. Rome outlawed CHRISTIANITY. For one reason, Christians seemed to bring out the worst in Jews, provoking Jews to react with mob violence. Also, NERO had apparently blamed Christians for starting the fire that burned down two-thirds of the capital city of Rome in AD 64. After that, Christians were fair game for arena GAMES.

Roman historian Tacitus (AD 56–120) described the PERSECUTION of Christians this way during the reign of Nero (AD 54–68):

> *Besides being put to death they [Christians] were made to serve as objects of amusement; they were dressed in the hides of beasts and torn to death by dogs. Others were crucified. Others were set on fire to serve to light the night when*

R

daylight ended. Nero had thrown open his grounds for the display, and was putting on a show in the circus.

Romans targeted Christians in waves, depending on who was emperor at the time. Some ignored them. Some were nasty to them. Notable nasties included Domitian (reigned AD 81–96) and Trajan (reigned AD 98–117).

Persecution ended when Emperor Constantine (reigned AD 306–337) not only legalized Christianity in AD 313, but declared it the empire's main religion. That's when Christians started building churches, such as:

- the Church of the Nativity, marking the birthplace of Jesus in BETHLEHEM
- the Church of the Holy Sepulchre in Jerusalem, marking the location of Jesus' execution and BURIAL

Over a century later, the Roman Empire collapsed under a tsunami of payback-minded tribal invaders from what is now Germany. The Germans deposed the last Roman Emperor in AD 476: Romulus Augustus—double-dipped in ironic names. Romulus was the legendary founder of Rome. Augustus was Rome's first emperor.

Rome had run full circle.

ROMAN EMPIRE: BIG EVENTS

753 BC	City of Rome founded by Romulus (Roman legend)
509 BC	Became senate-governed republic
241 BC	Added Sicily to empire
201 BC	Added much of Spain
146 BC	Added Greece, North Africa
133 BC	Added parts of Turkey, Syria
63 BC	Added Israel
44 BC	Julius Caesar assassinated after becoming dictator
31 BC	Civil war ended with Augustus defeating Mark Antony
27 BC	Republic ended; Augustus ruled as emperor dictator
AD 476	Last emperor deposed; empire collapsed

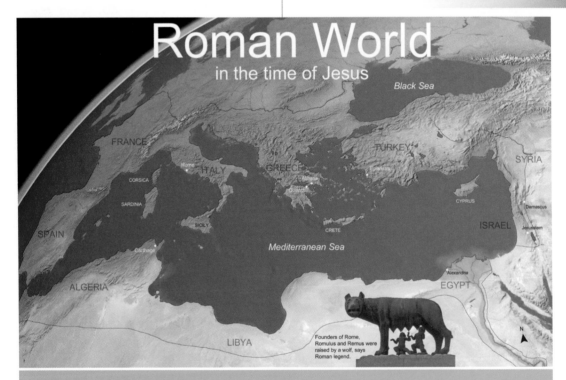

Roman World
in the time of Jesus

Founders of Rome, Romulus and Remus were raised by a wolf, says Roman legend.

ROME'S EMPIRE framed the Mediterranean Sea, which stretches about the distance of New York City to Spokane, some 2,200 miles (3,540 km).

ROME, from a pope's eye-view in the dome of St. Peter's Basilica in the Vatican. This is the church from which the pope sometimes greets crowds gathered below in St. Peter's square.

ROME   Map 2 D4

> When we arrived in Rome, Paul was permitted to have his own private lodging, though he was guarded by a soldier.
> Acts 28:16

- Capital of Roman Empire
- Where Paul, Peter were probably executed

THE ROMAN EMPIRE'S PRIMO CITY was home to an estimated one million souls when PAUL wrote his most famous LETTER to Christians there: the NEW TESTAMENT book of ROMANS.

Paul had never been to Rome, but he hoped to visit. So he wrote to introduce himself and his beliefs.

There were at least three synagogues in Rome at the time. Some of the JEWS there heard the story about Jesus and believed he was the MESSIAH. They apparently got into arguments with other Jews, because in AD 49 Emperor CLAUDIUS expelled all Jews from the city. Among them: Aquila and Priscilla, the couple who moved to CORINTH and ended up working with Paul. They made and repaired tents and apparently helped Paul start the Corinthian CHURCH.

Paul was arrested in JERUSALEM and sent to Rome for trial after his presence in the TEMPLE provoked the Jews to riot. The book of ACTS ends with a cliffhanger: Paul under arrest in Rome awaiting trial. No word about the outcome.

Many Bible experts speculate that Paul was released only to get arrested again and sent back to Rome. This time, as the theory goes, he was executed after Emperor NERO accused Christians of starting the fire in AD 64 that destroyed two-thirds of Rome.

Early church writers say the Romans executed Paul and PETER in Rome.

Today Rome hosts Vatican City, world headquarters of the Roman Catholic Church. More than four million people visit the Vatican each year.

R

ROOF

AN ANCIENT VERSION OF TODAY'S DECK or a porch, the roof was a place to relax, work on household chores, or sleep in the open air on a hot night.

Most roofs were flat. Builders often started with wooden beams. On top of the beams they would lay a thick mesh of branches. Then they coated the branches with a thick layer of clay, which they packed down with a stone roller.

By law, JEWS had to build a wall around the perimeter, to help keep people from falling off.

The roof was the setting for several famous Bible stories:

- RAHAB the Jericho PROSTITUTE hid two Jewish SPIES under a pile of FLAX she was drying on her roof (Joshua 2:6).
- King DAVID was taking a stroll on his roof when he caught sight of BATHSHEBA bathing below (2 Samuel 11:2).
- Four men dug a hole through a roof in CAPERNAUM so they could bypass the crowd and lower their sick friend to Jesus below; Jesus healed the man (Mark 2:1–12).

see painting, page 223

ROPE

ROPE MAKERS used everything from grass to animal hair when they wove ropes together. They also used fibers from plants such as reeds, PALM TREES, and flax. Some used LEATHER.

Ropes might be as thin as pencil lead or as thick as a man's arm.

People used ropes to:

TO MAKE ROPE, people spun plant fibers into strings, wove the strings into cords, and then wove the cords together.

- secure a TENT (Exodus 35:18)
- escape over a city wall (Joshua 2:15)
- lower workers into a mine (Job 28:4)
- whip people to drive them off (John 2:15)
- lower a BUCKET into a well (John 4:11)

RUBY

BIBLE TRANSLATORS GOT IT WRONG when they said SOLOMON, JOB, and ISAIAH wrote about rubies. So say many other Bible experts.

They say the HEBREW word *peninim*, translated "rubies," may mean something other than the deep red gemstone. Perhaps pearls. Or some other treasure. The reason: No rubies have yet been found among the ruins of Bible lands that date to OLD TESTAMENT times. The oldest is from the 200s BC, between the time of the Old and New Testament stories.

One counterpoint: keep looking. Another counterpoint: people would tend not to lose gems.

1100s BC

Ruth replied [to Naomi], "Don't try to make me leave you and go back. Where you go I'll go. Where you stay I'll stay. Your people will be my people. Your God will be my God."
Ruth 1:16 NIrV

- King David's great-grandmother
- Arab from Jordan

THE MOTHER OF ISRAEL'S GREATEST DYNASTY of KINGS was an Arab.

Ruth lived in MOAB, in what is now Jordan—an Arab country east of ISRAEL. She married a Jewish immigrant from BETHLEHEM. He and his FAMILY had moved there to escape a lingering drought in their homeland.

Tragically, he and his brother and his father died—leaving three widows. The elderly matriarch, NAOMI, decided to make the long trip home: about 100 miles (160 km). She hoped some Bethlehem relative would take her in.

Naomi told her daughters-in-law to go back to their fathers and get remarried.

Ruth refused. She insisted on staying with Naomi.

Destitute in Bethlehem with Naomi, Ruth found herself scrounging for HARVEST leftovers in the BARLEY fields of a man named BOAZ. He respected her devotion to old Naomi, and he told his harvesters to leave her some extra barley.

When Naomi found out about this, she morphed into Matchmaker Mode. She realized that Boaz was a distant relative and a potential "FAMILY REDEEMER" (Ruth 3:9). That's a relative who agrees to marry a WIDOW so she might have a SON to inherit her first husband's estate.

At Naomi's instruction, Ruth snuck under the covers of Boaz one night while he was camping out in his field, guarding his harvest. When he woke up, there was Ruth lying at his feet. Freshly bathed, scented with PERFUME, and dressed to entertain the eyeballs, Ruth proposed.

Boaz was one happy camper.

They had a son: OBED, father of JESSE and grandfather of King DAVID.

Famous sound bite: "Where you go I'll go. Where you stay I'll stay. Your people will be my people. Your God will be my God."
Ruth 1:16 NIrV

AN ARAB WIDOW from what is now Jordan, Ruth moves to BETHLEHEM with her widowed mother-in-law, NAOMI. There she meets and marries a Jewish farmer named BOAZ. They have a son who grows up to become the grandfather of ISRAEL's greatest dynasty of KINGS. The dynasty will start with King DAVID, and it will endure for more than 400 years.

- Writer: Unknown. Jewish tradition says the prophet Samuel wrote it.
- Time: Before Israel had a king, in the time of the heroic judges—perhaps 1100s BC
- Location: The story starts in Moab in what is now Jordan and ends in Bethlehem.

BIG SCENES

Back to Bethlehem. Naomi and her husband and two sons move from Bethlehem to MOAB to escape a DROUGHT. The sons marry, but all three men die. Naomi decides to go home to Bethlehem. One daughter-in-law goes with her: Ruth. *Ruth 1*

Ruth undercover. A wealthy farmer named Boaz respects Ruth's devotion to Naomi, and he lets her pick GRAIN from his BARLEY field at no cost. Naomi sees Boaz as husband material for Ruth. She tells Ruth to take a BATH, wear PERFUME, and put on her best clothes. When Boaz goes to sleep—outside protecting his HARVEST—Ruth is to crawl under the covers at his feet: "He will tell you what to do." When Boaz wakes up, pleasantly surprised, Ruth proposes. *Ruth 2–3*

It's a boy. Boaz, apparently an older man, is delighted to say, "I do." So he does. The couple has a son: OBED, father of JESSE and grandfather of King David. *Ruth 4*

R

SABBATH DAY

"You have six days each week for your ordinary work, but the seventh day must be a Sabbath day of complete rest, a holy day dedicated to the Lord." Exodus 31:15

- Day of rest and worship
- Observed from sunset Friday to sunset Saturday
- Sabbath in Hebrew is *Shabbat* (shuh BAHT): "Stop"

ONE OF THE 10 COMMANDMENTS—a short stack of laws that form the bedrock foundation on which all other Jewish laws are built—the Sabbath Day law requires JEWS to take a day off each week.

MOSES explained that Jews are to follow GOD's example. "For in six days the LORD made heaven and earth, but on the seventh day he stopped working and was refreshed" (Exodus 31:17).

Moses didn't define "work," other than to say, "You must not even light a fire in any of your homes on the Sabbath" (Exodus 35:3).

Jewish TEACHERS in Bible times added their view of what qualified as work. Jesus disagreed. When his DISCIPLES picked a snack of GRAIN while walking through a field on the Sabbath, Jesus' critics called it harvesting. And when Jesus healed the sick on the Sabbath, they called it practicing MEDICINE.

Jesus' comeback: "The Sabbath was made to meet the needs of people, and not people to meet the requirements of the Sabbath" (Mark 2:27).

SABBATH YEAR

"For six years plant your fields. . . . But the seventh year must be a sabbath for the land. The land must rest during it." Leviticus 25:3–4 NIrv

- A year not to plant crops

EVEN DIRT GETS A BREAK under GOD's law.

Every seventh year, Jewish farmers were to give their farmland a year to recover from six years of nourishing crops. No planting allowed. JEWS had to live off rations from the previous years and from any crops that might spring up on their own.

First-century Jewish historian, Josephus, reported that Julius CAESAR exempted Jews from taxes during the Sabbath year.

Some Jews in ISRAEL still observe the Sabbath year, most recently from September 2007–September 2008. Sabbath year next: 2014–15.

SACKCLOTH

Jacob tore his clothes, put on sackcloth and mourned for his son many days. Genesis 37:34 TNIV

- Rough burlap-like material
- Mourning attire

BLACK IS THE COLOR for MOURNING today. People wear black clothes at funerals and for other sad occasions. In Bible times, it wasn't about the COLOR of the CLOTHING. It was about the texture. People dressed in coarse, scratchy material often woven of CAMEL or GOAT hair—cheap fiber typically used to make GRAIN sacks.

SACRIFICES

"Build for me an altar made of earth, and offer your sacrifices to me—your burnt offerings and peace offerings, your sheep and goats, and your cattle." Exodus 20:24

- Animal and grain offerings presented to God
- Expressions of gratitude for blessings, regret for sin

THIS JEWISH GUIDEBOOK for how to WORSHIP God and live in PEACE with others starts with bad news for livestock.

LEVITICUS reports hundreds of laws and rituals GOD expects the JEWS to observe. But it starts with the most important ritual of all: ANIMAL sacrifice.

	NAME OF SACRIFICE	WHAT'S OFFERED	WHAT HAPPENS	REASON	FIND IT IN LEVITICUS
	BURNT	Rich people: bull* Others: sheep, goat Poor: dove or pigeon	The animal is cut up and burned on the altar.	Atones for sin and ritually cleans the worshiper	1:1–17 6:8–13
	GRAIN	Baked goods, roasted kernels	Priest burns some of it and keeps the rest as salary.	Thanks God for the harvest	2:1–16 6:14–23
	PEACE	Grain or livestock (sheep, goats, cattle)	Part of the offering is burned. Part goes to the priest as salary. Worshiper eats the rest with family and guests.	Thanks God for something noteworthy, such as birth of a child	3:1–17 7:11–36
	ACCIDENTAL SIN	Priest: bull Others: goat or female sheep	Priest burns the fat and keeps the meat as salary.	Purifies a person who sinned without meaning to.	4:1–5:13 6:24–30 16:3–22
	RESTITUTION (OR GUILT)	Ram (male sheep) or value of the ram, and value of property damaged plus 20 percent	Priest burns part of ram and keeps the rest along with the fine.	Makes restitution to God or a person. To God for desecration of something sacred. To a person for some wrongdoing.	5:14–6:7 7:1–7

All sacrificial animals must be free of disease or other obvious defects. Worshipers are often instructed to lay hands on the animal, to symbolically transfer their sins to the animal (see Leviticus 16:21). Some of the blood is poured on the altar, symbolizing spiritual cleansing of sin.

With detail fit for a butcher, Leviticus explains how to slice and dice SHEEP, GOATS, BULLS, and BIRDS and then how to burn the carcass parts on an ALTAR.

The first sacrifice Leviticus describes is called the burnt offering. In a sense, it's a sincere apology to God for SIN. The entire animal gets burned. With most other offerings, the worshiper gets to keep and eat part of the animal.

God explains why animals have to die for HUMANITY's sins.

In the eyes of a HOLY God, sin is a capital offense. But God says he will accept the death of animals as a substitute for humans.

"The life of each creature is in its blood. So I have given you the blood of animals to pay for your sin on the altar" (LEVITICUS 17:11 NIrv).

Killing an animal and burning it engages a wagon-load of senses:

- the sight of the animal's throat being cut
- the sound of its squeal
- the slippery touch of the BLOOD
- the barbecue aroma of burning meat

Each sense grips the soul in a graphic reminder that as far as God is concerned, sin is deadly serious.

NEW TESTAMENT writers introduced Jesus as the sacrifice to end all sacrifices: "JESUS CHRIST offered his body once and for all time" (Hebrews 10:10 NIrv). In fact, the Jewish system of animal sacrifices ended about 40 years later, when in AD 70 the Romans crushed a Jewish uprising by destroying the JERUSALEM Temple, which has never been rebuilt.

See also HUMAN SACRIFICE.

ANIMAL SACRIFICES were common throughout the Middle East in Bible times. Here, in a piece of ancient Roman art, a worshiper prepares to sacrifice a bull.

SADDUCEES

The Sadducees say there is no resurrection or angels or spirits, but the Pharisees believe in all of these. Acts 23:8

- One ancient branch of the Jewish religion
- From Hebrew word meaning "righteous ones"

JUST AS THERE ARE DIFFERENT GROUPS OF CHRISTIANS—such as Catholics, Baptists, and Methodists—there are different groups of JEWS, with distinctly different beliefs.

One group in NEW TESTAMENT times was the Sadducees. Now extinct, their heyday stretched over a couple of centuries—from the 100s BC until Romans destroyed the Jerusalem TEMPLE in AD 70.

The reason their fate was tied to the Temple is because their limited influence reached mainly to the Temple PRIESTS and a few wealthy families, according to Josephus, a first-century Jewish historian. With the Temple gone, the priests were out of a job, and the Sadducees slipped off history's page, into a footnote.

Key teachings of the Sadducees, as reported by Josephus and Bible writers:

- no life after DEATH
- no angels
- no need to observe manmade laws and TRADITIONS like the PHARISEES did.

They also encouraged students to aggressively challenge their TEACHERS instead of treating them like they're GOD's gift to intellectuals.

Though some Sadducees served on the top Jewish council, called the SANHEDRIN, Josephus says Sadducees weren't widely respected among average folks. But some scholars say that could merely mean they weren't widely respected by Josephus.

SAINTS

To all who are in Rome, beloved of God, called to be saints. Romans 1:7 NKJV

- A word describing followers of Jesus
- Greek, *hagioi*, "holy ones"

THERE'S A CHECKLIST FOR SAINTHOOD in the Catholic Church. Contenders who weren't martyred need to be credited with four posthumous healing MIRACLES from people praying to them.

Not so in Bible times. NEW TESTAMENT writers used the term to describe all Christians. Most modern Bible translations replace *saints* with phrases like "HOLY people" and GOD's "very own people."

Bible writers taught that people devoted to God were holy, not perfect, but sacred because they belonged to God.

SALAMIS   Map 3 K5

(SAL uh miss)

Barnabas and Saul were sent on their way by the Holy Spirit. They. . .sailed to Cyprus. They arrived at Salamis. There they preached God's word in the Jewish synagogues. Acts 13:4–5 NIrV

- Port on east coast of Cyprus
- First stop on Paul's first mission trip

PAUL'S FIRST STOP in his estimated 10,000 miles (16,000 km) of missionary journeys was the port city of Salamis, CYPRUS. PAUL, BARNABAS, and JOHN MARK preached their way across the island, traveling about 140 miles (225 km) from east coast to west coast. Afterward they sailed to Turkey.

SALOME

(suh LOH me)

First century AD

Mary Magdalene, Salome, and Mary the mother of James bought some spices to put on Jesus' body. Mark 16:1 CEV

1. FOLLOWER OF JESUS. Salome was one of several women who witnessed the CRUCIFIXION of Jesus, "watching from a distance" (Mark 15:40). She was also among the group of women who first saw the empty TOMB on Sunday morning.

2. DANCING FOR HEAD OF JOHN THE BAPTIST. A second Salome was HEROD ANTIPAS's stepdaughter. The BIBLE doesn't mention her by name. But first-century historian Josephus did. He confirms the Bible story that she danced so well for her stepfather's birthday that he granted her wish: the head of JOHN THE BAPTIST, who had insulted her mother, HERODIAS, by saying her marriage to Herod was INCEST (Matthew 14:1–12). By Jewish law, it was. She had DIVORCED her first husband, HEROD PHILIP, to marry her husband's brother.

HEAVY ON THE SALT, the Dead Sea is loaded with minerals. Some Israeli physicians recommend the water for certain skin conditions. Further south, an Israel mining company harvests minerals in evaporation beds.

SALT

"Have the qualities of salt among yourselves and live in peace with each other." Mark 9:50

WITH NO FRIDGES in the hot Middle East of Bible times, salt was an important preservative.

People got their best salt from salt mines. Not a good place to work. Romans sent slaves and prisoners there, which some writers described as a death sentence.

Jews got lower quality salt from the DEAD SEA.

S

STEPHEN M. MILLER'S ILLUSTRATED BIBLE DICTIONARY

They could chip it from the salt formations. Or they could simply scoop up some of the water and wait for it to evaporate, since the Dead Sea is roughly 25 percent salt, sometimes higher.

Bible writers used salt as a metaphor. Sometimes it meant preservation, as when Jesus told his DISCIPLES: "Be preservatives [salt] yourselves. Preserve the PEACE" (Mark 9:50 MSG). Other times it meant destruction, since a field salted by invaders wouldn't grow crops.

SALVATION

> Only Jesus has the power to save! His name is the only one in all the world that can save anyone. Acts 4:12 CEV
>
> ■ Rescue

ANYONE who comes to the rescue of someone else is a SAVIOR.

In the BIBLE, the person most likely to save is GOD. That's why JEWS praised him in PRAYERS and SONGS: "Save us, O God of our salvation!" (1 Chronicles 16:35).

In the OLD TESTAMENT, Jews were generally talking about salvation from their enemies. But in the NEW TESTAMENT, writers described Jesus as the savior who defeated the ultimate enemy: DEATH. "Everyone who believes in him will not perish but have ETERNAL LIFE" (John 3:16).

SAMARIA, CITY OF — Map 1 C5

> (suh MAIR ee uh)
>
> Omri bought the hill. . .for 150 pounds [68 kg] of silver. He built a city on it and called the city Samaria. 1 Kings 16:24
>
> ■ Capital of northern Jewish nation, Israel

NASTY KING AHAB—husband of nasty Queen JEZEBEL—inherited his dynasty and capital city from his father, OMRI.

Thinking like the soldier he was, Omri chose a great site for his capital: near a main ROAD but easy-

to-defend, sitting some 100 steep yards [91 m] above a valley.

Omri built the city of Samaria in about 885 BC. It lasted as long as the country did—about a century and a half. Assyrian invaders from what is now Iraq destroyed the city in 722 BC and deported most of the survivors.

The ruins lie in what is now the Arab city of Sebastiya, in the West Bank about 40 miles [64 km] north of JERUSALEM—a two-day walk.

SAMARIA, REGION OF — Map 1 D4

> (suh MAIR ee uh)
>
> The king of Assyria transported groups of people from Babylon. . .and resettled them in the towns of Samaria, replacing the people of Israel. 2 Kings 17:24
>
> ■ Area in central Israel

MANY JEWS HATED MIXED-RACE Samaritans who lived in a territory called Samaria—a plug of land in the middle of what is now ISRAEL.

The region stretched about 40 miles long, between GALILEE in the north and JUDEA with its capital of JERUSALEM in the south. Many JEWS refused to TRAVEL through this area. Instead, they took a long bypass around it.

Jesus was an exception to the rule. It was in Samaria that he taught a woman at a WELL about "living WATER" (John 4:10) that gives ETERNAL LIFE.

SAMARITANS

> (suh MAIR uh tons)
>
> The Samaritan woman, taken aback, asked, "How come you, a Jew, are asking me, a Samaritan woman, for a drink?" (Jews in those days wouldn't be caught dead talking to Samaritans.) John 4:9 MSG
>
> ■ Descendants of Iraqi settlers in Israel

A BIT LIKE EARLY AMERICAN SETTLERS driving out native Americans and taking their land,

Assyrian settlers from what is now Iraq did the same to the JEWS. ASSYRIA defeated the northern Jewish nation of ISRAEL, deported many survivors, and resettled the land with their own colonists.

The GENERATIONS that followed became known as Samaritans, after the name of the region: SAMARIA.

As the theory goes, many settlers married Jews still in the area. As a result, a Jewish-like religion developed. In time, Samaritans claimed to be descended from two of the Lost TRIBES OF ISRAEL—those named after Joseph's sons: MANASSEH and EPHRAIM. Jews begged to differ.

Samaritans had a few other ideas Jews didn't like:

- Short Bible. They considered only the first five books in the BIBLE as sacred—the Laws of MOSES.
- Edited Bible. They taught that the Jewish version of those five books had been edited to puff JERUSALEM as the place of WORSHIP. Jews countered by saying it was the Samaritans who had the edited Bible.
- Bypassing Jerusalem. Samaritans said MOUNT GERIZIM in Samaria was the sacred worship site, not Jerusalem.

A Samaritan starred in one of Jesus' most famous PARABLES. A "Good Samaritan" stopped to help a Jew who had been mugged—though two Jewish worship leaders had ignored the injured man, walking right past him (Luke 10:30–37). The parable was a lesson in how to be a good NEIGHBOR.

SAMSON

(SAM son)

About 1100–1050 BC

Samson fell in love with a woman named Delilah. Judges 16:4

- One of Israel's 12 heroes in the book of Judges
- Waged one-man war against Philistines
- Brought down by Delilah with scissors and a trim

IT'S HARD TO SAY ANYTHING NICE about Samson once you've read his story.

Everything the BIBLE says about him spins around the trouble he got into because of his attraction to three unsavory Philistine women: his BRIDE, a PROSTITUTE, and DELILAH—who cut him down to size by taking a little off the top.

Samson was born to an Israelite couple who thought they couldn't have CHILDREN. His parents—Manoah and his unidentified WIFE—lived in the hills of JUDEA in the tiny village of ZORAH. That's about 15 miles (24 km) west of JERUSALEM and a few miles from several Philistine villages on the coastal plain farther west.

An ANGEL appeared to Manoah's wife and told her she would have a son. Not just any son. "He will be dedicated to GOD as a NAZIRITE from birth. He will begin to rescue ISRAEL from the PHILISTINES" (Judges 13:5).

Nazirites were Hebrews who lived by unique rules, to show a devotion to God that was above and beyond the normal. There were three main rules:

- Don't eat GRAPES or drink WINE made from them.
- Don't go near a corpse—not even of a close relative.
- Don't cut your HAIR.

SAMSON'S WEAKNESS was the supposedly "gentler sex." He could kill a thousand Philistine warriors with the jawbone of a donkey. But one girlfriend could leave him looking dumber than the dumb critter—though nicely trimmed.

SAMSON'S SHORT MARRIAGE

Samson married a Philistine woman from a neighboring village 5 miles (8 km) west. But his honeymoon turned deadly. Samson bet his Philistine guests a change of clothes that they couldn't solve his RIDDLE about honey he found in the carcass of a lion: "Out of the one who eats came something to eat; out of the strong came something sweet" (Judges 14:14).

The guests threatened Samson's bride into nagging the answer out of him and telling them. Betrayed by his wife, Samson stormed off. He killed and stripped 30 Philistine men to pay his DEBT.

In his absence, the bride's father married his daughter off to the best man.

Livid about that, Samson burned Philistine fields and orchards. To retaliate, Philistines burned to death his ex-wife and father for starting the trouble.

Philistine soldiers launched a manhunt into Jewish territory. Judeans saw this invasion as the start of potentially worse consequences ahead. So they asked Samson to give himself up. In a rare selfless gesture, Samson agreed.

Bound with new ropes, Samson was turned over to the Philistines. Once in custody, however, he promptly broke free, picked up a DONKEY's jawbone, killed a thousand soldiers, and escaped.

DATE WITH A PROSTITUTE

Another woman generated the next scene in Samson's story. She was a prostitute in the Philistine coastal city of GAZA. When Samson came to her place of business, word of his arrival spread throughout the town.

Men surrounded the place and lay in wait, planning to kill Samson when he left in the morning, exhausted from SEX. But the surprise was on them. Samson left about midnight, energized. He tore off the city's massive front GATE—posts and all. Then he hauled it away on his shoulders. He lugged it some 40 miles (64 km) before setting it up on a hilltop in front of the Israelite village of HEBRON.

DELILAH, THE LOUSY GIRLFRIEND

Samson's most famous story begins with Delilah. He fell in love with her. But she loved MONEY more than him. Philistine leaders—probably from the five major Philistine cities—each promised to pay her 28 pounds

(12.7 kg) of SILVER if she coaxed out of him the secret of his strength. That was likely more than her weight in silver.

It took several days, but Delilah got him with this question, wrapped in guilt: "How can you tell me, 'I love you,' when you don't share your secrets with me?" (Judges 16:15).

"My hair has never been cut," Samson finally admitted, "for I was dedicated to God as a Nazirite from birth. If my head were shaved, my strength would leave me, and I would become as weak as anyone else" (Judges 16:17).

Samson took a nap. When he woke up, his clipped head lay on the lap of Delilah and his fate lay in the hands of Philistine soldiers she had called. They gouged out his eyes and led him to a PRISON mill where he ground GRAIN kernels into FLOUR.

For 20 years Samson had been on the Philistines' most wanted list. So they celebrated. With thousands of happy Philistines crowded into a temple, Samson was paraded in front of them. By this time his hair was growing back.

Samson asked the attendant leading him to let him rest by the support pillars, which in many temples were blocks of wood or stone piled on top of each another. Samson pushed against the columns, the temple collapsed, and he was crushed to death with more Philistines than he had killed in all the years before.

SAMSON'S LEGACY

The Bible doesn't say that God was orchestrating Samson's bad decisions. But the story of Israel's history shows that God was able to put those bad decisions to good use.

Before Samson came along, Israel was in danger of becoming assimilated into the stronger Philistine nation. But Samson drove a wedge between the two nations. What Samson started, King DAVID finished about 50 years later—crushing the Philistine ARMY. David made Israel the leading nation in the region. In time, the Philistines vanished from history, assimilated into other Middle East nations.

(SAM yoo uhl)

About 1100–1010 BC

Samuel passed on the LORD's warning to the people who were asking him for a king. . . . "The king will draft your sons. . .take away the best of your fields and. . .take a tenth of your grain." (1 Samuel 8:10–11, 14–15)

- Jewish prophet
- Anointed Israel's first two kings: Saul, David

SAMUEL'S PARENTS GAVE HIM AWAY. His previously infertile mother, HANNAH, had promised that if GOD gave her a SON she would give him back to God. So after Samuel was born, his parents took him to the WORSHIP center to be raised by the priest ELI.

Samuel grew up to become a PROPHET who led ISRAEL before the nation had a KING. In fact, he felt insulted when the JEWS asked him for a king. But he was old, and the Jews were afraid that his corrupt sons would take over.

God told Samuel not to take it personally, and that it was God the people were rejecting as king, not Samuel. So on God's order, Samuel ANOINTED Saul as Israel's first king. Years later, when SAUL let his power go to his head, Samuel followed God's order by secretly anointing young DAVID to be the next king, after Saul died.

Samuel died before Saul did. But on the night before the battle in which PHILISTINES killed Saul and his sons, Saul had a medium call Samuel from the realm of the dead. Saul wanted the prophet to give him God's insight about the coming battle. Samuel did. "Tomorrow," Samuel said, "you and your sons will be here with me" (1 Samuel 28:19).

SAMUEL, BOOKS OF 1–2 ▶

Famous sound bite: "How the mighty have fallen!" David's reaction to the death of King Saul and sons, 2 Samuel 1:19 TNIV

JEWS DON'T BOTHER WITH A KING for several GENERATIONS. They rely on GOD's help through heroic leaders like GIDEON and SAMSON, and from PROPHETS such as Samuel. But as Samuel grows old, they ask for a KING. SAUL is first; he's a DONKEY herder. Because he disobeys God, his dynasty is one and out (though one of his sons rules northern JEWS for a short time). Up next is DAVID, a SHEPHERD. He's the second king of the unified Jewish nation.

- Writer: Unknown. Scholars guess it was a writer after the time of Samuel and David because the writer talks about the two Jewish countries of Israel and Judah, which didn't exist until after Solomon died in the 900s BC.
- Time: 1000s BC.
- Location: Israel.

BIG SCENES

Good news for infertile mom: it's a boy. A Jewish woman named HANNAH pleads with God to cure her INFERTILITY. In return for a son, she promises to give the boy back to God. Samuel is born. By the time he is able to eat solid food, Hannah takes him to the WORSHIP center to be raised by the priest, ELI. *1 Samuel 1*

Losing the 10 commandments. Samuel ends up leading ISRAEL after Eli and his PRIEST sons die on the same day. Eli's sons take into battle the ARK OF THE COVENANT, Israel's most sacred relic. It's a chest that holds the 10 COMMANDMENTS. PHILISTINES defeat the Jews, take the chest, and kill Eli's sons. Old Eli dies when he gets the news, falling out of his chair and suffering a broken neck. *1 Samuel 4–6*

Donkey king. Samuel leads Israel as the prophet. But he has rotten sons, corrupt to the bone. So when he gets old, Israel's tribal leaders ask for a king. They don't want Samuel's boys running the country. God selects a donkey herder named Saul, who turns out to be a good warrior king. *1 Samuel 7–10*

Shepherd boy vs. Philistine champ. Armies of the Jews and Philistines are eyeballing each other across a contested valley a few miles/kilometers west of BETHLEHEM—hometown of a young shepherd named David. Samuel had already secretly ANOINTED him as Israel's future king. David shows up with a care package for his older brothers in the Jewish ARMY. He hears the Philistine champion GOLIATH challenge any Jew to mortal combat. Goliath stands almost 7 feet tall (2 m).

No takers. Until David. Young David kills the champion with a rock fired from a slingshot. Suddenly, David's a rock star. *1 Samuel 16–17*

Saul goes wacko jealous. Jewish women sing a SONG that drives King Saul crazy: "Saul has killed his thousands, and David his ten thousands!" (1 Samuel 18:6–7). Shepherd trumps donkey herder. Not a good thing for the donkey herder. Saul puts a hit out on David, who turns fugitive and develops a following of men disenchanted with Saul. *1 Samuel 18–22*

David: the dynasty begins. Saul seems to ignore the Philistine threat, focusing his resources on catching David. Meanwhile, the Philistines gather a massive army and invade. Saul and most of his sons die in the battle. Jews later rally around David and declare him king. It's the start of a FAMILY dynasty that will endure more than 400 years, until invaders from what is now Iraq erase the Jewish nation from the world map. *1 Samuel 21–2 Samuel 5*

Bathsheba and the wandering eye. While David's army is off fighting to push Israel's borders further into what is now Jordan, the king's eye catches a soldier's WIFE, BATHSHEBA. She's wearing nothing but skin, water, and sunshine. She's bathing away the ritual impurity of her menstrual period. Which means she's as fertile as all get out. The very married David—seven wives at least—calls Bathsheba to the PALACE for a command performance. She gets pregnant. David arranges for her husband, URIAH, to die in battle. Then David marries the grieving WIDOW. Prophet NATHAN calls him on it. David confesses. God forgives him. *2 Samuel 11–12*

Rapist and traitor in David's family. A great king, David is a stinker of a family man, as the BIBLE reports it. He doesn't punish his oldest son, AMNON, who rapes his own half sister, TAMAR. Tamar's full brother ABSALOM settles the score by arranging the assassination of Amnon. Then he attempts to dethrone his dad—and dies trying, in a failed coup. Turns out that David's SOLDIERS are better fighters than Absalom's. They've had more experience. *2 Samuel 13–19*

SANBALLAT

(san BAL at)

400s BC

Sanballat was very angry when he learned that we were rebuilding the wall. He flew into a rage and mocked the Jews. Nehemiah 4:1

- Arab governor of Samaria region
- Opposed Nehemiah rebuilding Jerusalem walls

ARABS didn't want to see the rebirth of a Jewish JERUSALEM. Babylonian invaders from what is now Iraq had erased the Jewish nation from the political map. But Persian invaders from Iran freed them to go home. When a Jew named NEHEMIAH arrived to rebuild the walls, Sanballat tried to stop him with intimidation and raids. No luck. JEWS finished the walls in a mere 52 days.

SANCTIFICATION

(SANK tuh fuh KAY shun)

It is God's will that you should be sanctified. . . . For God did not call us to be impure, but to live a holy life. 1 Thessalonians 4:3, 7 TNIV

- Reserving something for sacred use

JEWS USED RITUALS, such as sprinkling BLOOD on Temple BOWLS and other utensils, to dedicate them for sacred use only. No eating breakfast out of TEMPLE bowls.

For JEWS themselves, they considered themselves sanctified by observing the laws GOD gave them through MOSES.

Christian writers like PAUL taught that followers of Jesus were sanctified by devoting themselves entirely to him. That meant living as though they were in the reserves of God's army—ready to do whatever God commanded, whenever he commanded it.

It doesn't mean they're perfect, many scholars say. It means they're committed.

Even Paul admitted: "I have not yet been made perfect" (Philippians 3:12 NIrv). But he was committed enough to Jesus that he suffered through BEATINGS, STONING, imprisonment, and if early church writers are correct, execution.

SANCTUARY

"Have the people of Israel build me a holy sanctuary so I can live among them. You must build this Tabernacle and its furnishings exactly according to the pattern I will show you." Exodus 25:8–9

- Worship center, such as the Jewish Temple

A HOLY PLACE, the sanctuary was where JEWS worshiped GOD. During the EXODUS out of EGYPT, the sanctuary was a TENT sometimes called the TABERNACLE. In JERUSALEM it was the TEMPLE.

Sometimes *sanctuary* meant the entire WORSHIP center. Other times it referred to the most sacred room in the worship center: the HOLY OF HOLIES. That's where Jews kept their most sacred relic: the ARK OF THE COVENANT, a chest that held the 10 COMMANDMENTS. Only the HIGH PRIEST could enter this room, and only once a year: *Yom Kippur*, the DAY OF ATONEMENT—to sprinkle sacrificial BLOOD on the Ark, to atone for the sins of the nation.

SANDALS

I gave you the finest clothes and the most expensive robes, as well as sandals made from the best leather. Ezekiel 16:10 CEV

THE MOST POPULAR FOOTWEAR in the hot Middle East of Bible times, sandals let the feet breathe. And pick up dust. Which is why folks welcomed guests by giving them water to wash their feet.

Like shoes today, sandals could be cheap or expensive—made of fine LEATHER, such as goatskin. Or they could be cut from blocks of wood.

The prophet AMOS criticized rich people for selling the POOR into SLAVERY to recoup tiny DEBTS no higher than the price of "a pair of sandals" (Amos 8:6).

FOOTWEAR. This pair of leather sandals dating to the first Christian century were uncovered from Masada, a hilltop fortress where Jews committed mass suicide rather than surrender to the Roman army.

SANHEDRIN

(san HEE druhn)

The chief priests and the whole Sanhedrin were looking for false evidence against Jesus. Matthew 26:59 TNIV

- Jewish supreme court
- Tried Jesus
- Convinced Pilate to execute Jesus

GUARDIANS OF THE JEWISH WAY OF LIFE. That seemed to be the job description of the Sanhedrin, a council of PRIESTS, religion scholars, and other respected JEWS such as PHARISEES and SADDUCEES—convened by the HIGH PRIEST.

They judged matters involving Jewish law and TRADITIONS. They also punished offenders, though under Roman law were not allowed to execute anyone; only Roman officials could sentence someone to death.

That's why when the council found Jesus guilty of BLASPHEMY for dishonoring GOD, they had to take him to PILATE. The wanted Jesus dead. But only Pilate, Roman GOVERNOR of the region, could issue the death sentence.

Later the same council ordered Jesus' DISCIPLES to stop PREACHING about him. The disciples refused. The council felt powerless to do anything because the

S

disciples were performing MIRACLES and were enjoying widespread popularity.

One council member, GAMALIEL, offered this advice: "Let them go! If their plans and actions are only human, they will fail. But if their plans come from God, you won't be able to stop these men" (Acts 5:38–39 NIrV).

SAPPHIRA
(see ANANIAS AND SAPPHIRA)

SARAH
(SAIR uh)

2100s BC

The LORD said to Abraham, "Why did Sarah laugh? Why did she say, 'Can an old woman like me have a baby?' Is anything too hard for the LORD?" Genesis 18:13–14

- Abraham's wife
- Abraham's half sister
- Isaac's mother

THE MOTHER OF THE JEWISH NATION seemed to have every reason to laugh when GOD appeared in what seems to have been human form and told her she would have a son within the year. She was 89 years old. ABRAHAM was 99.

A year later, she gave BIRTH to ISAAC—a NAME that means "laughter."

Sarah's name was Sarai until God changed it as a way of sealing his promise to give her a son.

Abraham and Sarah had the same father, TERAH, but different mothers. When Sarah was 76, she gave up all hope of having CHILDREN. She told Abraham to use her maid, HAGAR, as a surrogate mother to produce an heir for the FAMILY. Hagar gave birth to ISHMAEL.

But after Sarah gave birth to ISAAC, she convinced Abraham to send Hagar and Ishmael away. God agreed to Sarah's request but promised Abraham that he would bless both of his sons. Many consider Isaac the ancestor of the JEWS and Ishmael the ancestor of the Arabs.

Sarah died at age 127. Abraham buried her in a cave called MACHPELAH, near HEBRON, a village about 20 miles (32 km) south of JERUSALEM. King HEROD

built a shrine to mark the location. Jews, Christians, and Arabs all visit the site thought to have been Abraham's family TOMB.

SARDIS
Map 3 F3

(SARR diss)

"You still have a few followers of Jesus in Sardis who haven't ruined themselves wallowing in the muck of the world's ways." Revelation 3:4 MSG

- One of seven churches addressed in Revelation
- City in western Turkey

DICTATING LETTERS addressed to seven churches, Jesus praised the community of FAITH in Sardis because they still had at least a few genuine Christians left. But warning that they were a dying CHURCH, Jesus told them to "Wake up!" (Revelation 3:2).

SARGON II
(SAR gon)

Ruled 722–705 BC

Sargon sent his highest commander to the city of Ashdod. He attacked it and captured it. Isaiah 20:1 NIrV

- King of Assyria (based in Iraq)
- Conquered northern Jewish nation of Israel

THE BIBLE MENTIONS HIM ONLY ONCE. But he was a big deal in Jewish history.

He finished the work of erasing the northern Jewish nation of ISRAEL from the world map—a job King SHALMANESER had started before he died. Sargon destroyed the Jewish capital city of SAMARIA, deported the Jewish survivors, and then resettled the Jewish homeland with colonists from what is now Iraq. Think of it as a racial makeover.

Descendants of these settlers became known as SAMARITANS—a race not particularly popular among Jews of Jesus' day.

(SAY ton)

Satan, who is the god of this world, has blinded the minds of those who don't believe.
2 Corinthians 4:4

- Hebrew for "Accuser"
- Boss of the demons
- Bad to the bone

A BIBLE LATECOMER, Satan makes his grand entrance into SCRIPTURE only when he arrives to tempt Jesus. That's the first time Satan shows up as a spiritual being.

Before that, *Satan* wasn't used as a person's name. It was just a HEBREW word that meant "ACCUSER" or "enemy." OLD TESTAMENT writers used that word to describe all kinds of people—including revered characters such as DAVID, SOLOMON, and even GOD when he angrily accused ISRAEL of SIN.

For example, one story told in two books reveals that "Satan" (the enemy of Israel at the moment) was actually "God."

- "Satan rose up against Israel and caused David to take a CENSUS of the people of Israel" (1 Chronicles 21:1).
- "The anger of the LORD burned against Israel, and he caused David to harm them by taking a census" (2 Samuel 24:1).

What about the talking SNAKE in the Garden of EDEN?

It was just that, as described in the CREATION story—a talking snake.

What about JOB's tormenter?

He was just "the Accuser," someone who addressed the heavenly council, accusing Job of being righteous only because God was his Sugar Daddy. Take away the sugar, Satan predicted, and Job would turn into a sour ball.

It took many centuries for Jewish and Christian writers to begin identifying the snake and Job's accuser as Satan—the incarnation of evil and the leader of a demonic coalition devoted to destroying humanity.

One end-time visionary best known for looking forward in time, JOHN OF REVELATION, also looked

SATAN doesn't show up as the Bible's bad guy until he arrives to tempt Jesus. Earlier references to Satan, scholars say, don't clearly describe Satan as a demon. Sometimes "Satan" actually referred to God. That's because *satan* is a Hebrew word that means "Accuser." And sometimes God was Israel's accuser.

backward and revealed the identity of Eden's snake: "the ancient serpent called the devil, or Satan" (Revelation 12:9).

Satan's first known appearance as an individual came a little more than a century before Jesus. A Jewish PHARISEE, writing sometime between 135–105 BC, looked forward to a utopian time when people would "live in PEACE and in joy, and there shall be no Satan or any evil destroyer" (Book of Jubilees 23:29).

In the centuries that followed, new insights about Satan continued to emerge in Jewish and Christian WRITINGS.

The Talmud, a collection of ancient Jewish teachings, presents an array of ideas about Satan:

- He came into the world with Eve, as a created being.
- He flies.
- He can assume various forms, such as a bird, a deer, or a beggar.

He shows up in early writings by various names: the devil, LUCIFER, Belial, BEELZEBUB, Apollyon.

NEW TESTAMENT writers described him as "the ruler of this world" (John 12:31). But they also doomed

S

him as history's biggest loser. In a VISION of the future, JOHN OF REVELATION reported that "the devil, who had deceived them, was thrown into the fiery lake of burning SULFUR, joining the beast and the FALSE PROPHET. There they will be tormented day and night forever and ever" (Revelation 20:10).

The evolution in humanity's understanding of Satan doesn't mean people invented him, many scholars argue. Jesus certainly spoke of Satan and other DEMONS as real spiritual entities. But the gradual emergence of information does suggest that for several millennia, Satan operated under the cloak of humanity's ignorance. It took Jesus to bring him into the light of day, revealing him as the evil creature he is.

Some Bible experts, however, say JEWS picked up the idea from Persian religion, which taught that there was a ruler over the forces of evil. One problem with that theory, others say, is what to do with New Testament stories of Jesus arguing with him: "Get out of here, Satan" (Matthew 4:10).

DEAD AND DYING, King Saul and his sons fall to the Philistines in the Battle of Mount Gilboa. Fatally wounded, Saul falls on his sword rather than be taken captive and perhaps tortured.

SAUL

About 1044–1004 BC

Saul was the most handsome man in Israel— head and shoulders taller than anyone else in the land. 1 Samuel 9:2

- Israel's first king
- Died in battle with Philistines

SAUL WAS A DONKEY HERDER who wanted nothing to do with being the first king of ISRAEL.

But SAMUEL the PROPHET insisted.

Samuel ANOINTED him with OLIVE OIL and told him, "I am doing this because the LORD has appointed you to be the ruler over Israel" (1 Samuel 10:1).

Though Saul was tall and handsome—apparently kingly looking—people didn't seem impressed. Especially the locals. Some folks in his hometown of GIBEAH, 3 miles (5 km) north of JERUSALEM, asked the logical question about the DONKEY herder: "How can someone like Saul rescue us from our enemies?" (1 Samuel 10:27 CEV).

They didn't want him as KING, and they refused to honor him with GIFTS.

They soon had to eat their words.

The BIBLE's first scene of Saul as king describes him walking behind a team of oxen, plowing a field. Not a kingly endeavor. But what happened next certainly was.

Ammonites in what is now Jordan had been oppressing the two tribes east of the JORDAN RIVER—GAD and REUBEN. AMMON's king ordered the right eyes of each Jew gouged out—to humiliate the nation. Some JEWS fled north to the city of Jabesh-gilead, but Ammonites followed. When the Jews offered to surrender, the merciless king said only if they agreed to lose their right eyes. With a week to think about whether or not depth perception was worth dying for, they sent messengers to Saul pleading for help.

"The Spirit of GOD came powerfully upon Saul, and he became very angry" (1 Samuel 11:6). He cut his oxen to pieces and sent them with messengers throughout Israel. The message was essentially this: Saul would do this to the oxen of anyone who didn't join him in battle.

More than 300,000 came, and Saul led his militia

on a surprise attack that slaughtered the Ammonites.

"Where are the men who said they didn't want Saul to be king?" the crowds cheered. "Bring them to us, and we will put them to death!" (1 Samuel 11:12 CEV). Saul vetoed the execution proposal and gave God credit for the victory.

SAUL'S BIG MISTAKES

Saul was usually at his best on the battlefield, but two battlefield blunders cost him his life and doomed his dynasty.

Instead of waiting for Samuel to offer a SACRIFICE so Saul's ARMY could attack the ever-growing Philistine army preparing for battle, Saul offered the sacrifice himself as though he were a PRIEST or a prophet.

"That was stupid!" Samuel said when he finally arrived. "You didn't obey the LORD your God. . .so the LORD won't choose anyone else from your FAMILY to be king" (1 Samuel 13:13–14 CEV).

His second mistake was to treat a Jewish hero as an enemy. Young DAVID killed the Philistine champion GOLIATH in one-on-one mortal combat. The Jews suddenly treated the boy like a rock star and Saul like a has-been. Insanely jealous, Saul declared David an outlaw. Saul invested so much of his time and resources in trying to hunt down and kill David, many scholars say, that he neglected his real enemy: the PHILISTINES.

In time, the Philistines assembled an overwhelming force and invaded Israel's breadbasket farmland in the JEZREEL VALLEY. Saul was so terrified that he consulted a medium and asked her to conjure up the SPIRIT of Samuel, who had died. Saul wanted God's advice, which only Samuel had been able to give him.

To the medium's shock and awe, Samuel's spirit appeared. Bad news, though. Samuel said that before the day ended, Saul and his sons would join him in the land of the dead.

Three of Saul's sons died in the fierce fighting: JONATHAN, Abinadab, and Malkishua. Wounded by archers, Saul asked his ARMOR bearer to finish him off before the Philistines could capture him. The armor bearer refused, so Saul fell on his SWORD.

Philistines cut off Saul's head and tied the bodies of him and his sons to the city walls of nearby BETH-SHAN.

It's unclear how long Saul served as king—

perhaps 25 years or more. However long it was, the people he saved in his first battle at Jabesh-gilead honored his memory. Some of their warriors made a nighttime, 20-mile (32 km) march to Beth-shan and took the bodies of Saul and his sons back to Jabesh-gilead, where they cremated them.

One of Saul's surviving sons became king: ISH-BOSHETH. But he was a wimpy, nervous king. Two years into his shaky reign, a couple of his commanders cut off his head and took it to David, who executed them both before becoming king himself.

SAVIOR

"The Savior—yes, the Messiah, the Lord— has been born today in Bethlehem, the city of David!" Luke 2:11

- One who saves someone from danger
- Description of God in the Old Testament
- Description of Jesus in the New Testament

MOST SAVIORS ARE HUMANS. At least when it comes to the Jewish Bible, which many Christians call the OLD TESTAMENT.

Savior is a word that Bible writers used to describe heroes and leaders GOD sent to help the JEWS fight off their enemies: "The LORD gave ISRAEL a savior, so that they escaped from the hand of the Arameans" (2 Kings 13:5 NRSV). These deliverers included warriors such as GIDEON and King DAVID.

The word also shows up in SONGS praising God, and in NEW TESTAMENT descriptions of Jesus as "the Savior of the world" (John 4:42).

S

> All of those buildings [Solomon's palace] were made out of blocks of very fine stone. They were cut to the right size. They were shaped with a saw on the back and front sides. 1 Kings 7:9 NIrV

> "You are like a trader who uses dishonest scales. You love to cheat others."
> Hosea 12:7 NIrV

▪ Tool for weighing objects

BY THE TIME KING SOLOMON built Israel's first Temple and his palace, construction workers had saws strong enough to cut stone. Those blades were probably crafted from iron, made from a procedure that was developed a couple centuries earlier, in about 1200 BC.

Jewish tradition says that nasty Jewish king Manasseh (reigned about 696–642 BC) had the prophet Isaiah cut in half with a wooden saw.

JUST AS WE USE SCALES to weigh fruit and veggies in the grocery store, people in ancient times used scales to weigh their merchandise as well as gold, silver, and other products used as currency.

They typically used balance scales, which worked a bit like a small teeter-totter. They would set an object on one side. And they would measure the weight by putting metal or stones of known weight on the other side.

Some merchants cheated by tampering with the balance or by using weights that didn't actually weigh what the merchant claimed.

Jewish law prohibited that: "Your scales and weights must be accurate" (Leviticus 19:36).

DON'T CHEAT the customer. Prophets and Proverbs say the same thing: use honest scales. "The Lord detests the use of dishonest scales" (Proverbs 11:1).

SCAPEGOAT ON THE RUN. Once a year, on *Yom Kippur*, Jews symbolically dumped all their sins onto a goat and ran it off. Good-bye, goat. Good-bye, sins.

SCAPEGOAT

"The goat chosen by lot as the scapegoat shall be presented alive before the LORD to be used for making atonement by sending it into the wilderness." Leviticus 16:10 TNIV

- Goat that symbolizes the nation's sins

ONE UNFORTUNATE GOAT got chased off into ISRAEL's badlands every autumn, on *Yom Kippur*, the DAY OF ATONEMENT. This was a national day of REPENTANCE for sins the people committed during the past year.

To atone for these sins, the HIGH PRIEST selected two GOATS. He sacrificed one. But he had different instructions for the second goat, famous as the scapegoat:

"He [the priest] will lay both of his hands on the goat's head and confess over it all the wickedness, rebellion, and sins of the people of Israel. In this way, he will transfer the people's sins to the head of the goat. Then a man specially chosen for the task will drive the goat into the WILDERNESS. As the goat goes into the wilderness, it will carry all the people's sins upon itself into a desolate land" (Leviticus 16:21–22).

SCHOOLS (see EDUCATION)

SCEPTER

The king. . .was happy to see Esther, and he held out the gold scepter to her. Esther 5:1–2 CEV

- King's ceremonial staff

A CLUB TO BEAT OFF ATTACKERS is how the royal scepter started, according to guesses by some historians. In time, it became an ornate symbol of power—often a rod layered with GOLD and studded in gems. Instead of using it to club the unwanted, kings held it out to welcome guests.

SCORPION

The LORD brought you out of Egypt. . . . He led you through that huge and terrible desert. It was a dry land. . . . It had poisonous snakes and scorpions. Deuteronomy 8:14–15 NIrv

A DOZEN SPECIES of these stinger-tail arachnids live in the Middle East. But the most common are yellowish critters know by the scientific name *Buthus quinquestriatus*. These particular creepy crawlers produce a neurotoxin that can cause a full-grown human to collapse in convulsions, PARALYSIS, and sometimes death.

A CREEPY CRAWLER, the desert scorpion can drop a man in his tracks and curl him into convulsions—perhaps even leaving him dead in the dirt.

S

STEPHEN M. MILLER'S ILLUSTRATED BIBLE DICTIONARY

Scorpions prefer the night. With POISON in their stinger tails they paralyze their prey: usually insects, spiders, and other scorpions, but sometimes lizards, SNAKES, and mice.

The average scorpion is about as long as a little finger—about 2.5 inches (6 cm).

SCRIBE

MANY PEOPLE COULDN'T READ OR WRITE in Bible times. So when they needed to send a message or write a CONTRACT, they hired scribes—people trained to read and write.

Some Bible writers dictated their messages, not necessarily because they couldn't write, but possibly because it was faster or because a trained writer could help them phrase themselves more clearly.

JEREMIAH dictated his prophecies to BARUCH. PAUL dictated his most respected LETTER: ROMANS. "I, Tertius, the one writing this letter for Paul, send my greetings, too" (Romans 16:22).

See also SCROLL.

SCRIPTURE

THE CHRISTIAN BIBLE isn't what PAUL was talking about when he wrote to TIMOTHY that "all Scripture is inspired by GOD" (2 Timothy 3:16). Paul was talking about their BIBLE at the time: the Jewish Bible, which

most Christians call the OLD TESTAMENT. There was no NEW TESTAMENT yet.

But by the time the last of the New Testament books were written, the early LETTERS of Paul were already being spoken of as Scripture: "Some things Paul writes are difficult to understand. Irresponsible people who don't know what they are talking about twist them

GETTING IT IN WRITING. A Jewish scribe in Morocco makes a new copy of the Torah, which is the Law section of the Jewish Bible—Genesis through Deuteronomy. The work is on commission from a synagogue. Scribes in Bible times also wrote for hire, since many folks couldn't read or write. Though Paul could do both, even he used a scribe for some of his most important letters, such as the book of Romans.

every which way. They do it to the rest of the Scriptures, too" (2 Peter 3:16 MSG).

Scripture comes from a Latin word the Romans used. It means "WRITING." But for JEWS and CHRISTIANS, the term came to mean their sacred writings.

See also WORD OF GOD.

SCROLL

> "Get a scroll, and write down all my messages against Israel, Judah, and the other nations." Jeremiah 36:2
>
> - Writing material, often leather or papyrus
> - Book made into a long roll instead of pages

BOOKS DIDN'T EXIST IN BIBLE TIMES—not the kind of page-by-page books we have today. Instead, people wrote stories and LETTERS on long rolls of material that look a bit like a roll of paper towels.

Two types of material, mainly:

- leather called parchment, made from the hide of GOATS, SHEEP, or CATTLE
- papyrus paper made from slices of spongy pith inside the stems of NILE RIVER reeds.

When scrolls began to fade or wear out, a SCRIBE meticulously copied the words onto new scrolls. That was apparently one of the jobs of the community of JEWS who produced the famous DEAD SEA SCROLLS, written a thousand years before the scrolls used to translate the King James Version of the BIBLE.

SCYTHIAN

(SITH ee uhn)

> It doesn't matter if you are a Greek or a Jew, or if you are circumcised or not. You may even be a barbarian or a Scythian.
> Colossians 3:11 CEV
>
> - Nomads from Iran who migrated to Russia

MENTIONED JUST ONCE IN THE BIBLE, PAUL used them as an example of barbarians. They had a reputation as fierce warriors who knew how to handle their horses on the battlefield.

SEA OF GALILEE

Map 4 D4

> As Jesus was walking by Lake Galilee, he saw two brothers, Simon (called Peter) and his brother Andrew. They were throwing a net into the lake because they were fishermen.
> Matthew 4:18 NCV

IT'S NOT A SEA. It's a freshwater lake. Shallow, too. No more than about 160 feet (49 m) at its deepest.

But it can churn up deadly storms in an eye blink. That's because of where it's located—at the bottom of a bowl. It's lower than the hills surrounding it. It's even lower than the nearby ocean. The Sea of Galilee squats 700 feet (213 m) below the MEDITERRANEAN SEA, some 30 miles (48 km) west. Mountain ravines on the lake's west side channel cool sea breezes toward it. When a burst of cool sea air crashes into hot air rising from the lake, the swirl of wind can churn up angry waves high enough to sink FISHING boats.

Jesus and his DISCIPLES may have gotten caught in such a storm one day while crossing the lake. "As they sailed across, Jesus settled down for a nap. But soon a fierce storm came down on the lake. The boat was filling with water, and they were in real danger" (Luke 8:23).

The disciples woke Jesus. He calmed the storm.

AN ISRAELI TOUR GUIDE holds up a fish named after a famous Galilean fisherman. Saint Peter's fish, as it's called, is a mild-tasting tilapia caught in the Sea of Galilee and served with its head intact.

S

Chorazin
Jesus denounced citizens for lack of faith

Bethsaida
Home of several disciples

Capernaum
Jesus' ministry HQ

Gennesaret
First-century fishing boat found

Magdala
Home of Mary Magdalene

Gergesa
Jesus cast demons into herd of pigs

Tiberias
Capital of Galilee

SEA OF GALILEE
AKA Harp Lake

HARP LAKE

Locals don't generally call this lake the Sea of Galilee. Some call it Lake Tiberias, after a city on the western shore. Others called it Harp Sea, as it would translate into English—or the Sea of Kinnereth, using the HEBREW word for harp.

That's because the lake is shaped like a HARP—a big harp about 13 miles (21 km) long and 7 miles (11 km) across at its widest point.

The lake functions like a reservoir along the JORDAN RIVER. The Jordan flows into the lake at the north and out of the lake at the southern tip.

In Jesus' time, fishing villages dotted the north shore. That's where he met most of his disciples, and that's where he set up his ministry headquarters, in CAPERNAUM.

Fishermen like PETER, ANDREW, JAMES, and JOHN worked in the thriving industry—as did crews of 230 fishing boats, according to first-century Jewish historian Josephus.

There was no other large lake in the country, and JEWS weren't fond of ocean fishing. The lake held three main kinds of fish. There were sardines—perhaps the "few small fish" Jesus used to feed a crowd of thousands (Matthew 15:34). There were barbels, named after the barb-looking feelers on their upper lips. And there were mild-tasting tilapia, which lakeshore restaurants today serve tourists. They call them St. Peter's fish.

Peter probably caught plenty of them.

THE BOAT

When a 1986 drought shrunk the massive lake, widening the shoreline by several yards (meters), two men on a walk noticed the outline of a boat in the mud.

It turned out to be a fishing boat from the time of Jesus—perhaps the same kind of boat Jesus sailed on with his disciples.

Experts quickly decided to get it out before the lake rose. It's now on display near where it was discovered. At about 26 feet (8 m) long and 8 feet (2 m) wide, it could have held 15 men—enough for Jesus and all 12 of his disciples.

SPECS: SEA OF GALILEE

Local name: Yam Kinneret, "Sea Harp"

Shape: Like a harp

Water: Fresh, not salty

Size: 13 by 7 miles (21 by 11 km)

Surface area: three Manhattan islands; 64 square miles (166 sq. km)

Depth: half a football field; 160 feet (49 m)

Elevation: two football fields below sea level; –700 feet (–213 m)

Water sources: snow from Mount Hermon, underground springs, rainwater runoff

SEAL

"The earth takes shape like clay pressed beneath a seal." Job 38:14

- Ancient version of a rubber stamp

ARTISTS CREATED SEALS by engraving words or pictures on a hard object, such as a small stone, a baked clay cylinder, or the head of a RING. The owner could press that seal into a soft plug of clay or wax, transferring the image. It served as a signature.

Also, if a LETTER writer wanted to make sure no one but the intended reader saw the message inside a SCROLL, the writer could tie the scroll with string and press a glob of clay or wax into the string. Then the writer would press the seal into a glob. Once the clay or wax hardened, a person had to break the seal to open the scroll.

Archaeologists have found what many say was the seal of BARUCH, a SCRIBE who wrote the prophecies that JEREMIAH dictated.

SEALS and signet rings had words or pictures etched into them. They worked a bit like a signature.

S

"You have six days each week for your ordinary work, but on the seventh day you must stop working, even during the seasons of plowing and harvest." Exodus 34:21

TWO SEASONS made up the year in Jesus' homeland.

We might call them winter and summer or perhaps rainy and dry. But Bible writers often spoke of them in FARMING terms:

- the season to plow the ground and plant seeds (October–May)
- harvesttime (April–September).

SECOND COMING

Let us clarify some things about the coming of our Lord Jesus Christ and how we will be gathered to meet him. 2 Thessalonians 2:1

- The return of Jesus Christ

JESUS IS COMING BACK. That's what he told his followers after explaining that he had to leave.

"When everything is ready, I will come and get you, so that you will always be with me where I am" (John 14:3).

Christians don't agree on when he will return or what his comeback will look like.

Some say it will be a two-part event. First a secret rapture—a snatching away of Christians—followed years later by a public and glorious return with all the godly people who ever lived. Others say both events will happen at the same time.

Bible writers said that once Jesus returns, godly people from throughout the ages will live with him forever.

JESUS MAKES A COMEBACK. Humble though his first coming was—born in what amounted to a barn—his second coming will look a bit different, Bible writers promise. "With a loud command and with the shout of the chief angel and a blast of God's trumpet, the Lord will return from heaven" (1 Thessalonians 4:16 CEV).

SECOND DEATH

> "The corrupt, murderers, the immoral. . .
> their fate is in the fiery lake of burning
> sulfur. This is the second death."
> Revelation 21:8

- Destiny of an evil soul or spirit

EVIL PEOPLE end up destroyed, some scholars speculate.

Wicked people won't suffer forever, those scholars say. Instead, it's the consequences that last forever: the wicked are annihilated. The scholars add that Jesus hinted of this when he said, "Don't be afraid of those who want to kill your body; they cannot touch your SOUL. Fear only GOD, who can destroy both soul and body in HELL" (Matthew 10:28).

Others say the second death is another name for hell, and that it's where evil souls will suffer forever.

SEIR
Map 2 J8

(SEER)

> Esau (also known as Edom) settled in the hill
> country of Seir. Genesis 36:8

- Also known as Edom, in what is now Jordan
- Hebrew for "hairy"

MOSES AND THE JEWS on the EXODUS out of EGYPT asked permission to pass through Seir on their way to the PROMISED LAND. Request denied. GOD told the Jews to go around Seir since the people living there were relatives: descendants of JACOB's brother ESAU.

SELAH

(SEE luh)

> LORD, you are the one who saves. May your
> blessing be on your people. Selah.
> Psalm 3:8 NIrV

- Mysterious word used in Psalms

THE WORD may have been an instruction to musicians—

a bit like *forte*, which means "get louder." But Bible experts say they aren't sure.

Selah shows up 74 times in the BIBLE—71 times in the Jewish hymnbook of PSALMS and three times in the poetic prophecy of HABAKKUK.

SELEUCIA
Map 3 L4

(suh LOO shuh)

> Barnabas and Saul were sent on their way by
> the Holy Spirit. They went down to Seleucia.
> From there they sailed to Cyprus.
> Acts 13:4 NIrV

- Syrian port city
- Where Paul set sail on first mission trip

WHEN PAUL AND BARNABAS, led by the HOLY SPIRIT, decided to take the story of Jesus on the road, they left the CHURCH they pastored at ANTIOCH in SYRIA and traveled to the nearby port city of Seleucia. From there they sailed to BARNABAS's homeland, the island of CYPRUS. After PREACHING their way across the island, they moved on to Turkey.

SENNACHERIB

(suh NACK ur rib)

Ruled 705–681 BC

> "I am King Sennacherib of Assyria, and I
> have Jerusalem surrounded. . . . Hezekiah
> your king is telling you that the LORD your God
> will save you from me. But he is lying."
> 2 Chronicles 32:10–11 CEV

- King of Assyria (Iraq)
- Destroyed many Jewish towns
- Besieged Jerusalem but didn't capture it

THE BIBLE PAINTS ONE PICTURE of what happened when King Sennacherib and his ARMY surrounded JERUSALEM. But Assyrian records paint quite another.

Bible version: He was a conquered coward who limped home.

Assyrian version: He was a conquering hero who gave the JEWS what for.

S

Oddly enough, when we read the two versions together, the story makes sense.

Sennacherib invaded the southern Jewish nation of JUDAH in 701 BC, when HEZEKIAH was KING there. Assyrians had already conquered the northern Jewish nation of ISRAEL about 20 years earlier.

In his campaign against Judah, Sennacherib captured most fortified cities. Then he surrounded Jerusalem. But the BIBLE says that before he could take the city, an ANGEL killed 185,000 Assyrians and sent the others running for home. A Greek historian named Herodotus, writing some 250 years later, said an infestation of rats stopped Sennacherib's army and killed many of his soldiers—perhaps a hint of bubonic plague.

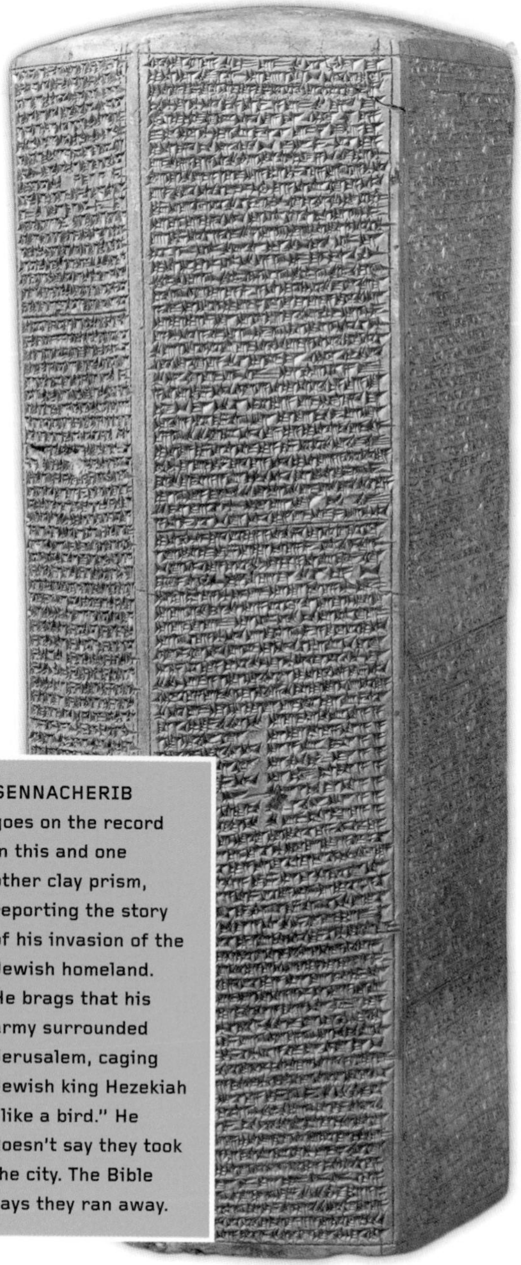

An Assyrian clay prism from Sennacherib's day confirms the invasion, reporting that Sennacherib conquered 46 cities. But it stops short of claiming victory over Jerusalem.

"As for Hezekiah," Sennacherib said in the record, "I made him a prisoner in Jerusalem, his royal residence, like a bird in a cage. I surrounded him."

When Sennacherib got home, two of his sons murdered him.

SENNACHERIB goes on the record in this and one other clay prism, reporting the story of his invasion of the Jewish homeland. He brags that his army surrounded Jerusalem, caging Jewish king Hezekiah "like a bird." He doesn't say they took the city. The Bible says they ran away.

SEPPHORIS
Map 4 C4

(SEFF uh riss)

- Capital of Galilee

THOUGH IT'S NOT MENTIONED IN THE BIBLE, Sepphoris may have been a town where carpenter JOSEPH and his sons spent a lot of time.

Two reasons:

- JEWS were rebuilding the city during much of Jesus' lifetime.
- Sepphoris was an easy walk 4 miles (6 km) northwest of Jesus' hometown of NAZARETH.

After King HEROD died in 4 BC, Jews in Sepphoris revolted against Rome. The Roman ARMY crushed the rebellion and destroyed the city. But the new ruler of the region—Herod's son, HEROD ANTIPAS—rebuilt the city and lived there for a time.

SEPTUAGINT

(sep TOO uh jint)

- First known Bible translation
- Translation of Jewish Bible from Hebrew into Greek

A BOOK LOVER, the king of EGYPT took such pride in his world-famous library at ALEXANDRIA that he not only collected books, he created them. King Ptolemy II Philadelphus (reigned 285–246 BC) wanted a copy of the sacred Jewish writings in GREEK, the international language of the day. So, as ancient historians tell the story, he brought in a team of 72 Jewish scholars to do the job.

Septuagint comes from the Greek word for "70."

Translators started with the first five books of the BIBLE, which contain the laws of MOSES. The translation process continued for decades, into the 100s BC.

Copies found among the DEAD SEA SCROLLS show that the translation was an ongoing work, being continually revised—a bit like Bible translations are today.

SERAIAH

(sir RAY uh)

Died 586 BC

Nebuzaradan arrested Seraiah the chief priest, Zephaniah his assistant, and three temple officials. . . . Nebuchadnezzar had them killed. 2 Kings 25:18, 21 CEV

- Jewish high priest executed by Nebuchadnezzar

A DOZEN PEOPLE in the BIBLE are named Seraiah. Most appear simply on lists of names. Perhaps the most notable was the HIGH PRIEST who saw Babylonian invaders from what is now Iraq destroy JERUSALEM and the TEMPLE. Babylonian King NEBUCHADNEZZAR then ordered him and his captured assistants executed.

SERAPHIM

(SAIR a fim)

Angel-seraphs hovered above him, each with six wings. With two wings they covered their faces, with two their feet, and with two they flew. Isaiah 6:2 MSG

ALSO CALLED SERAPHS, these celestial beings show up only in a VISION Isaiah said he had.

When GOD called ISAIAH to become a PROPHET, seraphim took part in a ceremony to purify him. One seraph flew to Isaiah, touched his lips with a burning coal, and said, "Your sins are forgiven" (Isaiah 6:7). This apparently prepared Isaiah for delivering God's HOLY messages to the people.

See also ANGEL.

SERGIUS PAULUS

(SIR gee uhs PAW luhs)

Sergius Paulus, an intelligent man. . .invited Barnabas and Saul in, wanting to hear God's Word firsthand from them. Acts 13:7 MSG

- Roman governor of Cyprus
- First Roman official to convert to Christianity

ON THEIR FIRST MISSION TRIP, PAUL and BARNABAS preached their way across the island of CYPRUS. When they reached the capital city of PAPHOS on the western coast, their words and MIRACLES convinced the GOVERNOR, Sergius Paulus, to become a follower of Jesus.

S

SERMON ON THE MOUNT

When Jesus saw the crowds, he went up on a hill and sat down. His followers came to him, and he began to teach them.

Matthew 5:1–2 NCV

- Jesus' most famous sermon
- Contains many of Jesus' key teachings

ON ONE OF THE GENTLY SLOPING HILLS near CAPERNAUM, Jesus preached what is perhaps the most famous sermon in history: the Sermon on the Mount.

The GOSPEL of LUKE lowers the elevation and shortens the sermon. He calls it the Sermon on the Plain. And he condenses MATTHEW's three chapters to just half a chapter.

But the gently rolling hills in the area could be described either way—hills or plain. And the sermon, many Bible experts say, sounds more like a series of talks: the Best of Jesus, a condensed version of all his most important teachings.

Jesus started his sermon with a famous section called the BEATITUDES—his prescription for spiritual happiness. What followed was anything but a promise of comfort or success in this world. Instead, Jesus assured his audience they would face discomfort and failure. But he urged them to press on anyway, humbly serving GOD and others—even when it hurts.

In a way, Jesus was flipping conventional wisdom upside down.

As Jesus told it, rich folks could afford the most expensive objects on earth, but "God blesses those who are POOR and realize their need for him, for the KINGDOM OF HEAVEN is theirs" (Matthew 5:3).

Aggressive go-getters might corner a tiny clump of success, but "God blesses those who are humble, for they will inherit the whole earth" (Matthew 5:5). The strength of a gentle soul catches the attention of HEAVEN and earth—and is honored in both.

SOUND BITES FROM THE SERMON

Golden Rule. "Do to others whatever you would like them to do to you. This is the essence of all that is taught in the law" (Matthew 7:12).

Anger. "Settle your differences quickly" (Matthew 5:25).

Revenge. "Do not resist an evil person!" (Matthew 5:39).

Judging. "The standard you use in judging is the standard by which you will be judged" (Matthew 7:2).

Enemies. "Love your enemies! Pray for those who persecute you!" (Matthew 5:44).

Charity. "Don't do your good deeds publicly, to be admired by others" (Matthew 6:1).

Money. "You cannot serve both GOD and MONEY" (Matthew 6:24).

Assets. "Don't store up treasures here on earth. . . . Store your treasures in heaven" (Matthew 6:19–21).

Worry. "I tell you not to worry about everyday life—whether you have enough food and drink, or enough clothes to wear" (Matthew 6:25, 32).

Prayer. "Don't babble on and on. . . . Your Father knows exactly what you need" (Matthew 6:7–8).

A MODEL OF JESUS teaching his disciples tops the Mount of the Beatitudes, where an ancient tradition says Jesus preached the Sermon on the Mount.

SERPENT

(see BRONZE SERPENT, SNAKE)

SERVANT

The king of Egypt. . .gave Abram sheep, cattle, male and female donkeys, male and female servants, and camels. Genesis 12:15–16 NCV

- Usually a slave, not a hired worker

THE BIBLE IS FULL of "servants," with more than 800 references to people working as a servant. In most cases, those workers weren't getting anything more than room and board and instructions on how high to jump.

They were slaves:

- captured in raids
- kidnapped while traveling
- sold to cover a DEBT they couldn't pay.

These slaves herded flocks, worked around the house—some even serviced the sexual needs of their masters. Two servant women who worked for JACOB's pair of wives ended up becoming surrogate mothers. These surrogates produced the ANCESTORS of four of ISRAEL's 12 tribes. LEAH's servant Zilpah gave BIRTH to GAD and ASHER. RACHEL's servant Bilhah gave birth to DAN and Naphtali.

Perhaps one of the BIBLE's most famous servants is the young woman who launched the apostle PETER into his most regrettable moment: As both awaited the outcome of Jesus' trial, the woman said: "You were one of those with Jesus the Galilean" (Matthew 26:69). Peter replied, "I don't know what you're talking about" (Matthew 26:70).

SETH

Before 4000 BC

Adam and his wife had another son. They named him Seth, because they said, "God has given us a son to take the place of Abel, who was killed by his brother Cain." Genesis 4:25 CEV

- Third son of Adam and Eve

ADAM AND EVE lost their first two sons. GOD banished their oldest son, CAIN, to a life of wandering after

Cain murdered his younger brother ABEL. Seth "lived 912 years" (Genesis 5:8).

SEVEN

"The seventh day must be a Sabbath day of complete rest. . . . For in six days the LORD made heaven and earth, but on the seventh day he stopped working and was refreshed." Exodus 31:15, 17

- Symbol of perfection or of job done

GOD RESTED ON DAY SEVEN after CREATION. Because of that, Bible writers took the number seven—and multiples of seven—and used them to represent completion and excellence, as in a job well done, to the max.

PETER asked Jesus if he should forgive people seven times, as though that's the full measure of FORGIVENESS. "No, not seven times," Jesus replied, "but seventy times seven!" (Matthew 18:22).

See also NUMBERS.

SEX

"Do not have sex with any of your close relatives." Leviticus 18:6 NIrV

WHEN IT CAME TO SEX, JEWS had a long list of to-dos and not-to-dos.

One law ordered Jews not to engage in sex with any close relatives. And then it identified who qualifies as a close relative. Kissing cousins are fair game, regardless of the blood relationship. But stepbrothers and stepsisters are not, apparently because the close relational connection trumps the distant blood connection.

The BIBLE is filled with warnings about the danger of sex sins. And there are plenty of stories about people who ignored those warnings. King DAVID, for example. Cue BATHSHEBA.

Notable Bible advice about sex:

- Cheap thrills. "Why would you trade enduring intimacies for cheap thrills with a whore?" (Proverbs 5:20 MSG).

S

- Hot pants. "If you build a fire in your pants, what makes you think you won't get burned?" (Proverbs 6:27 AUTHOR'S PARAPHRASE).

- Run away. "Run from sexual SIN! No other sin so clearly affects the body as this one does. For sexual IMMORALITY is a sin against your own body" (1 Corinthians 6:18).

See also INCEST.

SHADRACH, MESHACH, ABEDNEGO

(SHAD rack)(ME shack) (uh BED nee go)

About 600 BC

"Shadrach, Meshach, and Abednego. . .refuse to serve your gods." Daniel 3:12

- Survived execution in a furnace

BABYLONIAN SOLDIERS threw these three Jewish men into a blazing FURNACE. King NEBUCHADNEZZAR of BABYLON, in what is now Iraq, had brought them from their homeland to serve on his team of advisers. But he sentenced them to death when they refused to worship his idol. They survived, prompting the king to PRAISE their GOD.

SHALMANESER V

(SHALL muh NEE zur)

Ruled 727–722 BC

King Shalmaneser of Assyria attacked the city of Samaria and began a siege against it. Three years later. . .Samaria fell. 2 Kings 18:9–10

- Assyrian king
- Erased northern Jewish nation of Israel

WHEN ISRAEL stopped sending taxes to ASSYRIA, in what is now Iraq, King Shalmaneser came and took everything. His armies destroyed the capital city of SAMARIA, deported Jewish survivors, and repopulated the land with Assyrian settlers.

SHARON, PLAIN
Map 4 B4

(SHARE uhn)

I am the rose of Sharon, and the lily of the valleys. Song of Solomon 2:1 KJV

- Fertile coastland in Israel

SAND DUNES AND MARSHLAND made up some of the Sharon Plain in Bible times. Sharon was a strip of Mediterranean coastland about 10 miles wide and 30 miles long (16 by 48 km). But parts of it were ideal for grazing livestock, which is how the people used it.

SHAVE

Hanun arrested David's officials and had their beards shaved off on one side of their faces. . . . They were terribly ashamed. 2 Samuel 10:4–5 CEV

JEWS DIDN'T SHAVE in OLD TESTAMENT times. Not usually, it seems. Assyrian art shows Jewish men with full BEARDS and long HAIR.

Exceptions to the rule: They shaved their head while MOURNING or as part of a "PURIFICATION ceremony" (Acts 21:24).

See also RAZOR.

Mt. E

Mt. Gerizim

SHEBA

Map 2 L10

(SHE buh)

Long live the king! May the gold of Sheba be given to him. Psalm 72:15

- Arab nation

YEMEN is a common guess about where King SOLOMON's visitor, the QUEEN OF SHEBA, came from. If that guess is right, she drove her CARAVAN loaded with over 4 tons (4,000 kg) of GOLD some 1,500 miles (2,400 km) north to ISRAEL. That's nearly the distance from Washington DC to Denver.

SHECHEM

(SHECK come)

1800s BC

When. . .Shechem saw Dinah, he took her and raped her. Then his heart longed for Jacob's daughter Dinah. He fell in love with her. Genesis 34:2–3 NIrV

- Prince of city of Shechem
- Raped Jacob's daughter Dinah

PRINCE SHECHEM managed to get his city wiped out by JACOB's angry sons, SIMEON and LEVI.

First mistake: raping their only sister, DINAH.

Second mistake: asking to marry her.

Last mistake: agreeing to have all the men in the village get circumcised, out of respect for Jewish TRADITION.

While the men were still hurting from the surgery, Dinah's brothers killed them and looted the town. They took everything, including the women and children as slaves.

SHECHEM, CITY OF

Map 1 D5

(SHECK come)

Abram traveled through the land as far as Shechem. . . . Then the LORD appeared to Abram and said, "I will give this land to your descendants." Genesis 12:6–7

- Where God promised Israel to Abraham

SOME OF ISRAEL'S MOST IMPORTANT HISTORY took place in the valley where the city of Shechem grew up, at the end of a narrow pass between MOUNT GERIZIM and MOUNT EBAL:

1. first city ABRAHAM visited in what is now ISRAEL
2. where JOSHUA renewed Israel's CONTRACT with GOD after conquering the highlands (Joshua 24)
3. first capital of the north Jewish nation of Israel after the nation split (1 Kings 12:25).

SHECHEM village was nestled in the pass between two mountains where Joshua and the Jews renewed their pledge of allegiance to God.

Shechem ruins

NABLUS, WEST BANK

N

STEPHEN M. MILLER'S ILLUSTRATED BIBLE DICTIONARY

Nabal was a very rich man who lived in Maon. He owned three thousand sheep.
1 Samuel 25:2 CEV

- Money-making livestock

SHEEP EQUALED MONEY in Bible times, with herders measuring their net worth by counting their sheep.

Relatively easy to care for, sheep could graze on next to nothing, including the shortest plant nubs—nibbling them down to the roots. But they provided a rich return on the investment:

- a HARVEST of wool each spring
- MILK
- meat
- horns to hold OLIVE OIL or to serve as shofar horns
- skin for tents, WINESKINS, and CLOTHING

JEWS sacrificed sheep, too.

Most sheep in the area had fatty tails that could weigh up to 30 pounds (14 kg). Hungry Middle Easterners considered those tails a delicacy.

Jesus used sheep as symbols in his teachings PARABLES—including one story about a worried herder who left his 99 safe sheep to find the one lost sheep (Matthew 18:12–14).

SHEKEL

(SHECK uhl)

"The standard unit of weight will be the silver shekel." Ezekiel 45:12

- Almost half an ounce (11 g)
- Jewish silver coin

WEIGHING ABOUT AS MUCH as a 50-cent piece or almost as much as two Euro coins, a SILVER shekel in Bible times would pay the average worker's WAGES for four days. It equaled four denarii.

When Jewish men paid their annual half-shekel TAX to the Jerusalem TEMPLE, PRIESTS preferred the high-quality silver shekels and half-shekels stamped at TYRE, a city in what is now LEBANON. MONEY CHANGERS converted other currency into Tyre coins.

See also MONEY.

SHEM

Before 2500 BC

Noah was the father of three sons: Shem, Ham, and Japheth. Genesis 6:10

- Noah's oldest son
- Helped cover drunk, naked Noah

NOAHS' OLDEST SON, Shem helped him build the boat that weathered out the FLOOD. Afterward, when his brother HAM invited the other two to come and see their father drunk and naked, Shem and JAPHETH respectfully backed toward their father and covered him.

SHEMA

(shuh MAH)

"Israel, listen to me. The LORD is our God. The LORD is the one and only God. Love the LORD your God with all your heart and with all your soul. Love him with all your strength."
Deuteronomy 6:4–5 NIrv

- The bedrock foundation of all Jewish beliefs

JEWS DON'T HAVE A CREED like the Apostles' Creed that Christians use as a statement of FAITH, to separate heretics from genuine Christians. But if they did, Deuteronomy 6:4–9 would ring that bell.

JEWS call the passage the *Shema* because in HEBREW the word means "listen," which is how the passage begins.

The Jewish belief in one GOD—not three—is why most Jews in NEW TESTAMENT times rejected the teaching of fellow Jews who presented Jesus as God's Son and the HOLY SPIRIT as God at work among believers.

SHEMAIAH

(shuh MAY yuh)

900s BC

God told Shemaiah the prophet to give Rehoboam. . .this warning: "Don't go to war against the people from Israel—they are your relatives." 1 Kings 12:22–24 CEV

- Jewish prophet
- Helped avert a Jewish civil war

WHEN ISRAEL'S 10 NORTHERN TRIBES seceded from the union to start their own independent Jewish country, King REHOBOAM decided to go to WAR to keep ISRAEL united under his rule. Shemaiah advised against it, preventing the war.

SHEOL

(SHE ohl)

"You know also what Joab son of Zeruiah did to me. . . . Do not let his gray head go down to Sheol in peace." David to Solomon, 1 Kings 2:5–6 NRSV

- Place of the dead
- Hebrew word for Greek "Hades"

JEWS IN OLD TESTAMENT TIMES spoke of the dead going to a place called Sheol. The JEWS seemed to think of Sheol as underground, in some kind of hollow earth world—a place for both the good and the bad.

When a man named KORAH led a revolt against MOSES, the writer described the death of Korah and his followers: "The ground opens its mouth and swallows them up, with all that belongs to them, and they go down alive into Sheol" (Numbers 16:30 NRSV).

See also HADES.

SHEPHERD

The LORD cares for his nation, just as shepherds care for their flocks. He carries the lambs in his arms, while gently leading the mother sheep. Isaiah 40:11 CEV

- Herder of sheep, goats

A GOOD SHEPHERD puts his life on the line to protect his sheep. So said Jesus, comparing himself to a shepherd out to save the human flock.

S

TRAVELING HERDERS, shepherds were often on the move searching for pasture and WATER for their flocks of SHEEP and herds of GOATS.

The job required constant attention—especially keeping an eye out for strays and fighting off hungry predators.

Young DAVID, lobbying to fight GOLIATH, told King SAUL, "I take care of my father's sheep. And when one of them is dragged off by a lion or a bear, I go after it and beat the wild ANIMAL until it lets the sheep go. If the wild animal turns and attacks me, I grab it by the throat and kill it" (1 Samuel 17:34–35 CEV).

Jesus used shepherds who put their lives on the line as a way to describe his mission: "I am the good shepherd. The good shepherd sacrifices his life for the sheep" (John 10:11).

SHIBBOLETH

(SHIB uh leth)

They would tell him to say "Shibboleth." If he was from Ephraim, he would say "Sibboleth," because people from Ephraim cannot pronounce the word correctly. Judges 12:6

- A mysterious word that killed 42,000 Jews

NO ONE SEEMS TO KNOW what Shibboleth means. But the BIBLE says JEWS from the northern tribe of EPHRAIM couldn't pronounce the *h* in the word.

Instead of saying *SHIB uh leth* they would say *SIBB uh leth*.

A Jewish warrior named JEPHTHAH used that word to get even with the tribe—to punish them for refusing to help him fight off one of ISRAEL's enemies. When Ephraim Jews tried to cross the JORDAN RIVER at a shallow ford that had become a popular crossing, his men ordered them to pronounce the password. If they couldn't, they died trying.

SHIELD

Goliath walked out toward David with his shield bearer ahead of him. 1 Samuel 17:41

GOLIATH'S SHIELD may have been a full-body shield—or nearly so—since a shield bearer carried it for him. But most soldiers didn't seem to have the luxury of a shield holder. Many soldiers fought with both a shield and a SWORD or SPEAR.

Some shields were made of metal. But it seems

that most shields in Bible times were small and light-weight, made of LEATHER stretched over a wooden or metal frame. Soldiers had to keep that leather oiled so it wouldn't become dry and brittle.

SHILOH

Map 1 D5

(SHY low)

The LORD continued to appear at Shiloh and gave messages to Samuel there at the Tabernacle. 1 Samuel 3:21

- Israel's first capital
- Home of the tent worship center

WHEN JEWS SETTLED in what is now ISRAEL after JOSHUA led them in capturing the central highlands, they set up shop in Shiloh, a community about 30 miles (48 km) north of JERUSALEM.

Shiloh became both their political headquarters and their WORSHIP center. The prophet SAMUEL grew up there, working as a PRIEST in the TABERNACLE, a TENT version of what would later become the Jerusalem TEMPLE.

SHINAR

(see SUMER)

SHIP

Hiram sent experienced crews of sailors to sail the ships with Solomon's men. 1 Kings 9:27

JEWS WERE LANDLUBBERS. Mostly. They were herders and farmers who preferred dirt under their feet—more sea-fearing than seafaring. But they did get their feet wet from time to time.

They fished, mainly on small boats in the Disney World–sized lake called the SEA OF GALILEE.

The dilapidated frame of a first-century FISHING boat was discovered in the lake's mud in 1986. The boat, 8 by 26 feet (2 by 8 m), would have held about 15 men.

JEWS traveled, too, sailing on large ships built by neighboring nations. Phoenicians in what is now LEBA-NON were famous for their ships and sailors. Phoenician

SAILING, GREEK-STYLE. This picture from an ancient Greek dish shows a style of sailboat in the 500s BC. That's about the time the Jews returned to their homeland after 50 years of exile in what is now Iraq.

king HIRAM provided crews for King SOLOMON's fleet of trading ships. PAUL sailed thousands of miles on ships built by Phoenicians, Egyptians, and Romans—and getting shipwrecked several times.

There weren't really passenger ships. There were cargo ships that took passengers as cargo. Passengers probably slept on deck and brought their own food for the VOYAGE. They sailed under the power of the wind and a crew of oarsmen—often dozens of them.

There were warships, too. Some could carry about 200 soldiers.

Winter storms and fog kept most sailors in port from October through April. Exceptions: WAR, lots of MONEY—as a crew might get when hungry citizens of ROME were willing to pay a premium price for Egyptian GRAIN. It was on just such "an Egyptian ship from ALEXANDRIA that was bound for Italy" (Acts 27:6)—sailing in the risky season—that Paul got shipwrecked.

SHISHAK

(SHY shack)

Ruled 945–924 BC

King Shishak of Egypt came up and attacked Jerusalem. He ransacked the treasuries of the LORD's Temple and the royal palace; he stole everything. 2 Chronicles 12:9

- King of Egypt
- Attacked both Jewish nations: Israel, Judah
- Plundered Jerusalem's Temple
- Egyptian name: Shoshenq I

AN OPPORTUNIST, EGYPT's king invaded the Jewish homeland during one of ISRAEL's weak moments in history: shortly after the nation split into two countries.

That was a shock to the new king of the northern Jewish nation of Israel: JEROBOAM. Years earlier, Shishak had given him asylum from King SOLOMON, who wanted to kill him.

As for the southern Jewish nation of JUDAH, King REHOBOAM—Solomon's son—averted the destruction of his capital city of JERUSALEM by agreeing to pay TRIBUTE taxes to Shishak.

Reports of this invasion aren't limited to the BIBLE. They're posted as a brag on the wall of the king's temple at Karnak, with pictures of 156 captives.

PICTURES OF CAPTIVES from what is now Israel decorate the wall of the temple in Karnak. It commemorates Shishak's invasion, also reported in the Bible.

| SHITTIM | (see ACACIA GROVE) |

| SHOFAR | (see RAM'S HORN) |

| SHOWBREAD | (see BREAD OF THE PRESENCE) |

SHRINE

The people of Judah. . .built their own local shrines and stone images of foreign gods. . . on every hill and in the shade of large trees.
1 Kings 14:22–23 CEV

▪ A place to worship a god

PEOPLE WORSHIPED THEIR GODS in shrines as elaborate as a temple or as simple as a pile of ROCKS on a hilltop.

Those pagan shrines were everywhere, especially on hilltops—which seemed to get the worshiper as close to their heavenly god as possible.

JEWS, however, weren't supposed to WORSHIP just anywhere: "Be careful not to SACRIFICE your burnt offerings just anywhere you like. You may do so only at the place the LORD will choose within one of your tribal territories" (Deuteronomy 12:13–14).

GOD chose JERUSALEM, after King SOLOMON built the TEMPLE there.

Most Jewish KINGS, however, seemed to tolerate pagan shrines. Even Solomon.

But others didn't, including JOSIAH and HEZEKIAH: "Didn't Hezekiah tear down his shrines and altars and make everyone in JUDAH and Jerusalem worship only at the altar here in Jerusalem?" (2 Kings 18:22).

SHUNEM   Map 1 C4

(SHOO nuhm)

Philistines set up their camp at Shunem, and Saul gathered all the army of Israel and camped at Gilboa.
1 Samuel 28:4

▪ Where Elisha brought a dead boy to life

A VILLAGE some 7 miles (11 km) south of Jesus' hometown of NAZARETH, Shunem is best known for the BIBLE's report of what sounds like CPR.

Treating a seemingly dead boy, ELISHA "lay down on the child's body, placing his mouth on the child's mouth" (2 Kings 4:34). The child sneezed and opened his eyes.

Shunem was also the campground for the Philistine ARMY that defeated King SAUL's army, killing him and three of his sons.

SHUR DESERT
Map 2 I8

(SURE)

Moses led the people of Israel away from the Red Sea, and they moved out into the desert of Shur. They traveled in this desert for three days without finding any water. Exodus 15:22

- Somewhere in Sinai Peninsula

NO ONE KNOWS exactly where this DESERT was. Though MOSES led the Jewish refugees into this desert after crossing the RED SEA (literally "Sea of Reeds"), it's unclear what body of WATER they crossed. What seems likely, though, is that they were headed east into the Sinai badlands.

SHUSHAN
(see SUSA)

SIDON
Map 1 C3

(SI duhn)

Men of Tyre and Sidon had brought vast amounts of cedar to David. 1 Chronicles 22:4

- City in Lebanon
- 35 miles (56 km) north of Israel
- Arabic name: Sayda

LUMBERJACKS FROM SIDON in LEBANON cut CEDAR timber for King DAVID, who was stockpiling construction material for Jerusalem's TEMPLE. David's son and successor later built the Temple.

SIEGE

King Nebuchadnezzar came with his army to besiege Jerusalem. Two and a half years later, on July 18 in the eleventh year of Zedekiah's reign, the Babylonians broke through the wall, and the city fell. Jeremiah 39:1–2

- Military tactic of surrounding a city

WALLED CITIES were more than a speed bump for invading forces. Scaling defended walls cost a lot in blood. Many invaders opted to surround the target city and wait the defenders to death, starving them in a long siege.

IT WAS A WAITING GAME for many invasion forces when they came to a city protected by towering stone walls.

Invaders could expect high casualties if they stormed the walls. If they had the time, it was a smarter use of blood and guts to surround the city and cut off all sources of food, WEAPONS, and other supplies.

In Bible times, JERUSALEM was besieged by invaders from the empires of ASSYRIA and BABYLON in Iran and from ROME.

Assyrian king SENNACHERIB in 701 BC gave up after 185,000 of his soldiers were killed by what some scholars speculate was probably a PLAGUE, perhaps bubonic.

NEBUCHADNEZZAR of Babylon waited two and a half years before his troops broke through the walls and leveled Jerusalem in 586 BC.

One Jewish writer described how the JEWS suffered during their marathon wait:

S

- Starving children. "Little children and tiny babies are fainting and dying in the streets. . . . Even the jackals feed their young, but not my people" (Lamentations 2:11; 4:3).
- Emaciated nobles. "No one recognizes them in the streets. Their skin sticks to their bones; it is as dry and hard as wood" (Lamentations 4:8).
- Cannibal mothers. "Tenderhearted women have cooked their own children. They have eaten them to survive the siege" (Lamentations 4:10).

First-century Jewish historian Josephus reported more of the same when Roman general Titus, crushing a Jewish uprising, besieged Jerusalem in AD 68. The seige lasted for a couple of years—without much success. But in AD 70, Titus amped up the siege by building a trench around the city. By summertime, his men broke through the walls. They set fire to the city and destroyed the TEMPLE.

SIGN

"The Lord himself will give you the sign. Look! The virgin will conceive a child! She will give birth to a son and will call him Immanuel (which means 'God is with us')." Isaiah 7:14

- Miraculous event that shows God is involved

MIRACLES and predicted events coming true served as evidence that GOD was on the job.

That's how God described the 10 plagues of EGYPT: "my miraculous signs and wonders" (Exodus 7:3).

That's also how the GOSPEL of JOHN described the MIRACLES of Jesus. Sadly, the writer reported, "Despite all the miraculous signs Jesus had done, most of the people still did not believe in him" (John 12:37).

SIHON

(SI hon)

1400s or 1200s, debated

King Sihon would not let the Israelites pass through his country. He gathered his whole army together, and they marched out to meet Israel in the desert. Numbers 21:23 NCV

- King of Amorites in Jordan

REFUSING TO LET MOSES and the Jewish refugees pass peacefully through his land, King Sihon attacked them. He died in the battle, and the JEWS seized his land.

SILAS

(SI luhs)

First century AD

About midnight Paul and Silas were praying and singing praises to God, while the other prisoners listened. Suddenly a strong earthquake shook the jail. Acts 16:25–26 CEV

- Ministry associate of Paul
- Helped write 1 Peter

WHEN PAUL DECIDED to take a second missionary trip to Turkey, he took Silas with him as an associate. They ventured into Europe, going to what is now Greece. Both men were arrested in PHILIPPI but were freed by an EARTHQUAKE. Instead of fleeing, they stayed—an act that seemed to convince the jailer their FAITH was genuine. The jailer converted to CHRISTIANITY.

SILK

"I gave you expensive clothing of fine linen and silk." Ezekiel 16:10

- Fabric imported from China

CHINESE CATERPILLARS nicknamed "silkworms" spun silk fiber for their cocoons. The Chinese harvested these fibers from what are several species of moths.

They used the fiber to make fabric, which they exported throughout the world. It was a favorite of royalty—and it was beyond the sensible budget of most others.

SILOAM POOL
See Jerusalem, Map 4 C5

(si LOH uhm)

"The man they call Jesus made mud and spread it over my eyes and told me, 'Go to the pool of Siloam and wash yourself.' So I went and washed, and now I can see!" John 9:11

- Jerusalem's water reservoir

JERUSALEM GOT ITS WATER from Siloam pool, which was fed by the GIHON Spring in a cave outside the city walls.

King HEZEKIAH wanted to make sure JERUSALEM had all the WATER it needed when invaders surrounded the city. So he assigned miners to chisel a TUNNEL nearly 600 yards (550 m) through solid rock, from the spring to what became the Siloam Pool inside the city. This is the pool where Jesus sent a blind man to wash his eyes.

SILVER

Judas Iscariot, went to talk to the leading priests. He said, "What will you pay me for giving Jesus to you?" And they gave him thirty silver coins. Matthew 26:14–15 NCV

SILVER was one of the first metals people used, some 5,000 years ago. Folks loved its shiny look. And it was easy to work with—bending, hammering thin, and pulling into strings of wire.

Silver came from refining a lead ore called galena. There wasn't much galena in what is now ISRAEL, so JEWS had to import it from places such as CRETE, the Greek islands, and SPAIN.

People used silver to make coins, JEWELRY, musical instruments, and figurines. PAUL managed to start a riot because his PREACHING in the city of EPHESUS hurt the idol-making business of an influential silversmith named DEMETRIUS (Acts 19:23–41).

DEDICATING JESUS. "I have seen your salvation," the prophet Simeon says during the dedication of Jesus. "He is a light to reveal God to the nations" (Luke 2:30, 32).

SIMEON

(SIM ee uhn)

1. 1800s BC
2. About 6 BC

Simeon and Levi, who were Dinah's full brothers, took their swords and. . . slaughtered every male there [in Shechem]. Genesis 34:25

1. JACOB'S SECOND SON OF 12, Simeon is most famous for taking REVENGE on the entire city of SHECHEM after the PRINCE of the city raped his sister, DINAH. Simeon and his brother LEVI killed all the men. Then the rest of JACOB's sons helped plunder the city and enslave the women and children.

2. PROPHET AT DEDICATION OF JESUS. An elderly PROPHET in JERUSALEM, Simeon was at the TEMPLE when MARY and JOSEPH brought baby Jesus for the ritual of DEDICATION (Luke 2). The HOLY SPIRIT had promised that Simeon wouldn't die until he saw the MESSIAH.

S

SIMEON, TRIBE OF
Map 1 B7

(SIM ee uhn)

Simeon was the second tribe chosen to receive land, and the region for its clans was inside Judah's borders. Joshua 19:1 CEV

ON HIS DEATHBED, Jacob complained about his son Simeon's tendency toward violence. Jacob predicted that Simeon's ANCESTORS would become scattered. In fact, Simeon's tribe eventually got assimilated into the larger tribe of JUDAH.

SIMON

(SI muhn)

First century AD

As the soldiers were going out of the city with Jesus, they forced a man from Cyrene, named Simon, to carry the cross for Jesus.
Matthew 27:32 NCV

THERE ARE NEARLY A DOZEN men named Simon in the BIBLE, including Simon PETER, another DISCIPLE of Jesus, a leper, a PHARISEE, the CYRENE who carried Jesus' CROSS, a sorcerer, and a leatherworker.

SIMON PETER (see PETER)

SIN

"Do what is right. Then you will be accepted. If you don't do what is right, sin is waiting at your door to grab you. It longs to have you. But you must rule over it." God to Cain,
Genesis 4:7 NIrv

▪ Disobeying God

CHRISTIANS DON'T AGREE on what qualifies as sin.

Some say it's sin only if we know it's wrong, but we do it anyhow. The BIBLE seems to go further, some scholars say, suggesting that ignorance of GOD's law is no excuse. The evidence that some scholars cite: God created a SACRIFICE ritual to "purify you from your unintentional sin" (Leviticus 5:18).

Jesus said we can sin, too, when we don't act: "I was hungry. But you gave me nothing to eat. I was thirsty. But you gave me nothing to drink. I was a stranger. But you did not invite me in. I needed clothes. But you did

not give me any. I was sick and in PRISON. But you did not take care of me" (Matthew 25:42–43 NIrv).

The remedy for sin? See FORGIVENESS.

SIN, UNFORGIVABLE

"Anyone who speaks against the Holy Spirit will not be forgiven." Matthew 12:32 NIrv

▪ Unconfessed sin, according to some experts

JESUS TREATED THE HOLY SPIRIT like his little sister—or so it might seem to some Bible newcomers. Jesus said it's fixable to say bad things about him or about GOD the FATHER. Those sins can be forgiven. But if we diss the HOLY SPIRIT, we're toast. That is what it sounds like. BLASPHEMY is an eternal killer.

Most Bible experts agree that Jesus wasn't saying that at all.

The way to understand what Jesus meant, scholars say, is to look at what provoked him to say what he did. He had just healed a man triple-dipped in trouble: demon-possessed, blind, and unable to speak. Instead of attributing this MIRACLE to the power of God, the PHARISEES said, "No wonder he can cast out DEMONS. He gets his power from SATAN, the prince of demons" (Matthew 12:24).

Scholars interpret Jesus' warning to them in a variety of ways. Among the many theories about what the UNFORGIVABLE SIN is:

▪ giving the devil credit for God's work
▪ rejecting the work of the Holy Spirit, who is the one who calls us to God
▪ talking ourselves out of believing in Jesus.

Pharisees saw the proof of God's power with their own eyes but refused to believe it. God won't forgive people who refuse to admit their sin and repent, many scholars insist.

For people worried that they've committed the unforgivable sin, scholars say, their worry is evidence they haven't committed it. God forgives everyone who asks for FORGIVENESS.

Map labels: Mediterranean Sea · EGYPT · CANAAN (Israel) · Dead Sea · Nile River · SINAI PENINSULA · Gulf of Sinai · Gulf of Aqaba · △ Mt. Sinai 7,497 ft 2,285 m · N · Red Sea

SINAI PENINSULA

Map 2 I8

(SI ni)

Two months after the Israelites left Egypt, they arrived in the wilderness of Sinai.
Exodus 19:1

- Where Jews camped for a year at Mount Sinai
- Egyptian badlands the size of West Virginia

FROM ORBIT, the Sinai Peninsula looks like a wedge of rock pie splitting the top of the RED SEA into a couple of rabbit ears.

The Sinai stretches about 240 miles (386 km) from that southern tip north to the MEDITERRANEAN SEA. Covering some 24,000 square miles (about 62,000 square km), it's about the size of West Virginia—or double the size of ISRAEL.

The Sinai isn't kind to visitors. Looking a bit like the Dakota Badlands—or Mars in some spots—the Sinai is part of the Sahara and the Arabian DESERTS.

In a year's time, the arid southland is lucky to get over 2 inches (5 cm) of rain. That's the area where many say MOSES and the JEWS spent about a year.

It was there, at the foot of MOUNT SINAI, that

Moses was grazing flocks when he encountered GOD at a BURNING BUSH. This is also where he and the Jewish refugees on their EXODUS out of EGYPT camped while Moses received laws from God that organized the 12 TRIBES OF ISRAEL into a nation.

Israel captured the Sinai during the Six-Day War of 1967 but returned the land to Egypt in 1982.

SISERA

(SIS ur uh)

1100s BC

When Sisera fell asleep from exhaustion, Jael quietly crept up to him with a hammer and tent peg in her hand. Then she drove the tent peg through his temple and into the ground.
Judges 4:21

- Commander of a Canaanite army invading Israel
- Killed by a woman with a hammer and tent peg

SISERA LED HIS CHARIOT CORPS into battle against the JEWS commanded by a prophetess, DEBORAH. A rainstorm trapped the chariots in mud, forcing

S

Sisera and his men to run for their lives. Sisera found a resting place in the camp of a herder's family. The herder was gone, but his WIFE—JAEL—welcomed Sisera to rest in their TENT. Jael either favored ISRAEL or was a terribly inhospitable host, given what she did with her hammer and tent peg.

SLANDER

Never slander a worker to the employer, or the person will curse you, and you will pay for it. Proverbs 30:10

- A lie intended to hurt someone

FROM OLD TESTAMENT SAGES to New Testament APOSTLES, the BIBLE's message is consistent when it comes to telling lies that damage another person's character: don't.

"Now is the time to get rid of anger, rage, malicious behavior, slander, and dirty language" (Colossians 3:8).

SLAVERY

Masters, be just and fair to your slaves. Remember that you also have a Master—in heaven. Colossians 4:1

- Common throughout Bible times

SLAVERY WAS COMMON among GOD-loving JEWS and Christians as it was among Southern Christians in early American history. Most folks saw nothing wrong with it.

People got enslaved for many reasons:

- sold to pay a DEBT they couldn't cover
- sold when children to provide MONEY for the FAMILY
- captured in WAR
- kidnapped by pirates or raiders.

Founding fathers of ISRAEL had slaves. ABRAHAM and SARAH had HAGAR who became a surrogate mother for the couple, giving BIRTH to ISHMAEL. JACOB's two wives each had a personal slave who also served as a surrogate mother.

PHILEMON, the CHURCH leader in COLOSSE, had a runaway slave: ONESIMUS. PAUL apparently converted the slave and then ordered him to go back. But Paul also suggested that Philemon free Onesimus so he could help Paul.

Instead of lobbying for Christians to free all slaves—an act that might have prodded ROME into seeing CHRISTIANITY as a threat to their way of life—Paul urged mutual respect between master and slave. In the long haul, Paul may have realized, respect would unlock doors.

USING LOW-BUDGET ARTILLERY, slingers rained rocks on the enemy during battle.

SLING

Among all these soldiers there were seven hundred who were left-handed, each of whom could sling a stone at a hair and not miss. Judges 20:16 TNIV

- Weapon to propel a rock

WHEN DAVID DROPPED GOLIATH with a stone, he didn't use a forked slingshot powered by rubber bands. He used something more powerful: two strips of LEATHER with a wide pad in the middle.

David held the two ends of leather. Then he loaded a rock into the pad and swirled the sling above his head in a tight circle. When he released one strip of the leather, momentum could have driven the rock at about 100 yards (meters) a second. The force was so lethal that soldiers used slingshots as low-budget artillery.

SMYRNA   Map 3 E3

(SMUR nuh)

"To the church in Smyrna. . . "I know that you suffer and are poor. But you are rich!"
Revelation 2:8–9 NIrV

- West coast city in Turkey
- One of seven churches in Revelation

JESUS DICTATED LETTERS to seven churches in western Turkey. Only two got nothing but compliments: Smyrna and PHILADELPHIA. "Be faithful, even if it means you must die," Jesus told Christians at Smyrna. "Then I will give you a CROWN. The crown is life itself" (Revelation 2:10 NIrV).

SNAKE

The LORD sent poisonous snakes among the people, and many were bitten and died.
Numbers 21:6

POISONOUS SNAKES slink around the Bible lands—about half a dozen species, including the Egyptian cobra and the horned viper. So it's not surprising that MOSES and the Jewish refugees on their EXODUS out of EGYPT encountered what sounds like a nest of them.

The most famous snake in the BIBLE talked.

It talked Eve into eating FORBIDDEN FRUIT in the Garden of EDEN. It was just a talking snake in the first book in the Bible, GENESIS. But in the last book, it's "the ancient serpent, called the devil, or SATAN" (Revelation 12:9).

SOAP

"Scrub, using the strongest soaps. Scour your skin raw. The sin-grease won't come out. I can't stand to even look at you!"
Jeremiah 2:22 MSG

ANIMAL FAT AND ASHES. Those were the ingredients in the soap of Bible times—for those who used soap. Most probably didn't. In ISRAEL, where there was a lot of OLIVE OIL, they may have used that for the fatty base—adding SALT minerals or plant ashes for abrasives.

SODOM AND GOMORRAH   Map 1 E7

(SOD uhm) (guh MORE uh)

The LORD rained down fire and burning sulfur from the sky on Sodom and Gomorrah. He utterly destroyed them, along with the other cities and villages of the plain, wiping out all the people and every bit of vegetation.
Genesis 19:24–25

- Twin sin cities destroyed by fire

WHEN ABRAHAM AND LOT PARTED COMPANY, Lot picked what he thought was the better location: Sodom, with its "fertile plains. . .like the garden of the LORD" (Genesis 13:10).

Raiders liked it, too. They plundered Sodom and other cities of the plain, taking the citizens captive. ABRAHAM came to their rescue, chasing down the raiders and freeing the captives. But he wasn't able to save them from GOD's judgment later.

God told Abraham, "Their SIN is so bad that I will go down and see it for myself" (Genesis 18:20–21 NIrV).

God didn't like what he saw. He sent ANGELS to escort LOT and his FAMILY out of town. Then came the fireworks. Scholars speculate that a fire or lightning may have ignited one of the many pockets of gas in the area, unleashing a storm of searing SULFUR, SALT, and other minerals in the area.

It's uncertain where the cities were. But a persistent theory places them in what are now the southern shallows of the DEAD SEA. In Bible times, that may have

S

been a fertile plain that got flooded—perhaps by a quake in this quake-prone rift valley.

- or just got engaged (see Deuteronomy 20:5–8).

SOLDIERS

King Shishak of Egypt. . .attacked Jerusalem. . . with 1,200 chariots, 60,000 horses, and a countless army of foot soldiers. 2 Chronicles 12:2–3

- Volunteers, draftees, local warriors, foreign mercenaries

ISRAEL DIDN'T HAVE AN ARMY until they got a KING. They had a militia—volunteers and draftees who fought to defend their people.

ABRAHAM mustered his SERVANTS, who helped him fight raiders who had kidnapped LOT. And when JOSHUA led the conquest of what is now ISRAEL, most Jewish men who were able to fight were expected to do just that.

Exempt from military service, men who:

- were LEVITES (the tribe in charge of WORSHIP; see Numbers 1:49)
- just built a HOUSE
- just planted a vineyard

SAUL, Israel's first king, set up the country's first paid ARMY. As part of their pay, his soldiers probably got to keep some of the valuables they took from conquered towns.

DAVID added to Israel's army an elite force that served as his bodyguard: the Thirty, which apparently included the best of the best: the Three (2 Samuel 23:23).

SOLOMON

(SAH luh muhn)

Ruled about 970–930 BC

God said: Solomon. . .I'll make you wiser than anyone who has ever lived or ever will live. 1 Kings 3:11–12 CEV

- King of Israel
- Builder of the first Jewish Temple
- Son of David and Bathsheba
- Husband to 1,000 women
- Credited with writing 3,000 proverbs

FOR A WISE GUY, King Solomon did some incredibly stupid things. Like marrying 1,000 women, building shrines to their idol GODS, and then worshiping the IDOLS.

SOLOMON'S MOST FAMOUS judgment saves a baby. Two women claim the baby. When Solomon offers to split the baby in two, only the real mom objects. Case solved.

Because of it, he lost his kingdom. His dynasty over ISRAEL was one and out. When his son REHOBOAM came to power, the nation split in two. Ten tribes seceded from the union. All that was left for Rehoboam was his FAMILY tribe of JUDAH along with the tiny tribe of BENJAMIN, which got assimilated into Judah.

The PROPHET Ahijah had predicted it.

Quoting GOD, he told JEROBOAM, the man who would be king of the 10 northern tribes: "I am about to tear the kingdom from the hand of Solomon, and I will give ten of the tribes to you!" (1 Kings 11:31).

SOLOMON'S START: WEALTHY AND WISE

After Solomon became KING, he offered sacrifices to God. That night God came to him in a DREAM, inviting him to ask for anything.

"I am like a little child who doesn't know his way around," Solomon said. "Give me an understanding heart so that I can govern your people well" (1 Kings 3:7, 9).

Done. And then some. God promised him riches and fame, too.

Wisdom. One Bible story illustrates his WISDOM. Two PROSTITUTES each claimed a baby son as theirs. One had accidentally rolled onto her child in the night and suffocated him. Then she swapped babies with her roommate. Solomon offered to hack the living baby in two, giving each woman half. When the baby thief agreed, he knew she wasn't the MOTHER.

Riches. Solomon got rich on trade deals. He controlled Israel, the only popular land bridge between northern nations and African nations in the south. He built a fleet of trade ships that sailed the RED SEA and the Mediterranean. The QUEEN OF SHEBA came with what sounds like a CARAVAN of goods to trade: four and a half tons (4,000 kg) of GOLD, along with jewels and SPICES. "Each year Solomon received about 25 tons [23 metric tons] of gold. This did not include the additional revenue he received from MERCHANTS and traders, all the kings of ARABIA, and the GOVERNORS of the land" (1 Kings 10:14–15).

Fame. He is credited with writing "some 3,000 proverbs. . .1,005 songs" (1 Kings 4:32), including some attributed to him in the books of PROVERBS and PSALMS. He's also credited with writing the cerebral book of ECCLESIASTES—a quest for the meaning of life. Some

say he wrote the SONG OF SONGS—an erotic love song, though others say he had nothing to do with it.

Perhaps his most memorable feat was to build the first Jewish TEMPLE. God had not allowed King DAVID to build the Temple, perhaps because David was a man of WAR. But Solomon lived in a time of PEACE. He drafted nearly 200,000 men to build the Temple, a project that took seven years. But it was a Temple that would endure for about 400 years, until Babylonian invaders from what is now Iraq tore it to the ground in 586 BC.

Israel reached its peak in size, GLORY, and influence during Solomon's Golden Age. When he died, the glory died with him, and his son was left to rule a splinter of a nation.

SON

"Why are you crying, Hannah? . . . Why be downhearted just because you have no children? You have me—isn't that better than having ten sons?" 1 Samuel 1:8

JOB ONE FOR A WOMAN in Bible times was to produce kids—preferably sons. Only sons could inherit their FATHER's estate, unless the father had nothing but daughters. Every son got an equal share, except the first son. He got a double share.

Some Bible writers used the word *son* as a term of endearment. Writers in PROVERBS and ECCLESIASTES often addressed their student as "my son." In the NEW TESTAMENT, PAUL and PETER spoke of their associates—TIMOTHY and MARK—as "son" or "child."

SON OF GOD

Jesus is the Christ, the Son of God. If you believe this, you will have life because you belong to him. John 20:31 NIrV

- Nickname of Jesus
- Nickname of someone devoted to God

NEW TESTAMENT WRITERS introduced Jesus as more than just ISRAEL's MESSIAH and SAVIOR. They

S

identified him as GOD's one and only Son.

OLD TESTAMENT writers often spoke of Israel as God's children, too. "This is what the LORD says: Israel is my FIRSTBORN son" (Exodus 4:22). Same for Israel's righteous KINGS: "You are my son" (Psalm 2:7).

Used in the plural—sons of God—the phrase seems to describe either heavenly beings or perhaps earthly rulers:

- "The sons of God saw the beautiful women and took any they wanted as their wives" (Genesis 6:2).
- God to JOB: "Where were you when I laid the foundations of the earth? . . . When the morning stars sang together, and all the sons of God shouted for joy?" (Job 38:4, 7 NKJV).

SON OF MAN

"Passover begins in two days, and the Son of Man will be handed over to be crucified."
Matthew 26:2

- Jesus' favorite way of describing himself
- God's way of describing Ezekiel

THERE'S A REASON this was Jesus' favorite way of referring to himself. Scholars say the history of this title suggests Jesus used it because it pointed both to his HUMANITY and his divinity.

Humanity: About 600 years earlier, GOD used this title for the prophet EZEKIEL—as a way of reminding the prophet that Ezekiel was only human. "Stand up, son of man" (Ezekiel 2:1).

Divinity: But for the prophet DANIEL, the title seemed to point to the SECOND COMING of Jesus. Daniel had a VISION he described this way: "I saw someone like a son of man coming with the clouds of HEAVEN. . . . He was given authority, honor, and sovereignty over all the nations of the world, so that people of every race and nation and language would obey him. His rule is eternal—it will never end. His kingdom will never be destroyed" (Daniel 7:13–14).

SONG   (see MUSIC)

LOVERS in the Song of Songs might not be King Solomon and his queen-to-be. But given the sizzling love words they exchange, he's the king in her eyes and she rocks his world with "lips. . .sweet as nectar. . . . Honey and milk are under your tongue" (Song of Songs 4:11). This is a couple working up to something. And it's not a metaphor, most scholars agree.

SONG OF SONGS

Famous sound bite: Your love is sweeter than wine. Song of Songs 1:2

A YOUNG MAN AND WOMAN IN LOVE express their desire for each other in a sexually explicit song that most scholars agree is neither crude nor vulgar. Most scholars used to say this song was a metaphor about GOD's love for the JEWS or Christ's love for the CHURCH. Nobody seems to be buying that today. It's a love song, most agree.

- Writer: Unknown. It's a song "of Solomon." But that could mean by him, for him, or about him. One guess is that it was a love song performed at one of his weddings.
- Time: During Solomon's reign, about 970–930 BC.
- Location: Israel.

BIG SCENES

Love lingo. Sounding like the championship battle in a compliment contest, two lovers have at it:

- She: "Kɪss me—full on the mouth!" (1:2 msg).
- He: "Your lips are jewel red. . . . Your breasts are like fawns. . . . The kisses of your lips are honey, my love. . . . You're a secret garden. . .a whole orchard of succulent fruits" (4:3, 5, 12, 13 msg).
- She: "Let my lover enter his garden! Yes, let him eat the fine, ripe fruits" (4:16 msg).
- He: "Your full breasts are like sweet clusters of dates. I say, 'I'm going to climb that PALM TREE! I'm going to caress its fruit!' Oh yes! Your breasts will be clusters of sweet fruit to me" (7:7–8 msg). *Song of Songs 1, 4, 7*

Beyond "till death us do part." The woman gives her love, but she wants something in return—a one-woman man: "Wear my RING on your finger" (Song of Songs 8:6 msg). She wants her lover's love for a long, long time: "The passion of love bursting into flame is more powerful than DEATH, stronger than the grave" (Song of Songs 8:6 cev).

SONS OF THUNDER

James and John (the sons of Zebedee. . . Jesus nicknamed them "Sons of Thunder"). Mark 3:17

- Nicknames for James and John

IT'S A MYSTERY why Jesus nicknamed two of his DISCIPLES the "Sons of Thunder." They were brothers JAMES and JOHN.

Educated guesses from scholars:

- They were Zealots. Perhaps they were members of this Jewish freedom movement, which wanted to drive out the Roman occupiers.

- They had a fiery temper. When a SAMARITAN village refused to welcome Jesus, they asked if they should "call down fire from heaven to burn them up" (Luke 9:54). Jesus declined their offer.

SORCERY

A number of them [new believers] who had been practicing sorcery brought their incantation books and burned them at a public bonfire. The value of the books was several million dollars. Acts 19:19

- Casting spells or performing magic

MOSES HAD COMPETITION from Egypt's sorcerers when he unleashed the 10 plagues that pressured EGYPT to free the Jewish slaves.

When MOSES produced a frog stampede, Egypt's sorcerers did the same "with their enchantments" (Exodus 8:7 kjv).

In the end, Moses outdid the Egyptian sorcerers.

PAUL silenced a sorcerer in CYPRUS, too: Elymas, who was trying to prevent him from converting the Roman governor to CHRISTIANITY. Paul looked Elymas in the eye and said GOD would strike him blind. "Instantly mist and darkness came over the man's eyes, and he began groping around begging for someone to take his hand and lead him" (Acts 13:11). That convinced the GOVERNOR of Paul's power.

Sorcerers were magicians who used incantations and rituals in an attempt to conjure up good luck, cure sickness, or put a hex on someone. King BALAK of MOAB, in what is now Jordan, hired BALAAM to put a CURSE on the approaching JEWS, led by Moses (Numbers 22). Instead, at God's direction, Balaam blessed them and predicted victory for them.

Jewish law prohibited people from practicing any form of magic, including "FORTUNE-TELLING. . . sorcery. . . omens. . .witchcraft. . .spells. . .mediums or psychics" (Deuteronomy 18:10–11).

S

SOSTHENES

(SOSS thuh nees)

First century AD

The crowd then grabbed Sosthenes, the leader of the synagogue, and beat him right there in the courtroom. Acts 18:17

- Corinth synagogue leader
- Christian associate of Paul

HE'S MENTIONED TWICE, though the second reference might be about a second Sosthenes with CORINTH connections. In his first appearance, he's the leader of the SYNAGOGUE in Corinth. A mob of JEWS beat him in a courtroom, perhaps because he converted to CHRISTIANITY—as his predecessor Crispus had done (Acts 18:8). In his second appearance, he's in EPHESUS and he's sending greetings to the Corinth Christians (1 Corinthians 1:1).

SOUL

"You will not leave my soul among the dead." Acts 2:27

- Essence of a human

SOUL **MEANS BREATH** or life, at least in the original HEBREW language (*nephesh*). But Bible writers used the word in a variety of other ways, too.

Sometimes the writer was talking about the essence of a person that lives on after the body dies. Other times the writer was simply referring to people. *Nephesh* (soul) is the original word describing JACOB's descendants through RACHEL (Genesis 46:22): 14 souls. Most Bibles today translate the term with words such as "descendants" (NLT) or "persons" (NRSV).

Greeks taught that the soul is immortal. But most Bible experts say Christians expect more than a disembodied SPIRIT. They expect a soul with a spiritual body, perhaps like the body Jesus had after his RESURRECTION—able to touch, be touched, eat, levitate, and pass through walls.

SOVEREIGNTY OF GOD

(see FREE WILL)

SPAIN

Map 2 A5

I am planning to go to Spain, and when I do, I will stop off in Rome. Romans 15:24

- Western frontier of the Roman Empire

IT TOOK THE ROMANS about 200 years to pacify rebellious Spain and assimilate its citizens into the empire. In time, Spain would contribute soldiers and even emperors to the empire.

By PAUL's time, most of Spain was under Rome's control, and Paul hoped to take the story of Jesus there. It's unclear if he made it. He was arrested and sent to ROME for trial before he got a chance, at least as far as the BIBLE goes in telling the story.

But one early CHURCH leader named Clement wrote in about AD 97 that Paul eventually reached "the limit of the west." Some scholars interpret that to mean he was found not guilty in Rome, and after his release he went to Spain. Others say they doubt Clement's claim or that he didn't necessarily mean Spain.

SPEAR

Phinehas thrust the spear all the way through the man's body and into the woman's stomach. Numbers 25:8

SOLDIERS DIDN'T USUALLY THROW SPEARS. Lighter, shorter javelins were for throwing. Spears were for holding and thrusting into enemies during hand-to-hand combat.

In an attack, the first wave of soldiers often advanced behind a wall of SHIELDS with their spears sticking out to make first contact with the enemy. The opposite of a handshake.

Spearheads were often crafted into a metal triangle with a hole in the base for inserting the wooden shaft. Others spears had creative heads shaped like a pointed leaf or a barbed blade.

To confirm that Jesus was dead, a Roman soldier "pierced his side with a spear" (John 19:34).

SPICES

"Mix a gallon of olive oil with the following costly spices: twelve pounds of myrrh, six pounds of cinnamon, six pounds of cane, and twelve pounds of cassia [about 6 kg myrrh; 3 kg cinnamon, cane; 6 kg cassia]." Recipe for anointing oil, Exodus 30:23–24 CEV

- Active ingredients in perfume
- Added flavor for food

IMPORTED from as far away as India, aromatic spices added their fragrance to oils and creams—creating expensive PERFUMES and salves.

People used these as deodorant, MEDICINE, and sacrificial INCENSE, and to prepare the dead for BURIAL by masking the odor of decay.

Edible spices were added to food and drinks: "Cook the meat with many spices" (Ezekiel 24:10); "WINE mixed with spices" (Psalm 75:8).

SPICE IS NICE at a Middle Eastern bazaar. In Bible times, Jews used spice to liven up their food and to burn as incense. Some incense served as a worship offering. Other incense served as a nasal distraction until someone invented soap.

SPIES

"You are spies! You have come to see how vulnerable our land has become." Joseph to his brothers, Genesis 42:9

- Scouts in enemy territory

MOSES AND JOSHUA both used spies to scout their target land ahead.

MOSES sent a dozen spies to explore CANAAN, now ISRAEL. They came back with a mixed report. Two scouts, JOSHUA and CALEB, said the land was fertile and GOD would help them conquer the Canaanites. But the other 10 warned of walled cities defended by GIANTS. Terrified, the people refused to invade—and spent 40 years in the badlands.

When they were finally ready to invade, Joshua sent two spies to scout the first target city: JERICHO. They came back with good news: The locals were frightened by stories of how God had helped the JEWS defeat EGYPT and other enemies along the EXODUS trail.

SPIKENARD   (see NARD)

SPIRIT

"A spirit glided past my face. The hair on my body stood on end. Then the spirit stopped. But I couldn't tell what it was. Something stood there in front of me." Job 4:15–16 NIRV

- Soul of a person
- Supernatural being: God, angel, demon

BIBLE WRITERS use *spirit* in many ways, including to describe a person's character, a person's SOUL, a celestial being, GOD himself, or an evil being.

One Bible writer even seems to link it to depression—or at least to a spirit that causes depression: "The Spirit of the LORD had left SAUL, and the LORD sent a tormenting spirit that filled him with depression and fear" (1 Samuel 16:14).

The word literally means "blowing wind" or "breath."

S

That makes the word a wonderful fit for Luke's description of the Holy Spirit's arrival at Pentecost: "Suddenly, there was a sound from heaven like the roaring of a mighty windstorm, and it filled the house where they were sitting" (Acts 2:2).

SPIRITUAL GIFTS

A spiritual gift is given to each of us so we can help each other. To one person the Spirit gives the ability to give wise advice; to another the same Spirit gives a message of special knowledge. 1 Corinthians 12:7–8

- Abilities given by God, often reflected in character

EVERY SKILL WE HAVE is a gift from God, as the Bible teaches it. That's because he created us. But Paul said some gifts are unique because they're intended to help us strengthen our spiritual health. Included in his list:

- wisdom
- knowledge
- faith
- ability to heal people
- ability to perform miracles
- prophecy
- ability to tell if a teaching is from God or from another spirit
- ability to speak in other languages, including heavenly languages
- ability to interpret languages
- love—the greatest gift of all (1 Corinthians 12, 13)

SPIT

"If the man refuses to marry his brother's widow. . .the widow must walk over to him in the presence of the elders, pull his sandal from his foot, and spit in his face." Deuteronomy 25:7, 9

- Sign of disrespect
- Treatment used in healing

THERE'S NOTHING SUBTLE about spitting in the direction of someone or—worse—spitting in his face. This pucker is the opposite of a kiss.

When Jesus was beaten and crucified, the soldiers "spit in Jesus' face" (Matthew 26:67).

Oddly enough, spit was also an ingredient used by physicians. First-century Roman science writer Pliny recommended it: "To cure inflammation of the eyes, wash the eyes each morning with spit from your overnight fast" (*Natural History*, "Remedies from Living Creatures," book 28, chapter 10).

Jesus used spit to cure a blind man, perhaps as a way to strengthen the man's faith by employing a well-known treatment: "He spit on the ground, made mud with the saliva, and spread the mud over the blind man's eyes" (John 9:6). Then Jesus told the man to wash off the mud.

STAR OF BETHLEHEM

The star they [wise men] had seen in the east guided them to Bethlehem. It went ahead of them and stopped over the place where the child was. Matthew 2:9

- Astronomical event that directed magi to Israel

THERE ARE NOTHING BUT GUESSES about what exactly led the wise men to Bethlehem.

Clues in the Bible:

- It pointed toward Israel. The star led them initially to the capital of the Jewish homeland, not to Bethlehem: "Some wise men from eastern lands arrived in Jerusalem, asking, 'Where is the newborn king of the Jews? We saw his star as it rose, and we have come to worship him'" (Matthew 2:1–2).

- It took them two years to reach Jerusalem. King Herod ordered all boys in Bethlehem ages two and under executed "based on the wise men's report of the star's first appearance" (Matthew 2:16).
- It eventually guided them to Bethlehem. After Herod's scholars directed the wise men to Bethlehem, based on a prophecy that Israel's Messiah would be born there, the star seems to have made a comeback. It "guided them to Bethlehem" (Matthew 2:9).

One theory: The star was a celestial being perhaps a bit like the pillar of light that led Moses and the Jews during the Exodus out of Egypt.

Other theories: It was a comet or a supernova.

A popular theory today: It was an alignment of Jupiter and Saturn beside the Pisces constellation. Jupiter represented kings because this giant planet was named after Jupiter, the Roman king of gods. Greeks called him Zeus. Saturn represented Jews because Jews worshiped on the day of the week named after the god Saturn: Saturday. Pisces means "fish." As far as stargazers were concerned, it represented the land beside the Mediterranean Sea— which includes the Jewish homeland.

This rare alignment happened about every 20 years. But in 7 BC it happened three times. That triple alignment occurs about once in a millennium. As far as these ancients were concerned, it had never happened before.

If this is what happened, it wasn't just one star that got them to Bethlehem. It was a choir of stars and planets that sent the general message: Go to Israel. Look for a king.

AN ALIGNMENT of Saturn and Jupiter in the Pisces constellation would have looked like this, some say. This is the view looking south of Jerusalem in 7 BC.

STEPHEN

(STEVE uhn)

First century AD

As they stoned him, Stephen prayed, "Lord Jesus, receive my spirit." Acts 7:59

- Helped Jesus' disciples with food distribution ministry
- First known Christian martyr
- Was stoned to death by Jews

STEPHEN WAS ONE OF SEVEN men picked to run a food ministry for impoverished Christians in JERUSALEM.

Jesus' DISCIPLES had been running the program for

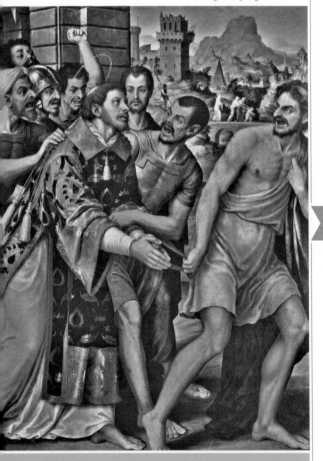

STONING STEPHEN is against the law, even in Jerusalem—and even if the Jewish high court ordered it. Romans had to sign off on any execution. That's why Jewish leaders took Jesus to Pilate. This Jewish mob, however, didn't follow protocol. It followed their adrenalin surge after Stephen's speech.

POOR folks, including widows without a FAMILY to look after them. But the disciples passed the job off to Stephen and others so the disciples could concentrate on teaching.

Stephen got in trouble when he opened his mouth.

He ended up in a debate with JEWS, probably about Jesus. At this time in CHURCH history, most Christians were Jews who still worshiped at the SYNAGOGUE. And that's where Stephen got in trouble.

Jews arrested Stephen and took him before the same high council that had orchestrated the execution of Jesus.

Stephen opened his mouth again. Fatal mistake this time.

He not only dissed the Jewish leaders, he blistered them: "You stiff-necked people. . . . Was there ever a PROPHET your ANCESTORS did not persecute? They even killed those who predicted the coming of the Righteous One. And now you have betrayed and murdered him" (Acts 7:51–52 TNIV).

Charged with MURDER, the Jews proved Stephen's point. They murdered him.

They stoned him to death. Holding the cloaks of the mob executioner was a zealous Jew named Saul, destined to become a zealous CHRISTIAN better known as PAUL.

STOCKS

The jailer put them [Paul, Silas] into the inner dungeon and clamped their feet in the stocks. Acts 16:24

SOME PRISONERS weren't just tossed in jail. As an extra precaution, they were secured in stocks: blocks of wood that secured their feet, or sometimes their neck and hands.

Prisoners put in stocks included:

- Hanani the seer, for speaking out against Jewish king ASA (2 Chronicles 16:10)
- Jeremiah the prophet, twice, for predicting the fall of JERUSALEM (Jeremiah 20:2; 29:26)
- Paul and Silas, for HEALING a demon-possessed girl, which left her unable to make MONEY for her masters by predicting the future (Acts 16:16–24).

STOICS

(STOH icks)

Paul was waiting for Silas and Timothy in Athens. . . . A group of Epicurean and Stoic thinkers began to argue with him. Acts 17:16, 18 NIrV

▪ Philosophers who taught emotional restraint

STARTED IN ATHENS, Stoic philosophy taught that everything in life is predetermined. So Stoic philosophers said that instead of getting all worked up when things aren't going well, we should simply accept it as fate. PAUL debated Stoics during his brief stay in ATHENS, on his way to CORINTH.

STONING

"We are stoning you because you did a terrible thing. You are just a man, and here you are claiming to be God!" John 10:33 CEV

▪ Most common form of execution among Jews

ISRAEL IS LOADED WITH ROCKS. Whenever an execution was in order, there were usually rocks nearby.

Jewish law allowed for stoning a person to death for many offenses, including ADULTERY, working on the SABBATH, and using mediums to consult the dead. For a long list, see Leviticus 20.

Bible experts seem to doubt that the JEWS consistently killed people for that long list of offenses, which included "Anyone who dishonors FATHER or MOTHER" (Leviticus 20:9).

But when they did execute, there needed to be at least two WITNESSES to the CRIME. "The witnesses must throw the first stones, and then all the people may join in. In this way, you will purge the evil from among you" (Deuteronomy 17:7).

Jesus halted the execution of a woman caught in adultery. He did it with his now famous invitation: "Let the one who has never sinned throw the first stone!" (John 8:7).

STRANGLING OF ANIMALS

"You should not eat any meat that still has the blood in it or any meat of any animal that has been strangled." Acts 15:29 CEV

STRANGLING AN ANIMAL to death instead of slitting its throat was a great way to keep the tasty BLOOD in the meat. Think: steak ordered up rare. Not KOSHER. JEWS couldn't even have a medium rare steak. No pink whatsoever.

Jews need to drain all the blood. That's because blood was sacred. It belonged to GOD. "The life of the body is in its blood. I have given you the blood on the ALTAR to purify you, making you right with the LORD. It is the blood, given in exchange for a life, that makes PURIFICATION possible" (Leviticus 17:11–12).

SIN was a capital offense. But God allowed people to sacrifice ANIMALS instead of themselves.

STREET (see ROAD)

SUCCOTH

Map 2 I8

(SUCK uhth)

Gideon went and got the elders of the town. Then he taught the men of Succoth a lesson. He tore their skin with thorns from desert bushes. Judges 8:16 NIrV

▪ City that refused to help Gideon

THERE ARE TWO CITIES named Succoth. MOSES and the Jewish refugees passed through one in EGYPT (Exodus 12:37). JACOB passed through another in what is now Jordan (Genesis 33:17). That's the same town that refused to feed GIDEON's 300-man militia as they hunted down raiders who had been stealing crops from the JEWS at harvesttime.

S

SULFUR

The Lord rained down fire and burning sulfur from the sky on Sodom and Gomorrah.
Genesis 19:24

- Flammable chemical now used in matches, gunpowder

CALLED *BRIMSTONE* in some older Bibles, highly flammable sulfur became a metaphor to describe what God would do to the wicked: destroy them. Sulfur is among the many chemicals and minerals that Israelis today still mine in the DEAD SEA area. That's where some speculate the twin sin cities of SODOM AND GOMORRAH once existed before God used an explosion of fiery sulfur to sear them out of existence.

SUMER

Map 2 M7

(SU mur)

- Original homeland of Abraham

NOT MENTIONED BY NAME in the BIBLE, Sumer (or Sumeria) was the first known civilization in the Middle East. It extended throughout what is now south Iraq, in the fertile plain between the TIGRIS and EUPHRATES rivers. ABRAHAM grew up there, in the riverside city of UR.

SUN WORSHIP

"When you look up into the sky and see the sun, moon, and stars—all the forces of heaven—don't be seduced into worshiping them." Deuteronomy 4:19

JEWS WERE SURROUNDED by nations and empires that worshiped the sun: EGYPT, PHOENICIA in what is now LEBANON, along with ASSYRIA and BABYLON in what is now Iraq. The most famous sun god was Egypt's Re, their top god. It must have made sense to them to treat Re as the king of GODS since the sun dominated life in this DESERT land.

Though JEWS weren't supposed to worship anyone but GOD, one PROPHET accused them of turning their backs on God at the Jerusalem TEMPLE: "They were facing east, bowing low to the ground, worshiping the sun!" (Ezekiel 8:16).

RISE AND SHINE. It's 7 a.m. in this modern take on an ancient idea for telling time. The shadow knows. Folks in Bible days made do with shadows of other stationary objects, too. Even shadows on stair steps.

SUNDIAL

The shadow on the sundial moved backward ten steps. Isaiah 38:8

- Tool to measure time by shadows

AS A SIGN to prove GOD would heal King HEZEKIAH, the prophet ISAIAH said God would make the sun's shadow on a sundial move backward. Many Bible experts suggest this particular tool wasn't a dial but was a staircase of some kind. As the sun moved from east to west, the shadow of a building or some other object moved from one stair step to another.

SUSA

Map 2 M7

(SU suh)

Esther, along with many other young women, was brought to the king's harem at the fortress of Susa. Esther 2:8

- Capital of Persian Empire
- Hebrew: *Shushan*
- Home of Queen Esther, prophet Daniel, Nehemiah

THREE FAMOUS JEWS lived in what is now Iran, near Iraq's eastern border. Deportations are likely what got them there.

Babylonian invaders from Iraq deported DANIEL out of JERUSALEM in around 600 BC. He ended up in Susa after Persians from Iran conquered BABYLON in 539 BC and drafted him as a royal adviser.

ESTHER and NEHEMIAH may have ended up there because their ANCESTORS were deported, too. Assyrians from Iraq had deported JEWS in what is now northern ISRAEL in 722 BC. Babylonians deported southland Jews in 586 BC. Many were taken captive to Iraq, but some made their way across the TIGRIS RIVER into Iran.

One of the oldest cities in the Middle East, Susa was already about 2,500 years old by the time the Persian Empire crushed the Babylonians. Today it's called Shush, a city of about 54,000 people some 40 miles (64 km) across the Iraqi border.

SWADDLING CLOTHES

"On the day you were born your navel cord was not cut, nor were you washed in water to cleanse you; you were not rubbed with salt nor wrapped in swaddling cloths." Ezekiel 16:4 NKJV

- Strips of cloth to wrap babies tightly

WHEN JESUS WAS BORN, his mother "wrapped him snugly in strips of cloth" (Luke 2:7). People in ancient times seemed to think this helped the arms and legs of the babies to grow straight.

See also BIRTH.

SWORD

David ran over and pulled Goliath's sword from its sheath. David used it to kill him and cut off his head. 1 Samuel 17:51

- Most common weapon mentioned in the Bible

THE FIRST SWORDS looked more like DAGGERS—usually shorter than a foot (30 cm). That's because BRONZE was too soft for longer blades. By the time of ABRAHAM and the other early GENERATIONS of JEWS,

ROMAN SWORDS were shorter than many earlier versions—easier to swing during an in-your-face fight.

S

swords were getting a makeover: curved blades that looked like a harvesting sickle. Those swords weren't for stabbing. They were for hacking.

By about 1200 BC, when PHILISTINES and Jews were competing for what is now ISRAEL, the Philistines figured out how to produce IRON. It became their secret weapon, allowing them to forge long, powerful double-edged swords about a meter long (roughly 3 feet).

Romans typically used shorter, well-balanced swords with blades about 2 feet (roughly 0.5 m). They were lighter and easier to stab and slash in close-quarter, hand-to-hand combat.

SYCAMORE TREE

Zaccheus was a short man and could not see over the crowd. So he ran ahead and climbed up into a sycamore tree. Luke 19:3 CEV

- Fig tree
- Prophet Amos grew them
- Tax collector Zacchaeus climbed one to see Jesus

A TREE-CLIMBER'S DELIGHT, sycamore trees often have low, thick branches—making them easy climbing even for diminutive souls like ZACCHAEUS. Sycamore trees grow in low areas, like the JERICHO oasis near the JORDAN RIVER. The prophet AMOS tended an orchard of sycamores to HARVEST their figs (Amos 7:14).

SYCHAR   Map 4 D5

(SY car)

In Samaria Jesus came to the town called Sychar. John 4:5 NCV

- Where Jesus met a woman at the city well

AFTER HIS BAPTISM and TEMPTATION in the Judean badlands, Jesus headed home to what is now northern ISRAEL. Along the way he stopped in Sychar, a village in the hills of central Israel. That's where he met a woman drawing WATER from a WELL in the heat

of the day—to avoid the crowds because she was a social outcast who had been married five times.

Jesus offered her "living water" (John 4:10)—a metaphor for the gift of ETERNAL LIFE.

The village was probably near SHECHEM, most scholars guess. That area today is the predominately Palestinian city of Nablus in the West Bank.

SYNAGOGUE

(SIN uh gog)

Jesus went to Capernaum, a town in Galilee, and taught there in the synagogue every Sabbath day. Luke 4:31

- Jewish worship center

IT WASN'T JUST A PLACE where JEWS met on the Sabbath to WORSHIP. Synagogues also served as a school,

STEPHEN M. MILLER'S ILLUSTRATED BIBLE DICTIONARY

a courtroom, a community center for meetings and celebrations, and a temporary home for travelers.

History experts say they aren't certain when Jews started worshiping in synagogues. But a common guess is that synagogues got their start in Iraq. Babylonians from what is now Iraq destroyed JERUSALEM and its TEMPLE in 586 BC, and then deported the Jewish survivors to Iraq. There the Jews began to meet in small groups to pray and read their SCRIPTURES.

The apostle PAUL, on his missionary trips, often went to the local synagogue to tell the Jews there that the MESSIAH had finally come. Some believed him, and church groups were started. But that's because most Jews kicked the Jesus-believers out of the synagogues.

LEADING JEWS IN WORSHIP, Rabbi Herschel Gluck of Walford Road Synagogue in London reads from the scroll of Esther. The community gathered during the springtime festival of Purim to remember how God used Queen Esther to avert a Jewish holocaust throughout the Middle East.

SYRACUSE
Map 2 D6

(SEAR uh cuse)

Three months after the shipwreck. . .we set sail on another ship. . . . Our first stop was Syracuse, where we stayed three days. Acts 28:11–12

- Port of call for Paul, sailing to Rome for trial

AFTER THE SHIP PAUL was sailing on ran aground at the island of MALTA, he was forced to winter there. Afterward, he caught another SHIP headed to ROME where he would stand trial in CAESAR'S COURT. Along the way he stopped at Syracuse, Sicily.

SYRIA
Map 1 F2

(SEER ee uh)

This was the first census taken when Quirinius was governor of Syria. Luke 2:2

- Israel's neighbor to the northeast
- Israel's sometimes ally, often times enemy

SYRIA in Bible times was mainly a reference to the DAMASCUS area—not to the modern-day country that's about seven times larger than ISRAEL.

Damascus, an oasis town, was the region's capital—just as it is the nation's capital today.

Israel's warrior king, DAVID, overpowered Syrian forces and made Damascus his subject city. Late in SOLOMON's reign, however, Syria broke free.

Throughout most of Bible history, Syria and Israel fought each other. They did team up once to drive back Assyrians from what is now Iraq. Later, however, Assyria crushed both nations.

Syria was the first place followers of Christ were called Christians, at a CHURCH pastored by PAUL and BARNABAS "at ANTIOCH" (Acts 11:26).

S

Map 1 C4

TAANACH

(TAY uh nack)

Canaanite kings fought us at Taanach by the stream near Megiddo—but they couldn't rob us of our silver. Judges 5:19 CEV

A WALLED CITY, Taanach guarded one of the main passes through ISRAEL's northern mountain range, the Carmel Mountains. It was near this city that a prophetess named Deborah led a Jewish militia to victory against an invading CHARIOT corp.

TABERNACLE

(TAB ur nack uhl)

"Set up the Tabernacle on the first day of the new year. Place the Ark of the Covenant inside, and install the inner curtain to enclose the Ark within the Most Holy Place." Exodus 40:2–3

- Tent worship center for Jews
- Used during the exodus out of Egypt

JEWS MADE A TENT WORSHIP CENTER during their EXODUS out of SLAVERY in EGYPT.

Surrounding the TENT was a wall of LINEN curtains, which produced a portable COURTYARD around the tent. This courtyard stretched about 50 yards (46 m) long and half as wide.

Inside the courtyard stood a bronze ALTAR placed in front of the tent. It looked a bit like a barbecue pit, hollow in the center for wood that burned sacrificial meat.

The tent sat at the back of the courtyard. It was shaped like a railroad boxcar, 15 yards long and 5 yards wide and high (14 by 4.5 m). The snap-together frame was ACACIA WOOD covered with plates of GOLD and SILVER.

Blanketing this frame were four layers of cloth and LEATHER. The inside layer, which formed the interior roof and walls, was crafted of fine linen and decorated with angelic beings: CHERUBIM. Only PRIESTS saw these, for only priests were allowed inside. And only the HIGH PRIEST was allowed in the back room—the holiest room in this sacred tent of GOD. It contained the ARK OF THE COVENANT, the chest that held the 10 COMMANDMENTS.

TABITHA

(see DORCAS)

A TABERNACLE, built to the size specs of the Jewish worship center in Moses' day, this reproduction in Israel gives visitors a sense of how Jews worshiped God during the Exodus.

TABLE

Bezalel made the table of acacia wood, 36 inches long, 18 inches wide, and 27 inches high [92 by 46 by 69 cm]. He overlaid it with pure gold and ran a gold molding around the edge. Exodus 37:10–11

SOME TABLES, like the sacred table Bezalel made for the Jewish WORSHIP center, stood about the size of many tables today. But tables used to serve food inside homes were often lower to the ground—more like coffee tables, suitable for eating while seated on a rug or cushion.

Sitting at the head of the table was the most honored spot. Jesus advised his followers not to sit there unless they were invited to do so. Otherwise the host might make you move so someone else can have that seat (Luke 14:9).

TAMAR

(TAY mar)

Judah was told, "Tamar, your daughter-in-law, has acted like a prostitute. And now, because of this, she's pregnant." Genesis 38:24

1. PREGNANT TAMAR (1800s BC). JUDAH's daughter-in-law was twice widowed by Judah's sons. But she had no boy to inherit her first husband's estate or to care for her in her old age. Judah failed to provide her with another husband, as Jewish law allowed. So Tamar disguised herself as a PROSTITUTE, had SEX with Judah, and gave BIRTH to twin sons.

Judah nearly had her executed when he found out she was pregnant. But when he discovered he was the father, he changed his mind.

2. RAPED TAMAR (about 1000 BC). DAVID's oldest son and heir to the throne, AMNON, lusted so much for his half sister Tamar that he raped her. Tamar moved out of the PALACE room for VIRGINS and moved in with her full brother ABSALOM. There's no indication she ever married. Raped WOMEN were considered damaged goods.

King David got angry about the RAPE but did nothing. Absalom, however, had Amnon assassinated.

TAMARISK TREE

Saul heard that David and his men had been discovered. And Saul was seated, spear in hand, under the tamarisk tree on the hill at Gibeah. 1 Samuel 22:6 TNIV

ONE OF MORE THAN 50 species of drought-resistant shrubs and low trees, the tamarisk is hearty enough to survive in places where other plants would wither, including salty DESERTS and badlands.

THE TAMBORINE MAN gets the beat on an instrument Jews used in their worship services.

TAMBOURINE

After David had killed Goliath. . . the women came out of all of the towns of Israel. . . . They danced and sang joyful songs. They played lutes and tambourines. 1 Samuel 18:6 NIRV

- Hand-held drum

AN EASY RHYTHM INSTRUMENT to play—at least compared to harps and FLUTES—the tambourine

T

was popular in ISRAEL. It showed up in WORSHIP services and impromptu outbursts of joy. MIRIAM took a tambourine and led the women in singing and DANCING after GOD saved them from the Egyptians by making an escape route through a body of WATER (Exodus 15:20).

TANNER

> Peter stayed a long time in Joppa, living with Simon, a tanner of hides. Acts 9:43

A STINKY JOB, the tanning of ANIMAL hides into soft LEATHER was something best done downwind of a city—so the smell would blow away. That's why SIMON the tanner lived outside of town "near the seashore" (Acts 10:6).

The smell came from soaking the hides for several weeks in a brew of berries, POMEGRANATE rinds, and other plants that smell quite nice—when they're not rotten.

JEWS considered tanners ritually unclean because tanners worked with some ritually unclean dead animals. Jewish law said, "If any of you touch the dead body of such an animal, you will be defiled until evening" (Leviticus 11:31). Tanners did that nearly every day.

see photo, page 294

TAR

> The valley of the Dead Sea was filled with tar pits. And as the army of the kings of Sodom and Gomorrah fled, some fell into the tar pits. Genesis 14:10

The oil-rich Middle East had tar pits scattered throughout the land. The DEAD SEA also had jellied globs of tar that would pop to the surface. Some were the size of FISHING boats. When locals noticed a floating glob, they rowed out to it and hacked it into chunks for sale.

People used tar, also called asphalt and BITUMEN, in waterproofing and as MORTAR that held BRICKS together. NOAH used it to waterproof his barge (Genesis 6:14). MOSES' mother used it to waterproof the BASKET that held baby Moses as he floated on the NILE RIVER (Exodus 2:3).

TARSHISH
Location Uncertain

(TAR shish)

> Jonah got up and went in the opposite direction to get away from the LORD. He went down to the port of Joppa, where he found a ship leaving for Tarshish. Jonah 1:3

- Jonah's mysterious destination

ORDERED TO NINEVEH, capital of ASSYRIA in what is now northern Iraq, JONAH booked passage on a SHIP headed to Tarshish. Many Bible experts speculate that he was headed to Tartessus, a kingdom in SPAIN—at the other end of the known world.

TARSUS
Map 3 K4

(TAR suhs)

> Paul replied, "I am a Jew and a citizen of Tarsus in Cilicia, which is an important city." Acts 21:39

- Paul's hometown in Turkey

PAUL GREW UP as a Roman CITIZEN because the people of his hometown—Tarsus, along Turkey's southern coast—had warmly welcomed the Romans when they arrived. In appreciation, Mark Antony of ROME declared the people citizens of Rome. As a citizen, PAUL had the right to a trial before being beaten. And if sentenced to death, he was to be given a swift execution.

TATTOO

> "Do not cut your bodies for the dead, and do not mark your skin with tattoos." Leviticus 19:28

JEWISH LAW prohibited tattoos. Romans tattooed slaves to help keep track of them. They also tattooed criminals, sometimes writing the CRIME on their forehead—as punishment. After CHRISTIANITY spread throughout Europe, tattoos were forbidden in many countries there.

> *To get the silver and gold demanded as tribute by Pharaoh Neco, Jehoiakim collected a tax from the people of Judah.*
> 2 Kings 23:35

> *Jesus was going through Jericho, where a man named Zacchaeus lived. He was in charge of collecting taxes and was very rich.*
> Luke 19:1–3 CEV

JEWS TAXED THEMSELVES. Romans taxed them, too.

MOSES raised nearly four tons of SILVER for building the TABERNACLE tent WORSHIP center by imposing a "tax collected from 603,550 men who had reached their twentieth birthday" (Exodus 38:26).

KINGS taxed their citizens to fund the government, pay for building projects, and to pay TRIBUTE to bullying superpowers such as EGYPT, ASSYRIA, and BABYLON. SOLOMON taxed the JEWS so much that they felt oppressed; it eventually split the country in two.

Each Jewish man also paid an annual half-SHEKEL tax to help fund the TEMPLE (Matthew 17:24). That was about two days of salary for the average working man in Roman times.

When Romans occupied a region, they brought with them a system of taxation. Sample taxes:

- personal tax on each person
- tax of land the people owned
- tolls for travelers
- import/export tax
- INHERITANCE tax, 5 percent
- emancipation tax for freeing a slave, 5 percent
- sale of a slave, 4 percent
- products bought at auction, 1 percent

When Jewish scholars asked Jesus if Jews should pay Roman taxes, he recognized it as a trick question. "Yes," would erode his popularity with the Jews. "No" could get him arrested. His savvy answer: He held up a Roman coin and asked whose picture was on it. When the scholars said CAESAR, Jesus replied: "Give to Caesar what belongs to Caesar, and give to GOD what belongs to God" (Matthew 22:21).

WHEN ROMANS OCCUPIED the Jewish homeland, they let locals bid on various government contracts, including the lucrative job of collecting taxes.

JEWS taxed their fellow Jews.

It wasn't a great way to make friends, because tax men were considered Roman collaborators. But it was a wonderful way to make MONEY. It was easy to get rich by overcharging people and keeping the extra.

That's why citizens of JERICHO were disturbed when Jesus decided to honor the local tax man, ZACCHAEUS, by spending the night at his HOUSE. By the next day, however, Zacchaeus was promising tax refunds.

Jesus chose a tax collector as one of his DISCIPLES: Levi, likely the nickname of MATTHEW (Luke 5:27).

> *Three days later they [Mary and Joseph] found Jesus [age 12] sitting in the temple, listening to the teachers and asking them questions.* Luke 2:46 CEV

READING, WRITING, AND ARITHMETIC wasn't the standard lesson material for Jewish CHILDREN in Bible times. Their Bible was.

Parents taught their children about Jewish laws and customs. The children learned, too, by taking part in Jewish observances, including the SABBATH and annual festivals such as PASSOVER.

Fathers taught their sons the FAMILY business or arranged for them to learn another trade. Mothers taught their daughters about COOKING, sewing, and other household chores.

By NEW TESTAMENT times, older Jewish boys could continue their Jewish studies in classes led by local RABBIS. PAUL bragged that he studied under one of the most famous rabbis of his day: GAMALIEL (Acts 22:3). LUKE called Gamaliel "an expert in religious law and respected by all the people" (Acts 5:34).

T

(tuh KOH uh)

These are the words of Amos. He was a
shepherd from the town of Tekoa.
Amos 1:1 NIrV

- Hometown of Amos
- Home of a wise woman in David's day

A SMALL VILLAGE about 6 miles (10 km) south of
BETHLEHEM, Tekoa was the ridgetop home of a SHEPHERD
God called into temporary duty as a prophet: AMOS.

Tekoa was also home to an unidentified woman
whom King DAVID's general, JOAB, recruited to talk some
sense into the king. The woman, known for her WISDOM,
told David a parable that convinced him to end the banishment of his son ABSALOM (2 Samuel 14:1–20).

TEMPLE, JERUSALEM

[Solomon said,] The LORD God promised my
father [David] that when his son became
king, he would build a temple for worshiping
the LORD. So I've decided to do that.
1 Kings 5:5 CEV

- Jewish worship center
- The place Jews offered sacrifices

ISRAEL'S MOST REVERED KING, David, didn't
get the honor of building ISRAEL's first permanent
WORSHIP center.

He wanted to. But as his son SOLOMON reported
later, "My father DAVID had to fight many battles. His
enemies attacked him from every side. So he couldn't
build a temple where the LORD his GOD would put his
NAME. That wouldn't be possible until the LORD had put
his enemies under his control" (1 Kings 5:3 NIrV).

That time came during Solomon's rule.

Solomon "began to construct the Temple of the
LORD. . .480 years after the people of Israel were rescued
from their SLAVERY in EGYPT" (1 Kings 6:1). For all that
time, the Jews had been worshiping God in a TENT that
some Bible translations call the TABERNACLE.

Building the Temple was a project that took an
army of about 200,000 drafted workers seven years
to complete. Solomon recruited 30,000 loggers to cut
CEDAR in LEBANON, 80,000 QUARRY workers and stone
cutters, 70,000 general laborers to haul the timber and
stone, and 3,600 foremen to manage the crews.

Surprisingly, the majestic Temple was a prefab-
ricated building that MASONS pieced together on site.
"The stones used in the construction of the Temple were
finished at the quarry, so there was no sound of hammer,
ax, or any other IRON tool at the building site" (1 Kings
6:7).

This may have been out of respect for what the
Jews knew would become their holiest spot on earth. Or

JERUSALEM'S TEMPLE and massive courtyard dominated the cityscape in Jesus' day. The view here is from
the east, hovering above the Mount of Olives.

perhaps the site was already sacred and used for SACRIFICES. Decades earlier, DAVID had bought a bedrock THRESHING floor on what some say became the Temple hilltop. Then he "built an ALTAR there to the LORD and sacrificed burnt offerings and peace offerings" (2 Samuel 24:25).

By today's standards, Solomon's Temple was a small building: 30 yards long, 10 yards wide, and 15 yards high (27 by 9 by 14 m). That's about as high as a four-story building. Inside, where only PRIESTS are allowed, there are three rooms:

- porch, an entrance room
- sanctuary, a cedar-paneled room where priests burned INCENSE, lit golden LAMPSTANDS, and set out 12 sacred loaves of BREAD each SABBATH—the bread representing Israel's 12 tribes and their devotion to God
- inner sanctuary, a GOLD-paneled, 10-yard (9 m) cube where Israel kept its holiest object: the ARK OF THE COVENANT, a chest that held the 10 COMMANDMENTS.

Outside in the COURTYARD, people brought their offerings. There they killed and butchered the ANIMALS. Priests burned the offerings on top of an altar 15 feet high (4.5 m).

TEMPTATION

God himself does not tempt anyone. But people are tempted when their own evil desire leads them away and traps them.
James 1:13–14 NCV

GOD TESTS PEOPLE, as he did ABRAHAM. God's intent, as Bible writers imply, is to showcase the person's character or perhaps to strengthen it. But Bible writers insist that GOD never lures people into doing something evil.

They say that temptation like that comes from within or—sometimes—from SATAN.

When Jesus was about to launch his ministry, Satan tried to derail him in a series of temptations. Each time Jesus responded by quoting scripture.

His response while tempted to:

- Eat during a fast: "People do not live by BREAD alone."
- Worship Satan in exchange for power: "You must WORSHIP the LORD your God and serve only him."
- Show off his invincibility: "You must not test the LORD your God" (Luke 4:4, 8, 12, quoting passages in Deuteronomy).

TEN COMMANDMENTS

The LORD told Moses to put these laws in writing. . . . And he wrote down the Ten Commandments, the most important part of God's agreement with his people.
Exodus 34:27–28 CEV

- Most basic Jewish laws

BEFORE MOSES gave the JEWS the hundreds of laws that fill the books of LEVITICUS, NUMBERS, and DEUTERONOMY, he started with the 10 bedrock laws on which all other Jews laws are built.

1. No other GODS, only me.
2. No carved gods.
3. GOD won't put up with the irreverent use of his NAME.
4. Observe the SABBATH day, to keep it HOLY. . . . Don't do any work.
5. Honor your FATHER and MOTHER.
6. No MURDER.
7. No adultery.
8. No stealing.
9. No lies about your NEIGHBOR.
10. Don't set your heart on anything that is your neighbor's.

EXODUS 20:3–17 MSG

T

TENT

Paul went to see Aquila and Priscilla. They were tentmakers, just as he was. So he stayed and worked with them. Acts 18:2–3 NIrv

MANY JEWS WERE HERDERS who traveled in search of WATER and fresh grazing pasture for their flocks and herds. They carried their homes with them: tents.

Many tents in Bible times were woven together of GOAT hair or stitched together with patches of LEATHER from goat, SHEEP, CAMEL, and CATTLE.

PAUL worked at least part of the time as a bivocational PASTOR, paying his way as a tentmaker. He probably learned that trade in his home region of CILICIA, known for *cilicium*, a goat hair cloth.

TERAH

(TER uh)

2200s BC

Terah decided to move from Ur to the land of Canaan. He took along Abram and Sarai and his grandson Lot. Genesis 11:31 CEV

▪ Abraham's father

IT WASN'T ABRAHAM who decided to leave his hometown of UR, in what is now southern Iraq, and move to CANAAN, now ISRAEL. It was his dad. Terah made it only about two-thirds of the way. He settled in HARAN, along Turkey's southern border with SYRIA. Only after Terah died did ABRAHAM finish the journey.

THADDAEUS

(THAD ee uhs)

First century AD

Here are the names of the twelve apostles. . . Thaddaeus. Matthew 10:2–3

▪ Disciple of Jesus

THIS DISCIPLE apparently went by three names. The other two names show up in various ancient copies of the GOSPELS: Lebbaeus and JUDAS, a relative of James.

THEATER

People were making trouble in the whole city. They all rushed into the theater. Acts 19:29 NIrv

GREEKS PLAYED PRETEND in their theaters. Romans preferred reality shows—spectacles such as gladiators fighting to the death, *Ben Hur*–style CHARIOT races, and slaves dancing with the lions.

Most theaters were amphitheaters, either carved out of the side of a hill or constructed to look like a hill. The action took place at the bottom, while spectators watched in seats that rose above the stage or the playing field. That's how we got the word *theater*. It comes from the GREEK *theatron*: "a place for seeing."

THEBES

Map 2 I9

(THEEBS)

"Are you any better than the city of Thebes, situated on the Nile River, surrounded by water? She was protected by the river on all sides. . . . Yet Thebes fell." Nahum 3:8, 10

▪ Capital of Egypt in its heyday

PROPHETS WARNED Assyrians in NINEVEH of impending disaster, citing the fall of Thebes—majestic capital of EGYPT during the height of Egyptian power, in the time of MOSES.

Located a little more than 400 miles (some 675 km) south of Cairo, Thebes (today: Luxor) covered some 36 square miles (93 square km)—about the size of Miami.

THEOPHILUS

(thee AH fuh luhs)

First century AD

In my first book [Gospel of Luke] I told you, Theophilus, about everything Jesus began to do and teach. Acts 1:1

▪ Intended reader for books of Luke and Acts

THE WRITER of LUKE and ACTS—physician Luke, according to early CHURCH writers—addressed both books to "most honorable Theophilus" (Luke 1:3).

That's a title fitting for a high-ranking Roman official. Perhaps, some scholars say, Luke was giving the Romans an inside look at CHRISTIANITY to show that it wasn't a threat to the empire.

Other guesses:

- Donor. Theophilus hired PAUL's associate, Luke, to preserve in writing the story of Jesus and the birth of the church.
- Christians. Theophilus represented all believers, since *theophilus* means "GOD's friend."

THESSALONIANS, LETTERS OF 1–2

Famous sound bite: The day of the Lord will come like a thief in the night.
1 Thessalonians 5:2 NIrv

AFTER RIOTING JEWS run him out of town, PAUL writes a couple letters of encouragement to the fledgling congregation he left behind.

- Writer: Paul.
- Time: Possibly written during Paul's second mission trip, between AD 49–51.
- Location: Possibly written from Corinth, Greece, to the church in Thessalonica, about a 300-mile (480 km) walk north.

BIG SCENES

Keep the faith, even when it hurts. When Paul gets word that Christians in Thessalonica are suffering, he urges them not to give up on Jesus. He reminds them that Jesus suffered and the first Christians in JERUSALEM suffered, too. "We are destined for such troubles," Paul adds. *1 Thessalonians 1–4:12*

Jesus is coming back. Under the gun of PERSECUTION, Christians in Thessalonica want to know when Jesus will come back. Paul says no one knows. But he says when it happens, believers dead and alive "will be caught up in the clouds to meet the LORD in the air." After that, they'll be with Jesus forever. *1 Thessalonians 4:13–2 Thessalonians 2*

THESSALONICA

Map 3 C3

(THESS uh loh NI kuh)

When some Jews in Thessalonica learned that Paul was preaching the word of God in Berea, they went there and stirred up trouble. Acts 17:13

- Greek town that ran Paul off

PAUL STARTED A CHURCH in this northern Greek town, using the SYNAGOGUE as a PREACHING platform. But once the Jewish leaders heard what he had to say about Jesus rising from the dead as the promised MESSIAH, they rioted and ran him out of town.

PAUL stayed in contact with believers through LETTERS and messengers. Ruins of the ancient FISHING town lie beneath modern Thessaloniki.

THOMAS

First century AD

Although Thomas the Twin was one of the twelve disciples, he wasn't with the others when Jesus [resurrected] appeared to them. John 20:24 CEV

- Disciple who doubted Jesus' resurrection

DOUBTING THOMAS was the nickname he earned. When Jesus' other DISCIPLES told him they had seen the resurrected Jesus, he didn't believe it.

He said, "I won't believe it unless I see the nail wounds in his hands, put my fingers into them, and place my hand into the wound in his side" (John 20:25).

Eight days later Jesus returned. Suddenly, Thomas was a believer.

Early CHURCH writers said Thomas started the church in India before he was martyred there. India's Syro-Malabar Catholic Church with nearly four million members claims him as founder.

T

THORN IN THE FLESH

I was given a thorn in my flesh, a messenger from Satan to torment me and keep me from becoming proud. 2 Corinthians 12:7

- Paul's mystery problem

SCHOLARS CAN ONLY GUESS about PAUL's thorn in the flesh.

Three popular theories:

- Corinthian Christians. They were a pain in Paul's posterior. The HEBREW version of the GREEK word Paul used for "thorn" describes the Canaanites that way: "thorns in your sides" (Numbers 33:55).
- Physical problem. Perhaps poor eyesight, EPILEPSY, or malaria picked up while traveling through coastal swamps in Turkey.
- Emotional problem. Maybe depression or anger.

THREE TAVERNS

Map 2 D5

Friends in Rome heard we were on the way and came out to meet us. . .at Three Taverns. Acts 28:15 MSG

- Rest stop on the road to Rome

HEADED TO ROME FOR TRIAL in CAESAR's supreme COURT, PAUL traveled the last leg north along a ROAD called the APPIAN WAY. Christians in ROME heard he was coming. Some went to meet him, reaching him at the Three Taverns rest area about 30 miles (about 50 km) south of Rome.

THRESHING

"Use boards from the threshing sleds for the wood. Use the wheat for the grain offering." 1 Chronicles 21:23 NIrV

- Separating grain kernels from chaff and stalks

KERNELS OF WHEAT and BARLEY grow at the top of stalks where they are each wrapped in thin fiber cocoons called CHAFF. Farmers cut the stalks at harvesttime. Then they have to peel away the chaff and straw stalks. The process is called threshing.

Often farmers lay the cut WHEAT on flat bedrock, which they called a "threshing floor." ANIMALS would drag wooden sleds over the wheat, scraping and loosening the chaff.

Afterward, on a windy day farmers would use pitchforks to toss the mess in the air. That's a process called winnowing. The wind would blow most of the light chaff and stalks away, while the heavy GRAIN kernels would fall back down onto the threshing floor.

THRONE

"All my people will take orders from you. Only I, sitting on my throne, will have a rank higher than yours." Pharaoh to Joseph, Genesis 41:40

- Seat for a king or queen

ROYAL THRONES were often large, extravagant, and elevated—to make it clear who's boss.

SOLOMON's taste in thrones:

"He made a large throne. It was decorated with IVORY. It was covered with fine GOLD. The throne had six steps. Its back had a rounded top. The throne had armrests on both sides of the seat. A statue of a lion stood on each side of the throne. Twelve lions stood on the six steps. There was one at each end of each step. Nothing like that throne had ever been made for any other kingdom" (1 Kings 10:18–20 NIrV).

THRESHING gives grain a thrashing. Farmers in Bible times pulled wooden sleds over the stalks to loosen the kernels. Then they tossed the mess into the air and let the wind blow away the light chaff. The kernels, which are heavier, fall back down in a pile.

THUMMIM

(see URIM AND THUMMIM)

THYATIRA

Map 3 F3

(THI uh TI ruh)

One of the listeners was a woman named Lydia from the city of Thyatira whose job was selling purple cloth. She. . .opened her mind to pay attention to what Paul was saying.
Acts 16:14 NCV

- Hometown of Lydia
- One of seven churches in Revelation

IN THE MESSAGE JESUS DICTATED to seven churches in REVELATION, the CHURCH at Thyatira drew praise and critique.

This city in western Turkey had a group of Christians who were growing in their FAITH and service to others. But Jesus warned that they needed to take a stand against a heretic in the church: a "JEZEBEL" who was apparently teaching a warped brand of CHRISTIANITY that advocated sex rituals and eating meat offered to IDOLS (Revelation 2:20).

A cloth MERCHANT named LYDIA came from Thyatira. She moved to PHILIPPI and helped PAUL start the first known church in Europe there, in what is now Greece.

TIBERIAS

Map 4 D4

(ty BEER ee us)

Several boats from Tiberias landed near the place where the Lord had blessed the bread and the people had eaten. John 6:23

- City beside Sea of Galilee

HEROD ANTIPAS, a son of HEROD THE GREAT, founded this lakeshore city in AD 20 to replace SEPPHORIS as his capital of GALILEE. JEWS avoided the city because it was built over a cemetery. Jews taught that walking over a grave would make them ritually unclean and unfit to WORSHIP until they had performed cleaning rituals.

T

TIBERIUS, CAESAR

Map 4 D4

(ty BEER ee us SEE zur)

Ruled AD 14–37

Tiberius Caesar had been ruling for 15 years. Pontius Pilate was governor of Judea. . . . At that time God's word came to John [the Baptist]. Luke 3:1–2 NIrV

- Roman emperor during Jesus' ministry
- Full name: Tiberius Julius Caesar Augustus

A GIFTED SOLDIER, Tiberius should have kept his day job. Roman historians say he was a rotten emperor: cruel and decadent.

Jesus referred to him only once, when asked if Jews should pay Roman taxes. Jesus pointed to the emperor's picture pressed into a coin and said, "Give to CAESAR what belongs to Caesar, and give to GOD what belongs to God" (Matthew 22:21).

TIGLATH-PILESER III

(TIG lath pi LEE zur)

Reigned 745–727 BC

When King Tiglath-pileser of Assyria arrived, he attacked Ahaz instead of helping him. 2 Chronicles 28:20

- King of Assyrian Empire based in Iraq
- Overran the Jewish homeland

WHEN TIGLATH-PILESER III got word that SYRIA and the northern Jewish nation of ISRAEL were making a move to break free of his Assyrian Empire, he crushed their armies, EXILED many of their citizens, and installed HOSHEA as a new Jewish king he kept on a short leash.

Tiglath-pileser had gotten word of the revolt from AHAZ, king of the southern Jewish nation of JUDAH. Instead of rewarding Ahaz, he stuck him with taxes so heavy that the JEWS had to strip GOLD from the Temple and PALACE to pay the tab.

TIGRIS RIVER

Map 2 L6

(TI gris)

As I was standing on the bank of the great Tigris River, I [Daniel] looked up and saw a man dressed in linen clothing, with a belt of pure gold around his waist. Daniel 10:4–5, 7

- Major river in Syria and Iraq
- About 1,200 miles (1,930 km) long

THE TIGRIS AND EUPHRATES RIVERS are the two biggest rivers in the heart of the Middle East. Both pour out of the Turkish mountains and flow south through Syria and Iraq before draining into the Persian Gulf. Civilization is said to have started there, in the land between the rivers.

see map, page 320

TIME OF DAY

About three o'clock in the morning [literally: fourth watch of the night] Jesus came toward them, walking on the water. Mark 6:48

WITHOUT CLOCKS, folks in Bible times used a variety of ways to talk about the time of day. Often they used descriptive words and phrases: morning, noon, heat of the day, evening, night.

By the time of NEHEMIAH (400s BC), JEWS spoke about four parts of the daylight hours: "They remained standing in place for three hours [literally: a quarter of a day] while the Book of the Law of the LORD their GOD was read aloud to them" (Nehemiah 9:3).

This may have been a predecessor to the 12-hour divisions that the Romans used. Their guards worked three-hour shifts: four shifts in a 12-hour day and four more in a 12-hour night. The fourth watch of the night, when the GOSPEL of MARK says Jesus walked on water, would have started about 3 a.m. and ended around 6 a.m. The first watch of the day began at 6 a.m.

TIMNAH

Map 1 B6

(TIM nuh)

Samson returned to Timnah for the wedding.
Judges 14:8 CEV

- Hometown of Samson's Philistine bride

SEVERAL JEWISH TOWNS were named Timnah, but the most famous was a small Philistine village about 20 miles (32 km) west of JERUSALEM. That's where SAMSON met the woman he married. The village didn't last. It's now a ruin called Tell el-Batashi. The marriage didn't last either. Never made it past the honeymoon.

TIMOTHY

(TIM uh thee)

First century AD
Believers in Lystra and Iconium respected Timothy. . . . Paul wanted Timothy to travel with him. **Acts 16:2–3** NCV

- Paul's most trusted associate
- Church troubleshooter, problem-solver
- Assigned to lead the Ephesus church

A BACHELOR, Paul seemed to think of Timothy as a "dear son" (2 Timothy 1:2). The two probably met during PAUL's first mission trip when Paul visited Timothy's home in LYSTRA, a city in Turkey. During Paul's second trip, he recruited Timothy as an associate.

Paul used Timothy as a messenger and spiritual doc who helped fix troubled churches: "I'm sending Timothy to you. He is like a son to me, and I love him. He is faithful in serving the LORD. He will remind you of my way of life in serving Christ Jesus" (1 Corinthians 4:17 NIrV).

When Paul heard about troubles erupting in the EPHESUS church, he assigned Timothy to go there and PASTOR the congregation. Early church leaders said Timothy became the bishop of Ephesus and was martyred there in AD 97 during a wave of PERSECUTION by the Romans.

See also EUNICE, LOIS.

TIMOTHY, LETTERS OF 1–2

Famous sound bite: Love of money is the root of all kinds of evil. 1 Timothy 6:10

PAUL HEARS OF TROUBLE at the EPHESUS church. So he assigns Timothy to PASTOR the people. PAUL then writes a couple letters of practical advice about how to lead the CHURCH.

- Writer: Paul.
- Time: In Paul's last years of ministry. Perhaps in about AD 63 or later.
- Location: Paul writes 2 Timothy from jail in Rome. He's apparently free when he writes 1 Timothy. Both letters are addressed to Timothy in Ephesus, on what is now Turkey's west coast.

BIG SCENES

Female etiquette in church. Some WOMEN are apparently causing trouble in the church. So Paul gives Timothy tips for dealing with the problem. Women—at least in this particular church and at this particular time—should dress modestly and keep quiet during the WORSHIP services. *1 Timothy 2*

To-do list for church leaders. Paul offers Timothy a list of character traits to look for when recruiting church leaders. Among them: integrity, good reputation, faithful to WIFE, not money-hungry. *1 Timothy 3*

Paul's last request. Paul writes as he awaits execution in ROME. "I have fought the good fight. I have finished the RACE. I have kept the FAITH. Now there is a CROWN waiting for me" (2 Timothy 4:7–8 NIrV). Paul asks Timothy to come and be with him at the end. *2 Timothy 4* NIrV

T

> *"Set aside a tithe of your crops—one-tenth of all the crops you harvest each year. Bring this tithe to the designated place of worship."* Deuteronomy 14:22–23

- A tenth of income to maintain the Jewish Temple

A FUND-RAISING TECHNIQUE God set up to support ISRAEL's WORSHIP center, tithing involved bringing a tenth of a FAMILY's income to the PRIESTS: "GRAIN, new WINE, OLIVE OIL, and the FIRSTBORN males of your flocks and herds" (Deuteronomy 14:23).

It's a confusing process, scholars say, apparently because JEWS practiced it differently at different times in their history.

In some cases, the tithe is described as the salary that belongs to the LEVITES, the tribe of Jews responsible for worship. The salary was to make up for the fact that they didn't receive an allotment of territory like the other tribes did (Numbers 18:24).

At other times, the Bible writers said the Jews ate their tithe at the worship center as an act of worship and that they gave it to the Levites only every third year, along with giving some to orphans and widows (Deuteronomy 14:28–29).

There's no mention in the NEW TESTAMENT of Christians tithing.

One Christian writer portrayed the Jewish law system as "obsolete. It is now out of date and will soon disappear" (Hebrews 8:13). PAUL seemed to agree. But he did accept at least some GIFTS to support his ministry (Philippians 4:15). And he collected offerings to give to the needy (2 Corinthians 8).

Church history scholars say that it wasn't until the 1800s that Christians started to tithe. That's when church leaders dusted off the Jewish system of tithing and started using it as a fund-raising tool. They did this when they were hurting financially after government officials rescinded tax laws that had funneled money to places of worship.

Many countries still fund religious institutions through taxes, apparently because they consider spirituality a vital part of a healthy nation.

(TI tuhs)

First century AD

> *If anyone asks about Titus, say that he is my partner who works with me to help you.* 2 Corinthians 8:23

- Gentile associate of Paul
- Director of Crete mission

A TEST-CASE GUINEA PIG, Titus was the first-known non-Jewish CHURCH leader who wasn't circumcised.

Like TIMOTHY, who was half Jewish, Titus was a ministry associate of PAUL. Apparently at Paul's request, Timothy was circumcised so JEWS would consider him kosher; CIRCUMCISION was required of all Jewish males. But Paul refused to require it of Titus—and church leaders in JERUSALEM, all of whom were Jews, backed him up.

Paul assigned Titus the job of finding PASTORS for congregations on the island of CRETE.

TITUS, LETTER OF

> *Famous sound bite: "The people of Crete are all liars, cruel animals, and lazy gluttons." Paul, quoting a Cretan writer, Titus 1:12*

AFTER GIVING TITUS THE JOB of finding PASTORS to lead churches in CRETE, PAUL writes him a letter to encourage him and to offer suggestions about what SPIRITUAL GIFTS and character traits to look for in a CHURCH leader.

- Writer: "This letter is from Paul" (Titus 1:1).
- Time: Perhaps in AD 63 or later, when Paul wrote 1, 2 Timothy.
- Location: Titus is starting the church on the island of Crete, about 100 miles (160 km) south of Greece.

BIG SCENES

Prerequisites for a pastor. On an island with a bad rep, Titus has to find a few good men to lead churches. Paul gives him a wish list of qualifications. Pastoral candidates must:

- have a good reputation
- be sensible
- be faithful to WIFE
- have well-behaved children (Paul is single, by the way)
- be friendly
- enjoy having company visit
- not be bossy, a bully, quick-tempered, or dishonest. *Titus 1*

Christian etiquette. Paul gives Titus some practical advice to pass along to various groups of Christians.

Older men: Be sensible and serious.

Older women: Don't GOSSIP or get drunk.

Young men: Work on self-control.

Young women: Take your cue from older women.

Slaves: Obey your masters.

Everyone: Be kind, earn the respect of others, and obey your leaders. *Titus 2–3*

> *Joseph. . .put Jesus' body in a new tomb that he had cut out of a wall of rock, and he rolled a very large stone to block the entrance of the tomb.* Matthew 27:59–60 NCV

A GRAVE IN THE GROUND is the best resting place most folks could afford in Bible times. Well-to-do people, however, often prepared rock tombs for themselves, just as some people today buy BURIAL lots ahead of time.

Some bought caves, which they converted into tombs. Others chiseled room-size tombs into the soft limestone of a hill and sealed the tombs closed with wheel-shaped rocks that rolled in a grooved track.

These tombs often served a FAMILY for GENERATIONS. The family would place the body on a ledge inside the tomb. A year or more later, they would take the bones off the ledge and put them in a small stone coffin called an ossuary. It's a bone box.

ROLLING STONES covered the doorways of many tombs. Some tombs, like this one, required more than one person to open the grave. That's because it's an uphill push to open and a downhill push to close.

STEPHEN M. MILLER'S ILLUSTRATED BIBLE DICTIONARY

Some scholars insist that the stone coffin of Caiaphas—the high priest who condemned Jesus—was found in Jerusalem in 1990. It dates to the first Christian century. It's ornately decorated—fitting for a high priest. And it has the name "Caiaphas" chiseled on it. It contained the bones of six people, including a man of about age 60.

TONGUES, SPEAKING IN

> I thank God that I [Paul] speak in tongues more than any of you. But in a church meeting I would rather speak five understandable words to help others than ten thousand words in an unknown language. 1 Corinthians 14:18–19

- a spiritual language most don't understand, including the speaker

SCHOLARS CALL IT by its Greek name: *glossolalia* (gloss oh LAY lee uh). To most listeners, the language sounds like gibberish. But Christians who speak in tongues say the Holy Spirit is speaking through them, praising God, praying, or delivering a message.

Christians who practice this are often described as charismatic, worshiping in Pentecostal churches.

Many Christian groups forbid people from speaking in tongues during worship services, arguing it can be disruptive and it calls attention to the speaker.

Bible writers, however, described it as a spiritual gift.

Paul did, however, warn that it can be misused. For that reason, he put limits on it in worship: "No more than two or three should speak in tongues. They must speak one at a time, and someone must interpret what they say" (1 Corinthians 14:27).

TOOLS

> Solomon did not want the noise of hammers and axes to be heard at the place where the temple was being built. So he had the workers shape the blocks of stone at the quarry. 1 Kings 6:7 CEV

TOOLS THAT FARMERS, herders, and builders used in early Bible times were generally made of wood, easy-to-sharpen flint, copper, and bronze.

With these they made plows, hammers, chisels, knives, saws, sickles, and pick-like adzes for digging.

In about the 1200s BC, when Philistines and Jews were competing for turf in what is now Israel, people figured out how to forge iron—which made for stronger, sharper, and more durable tools.

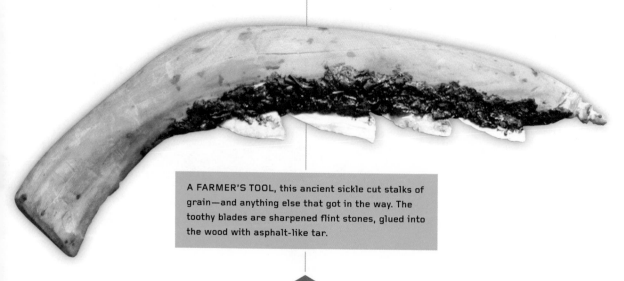

A FARMER'S TOOL, this ancient sickle cut stalks of grain—and anything else that got in the way. The toothy blades are sharpened flint stones, glued into the wood with asphalt-like tar.

TORAH

> "This is a statute of the law [Hebrew: torah] that the LORD has commanded."
> Numbers 19:2 NRSV

- Hebrew for "law"
- Name for the laws of Moses
- Nickname for first five books in the Bible

BIBLE WRITERS used this HEBREW word in many different ways. But most of the time it refers to the hundreds of laws that GOD gave MOSES to pass along to the JEWS.

These commandments are preserved in the WRITINGS traditionally credited to Moses, especially the book of DEUTERONOMY. That's a book that sums up the rules Jews are supposed to follow in return for God's continued BLESSING.

Those laws distinguished the Jews from other races because many of them are unique: such as the law requiring Jews to WORSHIP on the Saturday SABBATH and to circumcise their baby boys on the eighth day.

TORCH

> Gideon separated the 300 men into three companies. He put a trumpet and an empty jar into the hands of each man. And he put a torch inside each jar. Judges 7:16 NIRV

INSTEAD OF USING FLASHLIGHTS, people in Bible times lit the darkness with LAMPS and torches. Both burned oil, often OLIVE OIL.

To make a torch, people tied strips of cloth around the top of a pole. Then they dipped the cloth into oil and set it on fire.

Some torches in NEW TESTAMENT times, however, consisted of clay or metal lamps instead of cloth. Those torches looked like small lamps mounted on top of poles. Using a wick and oil, they could burn much longer than the typical torch.

TOWER

> Hezekiah worked hard repairing all of the broken parts of the [Jerusalem] wall. He built towers on it. He built another wall outside that one. 2 Chronicles 32:5 NIRV

- Defensive guard station, often in a city wall

FARMERS BUILT LOOKOUT TOWERS in their vineyards and fields so they could guard their crops during HARVEST season, when thieves were most likely to pick themselves a free lunch—or more.

Cities protected by walls often had towers built into those walls, especially beside the gates, where invaders would often concentrate their firepower.

TRADITION

> Pharisees and teachers of religious law asked him [Jesus], "Why don't your disciples follow our age-old tradition? They eat without first performing the hand-washing ceremony." Mark 7:5

- Customs passed down from generation to generation

MANY JEWS FOLLOWED MORE than the Jewish laws. They picked up on traditions recommended by Jewish scholars and RABBIS throughout the centuries. In time, some JEWS said those traditions were as important and binding as the laws written in the BIBLE.

For example, Jewish law says people shouldn't work on the SABBATH. Rabbis and scholars added traditions about what they thought constituted work. One tradition that emerged said it was work to treat the sick on the Sabbath, unless the person was in danger of dying.

Jesus said a tradition like that does more harm than good: "The Sabbath was made to serve us; we weren't made to serve the Sabbath" (Mark 2:27 MSG).

T

TRANSFIGURED into what sounds like a celestial being, Jesus glows "like the sun." Even his clothes seem to radiate light.

See Syria, Map 3 N6

TRANSFIGURATION

> He [Jesus] was transfigured before them. His face shone like the sun, and his clothes became as white as the light. Just then there appeared before them Moses and Elijah, talking with Jesus. Matthew 17:2–3 TNIV

- Jesus' appearance with Moses and Elijah

JESUS GLOWED on a hilltop, in an event that some scholars speculate revealed what he looks like in his heavenly form. The GREEK word for what happened is *metamorphoo*, from which we get *metamorphosis*.

Jesus took his three closest DISCIPLES and best friends—PETER, JAMES, and JOHN—to an unidentified mountain. While praying, he morphed into what sounds like a celestial being who ended up talking with two spirit beings from ISRAEL's distant past.

The writer of REVELATION describes Jesus in glowing terms, too: "The city has no need of sun or moon, for the GLORY of GOD illuminates the city, and the Lamb is its light" (Revelation 21:23).

TRANSJORDAN

> "Please give us this land [Transjordan]. Then it will belong to us. But don't make us go across the Jordan River." Numbers 32:5 NIrV

- Land east of the Jordan River (Syria, Jordan)

SYRIA AND JORDAN became a staging ground for the Jewish invasion of CANAAN, in what is now ISRAEL. MOSES led the JEWS north out of EGYPT, but instead of approaching Canaan from the south, he took them into Jordan, east of the JORDAN RIVER.

The Jews met resistance there but overwhelmed their enemies and seized the land.

The tribes of REUBEN and GAD, along with half the tribe of MANASSEH, realized that the grazing fields there were perfect for their livestock. So with the blessing of MOSES, that's where they settled.

I [Paul] have traveled on many long journeys. I have faced danger from rivers and from robbers. . . . I have faced danger in the cities, in the deserts, and on the seas.
2 Corinthians 11:26

WALKING was the most common mode of transportation in Bible times. On average, people could walk about 20 miles (32 km) a day. Same for riding a DONKEY or a CAMEL, except in an emergency, when they would pick up the pace.

Typically, JEWS didn't sail much. That's because they didn't have a natural harbor to protect ships from bad weather. HEROD THE GREAT (reigned 40–4 BC) built an artificial one at CAESAREA.

WALKING or riding a donkey, folks in what is now Israel could generally cover about 20 miles (32 km) a day. Not so much in the hilly badlands.

People tried to avoid travel during the winter months. That's when the MEDITERRANEAN SEA was its stormiest and the dirt roads were muddiest.

Romans made travel easier by building throughout the Middle East a network of rock-paved roads that were raised a tad in the middle so rainwater drained into gullies on each side of the ROAD. The apostle PAUL made excellent use of those roads, traveling an estimated 10,000 miles (16,000 km) during his missionary journeys.

TREE OF KNOWLEDGE

"You [Adam] may freely eat the fruit of every tree in the garden—except the tree of the knowledge of good and evil. If you eat its fruit, you are sure to die." Genesis 2:16–17

▪ Tree that produced the forbidden fruit

FRUIT FROM THIS TREE was the only FRUIT in the Garden of EDEN that ADAM AND EVE weren't allowed to eat—on threat of DEATH.

It's unknown what kind of fruit it was or why something as seemingly beneficial as "the knowledge of good and evil" would be lethal.

Perhaps, some say, the tree was a symbol of spiritual knowledge that Adam and Eve weren't yet mature enough to handle. Some also speculate that GOD had intended the couple to live forever, but that when they ate the toxic fruit they sealed their fate. (It was toxic spiritually, if not physically.) Adam died at age 930.

TREE OF LIFE

God said, "Look, the human beings have become like us, knowing both good and evil. What if they reach out, take fruit from the tree of life, and eat it? Then they will live forever!" Genesis 3:22

▪ Tree that symbolizes eternal life

IN THE BIBLE'S FIRST BOOK—in the CREATION story—this tree produces FRUIT that prolongs life. In the

T

Bible's last book, John talks about trees of life in New Jerusalem, where people no longer die.

Archaeologists have found pictures throughout the Middle East showing a sacred tree that represented life, IMMORTALITY, or fertility. Some speculate that the design of the menorah, the Jewish SEVEN-branch LAMPSTAND, was inspired by the tree of life.

TRIBES OF ISRAEL

These are the twelve tribes of Israel, and this is what their father said as he told his sons good-bye. He blessed each one with an appropriate message. Genesis 49:28

- Families descended from Jacob's 12 sons by four women

JEWS TRACE THEIR FAMILY HERITAGE to one of Jacob's dozen sons. Each son produced an extended family that grew into a tribe. When Moses led the Jews home from slavery in Egypt, he assigned each tribe its own territory. Levites were the exception. As Israel's worship leaders, they were scattered throughout the land in various cities.

There were actually 13 tribes. That's because Joseph's tribe spawned two tribes descended from each of his sons: Ephraim and Manasseh. But there were only a dozen tribes assigned plugs of territory. Those 12, along with the landless tribe of Levi:

Leah's kids: Reuben, Simeon, Levi, Judah, Issachar, Zebulun

Rachel's kid: Benjamin

Rachel's grandkids: Joseph's sons Ephraim and Manasseh

Zilpah's kids: Gad, Asher

Bilhah's kids: Dan, Naphtali

King Solomon busted up the tribal system, possibly to erode the influence of the tribal leaders. He divided the country into regions led by governors he appointed.

TRIBULATION

"These are the ones who died in the great tribulation. They have washed their robes in the blood of the Lamb and made them white."
Revelation 7:14

- Era of intense persecution

GOD'S PEOPLE would suffer through a period of intense PERSECUTION and martyrdom, wrote John of Revelation.

Some Christians say this will happen in the end times, before Jesus returns in the Second Coming. Daniel, they say, predicted as much: "a time of anguish greater than any since nations first came into existence" (Daniel 12:1).

Others say the tribulation has already happened because John was describing the Roman Empire's persecution of Christians.

TRIBUTE

King Mesha of Moab was a sheep breeder. He used to pay the king of Israel an annual tribute of 100,000 lambs and the wool of 100,000 rams. 2 Kings 3:4

- Required payment to a foreign ruler

THINK "LUNCH MONEY" STOLEN by the class bully. That's essentially what tribute was: giving the dominant ruler in the area whatever he wanted.

Jews had to pay tribute taxes to various nations and empires throughout Bible times. They paid in livestock, crops, GOLD, SILVER, gems, SPICES, slaves—and just about anything else of value.

King Hezekiah once had to empty his treasury and strip gold from the Temple doors to pay Assyria's demand of "more than eleven tons of silver and one ton of gold" (2 Kings 18:14).

Refusing to continue paying tribute is what destroyed both Jewish nations. Israel in the north halted payments to Assyria. Judah halted payments to Babylon.

Assyrians and Babylonians, each based out of Iraq, came to collect.

In the process, they erased each nation from the political map: Israel in 722 BC, Judah in 586 BC.

TRINITY

> *Jesus came to them. He said. . . "Go and make disciples of all nations. Baptize them in the name of the Father and of the Son and of the Holy Spirit." Matthew 28:18–19* NIrV

- Description of God the Father, Son, Holy Spirit

TRINITY ISN'T A WORD IN THE BIBLE. Most Bible experts, however, insist it's a teaching in the BIBLE.

- There's God the Father, to whom Jesus prays in the Garden of GETHSEMANE (Mark 14:36).
- There's Jesus, who says, "Anyone who has seen me has seen the FATHER!" (John 14:9).
- There's the Holy Spirit, whom Jesus promised would come to help the DISCIPLES after Jesus left (John 14:16–17).

From the beginning of CHRISTIANITY, it seems, scholars have tried to understand how we can have three Gods in one. No joy. In the end, the early scholars admitted they couldn't figure it out. Yet they said they believed it because it's in the Bible.

> *The Father is God, the Son is God, the Holy Spirit is God. . .yet we do not say that there are three gods, but one God, the most exalted Trinity.*
>   Augustine (about AD 354–430)

> *We don't understand the mystery of how this can be, or what causes it. But we trust the evidence of this truth.*
>   Ambrose (about AD 340–397)

TRIUMPHAL ENTRY

> *The people gave him a wonderful welcome. . . . They were calling out, "Hosanna! Blessed is he who comes in God's name!"*
> Mark 11:8–9 MSG

- Jesus' Palm Sunday ride into Jerusalem

ON THE SUNDAY BEFORE JESUS' CRUCIFIXION, Jews gave him a hero's welcome to JERUSALEM. Many seemed to think he was the promised MESSIAH. Some probably hoped he would lead ISRAEL to freedom and glory, driving out the occupying forces of Rome.

Jewish leaders also seemed to fear he would lead a doomed revolt against Rome. So they orchestrated his execution on charges of treason against CAESAR.

Sunday's hero became Friday's execution.

But Friday's execution became Sunday's hero. (See RESURRECTION.)

JERUSALEM GREETS JESUS as a messiah king on Sunday. By Friday, the city will see him executed.

T

TROAS
Map 3 D3

(TROH as)

They went down to Troas. During the night Paul had a vision. He saw a man from Macedonia standing and begging him. "Come over to Macedonia!" Acts 16:8–9 NIrv

- Turkish city of Paul's vision to go to Europe
- Where Paul revived a dead boy

ALONG THE NORTHEAST COAST of Turkey, PAUL reached the port city of Troas. He was on his second mission trip, spreading the story of Jesus throughout Turkey. But in what sounds like a vivid DREAM, he saw a man from GREECE calling him: "Help us!" Paul left for Greece the next day. There he started the first CHURCH in Europe, in the city of PHILIPPI.

Later Paul preached an all-night sermon in Troas, lulling a young man named EUTYCHUS to sleep. Eutychus fell off a window ledge and died. But Paul revived him and went back to PREACHING—"until dawn" (Acts 20:11).

TROPHIMUS

(TROF uh muhs)

First century AD

"He [Paul] has brought some Greeks into the Temple and has made this holy place unclean!" (They [the Jews] said this because they had seen Trophimus, a man from Ephesus, with Paul in Jerusalem.) Acts 21:28–29 NCV

- Associate of Paul

A CHRISTIAN FROM EPHESUS, Trophimus traveled with PAUL to JERUSALEM after Paul's third and last-known mission trip. Jerusalem JEWS mobbed Paul and falsely accused him of taking Trophimus, a GENTILE, into the Jews-only section of the TEMPLE.

TRUMPET

(see RAM'S HORN)

TUNNEL

He [King Hezekiah] built a pool and dug a tunnel to bring water into the city [Jerusalem]. 2 Kings 20:20

ONE OF THE MOST FAMOUS tunnels in the BIBLE is one rediscovered in JERUSALEM in 1880. King HEZEKIAH had it chiseled through nearly 600 yards [550 m] of solid rock.

It provided Jerusalem with WATER by tapping into GIHON Spring outside the city walls and channeling the water into a POOL inside the city. Hezekiah apparently did this because he anticipated ASSYRIA's attack and SIEGE of Jerusalem. The JEWS survived that siege.

TURBAN

He [Moses] placed the turban on Aaron's head, and on the front of the turban was the narrow strip of thin gold as a sign of his dedication to the LORD. Leviticus 8:9 CEV

▪ Head covering

To protect their head from the sun and RAIN, many people in Bible times wore turbans—head coverings made by winding together strips of cloth.

The Jewish HIGH PRIEST wore a turban. Hanging in the front, attached by a blue cord, was a GOLD medallion engraved with the words "HOLY TO THE LORD" (Exodus 28:36).

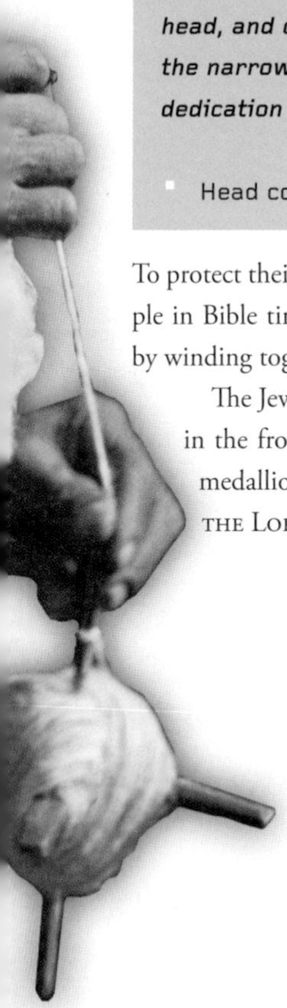

TURBAN-TOPPED, a man in what is now the West Bank Palestinian city of Ramallah spins wool at the turn of the 1900s. The turban keeps him warm in cool weather and protects him from the sun when it's hot.

TYCHICUS

(TICK ee cuss)

Tychicus will give you a full report about how I am getting along. He is a beloved brother and faithful helper who serves with me in the Lord's work. Colossians 4:7

▪ Associate of Paul

A TRUSTED MESSENGER and fellow MINISTER with PAUL, Tychicus seems to have delivered two of Paul's LETTERS: COLOSSIANS and EPHESIANS. He was also one of two possible ministry replacements for TITUS on the island of CRETE (Titus 3:12).

TYRE

Map 1 C3

(TIRE)

King Hiram of Tyre sent messengers to David, along with cedar timber, and stonemasons and carpenters to build him a palace. 1 Chronicles 14:1

▪ Seaport city in Lebanon
▪ Provided cedar and workers for Jewish Temple, palaces

ISRAEL AND ITS NEIGHBOR kingdom of Tyre had a good relationship in the early years of the Jewish nation when DAVID and SOLOMON were KINGS.

Tyre was a coastal kingdom in what is now the LEBANON city of Sur, about 15 miles (24 km) north of the Israeli border. Tyre's king HIRAM supplied both kings with Lebanon's prized CEDAR, along with carpenters and stonemasons to help build up JERUSALEM.

Some 400 years later, Jewish PROPHETS were predicting the fall of Tyre.

EZEKIEL said invaders would "destroy the walls of Tyre and. . .scrape away its soil and make it a bare rock!" (Ezekiel 26:4). ALEXANDER the Great did just that some 200 years later. He tore the city apart and used the debris to make a bridge to Tyre's last holdout: a fortress island 700 yards [640 m] offshore.

T

UNITY IN THE CHURCH

I [Paul] appeal to you, brothers and sisters. . . that there be no divisions among you, but that you be perfectly united in mind and thought. 1 Corinthians 1:10 TNIV

- Paul's persistent appeal to churches he founded

PAUL STARTED churches throughout Syria, Turkey, and Greece. Some were a little tougher to maintain than others.

Perhaps the Church of the Biggest Headache was in Corinth, Greece, where Paul spent one and a half years—more time than at any church before then. Possibly it's because he felt he needed to.

After Paul left, he got word that the church was arguing over who would lead them.

Paul pled for them to work out a compromise that would unite them. The call for unity in the church became one of Paul's trademarks. It may be because there was so much disunity, especially among Christian Jews clashing with Christian Gentiles. Many Jews argued that Gentiles had to follow Jewish laws to become Christian. Paul argued otherwise, insisting that Christ "united Jews and Gentiles into one people" (Ephesians 2:14).

UNLEAVENED BREAD

"Celebrate the Festival of Unleavened Bread. For seven days the bread you eat must be made without yeast." Exodus 23:15

- Tortilla-like flat bread made without yeast

WHEN THE JEWS enslaved in Egypt got word that they would be freed within hours, Moses told them to eat a meal to give them strength for the road. They wouldn't have time to let bread dough rise. So they skipped the yeast, which would have made the dough rise.

Every year afterward, Jews were to commemorate their freedom by reenacting the meal, which became known as the Passover meal.

UPPER ROOM

"The owner will take you upstairs and show you a large room ready for you to use. Prepare the meal there." Luke 22:12 CEV

- Where Jesus and disciples ate the Last Supper
- Where the Holy Spirit descended on the disciples

IN JERUSALEM, a man who was apparently a follower of Jesus allowed Jesus and his disciples to use an upper room in his house to eat the Passover meal. This meal became known as the Last Supper.

The disciples seemed to continue using the house as a meeting place. When Jesus ascended to heaven, he told them to wait in Jerusalem for the coming of the Holy Spirit. "They went up to the upper room where they were staying" (Acts 1:13 NASB).

ABRAHAM'S HOMETOWN of Ur was the New York City of its day—a busy waterfront town, and a center of business and culture.

UR   Map 2 M7

(URR, rhymes with her*) or (OOR, sounds like* oar*)*

The Lord said to Abram, "I brought you here from Ur in Chaldea, and I gave you this land." Genesis 15:7 CEV

- Abraham's hometown in Iraq

ABRAHAM GREW UP in the busy riverside city of Ur, just across the Euphrates River from Nasiriya, a hard-fought holdout during the 2003 war in which American and British troops ousted dictator Saddam Hussein.

In ABRAHAM's day, 4,000 years ago, Ur was the New York City of its time: the civilized world's hub of culture, wealth, and power.

URIAH

(your I uh)

About 1000 BC

David wrote a letter to Joab and sent it by Uriah. In the letter David wrote, "Put Uriah on the front lines where the fighting is worst and leave him there alone. Let him be killed in battle." 2 Samuel 11:14–15 NCV

- Bathsheba's husband
- Elite solider in King David's army

A SOLDIER IN DAVID'S strike force known as The Thirty, Uriah was off fighting a WAR when DAVID slept with Uriah's wife BATHSHEBA and got her pregnant.

To cover up his SIN, David called Uriah home, hoping he would sleep with Bathsheba and think the child was his.

Uriah refused, saying he couldn't indulge in SEX while his colleagues were dying in battle. So David arranged for him to die in battle, too.

URIM AND THUMMIM

(YOOR im) (THUM im)

The governor told them not to eat the priests' share of food from the sacrifices until a priest could consult the LORD about the matter by using the Urim and Thummim—the sacred lots. Ezra 2:63

- Sacred device Jews used to consult God

AARON and Jewish HIGH PRIESTS after him carried in their pocket what sounds like a couple of holy dice or stones.

No one seems to know exactly what the Urim and Thummin were. But PRIESTS used them to get a "yes" or "no" answer to questions they posed to GOD.

See also LOTS.

UZ

Location Uncertain

(UHZ, rhymes with *buzz*)

There once was a man named Job who lived in the land of Uz. . . .a man of complete integrity. Job 1:1

- Job's mysterious homeland

SADLY, the BIBLE never says where Uz was. The most common guess is EDOM, in what is now the Arab country of Jordan—ISRAEL's neighbor to the east.

UZZAH

(UHZ uh)

About 1000 BC

The LORD's anger was aroused against Uzzah, and he struck him dead because he had laid his hand on the Ark. 1 Chronicles 13:10

- Died transporting the Ark of the Covenant

ISRAEL'S MOST SACRED OBJECT, the ARK OF THE COVENANT, a chest that held the 10 COMMANDMENTS, was transported to JERUSALEM on an oxcart. Uzzah made the mistake of touching the chest to steady it so it didn't fall off when an OX stumbled.

He died. The Bible writer didn't say why. Guesses include that only PRIESTS were supposed to touch the Ark. Priests had carried it during the EXODUS out of EGYPT.

UZZIAH

(uh ZI uh)

Ruled about 792 BC–740 BC

Azariah—he was only sixteen years old at the time—was the unanimous choice of the people of Judah to succeed his father Amaziah as king. 2 Kings 14:21 MSG

- King of south Jewish nation of Judah
- Leprosy forced him to declare his son Jotham king

BIBLE WRITERS reported that King Uzziah strengthened JUDAH's ARMY and overpowered local enemies such as the PHILISTINES and Ammonites (2 Chronicles 26:2). He also built forts and watchtowers in the farmland to guard against raiders.

U

VASHTI

(VASH ty or VASH tee)

(VASH ty or VASH tee)

Husband ruled 486–465 BC

King Xerxes was feeling happy because of so much wine. And he asked his seven personal servants. . .to bring Queen Vashti to him. . . and let his people and his officials see how beautiful she was. . . . She refused."

Esther 1:10–12 CEV

- Queen of Persia, based in Iran
- Lost her job to Jewish woman: Esther

HER BEAUTY WAS THE BEAST that did her in. Queen Vashti was so gorgeous that when her husband, King XERXES, got drunk at a royal party for the guys, he decided to show her off.

Trophy WIFE.

Nothing doing, Vashti said.

She was hosting her own party for the ladies. And she wasn't going into a room full of gawking men at the end of a seven-day drunk.

Xerxes wasn't too drunk to realize he had been dissed by a woman.

He consulted his advisers. One man said, "The women in the kingdom will hear about this, and they will refuse to respect their HUSBANDS. They will say, 'If Queen Vashti doesn't obey her husband, why should we?'" (Esther 1:17 CEV).

The men decided to give Vashti what she wanted—forever. She would never again see the king. She was banished to the royal HAREM as just another desperate housewife craving attention.

The guys devised the perfect guy-plan to find a replacement queen: They'd have a beauty contest. ESTHER won.

VEIL

When Rebekah looked up and saw Isaac, she quickly. . .covered her face with her veil.

Genesis 24:64–65

- Cloth to cover a woman's face

SOME WOMEN in Bible times hid their faces from men outside their FAMILY—covering their face with cloth much like some WOMEN still do in parts of the world.

It wasn't Jewish law, but it did seem to be a custom.

PAUL insisted women wear a veil when they spoke in CHURCH: "Any woman who prays or prophesies with her head unveiled disgraces her head" (1 Corinthians 11:5 NRSV).

VINE

I am the vine, and you are the branches. If you stay joined to me, and I stay joined to you, then you will produce lots of fruit.

John 15:5 CEV

PLENTY OF PLANTS grew on vines in Bible lands: cucumbers, melons, squash. But Bible writers almost always used *vines* to talk about vineyards: vines that grow GRAPES.

The climate and land in ISRAEL and other parts of the Middle East are ideal for vineyards.

People:

- ate grapes as FRUIT
- dried some of the clusters into raisins—a perfect snack for the road
- boiled the juice into grape syrup
- stomped grapes in winepresses to make wine.

Newly planted vines took three to five years to produce fruit. That's why the PHILISTINES were so upset with SAMSON for setting fire to their vineyards (Judges 15:5).

Bible writers also used the word symbolically, sometimes to describe the Jewish nation—often in a sad way. JEREMIAH said GOD planted the JEWS from the "purest stock" but they grew into a "wild vine" (Jeremiah 2:21).

EZEKIEL said God would rip the Jews out of the ground, "roots and all!" (Ezekiel 17:9). Babylonian invaders did just that in 586 BC, defeating the nation and deporting many survivors to what is now Iraq.

Jesus compared himself to a vine that provides spiritual nourishment to everyone connected to him.

See also WINE.

VINEGAR

They put poison in my food and gave me vinegar to drink. Psalm 69:21 NCV

- Sour wine
- Common drink among the poor

PEOPLE DIDN'T DRINK pure vinegar; they used it to season food.

Many did, however, drink a cheap, sour WINE sometimes translated in English Bibles as vinegar. Hanging on the CROSS, Jesus was offered a sponge soaked in "wine vinegar" (Mark 15:36 TNIV). It was apparently to help deaden the pain.

VINEYARD   *(see VINE)*

VIRGIN

"The woman the high priest gets married to must be a virgin. He must not marry a widow or a woman who is divorced."
Leviticus 21:13–14 NIrV

- Woman who hasn't had sex with a man

IN THE MAN-RUN WORLD of Bible times, WOMEN were considered damaged goods if they met this combo criterion: unmarried, nonvirgin.

Even King DAVID's daughter, Princess TAMAR, seemed unable to find a husband after she was raped by her half brother AMNON. Tamar moved out of the PALACE residence for royal virgins. She "lived as a desolate woman in her brother ABSALOM's house" (2 Samuel 13:20).

Any BRIDE who presented herself as a virgin needed to be able to prove it during the honeymoon: blood on the bed sheet from the broken hymen—a thin membrane that partly covers the vaginal opening.

Some parents apparently kept the bed sheet as proof of their daughter's virginity in case the husband accused her of sleeping around before the WEDDING (Deuteronomy 22:17).

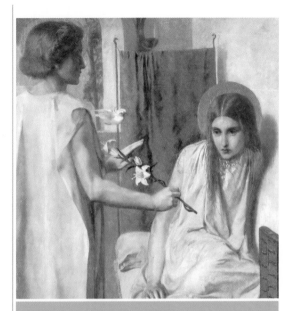

NEWS FLASH from Gabriel: Mary, while still a virgin, is going to become pregnant and give birth to Jesus. Pregnancy without having sex? Unbelievable to many, though mere human docs can work that miracle today.

VIRGIN BIRTH

"The virgin will conceive a child! She will give birth to a son, and they will call him Immanuel, which means 'God is with us.'"
Matthew 1:23

- Birth of Jesus, before Mary had sex with anyone

WHEN THE ANGEL GABRIEL told MARY she would have a baby, Mary objected.

"But how can this happen? I am a virgin" (Luke 1:34).

Mary was engaged to JOSEPH at the time, and the GREEK word Mary used for "virgin," *parthenos*, means she had never had SEX with anyone.

That is, however, not the word that the prophet ISAIAH used for the prophecy that the writer of MATTHEW linked to Mary. Pointing to Isaiah's prediction, the writer of Matthew said, "All of this occurred to fulfill the LORD's message through his prophet: 'Look! The virgin will conceive a child! She will give BIRTH to a son, and they will call him IMMANUEL,'" (Matthew 1:22–23).

Isaiah's "virgin" prophecy used the HEBREW word *almah*, which means "a young woman." Isaiah did not use

V

501

the Hebrew word *betulah*, which literally means "virgin."

Most scholars say Isaiah wasn't talking about Jesus—at least as far as he knew. He was talking about a child who would be born in his day as a divine SIGN to the king warning him not to sign an alliance with ASSYRIA. The king wanted Assyria's help to deal with a threat from neighboring nations. Isaiah said that by the time this "Immanuel" was old enough to eat solid food, the threatening nations would be defeated.

The writer of Matthew, however, apparently saw the prophecy pulling a double shift—working in Isaiah's day as well as in the birth of Jesus some 700 years later.

Two of the four GOSPEL stories about Jesus' life report the Virgin Birth: Matthew and LUKE.

In the AD 100s, Celsus, a critic of CHRISTIANITY, said *parthenos* wasn't a description of Mary as a virgin. Instead, it was a subtle code word identifying the name of Jesus' father: a soldier named Panthera. The Greek word for soldier is the similar-sounding *pandera*.

Most Christians by that time disagreed. They taught that Jesus was born to the Virgin Mary.

Some Christians today ask why it's hard to believe GOD could arrange for a virgin to have a child since physicians can do that now.

VISION

I [Paul] will reluctantly tell about visions and revelations from the Lord. . . . Whether I was in my body or out of my body, I don't know.
2 Corinthians 12:1-2

- apparition in a dream, trance, or another altered state

GOD SPOKE TO PROPHETS "in visions and DREAMS" (Numbers 12:6 CEV).

Trances, too. When several KINGS asked the prophet ELISHA to consult GOD about a coming battle, Elisha needed to be lulled into either a trance or a dreamlike state. He told the kings, "Bring me someone who can play the HARP" (2 Kings 3:15).

Often it's hard to tell the difference between *vision* and *dream*. The words seem to be used interchangeably. JOB told of God speaking "in dreams, in visions of the night" (Job 33:15).

PAUL experienced something that sounds even more dramatic than a vivid dream: "Only God knows whether I was in my body or outside my body. But I do know that I was caught up to PARADISE and heard things so astounding that they cannot be expressed in words, things no human is allowed to tell" (2 Corinthians 12:3–4).

VOW (see Oath)

VOYAGE

The weather was becoming dangerous for sea travel because it was so late in the fall, and Paul spoke to the ship's officers about it.
Acts 27:9

- Paul: "Three times I was shipwrecked" (2 Corinthians 11:25)
- Jonah: Thrown overboard for causing a "terrible storm" (Jonah 1:7)

THE CHURCH WAS BORN in the land that framed the MEDITERRANEAN SEA: ISRAEL in the east, ROME in the north, EGYPT in the south, SPAIN in the distant west. Sailing was one of the quickest ways to get from one place to another.

But there were two big threats: pirates and weather.

As far as weather was concerned, summer was the safest time to sail: late May through mid-September. Sailing got a bit dicey in the spring and fall. It was downright dangerous in the winter, from mid-November through early March. Folks needed a strong motivation to sail then:

- transport of soldiers and supplies for WAR
- transport of GRAIN for a well-paying client, such as hungry souls in ROME.

Under arrest and headed to Rome for trial in CAESAR's COURT, PAUL's military escort decided to set sail in late summer. Sailing into a prevailing headwind, they managed to get only about a fourth of the way by early October, landing at southern Turkey. But they pressed on. Big mistake. They got caught in a typhoon-like storm that pummeled the SHIP for two weeks before running it aground near the island of MALTA. Fortunately, no lives were lost.

WAGES

"If you hire poor people to work for you. . . pay them their wages at the end of each day, because they live in poverty and need the money to survive." Deuteronomy 24:14–15 CEV

WAGES WAFFLED throughout the 2,000 years of Bible history. There's no posted union rate in the BIBLE—or a union, for that matter. But there are some examples of payment.

Day laborer. In a PARABLE, Jesus told of a landowner who hired workers by the day, paying them each a DENARIUS. That was a Roman-stamped SILVER coin about 18 to 20 millimeters across—the size of a US, Canadian, or Euro dime.

Shepherd. JACOB, working as a SHEPHERD for his father-in-law LABAN, asked for "all the SHEEP and GOATS that are speckled or spotted, along with all the black sheep" (Genesis 30:32).

Travel consultant. SAUL, wanting to be pointed in the right direction, paid a man "one small silver piece" (1 Samuel 9:8). The coin weighed about a tenth of an ounce (3 g)—about the weight of a US or Canadian penny or a Euro two-cent piece.

Mercenaries. JUDAH's King Amaziah hired mercenaries for an upcoming battle, offering an average of 1.2 ounces (34 g) of silver per soldier (2 Chronicles 25:6). That's about the weight of a buck and a half in quarters, or almost 5 one-euro coins.

WALLED CITY

He [King Hezekiah] also conquered the Philistines. . .from their smallest outpost to their largest walled city. 2 Kings 18:8

MANY CITIES in Bible times were protected by massive walls—sometimes double walls running parallel. Cities often used the land in between for storage and housing.

The average city wall enclosed 5 to 10 acres, which is about the size of 5 to 10 football fields. The walls were often built of sunbaked mud BRICKS waterproofed with plaster, and rested on a stone foundation.

JERUSALEM CITY WALLS in 1919. In Bible times, many of the larger cities were protected by walls. Invaders often tried to starve out the people if they couldn't break through the city gates or walls.

STEPHEN M. MILLER'S ILLUSTRATED BIBLE DICTIONARY

JERICHO was the first known city in the region with walls. Jericho's earliest walls reportedly date to about 7000 BC. Built of stone, they were over six feet thick (about 2 m).

Some later walls were much thicker.

BABYLON's wall in what is now Iraq stood about four times thicker than Jericho's: some 25 feet (about 8 m).

WAR

> In the spring of the year, when kings normally go out to war, David sent Joab and the Israelite army to fight the Ammonites.
> 2 Samuel 11:1

LOVE OF RICHES was a big motivator for war in Bible times.

Raiders from small kingdoms would attack even smaller kingdoms, to steal the spring and summer HARVEST, along with anything else they could get their hands on. That's how LOT and his FAMILY got taken as slaves. Fortunately, his uncle ABRAHAM assembled a militia, caught up with the raiders, overpowered them, and "brought back his nephew Lot with his possessions and all the women and other captives" (Genesis 14:16).

Some larger kingdoms—such as Iraqi-based ASSYRIA and BABYLON, Iran-based PERSIA, along with GREECE and ROME—wanted to grow into superpowers. So they invaded weaker kingdoms and forced them to pay annual taxes. A bit like a bully stealing lunch money—but on an international scale.

When the smaller nations rebelled and stopped sending MONEY, the empires usually came to collect. That's how both Jewish nations got wiped off the map. ISRAEL in the north fell to Assyria in 722 BC. JUDAH in the south fell to Babylon in 586 BC.

The Jewish homeland was a popular target because it formed the favorite land bridge connecting southland people of EGYPT and ARABIA with northerners from Italy to Iran. If armies or MERCHANTS wanted to go north or south, they either had to pass through Jewish land or TRAVEL by the sea in the west or the DESERT in the east.

Wars often began in the spring after the land dried up from winter rains. It was hard to move an ARMY through mud trails in a day before paved roads. That's why Romans built a vast network of stone-paved roads—to make sure their army could go wherever needed whenever needed.

See also WEAPONS.

WASHING (see PURIFICATION)

WATCHTOWER (see TOWER)

WATER

> Moses led the people of Israel. . .out into the desert of Shur. . . . When they came to the oasis of Marah, the water was too bitter to drink. Exodus 15:22–23

ISRAEL IS NO MINNESOTA, a state nicknamed "Land of 10,000 Lakes." In fact, Minnesota has almost 12,000 lakes. ISRAEL, on the other hand, has:

- one lake, called the SEA OF GALILEE
- the JORDAN RIVER
- the DEAD SEA—lowest spot on earth, making it the drainage pit of the Middle East and too salty even for fish.

Farmers and herders depended on RAIN to water their crops and grazing pastures. To preserve rainwater, they dug cisterns: pits waterproofed with plaster. Rainwater drained into the pits and was stored there like artificial WELL water.

People dug wells—and fought over them. ISAAC dug three wells but lost two of them to competing herders who moved in on him (Genesis 26:19–22).

Water was so scarce that cities grew up around wells. It was in one such city that Jesus met a woman at the local well and offered her "living water" (John 4:10) to quench her spiritual thirst.

WAY, THE

I [Paul] persecuted the followers of the Way, hounding some to death, arresting both men and women and throwing them in prison.
Acts 22:4

- Nickname for Christian movement

BEFORE FOLLOWERS OF JESUS were called Christians, they were apparently known as people of "the Way." They may have adopted this nickname from something Jesus said: "I am the way, the truth, and the life. No one can come to the FATHER except through me" (John 14:6).

See also CHRISTIANITY.

WEAPONS

There were 120,000 troops armed with every kind of weapon. 1 Chronicles 12:37

DURING BIBLE TIMES, weapons used in combat included:

- Knives and daggers. These were often about a foot long (30 cm). (See also DAGGER.)
- Swords. Early ones common in what is now ISRAEL had BRONZE blades curved like sickles to cut WHEAT; great for slashing people. A Philistine invention made them obsolete: the double-edged, iron SWORD. It could slash and stab.
- Slingshots. Slingers added a dimension of artillery. They could launch baseball-sized stones like cannonballs, mowing down soldiers before the slingers could see the whites of their eyes.
- Bows and arrows. Acting as even longer-range artillerymen, archers could darken the sky with a cloud of arrows that would collapse a wave of soldiers more than a hundred yards (meters) away.

In SIEGE warfare, armies such as those fielded by the ROMAN EMPIRE attacked walled cities with:

- Shovels. Sappers dug TUNNELS under the city wall then collapsed the tunnel in hopes that part of the wall would drop into the hole.
- Rolling towers. This put invading archers at the same height as defenders on the city walls.
- Battering rams. Rolling on wheels, and sometimes tipped with metal, these logs were rammed into the wooden gates or into weak sections of the stone wall.
- Catapults. These launched artillery projectiles—anything the attackers could find: boulders, stones, metal fragments, logs, even corpses (which would spread DISEASE inside the city).

See also WAR.

DRESSED TO KILL, warriors in Bible times often armed themselves with swords and spears. Many wore some kind of body armor, such as leather or metal, and some fought with a shield to ward off arrows and slashing swords.

W

WEAVER

My life has been. . .cut short, as when a weaver cuts cloth from a loom. Isaiah 38:12

WEAVERS created cloth by crisscrossing threads of LINEN, wool, or some other fabric. They did this with a loom.

They hung the vertical threads, called the warp, from a top beam. These threads were held taut by weights at the bottom, often stones. Then the weavers pulled the horizontal threads, called the woof, through the vertical threads. They did this with a shuttle, which works a bit like a big wooden NEEDLE with a thread attached.

DELILAH did this to SAMSON's HAIR while he napped, hoping it would drain him of his strength so she could collect a reward for his capture. When he woke up, he "yanked his hair away from the loom and the fabric" (Judges 16:14).

WEDDING

Laban invited everyone in the neighborhood and prepared a wedding feast.
Genesis 29:22

JEWS GOT MARRIED IN A FEVER at the pepper-sprout peak of sexual desire—a great time for making babies. They were teenagers.

That's if they followed Middle Eastern customs of the day.

The BIBLE doesn't say when guys and gals got hitched. But Egyptian documents do. WOMEN often married between the ages of 12 and 14, after their menstrual periods started. Men married when they could shake a shekel and support a FAMILY: ages 14–20. For Romans, the minimum legal age: 12 for ladies, 14 for gents.

TALKING TURKEY, SHEEP, GOATS

Arranging a marriage was a bit like dickering for a car—preferably one never driven.

Typically, the FATHER of a young man or a young woman would approach the father of a potential spouse. If the two agreed that their CHILDREN would make a suitable couple, they negotiated the BRIDE fee and the DOWRY. The bride fee that some RABBIS recommended for a VIRGIN was about double the fee for a WIDOW. Low resale value.

JEWS preferred to marry not only fellow Jews, but Jews in their own tribe—their extended FAMILY. Kissing cousins. It was kosher. JACOB married his uncle LABAN's two daughters.

The father of the bride received a bride fee to compensate him for the loss of a helpful daughter. But this same man typically paid out more than he got. He usually had to provide his daughter with a dowry she could take into the marriage to help out financially: MONEY, jewels, livestock, clothes, or household supplies.

Once the groom-to-be paid the bride price—in a legally binding ceremony—he and the lady were engaged. But they weren't called fiancé and fiancée; they were HUSBAND and WIFE, without the SEX.

The engagement could last a year. If they changed their minds during that time, they'd have to get a DIVORCE. It was apparently during this engagement period that Joseph discovered MARY was pregnant by Someone Else.

WEDDING SINGER. Rabbi Dov Yonah Korn breaks out in song at a wedding in New York City. Weddings in Bible times were happy events, too. People partied long and hard—sometimes for a week or more if the food and wine held out.

TWO-WEEK RECEPTION

Jesus gave a few clues about weddings when he told the story of the ten bridesmaids (Matthew 25:1–13).

The bridesmaids waited at the bride's HOUSE for the groom to arrive with his entourage. After the groom got there, he led the bride and her family and friends back to where he was hosting the wedding festivities—often at the home of the groom or his parents.

Like wedding receptions today, guests brought GIFTS and expected to have a good time: plenty of food, MUSIC, and DANCING.

Unlike today's wedding receptions, the party could go on for days—even two weeks if the family had the money or wanted others to think they did.

GETTING IT IN WRITING

Some couples had marriage contracts drawn up.

Here's part of an ancient marriage CONTRACT between a bride named Demetria and a groom named Herakleides, from about 300 BC.

> Herakleides, a free man, takes Demetria, a free woman of Cos, as his legitimate wife from her father Leptines of Cos and from her mother Philotis, bringing clothing and jewelry (worth) 1000 drachmas. Let Herakleides provide to Demetria everything deserving to a free wife. . . .

> If Demetria is discovered doing any evil that would shame her husband Herakleides, let her be deprived of everything she brought (to the marriage); but let Herkleides prove whatever he sues Demetria about before three men on whom they both agree.

> Herakleides shall not be permitted to have an affair with another woman or have children by another woman. . . . If Herakleides is discovered doing any of these things and Demetria proves it before three men whom they both designate, Herakleides shall return the dowry of 1000 drachmas to Demetria which she brought and let him compensate her with 1000 additional drachmas of SILVER.

MARITAL PRIVILEGES

In case anyone had any doubts, Jewish law spelled out the rights of the wife. No need to spell out the rights of the HUSBAND. It was a man's world. By law, a husband had to provide his wife with:

- food
- clothing
- sex

If he didn't, "she may go free, and she owes him no money" (Exodus 21:11 NCV).

See also BRIDEGROOM, LEVIRATE MARRIAGE.

WEIGHTS (see MEASURES)

STOPPING AT A WELL, Jesus had to wait until someone came along with a bucket. In a land where water was scarce, villages did what they could to preserve the water.

WELL

> "Our ancestor Jacob dug this well for us, and his family and animals got water from it."
> John 4:12 CEV

IN THE DRY MIDDLE EAST, people depended on wells to supplement the winter rains.

Finding well WATER was something to sing about: "Spring up, O well! Yes, sing its praises! Sing of this well, which PRINCES dug, which great leaders hollowed out with their SCEPTERS and staffs" (Numbers 21:17–18).

W

Early wells were dug as dirt shafts in low-lying dry riverbeds.

Later, people began lining the shafts with stone, BRICK, or wood to keep the dirt from collapsing. People also started covering the wells with stones, to keep people and ANIMALS from falling in.

Many well shafts were about a couple feet across (0.5 m). That was wide enough for a miner to dig his way down and wide enough to drop in a BUCKET and haul water back up.

JACOB'S WELL, which may be the one Jesus visited in SYCHAR, is roughly 100 feet (30 m) deep. The woman Jesus met there said as much: "You don't even have a bucket, and the well is deep" (John 4:11 CEV).

One well dug in Palmyra, SYRIA, during Roman times dropped almost 250 feet (about 75 m).

All the flax and barley were ruined by the hail. . . . But the wheat and the emmer wheat were spared, because they had not yet sprouted from the ground. Exodus 9:31–32

TASTIEST and most popular GRAIN in Bible times, wheat was usually HARVESTED in late spring—after BARLEY, a blander and cheaper grain.

Farmers would separate the wheat kernels from the stalks. They could roast the kernels and eat them or grind them into FLOUR for BREAD.

PAYDAY. A farmer in the late 1800s pays workers for a day's labor: cutting wheat. The cutting tool, called a sickle or a scythe, is similar to the curved blades farmers used in Bible times

STEPHEN M. MILLER'S ILLUSTRATED BIBLE DICTIONARY

WHIRLWIND

Elijah went up to heaven in a whirlwind.
2 Kings 2:11 NCV

- Windstorm or tornado

ISRAEL sees its share of destructive windstorms, especially in the rainy SEASON of winter. Tornadoes, though rare, do occur from time to time, usually along the Mediterranean coast. ELIJAH seemed to experience one further inland, east of the JORDAN RIVER, in what is now the Arab country of Jordan. That's where a whirlwind lifted him into the sky.

WIDOW

"You must not exploit a widow or an orphan. If you exploit them in any way and they cry out to me [God], then I will certainly hear their cry." Exodus 22:22–23

PEOPLE AT GREATEST RISK in Bible times were widows, orphans, and immigrants. Jewish law warned people against taking advantage of them.

Widows were at risk because they were WOMEN in a man-run world. The FAMILY estate passed from FATHER to SON. If there was no son, it typically went to the closest male relative of the dead man, such as a brother or an uncle.

If the widow didn't have a son, Jewish law encouraged the closest relative of the dead man to marry the widow and try to provide her with a son who would inherit the dead man's estate and take care of his MOTHER in her old age. The Bible-time version of Social Security.

See also LEVIRATE MARRIAGE.

WIFE

A truly good wife is the most precious treasure a man can find! Proverbs 31:10 CEV

A WOMAN GETS THE LAST WORD in PROVERBS. She's the MOTHER of a mysterious king called Lemuel.

Lemuel's mother describes for her son the kind of things an ideal wife does:

- spins wool and FLAX (for LINEN)
- gets up before dawn to make breakfast
- plans the day's work for her daughters
- inspects and buys property
- plants a vineyard
- works late spinning thread
- makes clothes and sells them.

For all a wife like this does, Lemuel's mother said, the HUSBAND should praise her in public, saying things like, "There are many good women, but you are the best!" (Proverbs 31:29 CEV).

See also WEDDING, WOMEN.

WILDERNESS

Jesus was led by the Spirit into the wilderness to be tempted there by the devil. Matthew 4:1

- Dry badlands
- Deserted region

THE BIBLE'S "WILDERNESS" wasn't a forest.

Nor was it the typical "DESERT," as some Bibles translate the original HEBREW word *midbar* ("desolate and deserted") or the GREEK word *eremos* ("waterless").

Instead, it looked more like the Dakota Badlands or Mars: dirt, ROCKS. Great place for solitude. But not for a vacation.

WINE

Go ahead. Eat your food with joy, and drink your wine with a happy heart, for God approves of this! Ecclesiastes 9:7

WINE WAS A FAVORITE money maker among farmers in Bible times. ISRAEL's dry summers and wet winters were perfectly suited to vineyards. (See also VINE.)

Farmers harvested the GRAPES from August to September, clipping the clusters and dropping them into baskets. They would empty the baskets into a shallow, wide trough called a winepress. Stompers would dance on the grapes, sometimes to MUSIC, since harvesttime was payday for the farmer—a perfect time to celebrate.

Juice flowed out of an opening at the bottom of the press and into a vat. From there, harvesters would scoop up the grape juice and pour it into jars. They sealed the jars with cloth plugs to allow gases to escape during about six weeks of fermentation.

Finally, the wine was filtered into large clay storage jars that could hold as much as 10 gallons (38 l). The jars were stored in a cool place, often underground in cisterns or perhaps partly buried—which is why many of the recovered wine jars are pointed at the bottom, to rest in a hole.

At the LAST SUPPER, Jesus used a cup of wine to symbolize the BLOOD he would shed the next day during his CRUCIFIXION.

WINE STEWARD

I [Nehemiah] was the one who served wine to the king. Nehemiah 1:11 NCV

MORE THAN A WINE TASTER, the royal wine steward not only protected the king from bad wine—including poisoned wine—he sometimes served as an adviser.

Stewards usually saw the king every day. If the relationship developed, they could find themselves promoted.

Assyrian King SENNACHERIB promoted his steward to "chief of administration" (Tobit 1:22). Persian King

WINE JARS pointed at the bottom were perfect for storing partly buried in the cool ground. Dirt was the closest thing most folks had to a wine cooler.

WATERBOY OR WINE STEWARD. The goatskin bag would hold either drink. Milk, too. Because new wine produces gas as it continues to ferment, it needs to be stored in new wineskins that still have some stretch to them.

ARTAXERXES promoted NEHEMIAH to GOVERNOR of the Jewish province (Nehemiah 8:9).

WINNESKIN

> "No one puts new wine into old wineskins. For the wine would burst the wineskins."
> Mark 2:22

- Canteen

GOATSKIN was a favorite canteen for wine. With hair on the outside to provide insulation, the wine was stored inside the tightly sewn leather BAG.

New wine needed to go into new, still-pliable goatskin because the bag needed to expand as the wine continued to ferment and produce gases. Old, brittle wineskins would break under the pressure. But they could hold WATER.

WINNOWING (see THRESHING)

WISDOM

> Let your ears listen to wisdom. Apply your heart to understanding. Call out for the ability to be wise. Cry out for understanding.
> Proverbs 2:2–3 NIRV

THE TOP WISH of the wisest man who ever lived was, appropriately, for wisdom.

King SOLOMON: "Make me wise. Give me the knowledge I'll need to be the KING of this great nation of yours" (2 Chronicles 1:10 CEV).

GOD's reply: "I will give you what you asked for! I will give you a wise and understanding heart such as no one else has had or ever will have!" (1 Kings 3:12).

In the BIBLE, *wisdom* is a word that multitasks. It shows up in descriptions of artisans, politicians, and even in the everyday coping skills of average folks: "My son, pay attention to my wisdom. . . . The lips of an immoral woman are as sweet as honey. . . . But in the end she is as bitter as POISON" (Proverbs 5:1–4).

WISE MEN

> Wise men from eastern lands arrived in Jerusalem, asking, "Where is the newborn king of the Jews? We saw his star as it rose, and we have come to worship him." Matthew 2:1–2

- Sages, advisers, teachers

LIKE PROPHETS AND PRIESTS, wise men were their own snowflake—a unique class of people recognized for their WISDOM. They led tribes, settled COURT cases, taught school, and advised rulers.

BABYLON's king appointed the prophet DANIEL "chief over all his wise men" (Daniel 2:48).

The most famous wise men of the BIBLE were the ones who came to BETHLEHEM to WORSHIP baby Jesus. The Bible doesn't say how many there were. One tradition says three, perhaps because they brought three GIFTS: "GOLD, FRANKINCENSE, and MYRRH" (Matthew 2:11).

See also STAR OF BETHLEHEM.

WITNESS

> "Never put a person to death on the testimony of only one witness. There must always be two or three witnesses."
> Deuteronomy 17:6

IN A DEATH-PENALTY OFFENSE, Jewish law not only required two or more witnesses. It required that those witnesses do more than fire off accusations: "The witnesses must throw the first stones" (Deuteronomy 17:7).

In any kind of case, perjury was prohibited by one of the 10 COMMANDMENTS: "You must not testify falsely against your NEIGHBOR" (Exodus 20:16).

WOMEN

> This is how the holy women of old made themselves beautiful. They trusted God and accepted the authority of their husbands.
> 1 Peter 3:5

W

WOMEN LIVED IN A MAN-RUN WORLD in Bible times.

Some women rose to power and influence. But they were the rare exceptions, as Bible writers report it. A few notable leaders:

- MIRIAM, a prophetess and sister of MOSES
- DEBORAH, a prophetess, JUDGE, and military leader before ISRAEL had KINGS
- Priscilla, an associate of PAUL who helped educate a preacher named APOLLOS about Jesus.

Bible writers didn't seem especially interested in women's liberation, some scholars say. Even at the launch of the CHRISTIAN movement, bachelor Paul advised women to take a submissive role in the CHURCH—at least in the churches at CORINTH and EPHESUS, where some scholars speculate women may have been stirring up trouble that detracted from the church's mission.

Paul: "Women should learn quietly and submissively. I do not let women teach men or have authority over them" (1 Timothy 2:11–12).

WOMEN'S WORK included hauling milk to market, as these women are doing in Siloam, on the outskirts of Jerusalem at the turn of the 1900s.

Elsewhere, Paul commended women leaders, including PHOEBE, "a DEACON in the church" (Romans 16:1).

See also MOTHER, WIFE.

WORD OF GOD

> *While Jesus was standing beside Lake Galilee, many people were pressing all around him to hear the word of God.*
> **Luke 5:1** NCV

- Nickname for Bible
- Message from God

THE WORD OF GOD isn't usually the BIBLE—at least not as Bible writers use the phrase.

One exception: Jesus talking about his Bible, the OLD TESTAMENT. Complaining that Jewish scholars were bumping aside the laws of MOSES for their own new traditions, he said: "You make the word of GOD useless by putting your own teachings in its place" (Mark 7:13 NIRV).

Most of the time, though, "word of God" refers to a message from God—often delivered by a PROPHET, Jesus, or a preacher who was telling folks about Jesus.

See also SCRIPTURE.

WORKS, GOOD

> *Just as the body is dead without breath, so also faith is dead without good works.*
> **James 2:26**

IT'S NOT FAITH if we keep it to ourselves. CHRISTIAN faith, as the NEW TESTAMENT teaches it, isn't just a mental exercise. FAITH works up a sweat.

"You say you have faith, for you believe that there is one GOD," wrote JAMES, whom many scholars say was the brother of Jesus and leader of the JERUSALEM CHURCH. "Good for you! Even the DEMONS believe this, and they tremble in terror. How foolish! Can't you see that faith without good deeds is useless?" (James 2:19–20).

> *"Do not worship any god except me."*
> Exodus 20:3 CEV

- Showing reverence to God

IT'S THE FIRST and most important of the 10 COMMANDMENTS: Don't worship any god but GOD.

As if that's not clear enough, the second commandment seems like a ditto: And that includes IDOLS (Exodus 20:4–5).

JEWS worshiped God in OLD TESTAMENT times by learning the laws of MOSES and obeying them. One of their main acts of worship was to sacrifice ANIMALS—expressions of gratitude for their BLESSINGS or regret for their sins. After SOLOMON built the TEMPLE in JERUSALEM, the Temple became the only place Jews were allowed to offer SACRIFICES. It was their worship center.

Christians expressed their worship by meeting together and:

- singing (Ephesians 5:19)
- praying (1 Timothy 2:8)
- taking COMMUNION—eating BREAD and drinking WINE to commemorate Jesus' broken body and shed BLOOD at the CRUCIFIXION (Acts 2:42)
- teaching and PREACHING about Jesus and how to live the CHRISTIAN life (Acts 2:42)
- collecting offerings for the POOR (1 Corinthians 16:2).

Christians often met for worship in homes. At the beginning of the movement, they met in the Jerusalem Temple COURTYARD "each day" (Acts 2:46).

Later, as one writer reported it, "on the first day of the week, we gathered with the local believers to share in the LORD'S SUPPER" (Acts 20:7). That's Sunday, most scholars agree—the first day after the SABBATH day of rest.

WRITING

> *The LORD instructed Moses, "Write this down on a scroll as a permanent reminder."*
> Exodus 17:14

MOST PEOPLE DIDN'T READ OR WRITE in Bible times. Apparently, MOSES—raised as a prince in EGYPT—was an exception. Egyptians had been writing for many centuries before Moses.

By the time Moses showed up—sometime between 1550 and 1200 BC—people in the Middle East were using alphabets developed in what is now ISRAEL and LEBANON.

Before then, in the time of ABRAHAM (2100s BC), Sumerians in what is now Iraq were writing in cuneiform: wedge-shaped figures pressed into soft clay.

Egyptians developed a picture style of writing called hieroglyphics. One picture could represent a sound or various objects, depending on the context. For example, the picture of a crouching lion could represent the "L" sound. And a picture of a circle with a dot in the middle could mean "sun" or "Re," the sun god.

People chiseled their writing into stone. Some pressed letters into soft wax mounted into wooden boards. Others wrote with INK on POTTERY fragments, PAPYRUS paper, and LEATHER scrolls.

New Testament LETTERS and books were likely written on the leather SCROLLS made from the skin of GOATS and SHEEP. When scholars in recent years pieced together the jigsaw puzzle of fingernail-sized fragments of the famous DEAD SEA SCROLLS— 2,000-year-old copies of the OLD TESTAMENT and other Jewish writings—DNA testing helped them match the leather pieces.

ON THE RECORD. People in what is now Iraq once used wedge-shaped cuneiform symbols, which they pressed into soft clay or chiseled into stone. In this Babylonian stone monument from about 850 BC, a son commemorated his father. That's about the time Elisha saw Elijah ride a whirlwind to heaven.

XERXES I

(ZURK zees)

Ruled 486–465 BC

On the seventh day of the party, the king, high on the wine, ordered the seven eunuchs. . . to bring him Queen Vashti. . .to show off her beauty to the guests. Esther 1:10–11 MSG

- King of Persian Empire, based in Iran
- Husband of Esther

KING XERXES married a Jewish ORPHAN, Esther, after banishing from his presence the former queen, VASHTI.

Xerxes demoted Vashti after she made the mistake of refusing his request to come to his drinking party and show off her good looks—as a trophy WIFE.

To find his next trophy, Xerxes held an empire-wide beauty contest. ESTHER won. This was good for the JEWS, because Xerxes later helped Esther stop a plot to wipe out all Jews in the empire.

Bible writers called Xerxes by what seems to have been either the Persian or the HEBREW form of his NAME: Ahasuerus (uh has YOU air uhs).

YAHWEH

(YAH way)

*The L*ORD *God [Yahweh] made the earth and the heavens. Genesis 2:4*

- God's name

THE BIBLE'S MOST COMMON NAME for GOD is used about 7,000 times. It's from consonant-only shorthand in ancient SCROLLS: YHWH. Scholars have to guess about what vowels to fill in. Most Bibles translate the word with small capital letters: LORD.

See also I AM.

YOKED TOGETHER, an ox and a donkey plow a rocky field in the Holy Land about a century ago. The yoke and the plow are both made of wooden limbs.

YOKE

*The L*ORD *told me: "Jeremiah, make a wooden yoke with leather straps, and place it on your neck." Jeremiah 27:1* CEV

- Frame to link a team of animals for pulling something

A TEAM OF OXEN or other ANIMALS were linked by a yoke frame around their necks. This way, when they pulled a wagon or a PLOW, they would have to walk together. Yokes were made of wood, metal, or LEATHER.

YOM KIPPUR

(see DAY OF ATONEMENT)

ZACCHAEUS

(zuh KEE us)

First century AD

Jesus entered Jericho and was passing through. A man named Zacchaeus lived there. He was a chief tax collector and was very rich. Luke 19:1–2 NIRV

- Jericho tax collector

ZACCHAEUS WAS A TAX MAN who got rich, apparently by overcharging his own Jewish people for taxes required by the occupying forces of Rome.

Jews hated him, along with most TAX COLLECTORS. People considered them collaborators who worked with the enemy. Many Jews treated them as ritually unclean—like lepers, refusing to touch them or even take change back when paying taxes.

Jesus, however, had another approach. He chose one tax collector, MATTHEW, as a DISCIPLE. And when Jesus passed through JERICHO and saw short Zacchaeus up a tree, trying to catch a glimpse of him over the crowds, Jesus called him down and spent the night at his home.

The crowd grumbled. But Jesus' kindness changed Zacchaeus.

"I will give half my wealth to the poor," he told Jesus, "and if I have cheated people on their taxes, I will give them back four times as much!" (Luke 19:8).

Tax refund.

ZADOK

(ZAY doc)

900s BC

Zadok the priest brought some olive oil from the sacred tent and poured it on Solomon's head to show that he was now king.
1 Kings 1:39 CEV

- Jewish high priest in Jerusalem

ISRAEL'S HIGH PRIEST during the reigns of DAVID and SOLOMON, Zadok became the father of a dynasty of HIGH PRIESTS that lasted some 400 years—until 586 BC. That's when Babylonian invaders from what is now Iraq destroyed the Jerusalem TEMPLE. All high priests during that stretch came from his FAMILY tree.

ZAREPHATH

Map 1 C3

(ZAIR uh fath)

The LORD said to Elijah, "Go and live in the village of Zarephath, near the city of Sidon. I have instructed a widow there to feed you."
1 Kings 17:8–9

- Village in what is now Lebanon
- Where Elijah resurrected a widow's son

WHEN ISRAEL REJECTED GOD and the prophet ELIJAH, God sent a DROUGHT to punish the people. GOD told Elijah to wait out the drought in Zarephath, a village in what is now LEBANON, about 25 miles (40 km) north of the Israeli border.

There Elijah performed two MIRACLES for a WIDOW who was on the brink of starvation: her FLOUR and OLIVE OIL jars never emptied during the drought; and when her son died, Elijah brought him back to life.

Jesus managed to insult his hometown crowd in NAZARETH by reminding them of this story. When they rejected his teachings, Jesus said the JEWS had a long history of rejecting PROPHETS like himself. When they did, God found people elsewhere.

"There were many widows in ISRAEL," Jesus said, "yet Elijah was sent to none of them except to a widow at Zarephath" (Luke 4:25–26 NRSV). The hometown crowd responded by trying to throw Jesus off the nearest cliff.

ZEALOT

Here are the names of the 12 apostles. . . Simon the Zealot. Matthew 10:2, 4 NIRV

- Jew who resisted Roman occupation
- Religious or political extremist
- One of Jesus' disciples

ZEALOTS were a political group of patriotic JEWS in Jesus' day. Their goal: Drive out the Romans, who had been occupying the Jewish homeland for about a century.

One of Jesus' DISCIPLES was a zealot: SIMON. Scholars debate whether "zealot" means he was a member of this political group or was simply zealous about something else, such as the Jewish laws.

If he was a political Zealot, Jesus had quite the

assortment of disciples. MATTHEW the former TAX COLLECTOR would have been the opposite extreme: someone considered a Roman collaborator, since he collected taxes from fellow Jews and gave the MONEY to ROME.

ZEALOTS were patriotic Jews who wanted to oust the Roman occupying army. They got their wish in AD 66. But their freedom was short-lived and expensive. Romans came back and leveled Jerusalem, destroying the Temple. It has never been rebuilt.

ZEBEDEE

(ZEB uh dee)

First century AD

While Jesus was walking along the shore of Lake Galilee. . .he saw James and John, the sons of Zebedee. They were in a boat with their father, mending their nets. Matthew 4:18, 21 CEV

- Father of disciples James and John
- Fisherman

A FISHERMAN who worked with his sons on ISRAEL's northern lake called the SEA OF GALILEE, Zebedee was more than just the owner of a FAMILY business. He was successful enough to have hired men working with him, too.

Some Bible experts speculate that his WIFE was SALOME, a follower of Jesus who helped financially support his ministry and who witnessed his CRUCIFIXION.

ZEBULUN

(ZEBB yuh luhn)

1800s BC

When Leah had another son, she exclaimed, "God has given me a wonderful gift." . . . So she named the boy Zebulun [a word that sounds like "honor"]. Genesis 30:19–20 CEV

- Son of Jacob and Leah
- Founder of Israel's tribe of Zebulun

JACOB'S TENTH SON—number six by his wife LEAH—Zebulun produced a FAMILY whose descendants became one of the 12 TRIBES OF ISRAEL.

ZEBULUN, TRIBE OF

Map 1 C4

(ZEBB yuh luhn)

"Zebulun will settle by the seashore and will be a harbor for ships." Genesis 49:13

- One of Israel's 12 tribes

DESCENDANTS OF JACOB'S SON Zebulun got one of the smaller plots of land in ISRAEL.

Using a selection process a bit like drawing straws, they ended up with about a 20-mile-long (32 km) stretch of land between the Carmel mountain range and the Galilean hills. Between those highlands, however, lay the fertile valley of JEZREEL—Israel's best farmland.

Warriors of Zebulun joined DEBORAH's militia at the battle of MOUNT TABOR, routing a Canaanite CHARIOT corps that got bogged down in the valley during a rainstorm.

ZECHARIAH

(ZECK uh RYE uh)

Zechariah and Elizabeth were righteous in God's eyes. . . . They had no children because Elizabeth was unable to conceive, and they were both very old. Luke 1:6–7